HEGEL'S *AESTHETICS*

AESTHETICS

LECTURES ON FINE ART

BY

G. W. F. HEGEL

Translated by T. M. Knox

VOLUME II

CLARENDON PRESS · OXFORD

OXFORD
UNIVERSITY PRESS

Great Clarendon Street, Oxford OX2 6DP
United Kingdom

Oxford University Press is a department of the University of Oxford.
It furthers the University's objective of excellence in research, scholarship,
and education by publishing worldwide. Oxford is a registered trade mark of
Oxford University Press in the UK and in certain other countries

© Oxford University Press 1975

The moral rights of the author have been asserted

First published 1975
Reprinted 2014

All rights reserved. No part of this publication may be reproduced, stored in
a retrieval system, or transmitted, in any form or by any means, without the
prior permission in writing of Oxford University Press, or as expressly permitted
by law, by licence or under terms agreed with the appropriate reprographics
rights organization. Enquiries concerning reproduction outside the scope of the
above should be sent to the Rights Department, Oxford University Press, at the
address above

You must not circulate this work in any other form
and you must impose this same condition on any acquirer

Published in the United States of America by Oxford University Press
198 Madison Avenue, New York, NY 10016, United States of America

British Library Cataloguing in Publication Data
Data available

Library of Congress Cataloging in Publication Data
Data available

ISBN 978-0-19-824499-8

TRANSLATOR'S FOREWORD TO VOLUME TWO

IN this volume Hegel is surveying five different arts from his philosophical point of view and supporting his argument by numerous examples. Therefore it may be helpful to recall what his attitude is to his own 'speculative' thinking and the empiricism adopted by the scientific intellect (or the Understanding). Nature, history, art, religion, and even philosophy may all be studied as it were on the surface. Scientists and historians may discern or try to discern laws in all these fields, but their first task is to accumulate a vast array of facts. This is something that must be done, but it would all add up to a tale told by an idiot if it were not possible to penetrate below the surface of fact, and even law, and discern the truth or the Reason lying at the heart. Hegel believes that this is the task of philosophy, but it must be given the facts first; it cannot work *a priori*. Consequently, although this volume provides facts in plenty, it really contains a philosophy rather than a history of art. See the closing paragraphs of the Division of the Subject which follows the Introduction here.

The lectures in this volume do depend here and there on the work of art historians and critics, but the bulk of them rest on Hegel's own direct acquaintance with works of art. In a few footnotes I have referred to his personal knowledge of buildings, pictures, and operas. His letters to his wife when he travelled to the Low Countries, Austria, and Paris testify to his devotion to works of visual art and his eagerness to see them; he looked at them with a fresh eye. Also he listened to opera with delight, and he read poetry with care and insight.

Not all of his judgements, still less his speculative reasoning, will command general assent. Novels seem to have little interest for him—Scott he regarded as a recorder of trivialities instead of great events, and the praise he lavishes on Hippel has amazed German critics. Moreover he seems to me to have had little understanding of what he calls 'independent' music. Nevertheless, a reader who is interested in art must find fascinating this survey of five arts, and he may even envy its comprehensiveness.

Throughout, however, it is necessary to remember that Hegel died in 1831.

In a set of lectures as long as this some repetition is not unnatural. This has led to some repetition in footnotes, but this may be less irksome than more cross-references. Some notes in this volume have benefited from corrections and suggestions by Mr. T. J. Reed.

T. M. KNOX

Crieff, June 1973

CONTENTS OF VOLUME TWO

PART III. THE SYSTEM OF THE INDIVIDUAL ARTS	613
INTRODUCTION	613
DIVISION OF THE SUBJECT	621
SECTION I. ARCHITECTURE	630
INTRODUCTION	630
Chapter I. INDEPENDENT OR SYMBOLIC ARCHITECTURE	635
1. Architectural Works Built for National Unification	638
2. Architectural Works wavering between Architecture and Sculpture	640
(a) Phallic Columns	641
(b) Obelisks etc.	642
(c) Egyptian Temples	644
3. Transition from Independent to Classical Architecture	648
(a) Indian and Egyptian Subterranean Buildings	648
(b) Housing for the Dead, Pyramids, etc.	650
(c) Transition to Architecture in the Service of some Purpose	654
Chapter II. CLASSICAL ARCHITECTURE	660
1. General Character of Classical Architecture	661
(a) Subservience to a Specific End	661
(b) The Building's Fitness for its Purpose	661
(c) The House as the Fundamental Type	662
2. The Particular Determinants of the Architectural Forms	663
(a) Building in Wood and Stone	663
(b) The Specific Forms of the Temple	665
(c) The Classical Temple as a Whole	674
3. The Different Styles in Classical Architecture	676
(a) Doric, Ionic, and Corinthian Orders	676
(b) The Roman Construction of Arch and Vault	680
(c) General Character of Roman Architecture	682

CONTENTS

Chapter III. ROMANTIC ARCHITECTURE — 684

1. General Character of Romantic Architecture — 684
2. Particular Architectural Formations — 685
    (a) The Fully Enclosed House as the Fundamental Form — 685
    (b) The Form of the Exterior and the Interior — 687
    (c) Mode of Decorating — 695
3. Different Styles in Romantic Architecture — 697
    (a) Romanesque (pre-Gothic) Architecture — 697
    (b) Gothic Architecture Proper — 698
    (c) Secular Architecture in the Middle Ages — 698

SECTION II. SCULPTURE — 701

INTRODUCTION — 701

DIVISION OF THE SUBJECT — 708

Chapter I. THE PRINCIPLE OF SCULPTURE PROPER — 710

1. The Essential Content of Sculpture — 710
2. The Beautiful Sculptural Form — 713
    (a) Exclusion of Particulars — 716
    (b) Exclusion of Mien — 717
    (c) Substantive Individuality — 718
3. Sculpture as the Art of the Classical Ideal — 718

Chapter II. THE IDEAL OF SCULPTURE — 721

1. General Character of the Ideal Sculptural Form — 723
2. Particular Aspects of the Ideal Form in Sculpture — 727
    (a) The Greek Profile — 727
    (b) Position and Movement of the Body — 738
    (c) Draping [or Clothing] — 742
3. Individuality of the Ideal Sculptured Figures — 750
    (a) Attributes, Weapons, Adornment — 752
    (b) Differences of Age and Sex, and of Gods, Heroes, Men, and Animals — 756
    (c) Portrayal of the Individual Gods — 761

CONTENTS ix

Chapter III. THE DIFFERENT KINDS OF POR-
TRAYAL AND MATERIAL AND THE HISTORI-
CAL STAGES OF SCULPTURE'S DEVELOP-
MENT 765

1. Modes of Portrayal 765
    (a) The Single Statue 766
    (b) Groups 767
    (c) Reliefs 771
2. Materials for Sculpture 771
    (a) Wood 772
    (b) Ivory, Gold, Bronze, and Marble 773
    (c) Precious Stones and Glass 777
3. Historical Stages in the Development of Sculpture 778
    (a) Egyptian Sculpture 779
    (b) Greek and Roman Sculpture 784
    (c) Christian Sculpture 788

SECTION III. THE ROMANTIC ARTS 792

INTRODUCTION 792

Chapter I. PAINTING 797

INTRODUCTION 797

1. General Character of Painting 799
    (a) The Chief Determinant of the Subject-matter 802
    (b) The Sensuous Material of Painting 804
    (c) Principle of the Artistic Treatment 811
2. Particular Characteristics of Painting 814
    (a) The Romantic Subject-matter 814
    (b) More Detailed Characterization of the Sensuous Material of Painting 837
    (c) The Artist's Conception, Composition, and Characterization 850
3. Historical Development of Painting 869
    (a) Byzantine Painting 871
    (b) Italian Painting 872
    (c) Flemish and German Painting 882

Chapter II. MUSIC — 888

INTRODUCTION AND DIVISION OF THE SUBJECT — 888

1. General Character of Music — 893
    (a) Comparison with the Visual Arts and Poetry — 893
    (b) Musical Treatment of the Subject-matter — 901
    (c) Effect of Music — 904
2. Particular Characteristics of Music's Means of Expression — 910
    (a) Time, Bar, Rhythm — 913
    (b) Harmony — 919
    (c) Melody — 929
3. Relation between Music's Means of Expression and their Content — 933
    (a) Music as an Accompaniment — 937
    (b) Independent Music — 951
    (c) The Execution of Musical Works of Art — 955

Chapter III. POETRY — 959

INTRODUCTION — 959

A. THE POETIC WORK OF ART AS DISTINGUISHED FROM A PROSE WORK OF ART — 971

1. Poetic and Prosaic Treatment — 972
2. The Poetic and the Prose Work of Art — 979
3. The Poet's Creative Activity — 996

B. POETIC EXPRESSION — 1000

1. The Poetic Way of Imagining Things — 1001
2. Poetic Diction — 1007
3. Versification — 1011
    (a) Rhythmic Versification — 1014
    (b) Rhyme — 1022
    (c) Unification of Rhythmical Versification and Rhyme — 1031

C. THE DIFFERENT GENRES OF POETRY — 1035

Introduction and Division of the Subject — 1035

CONTENTS   xi

A. Epic Poetry   1040

   1. General Character of Epic   1040
   2. Particular Characteristics of Epic Proper   1050
     (a) The General World-Situation of Epic   1051
     (b) The Individual Epic Action   1062
     (c) The Epic as a Fully Unified Whole   1077
   3. The Historical Development of Epic Poetry   1093
     (a) The Oriental Epic   1094
     (b) The Classical Epic of Greece and Rome   1098
     (c) The Romantic Epic   1100

B. Lyric Poetry   1111

   1. General Character of Lyric   1113
   2. Particular Aspects of Lyric Poetry   1128
     (a) The Lyric Poet   1129
     (b) The Lyrical Work of Art   1132
     (c) The Kinds of Lyric Proper   1138
   3. Historical Development of Lyric   1147

C. Dramatic Poetry   1158

   1. The Drama as a Poetical Work of Art   1158
     (a) The Principle of Dramatic Poetry   1159
     (b) The Dramatic Work of Art   1164
     (c) Relation of the Dramatic Work of Art to the Public   1174
   2. The External Execution of a Dramatic Work of Art   1181
     (a) Reading Dramas and Reciting them   1182
     (b) The Actor's Art   1185
     (c) The Art of the Theatre more Independently of Poetry   1190
   3. The *Genres* of Dramatic Poetry and the Chief Features it has had in History   1192
     (a) The Principle of Tragedy, Comedy, and Drama   1193
     (b) Difference between Ancient and Modern Dramatic Poetry   1205
     (c) The Concrete Development of Dramatic Poetry and its *Genres*   1208

INDEX   1239

PART III

THE SYSTEM OF THE INDIVIDUAL ARTS

INTRODUCTION

The *first* part of the science we are studying was devoted to the general conception and the reality of beauty in nature and art: true beauty and true art or, in other words, the Ideal, in the still-undeveloped unity of its fundamental characteristics, independently of its particular content and its different modes of manifestation.

Secondly, this inherently solid unity of artistic beauty was unfolded within itself into an ensemble of forms of art. Their specific character was at the same time a specification of the content which the spirit of art had to frame from its own resources into an inherently articulated system of beautiful and general views of God and man.

What both of these spheres still lack is reality in the element of externality itself. For in the case of the Ideal as such and also of the particular forms of art—symbolic, classical, romantic—we did continually speak of the relation between (i) the meaning, as the inner side of the work of art, and (ii) its configuration in an external and phenomenal mode, or[1] of the complete conciliation of the two. But while this is so, nevertheless this realization of the Ideal amounted only to the still purely *inner* production of art within the sphere of the universal world-views into which it was elaborated. But it is implicit in the very conception of beauty that it shall make itself objective *externally* as a work of art presented to immediate vision, to sense and sensuous imagination. Consequently it is only through this existent, which is appropriate to itself, that beauty really explicitly becomes beauty and the Ideal.

---

[1] *oder* in Hotho's first edition has dropped out from the second, but I take this to be a misprint, as Bassenge does.

Therefore, *thirdly*, we still have to survey this sphere in which the work of art is actualized in the element of the sensuous. For only in virtue of this final configuration is the work of art genuinely concrete, an individual at once real, singular, and perfect.

The content of this third department of aesthetics can be afforded only by the Ideal, because what is objectified here is the Idea of the beautiful in the totality of the world-views implied by it. The work of art, therefore, is even now still to be regarded as an inherently articulated totality, yet as an organism. In the Second Part the different features of this organism were particularized as a group of essentially different world-views. But now they fall apart as separate members, each of which becomes on its own account an independent whole and in this individuality can bring into representation the totality of the different forms of art.[1] In itself, because of its essence, the ensemble of this new reality of art belongs to a *single* totality; but since it is in the sphere of what is present to sense that this totality is realized, the Ideal is now resolved into its factors or moments and gives them an independent subsistence, although they may interfere with one another, may have an essential relation to one another, and supplement each other. This real world of art is the system of the individual arts.

Now just as the particular art-forms, taken as a group, have in them a progress, a development from the symbolic into the classical and then the romantic, so on the one hand we find in the individual arts also a similar progress because it is precisely the art-forms themselves which acquire their determinate existence through the individual arts. Yet, on the other hand, the individual arts too, independently of the art-forms which they objectify, have in themselves a development, a course which, considered rather abstractly, is common to them all. Each art has its time of efflorescence, of its perfect development as an art, and a history preceding and following this moment of perfection. For the products of all the arts are works of the spirit and therefore are not, like natural productions, complete all at once within their specific sphere; on the contrary, they have a beginning, a progress, a perfection, and an end, a growth, blossoming, and decay.

Here at the very beginning, we will briefly indicate the course of these more abstract differences because it asserts itself similarly in

---

[1] See Vol. I, p. 72, note; p. 82, note.

III. INTRODUCTION

all the arts. These differences, usually under the name of severe, ideal, and pleasing style, are commonly described as the different artistic styles; these especially bear on the general mode of conception and portrayal in respect, for one thing, of the external form and its freedom, or lack of it, simplicity, overloading in details, etc., and in short on all the aspects in which the determinate content overflows into external appearance; for another thing, they concern the aspect of the technical manipulation of the sensuous material in which art brings its content into existence.

It is a common prejudice that art made its beginning with the natural and the simple. It is true that this can be granted in a certain sense: i.e. the crude and the savage, compared with the genuine spirit of art, are the simpler and the more natural. But what is natural, alive, and simple in art as fine art is quite different from this. Those beginnings which are simple and natural in the sense of being crude have nothing to do with art and beauty: as, for example, children make simple figures and with a few random strokes sketch a human form, a horse, etc. Beauty, as a work of the spirit, requires on the contrary even for its beginnings a developed technique, many sorts of experiment and practice; and the simple, as the simplicity of beauty, as ideal proportion, is rather a result which only after manifold intermediate steps has reached the point where multiplicity, variety, confusion, extravagance, and laboriousness have been overcome and where in this victory all preliminary studies and preparatory apparatus have been concealed or swept away; consequently only now does free beauty seem to have been produced wholly unhindered and as it were by a single cast.[1] This is like the manners of a cultured man: in everything he says and does he behaves quite simply, freely, and naturally, although he does not possess this simple freedom at all from the start but has acquired it only as a result of a thorough and perfect education.

Therefore in the nature of the case, and actually in history, art appears in its beginnings rather as *artificiality* and awkwardness, often copious in accessories, laborious in the elaboration of draperies and surroundings generally; and the more composite and varied these externals are, the simpler in that case is what is really expressive; this means that the truly free and living

[1] This metaphor from, e.g., the casting of a statue in bronze is occasionally used elsewhere. See, for example, Vol. I, p. 407, note 2.

III. INTRODUCTION

expression of the spirit in its forms and movements remains all the poorer.

In this regard, consequently, the earliest and oldest works of art in all the individual arts offer the most inherently abstract content, simple stories in poetry, seething theogonies with abstract thoughts and their imperfect development, individual saints in stone and wood, etc.; and the portrayal remains inflexible, uniform or confused, stiff, and dry. In visual art especially the facial expression is obtuse, with the peace of animal vacuity, not of spiritual and profound inner meditation, or else it is sharp and with an exaggeration of characteristic traits. Similarly too the forms and movements of the body are dead; the arms, for example, are glued to the body, the legs are not separated or they are moved unskilfully, angularly, with sharp edges; in other ways too the figures are shapeless, narrowly compressed or disproportionately thin and lengthened. On the other hand a great deal of love and industry is devoted to externals, to clothes, hair, weapons, and trappings of other sorts; but the folds of the dress, for instance, remain wooden and independent without being adapted to the limbs (as we can see often enough in the case of earlier images of the Virgin and saints); at one time they are set beside one another in uniform regularity, at another broken up variously in harsh angles, not flowing but laid broadly and amply round the figure. Similarly the first attempts at poetry are jerky, disconnected, monotonous, dominated abstractly by only one idea or feeling, or too they are wild, violent, in detail obscurely entangled, and in ensemble not yet bound together into a firm inner organic whole.

But [*first*], style, as we have to consider it here, consequently begins, after such preliminary studies, only with what is fine art proper. In fine art, style is indeed likewise still harsh at the start, but it is already softened more beautifully into severity. This severe style is that higher abstraction of beauty which clings to what is important and expresses and presents it in its chief outlines, but still despises charm and grace, grants domination to the topic alone, and above all does not devote much industry and elaboration to accessories. Thus the severe style still limits itself to reproducing what is present and available. In other words, while on the one hand, in *content* it rests, in respect of ideas and presentation, on the given, e.g. on the present sacrosanct religious tradition, on the other hand, for the external *form* it allows complete liberty to the topic and not to its own invention. For it is satisfied with the general grand effect of establishing the *topic* and therefore in its expressions it follows what is and is *there*. But similarly everything accidental is kept aloof from this style so that the caprice and freedom of the artist's personality does not seem to intrude through it. The motifs are simple, and, in the aims represented, few, and so after all no great variety appears in the details of the figure, or of muscles and movements.

Secondly, the ideal, purely beautiful style hovers in between the purely substantive expression of the topic and the complete emergence of what pleases. As the character of this style we may signalize supreme liveliness in a beautiful and still grandeur, like what we marvel at in the works of Phidias or in Homer. This is a liveliness of all points, forms, turns of phrase, movements, limbs; in it there is nothing meaningless or inexpressive; everything is active and effective, and it displays the stir and beating pulse of the free life itself, from whatever side the work of art is considered—a liveliness which essentially presents, however, only a whole, and is only an expression of *one* thing, of one individuality and one action.

Moreover in such true liveliness we find at the same time the breath of grace wafted over the whole work. Grace is an appeal to the listener or spectator which the severe style despises. Yet even if χάρις, grace, proves to be only an acknowledgement, a courtesy, to an audience, still in the ideal style it is altogether free from this eagerness to please. We can explain this in a more philosophical way. The topic is the substantial thing, concentrated and perfect in itself. But since it comes into appearance through art, it labours, so to say, to exist there for contemplation by others, and to pass over from its simplicity and inherent compression to particularization, partition, and dispersal. This progressive development into existence for others is to be explained on the part of the topic as if it were a complaisance, because it does not seem to need this more concrete existence for itself and yet pours itself completely into it for our sake. But such a grace should assert itself at this stage only if the substantial thing, as self-maintained, persists at the same time unweakened by the grace of its appearance, a grace that blossoms only in externals as an original sort of superfluity. Inner self-confidence's indifference to its external existence, as well as its inner peace, constitutes that beautiful neglect of grace which places no direct value on this its external appearance. At the same time it is precisely here that the *loftiness* of beautiful style is to be sought. Beautiful and free art is unconcerned in its external form; there it does not let us see any private reflection, any aim or intention; on the contrary, in every expression, every turn of phrase, it hints only at the Idea and soul of the whole. Only in this way does the Ideal of beautiful style maintain itself; this style is not harsh or severe, but is already mellowed into the serenity of beauty. No expression, no part of the whole is forced; each member appears on its own account and enjoys an existence of its own and yet at the same time it resigns itself to being only one factor of the whole. In this way alone is the grace of animation added to the depth and determinacy of individuality and character; on the one hand, it is solely the topic which dominates; but owing to the completeness of its exposition and the clear and yet full variety of the traits which make the appearance wholly determinate, distinct, living, and actual, the spectator is as it were liberated from the topic as such because he has its concrete life completely before him.

But, owing to this last point, so soon as the ideal style pursues still further this turning to the external side of the appearance, it passes over into the pleasing or agreeable style. Here it is obvious at once that something is intended other than the liveliness of the topic itself. Pleasing, an effect produced from without, is declared as an aim and becomes a concern on its own account. For example, the famous Belvedere Apollo does not itself belong exactly to the pleasing style, but it does at least belong to the transition from the lofty ideal to charm. In the case of such a kind of pleasing, it is no longer the one topic itself to which the whole external appearance refers; consequently in this way the particular details of this appearance become more and more independent, even if at first they still proceed from the topic itself and are necessitated by it. We feel that they are adduced and interpolated as decorations or contrived episodes. But just because they remain accidental to the topic itself and have their essential purpose solely in relation to the spectator or reader, they flatter the person for whom they have been devised. Virgil and Horace, for example, delight us in this respect by a cultivated style in which we perceive versatile intentions and an effort to please. In architecture, sculpture, and painting, the pleasing style produces the disappearance of simple and grand masses; everywhere we see little independent miniatures, decoration, ornaments, dimples on the cheeks, graceful coiffures, smiles, robes variously draped, attractive colours and forms, poses that are striking and difficult and yet unconstrained and alive. In what is called Gothic or German architecture, for example, when it passes over into a pleasing style, we find an infinitely elaborated gracefulness, so that the whole seems to be put together out of nothing but little columns superimposed on one another with the most varied decorations, turrets, pinnacles, etc. These are pleasing in themselves yet without destroying the impression of great proportions and unsurpassable masses.

But since this whole stage of art by[1] its presentation of the external makes straight for an exterior effect we may cite as its further general character the production of effects. This, as its means of making an impression, may make use of the unpleasing, the strained, the colossal (in which the tremendous genius of Michelangelo, for instance, often ran riot), abrupt contrasts, etc. Producing effects is in general the dominating tendency of turning to the public, so that the work of art no longer displays itself as peaceful, satisfied in itself, and serene; on the contrary, it turns inside out and as it were makes an appeal to the spectator and tries to put itself into relation with him by means of the mode of portrayal. Both, peace in itself and turning to the onlooker, must indeed be present in the work of art, but the two sides must be in the purest equilibrium. If the work of art in the severe style is entirely shut in upon itself without wishing to speak to a spectator, it leaves us cold; but if it goes too far out of itself to him, it pleases but is without solidity or at least does not please (as it should) by solidity of content and the simple treatment and presentation of that content. In that event this emergence from itself falls into the contingency of appearance and makes the work of art itself into such a contingency in which what we recognize is no longer the topic itself and the form which the nature of the topic determines necessarily, but the poet and the artist with his subjective aims, his workmanship and his skill in execution. In this way the public becomes entirely free from the essential content of the topic and is brought by the work only into conversation with the artist: for now what is of special importance is that everyone should understand what the artist intended and how cunningly

[1] Omitting *und*, with Hotho's first edition.

and skilfully he has handled and executed his design. To be brought thus into this subjective community of understanding and judgement with the artist is the most flattering thing. The reader or listener marvels at the poet or composer, and the onlooker at the visual artist, all the more readily, and finds his own conceit all the more agreeably satisfied, the more the work of art invites him to this subjective judgement of art and puts into his hands the intentions and views of the artist. In the severe style, on the other hand, it is as if nothing at all were granted to the spectator; it is the content's substance which in its presentation severely and sharply repulses any subjective judgement. It is true that this repelling may often be a mere hypochondria of the artist who inserts a depth of meaning into his work but will not go on to a free, easy, serene exposition of the thing; on the contrary, he deliberately intends to make things difficult for the spectator. But in that case such a trading in secrets is itself only an affectation once more and a false contrast to the aim of pleasing.

It is the French above all who aim in their works at flattery, attraction, and plenty of effects; therefore they have developed as the chief thing this light-hearted and pleasing turning to the public, because they look for the real value of their works in the satisfaction which these give to others whom they want to interest and on whom they want to produce an effect. This tendency is especially marked in their dramatic poetry. For example Marmontel tells the following story about the production of his *Denis-le-Tyran*: The decisive moment was a question put to the tyrant. Clairon had to put this question. As the important moment approached, while addressing Denis, she took a step forward at the same time towards the audience and so apostrophized them. This action decided the success of the whole piece.[1]

We Germans, on the other hand, make too strong a demand for a content in works of art in the depths of which the artist is then to satisfy himself, unconcerned about the public which must look after itself, give itself trouble and help itself in any way it likes or can.

[1] In Book ii of his *Memoirs* Marmontel does not tell this story, but he does say that an actor achieved this effect in the production of *Aristomène*.

III. INTRODUCTION

DIVISION OF THE SUBJECT

As for the more detailed division of our third Part, after these general indications of stylistic differences common to all the arts, it is especially the one-sided Understanding that has hunted around everywhere for the most varied kinds of bases for classifying the individual arts and sorts of art. But the genuine division can only be derived from the nature of the work of art; in the whole of the genres of art the nature of art unfolds the whole of the aspects and factors inherent in its own essence. In this connection the first thing that presents itself as important is the consideration that, since artistic productions now acquire the vocation of issuing into sensuous reality, art too is now there for apprehension by the senses, so that, in consequence, the specific characterization of the senses and of their corresponding material in which the work of art is objectified must provide the grounds for the division of the individual arts. Now the senses, because they are *senses*, i.e. related to the material world, to things outside one another and inherently diverse, are themselves different; touch, smell, taste, hearing, and sight. To prove the inner necessity of this ensemble and its articulation is not our business here: it is a matter for the philosophy of nature where I have discussed it [in §§ 358 ff.]. Our problem is restricted to examining whether all these senses—or if not all, then which of them—are capable by their nature of being organs for the apprehension of works of art. In this matter we have already [in Vol. I, Introduction, pp. 38-9] excluded touch, taste, and smell. Böttiger's[1] fondling of the voluptuous parts of marble statues of female goddesses has nothing to do with the contemplation or enjoyment of art. For by the sense of touch the individual subject, as a sensuous individual, is simply related to what is sensuously individual and its weight, hardness, softness, and material resistance. The work of art, however, is not purely sensuous, but the spirit appearing in the sensuous. Neither can a work of art be tasted as such, because taste does not leave its object free and independent but deals with it in a really practical way, dissolves and consumes it. A cultivation and refinement of

[1] K. A. Böttiger, 1760–1835; amongst his voluminous writings I have been unable to identify this quotation. Hegel met him and attended a lecture of his in Dresden in 1824.

taste is only possible and requisite in respect of foods and their preparation or of the chemical qualities of objects. But the *objet d'art* should be contemplated in its independent objectivity on its own account; true, it is there for our apprehension but only in a theoretical and intellectual way, not in a practical one, and it has no relation to desire or the will. As for smell, it cannot be an organ of artistic enjoyment either, because things are only available to smell in so far as they are in process and [their aroma is] dissipated through the air and its practical influence.

Sight, on the other hand, has a purely theoretical relation to objects by means of light, this as it were non-material matter. This for its part lets objects persist freely and independently; it makes them shine and appear but, unlike air and fire, it does not consume them in practice whether unnoticeably or openly. To vision, void of desire, everything is presented which exists materially in space as something outside everything else, but which, because it remains undisturbed in its integrity, is manifest only in its shape and colour.

The other theoretical sense is hearing. Here the opposite comes into view. Instead of with shape, colour, etc., hearing has to do with sound, with the vibration of a body; here there is no process of dissolution, like that required by smell; there is merely a trembling of the object which is left uninjured thereby. This ideal movement in which simple subjectivity, as it were the soul of the body, is expressed by its sound, is apprehended by the ear just as theoretically as the eye apprehends colour or shape: and in this way the inner side of objects is made apprehensible by the inner life [of mind].

To these two senses there is added, as a third element, *ideas*, sense-perceptions, the memory and preservation of images, which enter consciousness singly by a separate act of perception, and, now subsumed under universals, are put by imagination into relation and unity with these. The result is that now on the one hand external reality itself exists as inward and spiritual, while on the other hand the spiritual assumes in our ideas the form of the external and comes into consciousness as a series of things outside and alongside one another.

This threefold mode of apprehension provides for art the familiar division into (i) the visual arts which work out their content for our sight into an objective external shape and colour,

(ii) the art of sound, i.e. music, and (iii) poetry which, as the art of speech, uses sound purely as a sign in order by its means to address our inner being, namely the contemplation, feelings, and ideas belonging to our spiritual life. Yet if we propose to go no further than this sensuous side of art as the final basis of division, we at once run into a perplexity in relation to principles in detail, since instead of being drawn from the concrete concept of the thing at issue the bases of division are drawn only from the thing's most abstract aspects. Therefore we must look around again for the mode of division which has deeper grounds, and which has already been indicated in the Introduction [pp. 82–3] as the true and systematic articulation of this Third Part. Art has no other mission but to bring before sensuous contemplation the truth as it is in the spirit, reconciled in its totality with objectivity and the sphere of sense. Now since this is to come about at this stage in the medium of the external reality of artistic productions, the totality which is the Absolute in its truth falls apart here into its different moments.

In the middle here, the really solid centre, is the presentation of the Absolute, of God himself as God in his independence, not yet developed to movement and difference, not yet proceeding to action and self-particularization, but self-enclosed in grand divine peace and tranquillity: the Ideal shaped in a way adequate to itself, remaining in its existence identical and correspondent with itself. In order to be able to appear in this infinite independence, the Absolute must be grasped as spirit, as subject, but as subject having in itself at the same time its adequate external appearance.

But as divine subject [or person], entering upon actual reality, it has confronting it an external surrounding world which must be built up, adequately to the Absolute, into an appearance harmonizing with the Absolute and penetrated by it. This surrounding world is in one aspect objectivity as such, the basis and enclosure of external nature which in itself has no spiritual absolute meaning, no subjective inner life, and therefore while it is to appear, transformed into beauty, as an enclosure for the spirit, it can express the spirit only allusively.

Contrasted with external nature there stands the subjective inner life, the human mind as the medium for the existence and appearance of the Absolute. With this subjective life there enters at once the multiplicity and variety of individuality, particularization, difference, action, and development, in short the entire and variegated world of the reality of the spirit in which the Absolute is known, willed, felt, and activated.

It is clear already from this hint that the differences, into which the total content of art is broken up, correspond essentially, in respect of artistic apprehension and portrayal, with what we considered in Part Two under the name of the symbolic, classical, and romantic forms of art. For symbolic art does not reach the identity of content and form but only a relationship of the two and a mere indication of the inner meaning in an appearance external alike to that indication and the content which it is supposed to express. Thus it provides the fundamental type of the art which has the task of working on the objective as such, on the natural surroundings, and making them a beautiful artistic enclosure for spirit, and of picturing the inner meaning of spirit in an allusive way in this external sphere. The classical Ideal, on the other hand, corresponds to the portrayal of the Absolute as such, in its independently self-reposing external reality, while romantic art has for both its content and form the subjectivity of emotion and feeling in its infinity and its finite particularity.

On this basis of division the system of the individual arts is articulated in the following way.

First, architecture confronts us as the beginning of art, a beginning grounded in the essential nature of art itself. It is the beginning of art because, in general terms, at its start art has not found for the presentation of its spiritual content either the adequate material or the corresponding forms. Therefore it has to be content with merely *seeking* a true harmony between content and mode of presentation and with an external relation between the two. The material for this first art is the inherently non-spiritual, i.e. heavy matter, shapeable only according to the laws of gravity; its form is provided by productions of external nature bound together regularly and symmetrically to be a purely external reflection of spirit and[1] to be the totality of a work of art.

The *second* art is sculpture. For its principle and content it has spiritual individuality as the classical ideal so that the inner and spiritual element finds its expression in the bodily appearance immanent in the spirit; this appearance art has here to present in an actually existent work of art. On this account, for its material it

---

[1] With Hotho's first edition I retain *und*.

III. INTRODUCTION 625

likewise still lays hold of heavy matter in its spatial entirety, yet without regard to its weight and natural conditions and without shaping it regularly in accordance with inorganic or organic forms; nor in respect of its visibility does it degrade it to being a mere show of an external appearance or particularize it within in an essential way. But the form, determined by the content itself, is here the real life of the spirit, the human form and its objective organism, pervaded by spirit, which has to shape into an adequate appearance the independence of the Divine in its lofty peace and tranquil greatness, untouched by the disunion and restriction of action, conflicts, and sufferings.

Thirdly we must group together into a final ensemble the arts whose mission it is to give shape to the inner side of personal life.

This final series *begins* with painting, which converts the external shape entirely into an expression of the inner life. Within the surrounding world, painting[1] does not only [as sculpture does] present the ideal self-sufficiency of the Absolute but now brings the Absolute before our vision as also inherently subjective in its spiritual existence, willing, feeling, and acting, in its operation and relation to what is other than itself, and therefore too in suffering, grief, and death, in the whole range of passions and satisfactions. Its object, therefore, is no longer God as God, as the *object* of human consciousness, but this consciousness[2] itself: God either in his actual life of subjectively living action and suffering, or as the spirit of the community, spirit with a sense of itself, mind in its privation, its sacrifice, or its blessedness and joy in life and activity in the midst of the existing world. As means for presenting this content painting must avail itself in general, so far as *shape* goes, of what appears externally, i.e. both of nature as such and of the human organism because that permits the spiritual to shine clearly through itself. For *material*, however, it cannot use heavy matter and its existence in the three dimensions of space, but instead must do with this material what it does with shapes [in nature], namely inwardize or spiritualize it. The first step whereby the sensuous is raised in this respect to approach the spirit consists (*a*) in cancelling the *real* sensuous appearance [*Erscheinung*], the

---

[1] In Hegel's text the subject of this sentence is not 'painting' but 'the inner life'. However, that Hegel *means* 'painting' seems clear from the fact that the first word in his following sentence is *Ihr*.
[2] *Bewusstseins* (the genitive) in Hotho's second edition must be a misprint.

visibility of which is transformed into the pure *shining* [*Schein*] of art, and (*b*) in colour, by the differences, shades, and blendings of which this transformation is effected. Therefore, for the expression of the inner soul painting draws together the trinity of spatial dimensions into a surface as the first inwardizing of the external, and presents spatial intervals and shapes by means of the sheen of colour. For painting is not concerned with making visible as such but with the visibility which is both self-particularizing and also inwardized. In sculpture and architecture the shapes are made visible by light from without. But, in painting, the material, in itself dark, has its own inner and ideal element, namely light. The material is lit up in itself and precisely on this account itself darkens the light. But the unity and mutual formation of light and darkness is colour.[1]

Now *secondly* the opposite of painting in one and the same sphere is music. Its own proper element is the inner life as such, explicitly shapeless feeling which cannot manifest itself in the outer world and its reality but only through an external medium which quickly vanishes and is cancelled at the very moment of expression. Therefore music's *content* is constituted by spiritual subjectivity in its immediate subjective inherent unity, the human heart, feeling as such; its *material* is sound, while its *configuration* is counterpoint, the harmony, division, linkage, opposition, discord, and modulation of notes in accordance with their quantitative differences from one another and their artistically treated tempo.

Finally, the *third* art after painting and music is the art of speech, poetry in general, the absolute and true art of the spirit and its expression as spirit, since everything that consciousness conceives and shapes spiritually within its own inner being speech alone can adopt, express, and bring before our imagination. For this reason poetry in its content is the richest and most unrestricted of the arts. Yet what it wins in this way on the spiritual side it all the same loses again on the sensuous. That is to say, it works neither for contemplation by the *senses*, as the visual arts do, nor for purely ideal *feeling*, as music does, but on the contrary tries to present to *spiritual* imagination and contemplation the spiritual meanings which it has shaped within its own soul. For this reason the material through which it manifests itself retains for it only the value of a *means* (even if an artistically treated means) for the

---

[1] Another allusion to Goethe's theory of colour.

III. INTRODUCTION

expression of spirit to spirit, and it has not the value of being a sensuous existent in which the spiritual content can find a corresponding reality. Amongst the means hitherto considered, the means here can only be sound as the sensuous material still relatively the most adequate to spirit. Yet sound does not preserve here, as it does in music, a value on its own account; if it did, then the one essential aim of art could be exhausted in its manipulation. On the contrary, sound in poetry is entirely filled with the spiritual world and the specific objects of ideas and contemplation, and it appears as the mere external designation of this content. As for poetry's mode of configuration, poetry in this matter appears as the total art because, what is only relatively the case in painting and music, it repeats in its own field the modes of presentation characteristic of the other arts.

What this means is that (i) as *epic* poetry, poetry gives to its content the form of *objectivity* though here this form does not attain an external existence, as it does in the visual arts; but still, objectivity here is a world apprehended under the form of something objective by imagination and objectively presented to inner imagination. This constitutes speech proper as speech, which is satisfied in its own content and the expression of that content in speech.

(ii) Yet conversely poetry is, all the same, subjective speech, the inner life manifesting itself as inner, i.e. *lyric* which summons music to its aid in order to penetrate more deeply into feeling and the heart.

(iii) Finally, poetry also proceeds to speech within a compact action which, when manifested objectively, then gives external shape to the inner side of this objective actual occurrence and so can be closely united with music and gestures, mimicry, dances, etc. This is *dramatic* art in which the whole man presents, by reproducing it, the work of art produced by man.

These five arts make up the inherently determinate and articulated system of what art actually is in both essence and reality. It is true that outside them there are other imperfect arts, such as gardening, dancing, etc., which however we can only mention in passing. For a philosophical treatment has to keep to differences determined by the essence of art and to develop and comprehend the true configurations appropriate to them. Nature, and the real world in general, does not abide by these fixed delimitations but has a wider freedom to deviate from them; and in this connection we often enough hear praise given to productions of genius precisely because they have to rise above such clear distinctions. But in nature the hybrids, amphibia, transitional stages, announce not the excellence and freedom of nature but only its impotence; it cannot hold fast to the essential differences grounded in the thing itself and they are blurred by external conditions and influences. Now the same is true of art with its intermediate kinds, although these may provide much that is enjoyable, graceful, and meritorious, even if not really perfect.

If, after these introductory remarks and summaries, we propose to proceed to a more detailed consideration of the individual arts, we are at once met in another way by a perplexity. This is because, after concerning ourselves up to this point with art as such, with the ideal and the general forms into which it was developed in accordance with its essential nature, we now have to approach the concrete existence of art, and this means treading on the ground of the empirical. Here it is much the same as it is in nature: its general departments are comprehensible in their necessity, but in what actually exists for our senses single productions and their species (both in their existent shape and in the aspects they offer for our consideration) have such a wealth of variety that (*a*) the most varied ways of treating them are possible and (*b*) if we want to apply the criterion of the simple differences entailed by the philosophical Concept of nature, this Concept cannot cover the ground, and thinking in terms of that Concept seems unable to get its breath amid all this fullness of detail. Yet if we content ourselves with mere description and reflections that only skim the surface, this again does not accord with our aim of developing the subject philosophically and systematically.

Then moreover there is added to all this the difficulty that each individual art now demands for itself a philosophical treatment of its own, because with the steadily growing taste for it the range of connoisseurship has become ever richer and more extended. The fondness that dilettanti have for connoisseurship has become a fashion under the influence of philosophy,[1] in our day, ever since the time when it was proposed to hold that in art the real religion,

---

[1] This may be an allusion to the closing passages of Schelling's *System of Transcendental Idealism*, or to his lectures on the Philosophy of Art.

the truth, and the Absolute was to be found and that art towered above philosophy because it was not abstract but contained the Idea in the real world as well and presented it there to concrete contemplation and feeling. On the other hand it is a mark of superiority in art nowadays to equip oneself with a superfluity of the most minute details and everyone is expected to have noticed something new. Occupation with such connoisseurship is a sort of learned idleness which does not need to be all that hard. For it is in a way very agreeable to look at works of art, to adopt the thoughts and reflections which may occur in consequence, to make easily one's own the views that others have had about them, and so to become and to be a judge and connoisseur of art. Now the richer are the facts and reflections produced by the fact that everyone thinks he has discovered something original of his very own, the more now does every art—indeed every branch of it—demand a complete treatment of its own. Next, moreover, alongside this, history enters of necessity. In connection with the consideration and assessment of works of art it carries matters further and in a more scholarly way. Finally, in order to discuss the details of a branch of art a man must have seen a great deal, a very great deal, and seen it again. I have seen a considerable amount, but not all that would be necessary for treating this subject in full detail.

All these difficulties I will meet with the simple explanation that it does not fall within my aim at all to teach connoisseurship or to produce historical pedantries. On the contrary my aim is simply to explore philosophically the essential general views of the things at issue and their relation to the Idea of beauty in its realization in the sensuous field of art. In pursuit of our aim we should not be embarrassed by the multifariousness of artistic productions which has been indicated above. After all, despite this variety the guiding thread is the essence of the thing itself, the essence implied by the Concept. And even if, owing to the element of its realization, this is frequently lost in accident and chance, there are still points at which it emerges clearly all the same, and to grasp these and develop their philosophical implications is the task which philosophy has to fulfil.

SECTION I

ARCHITECTURE

INTRODUCTION

By making its content emerge into a determinate existence in the real world, art becomes a *particular* art and therefore we can now speak for the first time of art *realized* and so of the actual beginning of art. But since particularization is to bring about the objectivization of the Idea of beauty and art, there is at once present along with it, as the Concept requires, a *totality* of particulars. If therefore in the series of particular arts architecture is treated first, this must not merely mean that it is presented as the art offering itself for treatment first on the strength of its being so determined by the nature of art; on the contrary, it must equally clearly be seen to be the art coming first in the existence of art in the world. Yet in answering the question of where art has begun alike in conception and in reality, we must throughout exclude both the empirical facts of history and also the external reflections, conjectures and natural ideas that are so easily and variously propounded about it.

There is a common urge, namely, to visualize a thing in its beginnings, because the beginning is the simplest mode in which the thing is to be seen. In the background of this there is retained the dim idea that this simple mode reveals the thing in its essential nature and origin, and then that the development of this beginning up to the stage really in question is to be understood, equally easily, by the trivial reasoning that this progress has *gradually* brought art up to this stage. But the simple beginning is something so insignificant in itself, so far as its content goes, that for philosophical thinking it must appear as entirely accidental, even if precisely for this reason origination is regarded in this way by people's ordinary minds as so much the more intelligible. So, for example, to explain the origin of painting there is a story told of a girl who traced the outline of her sleeping lover's shadow.[1] Similarly for the beginning of architecture there are cited now a cavern, now

---

[1] Pliny: *Nat. Hist.* xxxv. 5; and 43.

a tree-trunk, etc. Such beginnings are so intelligible in themselves that the origin seems to need no further explanation. The Greeks especially have invented many charming tales to explain the beginnings not only of fine art but also of ethical institutions and other relationships of their life. With these tales they satisfied the need to bring the earliest origin before their minds in a picture. Historical such beginnings are not and yet they are not supposed to have the aim of making the mode of origin intelligible by deriving it from the *Concept* of the thing: on the contrary, this mode of explanation is supposed to keep to the pathway of history.

What *we* have to do is to establish the beginning of art by so deriving it from the Concept or essential nature of art itself that we can see that the first task of art consists in giving shape to what is objective in itself, i.e. the physical world of nature, the external environment of the spirit, and so to build into what has no inner life of its own a meaning and form which remain external to it because this meaning and form are not immanent in the objective world itself. The art on which this task is imposed is, as we have seen, architecture which originally began to be developed earlier than sculpture or painting and music.

Now if we turn to the earliest beginnings of architecture, the first things that can be accepted as its commencement are a hut as a human dwelling and a temple as an enclosure for the god and his community. Next, in order to determine this starting-point more precisely, people have seized on the difference between materials that could be used for building, and it is disputed whether architecture begins in building with wood—the opinion of Vitruvius [ii. 1–4] whom Hirt had in view when he maintained the same—or with stone. This contrast is important of course because it does not merely affect the external material but also, essentially connected with it, the fundamental architectural forms and the manner of their embellishment. Nevertheless we can leave this whole difference aside as a purely subordinate matter affecting rather what is empirical and accidental, and we can turn our attention to a point of greater importance.

In the case of a house and a temple and other buildings the essential feature which interests us here is that such erections are mere *means*, presupposing a purpose external to them. A hut and the house of god presuppose inhabitants, men, images of the gods, etc. and have been constructed for them. Thus in the first place a need is there, a need lying indeed outside art, and its appropriate satisfaction has nothing to do with fine art and does not evoke any works of art. Men also take pleasure in leaping and singing and they need the medium of speech, but speaking, jumping, screaming, and singing are not yet, for this reason, poetry, the dance, or music. But even if, within architecture's adaptability to the satisfaction of specific needs, whether of daily life, religious worship, or the state, the urge for artistic form and beauty becomes conspicuous, we nevertheless have on our hands immediately a *division* in the case of this art of architecture. On the one side stands man, the subject, or the image of the god as the essential purpose for which, on the other side, architecture provides only the means, i.e. the environment, the enclosure, etc. With such an inherent division we cannot make a beginning, for in its nature the beginning is something immediate and simple, not a relativity and essential connection like this. Instead we must look for a point at which such a difference does not yet arise.

In this connection I have already said earlier that architecture corresponds to the *symbolic* form of art, and, as a particular art, realizes the principle of that form in the most appropriate way, because the meanings implanted in architecture it can in general indicate only in the externals of the environment that it creates. But should there be absent at the beginning the difference between (*a*) the aim, explicitly present in man or the temple-image, of seeking an enclosure and (*b*) the building as the fulfilment of this aim, then we will have to look around for buildings which stand there independently in themselves, as it were like works of sculpture, and which carry their meaning in themselves and not in some external aim and need. This is a point of supreme importance which I have not found emphasized anywhere although it is implicit in the concept of the thing and can alone provide an explanation of the varied external shapes of buildings and a guiding thread through the labyrinth of architectural forms. But all the same such an independent architecture is distinguished again from sculpture by reason of the fact that, as architecture, it does not produce constructions the meaning of which is the inherently spiritual and subjective and has in itself the principle of its appearance which throughout is adequate to the inner meaning. On the contrary, what this architecture produces is works which can stamp the meaning on their external shape only symbolically. For this reason, then, this kind of architecture is of a strictly symbolic kind both in its content and in its mode of presenting it.

What has been said about the principle of this stage applies equally to its mode of presentation. Here too the mere difference between building in wood and in stone will not suffice because it points to the means of delimiting and enclosing a space devoted to particular religious or other human purposes, as is the case with houses, palaces, temples, etc. Such a space can be formed either by hollowing out masses already fixed and solid in themselves or, conversely, by constructing surrounding walls and roofs. With neither of these can independent architecture begin and consequently we may call it an inorganic sculpture because although it erects independently existent productions it does not pursue at all the aim of creating free beauty and an appearance of the spirit in a bodily shape adequate to it; on the contrary, in general it sets before us only a symbolic form which is to indicate on itself and express an idea.

Yet at this *starting-point* architecture cannot remain. For its vocation lies precisely in fashioning external nature as an enclosure shaped into beauty by art out of the resources of the spirit itself, and fashioning it for the spirit already explicitly present, for man, or for the divine images which he has framed and set up as objects. Its meaning this enclosure does not carry in itself but finds in something else, in man and his needs and aims in family life, the state, or religion, etc., and therefore the independence of the buildings is sacrificed.

From this point of view we can put the *progress* of architecture in the fact that it makes the above-mentioned difference between end and means emerge as a separation of the two, and for man, or for the individual anthropomorphic shape of the gods which sculpture has worked out in objects, builds an architectonic receptacle analogous to the meaning of these, i.e. builds palaces, temples, etc.

Thirdly, the *final* stage unites both factors and therefore appears within this cleavage as independent at the same time.

These considerations give us for the division of the entirety of architecture the following parts which comprise both the differences entailed in the Concept of the thing at issue and also the historical development of architecture:

(i) strictly *symbolic* or independent architecture;

(ii) *classical* architecture which gives shape to the individual spirit but divests architecture of its independence and degrades it to providing an artistically formed inorganic environment for the spiritual meanings that for their part have now been independently realized;

(iii) *romantic* architecture, so-called Moorish, Gothic, or German, in which houses, churches, and palaces are indeed likewise only the dwellings and assembly-places for civil and religious needs and for spiritual occupations, but, conversely, undisturbed as it were by this purpose, are framed and erected on their own account and independently.

While therefore architecture in its fundamental character remains throughout of a symbolic kind, still the artistic forms, the strictly symbolic, the classical, and the romantic, are its determinants at different stages and are here of greater importance than they are in the other arts. For the entire principle of sculpture is so deeply penetrated by the classical form, and that of painting and music by the romantic form, that only a more or less narrow room is left for the development in these arts of the typical character of the other art-forms. Although poetry, lastly, can stamp on works of art in the most complete way the whole series of art-forms, we nevertheless will not have to divide it according to the difference between symbolic, classical, and romantic poetry but instead according to the systematic arrangement specific to poetry as a particular art, namely its division into epic, lyric, and drama. Architecture on the other hand is the art whose medium is purely external, so that here the essential differences depend on whether this external object has its meaning within itself or whether, treated as a means, it subserves an end other than itself, or whether in this subservience it appears at the same time as independent. The first case coincides with the symbolic form as such, the second with the classical because here the meaning proper attains portrayal on its own account and then the symbolic is tacked on to it as a purely external environment, and this is implicit in the principle of classical art. But the union of the two runs parallel with the romantic, because romantic art does use the external as a means of expression, but it withdraws into itself out of this external reality and therefore can leave the objective existent free to be shaped independently.

Chapter I

INDEPENDENT OR SYMBOLIC ARCHITECTURE

The primary and original need of art is that an idea or thought generated by the spirit shall be produced by man as his own work and presented by him, just as in a language there are ideas which man communicates as such and makes intelligible to others. But in a language the means of communication is nothing but a sign and therefore something purely external and arbitrary; whereas art may not avail itself of mere signs only but must give to meanings a corresponding sensuous presence. That is to say, on the one hand, the work of art, present to sense, should give lodgement to an inner content, while on the other hand it should so present this content as to make us realize that this content itself, as well as its outward shape, is not merely something real in the actual and immediately present world but a product of imagination and its artistic activity. If, for instance, I see a real living lion, its individual shape gives me the idea 'lion' just as a picture of it does. But in the picture something more is implicit: it shows that the shape has been present in idea and found the origin of its being in the human spirit and its productive activity, so that now we have no longer acquired merely the idea of an object, but the idea of a man's [i.e. the artist's] idea. But for a lion, a tree as such, or some other single object to be reproduced in this way there is no original need for art. On the contrary, we have seen that art, and especially visual art, comes to an end when the representation of such objects has the aim of displaying the artist's subjective skill in producing semblances of them. The original interest [of art] depends on making visible to themselves[1] and to others the original objective insights and *universal* essential thoughts. Yet such national insights are abstract at first and indefinite in themselves, so that in order to represent them to himself man catches at what is equally abstract, i.e. matter as such, at what has mass and weight.

[1] So the text. But the meaning is to make these views and thoughts visible in art to those who see or think them.

This is capable of acquiring a definite form, but not an inherently concrete and truly spiritual one. On this account the relation between the meaning and the sensuous reality whereby the meaning is to issue from [the artist's] conception into the spectator's can be only of a purely symbolical kind. But at the same time a building which is to reveal a universal idea to spectators is constructed for no other purpose than to express this lofty idea in itself, and therefore it is an independent symbol of an absolutely essential and universally valid thought, or a language, present for its own sake, even if it be wordless, for apprehension by spiritual beings. Thus the productions of this architecture should stimulate thought by themselves, and arouse general ideas without being purely a cover and environment for meanings already independently shaped in other ways. But in these circumstances the form that lets such a content shine through it may not count as merely a sign in the way that, for instance, crosses are erected as signs on graves, or cairns in memory of a battle. For although a sign of this kind is suitable for stimulating ideas, a cross and a cairn do not themselves indicate the idea which their erection aimed at arousing, for they can just as easily recall all sorts of other things. These considerations give us the general nature of architecture at this stage.

With this in view, it may be said that whole nations have been able to express their religion and their deepest needs no otherwise than by building, or at least in the main in some constructional way. However, as is clear from what I have said already in the course of discussing the symbolic art-form, this is essentially true only in the East; in particular, the constructions of the older art in Babylonia, India, and Egypt, now partly in ruins, which have been able to brave all periods and revolutions and which excite our wonder and astonishment as well by their fantastic appearance as by their colossal massiveness, either bear this character entirely or else are for the most part its product. The building of such works exhausts the entire life and activity of nations at certain times.

Yet if we ask for a more detailed systematic arrangement of this chapter and the chief productions belonging to this context, we cannot in the case of this architecture, as we can in that of the classical and romantic kinds, start from specific forms, e.g. for a house; for here there cannot be cited any explicitly fixed meaning,

INDEPENDENT OR SYMBOLIC ARCHITECTURE 637

or, therefore, any fixed mode of configuration, as a principle which then in its further development is applicable to the range of different buildings. In other words, the meanings taken as content here, as in symbolic art generally, are as it were vague and general ideas, elemental, variously confused and sundered abstractions of the life of nature, intermingled with thoughts of the actual life of spirit, without being ideally collected together as factors in a *single* consciousness. This absence of connection makes them extremely varied and mutable, and the aim of architecture consists exclusively in visibly setting forth now this and now that aspect for contemplation, in symbolizing them, and by human labour making them pictorial. In view of the manifold character of *this* content, there therefore cannot be any intention of treating it exhaustively or systematically and I have therefore to restrict myself to connecting together into a rational classification, so far as that is possible, only the most important material.

The guiding considerations are, in brief, the following:

For content we demanded purely universal views in which individuals and nations have an inner support, a unifying point of their consciousness. Consequently the *primary* purpose behind such explicitly independent buildings is only the erection of something which is a unifying point for a nation or nations, a place where they assemble. Yet along with this there is the subordinate aim of making obvious, by the mode of configuration, what does in general unify men: the religious ideas of peoples. These then provide at the same time a more specific content for such works to express symbolically.

But, in the *second* place, architecture cannot stop at this original feature determining it as a *whole*; for the symbolic productions become individualized, the symbolic content of their meanings is determined in more detail and therefore permits their forms to be more clearly distinguished from one another, as, for example, in the case of *lingam*-pillars, obelisks, etc. On the other hand, in such individualized independence within itself, architecture presses on towards a transition to sculpture, i.e. to the adoption of organic animal shapes and human figures. Yet it tends to extend these into massive and colossal constructions and to set them in rows alongside one another; partitions, walls[1], gates, passages are added, and

---

[1] *Wände, Mauern.* These words are used frequently below. They both mean 'walls', but *Wand* is a wall considered as a surface, e.g. the north face of the

therefore what is like sculpture on them is treated purely architecturally. The Egyptian sphinxes, Memnons, and enormous temples belong to this category.

Thirdly, symbolic architecture begins to show a transition to classical by excluding sculpture and beginning to become a structure for other meanings, not those directly expressed architecturally.

In order to elucidate these stages further I will refer to a few familiar masterpieces.

1. *Architectural Works built for National Unification*

'What is holy?' Goethe asks once in a distich, and answers: 'What links many souls together.' In this sense we may say that the holy with the aim of this concord, and as this concord, has been the first content of independent architecture. The readiest example of this is provided by the story of the Tower of Babylonia. In the wide plains of the Euphrates an enormous architectural work was erected; it was built in common, and the aim and content of the work was at the same time the community of those who constructed it. And the foundation of this social bond does not remain merely a unification on patriarchal lines; on the contrary, the purely family unity has already been superseded, and the building, rising into the clouds, makes objective to itself this earlier and dissolved unity and the realization of a new and wider one. The ensemble of all the peoples at that period worked at this task and since they all came together to complete an immense work like this, the product of their labour was to be a bond which was to link them together (as we are linked by manners, customs, and the legal constitution of the state) by means of the excavated site and ground, the assembled blocks of stone, and the as it were architectural cultivation of the country. In that case, such a building is symbolic at the same time since the bond, which it is, it can only hint at; this is because in its form and shape it is only in an external way that it can express the holy, the absolute unifier of men. The fact that the centre of unification in such a building was

---

Eiger is in German the north 'wall', while *Mauer* is a thick structure, like a city wall. At this point Hegel distinguishes between the two words (a wooden partition must be *Wand* and not *Mauer*), but elsewhere he uses them as synonyms, and the translation has followed him there.

INDEPENDENT OR SYMBOLIC ARCHITECTURE 639

forsaken again by the peoples and that they separated is likewise reported in this tradition.[1]

Another more important building, for which the historical grounds are more secure, is the Tower of Bel [in Babylon] of which Herodotus gives an account (i. 181). We will not examine here the question of what relation this tower has to the one in the Bible. This whole building we cannot call a temple in our sense of the word, but rather a temple precinct; it was an enclosure two furlongs square with brazen entry gates. In the middle of this sanctuary, we are told by Herodotus who had seen this colossal structure, there was a tower of solid masonry (not hollow inside but solid, a πύργος στερεός) a furlong in length and breadth; on top of this was a second tower, on that a third, and so on up to eight. On the outside is a path winding round the eight towers up to the very top. About halfway up there is a halting-place with benches where those making the ascent take a rest. On the topmost tower there is a spacious temple, and in the temple there is a huge bed richly caparisoned and in front of it a golden table. Yet there is no statue set up in the temple and no one sleeps there at night except one of the native women selected from them all by the god, according to the Chaldaeans, the priests of this god. The priests also maintain (ch. 182) that the god visits the temple himself and reposes on the bed. Herodotus also relates (ch. 183) that below, in the sanctuary there is still another temple in which there is a large sitting-figure of the god, all of gold, with a large gold table in front of it. In the same chapter he mentions two altars outside the temple on which sacrifices are offered. In spite of all this, however, we cannot put this gigantic structure on a par with temples in the Greek or modern sense. For the first seven cubes are entirely solid and only the top storey, the eighth, is a habitation for the invisible god who enjoys up there no worship from priests or congregation. The statue was below, outside the building, so that the whole structure rises really independent by itself and serves none of the ends of worship, although what we have here is no longer a mere abstract point of unification but a sanctuary. The form here is still left a matter of accident and is made square only for the material reason that a cube is stable. But at the same time it occurs to us to demand that we should seek for a meaning which,

[1] The Tower of Babel. Genesis 11: 1–9, partly an attempt to explain the ziqqurats, temple-towers in the Tigris–Euphrates valley.

taken for the work as a whole, may provide a more fundamental determinant, a symbolic one, for the form. We must find this, although Herodotus does not mention this in so many words, in the number of the solid storeys. There are seven of them, with the eighth above them for the nightly visit of the god. But the number seven probably symbolizes the seven planets and heavenly spheres.

In Media too there are cities built in accordance with such a symbolism, as, e.g., Ecbatana with its seven encircling walls. Of these Herodotus relates (i. 98) that each is made higher than its neighbour below, partly because the rising ground on the slope of which they are built favoured this arrangement but partly deliberately and skilfully; and the ramparts are differently coloured: white on the first wall, black on the second, purple on the third, blue on the fourth, orange on the fifth; but the sixth is coated with silver and the seventh with gold. The royal palace and the treasury are within the last. In connection with this sort of building Creuzer says (*Symbolik*, i. 469), 'Ecbatana, the city of the Medes, with the royal palace in the centre, represents, with its seven encircling walls and seven different colours on their battlements, the heavenly spheres surrounding the palace of the sun.'

2. *Architectural Works wavering between Architecture and Sculpture*

The next advance which we must proceed to consider is this, that architecture adopts more *concrete* meanings as its content, and for their more symbolical representation has recourse to *forms* which are also more concrete, though whether it uses them in isolation [for monoliths] or assembles them into great buildings, it does not employ them in a sculptural way but in an architectural one in its own independent sphere. In dealing with this stage we must descend to details although here there can be no question of completeness or a development of the subject *a priori* because when art advances in its works to the wide field of actual historical views of life and religious pictorial ideas, it loses itself there in what is accidental and contingent. The fundamental character here is that architecture and sculpture are confused, even if architecture remains the decisive element.

(a) Phallic columns

Our previous treatment of symbolic art gave us occasion to mention that in the East what was emphasized and worshipped was the universal force of life in nature, not the spirituality and power of consciousness but the productive energy of procreation. This worship was general, especially in India, but it was propagated also in Phrygia and Syria under the image of the Great Goddess, goddess of fecundity, a pictorial idea adopted even by the Greeks. In particular the conception of the universal force of nature was represented and sanctified in the shape of the animal generative organs, i.e. in the phallus or the *lingam*. This cult was principally disseminated in India, but even the Egyptians were not strangers to it, as Herodotus relates (ii. 48). Something similar at least occurred at Dionysiac festivals: 'only instead of phalli the Egyptians have invented other images, a cubit long; pulled by a thread, women take them round to the villages; the *pudendum* is always bent forward and is not much smaller than the rest of the body.' The Greeks likewise adopted a similar cult, and Herodotus expressly informs us (ch. 49) that Melampus, not unacquainted with the Egyptian Dionysiac sacrificial festival, introduced the phallus which was carried in procession in honour of the god.

Especially in India this kind of worship of procreative force in the shape of the generative organs gave rise to buildings in this shape and with this meaning: enormous columnar productions in stone, solidly erected like towers, broader at the foot than above. Originally they were ends in themselves, objects of veneration, and only later did people begin to make openings and hollow chambers in them and to place images of the gods in these, a practice still maintained in the Greek *Hermae*, small portable temples.[1] But in India this cult started with solid phallic columns; only later was there a division between an inner kernel and an outer shell, and they became pagodas. The genuine Indian pagodas must be essentially distinguished from later Mohammedan and other imitations, because in their construction they do not originate from the form of a house; on the contrary, they are slender and

[1] There is some confusion here. In Greek religion there is no trace of hollowed columns. Herms were pillars with bearded heads and *membro erecto*, standing at doors or marking boundaries. They were sacred and their mutilation at Athens in B.C. 415 created great scandal. 'Small portable temples' must be wrong: the Greeks had no such thing. 'Small sanctuaries at doors' might pass as a description of Herms, although they were not exactly sanctuaries, but only sacred.

high and their original basic form is derived from these column-like structures. The same meaning and form is present in the conception, enlarged by imagination, of the hill Meru which is represented as a whorl in the Milky Way from which the world was born. Similar columns Herodotus mentions also, in the form partly of the male generative organ, partly of the female *pudendum*. He ascribes the construction of them to Sesostris (ii. 102[1]) who in his wars set them up everywhere amongst the peoples he conquered. Yet in the time of Herodotus most of these columns no longer existed; only in Syria had he seen them himself (ch. 106). But his ascription of them all to Sesostris of course has its basis only in the tradition he followed; besides he expresses himself entirely in the sense of the Greeks because he transforms the naturalistic meaning into one concerned with ethical life and says [ch. 102]:

In the countries where the people were brave in battle against Sesostris during his wars, he erected columns on which he inscribed his own name and country and how he had here reduced these peoples to subjection; where, on the contrary, they submitted without a struggle he added to this inscription on the pillar a female *pudendum* to indicate that they had been cowardly and unwarlike.

(*b*) *Obelisks etc.*

Further similar works intermediate between architecture and sculpture are to be found especially in Egypt. Amongst these are obelisks which do not derive their form from the living organic life of nature, from plants and animals or the human form; on the contrary they have a purely regular shape, though they do not yet have the purpose of serving as houses or temples; they stand freely on their own account and independently and are symbols meaning the rays of the sun. Creuzer (*Symbolik*, i. 469) says 'Mithras, the Mede or the Persian, rules in the sun-city of Egypt (On-Heliopolis) and is advised there in a dream to build obelisks, the sun's rays in stone, so to speak, and to engrave on them the letters called Egyptian.' Pliny (*Nat. Hist.* xxxvi. 14) had already ascribed this meaning to obelisks.[2] They were dedicated to the

---

[1] '162' in all editions may be a misprint.

[2] 'An obelisk is a symbolic representation of the sun's rays.' In the German text a reference is added to xxxvii. 8, but this seems to be a mistake.

sun-god whose rays they were to catch and represent at the same time. In Persian monuments too flashes of fire occur, rising out of columns (Creuzer, ibid., i. 778).

Next to the obelisks, we must make special mention of Memnons. The huge Memnon statues at Thebes had a human form; Strabo[1] saw one of them preserved, chiselled out of a single stone, while the other which gave a sound at sunrise was mutilated in his time. These were two colossal human figures, seated, in their grandiose and massive character more inorganic and architectural than sculptural; after all, Memnon columns occur in rows and, since they have their worth only in such a regular order and size, descend from the aim of sculpture altogether to that of architecture. Pausanias[2] says that the colossal sounding statue was regarded by the people of Thebes as an image of Phamenoph. But Hirt (*Geschichte der Baukunst bei den Alten*—History of ancient architecture—Berlin, 1821–7, i. 69) refers this statue not to a divinity but rather to a king who had his memorial here, like Ozymandias and others. Nevertheless, these huge constructions should really convey a more or less distinct idea of something universal. The Egyptians and Ethiopians worshipped Memnon, the son of the dawn, and sacrificed to him when the sun sent forth its first rays, and in this way the image greeted the worshippers with its voice. Thus by sounding and giving voice it is not of importance or interest on the strength of its shape, but because in its existence it is living, significant, and revealing, even if at the same time it indicates its meaning only symbolically.

What is true about the Memnon statues is true too about the sphinxes which I have discussed already in connection with their symbolic meaning. Sphinxes are found in Egypt not only in enormous numbers but of the most stupendous size. One of the most famous of them is the one standing near the group of pyramids at Cairo. It is 148 feet long, the height from the claws to the head is 65 feet, the feet extended in front are 57 feet from the breast to the point of the claws, and the claws are 8 feet high. Yet this enormous mass has not first been hewn at all and then transported to the place it now occupies; on the contrary, excavation at its base has discovered that its foundation is limestone so that it became obvious that this immense work had been hewn from one rock of which it still only forms a part. In its most colossal proportions

[1] 17. i. 46.   [2] i. 42. 2.

it approaches sculpture proper more nearly; but all the same the sphinxes were set alongside one another in avenues, and this at once gives them a completely architectural character.

(c) *Egyptian Temples*

Now independent formations like these do not as a rule stand separate from one another but become multiplied to form huge temple-like buildings, labyrinths, and subterranean excavations, and are used *en masse*, surrounded by walls, etc.

In the first place, as regards the Egyptian temple-precincts, the fundamental character of this huge architecture has been made familiar to us recently principally by French scholars. It consists in the fact that they are open constructions, without roofing, gates, or passages between partitions, especially between porticos and whole forests of columns. There are works of enormous extent outside and variety inside. In their purely independent effect, without serving as a habitation and enclosure for a god or the worshipping community, they amaze us by their colossal proportions and mass, while at the same time their individual forms and shapes engross our whole interest by themselves because they have been erected as symbols for purely universal meanings or are even substitutes for books since they manifest the meanings not by their mode of configuration but by writings, hieroglyphics, engraved on their surface. In a way these gigantic buildings might be called a collection of sculptures, yet they generally occur in such a number and such repetition of one and the same shape that they become rows and thereby only in this ordering in rows acquire their architectural character, but then this ordering becomes an end in itself again and is not at all just a support for architraves and roofs.

The larger buildings of this kind start with a stone-paved avenue a hundred feet wide, Strabo says,[1] and three or four times as long. On either side of this walk (δρόμος) there stand sphinxes in rows of fifty to a hundred, twenty to thirty feet high. Then follows a huge ceremonial entrance (πρόπυλον), narrower above than below, with pylons, and pillars of prodigious size, ten to twenty times higher than a man, some of them standing free and independently, others grouped in walls or as magnificent jambs; these, being likewise broader at the base than above, rise in a slant,

---

[1] The first two-and-a-half sentences of this description are from 17. i. 28.

freely, and independently to the height of fifty or sixty feet; they are unconnected with transverse walls and carry no beams and so do not form a house. On the contrary, their distinction from perpendicular walls which hint at the purpose of carrying beams shows that they belong to independent architecture. Here and there Memnons lean against the sloping walls which also form galleries and are bedecked all over with hieroglyphics or enormous pictures in stone so that they appeared to the French scholars who saw them recently as if they were printed calico. They can be regarded like the pages of a book which by this spatial limitation arouse in mind and heart, as the notes of a bell do, vague astonishment, meditation, and thought. Doors follow one another at frequent intervals, and they alternate with rows of sphinxes; or we see an open square surrounded by the main wall, with pillared galleries leading to these walls. Next comes a covered square which does not serve as a dwelling but is a forest of columns; the columns do not support a vault but only flagstones. After these sphinx-avenues, rows of columns, partitions with a surfeit of hieroglyphics, after a portico with wings in front of which obelisks and couching lions have been erected, or again only after forecourts or surrounded by narrower passages, the whole thing ends with the temple proper, the shrine (σηκός), of massive proportions, according to Strabo,[1] which has in it either an image of the god or only an animal statue. This shrine for the god was now and again a monolith, as, e.g., Herodotus (ii. 155) relates of the temple at Buto that 'it was constructed from one stone, equal in height and length, each wall being forty cubits square, and its roof was again one stone projecting four cubits over the eaves'. But in general the shrines are so small that there was no room for a congregation; but a temple requires a congregation or otherwise it is only a box, a treasury, a receptacle for keeping sacred images, etc.

In this way such buildings go on indefinitely with rows of animal shapes, Memnons, immense gates, walls, colonnades of the most stupendous dimensions, now wider, now narrower, with individual obelisks, etc. We can wander about amid such huge and astonishing human works which in part have only a more restricted purpose in the different acts of worship and we can leave these towered masses of stone to utter and reveal what they like of the nature of the

[1] 17. i. 28. But what Strabo says is that there is no statue in the form of a human figure but only of an animal one.

III. I. ARCHITECTURE

Divine. For when these buildings are looked at more closely, symbolical meanings are clearly interwoven with them throughout, so that the number of the sphinxes and Memnons and the position of the pillars and the passages, are related to the days of the year, the twelve signs of the zodiac, the seven planets, the chief phases of the moon, and so on. Here sculpture has not worked itself free from architecture; while on the other hand really architectonic features, proportion, distances, number of columns, walls, storeys, etc. are so treated that these relations do not have their proper purpose in themselves, in their symmetry, rhythm,[1] and beauty, but are determined symbolically. For this reason this building and constructing is seen to be an end in itself, as itself a cult in which King and people are united. Many works like canals, Lake Moeris,[2] waterworks in general, are related to agriculture and the inundations of the Nile. For example, Sesostris, according to Herodotus (ii. 108), had the whole country, hitherto used by horses and carriages, cut up by canals for the sake of a water-supply and thereby made horses and carriages useless. But the chief works are still those religious buildings which the Egyptians piled up on high in the same instinctive way in which bees build their cells. Their property was regulated,[3] their other concerns likewise, the soil was infinitely fertile and needed no laborious cultivation, so that work consisted almost wholly in sowing and reaping. Few of the interests and occupations engrossing other peoples occur here, and apart from priestly stories about the maritime undertakings of Sesostris [Herodotus, ii. 102], there are no reports of sea voyages. On the whole the Egyptians were restricted to this building and constructing in their own country. But the independent or symbolic architecture affords the fundamental type for their colossal works, because here the inner and spiritual life of man has not yet apprehended itself in its aims and external formations or made itself the object and product of its free activity. Self-consciousness has not yet come to fruition, is not yet explicitly complete; it pushes on, seeks, divines, and produces on and on

---

[1] i.e. 'Eurhythmy, a suitable display of details in their context. The details must be of a height suitable to their breadth, and everything is symmetrical' (Vitruvius, i. 2. iii). The meaning of these terms in Vitruvius is discussed in E. Panofsky, op. cit., pp. 96–7.

[2] Herodotus, ii. 149.

[3] By Sesostris who assigned square plots of land, equal in size, to all Egyptians (Herodotus, ii. 109).

INDEPENDENT OR SYMBOLIC ARCHITECTURE 647

without attaining absolute satisfaction and therefore without repose. For only in the shape adequate to spirit is spirit in its completeness satisfied and then only does it impose limits on its productive activity; whereas the symbolic work of art is always more or less limitless.

In the same category with such productions of Egyptian architecture are the so-called labyrinths—courts with avenues of columns round which are passages enigmatically interwoven between walls; yet their twistings and turnings are not designed for the silly problem of finding the way out, but for an intelligent wandering amongst symbolic riddles. For the course of these passages, as I have indicated already, is intended to imitate and picture the course of the heavenly bodies. Some of these labyrinths are built above ground, others below; apart from paths, they are equipped with enormous rooms and halls, the partitions of which are covered with hieroglyphics. The largest labyrinth which Herodotus saw himself (ii. 148), was the one in the neighbourhood of Lake Moeris. He found it beyond description and surpassing even the pyramids. He ascribes its construction to twelve Kings, and sketches it in the following way. The entire building, surrounded by a single wall, consisted of two storeys, one above ground and the other below. Altogether they contained 3,000 rooms, 1,500 in each storey. The upper storey, the only one that Herodotus was allowed to examine, was divided into twelve courts beside one another, with gates opposite to one another, six facing north and six south. Each court was surrounded by a colonnade built of white stones closely fitted together. Herodotus goes on to say that from courts he went into chambers, out of these into halls, out of these into other rooms, and again from these into courts. Hirt (op. cit., i. 75) thinks that Herodotus makes this last remark only to make it clearer that the chambers open directly on to the courts. Of the paths in the labyrinth Herodotus says that the numerous paths through the decorated rooms and the varied windings of the paths across the courts filled him with infinite amazement. Pliny (*Nat. Hist.* xxxvi. 19) describes these paths as dark and, for a stranger, exhausting in their windings, and he says that when the doors are opened there is a noise like thunder; and it is clear too from Strabo [17. i. 37], who is important as an eyewitness like Herodotus, that the labyrinthine passages encircled the spaces formed by the courts. It was principally the Egyptians who built

648   III. I. ARCHITECTURE

labyrinths like this, but a similar, though smaller, one, an imitation of the Egyptian, occurs in Crete, and also in Morea and Malta.[1]

But this architecture by its chambers and halls is already approaching something like a house, while, on the other hand, according to what Herodotus reports, the subterranean part of the labyrinth, which he was not allowed to enter, was designed for the graves of the builders and the sacred crocodiles. Here, therefore, it is only the labyrinthine paths which have a really independent symbolical meaning. Consequently we may find in these works a transition to the form of symbolic architecture, which of itself already begins to approach the classical form.

3. *Transition from Independent to Classical Architecture*

However astonishing the buildings are which we have just considered, the *subterranean* architecture of the Indians and Egyptians, which is common in many ways to eastern peoples, must seem to us to be even more prodigious and wonderful. Whatever great and excellent structures we find built on the surface, they cannot compare with what exists below the soil in India, in Salsette (an island off Bombay) and Ellora, and in upper Egypt and Nubia. In these marvellous excavations there is obvious first of all the immediate need for an enclosure. People looked for protection in caves and lived there, and whole tribes had no other dwelling; and this arose from imperious necessity. Cave dwellings of this kind existed in the mountains of Judea, where there were thousands in many storeys. So too in the Harz mountains, near Goslar, in Rammelsberg there were rooms into which people crept and where they took refuge with their goods.

(a) *Indian and Egyptian Subterranean Buildings*

But the Indian and Egyptian subterranean buildings that have been mentioned are quite different from these. They served as places of assembly, as subterranean cathedrals, and are constructions built for religious wonder and spiritual assembly, with arrangements and indications of a symbolical kind, colonnades,

---

[1] Crete: Since the labyrinth there had not been excavated in Hegel's day, he is simply assuming the truth of the familiar Greek story of Theseus and Ariadne. Morea: The reference is probably to the ruins of the sanctuary at Epidaurus. Malta: The reference is probably to the impressive megalithic structures on the island of Gozo. No labyrinth was discovered in Malta until 1915.

sphinxes, Memnons, elephants, colossal idols, hewn from the rock and left growing out of the unworked mass of the stone, just as the columns were left in these excavations. At the front of the wall of rock these buildings were entirely opened here and there, others were partly dark and lit only by torches, partly perhaps with an opening above.

In comparison with the buildings on the surface such excavations seem to be earlier, so that the enormous erections above ground may be regarded as imitations and above-ground blossomings of the subterranean. For in excavations there is no question of positive building but rather of the removal of a negative. To make a nest in the ground, or to burrow, is more natural than to dig up the ground, look for material and then pile it up together and give shape to it. In this matter we may picture caves as arising earlier than huts. Caves are an expansion rather than a limitation, or an expansion which becomes a limitation and an enclosure, in which case the enclosure is there already. Therefore subterranean building begins rather with what is present already, and, since it leaves the main mass alone as it is, is not erected yet with the freedom inherent in construction above ground. But for us, however symbolical these buildings may also be, they already belong to a further sphere because they are no longer so independently symbolical; they have the purpose of enclosing, providing walls and roofs within which the more symbolical productions are set up as such. Something like a temple or a house, in the Greek and more modern sense, is visible here in its most natural form.

Further, the Mithras caves are to be included in this category although they are found in a totally different locality. The worship and service of Mithras was native to Persia but a similar cult was propagated in the Roman Empire too. In the Louvre in Paris, for instance, there is a very famous bas-relief depicting a youth plunging a dagger into a bull's neck; it was found on the Capitol in a deep grotto underneath the temple of Jupiter. In these Mithras caves too there were vaultings and passages which seem to have been devised to hint symbolically at the course of the stars or (as happens still today in Masonic Lodges where you are led along many passages, must see many sights, etc.) at the ways the soul has to traverse during its purification, even if this meaning is better expressed in sculptures and work of other kinds than it is where architecture has been made the chief thing.

In a similar connection we may mention also the Roman catacombs, the original intention of which was certainly not that of serving as aqueducts, graves, or sewers.

(b) *Housing for the Dead, Pyramids, etc.*

Secondly, a more specific transition from the independent architecture to the one that serves some end beyond itself may be sought in those buildings which are erected as mausoleums, whether subterranean or on the surface.

Especially among the Egyptians, building works whether below or above ground are linked with a realm of the dead, as in general a realm of the invisible makes its home and occurs in Egypt for the first time. The Indians burn their dead or let their bones lie and rot on the ground; according to Indian conceptions, men are or become god or gods (express it as you like), and this firm distinction between the living and the dead as such is not reached by the Indians. On this account, in cases where Mohammedanism is not to be credited with the origin of Indian buildings, they are not habitations for the dead and they seem on the whole, like the enormous excavations mentioned above, to belong to an earlier period. But in the case of the Egyptians the opposition between the living and the dead is strongly emphasized; the spiritual begins in itself to be separated from the non-spiritual. It is the rise of the individual concrete spirit which is beginning. The dead are therefore preserved as something individual and in this way are fortified and preserved against the idea of absorption into nature, i.e. against dissolution, against being swept away by a universal tide. Individuality is the principle underlying the independent idea of spiritual life, because the sprit can exist only as individual and personal. Consequently the honouring and preservation of the dead must count for us as the first important constituent in the existence of spiritual individuality, because here, instead of being sacrificed, individuality appears as preserved, inasmuch as the body, at any rate, as this natural and immediate individuality, is treasured and respected. As was mentioned earlier, Herodotus reports [ii. 123] that the Egyptians were the first to say that the souls of men were immortal. However imperfect the preservation of spiritual individuality is when it is maintained that the deceased has for 3,000 years to go through the whole series of animals inhabiting land, water, and air, and only thereafter migrate into a human body again, still there is implicit in this idea and in the embalming of the body a firm hold on corporeal individuality and an independent existence separated from the body.[1]

Thus after all it is of importance for architecture that here there ensues the separation out, as it were, of the spiritual as the inner meaning which is portrayed on its own account, while the corporeal shell is placed round it as a purely architectural enclosure. In this sense the Egyptian mausoleums form the earliest temples; the essential thing, the centre of worship, is a person, an objective individual who appears significant on his own account and expresses himself in distinction from his habitation which thus is constructed as a purely serviceable shell. And indeed it is not an actual man for whose needs a house or a palace is constructed; on the contrary, it is the dead, who have no needs, e.g. Kings and sacred animals, around whom enormous constructions are built as an enclosure.

Just as agriculture ends the roving of nomads and gives them secure property in fixed sites, so cemeteries, tombstones, and the cult of the dead unite men and give to those who otherwise have no fixed abode, no determinate property, a rallying point and sacred places which they defend and from which they are not willingly torn. So, for example, as Herodotus tells (iv.[2] 126–7), the Scythians, this nomadic people, retreated everywhere before Darius. Darius sent a message to their King: 'If the King deems himself strong enough to make resistance, let him prepare for battle. Otherwise let him recognize Darius as his lord and master.' To this message Idanthyrsus [the Scythian King] replied:

We have neither towns nor cultivated lands and have nothing to defend, for there are none that Darius can devastate. But if Darius is concerned to have a battle, we have the tombs of our fathers and if Darius seeks them out and ventures to meddle with them, then he will see whether or no we would fight for the tombs.

The oldest grandiose mausoleums we find in Egypt in the shape of the pyramids. What at the first sight of these amazing constructions

---

[1] i.e. embalming implies the individuality of the deceased's *body*, while transmigration through other forms implies the continuity of *spiritual* existence distinct from those particular forms.

[2] Not ii, as all editions read.

may arouse our wonder is their colossal size which at once prompts reflection on the length of time and the variety, abundance, and persistence of human powers required for the completion of such immense buildings. In their form, however, they present nothing else to arrest our attention; the whole thing is surveyed and grasped in a few minutes. In regard to the simplicity and regularity of their shape there has long been a dispute about their purpose. The Greeks, e.g. Herodotus [ii. 148] and Strabo[1], long ago adduced the purpose that they actually subserved, but, even so, travellers and writers, old and new, have excogitated on this subject a great deal that is fabulous and untenable. The Arabs tried to force a way in because they hoped to find treasures inside the pyramids, but instead of achieving their aim these breaches in the structure only destroyed a great deal without reaching the actual passages and chambers. Modern Europeans amongst whom Belzoni of Rome and, later, Caviglia of Genoa[2] are especially outstanding, have at last succeeded in becoming acquainted with the interior of the pyramids with more precision. Belzoni uncovered the king's grave in the pyramid of Chephren. The entrances to the pyramids were closed most securely with ashlar masonry, and the Egyptians tried in the course of building so to arrange matters that the entrance, even if known to exist, could be rediscovered and opened only with great difficulty.[3] This proves that the pyramids were to remain closed and not to be used again. Within them chambers have been found as well as passages (indicating the ways which the soul traverses after death in its circulation through its changes of shape), great halls, and subterranean ducts which sometimes rose, sometimes descended. The king's grave discovered by Belzoni, for instance, runs in this way, hewn in the rock for a distance of a league. In the principal hall there stood a sarcophagus of granite, sunk into the ground, but all that was found in it was the remains of the bones of a mummified animal, an Apis

---

[1] 'The tombs of Kings', 17. i. 33.

[2] G. B. Belzoni, 1778–1823: *Narrative . . . of recent Discoveries in Egypt and Nubia* (London, 1820). G. B. Caviglia (1770–1845) was the Genoese master and owner of a merchantman which, with Malta as a base, sailed the Mediterranean under the British flag. He started his work on the pyramids in 1816. He does not seem to have published any book himself, but his explorations were well known to archaeologists. Belzoni mentions him in his *Narrative*.

[3] According to Strabo (loc. cit.) the entrance was halfway up the pyramid, not at ground level. It was a movable stone so tightly fitted that it could be found only with difficulty, even if it were known to exist.

INDEPENDENT OR SYMBOLIC ARCHITECTURE 653

probably. But the whole structure manifestly and undoubtedly had the purpose of serving as a house for the dead.

In age, size, and shape the pyramids differ. The oldest appear to be only stones piled upon one another to form something like a pyramid; the later ones are constructed regularly; some are flattened to some extent on top, others rise steadily to a point. On others there are steps, explicable, according to Herodotus' description of the pyramid of Cheops (ii. 125), by the Egyptian procedure in the building of such works. For this reason Hirt (op. cit., i. 55) includes this pyramid amongst those unfinished.[1] According to the latest French reports, the chambers and passages were more intricate in the older pyramids, simpler in the later ones, but entirely covered with hieroglyphics so that to transcribe these completely would take several years.

In this way the pyramids though astonishing in themselves are just simple crystals, shells enclosing a kernel, a departed spirit, and serve to preserve its enduring body and form. Therefore in this deceased person, thus acquiring presentation on his own account, the entire meaning is concentrated; but architecture, which previously had its meaning independently in itself as architecture, now becomes separated from the meaning and, in this cleavage, subservient to something else; while sculpture acquires the task of giving form to what is strictly inner, although at first the individual creation is retained in its own immediate natural shape as a mummy. Therefore, in considering Egyptian architecture as a whole, we find independent symbolic buildings on the one hand, and yet, on the other hand, especially in everything relating to mausoleums, there comes clearly to the front the special purpose of architecture, namely to furnish an enclosure merely. This essentially implies that architecture does not merely excavate and form caves but is manifest as an inorganic nature built by human hands where necessary for achieving a human aim.

Other peoples too have erected similar memorials to the dead, sacred buildings as dwellings for a dead body over which they are raised. The tomb of Mausolus in Caria, for example, and, later,

[1] 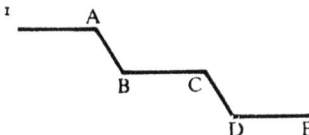 The triangular spaces ABC and CDE were afterwards filled in to give the side of the pyramid a continuous smooth surface from A to E. Hence when the steps remain, this may be a sign that the work was unfinished.

Hadrian's tomb (now the castle of San Angelo in Rome), a palace carefully constructed for a grave, were famous works even in antiquity. In the same category, according to Uhden (Wolff and Buttmann: *Museum* i. 536), are memorials (of a sort) to the dead which in their arrangement and surroundings imitated on a smaller scale temples dedicated to the gods. A temple of this kind had a garden, an arbour, a spring, a vineyard, and then chapels in which portrait-statues in the shape of gods were erected. It was especially under the [Roman] Empire that such memorials were built, with statues of the deceased in the form of divinities like Apollo, Venus, and Minerva. These figures, and the whole construction, therefore acquired at the same period the meaning of an apotheosis and a temple of the deceased,[1] just as in Egypt the embalming, the emblems, and the sarcophagus indicated that the deceased had become Osiris.

Nevertheless the simplest but grandiose constructions of this sort are the Egyptian pyramids. Here there enters the line proper and essential to architecture, the straight one, and, in general, regularity and abstract [i.e. geometrical] forms. For architecture as a mere enclosure and as inorganic nature (nature not in itself individualized and animated by its indwelling spirit) can be shaped only in a way external to itself, though the external form is not organic but abstract and mathematical. But however far the pyramid already begins to have the purpose of a house, still the right-angle is not dominant everywhere, as it is in a house proper; on the contrary, the pyramid has a character of its own which is not subservient to any mere purpose, and which therefore is self-enclosed in a line running directly and gradually from the base to the apex.

(c) *Transition to Architecture in the Service of Some Purpose*

From this point we can make the transition from independent architecture to architecture proper, the kind that is subservient to some purpose.

To the latter, two points of departure are available, one is symbolic architecture, the other is need and the appropriateness

---

[1] Hegel's description is drawn entirely from the article which he quotes, namely *Das Grab der Claudia Semne* by W. Uhden. The memorial in question was discovered near the Appian Way, not far from Rome, in 1792. It was probably constructed in Trajan's reign.

of means to satisfy it. In the case of symbolic formations, as we have noticed in considering them previously, an architectural purpose is purely an accessory and only a matter of external arrangement. The extreme opposite of this is the house, where elementary need demands a house with wooden columns or perpendicular walls with beams set over them at right angles, and a roof. There is no question but that the need for this strict appropriateness arises automatically; but the essential point in question is whether architecture proper, in the sense in which we are about to consider it in its classical form, begins from need only or whether it is to be derived from those independent and symbolic works which led us by themselves to buildings serving a purpose.

(a) Need introduces into architecture forms which are wholly and entirely purposeful and belong to the [mathematical] intellect, viz. the straight line, the right angle, level surfaces. For when architecture serves a purpose, the real purpose is there independently as a statue or, more particularly, as human individuals assembled as a community or nation for ends which are universal, i.e. religious or political, and which do not now issue from the satisfaction of physical needs. In particular, the primary need is to frame an enclosure for the image or statue of the gods, or generally for something sacred which is presented on its own account and actually available. Memnons, for instance, sphinxes, etc. stand in open spaces or in a grove; nature is their external environment. But such productions, and still more the humanly shaped figures of the gods, are derived from a sphere other than that of nature in its immediacy; they belong to the realm of imagery and are called into being by human artistic activity. Consequently a purely natural environment is insufficient for them. On the contrary, for what is outside them they require a ground and an enclosure which has the same origin as themselves, i.e. which is likewise the product of imagination and has been formed by artistic activity. Only in surroundings produced by art do the gods find their appropriate element. But in that case this external frame does not now have its end in itself; it serves an essential end other than its own and therefore falls subject to the rule of purposiveness.

But if these primarily purely useful forms are to rise to beauty, they must not remain at their original abstractness but must go beyond symmetry and eurhythmy to the organic, the concrete, the varied, and the self-complete. But in that event there enters as it were a reflection on differences and characteristics, as well as an express emphasis on and formation of aspects which for pure purposiveness is wholly superfluous. A beam, for example, in one aspect goes on in a straight line, but at the same time it stops at both ends; similarly a stanchion, which has to carry a beam or a roof, stands on the ground and terminates where the beam rests on it. Useful architecture displays differences of this kind and shapes them artistically, whereas an organic production, like a plant or a man, of course has its above and below but from the very beginning it is formed organically and therefore has the distinctions of foot and head, or, in the plant, of root and corolla.

(β) Symbolic architecture, conversely, takes its starting-point more or less from such organic formations, as in sphinxes, Memnons, etc. Yet it cannot altogether get rid of straight lines and regular intervals in walls, gates, beams, obelisks, etc., and when it intends to set up these sculptural colossi in something of an architectural way, and in rows beside one another, it must have recourse to equality of size and of distances from one another, to a rectilinear arrangement of the rows, and in general to the order and regularity of architecture proper. Thus it has in itself both the principles unified in the architecture which is at once useful and beautiful, though in symbolic architecture these are not built into one but still lie outside one another.

(γ) Therefore we may so conceive the transition that on the one hand the previously independent architecture must modify organic forms mathematically into regularity, and pass over to purposiveness, while conversely mere purposiveness of form has to move towards the principle of the organic. Where these two extremes meet and mutually interpenetrate, really beautiful classical architecture is born.

Now this unification can be clearly recognized, as it were in its real origin, in the initial transformation of what we have already seen in the architecture previously considered, i.e. of columns. Walls are of course necessary for an enclosure. But as has been shown in examples already, walls can also stand independently without completely forming an enclosure, for which a roof above is essential and not merely an enclosure of side-spaces. But such a roof must be carried. The simplest means for this consists of columns, the essential and also strict function of which in this

INDEPENDENT OR SYMBOLIC ARCHITECTURE 657

connection is to be load-bearing. For this reason, when it is a mere matter of load-bearing, walls are strictly a superfluity. For load-bearing is a mechanical relation and belongs to the province of gravity and its laws. Now here the gravity or weight of a body is concentrated at its centre of gravity; it is to be supported at this centre so that it rests level without falling. This support is what the column provides so that by it the force of support appears reduced to the minimum of external means. What a wall does at huge cost a few columns achieve, and it is a great beauty in classical architecture not to erect more columns than are necessary in fact for carrying the load of beams and what rests on them. In architecture proper there is no true beauty in columns used for adornment merely. For this reason too a column set up independently by itself does not fulfil its function. It is true that triumphal columns have been erected, e.g. the famous ones of Trajan and Napoleon, but these are as it were only a pedestal for a statue, clad in addition with carvings to commemorate and celebrate the hero whose statue the column carries.

It is especially remarkable how, in the course of architectural development, the column has to tear itself away from a concrete natural shape in order to attain a shape that is more abstract but alike purposeful and beautiful.

($\alpha\alpha$) Since independent architecture begins from organic formations it can seize on human figures; as in Egypt, for instance, use is made of figures still partly human, Memnons e.g., for columns. But this is a purely superfluous use of these figures because their real purpose is not load-carrying. In a different way caryatids occur in Greece; they serve the end of supporting beams in a more rigorous way, but they can only be used in small structures. Besides we must regard it as a misuse of the human form to compress it under such a load and thus the caryatids after all have this character of being pressed down, and their costume indicates the slavery which is burdened with the carrying of such burdens.

($\beta\beta$) The more natural organic form for stanchions and pillars that are to be load-bearing is therefore the tree or, in general, a plant, a trunk, a slender stem rising perpendicularly. The tree trunk naturally carries its corolla, the blade the ear, the stem the flower. These forms are drawn directly from nature by Egyptian architecture which has not yet gained freedom to formulate its intentions abstractly. In this respect the grandiose style of the

Egyptian palaces or temples, the colossal character of rows of columns and their vast number, and, in short, the gigantic proportions of the whole, have in all ages excited the astonishment and admiration of spectators. We see columns originating in the greatest variety from plant-formations; lotus plants and others are stretched up and lengthened into columns. In the colonnades, for example, all the columns do not have the same form; the form changes once, twice, or thrice. In his work on his Egyptian expedition, Denon[1] has assembled a great number of such forms. The whole column is not mathematically regular in form, because the pedestal is onion-shaped, the leaf rises from the bulb like a reed, or in other cases there is a cluster of radical leaves, as in various plants. Then out of this pedestal the slender stem rises up or mounts up, intricately interwoven, as a column. The capital again is a flower-like separation of leaves and branches. Yet the imitation is not true to nature; on the contrary; the plant-forms are distorted architecturally, brought nearer to the circle, the straight line, and what is mathematically regular. The result is that these columns in their entirety are like what are generally called arabesques.

(γγ) This then is the place to discuss the arabesque in general because it falls by its very conception into the transition out of a natural organic form used by architecture to the more severe regularity of architecture proper. But when architecture freely fulfils its purpose it degrades arabesques to a decoration and ornament. In that case they are principally distorted plant-forms and animal and human forms growing out of plants and intermingled with them, or animal shapes passing over into plants. If they are to shelter a symbolic meaning, then the transition from one natural kingdom to another may pass for it; without such a significance they are only plays of imagination in its assembly, connection, and ramification of different natural formations. In the invention of such architectural decoration imagination may indulge in the most varied friezes of every kind, in wood, stone, etc., and in borders even on furniture and clothing, and the chief characteristic and basic form of this decoration is that plants, leaves, flowers, and animals are brought nearer to the inorganic and geometrical. For this reason we often find that arabesques have become stiff and untrue to the organic, and therefore they are often criticized and art

[1] D. V., Baron Denon, 1747–1825: *Voyage dans la basse et la haute Égypte* (Paris, 1802).

is reproached for making use of them. Painting especially is so reproached, although Raphael himself ventured to paint arabesques on a large scale and with extreme grace, depth of spirit, variety, and charm. No doubt arabesques, whether in relation to organic forms or the laws of mechanics, run counter to nature, but this sort of contrariety is not only a right of art as such but is even a duty in architecture, since only by this means are the organic forms, otherwise unfit for architecture, adapted to and made harmonious with the truly architectural style. Nearest at hand for this adaptation is especially the plant kingdom which is used profusely for arabesques in the East too. The reason is that plants are not yet individuals who feel but they offer themselves in themselves for architectural purposes because they form protective roofing and shadow against rain, sunshine, and wind, and on the whole lack the swinging of lines which is free from conformity to mathematical law. When used architecturally, their otherwise already regular leaves are regulated into more definite curves and straight lines, so that in this way everything that might be viewed as a distortion, an unnaturalness and stiffness in the plant-forms [used in arabesques] is essentially to be regarded as an appropriate transformation for strictly architectural purposes.

Thus in the column architecture proper leaves the purely organic to enter the sphere of geometrically ordered purposiveness and then out of this into an approach to the organic again. It has been necessary here to mention this double starting point of architecture from (*a*) real needs and (*b*) purposeless independence, because the truth is the unity of these two principles. The beautiful column arises from a form borrowed from nature which then is reshaped into a stanchion, into a regular and geometrical form.

Chapter II

CLASSICAL ARCHITECTURE

When architecture acquires the place belonging to it in accordance with its own essential nature, its productions are subservient to an end and a meaning not immanent in itself. It becomes an inorganic surrounding structure, a whole built and ordered according to the laws of gravity. The forms of this whole are subject to what is severely regular, rectilinear, right-angled, circular, to relations depending on specific number and quantity, to inherently limited proportions and fixed conformity to law. The beauty of classical architecture consists precisely in this appropriateness to purpose which is freed from immediate confusion with the organic, the spiritual, and the symbolic; although it subserves a purpose, it comprises a perfect totality in itself which makes its one purpose shine clearly through all its forms, and in the music of its proportions reshapes the purely useful into beauty. Architecture at this stage, however, does correspond with its real essential nature because it cannot entirely endow the spiritual with an adequate existence and therefore can only frame the external and spiritless into a reflection of the spiritual.

In considering this architecture which is alike beautiful and useful we will take the following route:

First, we have to settle its *general* nature and character in more detail;

Secondly, to cite the *particular* fundamental characteristics of the architectural forms arising from the purpose for which the classical work of art was built;

Thirdly, we may cast a glance at the actual and concrete developments achieved by classical architecture.

In none of these sections will I enter into detail but will confine myself wholly to the most general considerations, which are simpler here than they were in the case of symbolic architecture.

1. General Character of Classical Architecture

(a) Subservience to a Specific End

In line with what I have maintained more than once already, the fundamental character of architecture proper consists in the fact that the spiritual meaning does not reside exclusively in the building (for, if it did, the building would become an independent symbol of its inner meaning) but in the fact that this meaning has already attained its existence in freedom outside architecture. This existence may be of two kinds, namely whenever another more far-reaching art and, in the strictly classical sphere, sculpture especially, gives shape to this meaning and presents it independently, or when man contains in himself and gives practical proof of this meaning in a living way in his immediate actual life. Moreover, these two sides may meet. In other words, the eastern architecture of Babylonia, India, and Egypt either shaped symbolically into productions, valid in themselves, whatever counted to these nations as the Absolute and the truth, or surrounded what, despite death, remained of a man in his external natural form. Now, however, the spirit, either in its immediate living existence or by means of art, is *separated* from the building and independent of it, and architecture betakes itself to the service of this spirit which is its proper meaning and determining purpose. In this way this purpose now becomes what rules, what dominates the entire work, and determines its fundamental shape, its skeleton as it were; and neither physical materials nor the fancy and caprice of the architect are allowed to go their own way independently, as happens in symbolic architecture, or to develop, beyond utility, a superfluity of various parts and forms, as in romantic architecture.

(b) *The Building's Fitness for its Purpose*

The first question in the case of a building of this sort is about its purpose and function, as well as about the circumstances in which it is to be erected. The good sense and genius of the architect has to show itself in the complete fulfilment of a general task, namely to make his building fit the circumstances, to have regard to climate, position, the environing natural landscape, and, while attending to all these points and keeping the purpose of the building in view, to produce at the same time a freely co-ordinated and unified whole. In the case of the Greeks the principal architectural subjects were public buildings—temples, colonnades, and porticos for resting and strolling in during the day, and avenues like, for instance, the famous approach up to the Acropolis at Athens, whereas their private houses were very simple. In the case of the Romans, on the other hand, what is conspicuous is the luxury of private houses, especially villas, as well as the magnificence of imperial palaces, public baths, theatres, circuses, amphitheatres, aqueducts, fountains, etc. But in such buildings utility remains prevalent and dominant throughout so that there can be room for beauty only more or less as a decoration. In this sphere, therefore, the freest purpose is that of religion, i.e. the construction of a temple to be an enclosure for a person who himself belongs to fine art and is set up by sculpture as a statue of the god.

(c) The House as the Fundamental Type

In virtue of these purposes, architecture proper seems to be freer than it was at the previous stage, the symbolic, which adopted organic forms from nature; freer indeed than sculpture which, compelled to adopt the human form that is there already, is bound down to it and its given general proportions. Classical architecture, on the other hand, devises the substance of its plan and figuration in the light of spiritual purposes, while its shape is the product of the human intellect and has no direct model. This greater freedom is to be admitted to some extent, but its scope remains restricted, and the classical treatment of architecture is on the whole abstract and dry because of the intellectual [i.e. mathematical] character of its forms. Friedrich von Schlegel[1] has called architecture 'frozen music', and indeed the two arts do rest on a harmony of relations which can be reduced to numbers and for this reason can easily be grasped in their fundamental characters. The house, as has been said, provides the chief determinant [in architecture] for these characters and their simple relations whether these be severe and large-scaled or more graceful

---

[1] 'Schlegel' seems to be a mistake for 'Schelling' who in his lectures on the Philosophy of Art, § 117, described architecture as *erstarrte* music. Hegel's word is *gefrorene* and this is the one that generally occurs in quotations of this familiar aphorism. So far as I can discover, it is nowhere else ascribed to Schlegel. It is possible, however, that Schlegel did say this in conversation at Jena and that he was overheard by both Schelling and Hegel.

and elegant: walls, pillars, beams, assembled in wholly mathematical and crystalline forms. Now what these relations are cannot be reduced to settlement by numerical proportions with perfect precision. For, e.g., an oblong with right angles is more pleasing than a square because in the equality of an oblong there is inequality too. If the breadth is half the length we have a pleasing proportion, whereas something long and thin is unpleasing. But in that case the mechanical relation between what bears and what is borne must be maintained in its genuine proportion and law; e.g. a heavy beam should not rest on thin and graceful columns, nor, conversely, should great carrying structures be erected to carry in the end something quite light. In all these matters, in the relation of the breadth to the length and height of the building, of the height of columns to their diameter, in the intervals and number of columns, in the sort of variety or simplicity in decoration, in the size of the numerous cornices, friezes, etc., there dominated in classical times a secret eurhythmy, discovered above all by the just sense of the Greeks. The Greeks did deviate from this in individual instances here and there, but on the whole they had to abide by these fundamental relationships in order to remain within the bounds of beauty.

2. *The Particular Determinants of the Architectural Forms*

(a) *Building in Wood and Stone*

It has already been mentioned earlier that there has been a long dispute about whether what was original was building in wood or in stone, and whether architectural forms derived from this difference. In architecture proper it is purpose that dominates, and the fundamental type of the house is developed into beauty, and for this reason wooden construction may be assumed to be the earlier.

This Hirt assumed, following Vitruvius [ii. 1–4], and he has often been criticized. My own view on this disputed question I will state briefly. The usual way of proceeding is to find an abstract and simple law for some concrete existent thing which is taken for granted. In this sense Hirt looks for a basic model for Greek buildings, as it were for the theory of them, their anatomical structure, and he finds it, its form and corresponding material, in the house and in building in wood. Now of course a house as such is built principally as a dwelling, as a protection against wind, rain, weather, animals, and men, and it requires a complete enclosure where a family or a larger community can assemble, shut in by themselves, and pursue their needs and concerns in this seclusion. A house is an entirely purposeful structure, produced by men for human purposes. So the builder has many aims and concerns in the course of his work. In detail the frame, in order to be supported and stable, has to connect various joints and thrusts together in line with mechanical principles, and observe the conditions imposed by weight and the need for stabilizing the structure, closing it, supporting its upper parts, and, in general, not merely carrying these but keeping the horizontal horizontal and binding the structure together at recesses and corners. Now a house does demand a total enclosure for which walls are the most serviceable and safest means, and from this point of view building in stone seems to be more appropriate, but a sort of wall can equally well be constructed from stanchions set alongside one another on which beams rest and these at the same time bind together and secure the perpendicular stanchions by which they are supported and carried. Finally, on top of these is the ceiling and the roof. Apart from all this the chief point in the temple, god's house, on which everything turns is not the enclosure but the carrying beams and what they carry. For this mechanical matter building in wood proves to be the first and the most appropriate to nature. For here the basic determinants are (i) the stanchion as load-bearing, and (ii) the cross-beams which provide the simultaneously necessary binding of stanchions together. But (*a*) this separation of the stanchions and (*b*) the linking of them together, as well as the appropriate dovetailing of (*a*) and (*b*) is essentially akin to building in wood which finds its material directly in the tree. Without any need for extensive and difficult workmanship, the tree affords both stanchions and beams, because wood has already in itself a definite formation; it consists of separate linear pieces, more or less rectangular, which can be directly put together at right, acute, or obtuse angles, and so provide corner-columns, supports, cross-beams, and a roof. On the other hand, stone does not have from the start such a firmly specific shape, but, compared with a tree, is a formless mass which, for some purpose, must be split and worked on before the separate stones can be brought together and piled on one another, and before they can be built together into a unity again. Operations of many kinds are required before it can have the shape and utility that wood has in and by itself from the start. Apart from this, stone in huge blocks invites excavation rather, and, in general, being relatively formless at the start, it can be shaped in any and every way and therefore it affords manageable material not only for symbolic but also for romantic architecture and its more fantastic forms; whereas wood owing to its natural form with rectilinear stems is directly more serviceable for the severer purposiveness and mathematical proportions that are the basis of classical architecture. From this point of view, building in stone is especially predominant in independent architecture, although even in the case of the Egyptians, for example, in their colonnades overlaid with entablatures, needs arise which building in wood can satisfy more easily and basically. But, conversely, classical architecture does not stop at all at building in wood but proceeds on the contrary, where it develops into beauty, to build in stone, with the result that while in its architectural forms the original principle of building in wood is still always recognizable, specific characteristics nevertheless enter which are not inherent in building in wood as such.

(b) *The Specific Forms of the Temple*

As for the chief particular points concerning the house as the fundamental model for the temple, the most essential things to be mentioned here are limited in brief to what follows.

If we look more closely at a house and examine its mechanical proportions, we have, as was said above, on the one hand architecturally formed masses carrying a load, and, on the other, those being carried, both being bound together to give support and stability. To these is added, thirdly, the purpose of enclosing, and partitioning, in the three dimensions of length, breadth, and height. Now by being an interconnection of different specific characteristics, a construction is a concrete whole, and this it must display on itself. Thus essential differences arise here, and they have to appear both in their particularization and specific development and also in their being fitted together on intelligent [i.e. mathematical] principles.

(α) The first thing of importance in this connection affects load-bearing. As soon as load-bearing masses are mentioned, we generally think first, in view of our present-day needs, of a wall as the firmest and safest support. But, as we said already, a wall as such does not have supporting as its sole principle, for on the contrary it serves to enclose and connect and for this reason is a preponderating feature in romantic architecture. The peculiarity of Greek architecture is at once seen to consist in the fact that it gives shape to this supporting as such and therefore employs the column as the fundamental element in the purposiveness of architecture and its beauty.

(aa) The column has no other purpose but to be a support and, although a row of columns set up beside one another in a straight line marks a boundary, it does not enclose something as a solid wall or partition does but is moved in front of a proper wall and placed by itself independently. Where the aim is exclusively that of serving as a support, it is above all important that in relation to the load resting on it the column should have the look of being there for a purpose and therefore should be neither too weak nor too strong, should neither appear compressed nor rise so high and easily into the air as merely to look as if it were playing with its load.

($\beta\beta$) Just as the column is distinguished on one side from an enclosing wall and a partition, so on the other side it is distinguished from a mere stanchion. The stanchion is planted directly on the ground and ends just as directly where the load is placed on it. Therefore its specific length, its beginning and end seem as it were to be a negative limitation imposed by something else, or to be determined accidentally in a way not belonging to it on its own account. But beginning and ending are determinations implicit in the very nature of a column as a support and on this account must come into appearance on it as constituent features of its own. This is the reason why developed and beautiful architecture supplies the column with a pedestal and a capital. It is true that in the Tuscan Order[1] there is no pedestal so that the column rises directly from the ground; but in that case its length is something fortuitous for the eye; we do not know whether the column has been pressed so and so deeply into the ground by the weight of the mass supported. If the beginning of the column is not to seem vague and accidental, it must be given on purpose a foot on which it

[1] A good illustration of the Orders, and of the technical terms involved, taken from the *Oxford Illustrated Dictionary*, s.v. order, is reproduced here.

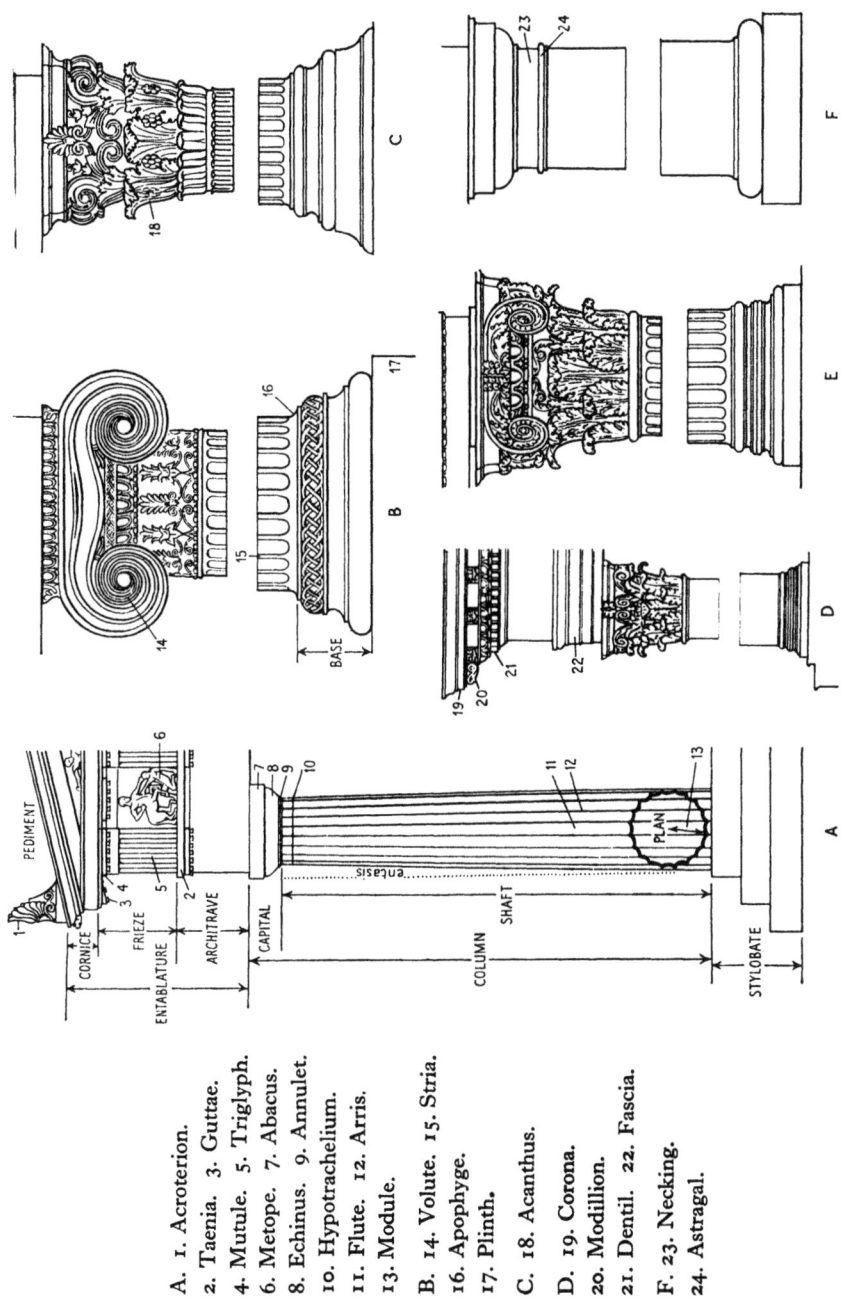

Orders of Architecture: A. Greek Doric. B. Greek Ionic. C. Greek Corinthian. D. Roman Corinthian. E. Composite. F. Tuscan.

A. 1. Acroterion.
2. Taenia. 3. Guttae.
4. Mutule. 5. Triglyph.
6. Metope. 7. Abacus.
8. Echinus. 9. Annulet.
10. Hypotrachelium.
11. Flute. 12. Arris.
13. Module.
B. 14. Volute. 15. Stria.
16. Apophyge.
17. Plinth.
C. 18. Acanthus.
D. 19. Corona.
20. Modillion.
21. Dentil. 22. Fascia.
F. 23. Necking.
24. Astragal.

stands and which expressly reveals the beginning to us as a beginning. By this means art intends, for one thing, to say to us: 'Here the column begins', and, for another thing, to bring to the notice of our eye the solidity and safety of the structure and, as it were, set our eye at rest in this respect. For the like reason art makes the column end with a capital which indicates the column's real purpose of load-bearing and also means: 'Here the column ends.' This reflection on the intentionally made beginning and end provides the really deeper reason for having a pedestal and a capital. It is as if, in music, there were a cadence without a firm conclusion, or if a book did not end with a full stop or begin without the emphasis of a capital letter. In the case of a book, however, especially in the Middle Ages, large decorative letters were introduced [at the beginning] and decorations at the end to give objectivity to the idea that there was a beginning and an end. Consequently, however far the existence of a pedestal and a capital is due to more than mere need, still we are not to regard them as a superfluous ornament, nor should we attempt to derive them from the example of Egyptian columns which still take the plant kingdom as their typical model. Organic products, as they are portrayed by sculpture in the shape of animals and men, have their beginning and end in their own free outlines, because it is the rational organism itself which settles the boundaries of its shape from within outwards. For the column and its shape, however, architecture has nothing but the mechanical determinant of load-bearing and the spatial distance from the ground to the point where the load to be carried terminates the column. But the particular aspects implicit in this determinant belong to the column, and art must bring them out and give shape to them. Consequently the column's specific length, its two boundaries above and below, and its carrying power should not appear to be only accidental and introduced into it by something else but must be displayed as also immanent in itself.

As for further details about the shape of the column beyond the pedestal and capital, the *first* point is that it is round, like a circle, because it is to stand freely, closed in on itself. But the circle is the simplest, firmly enclosed, intelligibly determinate, and most regular line. Therefore by its very shape the column proves that it is not intended, set up with others in a thick row, to form a flat surface in the way that stanchions, cut square and set alongside one another, make up walls and partitions, but that its sole purpose is, within its own self-limitation, to serve as a support. *Secondly*, in its ascent the shaft of the column tapers slightly, usually from a third of its height; it decreases in circumference and diameter because the lower parts have to carry the upper, and this mechanical relation between parts of the column must be made evident and perceptible. *Finally*, columns are usually fluted perpendicularly, partly to give variety to the simple shape in itself, partly, where this is necessary, to make them look wider owing to this division of the shaft.

(γγ) Now although a column is set up singly on its own account, it nevertheless has to show that it is not there for its own sake but for the weight it is to carry. Since a house needs to be bounded on every side, a single column is insufficient; others are placed alongside it and hence arises the essential requirement that columns be multiplied or form a row. Now if several columns support the same weight, this carrying a weight in common determines their common and equal height, and it is this weight, the beam, which binds them together. This leads us on from load-carrying as such to the opposite constituent, the load carried.

(β) What the columns carry is the entablature laid above them. The first feature arising in this connection is the right angle. The support must form a right angle alike with the ground and the entablature. For by the law of gravity, the horizontal position is the only one secure and adequate in itself, and the right angle is the only fixedly determinate one, while the acute and obtuse angles are indeterminate, variable, and contingent in their measurement.

The constituent parts of the entablature are organized in the following way:

(αα) On the columns of equal height set up beside one another in a straight line there immediately rests the architrave, the chief beam which binds the columns together and imposes on them a common burden. As a simple beam it requires for its shape only four level surfaces, put together at right-angles in all dimensions, and their abstract regularity. But although the architrave is carried by the columns, the rest of the entablature rests on it, so that it in turn is given the task of load-carrying. For this reason, architecture in its advance presented this double requirement on the main beam by indicating through projecting cornices, etc., the load-carrying function of its upper part. So regarded, the main beam, in other words, is related not only to the load-bearing columns but just as much to the other loads resting on it.

(ββ) These loads are first of all the frieze.[1] The band or frieze consists of (*a*) the ends of the roof-beams lying on the main beams and (*b*) the spaces between these. In this way the frieze contains more essential differences in itself than the architrave has and for this reason has to emphasize them in a more salient way, especially when architecture, though carrying out its work in stone, still follows more strictly the type of building in wood. This provides the difference between triglyph and metope. Triglyphs, that is to say, are the beam-ends which were cut thrice on the frieze, while metopes were the quadrangular spaces between the individual triglyphs. In the earliest times these spaces were probably left empty but later on they were filled, indeed overclad and adorned with bas-reliefs.[2]

(γγ) The frieze which rests on the main beam carries in turn the crest or cornice. This has the purpose of supporting the roofing which ends the structure at the top. At once the question arises about the sort of thing that this final boundary must be. For in this matter a double kind of boundary may occur, a right-angled horizontal one or one inclined at an acute or obtuse angle. If we look at requirements, it appears that southerners who have to suffer very little from rain or stormy winds need protection from the sun only, so that they can be satisfied with a horizontal and right-angled roof for a house. Whereas northerners have to protect themselves from rain which must be allowed to run off, and from snow which should not be allowed to become too heavy a load; consequently they need sloping roofs. Yet architecture as a fine art cannot settle the matter by requirements alone; as an art it has also to satisfy the deeper demands of beauty and attractiveness. What rises upwards from the ground must be presented to us with a base, a foot, on which it stands and which serves as a support; besides, the columns and walls of architecture proper give us materially the vision of load-carrying. Whereas the top, the roof, must no longer support a load but only be supported, and this character of *not* supporting must be visible on itself, i.e. it must be so constructed that it *cannot* now support anything and must

---

[1] The cornice rests on the frieze, the frieze on the architrave. All three form the entablature. See the illustration on p. 667, above.

[2] See the same illustration.

therefore terminate at an angle, whether acute or obtuse. Thus the classical temples have no horizontal roof, but roof surfaces meeting at an obtuse angle, and the termination of the building in this way is in conformity with beauty. For horizontal roofs do not give the impression of a completed whole, for a horizontal surface at the top can always carry something else, whereas this is not possible for the line in which sloping roof-sides meet. What satisfies us in this respect is the pyramidal form which is satisfying in painting too, e.g., in the grouping of its figures.

(γ) The final point for our consideration is enclosure, i.e. walls and partitions. Columns are indeed load-carrying and they do form a boundary, but they do not enclose anything; on the contrary, they are the precise opposite of an interior closed on all sides by walls. Therefore if such a complete enclosure is required, thick and solid walls must be constructed too. This is actually done in the building of temples.

(αα) About these walls there is nothing further to mention except that they must be set up straight and perpendicular to the ground, because walls rising at acute or obtuse angles give the eye the impression of impending collapse, and they have no once and for all settled direction because it may appear to be a matter of chance that they rise at this or that acute or obtuse angle and no other. Adaptation to a purpose and mathematical regularity alike demand a right-angle here once again.

(ββ) Walls can both enclose and support, while we restricted to columns the proper function of supporting only. Consequently this at once suggests the idea that, when the different needs of enclosure and support are both to be satisfied, columns could be set up and unified into walls by thick partitions, and this is the origin of half- [or embedded-] columns. So, for instance, Hirt, following Vitruvius [ii. 1. iv], begins his original construction with four corner-posts. Now if the necessity of an enclosure is to be satisfied, then of course, if columns are demanded at the same time, they must be embedded in the walls, and this can make clear too that half-columns are of very great antiquity. Hirt, e.g., says (*Architecture on Greek Principles* [Berlin, 1808] p. 111) that the use of half-columns is as old as architecture itself, and he derives their origin from the fact that columns and pillars supported and carried ceilings and roofs, but necessitated intervening partitions as a protection against the sun and bad weather. But, he continues, since the columns were already sufficient to support the building, it was unnecessary to make the partitions and walls as thick or of such solid material as the columns, and therefore the latter jutted out as a rule. This may provide a reason right enough for the origin of half-columns, but nevertheless half-columns are simply repugnant, because in them two different opposed purposes stand beside one another without any inner necessity and they are confused with one another. It is true that half-columns can be defended on the ground that even a column began so strictly from building in wood that it became the fundamental thing in the construction of an enclosure. But if walls are thick, the column has no sense any longer but is degraded to being a mere stanchion. For the real column is essentially round, finished in itself, and expresses precisely by this perfection that it is a contradiction to continue it with a view to making a level surface, and therefore a wall, out of it. Consequently, if supports are wanted in walls, they must be level, not round columns but flat things which can be prolonged to form a wall.

On these lines, in his early essay (1773) 'On German Architecture', Goethe passionately exclaims:

What is it to us, you expert with your up-to-date French philosophical ideas, that you[1] tell us that the first man, devising something for his needs, rammed four stakes into the ground, tied four sticks on top of them and covered them with branches and moss.... And in addition it is false too that your hut was the earliest in the world. Two sticks crossing one another at the top in front and two behind, with another transverse one as a coping, are and remain, as you can see any day in constructions for protecting crops and vines, a far more primitive invention, from which you cannot derive a principle even for your pig-sty.

In this way Goethe seeks to prove that, in buildings solely designed for protection, columns embedded in walls are senseless. It is not as if he intended to disparage the beauty of the column. On the contrary, he praises it highly and adds: 'Beware of using it inappropriately: its nature is to stand *freely*. Woe to those miserable characters who have hammered its slender build on to fat walls.'

---

[1] Eighteenth-century French scholars may have said this, but they were following Vitruvius, II. ii. 3–4.

Then he proceeds to properly medieval and contemporary architecture, and says:

A column is no constituent part of all of our habitations, rather does it contradict the essence of all our buildings. Our houses do not originate from four columns in four corners; they originate from four walls on four sides which stand instead of any columns, exclude all columns, and where columns are foisted on the walls they are a superfluous load-carrier. The same applies to our palaces and churches, with a few exceptions which I do not need to notice.

The correct principle of the column is expressed here in this statement produced by a free and factually appropriate insight. The column must have its foot in front of the wall and come forward independently of it. In modern architecture we do often have the use of pilasters,[1] but these have been regarded as a repeated shadow of earlier columns and have been made not round but flat.

(γγ) Hence it is clear that although walls can also carry, still, since the task of carrying is already borne by columns, they have, on their part, in developed classical architecture, to make enclosure their essential aim. If they carry, as columns do, then these different purposes [of enclosing and carrying] are not carried out as they should be by different parts, and our idea of what walls are supposed to do is murky and confused. For this reason we find even in temple-building that the central hall, where there stands the image of the god which it was the chief purpose of the temple to enclose, is often open overhead. But if a covering roof is needed, the higher claims of beauty require that it shall itself be carried independently [of walls]. For the direct placing of entablature and roof on the enclosing walls is only a matter of need and requirement, not of free architectural beauty, because in classical architecture no exterior or interior walls are needed as supports; rather would they be inappropriate, because, as we have seen earlier, they are arrangements and an expense beyond what is necessary for carrying the roof.

These are the chief points which have to arise in the particular characteristics of classical architecture.

[1] Flat half-columns.

(c) *The Classical Temple as a Whole*

While we may lay it down as a fundamental law that, on the one hand, the differences briefly indicated just above must come into appearance *as* differences, on the other hand it is equally necessary for them to be united into a whole. In conclusion we will cast a brief glance at this unification which in architecture cannot be more than a juxtaposition, and an association, and a thoroughgoing eurhythmy of proportion.

In general the Greek temples present us with an aspect which is satisfying, and, so to say, more than satisfying.

(α) There is no upward emphasis; the whole stretches out directly in breadth and width without rising. Confronted by it the eye scarcely needs to direct its glance upwards; on the contrary it is allured by the breadth, while the medieval German [i.e. Gothic] architecture almost struggles upwards immeasurably and lifts itself to the sky. With the Greeks the chief thing remains the breadth as a firm and convenient foundation on the ground, and the height is drawn rather from a man's height, but increased with the increased breadth and width of the building.

(β) Moreover, the ornamentation is so introduced that it does not impair the impression of simplicity. After all, a lot depends on the mode of ornamentation. The ancients, especially the Greeks, kept to the most beautiful proportions in this matter. Wholly simple lines and big surfaces, for example, appear in this undivided simplicity not so big as when some variety or interruption is introduced into them, with the result that the eye is only then presented with a more specific proportion. But if this division and its decoration is developed into minutiae, so that we have nothing in view except a multiplicity and its details, even the very greatest proportions and dimensions crumble and are destroyed. On the whole the Greeks did not labour by this means to make their buildings and their proportions seem just bigger than they were in fact, nor did they so divide the whole by interruptions and decorations that, because all the parts are small and a decisive unity bringing them all into a whole again is lacking, the whole too seems small likewise. Neither did their perfectly beautiful works lie pressed down on the ground in a compact mass nor did they tower upwards to an extent out of proportion to their breadth. On the contrary, in this matter too they kept to a beautiful mean and in their simplicity gave at the same time the necessary scope to well-proportioned variety. But, above all, the fundamental character of the whole and its simple details shines with complete clarity through every feature; it controls the individuality of the design in just the same way in which, in the classical ideal, the universal substance remains powerful enough to master and bring into harmony with itself the contingent and particular sphere in which it has its life.

(γ) What is to be noticed in respect of the arrangement and the separate parts of the temple is (*a*) a great series of stages of development and (*b*) much that remained traditional. The chief characteristics which may be of interest to us here are limited to the ναός (the cell of the temple, surrounded by walls and containing the images of the gods), the πρόναος (the forecourt [i.e. the first room of the temple through which one entered the cell]), the ὀπισθόδομος (the room behind the cell), and the colonnades surrounding the whole building. The kind that Vitruvius called ἀμφιπρόστυλος [with columns both back and front] originally had a room in front of the cell and another at the back with a row of columns in front of both. Next, in the περίπτερος [with a single row of columns] there is a row of columns in front of all four sides, until, finally, the highest degree is reached when this row of columns is doubled all round in the δίπτερος temple, and in the ὕπαιθρος [open to the sky] there are added, in the cell, colonnades with columns in two storeys, set apart from the walls, and so providing round the cell a walk similar to that provided by the outside colonnades. For this kind of temple the examples cited by Vitruvius are the eight-columned temple of Athene in Athens and the ten-columned one of the Olympian Zeus (Hirt, *History of Ancient Architecture*, iii. 14–18 and ii. 151).[1]

Detailed differences in respect of the number of columns, and their distances from one another and from the walls, we will pass over here and notice only the special significance which rows of columns, entrance halls, etc., have in general in the construction of Greek temples.

In these prostyles and amphiprostyles, i.e. these single and double colonnades, which led directly to the open air, we see people wandering freely and openly, individually or in accidental groupings; for the colonnades as such enclose nothing but are the boundaries of open thoroughfares, so that people walking in them are

---

[1] References in this paragraph to Vitruvius are to iii. 2, but there is more here than what he says himself.

half indoors and half outside and at least can always step directly into the open air. In the same way the long walls behind the columns do not admit of any thronging to a central point to which the eye could turn when the passages were crowded; on the contrary, the eye is more likely to be turned away from such a central point in every direction. Instead of having an idea of an assembly with a single aim, we see a drift outwards and get only the idea of people staying there cheerfully, without serious purpose, idly, and just chatting. Inside the enclosure a deeper seriousness may be surmised, but even here we find a precinct more or less (or entirely, especially in the most perfectly developed buildings) open to the external surroundings, which hints at the fact that this seriousness is not meant so very strictly. After all, the impression made by these temples is of simplicity and grandeur, but at the same time of cheerfulness, openness, and comfort, because the whole building is constructed for standing about in or strolling up and down in or coming and going rather than for assembling a collection of people and concentrating them there, shut in on every side and separated from the outside world.

3. *The Different Styles in Classical Architecture*

If in conclusion we cast a glance at the different forms of building which are typical of classical architecture throughout, we may emphasize the following differences as being the more important.

(a) *Doric, Ionic, and Corinthian Orders*

Primarily noticeable in this connection are those architectural styles whose difference comes out in the most striking way in the columns. For this reason I will confine myself here to citing the principal characteristic marks of the columnar Orders.

The most familiar Orders are the Doric, Ionian, and Corinthian. Neither earlier nor later was anything discovered more architecturally beautiful or appropriate to its purpose. For the Tuscan Order, or, according to Hirt (op. cit., i. 251), early Greek architecture also, belongs in virtue of its unadorned poverty to the originally simple building in wood, but not to architecture as a fine art. The so-called Roman Order is of no moment because it is merely the Corinthian with increased decoration.

The chief points of importance are the relation between the

height and the diameter of the columns, the different sorts of pedestal and capital, and the greater or lesser distances between the columns. As for the first point, the column seems heavy and compressed if its height is not at least four times the diameter, and if it rises to ten times the diameter the column looks to the eye too thin and slender for its purpose of supporting. But the distance of the columns from one another is closely related to this; for if the columns are to look thicker, they must be placed closer to one another, but, if they are to look slimmer and thinner, their distances must be wider. It is of equal importance whether the column has a pedestal or not, whether the capital is higher or lower, unadorned or decorated, because by the choice of one or other of these alternatives the whole character of the column is altered. But the rule for the shaft is that it must remain plain and undecorated, although it does not rise with the same thickness throughout but becomes a little thinner above than it is below and in the middle; for this reason there is a swelling in the middle which must be there even though it is almost imperceptible.[1] It is true that later, at the close of the Middle Ages, when the old columnar forms were applied again in Christian architecture, the plain columnar shafts were found too cold and therefore were surrounded by wreaths of flowers, or the columns were made to rise like spirals; but this is inadmissible and contrary to genuine taste, because the column has nothing to do but fulfil the task of supporting, and in fulfilling it to rise firm, straight, and independent [of decoration and anything else]. The only thing which the Greeks used on the shaft of the column was fluting; by this means, as Vitruvius says [iv. 4. iii], the columns appear broader than they would be if left quite smooth. Such flutings occur on the largest scale.

Of the more detailed differences between the Doric, Ionic, and Corinthian Orders in columns and architectural style, I will cite only the following principal points.

(α) In the earliest buildings the fundamental consideration is the security of the building, and architecture does not go beyond this. For this reason it does not yet risk elegant proportions and their bolder lightness but is content with heavy forms. This

---

[1] It is curious that Hegel does not seem to have realized that this swelling is required in order to make the column *look* straight. On the columns of the Parthenon at Athens, e.g., a plumb-line would reveal the swelling which the eye (untrained at least) does not notice at first.

happens in Doric architecture. In it the material with its load-carrying weight retains the chief influence and it comes especially into appearance in connection with breadth and height. If a building rises light and free, then the load of heavy masses seems to have been overcome, whereas, if it lies broader and lower, the chief thing it displays is, as in the Doric style, firmness and solidity, dominated by the law of gravity.

Conformably with this character, Doric columns, contrasted with the other Orders, are the broadest and lowest. The older of them do not exceed six times the height of their lower diameter, and are commonly only four times as high as their diameter, and therefore in their heaviness give the impression of a simple, serious, and unadorned masculinity, exemplified in the temples at Paestum and Corinth. But in the later Doric columns the height is raised to equal seven diameters, and for buildings other than temples Vitruvius adds half a diameter.[1] In general, however, the distinctive character of the Doric style is that it is still nearer the original simplicity of building in wood, although it is more susceptible of decorations and adornments than the Tuscan is. Yet the columns almost always have no pedestal but stand directly on the foundation, and the capital is put together in the simplest way out of an abacus and an echinus. The columns were sometimes left smooth, sometimes fluted with twenty drills left shallow in the lower third as a rule but hollowed out above (Hirt, *Architecture on Greek Principles*, p. 54). As for the distance between columns, in the older monuments this amounts to the width of twice the thickness of the columns, and in only a few cases is this increased to between two and two-and-a-half times the thickness.

Another peculiarity of Doric architecture in which it comes nearer to using building in wood as its model consists of the triglyphs and metopes. By prismatic incisions the triglyphs indicate on the frieze the heads of the roof beams that lie on the architrave, while the metopes fill the space between one beam and another and in Doric building keep the form of a square. They were commonly covered with bas-reliefs as a decoration, while on the architrave under the triglyphs, and above on the under-surface of the cornice, six small conical bodies, the drops [*guttae*—Vitruvius, iv. 3], served as ornaments.

[1] Although Vitruvius discourses on Doric columns in iv. 1 (seven diameters) and especially in iv. 3, this addition does not appear to be there.

(β) While the Doric style already develops into a character of pleasing solidity, Ionic architecture, though still simple, rises to what is typically slender, graceful, and elegant. The height of the columns varies between seven and ten times the length of their lower diameter. According to Vitruvius [iii. 3 and 5] the height is principally determined by the distance between the columns; for, the greater this is, the thinner and therefore taller do the columns appear, while if the intervening distance is less they appear thicker and lower. For this reason, in order to avoid excessive thinness or heaviness, the architect is compelled in the first case to lessen the height, in the second to increase it. Consequently if the distance between the columns exceeds three diameters, the height of the columns amounts to only eight, while if the distance is between two-and-a-quarter and three diameters, the height is eight-and-a-half. But if the columns are only two diameters apart, the height rises to nine-and-a-half, and even to ten when the distance is at its narrowest, i.e. one-and-a-half. Yet these last cases occur only very seldom, and, to judge from the surviving monuments of Ionic architecture, the Greeks made little use of proportions demanding higher columns.

Further differences between the Ionic and the Doric style are to be found in the fact that Ionic columns, unlike the Doric, do not have their shaft rising straight from the sub-structure, but are set up on a pedestal with many mouldings. From this they rise, gradually diminishing in girth to a slender summit; the shaft is deeply hollowed out with twenty-four broad flutes. In this matter the Ionic temple at Ephesus is especially contrasted with the Doric one at Paestum. Similarly the Ionic capital gains in variety and grace. It has not only an incised abacus, astragal, and echinus, but on the left and right it has in addition a shell-like curve and on the sides an ornament in the shape of a pillow; this gives this capital the name of 'pulvinated' capital. The shell-like curves on the pillow indicate the end of the column which could rise still higher but at this point of possible extension it curves back into itself.

Granted this attractive slenderness and decoration of the columns, Ionic architecture now demands a bearing architrave which is less heavy and therefore is applied to making the building more graceful. For the same reason, it no longer, like Doric, is indicative of a derivation from building in wood. Therefore in the flat frieze triglyphs and metopes disappear, and instead the chief decorations are now the skulls of sacrificial animals bound together with wreaths of flowers, and, in place of mutules, dentils are introduced (Hirt, *History of Ancient Architecture*, i. 254).

(γ) Finally, the Corinthian style abides fundamentally by the Ionian but, keeping the same slenderness, it develops it into a tasteful brilliance and reveals the final wealth of decoration and ornament. Content, as it were, with deriving its several and specific divisions from building in wood, it emphasizes them by decorations without letting this first origin glint through them and expresses a vigorous preoccupation with attractive differences by the various fillets and bands on cornices and beams, by troughs and weather moulds, by pedestals divided in various ways, and richer capitals.

The Corinthian column is not loftier than the Ionic, because usually, with similar fluting, its height is only eight or eight-and-a-half times the diameter of its lower part, yet owing to a higher capital it appears more slender and, above all, richer. For the capital's height is one-and-an-eighth times the lower diameter and has on all four corners thinner spirals with no pillows, and the part below these is adorned with acanthus leaves. The Greeks have a charming story about this [in e.g. Vitruvius iv. 1]. A remarkably beautiful girl, the story goes, died; her nurse then collected her toys in a basket and put it on her grave where an acanthus was beginning to grow. The leaves soon surrounded the basket and this gave rise to an idea for the capital of a column.

Of further differences between the Corinthian style and the Doric and Ionic I will mention only the charmingly chamfered mutules under the cornice, the projection of the *guttae*, and the dentils and corbels on the entablature.

(b) *The Roman Construction of Arch and Vault*

Secondly, Roman architecture can be regarded as a middle form between Greek and Christian because what especially begins in it is the use of the arch and vaultings.

It is not possible to determine with precision the period in which the construction of an arch was first discovered, but it seems certain that the arch and the vault were unknown to the Egyptians, no matter how far they progressed in the art of building, as well as to the Babylonians, Israelites, and Phoenicians. At least the monuments of Egyptian architecture show merely that when the Egyptians came to build a roof over the interior of their buildings, they could use nothing but massive columns on which flagstones were placed horizontally as beams. But when wide entrances and bridge-arches had to be vaulted, the only expedient which the Egyptians understood was to make a stone protrude inwards on either side and place another on top of it protruding further, so that as the side walls rose the distance between them grew gradually less until finally only one stone was needed to close the gap. Where they did not use this expedient, they covered the spaces with huge stones joined to one another like chevrons.

Among the Greeks we do find, though seldom, monuments in which an arch construction is used, and Hirt, whose volumes on the architecture of the Greeks and its history are of the first importance,[1] states that not one of them can be safely regarded as built before the Periclean age. In other words what is characteristic of Greek architecture, and developed to the full, is the column and the entablature superimposed on it horizontally, so that the column is little used in Greece for anything but its proper purpose of supporting beams. But a vaulted arch linking two pillars or columns, and the cupola formation, has a wider implication because here the column is already beginning to lose its purpose of being merely a support. For the arch in its rise, its curve, and its fall is related to a central point which has nothing to do with a column and its support. The different parts of the arch mutually carry, support, and continue one another, so that they are exempt from the aid of a column to a far greater extent than a superimposed beam is.

In Roman architecture, as I said, the construction of arches and vaults is very common; indeed, if full confidence can be placed in later testimonies, a few remains have to be ascribed to the period of the Roman kings. Of this sort are the catacombs and the cloaca which had vaults, but they have to be regarded as works restored at a later date.

The invention of the vault is ascribed with the greatest probability to Democritus[2] [in the fifth-century B.C.] who concerned

---

[1] Hirt may have been the best authority on the subject in Hegel's day, but he is subject to correction by modern scholars.

[2] Hegel cites Seneca, *Ep.* 90, for this, but Seneca says that Posidonius is the author of this ascription to Democritus and adds that for his part he thinks it false.

himself too with various mathematical subjects and is reputed to be the inventor of the art of the lapidary.

One of the most outstanding productions of Roman architecture, where the semicircle is the predominant model, is the Pantheon of Agrippa, dedicated to Jupiter Ultor, which was built to contain, in addition to the statue of Jupiter, in six other niches colossal images of Mars, Venus, the deified Julius Caesar, and three others that cannot be precisely determined. On each side of these niches were two Corinthian columns, and over the whole there was the most majestic vaulted roof in the form of a half globe, imitating the vault of heaven. In the matter of technique, it must be noticed that this roof is not vaulted in stone. What the Romans did in most of their vaults was first to make a wooden construction in the form of the vault they intended to build, and then they poured over it a mixture of chalk and pozzolana-cement made from light tufa and broken bricks.[1] When this mixture dried out the whole formed a single mass, so that the wooden framework could be discarded, and owing to the lightness of the material and the stability of its cohesion the vault exerted only a little pressure on the walls.

(c) General Character of Roman Architecture

Now quite apart from this novelty of arch-construction, Roman architecture, to speak generally, had a totally different range and character from the Greek. While keeping throughout to the purpose of their buildings, the Greeks were distinguished by their artistic perfection in the nobility and simplicity of their architecture as well as in the easy gracefulness of their decorations. Whereas the Romans are skilful in the mechanics of building, and although their buildings are richer and more magnificent, they have less nobility and grace. Moreover in their case a variety of purposes, unknown to the Greeks, arise for architecture. For, as I said at the beginning, the Greeks devoted the splendour and beauty of art only to public buildings; their private houses remained insignificant. Whereas in the case of the Romans, not only was there an enlarged range of public buildings where the purposiveness of their construction was allied with grandiose magnificence in theatres, amphitheatres for gladiators, and other works for the

---

[1] Or, rather, from volcanic ash found near Pozzuoli (anc. Puteoli).

public amusement, but architecture was also directed to the requirements of private life. Especially after the civil wars [end of first century B.C.], villas, baths, avenues, stairs, etc. were built with extreme luxury at enormous expense, and this opened a new sphere to architecture; this drew horticulture in its train and was perfected in a very ingenious and tasteful way. A brilliant example is the villa of Lucullus.[1]

The type of this Roman architecture has served in many ways as a model for later Italians and Frenchmen. In Germany we have long followed the Italians or the French, until now at last we have turned to the Greeks again and taken classical art in its purer form as our model.

[1] He lived 110 B.C.–47 B.C. The villa is therefore a little earlier than Hegel indicates. After distinguished service as a general in Asia Minor Lucullus retired to Rome. See Plutarch's *Life*. He had enormous wealth and his profusion has been no better pictured than in G. E. Stevens' *Monologues of the Dead* (London, 1896).

Chapter III

ROMANTIC ARCHITECTURE

The Gothic architecture of the Middle Ages which is the real centre of the properly romantic style was regarded as something crude and barbaric for a long time, especially since the spread and domination of French artistic taste. In more recent times it was chiefly Goethe who took the lead in bringing it into honour again when he looked on nature and art with the freshness of youth and in a way opposed to the French and their principles. Nowadays more and more efforts have been made to get to value in these grand works both a peculiar appropriateness to Christian worship and also a correspondence between architectural configuration and the inmost spirit of Christianity.

1. *General Character of Romantic Architecture*

As for the general character of these buildings, in which their religious function is to be particularly stressed, we saw already in the Introduction that here the architecture which is independent is united with that which serves a purpose. But this unification does not consist at all in a fusion of Eastern and Greek forms; it is to be found rather in the fact that, on the one hand, enclosure provides the fundamental type to a greater extent than is the case in Greek temple-building, while, on the other hand, mere utility and adaptation to an end is transcended all the same and the house [of God] is erected freely, independently, and on its own account. Thus these buildings and houses of God do prove, as was said, to be entirely suitable for worship and other uses, but their real character lies precisely in the fact that they transcend any specific end and, as perfect in themselves, stand there on their own account. The work stands there by itself, fixed, and eternal. Therefore no purely abstractly intellectual [or mathematical] relation determines the character of the whole; the interior does not have the box-like form of our Protestant churches which are built only to be filled by a congregation and have nothing but pews like stalls in a stable. Externally the [medieval] building rises freely to a pinnacle, so that, however appropriate it is to its purpose, the purpose disappears again and the whole is given the look of an independent existent. No one thing completely exhausts a building like this; everything is lost in the greatness of the whole. It has and displays a definite purpose; but in its grandeur and sublime peace it is lifted above anything purely utilitarian into an infinity in itself. This elevation above the finite, and this simple solidity, is its *one* characteristic aspect. In its other it is precisely where particularization, diversity, and variety gain the fullest scope, but without letting the whole fall apart into mere trifles and accidental details. On the contrary, here the majesty of art brings back into simple unity everything thus divided up and partitioned. The substance of the whole is dismembered and shattered into the endless divisions of a world of individual variegations, but this incalculable multiplicity is divided in a simple way, articulated regularly, dispersed symmetrically, both moved and firmly set in the most satisfying eurhythmy, and this length and breadth of varied details is gripped together unhindered into the most secure unity and clearest independence.

2. *Particular Architectural Formations*

In proceeding now to the particular forms in which the specific character of romantic architecture is developed, we will confine our discussion, as we have already noticed earlier, to Gothic architecture proper and mainly to Christian churches in distinction from Greek temples.

(a) *The Fully Enclosed House as the Fundamental Form*

(α) Just as the Christian spirit concentrates itself in the inner life, so the building becomes the place shut in on every side for the assembly of the Christian congregation and the collection of its thoughts. The spatial enclosure corresponds to the concentration of mind within, and results from it. But the worship of the Christian heart is at the same time an elevation above the finite so that this elevation now determines the character of the house of God. In this way architecture acquires elevation to the infinite as the significance which it is driven to express in architectonic forms, a significance independent of mere purposiveness. The impression, therefore, which art now has to produce is, on the one hand, in distinction from the cheerful openness of the Greek temple, the impression of this tranquillity of the heart which, released from the external world of nature and from the mundane in general, is shut in upon itself, and, on the other hand, the impression of a majestic sublimity which aspires beyond and outsoars mathematical limitation. Thus, while the buildings of classical architecture in the main lie on the ground horizontally, the opposite romantic character of Christian churches consists in their growing out of the ground and rising to the sky.

(β) Enclosure was to give effect to this forgetting of the external world of nature and the distracting activities and interests of finite existence. Adieu therefore to *open* entrance halls and colonnades, etc.; in their openness they are connected with the world and so they are now given instead in a totally different way a position *inside* the building. For the same reason the light of the sun is excluded or it only glimmers dimly through windows of the stained glass necessary for complete separation from the world outside. What people need here is not provided by the world of nature; on the contrary they need a world made by and for man alone, for his worship and the preoccupations of his inner life.

(γ) But as the decisive type assumed by the house of God in general and in its particular parts we may fix the free rising and running up into pinnacles whether these are formed by arches or by straight lines. In classical architecture the basic form was provided by columns or stanchions with superimposed beams, so that the chief thing was rectangularity and therefore support. For a weight resting at a right angle shows clearly that it is supported. And even if the beams themselves are in turn supports for a roof, their surfaces incline at an obtuse angle to one another. Here there is strictly no question of rising or coming to a pinnacle, but only of resting and supporting. In the same way even a round arch, which proceeds from one pillar to another in a uniformly curved line and is described from one and the same central point, likewise rests on its supporting substructure. But in romantic architecture the basic form is no longer afforded by supporting as such and therefore by rectangularity; on the contrary, these are cancelled because surrounding walls shoot upwards on their own account within and outside, and they meet at a point without the fixed and express difference between a load and its support. This predominant free striving upwards and the inclination of the sides culminating in the apex is here the essential determinant for the origin of the pointed arches or acute-angled triangles with a narrower or broader base which indicate the character of Gothic architecture in the most striking way.

(b) The Form of the Exterior and the Interior

Engaging in heartfelt devotion and elevation of soul has, as worship, a variety of particular features and aspects which cannot be carried out in open halls or in front of temples, but have their place in the interior of God's house. Therefore while in the temples of classical architecture the external form is the chief thing and, owing to the colonnades, remains independent of the construction of the interior, in romantic architecture the interior of the building not only acquires a more essential importance because the whole thing is meant to be an enclosure only, but the interior glints also through the shape of the exterior and determines its form and arrangement in detail.

In this connection, in order to examine the matter in more detail, we will first step into the interior and so thereafter become clear about the form of the exterior.

(α) As the principal determinant of its interior I have already cited the fact that the church is meant to enclose a space for the congregation, and all the aspects of its spiritual worship, as a protection partly from inclement weather, partly from the troubles of the external world. The space inside therefore becomes totally enclosed whereas the Greek temples often had open cells in addition to open colonnades and halls.

But Christian worship is both an elevation of soul above the restrictions of existence and also a reconciliation of the individual with God. This therefore essentially implies a reconciliation of differences into a single unity that has become inherently concrete. At the same time, romantic architecture constructs a building which exists as an enclosure for the spirit, and consequently it is its business, so far as is architecturally possible, to make spiritual convictions shine through the shape and arrangement of the building and so determine the form both of its interior and exterior. This task has the following implications.

(αα) The space of the interior must not be an abstractly uniform and empty one that has no differences and their intermediation; what is required on the contrary is a formation differentiated in length, breadth, height, and the character of these dimensions. The circle, the square, the oblong, with the equality of their enclosing walls and roofing are unsuitable. The movement of the spirit with the distinctions it makes and its conciliation of them in the course of its elevation from the terrestrial to the infinite, to the loftier beyond, would not be expressed architecturally in this empty uniformity of a quadrilateral.

(ββ) It is at once a corollary of this that in Gothic architecture the purposiveness of a house, whether in respect of its enclosure by means of side walls and roof or in regard to beams and columns, is only an incidental so far as the formation of the whole building and its parts is concerned. Consequently, as was already explained above, the strict difference between load and support has disappeared; the no longer purely appropriate form of the right angle is cancelled and a return is made instead to a form analogous to one in nature, and this must be the form of an enclosure for a freely aspiring assembly. Enter the interior of a medieval cathedral, and you are reminded less of the firmness and mechanical appropriateness of load-carrying pillars and a vault resting on them than of the vaultings of a forest where in lines of trees the branches incline to one another and quickly meet. A purlin needs a fixed point of support and a horizontal position. Whereas in Gothic architecture the walls rise upwards freely and independently; so do the pillars, which branch out above apart from one another in several directions and meet as if accidentally; i.e. although the vault does in fact rest on pillars, their purpose of supporting the vault is not expressly emphasized and presented independently. It is as if they were not supports at all; compare a tree—its boughs do not seem to be carried by the trunk; on the contrary in their form, rather like an easy curve, they look like a continuation of the trunk and with the leaves of other trees form a roof of foliage. The cathedral presents a vault like this, one meant for reverie, this place of dread which invites to meditation, because the walls and the forest of pillars meet freely at the apex. But this is not to say that Gothic architecture has taken trees and forests as the actual model for the forms it uses.

While tapering to a point provides in general a fundamental

form for Gothic, in the interior of the churches this form takes the special character of a pointed arch. This gives columns in particular a totally different purpose and shape.

As total enclosures, the wide Gothic churches need a roof which owing to that width is a heavy load necessitating support underneath. So here columns seem to be properly in place. But because the way the building strives upwards precisely converts load-carrying into the appearance of free ascending, columns cannot occur here in the significance they have in classical architecture. On the contrary they become pillars which, instead of purlins, carry arches in such a way that the arches seem to be a mere continuation of the pillars and rise to a point as it were unintentionally. We can indeed represent the way in which two pillars standing apart from one another necessarily end at a point as analogous to the way in which, e.g., a gabled roof can rest on corner posts, but when we look at the sides of the roof, then, even if they are set on the pillars at wholly obtuse angles and incline to one another at an acute angle, in that case we nevertheless get the idea of a load on the one hand and a support on the other. Whereas the shoulders of the pointed arch seem at first sight to rise at a right angle to the pillar and to curve only unnoticeably and slowly, so that each inclines gradually to the other; only then does this completely give us the idea that the shoulder is nothing at all but a continuation of the pillar which comes together with another to form an arch. In contrast to the column and the beam, the pillar and vault appear as one and the same construction, although the arches rest on and rise from capitals. Yet the capitals are absent altogether, e.g. in many Netherlands churches, and in this way that undivided unity is made clearly visible.

Since the striving upwards is meant to be manifest as the chief characteristic, the height of the pillars exceeds the breadth of their base to an extent which the eye cannot compute. The pillars become thin and slender and rise so high that the eye cannot take in the whole shape at a single glance but is driven to travel over it and to rise until it begins to find rest in the gently inclined vaulting of the arches that meet, just as the worshipping heart, restless and troubled at first, rises above the territory of finitude and finds rest in God alone.

The final difference between pillars and columns is that peculiarly Gothic pillars, once developed in their specific character, do not remain, like columns, circular, stable in themselves, one and the same cylinder, but already form, reed-like, at their base a coil or bundle of threads which then above are variously disentangled and radiate in numerous continuations on every side. In classical architecture a progress is visible in columns from heaviness, simplicity, and solidity to slenderness and decoration; so too something similar occurs in the pillar which, rising in greater slenderness, is less and less susceptible of fulfilling the purpose of support and floats freely upwards, though it closes at the top.

The same form of pillars and pointed arches is repeated in windows and doors. The windows especially, both the lower ones on the side-aisles and still more the upper ones of the nave and the choir, are of colossal size so that the eye that rests on their lower parts does not immediately take in the upper ones but is now drawn upwards, as happened in the case of the vaultings. This generates that restlessness of aspiration which is to be communicated to the spectator. Moreover the window-panes, as was mentioned above, are only half-transparent owing to the stained glass. Sometimes they display sacred stories; sometimes they are simply coloured to increase the twilight effect and leave candlelight to provide illumination; for here it is a day other than the day of nature that is to provide light.

(γγ) Coming now finally to the whole interior arrangement of Gothic churches, we have seen already that the different parts must be formed differently in height, breadth, and length. The next point here is the difference of the *chancel, transepts,* and long *nave* from the surrounding aisles. On the outer side these aisles are formed by the edifice's enclosing walls in front of which pillars and arches project, and on the inner side by pillars and pointed arches open to the nave because they have no walls connecting them. Thus the position of these aisles is the converse of that of the Greek temple colonnades which are open on the outside but closed on the inner side; whereas in Gothic churches free passageways are left open from the nave through between the pillars into the side-aisles. Sometimes there are two of these side-aisles alongside one another; indeed in Antwerp cathedral there are three on each side of the nave.[1]

The nave itself soars up above the aisles; it is enclosed by walls

---

[1] Hegel visited this cathedral in October 1822 and in a letter commented then on this triplicity.

varying in height compared with the aisles, being sometimes twice their height, sometimes less. The walls are so broken by colossal long windows that they become themselves as it were slender pillars which meet at the top in pointed arches and form vaults. Nevertheless, there are also churches where the aisles have the same height as the nave, as, for instance, in the later choir of St. Sebald's in Nürnberg [where Hegel lived for a few years]; this gives the whole church a character of sublime, free, and open slenderness and elegance.

In this way the whole church is divided and articulated by rows of pillars which resemble a forest in running together above in flying arches like boughs. In the number of these pillars, and in the numerical relations of the interior generally, it has been proposed to find much mystical meaning. Of course at the time when Gothic architecture blossomed most beautifully, e.g. at the time [1248] of Cologne cathedral, great importance was laid on such numerical symbolism since the still rather dim inkling of reason easily lapsed into external considerations like this; but, by such always more or less arbitrary games of an inferior symbolism, architectural works of art are given neither a deeper meaning nor a more exalted beauty, because their proper significance and spirit is expressed in forms and configurations quite otherwise than in the mystical meaning of numerical differences. We must therefore be very cautious not to go too far in the hunt for such meanings, because to try to be too profound and see a deeper significance everywhere is just as petty and superficial as the blind pedantry which passes over, without grasping it, the profound meaning which is clearly expressed and presented.

Finally, on the distinctive character of the chancel and the nave I will confine myself to the following remarks. The high altar, this real centre of worship, is placed in the chancel which is thus the place devoted to the clergy in contrast to the congregation which has its place, along with the pulpit, in the nave. Steps, more or less numerous, lead to the chancel, so that this whole part of the building, and what goes on there, is visible from every point. So too the chancel is more elaborately decorated and yet in comparison with the long nave it is more grave, solemn, and sublime, even when the height of the vaults is the same. At this point the whole building is finally enclosed: the pillars are thicker and closer together, with the result that the width is continually diminished, and everything seems to rise higher and more tranquilly, whereas the transepts and nave with their entrance and exit doors still permit of a connection with the outside world.—As for orientation, the chancel points to the east, the nave to the west, the transepts to north and south. There are also churches, however, with a double chancel, one at the east and the other at the west end, and the main entrances are into the transepts.—The font for baptism, for this consecration of entry to the company of the faithful, is erected in a porch beside the main entry to the church.—Finally, for private worship or special occasions there are set up round the whole building, especially round the chancel and the nave, smaller chapels each of which forms by itself as it were a new church.— This may suffice as a description of the arrangement of the parts of the whole.

In such a cathedral there is room for an entire community. For here the whole community of a city and its neighbourhood is to assemble not round the building but inside it. For this reason all the various interests of life which touch religion in any way have their place alongside one another. The wide space is not divided and narrowed by series of rows of pews; everyone goes and comes unhindered, hires or takes a chair for his present use, kneels down, offers his prayer, and departs again. If it is not the time for high mass, the most varied things go on simultaneously without inconvenience. Here there is a sermon: there a sick man is brought in. Between the two a procession drags slowly on. Here there is a baptism, there a bier. At another point again a priest reads mass or blesses a couple's marriage. Everywhere people wander like nomads, on their knees before some altar or holy image or other. All these varied activities are included in one and the same building. But this variety of occupations and their separate individuality with their continual alteration disappears all the same in face of the width and size of the building; nothing fills it entirely, everything passes quickly; individuals and their doings are lost and dispersed like points in this grandiose structure; the momentary event is visible only in its passing away; and over everything these infinite spaces, these gigantic constructions, rise in their firm structure and immutable form.

These are the chief characteristics of the interior of Gothic churches. Here we have not to look for purposiveness as such but only for appropriateness to the subjective worship of the heart as it immerses itself in its own inmost privacy and lifts itself above everything individual and finite. In short, these buildings are sombre, separated from nature by walls closing them in all round, and nevertheless carried out to the last detail as aspiring sublimely and illimitably.

(β) If we turn now to consider the exterior, the point has already been made that, in distinction from the Greek temple, in Gothic architecture the external shape, the decoration and arrangement of walls, etc., are determined from within outwards, since the exterior is to appear as only an enclosing of the interior.

In this context the following points need special emphasis.

(αα) First, the entire external cruciform shape in its fundamental outline makes recognizable the similar construction of the interior because it allows for the separation between the transepts and the nave and chancel, and besides makes clearly visible the different heights of the aisles and the nave and chancel.

In more detail, the chief façade, as the exterior of the nave and aisles, corresponds in its portals to the construction of the interior. A higher main door, leading to the nave, stands between two smaller entrances to the side-aisles and hints by the narrowing due to perspective that the exterior has to shrink, contract, and disappear in order to form the entrance. The interior is the already visible background in which the exterior is immersed just as the heart, retreating into itself, has to immerse itself in its own inner life. Next, over the side-doors there rise, likewise in the most immediate connection with the interior, colossal windows, just as the portals are carried up to pointed arches similar to those serviceable for the special form of vaulting in the interior. Over the main door, between the windows over the side-doors, a great circle opens, the rose-window, a form likewise belonging quite peculiarly to this architectural style and suitable only to it. Where such rose-windows are missing there is substituted a still more colossal window culminating in a pointed arch.—The façades of the transepts are divided similarly, while the walls of the nave, the chancel, and the aisles follow entirely in the windows and the form of these, as well as in the bearing walls between them, the appearance of the interior and display that externally.

(ββ) But secondly, in this close tie with the form and arrangement of the interior, the exterior begins nevertheless to have an independence of its own, because it has tasks of its own to fulfil.

694   III. I. ARCHITECTURE

In this connection we may mention the *buttresses*. They take the place of the various pillars in the interior, and they are necessary as *points d'appui* for the elevation and stability of the whole. At the same time they make clear in their intervals, number, etc. on the outside the division of the rows of pillars within, although they do not precisely imitate the form of the inner pillars but, on the contrary, the higher they rise the more are the intervals [like steps] at which they diminish in strength [or depth].[1]

(γγ) Thirdly, however, while the interior is meant to be in itself a complete enclosure, this feature is lost in the aspect of the exterior and gives place completely to the single character of rising upwards. For this reason the exterior acquires a form quite independent of the interior, a form manifest especially in striving upwards on all sides into projections and pinnacles and breaking out into apex on apex.

To this striving upwards there belong the high-mounting triangles which, beyond the pointed arches,[2] rise above the portals, especially those of the main façade and, above the colossal windows of the nave and chancel; to this same feature there also belong (*a*) the slenderly pointed form of the roof, the gable of which comes into view especially on the façades of the transepts, and (*b*) the buttresses which everywhere run up to small peaked towers and therefore, just as in the interior the rows of pillars form a forest of trunks, branches, and vaults, so here on the exterior a forest of pinnacles is raised on high.

As the most sublime summits of the structure the *towers*[3] rise in

[1] 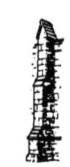 Gothic buttress as illustrated in *Oxford Illustrated Dictionary*.

[2] 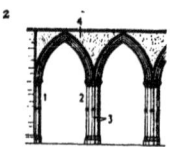 Hegel is referring here to the spandrels, i.e. to 4 in this illustration from *O.I.D.* s.v. Arcade.

[3] *Türme*: the word may mean either 'tower' or 'steeple'. A steeple is a tower surmounted by a spire, and Hegel's insistence on 'points' and 'striving upwards' might suggest that he has steeples in mind here, but wrongly because some cathedrals have towers and no spires, and therefore no steeples, and some towers have belfries.

the most independent fashion. That is to say that in them the whole mass of the building is as it were concentrated; in its main towers the mass is lifted up unhindered to a height that the eye cannot calculate, while its character of peace and solidity is not lost. Such towers stand in the main façade over the two aisles while a third and thicker main tower rises from the point at which the vaults of the chancel, nave, and transepts meet; alternatively, a single tower forms the main façade and rises over the whole breadth of the nave. These at any rate are the commonest positions. For worship the towers provide belfries because a peal of bells peculiarly belongs to Christian services. This simple and vague sound is a solemn stimulus to inner meditation, but it is primarily only a preparative, coming from without, whereas the articulated sound, expressive of what is felt or conceived, is song, which is heard only in the interior of the church. Inarticulate sounds, however, can have their place only outside the building and they ring out down from the towers, because they are meant to resound from these pure heights far and wide over the country.

(c) *Mode of Decorating*

In this third matter the chief characteristics were already indicated at the start.

(α) The first point to be emphasized is the importance of decoration as such for Gothic architecture. On the whole, classical architecture preserves a wise proportion in the adornment of its buildings. But since it is especially important for Gothic architecture to make the masses that it builds seem greater and, above all, higher than they are in fact, it is not content with simple surfaces, but divides them throughout, particularly in forms indicative themselves once more of striving upwards. Pillars, pointed arches, and acute-angled triangles rising above them, for example, occur in the decorations too. In this way the simple unity of the huge masses is split up and elaborated down to the last particular detail, and the whole now presents in itself the most tremendous contrast. The eye sees, on the one hand, the most obvious outlines clearly ordered, though in immense dimensions, and, on the other hand, an unsurveyable abundance and variety of decorative ornamentation, so that what is most universal and simple faces the most-diversified particularity of detail. Christian worship involves a similar contrast: the heart that worships is nevertheless immersed in finitude and habituated to pettiness and minutiae. This disunion should stimulate reflection, and this striving upwards invites a sense of the sublime. For in this sort of decoration the chief thing is not to destroy or conceal the outlines by the mass and diversity of ornamentation but to let them, as the essential thing on which all depends, permeate this variety through and through and completely. Only in this event, especially in Gothic buildings, is the solemnity of their grandiose seriousness preserved. Just as religious devotion should penetrate all the recesses of the soul and every relation in the life of individuals and engrave indelibly on the heart the most universal and unchanging ideas, so also the simple architectural types must always bring back again to these main outlines the most varied divisions, carvings, and decorations and make them disappear in face of those outlines.

(β) A second aspect in decorations is connected similarly with the romantic form of art as such. Romanticism has as its principle the inner life, the return of the intellectual life into itself, but the inner life is to be reflected in the external world and to withdraw into itself out of that world. Now in architecture it is the visible, material, and spatial mass on which the inmost heart itself is so far as possible to be brought before contemplation. Given such a material, nothing is left to the artistic representation but to refuse validity to the material and the massive in its purely material character and to interrupt it everywhere, break it up, and deprive it of its appearance of immediate coherence and independence. In this connection the decorations, especially on the exterior (which has not to manifest enclosing as such), acquire the character of carving everywhere, or, on surfaces, of a network. There is no architecture which along with such enormous and heavy masses of stone and their firmly mortised joints has still preserved, so completely [as Gothic architecture has done], the character of lightness and grace.

(γ) Thirdly, on the configuration of the decorations the only remark necessary is that apart from pointed arches, pillars, and circles, the forms here once again recall what is properly organic. This is already indicated by the carvings in and the reliefs protruding from the mass. But, more strikingly, there explicitly occur leaves, rosettes, and, intertwined like arabesques, animal and human forms, now true to life, now fantastically juxtaposed. In this way romantic fancy displays even in architecture its wealth of invention and extraordinary links between heterogeneous elements. On the other hand, however, at least at the time when Gothic architecture was at its purest, a steady return of the same simple forms is preserved even in decorations, e.g. in the pointed arches of the windows.

3. *Different Styles in Romantic Architecture*

The last matter on which I will add a few remarks concerns the chief forms into which romantic architecture has developed in different periods, although here there cannot be any question at all of providing a history of this branch of art.

(a) *Romanesque (pre-Gothic) Architecture*

From Gothic architecture, as sketched above, the Romanesque is of course to be distinguished; it was developed from the Roman.

The oldest form of Christian churches is that of the *basilica*, so-called because they originated from public imperial buildings, huge oblong halls with wooden roof framework, such as Constantine made available to Christians. In such halls there was a tribune; when congregations assembled for worship, the priest went to it to intone or speak or lecture, and the idea of the chancel may have arisen from this.[1] Similarly, Christian architecture took from Roman, especially in the Western Empire, its other forms such as the use of columns with round arches, domes, and the whole manner of decoration, while in the Eastern Empire it seems to have remained true to this style up to Justinian's time. Even the Ostrogothic and Lombard buildings in Italy retained the Roman basic character in essentials.—Nevertheless in the later architecture of the Byzantine Empire several changes were introduced. The centre was formed by a dome on four great pillars, then various sorts of construction were added for the particular purposes of the Greek, as distinct from the Roman, rite. But with this architecture that strictly belongs to the Byzantine Empire we must not confuse that kind generally called Byzantine which was employed in Italy, France, England, Germany, etc. up to towards the end of the twelfth century.

[1] Hegel may have in mind the basilica of Constantine at Trier which he visited in 1827.

(b) Gothic Architecture Proper

Later, in the thirteenth century, Gothic architecture developed in its own special form; its distinctive character I have described above in detail. Today this is denied to the Goths and the style is called German or Germanic. Nevertheless we may retain the older and commoner name, even if only because in Spain there are very old traces of this style which indicate a connection with historical events, because Gothic kings, driven back into the hills of Asturias and Galicia, maintained their independence there. For this reason this seems to make probable a closer relationship between Gothic and Arabic architecture, but the two are essentially distinct. For what is characteristic of medieval Arabic architecture is not the pointed arch but the so-called horse-shoe arch; and, apart from this, Arabic buildings are designed for a totally different religion and display an oriental profusion and magnificence, plant-like ornamentation, and other decorations in which the Roman and medieval styles are mixed up unblended.

(c) Secular Architecture in the Middle Ages

Secular architecture runs parallel with this development of religious architecture, and it repeats and modifies from its own point of view the character of the religious buildings. But in secular architecture, art has less scope, because here narrower aims and a variety of needs demand a precisely corresponding satisfaction and there is no room for beauty except as a decoration. Except in a general eurhythmy of form and proportion, art can only appear to any extent in the embellishment of façades, steps, staircases, windows, doors, gables, towers, etc., but, even so, only in such a way that utility remains the real decisive determinant of the structure. In the Middle Ages the fundamental type which is most prominent is the stronghold character of fortified dwellings placed not only in isolation on mountain sides or summits but also in cities where every palace, every family house, e.g. in Italy, took the form of a small fortress or stronghold. Walls, doors, towers, bridges, etc., are dictated by need and are decorated and beautified by art. Strength and security, along with grand magnificence and the living individuality of single forms and their harmony, are the essential determinant here, but its detailed analysis at this point would take us too far afield.

Lastly, by way of appendix, we may make a brief mention of the art of horticulture. Not only does it create afresh, *de novo*, an environment, like a second external nature, for the spirit, but it draws into its sphere and reshapes the natural landscape itself, treating it architecturally as an environment for buildings. As a familiar example I need only cite here the extremely magnificent park of Sans Souci [i.e. Frederick the Great's palace at Potsdam, *c*. 1745].

In considering horticulture proper we must of course distinguish between its picturesque and its architectural elements. A park, that is to say, is not architectural; it is not a building constructed out of free natural objects. On the contrary, it is a painting which leaves these objects as they naturally are and tries to imitate nature in its greatness and freedom. It hints in turn at everything that delights us in a landscape, at crags and their huge free masses, at valleys, woodlands, meadows, greensward, winding brooks, wide rivers with busy banks, calm lakes festooned with trees, roaring waterfalls, and whatever else.[1] All this is brought together into one whole, as in a picture. In this way Chinese horticulture comprises whole landscapes with lakes and islands, streams, vistas, rockeries, etc.

In a park like this, especially in modern times, everything should preserve the freedom of nature itself and yet at the same time be transformed and fashioned artistically; it is also conditioned by the existing terrain. The result is a discord which cannot be completely resolved. In this matter, nothing is in the main more tasteless than to make visible everywhere an intention in what has none or such a constraint on what is in itself free from constraint. But, this apart, in such an instance the proper character of a garden disappears, because the purpose of a garden is to provide, for diversion and the pleasure of strolling, a place which is no longer nature as such but nature transformed by man to meet his need for an environment created by himself. Whereas a huge park, especially if rigged out with Chinese pagodas, Turkish mosques, Swiss chalets, bridges, hermitages, and goodness knows what other curiosities, claims our attention on its own account; it pretends to be and to mean something in itself. But our allurement vanishes as soon as it is satisfied, and we can hardly look at this sort of thing twice,

[1] Hegel's dislike of hills (see above in Vol. I, pp. 132, 158) is evidenced again by their absence from this list.

because these trimmings offer to the eye nothing infinite, no indwelling soul, and besides they are only wearisome and burdensome when we want recreation and a stroll in conversation with a friend.

A garden as such should provide no more than cheerful surroundings, i.e. surroundings merely, worth nothing in themselves and so never distracting us from human affairs and our inner life. Here architecture with its mathematical lines, with its order, regularity, and symmetry has its place and it orders natural objects themselves architecturally. This is the type preferred in the horticultural art of the Mongols beyond the Great Wall, in Tibet, and in the Persian paradises. These are no English parks, but halls, with flowers, springs, fountains, courts, palaces, constructed for a stay in nature on a magnificent and grandiose scale at extravagant expense to meet human needs and comfort. But the architectural principle has been carried furthest in French horticulture, where gardens are usually attached to great palaces; trees are planted in a strict order beside one another in long avenues, they are trimmed, and real walls are formed from cut hedges; and in this way nature itself is transformed into a vast residence under the open sky.[1]

[1] Hegel recalls his visit to Versailles. He described the garden in a letter to his wife, 30 September 1827.

SECTION II

SCULPTURE

INTRODUCTION

In contrast to the inorganic nature of spirit which is given its appropriate artistic form by architecture, the spiritual itself now enters so that the work of art acquires and displays spirituality as its content. We have already seen the necessity for this advance; it is inherent in the very nature of the spirit which differentiates itself into its subjective self-awareness and its objectivity as such. Architectural treatment does make the inner subjective life glint in this externality but without being able to make it permeate the external through and through or to make the external into that completely adequate expression of spirit which lets nothing appear but itself. Art therefore withdraws out of the inorganic, which architecture, bound as it is to the laws of gravity, labours to bring nearer to an expression of spirit, into the inner and subjective life, and this life now enters on its own account in its higher truth and not intermingled with the inorganic. It is along this road of spirit's return into itself out of matter and mass that we encounter sculpture.

But the first stage in this new sphere is not yet spirit's reversion into its *inner* self-conscious life as such, at which point the presentation of the inner life would require expression in an *ideal* mode; on the contrary, here the spirit grasps itself at first only by still expressing itself in *bodily* form and in that form possesses an existence homogeneous with itself. The art which takes this level of the spirit as its content is called upon to shape spiritual individuality as an appearance in matter and indeed in what is material properly and directly. Speech, after all, or language is a self-manifestation of spirit in externality, but in an objectivity which, instead of counting as something directly and concretely material, is a communication of spirit only as sound, as the movement and vibration of a whole body and the abstract element, i.e. air. Whereas what is directly corporeal is spatial matter, e.g. stone, wood, metal, clay in complete three-dimensional space; but the shape appropriate to spirit is, as we have seen, its own body through which sculpture actualizes the spirit in all the spatial dimensions.

From this point of view sculpture is at the same stage as architecture in so far as it gives shape to the perceptible as such, to matter in its material and spatial form. But all the same it differs from architecture in that it does not remould the inorganic, as the opposite of spirit, into a spiritually created purposeful environment with forms which have their purpose outside themselves; on the contrary, it gives to spirit itself, purposive as it is and independent in itself, a corporeal shape appropriate to the very nature of spirit and its individuality, and it brings both—body and spirit—before our vision as one and the same indivisible whole. The sculptured shape is therefore emancipated from the architectural purpose of serving as a mere external nature and environment for the spirit and it exists simply for its own sake. But despite this freedom, a sculpture does nevertheless remain essentially connected with its surroundings. Neither a statue nor a group, still less a relief, can be fashioned without considering the place where the work of art is to be put. A sculptor should not first complete his work and only afterwards look around to see whither it is to be taken: on the contrary, his very conception of the work must be connected with specific external surroundings and their spatial form and their locality. For this reason sculpture retains a permanent relation with spaces formed architecturally. For the earliest purpose of statues was to be images in temples and set up in the interior of the cell, just as in Christian churches painting for its part provided altar-pictures; and in Gothic architecture too the same connection appears between sculptures and their position. Yet temples and churches are not the sole place for statues, groups, and reliefs; halls, staircases, gardens, public squares, gates, single columns, triumphal arches, etc., are likewise animated and, as it were, peopled by works of sculpture, and, quite independently of this wider environment, each statue demands a pedestal of its own to mark its position and terrain. On the connection between architecture and sculpture this may suffice.

If we go on to compare sculpture with the other arts, it is especially painting and poetry that come into consideration. Both single statues and groups present us with man as he is, with spirit completely in the shape of the body. Thus sculpture seems to have the mode truest to nature for representing the spirit, while painting and poetry seem to be unnatural because painting uses only flat surfaces instead of the three visible spatial dimensions which the human form and other things in nature actually occupy; and still less does speech express the corporeal, for by its utterance it can communicate only ideas of it.

Nevertheless, the truth is precisely the opposite. While a sculpture does indeed seem to have the advantage on the score of naturalness, this naturalness and corporeal externality presented in terms of heavy matter is precisely not the nature of spirit as spirit. As spirit, its own proper existence is its expression in speech, deeds, actions which are the development of its inner life and disclose to it what it is.

In this regard, sculpture must retire in favour of poetry especially. It is true that in visual art the corporeal is brought before our eyes in plastic clarity, but poetry too can describe the outlines of the human form, hair, brow, cheeks, build, clothing, posture, etc., though, true, not with the precision and exactitude of sculpture. But this deficiency is made up by imagination which does not need such definitive and detailed accuracy for producing a plain idea of an individual. Besides, imagination brings the man before us above all in *action*, with all his motives, the complications of his fate and circumstances, all his feelings and speech, with a disclosure of his thoughts as well as what happens to him in the world. This is what sculpture is incapable of doing except in a very imperfect way, because it can portray neither the subjective inner life in its own private depth of feeling and passion, nor, as poetry can, a series of its expressions, but only the universal element in an individual so far as the body can express that; it provides only a specific moment with nothing to follow it, something motionless without the progress of a living action.

In these respects sculpture is inferior to painting too. For, in painting, the expression of spirit acquires a superior and more definite accuracy and vividness, owing to the colour of the face and its light and shadow, not only in the natural sense of a purely material exactitude but above all in the sense of affording an appearance of facial and emotional significance. Therefore we could suppose at first sight that sculpture would need, with a view to coming nearer to perfection, to combine its own advantage of being three-dimensional with the different advantages of painting: is it just a caprice to have decided to give up painting's colour? Is it an inadequacy or unskilfulness in execution which confines itself to one feature of externality, i.e. its material form, and abstracts from the rest, just as, e.g., silhouettes or engravings are a mere *pis-aller*? The answer is that there can be no question of any such caprice in true art. The shape which is the subject of sculpture remains in fact only one abstract aspect of the concrete human body; its forms lack any variety of particular colours and movements. Nevertheless this is no accidental deficiency, but a restriction of material and mode of portrayal imposed by the very conception of art. For art is a product of the spirit, and indeed of the spirit in its higher level as thinking, and the subject-matter imposed on itself by a work of art like sculpture is a specific content and therefore requires a mode of presentation abstracted from other sorts of artistic realization. It is with art here as it is with the different sciences: the sole subject-matter of geometry is space, of jurisprudence law, of philosophy the unfolding of the eternal Idea and its existence and self-awareness in things; philosophy alone develops these topics in their difference and different forms, while none of the sciences mentioned brings completely before us what is called 'concrete actual existence' in the ordinary sense of these words.

Now art, as shaping what originates in the spirit, proceeds gradually, and separates what is separated in thought, in the real nature of the thing, but not in its existence. Therefore it maintains each of its stages fixedly in order to develop it in its own peculiar character. So in the conception of what is material and spatial, the element of visual art, we must distinguish and separate the corporeal as a three-dimensional totality from its abstract form, i.e. the human *shape* as such, and its more detailed particular character in relation to the variety of its colouring. In relation to the human form the art of sculpture stops at the first of these stages, for it treats that form as a stereometrical body in its three-dimensional shape. Now the work of art, belonging as it does to the field of what is sensuously perceived, must exist for someone's apprehension, and particularization begins at once with this. But the first art concerned with the form of the human body as an expression of spirit gets no further with this existence for someone's apprehension than the first still universal mode of existence in nature, i.e. pure visibility and what is in general illuminated,

INTRODUCTION

without bringing into the presentation that bearing on darkness where the visible is inherently particularized and becomes colour.[1] It is here, in the necessary course of art, that sculpture stands. For while poetry can embrace the totality of appearance in one and the same element, i.e. in our ideas, visual art must accept the separation of this totality into its parts.

Therefore on the one side we have *objectivity* which, not being the proper shape of the spirit, confronts it as inorganic nature. This object is changed by architecture into a merely indicative symbol, and the spiritual meaning which it indicates lies outside it. The extreme opposite of objectivity is *subjectivity*, the heart, feeling in the entire range of all its particular agitations, moods, passions, inner and outer movements, and deeds. Between these two extremes we meet with spiritual *individuality* which at this stage is definite indeed but not yet deep enough to comprise the inwardness of the subjective heart. What preponderates in individuality here is not personal individuality but the substantive universal element in the spirit and its aims and characteristics. In its universality it is not yet absolutely driven back into itself as a single spiritual unit, for as this middle term, issuing from the objective, from inorganic nature, it has the corporeal within itself as the proper existence of the spirit in the body belonging to it and manifesting it. In this external object which is no longer the mere opposite of the inner life, spiritual individuality is to be presented, yet not as a living body, i.e. one continually referred back to the point of unity implied in the spiritual individual, but as a form envisaged and presented as external; into this mould the spirit is poured, yet without coming out of this externality to appear in its withdrawal into itself as something inward.

These considerations determine the two points mentioned above: instead of taking for its expression in a symbolic way modes of appearance merely *indicative* of the spirit, sculpture lays hold of the human form as the *actual* existence of the spirit. Nevertheless, however, as the representation of unfeeling subjectivity and of emotion not yet particularized, sculpture is content with the *shape* as such in which the point of subjectivity is spread out. This is also the reason why sculpture does not present the spirit in action in a series of movements which have and accomplish a purpose or in undertakings and deeds in which character is displayed; and why,

[1] Once again, Goethe's theory of colour as a synthesis of light and dark.

on the contrary, it presents the spirit as it were remaining objective and therefore, principally, in a repose of form in which movement and grouping is only the first and easy beginning of action but not a complete presentation of a person drawn into all the conflicts of inner and outer struggles or involved with the external world in so many ways. Therefore since a sculpture after all brings before our eyes the spirit which, though immersed in the body, must be visibly manifest throughout the whole shape, it lacks the point where the person appears as person, i.e. the concentrated expression of soul as soul, the flash of the eye, as will be explained in more detail later. On the other hand, the subject of sculpture—individuality with its inner side not yet differentiated and particularized in a variety of ways—does not yet need for its appearance the painter's magic of colour which by the delicacy and variety of its shades can make visible the whole wealth of particular characteristics, the entire emergence of the spirit in its inner life, and the whole concentration of mind in the glance of the eye that reveals the soul. Sculpture must not adopt material unnecessary for the specific stage at which it stands. Consequently it avails itself not of a painter's colours but only of the spatial forms of the human body. On the whole a sculpture is uniformly coloured, hewn from white marble and not from something variously coloured; it also has metals at command as material, this original matter, self-identical, undifferentiated, a so-to-say congealed light without opposition and without the harmony of different colours.

It is the great spiritual insight of the Greeks to have grasped and firmly retained this position.[1] It is true that there do occur even in Greek sculpture, to which we must confine ourselves in the main, examples of polychrome statues, but in this matter we must distinguish art as it begins and ends from what it has achieved at its real summit. In the same way we must discount what religious tradition has dragged into this art and what does not properly belong to it. We have already seen in the case of the classical form of art that it did not immediately portray the finished ideal which

---

[1] Hegel is mistaken (deceived by Meyer) in thinking that the practice of colouring statues had ceased in the age when Greek sculpture was at its zenith. 'Greek sculpture throughout its career was painted.... Unpainted sculpture is a recent taste.... It was only in the Renaissance that unpainted figures were produced' (G. M. A. Richter, *The Sculpture and Sculptors of the Greeks* (New Haven and London, 1950), pp. 148–9. This book with its wealth of plates is a valuable aid to following Hegel's section on Sculpture.)

provided its fundamental determinant but had first to strip away much that was inappropriate and foreign to it. The same is true about sculpture. It must go through many preliminary stages before coming to perfection and its beginning differs in many ways from the summit it reaches. The oldest sculptures are painted wood, like the Egyptian idols, and the same is true even in the case of the Greeks. But things of this kind must be excluded when it is a matter of keeping to the fundamental nature of sculpture. Therefore it cannot be denied at all that many examples of painted statues occur, but the purer artistic taste became, the more did it 'give up that display of colour which was inappropriate to it; instead with wise deliberation it used light and shade in order to meet the spectator's eye with greater suppleness, repose, clarity, and pleasure' (Meyer, op. cit., i. 119). In contrast to the purely uniform colour of marble, not only may many bronze statues be cited of course, but, still more important, the greatest and finest works which, like, e.g., the Zeus of Phidias, were polychromatic [because chryselephantine]. Yet I am not discussing the abstraction of a complete *absence* of colour; ivory and gold are always coloured without the use of a painter's colour. And, in general, different productions of a specific kind of art do not always keep in fact to the fundamental nature of that art in abstract immutability, for they come into living relation with varied purposes, acquire local positions of various kinds and therefore become connected with external circumstances which once again modify the basic type. So, for instance, sculptures were often made from rich materials like gold and ivory; they were placed on magnificent thrones or stood on pedestals framed artistically and with prodigal luxuriousness and were provided with costly ornamentation in order to give the people who looked at such magnificent works an enjoyment of their power and richness. In particular, while sculpture is in and by itself a more abstract art, it does not always remain in this abstraction but brings with it incidentally from its origin much that is traditional, hidebound, and localized, but it is also adapted to the living needs of the people: for an active man requires an entertaining variety and wants employment in many directions for his vision and ideas. It is the same with a *reading* of Greek tragedies which also gives us the work of art in its more abstract form. When they are given a further existence externally, then performance is added with living characters, costume, stage decorations, dances, and music. In a similar way a sculpture in its real external appearance is not destitute of varied accessories; but here we are concerned only with sculpture proper as such, for those externals ought not to hinder us from becoming conscious of the inmost nature of the thing itself in its specific determinate character and in abstraction from anything superadded.

DIVISION OF THE SUBJECT

Proceeding now to the detailed division of this section, we find that sculpture is so much the centre of the classical form of art that here we cannot accept, as we could in the case of architecture, the symbolic, classical, and romantic as decisive differences and the basis of our division. Sculpture is the art proper to the classical ideal as such: of course sculpture too has stages at which, e.g. in Egypt, it is invaded by the symbolic form of art; but these are really only historical preliminaries, not differences inherent in the real conception and essence of sculpture, because owing to the manner of their placing and the use made of them these productions rather devolve on architecture than belong to the proper purpose of sculpture. In a similar way sculpture transcends itself when it becomes an expression of the romantic art-form, and only when it took to imitating Greek sculpture did it acquire its proper plastic type again. Consequently we must look elsewhere for a division.

In view of what has been said already, the centre of our treatment is derived from the manner in which it is through sculpture that the Greek ideal attains its most adequate realization. But before we can get to this development of ideal sculptures, we must first show what content and what form properly pertain to the character of sculpture as one of the particular arts and which therefore lead it to present the classical ideal in the spiritually permeated human figure and its abstractly spatial form. On the other hand the classical ideal rests on individuality, substantive indeed but nevertheless essentially particularized, with the result that sculpture takes for its content not the ideal of the human figure *in general* but the *determinate* ideal, and so separates into different modes of portrayal. These differences affect, partly the treatment and portrayal as such, partly the material in which the treatment is carried out and which by its varying character introduces new and

INTRODUCTION

further particular differences into the art, and with these there is then connected a final difference, namely the stages in the historical development of sculpture.

In the light of these considerations our inquiry will take the following course:

First, we are concerned solely with the general determinants of the essential nature of the content and form employed: these determinants arise from the very conception of sculpture.

Secondly, the classical ideal is analysed in more detail in so far as it attains by sculpture its most artistically appropriate existence.

Thirdly, and lastly, sculpture expands into the use of different kinds of portrayal and material, and opens out into a world of separate works in which in one way or another the symbolic and romantic art-forms assert themselves too, while in the middle between them the classical form is the genuinely plastic one.

Chapter I

THE PRINCIPLE OF SCULPTURE PROPER

Sculpture in general comprises the miracle of spirit's giving itself an image of itself in something purely material. Spirit so forms this external thing that it is present to itself in it and recognizes in it the appropriate shape of its own inner life.

What we have to consider in this connection concerns

First, the question what manner of spiritual life is capable of portraying itself in this element of a purely visible and spatial shape;

Secondly, how spatial forms must be shaped in order to make the spiritual known in a beautiful and corporeal figure; what we have to see in general is the unity of the *ordo rerum extensarum* and the *ordo rerum idealium*, the first beautiful unification of soul and body, in so far as the spiritual inner life expresses itself in sculpture only in its existence as body.

Thirdly, this unification corresponds with what we have already come to know as the ideal of the classical art-form, so that the plasticity of sculpture turns out to be the real and proper art of the classical ideal.

1. *The Essential Content of Sculpture*

The element in which sculpture creates its productions is, as we have seen, spatial matter in its original and still universal existence; in this material no particularization is employed for artistic use except the three universal spatial dimensions and the elementary spatial forms which those dimensions are capable of receiving when they are being shaped in the most beautiful way. To this more abstract aspect of the visible material there peculiarly corresponds, as content, the objectivity of spirit in its self-repose, i.e. the stage at which spirit has not distinguished itself either from its universal substance or its existence in body and therefore has not withdrawn into the self-awareness of its own subjectivity. Here there are two points to distinguish.

(*a*) Spirit as spirit is always subjectivity, inner self-knowledge, the ego. But this self can detach itself from what in knowing, willing, imagining, feeling, acting, and accomplishing constitutes the universal and eternal content of the spirit, and retain a hold on its own particular and fortuitous character. In that event it is subjectivity itself which comes into view because it relinquishes the objective and true content of the spirit and relates itself to itself as spirit in only a formal way, with no content. For example, in the case of self-satisfaction I can of course in a way regard myself quite objectively and be content with myself for doing a moral action. Yet, as self-satisfied, I am already ignoring what the action concretely was; as this individual, this self, I am abstracting myself from the universality of the spirit in order to compare myself with it. In this comparison, the concurrence of myself with myself produces the self-satisfaction in which this determinate self, precisely as this unit, rejoices in itself. A man's own ego is present in everything that he knows, wills, and carries out; only it makes a great difference whether in his knowing and acting his prime concern is his own particular self or what constitutes the essential content of consciousness, whether a man is immersed with his whole self undividedly in this content or lives steadily dependent on his own subjective personality.

(α) If what is substantive is thus disdained, a person, as subject, succumbs to the world of inclination where everything is abstract and separate, to the caprice and fortuitousness of feeling and impulse; the result is that, involved in the perpetual movement from one specific action or deed to another, he is a victim of dependence on specific circumstances and their changes and, in short, cannot avoid being tied to other persons and things. It follows that the person in these circumstances is purely finite and contrasted with the true spirit. Now if nevertheless he persists in this opposition, and the consciousness of it in his knowing and willing, and so clings to his subjective life alone, then, apart from the emptiness of his fancies and his image of himself, he falls into the ugliness of passions and idiosyncrasy, into viciousness and sin, into malice, ill-will, cruelty, spite, envy, pride, arrogance, and all the other perversities of human nature and its empty finitude.

(β) This whole sphere of subjective life is *eo ipso* excluded from sculpture which belongs solely to the objective side of spirit. By 'objective' here we are to understand what is substantial, genuine, imperishable, the essential nature that the spirit has without giving way to what is accidental and perishable, to that sphere to which the person surrenders himself if he relates himself exclusively to himself alone.

(γ) Yet the objective spirit cannot, as spirit, acquire reality without self-consciousness. For the spirit is spirit only as subject or person. But the position of the subjective within the spiritual content of sculpture is of such a kind that this subjective element is not expressed on its own account but shows itself as entirely permeated by what is substantive and objective and is not reflected back out of it into itself. Therefore the objective does have self-consciousness but a self-knowledge and volition not freed from the content which fills it but forming with it an inseparable unity.

The spiritual in this completely independent perfection of what is inherently substantial and true, this undisturbed and unparticularized being of the spirit, is what we call divinity in contrast to finitude as dispersal into fortuitous existence, differentiation, and fluctuating movement. From this point of view, sculpture has to present the Divine as such in its infinite peace and sublimity, timeless, immobile, without purely subjective personality and the discord of actions and situations. If sculpture does proceed to give closer definition to a man's figure or character, then in this event it must lay hold simply on what is unalterable and permanent, i.e. the substance, and only the substance, of his determinate characteristics; it must not choose for its content what is accidental and transient, because in its objectivity the spirit does not enter this changing and fleeting world of particulars which comes on the scene with a subjectivity conceived as individuality and no more. In a biography, for example, which relates the various fortunes, adventures, and acts of an individual, this history of diverse complications and arbitrariness usually ends with a character-sketch which summarizes this extensive detail in some such general quality as 'goodness, honesty, bravery, intellectual excellence' etc. Descriptions like these report what is permanent in an individual, whereas the additional particular details belong only to the accidents of his career. This permanent element is what sculpture has to portray as the one and only being and existence of individuality. Yet out of such general qualities it does not make mere allegories at all, but forms individuals whom it treats and shapes in their *objective* spiritual character as complete and perfect in themselves, in independent repose, exempt from relation to anything else. In sculpture the essential basis in every individual figure is what is substantive, and neither subjective feeling and self-knowing nor any superficial and alterable characteristic may gain the upper hand anywhere; what must be brought before our eyes in undimmed clarity is the eternal element in gods and men, divested of caprice and accidental egotism.

(*b*) The other point to be mentioned is this: since the sculptor's material makes the portrayal necessarily an external one in a three-dimensional solid, the content of sculpture cannot be spirit as such, i.e. the inner life, immersed in itself and reverting out of the object to close with itself alone, but the spirit which in its opposite, the body, is just beginning to become conscious of itself. The negation of the external is part and parcel of the inner subjective life, and therefore it cannot enter here where the divine and the human are adopted as the content of sculpture only in their objective character. And only this objective spirit, immersed in itself, without any inner subjective life as such, gives free scope to externality in all its dimensions and is bound up with this totality of space. But, for this reason, sculpture must take, as its subject matter, out of the objective content of spirit only that aspect which can be completely expressed in something external and corporeal, because otherwise it selects a content which its material cannot adopt or bring into appearance in an adequate way.

2. *The Beautiful Sculptural Form*

Now, given such a content, the second question is about the bodily forms called upon to express it.

Just as, in the case of classical architecture, the house is as it were the available anatomical skeleton to which art has to give further form, so sculpture for its part finds the human figure available as the fundamental type for its productions. But while the house itself is already a human, if not artistic, invention, the structure of the human frame appears as a product of nature, independently of man. The fundamental type is therefore *given* to sculpture, not devised by it. But to say that the human form belongs to nature is to use a very vague expression which we must explain more clearly.

In nature, as we saw in our consideration of the beauty of nature, it is the Idea which gives itself its first and immediate existence and it acquires its adequate *natural* existence in animal life and its complete organization. Thus the organization of the animal body is a product of the Concept in its inherent totality which exists in this corporeal existent as its soul. But as this soul, as the life of the animal merely, the Concept modifies the animal body into extremely varied particular types even if it always regulates the character of each specific type. However, it is a matter for the philosophy of nature to comprehend the correspondence between the Concept and the shape of the body or, more precisely, between soul and body. It would have to show[1] that the different types of the animal body in their inner structure, shape, and connection with one another, and the different specific organs within the body, conform to the moments of the Concept, so that it would be clear how far it is only the necessary particular aspects of the soul itself which are realized at this stage. Still, to prove this conformity is not our business in this context.

But the human form, unlike the animal, is the body not only of the soul, but of the spirit. Spirit and soul must be essentially distinguished from one another.[2] For soul is only this ideal simple self-awareness of the body as *body*, while spirit is the self-awareness of conscious and self-conscious life with all the feelings, ideas, and aims of this conscious existent. Granted this enormous difference between purely animal life and the consciousness of spirit, it may seem surprising that spirit's corporeality, the human body, nevertheless proves to be homogeneous with the animal one. We can remove amazement at such a similarity by recalling that determinate character which spirit decides to give to itself in accordance with its own essential nature, that character in virtue of which it is alive and therefore in itself simultaneously soul and natural existent. Now, as a living soul, spirit by virtue of the same Concept which is immanent in the animal soul gives itself a body which in its fundamental character generally matches the living animal organism. Therefore, however superior spirit is to mere life, it makes for itself its body which appears articulated and ensouled by one and the same Concept as that of the animal body. Further, however, spirit is not only the Idea existent, i.e. the Idea as nature

---

[1] Hegel's attempt to show this may be found in his *Philosophy of Nature*, §§ 350 ff. See also above in Vol. I, pp. 118–19, 434.

[2] For this distinction in detail and Hegel's doctrine of the soul in its various aspects (or stages) see his *Philosophy of Mind*, §§ 388 ff. (tr. by W. Wallace and A. V. Miller, Oxford, 1971).

THE PRINCIPLE OF SCULPTURE PROPER 715

and animal life, but the Idea present to itself as Idea in its own free element of the inner life, and so the spirit fashions its proper objectivity beyond perceptible life—i.e. in philosophy which has no other reality save that of thought itself. Apart from thinking and its philosophical and systematic activity, the spirit does still nevertheless lead a full life in feeling, inclination, imagination, fancy, etc.; this stands in more or less close connection with spirit's existence as soul and body and therefore has reality in the human body. The spirit makes itself living likewise in this reality appropriate to itself, it glints in it, pervades it, and through it becomes manifest to others. Therefore because the human body remains no merely natural existent but in its shape and structure has to declare itself as likewise the sensuous and natural existence of the spirit, it still, as an expression of a higher inner life, must nevertheless be distinguished from the animal body, no matter how far in general the human body corresponds with the animal. But since the spirit itself is soul and life, an animal body, there are and can be only modifications which the spirit, immanent in a living body, introduces into this corporeal sphere. Therefore, as an appearance of the spirit, the human form does differ from the animal in respect of these modifications, although the differences between the human and the animal organism belong to the unconscious creative work of the spirit, just as the animal soul forms its body by unconscious activity.

This is our point of departure in this matter. The human form as an expression of spirit is *given* to the artist, but he does not just find it generalized; on the contrary, in particular details the model for mirroring the spiritual inner life is presupposed in the shape, specific traits, posture, and demeanour of the body.

As for the more precise connection between spirit and body in respect of particular feelings, passions, and states of mind, it is very difficult to reduce it to fixed categories. Attempts have indeed been made in pathognomy[1] and physiognomy to present this connection scientifically, but so far without real success. Physiognomy alone can be of any importance to us because pathognomy is concerned only with the way that specific feelings and passions come alive in certain organs. So, for instance, it is said that anger has its seat in bile, courage in the blood. Said incidentally, this is

[1] This word, meaning the study of passions and emotions or of signs and expressions of them, was first used in English in 1793 in a summary of Lavater.

at once a false expression. For even if the activity of particular organs corresponds to particular passions, still anger does not have its *seat* in bile; on the contrary in so far as anger is corporeal, it is primarily in bile that its activity appears. This pathognomy, as I said, does not concern us here, for sculpture has to deal only with what passes over from the spiritual inner life into the external element of shape and makes the spirit corporeal and visible there. The sympathetic vibration of the inner organism and conscious feelings is not a topic for sculpture, and sculpture also cannot harbour a great deal that does appear in the external shape, e.g. the shaking of the hand and the whole body at an outburst of wrath, the twitching of the lips, etc.

About physiognomy I will only mention here that if the work of sculpture, which has the human figure as its basis, is to show how the body, in its bodily form, presents not only the divine and human substance of the spirit in a merely general way but also the particular character of a specific individual in this portrayal of the Divine, we would have to embark on an exhaustive discussion of what parts, traits, and configurations of the body are completely adequate to express a specific inner mood. We are instigated to such a study by classical sculptures to which we must allow that in fact they do express the Divine and the characters of particular gods. To admit this is not to maintain that the correspondence between the expression of spirit and the visible form is only a matter of accident and caprice and not something absolutely necessary. In this matter each organ must in general be considered from two points of view, the purely physical one and that of spiritual expression. It is true that in this connection we may not proceed after the manner of Gall[1] who makes the spirit into a bump on the skull.

(a) *Exclusion of Particulars*

Owing to the content which it has the vocation of portraying, we must go no further in the case of sculpture than to investigate how the spirit, both as substance and at the same time as individual within this universality, adopts a body and therein gains existence and form. In other words, owing to the content which is adequate for genuine sculpture, on the one hand the accidental particularity

---

[1] F. J., 1758–1828, the inventor of phrenology.

of the external appearance, whether of body or spirit, is excluded. What sculpture has to present is only the permanent, universal, and regular elements in the form of the human body, even if there is a demand so to individualize this universal element that what is put before our eyes is not only abstract regularity but an individual figure most closely fused with it.

(b) Exclusion of Mien

On the other hand, sculpture, as we saw, must keep itself free from the accidents of personality and its expression in its own independent inner life. Consequently the artist is forbidden, so far as the face is concerned, to propose to go as far as presenting the mien [or a facial expression]. For mien is nothing but simply what makes visible the subject's own inner life and his particular feeling, imagining, and willing. In his mien a man expresses only himself as he feels inwardly, precisely as this individual as he accidentally is, whether he is concerned only with himself or whether his feeling is a reflection from his relation to external objects or other persons. So, for instance, on the street, especially in small towns, we see by their features and mien that many people, indeed most people, are concerned only with themselves, their clothes and finery, in general with their subjective personality or, alternatively, with other passers-by and their accidental peculiarities and eccentricities. To this context there belong the miens of pride, envy, self-satisfaction, disdain, etc. But then further a mien may have its source in the feeling of what is substantive and in the comparison of that with my private personality. Humility, scorn, menacing, fear, are miens of this kind. Such comparison leads at once to a separation between the subject as such and the universal, and then reflection on what is substantive always reverts to introspection, so that this and not the substance remains the predominant thing. But neither that separation nor this predominance of the subjective ought to find expression in the shape that remains strictly true to the principle of sculpture.

Finally, apart from miens proper, the facial expression contains much that merely flits over the countenance and indicates a man's situation: a momentary smile, the sudden flash of an angry man's eye, a quickly effaced streak of mockery, etc. In this respect it is the mouth and the eye that have the most mobility and the greatest capacity to seize and make apparent every nuance of an emotional mood. Changes of this character, which are a suitable subject for painting, sculpture has to waive. It must on the contrary direct itself to the permanent features of the spiritual expression and concentrate on and reproduce these whether facially or in the posture and forms of the body.

(c) *Substantive Individuality*

Thus it turns out that the task of sculpture essentially consists in implanting in a human figure the spiritual substance in its not yet subjectively particularized individuality, and in setting this figure and this substance in a harmony in which what is emphasized is only the universal and permanent element in the bodily forms corresponding to the spirit, while the fortuitous and the transient is stripped away, although at the same time the figure must not lack individuality.

Such a complete correspondence of inner with outer, the goal of sculpture, leads us on to the third point which is still to be discussed.

3. *Sculpture as the Art of the Classical Ideal*

The first inference from the foregoing considerations is that sculpture more than any other art always points particularly to the Ideal. That is to say, on the one hand it is beyond the symbolic sphere alike in the clarity of its content, which is now grasped as spirit, and in the fact that its presentations are perfectly adequate to this content; on the other hand, it still ignores the subjectivity of the inner life to which the external shape is a matter of indifference. It therefore forms the centre of classical art. True, symbolic and romantic architecture and painting are conformable to the classical ideal, but the ideal in its proper sphere is not the supreme law for the symbolic and romantic art-forms or for architecture and painting, because these, unlike sculpture, do not have as their subject-matter substantive individuality, entire objective character, beauty at once free and necessary. But the sculptured figure must proceed throughout from the spirit of the thoughtful imagination which abstracts from all the accidents of the bodily form and spirit's subjective side, and which has no predilection for idiosyncrasies, or any feeling, pleasure, variety of impulses, or sallies of wit. For what is within the sculptor's reach for his supreme productions is, as we have seen, only spirit's body in what are the purely universal forms of the build and organization of the human figure; and his invention is limited partly to portraying the equally universal correspondence between inner and outer, and partly to giving an appearance to the individuality which, albeit unobtrusively, is accommodated to and interwoven with the universal substance. Sculpture must configurate in the way that within their own sphere the gods create according to eternal Ideas, while abandoning everything else in the rest of reality to the freedom and self-will of the creature. Similarly, theologians distinguish between what God does and what man accomplishes by his folly and caprice; but the plastic ideal is lifted above such questions because it occupies this milieu of divine blessedness and free necessity,[1] and for this milieu neither the abstraction of the universal nor the caprice of the particular has any validity or significance.

This sense for the perfect plasticity of gods and men was preeminently at home in Greece. In its poets and orators, historians and philosophers, Greece is not to be understood at its heart unless we bring with us as a key to our comprehension an insight into the ideals of sculpture and unless we consider from the point of view of their plasticity not only the heroic figures in epic and drama but also the actual statesmen and philosophers. After all, in the beautiful days of Greece men of action, like poets and thinkers, had this same plastic and universal yet individual character both inwardly and outwardly. They are great and free, grown independently on the soil of their own inherently substantial personality, self-made, and developing into what they [essentially] were and wanted to be. The Periclean age was especially rich in such characters: Pericles himself, Phidias, Plato, Sophocles above all, Thucydides too, Xenophon, Socrates—each of them of his own sort, unimpaired by another's; all of them are out-and-out artists by nature, ideal artists shaping themselves, individuals of a single cast, works of art standing there like immortal and deathless images of the gods,

---

[1] Blessedness is the character normally ascribed to the gods in Homer. The artist works in freedom and yet, when what he produces is a beautiful work of art, it is necessitated. It could not be otherwise than it is without departing from the ideal.

in which there is nothing temporal and doomed. The same plasticity is characteristic of the works of art which victors in the Olympic games made of their bodies, and indeed even of the appearance of Phryne,[1] the most beautiful of women, who rose from the sea naked in the eyes of all Greece.

[1] The famous courtesan who was the model for Apelles' picture of Aphrodite rising from the sea.

Chapter II

THE IDEAL OF SCULPTURE

In proceeding to consider the ideal style of sculpture we must once again recall that perfect art is necessarily preceded by imperfect, not merely in technique, which is not our prime concern here, but in the conception of the universal Idea and the manner of portraying it ideally. The art which is still seeking we have called, in general terms, the symbolic. Consequently even pure sculpture has a symbolic stage as its presupposition, not at all a symbolic stage in general, i.e. architecture, but a sculpture in which the character of the symbolic is still immanent. That this occurs in Egyptian sculpture we will have an opportunity of seeing later in Chapter III.

Here, in a quite abstract and formal way, taking the standpoint of the ideal, we may take the symbolic in art to be the imperfection of each specific art. Consider, for instance, a child's attempt to draw a human figure or to mould it in wax or clay; what he produces is a mere symbol because it only indicates the living man it is supposed to portray while remaining completely untrue to him and his significance. So art at first is hieroglyphic, not an arbitrary and capricious sign but a rough sketch of the object for our apprehension. For this purpose a bad sketch is adequate, provided that it recalls the figure it is supposed to mean. It is in a similar way that piety is satisfied with bad images, and in the most bungled counterfeit still worships Christ, Mary, or some saint, although such figures are recognized as individuals only by particular attributes like, for example, a lantern, a gridiron, or a millstone.[1] For piety only wants to be reminded of the object of worship in a general way; the rest is added by the worshipper's mind which is supposed to be filled with the idea of the object by means of the image, however unfaithful it may be. It is not the living expression

---

[1] Examples are: Lantern—St. Lucia and St. Gudule (her church in Brussels contained the finest stained glass that Hegel had ever seen. Letter, 8. viii. 1822). Gridiron—St. Laurence (because he was roasted on one). Millstone—fairly common, e.g. especially St. Florian and St. Vincent who were drowned with millstones round their necks.

of the object's presence which is demanded; it is not something present which is to fire us by itself; on the contrary the work of art is content simply to arouse a general idea of the object by means of its figures, however little they correspond with it. But our ideas are always abstractions. I can very easily have an idea of something familiar like, for instance, a house, a tree, a man, but although here the idea is engaged with something entirely specific it does not go beyond quite general traits, and, in general, it is only really an idea when it has obliterated from the concrete perception of the objects their purely immediate individuality and so has simplified what is seen. Now if the idea which the work of art is meant to awaken is an idea of the Divine and this idea is to be recognizable by everyone, by a whole people, this aim is achieved *par excellence* when no alteration at all is admitted into the mode of portrayal. In that case the result is that art becomes conventional and hidebound, as has happened not only with the older Egyptian art but with the older Greek and Christian art too. The artist had to keep to specific forms and repeat their type.

The great transition to the awakening of fine art we can only seek where the artist first works in freedom according to the ideal as he conceives it, where the lightning flash of genius strikes the tradition and imparts freshness and vivacity to the presentation. Only in that case is a spiritual tone given to the entire work of art which is now no longer restricted to bringing some idea into consciousness in a general way and reminding the spectator of a deeper meaning which he carries in his head already otherwise. On the contrary it proceeds to portray this meaning as wholly alive and graphic in an individual figure. Therefore it does not confine itself to the purely superficial universality of forms nor in respect of closer definition does it cling to traits available in the ordinary world.

Pressure to reach this stage is the necessary presupposition for the emergence of ideal sculpture.

The following are the points to be made about ideal sculpture.

First, it is a matter of considering, in contrast to the stages just mentioned, the *general* character of the ideal figure and its forms.

Secondly, we must cite the *particular* aspects of importance, the sort of facial characteristics, drapery, pose, etc.

Thirdly, the ideal figure is not a purely universal form of beauty in general, but, owing to the principle of individuality which belongs to the genuine and living ideal, it essentially includes differences and their definition; this widens the sphere of sculpture into a cycle of individual images of gods, heroes, etc.

1. *General Character of the Ideal Sculptural Form*

We have already seen in detail what the general principle of the classical ideal is. Here therefore it is only a question of the manner in which this principle is actualized by sculpture in the form of the human figure. A higher standard of comparison [between what represents the ideal and what does not] may be afforded by the difference between the human attitude and face, which is expressive of the spirit, and that of the animal which does not go beyond an expression of animated natural life in its firm connection with natural needs and with the animal organism's structure that is designed for their satisfaction. But this criterion still remains vague, because the human form as such is not from the start already completely of an ideal kind either as body or as an expression of the spirit. Whereas we come closer to a criterion by our ability to acquire from the beautiful masterpieces of Greek sculpture a perception of what the sculptural ideal has to accomplish in the spiritually beautiful expression of its figures. Amongst those with this knowledge and with an insight into Greek art and a burning love of it, it is Winckelmann above all who with the enthusiasm of his reproductive insight[1] no less than with intelligence and sound judgement put an end to vague chatter about the ideal of Greek beauty by characterizing individually and with precision the forms of the parts [of Greek statuary]—the sole undertaking that was instructive. To the result he achieved it is true that there must be added many acute comments on details, as well as exceptions and the like, but we must beware of being so led astray by such further details and the occasional errors into which he fell as to become oblivious of his main achievement. Whatever the increase in our knowledge of the facts, that achievement of his must lead the way by providing the essence of the matter. Nevertheless, it cannot be gainsaid that since Winckelmann's death our acquaintance with works of ancient sculpture has been essentially enlarged, and not only in respect of their number; on the contrary in respect of their style and our

[1] The artist's vision and imagination is productive, the scholar's only reproductive of what the artist has produced.

estimate of their beauty, it has been placed on a firmer basis. Winckelmann had of course a great number of Egyptian and Greek statues in view, but more recently we can see Aeginetan sculptures as well as masterpieces ascribed to Phidias or necessarily recognized as belonging to his period and chiselled by his pupils. In short, we have now acquired a closer familiarity with a number of sculptures, statues, and reliefs which, when we think of the severity of the ideal style, must be placed in the period of the supreme blossoming of Greek art. These marvellous memorials of Greek sculpture we owe, as is well known, to the activities of Lord Elgin[1] who, as English ambassador to Turkey, took to England from the Parthenon at Athens, and from other Greek cities, statues and reliefs of supreme beauty. These acquisitions have been signalized as sacrilege and sharply criticized, but in fact what Lord Elgin did was precisely to save these works of art for Europe and preserve them from complete destruction, and his enterprise deserves recognition through all time. Apart from the opportunity thus given, the interest of all connoisseurs and friends of art has been engrossed by that epoch of Greek sculpture and its mode of portrayal which in the still rather solid severity of its style constitutes the real greatness and sublimity of the ideal. What the public mood has appreciated in the works of this epoch is not any attractiveness and grace in their forms and attitude, nor the charm of expression which is visible already after the time of Phidias and which aims at giving pleasure to spectators, nor the elegance and audacity of the execution; on the contrary, universal praise is given to the expression of independence, of self-repose, in these figures, and especially has our admiration been intensified to an extreme by their free vivacity, by the way in which the natural material is permeated and conquered by the spirit and in which the artist has softened the marble, animated it, and given it a soul. In particular, whenever that praise is exhausted, its comes back ever anew to the figure of the recumbent river-god which is amongst the most beautiful things preserved to us from antiquity.[2]

(*a*) The liveliness of these works is due to their having been

[1] The seventh Lord Elgin (1766–1841) was Ambassador to the Porte, 1799–1803. He arranged for the transfer of the 'Elgin Marbles' to England, 1803–12, and sold them to the nation in 1816.

[2] Since the Elgin marbles have just been mentioned, this is probably a reference to the Ilissus on the Parthenon west pediment. If so, Hegel's encomium may seem excessive.

created freely out of the spirit of the artist. At this stage the artist is not content to use general and fortuitous outlines, allusions, or expressions in order to provide an equally general idea of what he is supposed to be portraying; nor does he adopt, for portraying an individual or some single characteristic, the forms as he has received them by chance from the external world. For this reason he does not reproduce them for the sake of fidelity to this accidental detail; on the contrary, by his own free creative activity he can set the empirical detail of particular incidents in complete and, once more, individual harmony with the general forms of the human figure. This harmonious unity appears completely permeated by the spiritual content of what it is its vocation to manifest, while at the same time it reveals its own life, conception, and animation as given to it by the artist. The universal element in the content is not the artist's creation; it is given to him by mythology and tradition, just precisely as he is confronted by the universal and individual elements of the human form. But the free and living individualization which he gives to every part of his creation is the fruit of his own insight, is his work and his merit.

(*b*) The effect and magic of this life and freedom is only achieved by the exactitude and scrupulous fidelity with which every part is worked out, and this demands the most precise knowledge and vision of the character of these parts whether they are at rest or in movement. The manner in which the different limbs, in every situation of rest or movement, are posed or laid, rounded or flattened, etc., must be expressed with perfect accuracy. This thorough elaboration and exhibition of every single part we find in all the works of antiquity, and their animation is only achieved by infinite care and truth to life. In looking at such works the eye cannot at first make out a mass of differences and they become evident only under a certain illumination where there is a stronger contrast of light and shade, or they may be recognizable only by touch. Nevertheless although these fine nuances are not noticed at a first glance, the general impression which they produce is not for this reason lost. They may appear when the spectator changes his position or we may essentially derive from them a sense of the organic fluidity of all the limbs and their forms. This breath of life, this soul of material forms, rests entirely on the fact that each part is completely there independently and in its own particular character, while, all the same, owing to the fullest richness of the transitions, it remains in firm connection not only with its immediate neighbour but with the whole. Consequently the shape is perfectly animated at every point; even the minutest detail has its purpose; everything has its own particular character, its own difference, its own distinguishing mark, and yet it remains in continual flux, counts and lives only in the whole. The result is that the whole can be recognized in fragments, and such a separated part affords the contemplation and enjoyment of an unbroken whole. Although most of the statues are damaged now and have their surface weathered, the skin seems soft and elastic and, e.g. in that unsurpassable horse's head,[1] the fiery force of life glows through the marble.—It is the way that the organic lines flow gently into one another, along with the most conscientious elaboration of the parts without forming regular surfaces or anything merely circular or convex, that alone provides the atmosphere of life, that delicacy and ideal unity of all the parts, that harmony which pervades the whole like a spiritual breath of ensoulment.

(c) But however faithfully the forms are expressed either generally or individually, this fidelity is no mere copying of nature. For sculpture is always concerned solely with the abstraction of form and must therefore on the one hand abandon what is strictly natural in the body, i.e. what hints at merely natural functions, while on the other hand it may not proceed to particularize the most external details; for example, the treatment and presentation of hair must be confined to the more general element in the forms. In this way alone does the human figure appear, as should be the case in sculpture, not as a merely natural form but as the figure and expression of the spirit. As a corollary of this there is a further consideration, namely that while the spiritual content is expressed by sculpture in the body, in the case of the genuine ideal it does not enter something external to such an extent that the pleasure of the spectator could be wholly or mainly derived from this external object itself with its grace and charm. On the contrary, while the genuine and more severe ideal must of course give a *body* to the spirit and make the spirit visible only through the figure and its expression, the figure must nevertheless always appear upheld, borne, and completely penetrated by the spiritual content. The swelling of life,[2] the softness and charm or the sensuous wealth

---

[1] Probably one of those on the Parthenon frieze.
[2] *Turgor vitae*: cf. Vol. I, p. 146, note.

and beauty of the bodily organism must not in itself be what the portrayal aims at; neither may the individual element in the spirit go so far as to become an expression of something subjective more nearly akin and approximating to the spectator's own purely personal character.

2. Particular Aspects of the Ideal Form in Sculpture

If we turn now to consider in more detail the chief features of importance in connection with the ideal sculptural form, we will follow Winckelmann in the main; with the greatest insight and felicity he has described the particular forms and the way they were treated and developed by Greek artists until they count as the sculptural ideal. Their liveliness, this deliquescence, eludes the categories of the Understanding which cannot grasp the particular here or get to the root of it as it can in architecture [mathematically]. On the whole, however, as we have seen already, a connection can be adduced between the free spirit and bodily form.

The first general distinction which we can make in this connection affects the purpose of sculpture in general, i.e. to make the human form express something spiritual. Although the expression of spirit must be diffused over the appearance of the entire body, it is most concentrated in the face, whereas the other members can reflect the spirit only in their position, provided that that has been the work of the inherently free spirit.

Our consideration of the ideal forms will begin with the head; then, secondly, we will go on to discuss the position of the body, and then we end with the principle for the drapery.

(a) The Greek Profile

In the ideal formation of the human head, we are confronted above all by the so-called Greek profile.

(α) This profile depends on a specific connection between forehead and nose: in other words on the almost straight or only gently curved line on which the forehead is continued to the nose without interruption; and, in more detail, on the vertical alignment of this line to a second one which if drawn from the root of the nose to the auditory canal makes a right angle with the forehead–nose line. In ideal and beautiful sculpture forehead and nose are related together by such a line and the question arises whether this is a physical necessity or merely a national or artistic accident.

Camper in particular, the well-known Dutch physiologist, has characterized this line more precisely as the line of beauty in the face since he finds in it the chief difference between the formation of the human face and the animal profile, and therefore he pursues the modification of this line in the different races of mankind, a point on which Blumenbach, it is true, contradicts him.[1] But, in general, this line does in fact provide a very significant distinction between the human and animal appearance. In animals the mouth and the nasal bone do form a more or less straight line, but the specific projection of the animal's snout which presses forward as if to get as near as possible to the consumption of food is essentially determined by its relation to the skull on which the ear is placed further upward or downward, so that the line drawn to the root of the nose or to the upper jaw (where the teeth are inset) forms with the skull an acute angle, not a right angle as is the case in man. Everyone by himself can have a general sense of this difference which of course may depend on more definite considerations.

(αα) In the formation of the animal head the predominant thing is the mouth, as the tool for chewing, with the upper and lower jaw, the teeth, and the masticatory muscles. The other organs are added to this principal organ as only servants and helpers: the nose especially as sniffing out food, the eye, less important, for spying it. The express prominence of these formations exclusively devoted to natural needs and their satisfaction gives the animal head the appearance of being merely adapted to natural functions and without any spiritual ideal significance. So, after all, we can understand the whole of the animal organism in the light of these tools in the mouth. In other words, the specific kind of food demands a specific structure of the mouth, a special kind of teeth, with which there then most closely correspond the build of the jaws, masticatory muscles, cheek-bones, and, in addition, the spine, thigh-bones, hoofs, etc. The animal body serves purely natural purposes and acquires by this dependence on the merely material aspect of nourishment an expression of spiritual absence.

---

[1] P. Camper, 1722–89. His rectorial oration, *De pulchro physico*, was delivered at Gröningen in 1766. J. F. Blumenbach (1752–1840) published his doctoral dissertation, *De generis humani varietate nativa*, at Göttingen in 1775. Hegel cites § 60 of this work.

Now if the human appearance in its bodily form is to bear an impress of the spirit, then those organs which appear as the most important in the animal must be in the background in man and give place to those indicative not of a practical relation to things but of an ideal or theoretical one.

(ββ) Therefore the human face has a second centre in which the soulful and spiritual relation to things is manifested. This is in the upper part of the face, in the intellectual brow and, lying under it, the eye, expressive of the soul, and what surrounds it. That is to say that with the brow there are connected meditation, reflection, the spirit's reversion into itself while its inner life peeps out from the eye and is clearly concentrated there. Through this emphasis on the forehead, while the mouth and cheek-bones are secondary, the human face acquires a spiritual character. The fact that the forehead comes into the foreground determines of necessity the whole structure of the skull which no longer falls back, forming one leg of an acute angle, the extreme point of which is the mouth now drawn forward; on the contrary, a line can be drawn from the forehead through the nose to the point of the chin which forms a right angle, or approximately one, with a second line drawn from the back of the skull to the apex of the forehead.

(γγ) Thirdly, the transition from the upper to the lower part of the face, from the purely theoretical and spiritual brow to the practical organ of nourishment, and the connection between them, is the nose which even in its natural function as the organ of smell stands in between our theoretical and practical relation to the external world. In this central position it does still belong to an animal need, for smelling is essentially connected with taste and this after all is why in the animal the nose is there in the service of the mouth and feeding; but smelling itself is still not an actual practical devouring of things, like eating and tasting, but takes up only the result of a process in which things mingle with air and its secret and invisible volatilizing. Now if the transition from forehead to nose is so made that the forehead curves outwards and withdraws next the nose, while the nose on its side remains pressed in next the forehead and only subsequently is projected, the result is that the two parts of the face, the theoretical one, the forehead, and the one indicative of practical activity, the nose and the mouth, form a marked contrast, the effect of which is to draw the nose which belongs as it were to both parts, down from the forehead to the mouth. In that event the forehead in its isolated position acquires a look of severity and obstinate spiritual self-concentration contrasted with the eloquent communication of the mouth. The mouth then becomes the organ of nutrition and at once makes a servant of the nose as a tool for smelling and so for stimulating desire and shows how it is directed on a physical need. Further, there is connected with this the contingency of the indeterminable modifications of form which forehead and nose can consequently adopt. The sort of curve and the projection or retreat of the forehead loses any fixed determinacy, and the nose may be flat or pointed, drooping, arched, or snub and retroussé.

By softening and smoothing the lines, the Greek profile introduces a beautiful harmony into the gentle and unbroken connection between the forehead and the nose and so between the upper and lower parts of the face. The effect of this connection is that the nose is made more akin to the forehead and therefore, by being drawn up towards the spiritual part, acquires itself a spiritual expression and character. Smelling becomes as it were a theoretical smelling—becomes a keen nose for the spiritual; after all, in fact when one screws up one's nose, etc., however insignificant such movements may be, this is an extremely quick way of expressing spiritual judgements and kinds of feeling. So we say, for example, of a proud man that he looks down his nose, or we may call a young girl saucy when she tosses up her little nose.

Something similar is true of the mouth too. It does have the purpose of being a tool for satisfying hunger and thirst, but it does also express spiritual states, moods, and passions. Even in animals it serves in this respect for ejaculations, but in man for speech, laughter, sighing, etc., and in this way the lines of the mouth already have a characteristic connection with the eloquent communication of spiritual states or of joy, grief, etc.

It is said, it is true, that such a facial formation has occurred to the Greeks alone as the really beautiful one, while the Chinese, Jews, and Egyptians regarded other, indeed opposite, formations as just as beautiful or more so and that, therefore, verdict against verdict, there is no proof that the Greek profile is the model of genuine beauty. But this is only superficial chatter. The Greek profile is not to be regarded as an external and fortuitous form; it belongs to the ideal of beauty in its own independent nature because (i) it is that facial formation in which the expression of the spirit puts the merely natural wholly into the background, and (ii) it is the one which most escapes fortuitousness of form without exhibiting mere regularity and banning every sort of individuality.

(β) Out of the abundant detail in the individual forms I will select for mention here only a few points of importance. Accordingly we may deal first with the forehead, the eye, and the ear as the parts of the face more related to the spirit and the theoretical life; then secondly, with the mouth, nose, and chin as the formations belonging, more or less, rather to the practical sphere; and thirdly we have to mention the hair as an external setting rounding off the head to a beautiful oval.

(αα) In the ideal figures of classical sculpture the forehead is neither curved outwards nor, in general, high, because, although the spirit is meant to appear in the build of the face, what sculpture has to represent is not spirituality as such but individuality wholly expressed in a corporeal form. In heads of Hercules, for example, the forehead is particularly low because he possesses the muscular vigour of the body directed on external objects rather than an introspective vigour of mind. Elsewhere the forehead is variously modified, lower in charming and youthful female figures, higher in those more dignified and spiritual and more intellectual. Towards the temples it does not fall away at an acute angle; it does not sink into the temples but is rounded ovally in a soft curve and overgrown with hair. For the acute hairless angles and deep sinkings into the temples befit only the weakness of advancing years and not the eternal bloom of youth in ideal gods and heroes.

In regard to the eye, [*first,*] we must at once make it clear that the ideal sculptural figure not merely lacks what is properly the colour of painting but also the glance of the eye. Attempts have no doubt been made to prove historically that the Greeks did paint the eye on some temple-figures of Athene and other divinities, on the strength of the fact that traces of paint have still been found on some statues, but in the case of sacred images the artists often kept so far as possible to what was traditional, in defiance of good taste. In other cases it seems that the statues must have had precious stones inset as eyes. But then this proceeds from what I have mentioned before, the desire to decorate the images of the gods as richly and magnificently as possible. And, on the whole, this colouring belongs to the beginnings of art, or to religious traditions, or is an exception; besides, colouring does not ever give to the eye that self-concentrated glance which alone makes the eye completely expressive. Therefore we can take it here as incontestable that the iris and the glance expressive of the spirit is missing from the really classic and free statues and busts preserved to us from antiquity. For although the iris is often delineated in the eyeball or indicated by a conical depth and turn which expresses the brilliance of the iris and therefore a sort of glance, this still remains only the wholly external shape of the eye and is not its animation, not a real glance, the glance of the inner soul.

It is therefore easy to suppose that it must cost the artist a lot to sacrifice the eye, this simple expression of the soul. Do we not look a man first of all in the eye in order to get a support, a point, and a basis for explaining his entire appearance which in its greatest simplicity can be understood from this point of unity in his glance? His glance is what is most full of his soul, the concentration of his inmost personality and feeling. We are at one with a man's personality in his handshake, but still more quickly in his glance. And it is just this clearest expression of a man's soul that sculpture must lack, whereas in painting what appears by means of the shades of colour is the expression of the man's personality either in its whole inwardness of feeling or in his varied contact with things outside and the particular interests, feelings and passions which they evoke. But in sculpture the sphere of the artist is neither the inner feeling of the soul, the concentration of the whole man into the one simple self which appears in a glance as this ultimate point of illumination, nor with the personality diffused in the complications of the external world. Sculpture has as its aim the entirety of the external form over which it must disperse the soul, and it must present it in this variety, and therefore it is not allowed to bring back this variety to one simple soulful point and the momentary glance of the eye. The work of sculpture has no inwardness which would manifest itself explicitly as this ideal glance, in distinction from the rest of the body or thus enter the opposition between eye and body; on the contrary, what the individual is in his inner and spiritual life is effused over the entirety of the sculptural form, and is grasped as a whole only by the spirit, the spectator, contemplating it. *Secondly*, the eye looks out into the external world; by nature it looks at something and therefore displays man in his relation to a varied external sphere, just as in feeling he is related to his environment and what goes on there. But the genuine sculptural figure is precisely withdrawn from this link with external things and is immersed in the substantial nature of its spiritual content, independent in itself, not dispersed in or complicated by anything else. *Thirdly*, the glance of the eye acquires its developed meaning through what the rest of the body expresses in its features and speech, although it is distinguished from this development by being the purely formal point at which the subjective personality is concentrated and in which the whole variety of the figure and its environment is brought together. Such breadth of detail, however, is foreign to plastic art and so the more particular expression in the eye's glance, which does not find its further corresponding expansion in the whole of the figure, is only something accidental and fortuitous which sculpture must keep at arm's length.

For these reasons sculpture not only loses nothing by the sightlessness of its figures but *must*, in virtue of its whole nature, dispense with this expression of soul. Thus once again we see the great insight of the Greeks in realizing the limits and boundaries of sculpture and remaining strictly true to this abstraction. This is their higher intellect in the fullness of their reason and the entirety of their vision. It is true that even in their sculpture there are instances of the eye looking at something specific, as for example in the statue of the faun, mentioned already twice,[1] which looks down at the young Bacchus. This smile is soulfully expressed, but even here the eye is not seeing, and the real statues of the gods in their simple situations are not presented with a turning of the eye and the glance in some specific direction.

As for the appearance of the eye in ideal sculptures, in its form it is big, open, oval, while in position it is deepset and lying at right angles to the line of the forehead and nose.

The bigness of the eye counts as beauty for Winckelmann (*Werke*, vol. iv, bk. 5, ch. v, § 20, p. 198)[2] on the ground that a big light is more beautiful than a small one. He continues: 'The size,

---

[1] In Vol. I. See p. 202, n. 4.

[2] This like Hegel's other references is to the edition of Winckelmann's *Works* edited by C. L. Fernow, 8 vols., Dresden, 1808–20. This splendid edition with a vast wealth of scholarly notes and many plates is not available everywhere and therefore I have given references in a way which makes it possible to identify them in other editions. This reference is to Winckelmann's *Geschichte der Kunst des Altertums* (History of Art in Antiquity), abbreviated below as *K.d.A.*; and here a reference to bk. 5, ch. v, § 20, is sufficient.

however, is proportionate to the orbit or its cavity and is expressed in the cut and opening of the eyelids of which, in beautiful eyes, the upper describes a rounder curve in relation to the internal recess than the lower does.' In profile heads of sublime workmanship the eyeball forms a profile itself and acquires precisely through this abrupt opening a majesty and an open glance, the light of which, according to Winckelmann, is made visible similarly on coins by a point on the upper part of the eyeball. Yet not all large eyes are beautiful, for they become so only, on the one hand, owing to the curve of the eylids and, on the other hand, owing to their being more deeply set. The eye, that is to say, should not protrude or, as it were, project itself into the external world, for this relation to the external world is remote from the ideal and is exchanged for [what the ideal requires, namely] the self's withdrawal into itself, into the substantive inner life of the individual. But the prominence of the eye at once reminds us that the eyeball is now pressed forward, now withdrawn again, and, in particular, when a man is goggle-eyed this only shows that he is beside himself, either staring thoughtlessly or just as absent-mindedly absorbed in gazing at some physical object.

In the ancient ideal sculptures the eye is set even deeper than it is in nature (Winckelmann, loc. cit., § 21). Winckelmann gives as a reason for this that in larger statues standing further away from the spectator's view the eye would have been meaningless and as it were dead without this deeper setting, especially because in addition the eyeball was usually flat; but the greatness of the orbits amplified the play of light and shade and so made the eye more effective. Yet this deepening of the eye has still another significance, namely that, if in consequence the forehead protrudes more than it does in nature, the intellectual part of the face predominates and its expression of spirit leaps to the eye more clearly, while the strengthened shadow in the orbits gives us of itself a feeling of depth and undistracted inner life, blindness to external things, and a withdrawal into the essence of individuality, the depth of which is suffused over the entire figure. On coins of the best period too the eyes are deeply set and the bones of the eye-socket are emphasized; whereas the eyebrows are not expressed by a broader arch of small hairs but only indicated through the sharply cut outline of the orbits which, without interrupting the continuous form of the forehead as eyebrows do by their colour and relative loftiness, form a sort of elliptical wreath round the eyes. The higher and therefore more independent curving of the eyebrows has never been regarded as beautiful.

About ears Winckelmann says (ibid., § 29) that

the ancients expended the greatest care on their elaboration, so that, e.g., in the case of engraved stones lack of care in the execution of the ear is an unequivocal sign of the work's inauthenticity. Portrait statues in particular often reproduced the peculiarly individual shape of the ear. Therefore from the form of the ear we can often guess the person portrayed, if he is someone well known, and from an ear with an unusually large inner opening we can infer that he is a Marcus Aurelius. Indeed the ancients have indicated even a malformation.

As one special kind of ear on ideal heads, Winckelmann cites on some Hercules statues ears that are flattened and then thickened at the cartilaginous parts. They indicate a wrestler and pancratiast, since after all Hercules carried off the pancratiast's prize at the games in honour of Pelops at Elis (ibid., § 34).[1]

(ββ) In connection with that part of the face which, viewed in its natural function, is related rather to the practical side of the senses, we have to mention, secondly, the more specific form of the nose, the mouth, and the chin.

The difference in the form of the nose gives to the face the most varied appearance and the most manifold differences of expression. A sharp nose with thin wings, for example, we are accustomed to associate with a sharp intellect, while a broad and pendant one or one snubbed like an animal's is indicative to us of sensuality, stupidity, and bestiality. But sculpture must keep itself free from both these extremes as well as from the intermediate stages of form and expression; it therefore avoids, as we saw in the case of the Greek people, not only the nose's separation from the forehead but also any upper or lower curvature, a sharp point or too rounded an appearance, either a rise in the middle or a fall towards forehead or mouth, in short a nose either sharp or thick; for in place of these numerous modifications sculpture substitutes as it were an indifferent form though one always faintly animated by individuality.

[1] A 'cauliflower' ear is associated with boxers, but the pancratiast boxed as well as wrestled. Hercules celebrated (some say founded) the Olympic games in Elis. For his victory see, for instance, Pausanias, v, 8, iv. Pelops was held in great honour at Olympia (ibid., 13, i), and it is possible that the games were originally instituted in his honour (or by him).

After the eye the mouth is the most beautiful part of the face, provided that it is shaped according to its spiritual significance and not to its natural purpose of serving as a tool for eating and drinking. So shaped, it is inferior in variety and wealth of expression to the eye alone, although it can vividly present the finest shades of derision, contempt and envy, the whole gamut of grief and joy, by means of the faintest movements and their most active play; similarly, in repose it indicates charm, seriousness, sensitiveness, shyness, surrender, etc. But sculpture uses it less for the particular nuances of the expression of spirit, and above all it has to remove from the shape and the cut of the lips what is purely sensuous and indicative of natural needs. Therefore it so forms the mouth as to make it, in general, neither over-full nor tight, for lips that are all too thin are indicative of parsimony of feeling too; so sculpture makes the lower lip fuller than the upper one, as was the case with Schiller; in the formation of his mouth it was possible to read the significance and richness of his mind and heart. This more ideal form of the lips, in contrast to the animal's snout, gives the impression of a certain absence of desire, whereas when the upper lip protrudes in an animal we are at once reminded of dashing for food and seizing on it. In man the mouth in its spiritual bearing is especially the seat of speech, i.e. the organ for the free communication of what we know, just as the eye expresses what we feel. The ideal sculptures, moreover, do not have the lips tightly closed; on the contrary, in works from the golden age of art (Winckelmann, loc. cit., § 26) the mouth remains somewhat open though without making the teeth visible, for these have no business with the expression of the spirit. This can be explained by the fact that when the senses are active, especially when our sight is firmly and strictly concentrated on specific objects, the mouth is closed, whereas when we are freely sunk in ourselves without looking at anything, it is slightly opened and the corners of the mouth are bent only a little downwards.

Thirdly, the chin completes in its ideal form the spiritual expression of the mouth, unless as in animals it is missing altogether or, as in Egyptian sculptures, it is pressed back and meagre. The ideal chin is itself drawn further down than is usual, and now, in the rounded fullness of its arched form, its size is still greater, especially if the lower lip is shorter. A full chin gives the impression of a certain satiety and repose; whereas old and restless women shuffle along with their weak chins and feeble muscles, and Goethe, for instance, compares their chaps to a pair of tongs that want to grip. But all this unrest disappears when the chin is full. But a dimple, now regarded as something beautiful, is just something casually charming without having any essential connection with beauty; but in lieu of this a big rounded chin counts as an authentic sign of Greek heads. In the Medici Venus the chin is smaller, but this statue has been discovered to be mutilated.[1]

(γγ) In conclusion, it now only remains for us to discuss the hair. Hair as such has the character of a plant production rather than of an animal one. It is a sign of weakness rather than a proof of the organism's strength. The barbarians let their hair hang flat or they wear it cut all round, not waved or curled, whereas the Greeks in their ideal sculptures devoted great care to the elaboration of the locks, a matter in which modern artists have been less industrious and less skilled; it is true that the Greeks too, when they worked in stone that was all too hard, did not make the hair hang freely in wavy curls but (Winckelmann, ibid., § 37) represented it as cut short and then finely combed. But in marble statues of the great period the hair is curled and, in male heads, kept long. In female heads it is stroked upwards and caught together *en chignon*. Here, at least according to Winckelmann (ibid.), we see it serpentine, with emphatic deepening between the locks to give them a variety of light and shade which cannot be produced by shallower drills. Moreover, the fall and arrangement of the hair differs in different gods. In a similar way Christian painting too makes Christ recognizable by a specific sort of locks and their parting, and the adoption of this example as a fashion today gives to many men the look of our Lord.

(γ) Now these particular parts [of the face] have to have their form harmonized into the head as into one whole. Here the beautiful shape is determined by a line which most nearly approaches an oval, and therefore anything sharp, pointed, or angled is dissolved into a harmony and a continuous soft connection of form, but without being purely regular and abstractly symmetrical or running away into a manifold variety of lines and their turning

---

[1] 'The affected gesture of the right arm is a restoration, and the head has been broken and re-set at the wrong angle' (K. Clark, *The Nude*, Pelican edition, p. 370. The statue is illustrated and severely criticized in the same book, pp. 79–81.) Cf. what Hegel says in Vol. I, p. 564.

and bending as happens with the other parts of the body. To the formation of this oval line (which returns into itself like a circle) the chief contribution, especially for a front view of the face, is made by the beautiful free swing from chin to ear, as well as the line, already mentioned, described by the forehead along the eye-sockets, together with the curve of the profile from the forehead over the point of the nose down to the chin, and the convexity of the occiput down to the nape of the neck.

This is as much as I wanted to describe about the ideal shape of the head, without entering into further detail.

(b) *Position and Movement of the Body*

The other parts of the body—neck, chest, back, trunk, arms, hands, legs, and feet—are organized on a different principle. In their form they can be beautiful, but beautiful only sensuously and in a living way without immediately expressing the spirit in their shape as the face does in its. Even in the shape of these members and its elaboration the Greeks have given proof of their supreme sense of beauty, yet in genuine sculpture these forms should not be asserted as simply the beauty of the living being, but must, as members of the *human* figure, give us a glimpse of the spirit, so far as the body as such can provide it. For otherwise the expression of the inner life would be concentrated solely in the face, while in the plasticity of sculpture the spirit should appear precisely as effused over the whole figure and not independently isolated and contrasted with the body.

Now if we ask by what means chest, trunk, back, and our extremities can work together into an expression of the spirit and therefore, apart from their beautiful vitality, receive in themselves the breath of a spiritual life, the means are the following:

first, the position into which the members are brought relatively to one another, in so far as this position emanates from and is freely determined by the inner life of the spirit;

secondly, movement or repose in its complete beauty and freedom of form;

thirdly, this sort of position and movement in their specific appearance and expression provides more clearly the situation in which the ideal, which can never be merely ideal *in abstracto*, is apprehended.

THE IDEAL OF SCULPTURE

On these points too I will add a few general remarks.

(α) The first point which offers itself for even superficial consideration about *position* is man's upright posture. The animal body runs parallel with the ground, jaws and eye pursue the same direction as the spine, and the animal cannot of itself independently annul this relation of itself to gravity. The opposite is the case with man, because the eye, looking straight outwards, has its natural direction always at right angles to the line of gravity and the body. Like the animals, man can go on all fours and little children do so in fact; but as soon as consciousness begins to awaken, man tears himself loose from being tied to the ground like an animal, and stands erect by himself. This standing is an act of will, for, if we give up willing to stand, our body collapses and falls to the ground. For this very reason the erect position has in it an expression of the spirit, because this rising from the ground is always connected with the will and therefore with the spirit and its inner life; after all it is common parlance to say that a man 'stands on his own feet' when he does not make his moods, views, purposes, and aims depend on someone else.

But the erect position is not yet beautiful as such; it becomes so only when it acquires freedom of form. For if in fact a man simply stands up straight, letting his hands hang down glued to the body quite symmetrically and not separated from it, while the legs remain tightly closed together, this gives a disagreeable impression of stiffness, even if at first sight we see no compulsion in it. This stiffness here is an abstract, almost architectural, regularity in which the limbs persist in the same position relatively to one another, and furthermore there is not visible here any determination by the spirit from within; for arms, legs, chest, trunk—all the members—remain and hang precisely as they had grown in the man at birth, without having been brought into a different relation by the spirit and its will and feeling. (The same is true about sitting.) Conversely, crouching and squatting are not to be found on the soil of freedom because they indicate something subordinate, dependent, and slavish. The free position, on the other hand, avoids abstract regularity and angularity and brings the position of the limbs into lines approaching the form of the organic; it also makes spiritual determinants shine through, so that the states and passions of the inner life are recognizable from the posture. Only in this event can the posture count as a sign of the spirit.

Yet in using postures as gestures sculpture must proceed with great caution and in this matter has many difficulties to overcome. For (i) in such a case the reciprocal relation of the parts of the body is indeed derived from the inner life, i.e. from the spirit, but (ii) this determination by the inner must not place the individual parts in such a way as to contradict the structure of the body and its laws and so give them the look of having suffered violence or put in opposition to the heavy material in which it is the sculptor's task to carry out his ideas. (iii) The posture must appear entirely unforced, i.e. we must get the impression that the body has adopted its position by its own initiative, because otherwise body and spirit appear different, parting from one another and entering a relation of mere command on one side and abstract obedience on the other, while in sculpture both should constitute one and the same directly harmonious whole. In this respect the absence of constraint is a prime requirement. The spirit, as what is inward, must entirely permeate the members, and these must adopt into themselves as the content of their own soul the spirit and its determining characteristics. (iv) As for the sort of gesture which the posture in ideal sculpture can be commissioned to express, it is clear from what has been said already that it should not be simply something caught at a moment and therefore alterable. Sculpture must not portray men as if, in the middle of a movement or an action, they had been frozen or turned to stone by a Gorgon's head.[1] On the contrary, although the gesture may hint in every case at a characteristic action, it must still express only the beginning and preparation of an action, an intention, or it must indicate the cessation of action and a reversion to repose. What is most suitable for a sculptured figure is the repose and independence of the spirit which comprises in itself the potentiality of an entire world.

(β) Secondly, it is the same with movement as it was with position. As movement proper it has a smaller place in sculpture as such, because sculpture does not advance of its own accord to a mode of portrayal approximating to that of a more advanced art. The chief task of sculpture is to present the peaceful divine image in its blessed perfection without any inner struggle. Variety of

---

[1] Hegel says 'Hüon's horn'—this is a reference to Wieland's *Oberon*. But this magic horn compelled those who heard it to dance, and this stood Hüon in good stead in moments of danger. The Gorgon's head seems more appropriate in this context, although Hegel may mean that people set in motion by the horn are then frozen or turned to stone.

movement therefore automatically disappears; what is presented is rather a standing or recumbent figure immersed in itself, something pregnant with possibilities but at this stage not proceeding to any definite action, and therefore not reducing its strength to a single moment or regarding that moment, instead of peaceful and even duration, as the essential thing. We must be able to have the idea that the divine image will stand eternally so in that same position. Self-projection into the external world, involvement in the midst of some specific action and its conflicts, the momentary strain that neither can nor want to persist—all these are opposed to the peaceful ideality of sculpture and occur only in groups and reliefs where particular features of an action are brought into the representation in a way reminiscent of the principle of painting. The spectacle of powerful emotions and their passing outburst does produce its immediate effect, but in that case it is over and done with and we do not willingly return to it. For what is conspicuous in such a spectacle is a matter of a moment which we see and recognize equally in a moment, while in such a case what is relegated to the background is precisely the fullness and freedom of the inner life, the infinite and eternal, in which we can immerse ourselves for ever.

(γ) But this is not to say that, where sculpture adheres to its severe principle and is at its zenith, it has to exclude an attitude of movement altogether, for if it did it would portray the Divine only in its vagueness and absence of difference. On the contrary, since it has to apprehend the divine substance as individuality and bring it before our eyes in a corporeal form, the inner and outer situation which sculpture imprints on the subject-matter and its form must also be individual. Now it is this individuality of a specific situation which is principally expressed in the posture and movement of the body. Yet just as substance is the chief thing in sculpture, and individuality has not yet won its way out of this into particular independence, so the particular determinate character of the situation too must not be of such a kind as to blur or cancel the simple solidity of that substantial element by inveigling it in one-sidedness and the clash of collisions, or, in short, by carrying it entirely into the preponderating importance and variety of particular events. On the contrary, this determinate character must rather remain one which, taken by itself, is less essential or is even a cheerful play of harmless liveliness on the surface of individuality, the substantiality of which therefore loses nothing of its depth, independence, and repose. This, however, is a point which I have mentioned already,[1] with continual reference to the ideal of sculpture, in dealing with the situation in which the ideal may enter the representation in its specific character, and therefore I will pass it over here.

(c) Draping [or Clothing]

The final important point, the one to be considered now, is the question of drapery in sculpture. At first sight it may seem that the nude form and its spiritually permeated and sensuous beauty of body in its posture and movement is what is most appropriate to the ideal of sculpture and that drapery is only a disadvantage. From this point of view, we hear again, nowadays especially, the complaint that modern sculpture is so often compelled to clothe its figures, on the ground that no clothing can match the beauty of the form of the human body. As a corollary of this there rises at once the further regret that so little opportunity is given to our artists to study the nude which the Greeks had always standing before their eyes. In general it need only be said on this matter that from the point of view of sensuous beauty preference must be given to the nude, but sensuous beauty as such is not the ultimate aim of sculpture, and so it follows that the Greeks did not fall into error by presenting most of their male figures nude but by far the majority of the female ones clothed.

(α) The reason for clothing in general lies, apart from artistic purposes, for one thing in the need for protection from the weather, since nature has given man this concern while exempting animals from it by covering them with fur, feathers, hair, scales, etc. For another thing, it is a sense of shame which drives men to cover themselves with clothes. Shame, considered quite generally, is the start of anger against something that ought not to be. Man becomes conscious of his higher vocation to be spirit and he must therefore regard what is animal as incompatible with that and struggle to conceal, as incompatible with his higher inner life, especially those parts of his body—trunk, breast, back, and legs—which serve purely animal functions or point to the purely external and have no directly spiritual vocation and express nothing spiritual. Amongst

---

[1] See Vol. I, pp. 201–3. 'Harmless' is explained there.

all peoples who have risen to the beginning of reflection we find therefore in a greater or lesser degree the sense of shame and the need for clothing. As early as the story in Genesis this transition is most sensitively expressed. Before they ate of the tree of knowledge Adam and Eve walked innocently naked in Paradise, but scarcely has a consciousness of spirit awakened in them than they see that they are naked and are ashamed of their nakedness. The same sense is dominant amongst the other Asiatic nations. So, e.g., Herodotus (i. 10), in telling the story of how Gyges came to the throne, says that 'among the Lydians, and indeed among the barbarians generally, it is reckoned a deep disgrace, even to a man, to be seen naked', a proof of which is the story of the wife of King Candaules of Lydia. Candaules gave Gyges, a favourite of his and one of his bodyguard, freedom to see his wife naked, in order to prove to him that his wife was of surpassing beauty. This was to have been kept secret from her, but she became aware of the outrage all the same by seeing Gyges, who had been hidden in her bedroom, slip out at the door. Incensed, she summoned Gyges the next day and told him that since the King had done this to her and Gyges had seen what he should not have seen, he could only have a choice: 'Either slay the King as a punishment and then possess me and the kingdom, or else die.' Gyges chose the former and after the King's murder mounted the throne and the widow's bed.

On the other hand, the Egyptians frequently or even usually displayed their statues naked, so that the male figures had only a small apron, and on the figure of Isis clothing is indicated only by a transparent and scarcely noticeable skirt round the legs. This was due neither to a lack of shame nor to a sense for the beauty of organic forms. For, given their symbolic outlook, we may say, they were not concerned with creating an appearance appropriate to the spirit, but with the meaning, the essence, and the idea of what the figure was to bring home to the spectator's mind, and consequently they left the human body in its natural form, without any reflection on its greater or lesser appropriateness to spirit; this form they did copy with great fidelity.

(β) In the case of the Greeks, finally, we find both nude and clothed figures. And thus they clothed themselves in fact, while at the same time they counted it an honour to have been the first to compete nude [in the games]. The Spartans in particular were the first to wrestle in the nude.[1] But in their case this did not occur at all out of a sense for beauty but from a rigid indifference to the delicate and spiritual element in modesty. In the Greek national character the feeling of personal individuality just as it immediately exists, and as spiritually animated in its existence, is as highly intensified as the sense for free and beautiful forms. Therefore there had to be an advance to giving form on its own account to the human being in his immediacy, to the body as it belongs to man and is permeated by his spirit, and to respect above everything else the human figure as a figure, just because it is the freest and most beautiful one. In this sense of course they discarded that shame or modesty which forbids the purely human body to be seen, and they did this, not from indifference to the spiritual, but from indifference to purely sensual desire, for the sake of beauty alone. For this reason a great number of their sculptures are presented naked from deliberate intention.

But neither could this lack of every kind of clothing be allowed to prevail throughout. For, as I remarked before in dealing with the difference between the head and the other parts of the body, it cannot in fact be denied that spiritual expression in the figure is limited to the face and the position and movement of the whole, to gestures expressed principally through the arms and hands and the position of the legs. For these members which are active in an outward direction serve best, through their sort of position and movement, to manifest an expression of spirit. Whereas the rest of the body is and remains capable of only a sensuous beauty, and the differences visible there can only be those of bodily strength, muscular development, or muscular suppleness and placidity, as well as differences of sex and of age, youth, and childhood. Therefore, so far as the expression of spirit in the figure is concerned, the nudity of these parts is a matter of indifference even from the point of view of beauty, and it accords with decency to cover those parts of the body [in a statue] if, that is to say, the preponderating thing in view is to represent the spiritual element in man. What ideal art does at every single point, namely extinguish the deficiency of animal life in its detailed organization—its little veins, wrinkles, little hairs on the head, etc.—and emphasize only the spiritual treatment of the form in its living outline, this is what clothing

[1] e.g. Thucydides, i. 6. He says that the practice of competing nude was a comparatively recent innovation.

does here. It conceals the superfluity of the organs which are necessary, it is true, for the body's self-preservation, for digestion etc., but, for the expression of the spirit, otherwise superfluous. Therefore it cannot be said without qualification that the nudity of sculptures is evidence throughout of a higher sense of beauty, a greater moral freedom and innocence. Here too the Greeks were guided by a truer and more spiritual insight.

The Greeks exhibited in the nude (*a*) children, e.g. Eros, for in them the bodily appearance is wholly naïve, and spiritual beauty consists precisely in this entire naïveté and ingenuousness; (*b*) youth, gods of youth, heroic gods and heroes like Perseus, Heracles, Theseus, Jason, for in them the chief thing is heroic courage, the use and development of the body for deeds of bodily strength and endurance; (*c*) wrestlers in contests at the national games, where the sole thing that could be of interest was not what they did, or their spirit and individual character, but the body's action, the force, flexibility, beauty, and free play of the muscles and limbs; (*d*) fauns and satyrs and bacchantes in the frenzy of their dance; (*e*) Aphrodite, because in her a chief feature is the sensuous charm of a woman. Whereas we get drapery where a higher intellectual significance, an inner seriousness of the spirit, is prominent and, in short, where nature is not to be made the predominant thing. So, for example, Winckelmann cited[1] the fact that out of ten statues of women scarcely one was nude. Amongst goddesses it is especially Pallas, Juno, Vesta, Diana, Ceres, and the Muses who are robed, and, amongst the gods, Zeus especially, the bearded Bacchus Indicus, and some others.

(γ) The rationale of clothes is a favourite topic so much discussed as to have become to some extent banal. I will therefore make on it only the following brief remarks.

On the whole we need not regret that our sense of propriety fights shy of making figures entirely nude; for if clothing, instead of concealing the posture, simply makes it shine through completely, then not only is nothing lost but, on the contrary, the clothing is simply what really emphasizes the posture and in this respect is to be regarded as an advantage because it deprives us of an immediate view of what, as purely sensuous, is without significance, and shows us only what is related to the situation expressed by posture and movement.

[1] In *K.d.A.*, bk. 6, § 33, Winckelmann says that only one in fifty was nude.

(αα) If we accept this principle, it may seem that that clothing is most advantageous of all for artistic treatment which conceals the shape of the limbs, and therefore the posture, as little as possible, and this is the case with our closely-fitting modern clothes. Our narrow sleeves and trousers follow the outlines of the figure, and therefore are the least hindrance because they make visible the whole form of the limbs as well as a man's walk and his gestures. The long wide robes and baggy trousers of the Orientals, on the other hand, would be wholly incompatible with our vivacity and varied activities and they only suit people who, like the Turks, sit all the day long with their legs crossed beneath them or who only walk about slowly and extremely solemnly.

But at the same time we know, and our first best glance at modern statues or pictures can prove to us, that our modern clothing is wholly inartistic: this is because what we really see in it, as I have already explained in another place,[1] is not the fine, free, and living contours of the body in their delicate and flowing development but stretched out sacks with stiff folds. For even if the most general character of the bodily forms remains, still the beautiful organic undulations are lost and what we see close at hand is something produced for an external purpose, something cut, sewn together here, folded over there, elsewhere fixed, and, in short, purely unfree forms, with folds and surfaces positioned here and there by seams, buttons, and button-holes. In other words, such clothing is in fact just a covering and a veil which throughout lacks any form of its own but, in the organic formation of the limbs which it follows in general, precisely conceals what is visibly beautiful, namely their living swelling and curving, and substitutes for them the visible appearance of a material mechanically fashioned. This is what is entirely inartistic about modern clothes.

(ββ) The principle for the artistic kind of drapery lies in treating it as if it were architectural. An architectural construction is only an environment in which we can nevertheless move freely and which on its side, being separated from what it encloses, must display in its formation the fact that it has a purpose of its own. Moreover, the architectural character of supporting and being supported must be formed on its own account according to its own mechanical nature. A principle of this kind is followed by the sort of drapery which we find used in the ideal sculpture of the Greeks.

[1] In vol. I, pp. 165-6.

THE IDEAL OF SCULPTURE 747

The mantle especially is like a house in which a person is free to move. It is carried indeed, but fastened at only one point, e.g. the shoulder, but otherwise it develops its own particular form according to its own special weight; it hangs, falls, and runs into folds spontaneously, and the particular modifications of this free formation depend solely on the pose of the wearer. Similar falling freely is little impaired essentially by other parts of Greek clothing, and it is this which is precisely appropriate to art, because in that case alone do we see nothing tight and manufactured and displaying by its form some purely external force and necessitation, but something formed on its own account yet taking its origin from the spirit by way of the pose of the figure. Therefore the dress of the Greeks is held up by the body, and determined by its pose, only to the extent necessary to prevent its falling, but otherwise it hangs down freely, and even in being moved along with the movement of the body it always abides by this principle. This is absolutely necessary, for the body is one thing, the clothing another, and the latter must come into its own independently and appear in its freedom. Whereas modern clothes, on the contrary, are either entirely carried by the body and are so subservient to it that they express the pose too predominantly and yet merely disfigure the forms of the limbs, or where, in the fall of the folds, etc., they might acquire a shape of their own, it is just the tailor over again who produces this shape according to the caprice of fashion. The material is dragged hither and thither partly by the different limbs and their movements, partly by its own stitching.—For these reasons the Greek clothing is the ideal model for sculptures and is to be preferred by far to the modern. On the form and details of the Greek manner of clothing, classical scholars have written *ad infinitum*; for although men have otherwise no right to talk about fashion in clothes, the sort of materials, trimmings, cut, and all the other details,[1] nevertheless research has provided a more respectable reason for treating these trivialities as important, and discussing them at length, than what women are allowed to have in this field.

(γγ) But we must bring up here a totally different consideration, namely whether modern clothes, or any kind of clothes except the Greek, should always and in every case be rejected. This question becomes important especially in the case of portrait statues, and we

[1] This reflection did not deter Hegel from writing at length to his wife about the fashion for ladies' hats in Paris (20 Sept. 1827).

will treat it here at some length because its main interest affects a principle for present-day art.

If today a portrait is to be made of an individual belonging to his own time, then it is essential that his clothing and external accessories be taken from his own individual and actual environment; for, precisely because he is an actual person who here is the subject of the work of art, it is most necessary that these externalities, of which clothes are essentially one, be portrayed faithfully and as they actually are or were. This requirement is especially to be followed when it is a matter of placing before our eyes, as individuals, definite characters who have been great and effective in some *special* sphere. In a painting or in marble the individual comes before our direct view in bodily form, i.e. conditioned by externals, and to propose to lift the portrait above these conditions would be all the more contradictory because it would imply that the individual had something downright untrue in himself; for the merit and peculiar excellence of actual men consists precisely in their activity in the real world, in their life and work in the specific spheres of their vocation. If this individual activity is to be made visible to us, the surroundings given to him must not be of the wrong kind or disturbing. A famous general, for instance, has existed as a general in his immediate environment amidst cannon, guns, and gunpowder, and if we want to picture him in his activity we think of how he gave commands to his officers, ordered the line of battle, attacked the enemy, and so on. And furthermore such a general is not *any* general but is especially marked by his special kind of weapons, etc.; he may be an infantry commander or a bold hussar or whatever. No matter what he is, he always has his particular uniform, appropriate to these differing circumstances. Moreover, he is a famous general—a famous general and therefore not a legislator, or a poet, or perhaps not even a religious man, nor has he been a king, etc.; in short he is not everything, and only what is *totum atque rotundum*[1] has the stamp of the ideal and divine. For the divinity of the ideal sculptures is precisely to be sought in the fact that their character and individuality are not incident to particular circumstances and branches of activity, but are exempt from this dispersion, or, if the idea of such circumstances is aroused, are so presented that we must believe of these individuals that in all circumstances they can achieve anything and everything.

[1] Horace, *Satires*, ii. 7. 86.

THE IDEAL OF SCULPTURE

For this reason it is a very superficial requirement that the heroes of our day, or of the most recent past, whose heroism is restricted to their own time, should be represented in ideal clothing. This requirement does betray an enthusiasm for the beauty of art, but an unintelligent enthusiasm, which from love of antiquity overlooks the fact that the greatness of the Greeks lay essentially at the same time in a profound understanding of everything that they did, because while they portrayed what was ideal in itself they never intended to impress an ideal form on what was nothing of the kind. If the whole life and circumstances of an individual are not ideal, neither should his clothing be; and just as a powerful, determined, and resolute general does not for this reason have a face betraying the visage of Mars, so here the clothes of Greek gods would be the same mummery as putting a bearded man in a girl's clothes.

Apart from all this, modern clothes create a further mass of difficulties because they are subject to fashion and unquestionably alterable. For the rationality at the basis of fashion is that it has the right, over against mere temporal duration, of continually altering. A coat cut in one way is soon out of fashion again and therefore in order to please it must be in fashion. But when the fashion passes, familiarity with it is at an end, and what still pleased a year or two ago is now at once ridiculous. Therefore there should be retained for statues only those types of clothing which have a more permanent type stamped on the specific character of an age, but in general it is advisable to find a middle way as our modern artists do. Yet on the whole it is still always a mistake to give modern clothes to portrait statues unless they are small or the intention is only to present the subject in a familiar guise. It is best therefore to produce busts only, stopping at the neck and chest, for these after all can be kept to the ideal more easily, because here the head and face are the chief thing and the rest is as it were only an insignificant accessory. In big statues, on the other hand, especially when the figures are in repose, we see at once what they have on, just because of this repose, and full size masculine figures, even in portraits, can in their modern dress hardly rise above insignificance. Take, e.g., Herder and Wieland painted, at full length and seated, by the elder Tischbein[1] and in engravings by good

---

[1] It is not clear to which Tischbein Hegel refers. The oldest was J. H., 1722–89. There were two others, his relatives J. F. A., 1750–1812, and J. H. W.,

artists—we feel at once something dull, dreary, and superfluous when we see their trousers, stockings, and shoes and, in short, their comfortable, self-satisfied attitude on a sofa with their hands cosily crossed together over their stomachs.

But it is different with portrait statues of individuals whose period of activity is far before our time or whose greatness is inherently of an ideal kind. For what is old has become as it were timeless and has retreated into the region of general and vaguer ideas, with the result that, released from its particular actual world, it becomes capable of ideal portrayal even in its clothing. This is still more true in the case of individuals who through their independence and the plenitude of their inner life are exempt from the plain restrictedness of a specific profession and from effectiveness only in a specific period and who thus constitute a free totality in themselves, a whole world of relationships and activities; for this reason they must appear, even in their clothing, raised above the familiarity of day to day life in the external world habitual to them in their own age. Even in the case of the Greeks there are portrait statues of Achilles and Alexander in which the more individual traits are so little pronounced that we might suppose them to be statues of young divinities rather than men. In Alexander, the great-hearted youth of genius, this is entirely in place. But in a similar way Napoleon has such a high standing and is such a universal genius that there is no objection to giving him ideal clothing on his statue; similar clothing would not be inappropriate for Frederick the Great if it were a matter of honouring him in all his greatness. Here too of course the size of statues is an essential consideration. On *small* figures, which have something familiar about them, we are not at all disturbed by Napoleon's little triangular hat, the familiar uniform, and the folded arms; and if we want to see Frederick the Great confronting us as 'auld Fritz', he can be portrayed with his hat and stick, as he is on snuff-boxes.

3. *Individuality of the Ideal Sculptured Figures*

Up to now we have considered the ideal of sculpture both in its general character and also in the detailed forms of its particular

---

1751–1829. The former of these made a portrait of Herder, and the reference is probably to him as being older than the third; Herder lived until 1803 and Wieland to 1813.

differentiations. *Thirdly*, it now only remains to us to emphasize that while ideal sculptures have to display, in their *content*, inherently substantial individuals, in their *form* the human body, they must also proceed to give them the appearance of distinguishable particular persons. Therefore they form a group of particular individuals which we already recognize from our study of the classical art-form as the group of the Greek gods. Someone might have the idea that there should be only *one* supreme beauty and perfection which could be concentrated in its entirety in a single statue, but this idea of an ideal as such is simply foolish and absurd. For the beauty of the ideal consists precisely in its not being a purely universal norm but in essentially having individuality and therefore particularity and character. In this way alone are sculptures vitalized, and the one abstract beauty is broadened into an ensemble of inherently specific shapes. Yet on the whole the content of this group is restricted because there are wanting in the genuine ideal of sculpture a number of categories which, for example, in our Christian outlook, we are accustomed to use when we want to give expression to human and divine qualities. So, for instance, the moral dispositions and virtues which the Middle Ages and the modern world have assembled into a group of duties, modified again and again from epoch to epoch, have no sense in the case of the ideal gods of sculpture, and for these gods they do not exist. Therefore we cannot expect here the portrayal of sacrifice or of selfishness conquered, the battle against the flesh, the victory of chastity, etc., nor any expression of the deep feeling of love, immutable fidelity, honour and modesty in men and women, religious humility, submission, and blissfulness in God. For all these virtues, qualities, and situations rest partly on the breach between the body and the spirit; partly they transcend the corporeal and retire into the pure inwardness of the heart; or they display the individual's subjective character in separation from his absolute substance as well as in his struggle for a reconciliation with that. Moreover, the group of these gods proper in sculpture is certainly an ensemble but, as we saw in our consideration of the classical art-form, it is not a whole the elements of which rigorously correspond with conceptual differences. Yet the single figures are to be distinguished from one another by each of them being a finished and specific individual, although they are not set apart from one another by abstractly marked traits of character, since on the contrary they retain much in common with one another in virtue of their ideality and divinity.

We can go through these differences in more detail under the following heads.

First to be considered are purely external marks of recognition—attributes set beside the gods, sort of clothing, weapons, and the like. Winckelmann especially has detailed these marks more specifically and at great length.

Secondly, however, the chief differences lie not only in such *external* indications and features but in the individual build and carriage of the entire figure. The most important thing in this connection is the difference of age and sex as well as of the various spheres from which the statues take their content and form, because there has been an advance from statues of gods to those of heroes, satyrs, and fauns, as well as to portrait-statues, and portrayal finally lost itself in adopting even animal shapes.

Thirdly, and lastly, we shall cast a glance at the individual figures in which sculpture has transformed those more general differences into the form of an individual. Here above all it is the widest detail that presses on us and we can allow ourselves to cite only some examples of individual figures, since in any case this is a sphere which in many ways issues in what is merely empirical.

(a) *Attributes, Weapons, Adornment*

As for attributes and other external accessories, sort of adornment, weapons, tools, vessels, in short, things connected with some relation to the environment, these externals are, in the great works of sculpture, kept simple, moderate, and limited, so that there is nothing of that kind except what is required to let us understand the work and identify its subject. For it is the figure in itself, its expression, and not the external accessory, which is to provide the spiritual meaning and our sight of it. Even so, however, such indications are necessary to enable us to recognize the individual gods. This is because universal divinity, which in each individual god affords the substantial element in the portrayal, produces, in virtue of this common foundation, a close kinship between the various figures of the gods and their expression. The result is that each god is deprived again of his particular character and so can enter situations and modes of representation other than those otherwise belonging to him. In this way his particular characteristics as such are not visible in him throughout in good earnest, and often only those externalities are left which are needed to make him recognizable. Of these indicative marks I will mention only the following:

(α) Attributes proper I have already discussed in connection with the classical form of art and its gods.[1] In sculpture these lose their independent and symbolic character still more, and they only retain the right of appearing on or beside the figure, which represents itself alone, as an external indication closely related to one or other aspect of the specific gods. Frequently they are drawn from animals, as Zeus, for instance, is portrayed with an eagle, Juno with a peacock, Bacchus with a tiger and a panther drawing his car (because, as Winckelmann says (op. cit., ii, p. 503),[2] the latter animal has a persistent thirst and is crazy for wine), Venus with a hare or a dove.—Other attributes are utensils or tools with a bearing on the activity and the actions ascribed to each god appropriately to his specific individuality. So, for example, Bacchus is portrayed with the thyrsus encircled with fillets and ivy-leaves, or he has a laurel-wreath to indicate him as a conqueror on his journey to India,[3] or again a torch with which he lighted Ceres.[4]

Such associations, of which I have of course mentioned here only the best known of all, have stimulated the acuteness and pedantry of antiquaries and have reduced them to a commerce in petty details which then, it is true, often goes too far and sees a significance in things where there is none. So, for example, two famous figures, in the Vatican and the Villa Medici, of reclining women have been taken to represent Cleopatra simply because they wear a bracelet shaped like a viper; the first thing that occurred to an archaeologist on seeing the snake was the death of Cleopatra, just as the first thought of a pious clergyman might have been of the first snake that seduced Eve in Paradise. But it was the general practice of Greek women to wear bracelets like the coils of a snake,

---

[1] In Vol. I, pp. 495 ff.
[2] i.e. *Versuch einer Allegorie*, ch. 2.
[3] This alleged conquest of India is described at length in the *Dionysiaca* of Nonnus (fifth-century A.D.). But the representation of Dionysus the conqueror is not infrequent on Roman sarcophagi.
[4] i.e. when she was seeking her daughter Proserpine (Pausanius, i. 2. 4). Hegel is still quoting the Winckelmann passage last referred to.

and the bracelets themselves are called 'snakes'. After all, Winckelmann, who had more sense, had already seen that these figures were not Cleopatras (op. cit., bk. v. 6, ii, p. 56, and vi. 11, ii, p. 222),[1] and Visconti[2] (Museo Pio-Clementino, ii, 89–92) has now finally definitely identified them as figures of Ariadne who had sunk down in sleep through grief at the departure of Theseus.— Now, however often people have been led astray in such matters and however petty the sort of acuteness seems which ends in the study of such insignificant externals, still this kind of research and criticism is necessary because often it is only by this means that the identification of a statue can be precisely determined. Yet even so here again the difficulty arises that the attributes, like the figure, do not every time serve to identify one god only, because they are common to several. For example, we see a cup beside Jupiter, Apollo, Mercury, Aesculapius, as well as Ceres and Hygiea; Juno, Venus, and Spes carry a lily; similarly, several goddesses have an ear of corn; and even the lightning indicates not only Zeus but also Pallas who is not alone, for her part, in carrying the aegis but shares it equally with Zeus, Juno, and Apollo (Winckelmann, op. cit., ii, p. 249). In origin the individual gods had a common, rather vague and universal significance, and this itself carries with it ancient symbols which belonged to this more general and therefore common nature of the gods.

(β) Other accessories, arms, vases, horses, etc., are more in place in such works as abandon the simple repose of the gods and proceed to represent actions, i.e. in groups or rows of figures as may occur in reliefs, and therefore can make more extended use of various external associations and indications. On votive offerings, too, which consisted of works of art of all kinds, especially statues, on the statues of Olympic victors, but especially on coins and engraved gems, the creative ingenuity of Greek invention had a huge scope for applying symbolic and other allusions, for example, to the locality of the city, etc.

(γ) External characteristics more deeply associated with the individual gods are such as belong to the determinate individual figure itself and are an integral part of it. Amongst these are included the specific kind of clothing, weapons, hair-dress, ornaments etc.,

---

[1] i.e. K.d.A., bk. 6, ch. ii, § 17, and bk. 11, ch. ii, § 7.
[2] E. Q., 1751–1818. The reference is to the catalogue of engravings in this Gallery.

and for their further explanation I will content myself here, however, with a few quotations from Winckelmann who was remarkably acute in seizing such differences. Amongst the particular gods, Zeus is principally to be recognized by the arrangement of his hair, so that Winckelmann affirms (vol. iv. 5, § 29)[1] that by the hair over its forehead or by its beard, a head could be recognized without doubt as Zeus's even if nothing else survived. 'Over the forehead,' he says (§ 31), 'the hair rises upwards and its different partings fall down again bent in a narrow curve' [i.e. over the sides of the head]. And this sort of hair-dress was so decisive that it was retained for the sons and grandsons of Zeus. In this regard the head of Zeus is scarcely to be distinguished from that of Aesculapius, but for this reason the latter has a different beard: the hair on the upper lip is the chief difference, it lies in a curve on Aesculapius [§ 32] whereas 'in Zeus it is all at once drawn down and cut into angles at the corners of the mouth and then fused with the beard on the chin'.[2] The beautiful head of a statue of Neptune in the Villa Medici, later in Florence, Winckelmann [§ 36 and note *ad loc.*] recognized by its more frizzled beard, which besides is thicker over the upper lip, and by the more curly hair on the head which distinguishes it from heads of Zeus. Pallas, in complete distinction from Diana, wears her hair long, tied at the back just beneath the head, and then hanging down in a series of curls; whereas Diana wears hers stretched upwards on all sides and fastened in a knot on the crown of the head. Ceres covers the back of her head with her robe, and besides carrying ears of corn wears a diadem 'in front of which', as Winckelmann remarks (vol. iv, book 5, ch. ii, § 10),[3] 'the hair rises dispersed in a charming confusion so that in this way there is perhaps to be indicated here distress at the rape of her daughter Proserpine'. A similar individuality is marked by other externals, as, for instance, Pallas is to be recognized by her helmet and its specific shape, by her sort of dress, etc.

[1] i.e. *K.d.A.*, bk. 5, ch. i, § 29.
[2] There is a confusion here. What is attributed to Aesculapius belongs to Zeus and vice versa. This is clear, for example, in illustrations in the latest edition of Smith's *Classical Dictionary*.
[3] i.e. *K.d.A.*, bk. 5, ch. ii, § 10.

(b) Differences of Age and Sex, and of Gods, Heroes, Men, and Animals

Truly living individuality is meant to be marked out in sculpture by the free and beautiful form of the body. It therefore may not be manifested simply by such accessories as attributes, chevelure, weapons and other tools, club, trident, bushel, etc., but must penetrate both the figure itself and its expression. In this individualizing of the figures the Greeks were all the more subtle and creative as the figures of the gods had in common an essential universal basis out of which, though without being cut adrift from it, the characteristic individual figure had to be so elaborated that this basis remained essentially living and present in it. What is especially to be admired in the best sculpture of antiquity is the keen attention with which the artists took care to bring each of the tiniest traits of the figure into harmony with the whole, an attention which in that case alone produces this harmony.

If we ask further about the chief general differences which can be properly regarded as the fundamental bases for the more specific individualization of the forms of the body, and their expression,

(α) the first is the difference between the forms of childhood and youth and those of later years. In the genuine ideal, as I have said earlier, every trait and every single part of the figure is expressed, and at the same time the straight line that goes on and on, abstract even surfaces, circles, and rigidly geometrical curves are avoided everywhere, and instead there is elaborated in the most beautiful way the living variety of lines and forms in the nuances linking their transitions together. In childhood and youth the boundaries of the forms flow into one another rather unnoticeably and they fade into one another so delicately that, as Winckelmann says (vol. vii, p. 78),[1] one might compare them with the surface of a sea unruffled by the winds, of which one could say that although it is in constant movement it is nevertheless calm. On the other hand, at a more advanced age the distinctions appear more markedly and must be elaborated into a more definite characterization. For this reason excellent statues of grown men please us more at a first glance, because everything is expressive and we learn all the more quickly to admire the knowledge, shrewdness, and skill of the artist. For owing to their tenderness and the smaller number of

---

[1] *Vorläufige Abhandlung von der Kunst der Zeichnung der alten Völker*, ch. iv, § 10.

differences youthful figures do seem easier [to produce], but in fact the opposite is the case. For since 'the formation of the parts is left vague as it were between the beginning and the perfection of growth' (ibid., p. 80), the joints, bones, sinews, and muscles must be softer and more delicate, but indicated all the same. In this matter Greek art celebrates its triumph, because even in the most delicate figures all the parts and their definite organization in almost invisible nuances of projection and depth are every time made noticeable in a way whereby the knowledge and virtuosity of the artist are appreciated only by an observer who examines the work with closest attention. If, for example, in a delicate masculine figure, like that of the young Apollo, the entire structure of the male form were not actually and thoroughly indicated with consummate but half-concealed judgement, the limbs would doubtless appear round and full but at the same time flaccid, inexpressive, and uniform, so that the whole figure could hardly be pleasing. As a most striking example of the difference between the bodies of youths and those of older men, the boys and their father in the Laocoon group may be cited.

But, on the whole, for the portrayal of their ideal gods in sculpture the Greeks preferred models that were still youthful, and even in heads and statues of Zeus or Neptune there is no indication of old age.

(β) A second and more important difference is that of sex, i.e. that between the portrayal of male and female figures. In general the same may be said about the latter as what I advanced earlier about the difference between youth and age. The feminine figures are more delicate and weaker, the sinews and muscles are less indicated although they must be there, the transitions from one of these to the other are softer and flow more easily, and yet there are many nuances and variations in the different expressions, ranging from serious repose, severe and sublime power, to the softest grace and charm that inspires love. The same wealth of forms occurs in the masculine figures, in which there is added besides the expression of developed bodily strength and courage. But the serenity of delight remains common to them all, a joy and a blissful indifference soaring away above everything particular, yet linked at the same time with a peaceful trait of mourning, that laughter in tears which becomes neither laughter nor tears.

In this matter, however, no strict line is to be drawn throughout between male and female characters, for the more youthful divine figures of Bacchus and Apollo often slip into the delicacy and weakness of feminine forms, indeed often acquire single traits of the female body; why, there are even statues of Hercules in which he is framed so youthfully that he has been confused with his beloved Iole! Not merely a passing of male into female forms but an actual connection of the two the Greeks have explicitly represented in hermaphrodites.

(γ) Thirdly, and lastly, we may inquire about the chief differences introduced into the sculptural form by reason of the fact that it belongs to one of the specific spheres constituting the content of the ideal world-view adapted to sculpture.

The organic forms of which sculpture can avail itself in its plasticity are both human and animal. So far as the latter is concerned, we have seen already that, at the peak of more severe art, it may appear only as an attribute alongside the figure of the god, as, for instance, we find a hind beside Diana the huntress and an eagle beside Zeus. In the same category are the panther, griffin, and similar animal shapes. But apart from attributes proper, animal forms acquire a value of their own, partly independently, partly mixed with human forms. But their sphere in sculptural figures is restricted. Apart from roe deer, it is principally the horse whose beauty and fiery life makes an entry into plastic art whether associated with the human form or in its own completely free shape. The horse, to explain, stands in close connection with the mettle, bravery, and dexterity of masculine heroism and heroic beauty, while other animals, the lion, etc., which Hercules slew, as Meleager did the boar, are themselves the object of these heroic deeds, and for this reason have the right of inclusion in the sphere of sculptural portrayal when this is expanded in reliefs and groups into situations and actions with more movement.

The human form, for its part, because in its form and expression it is apprehended as the pure ideal, provides the appropriate shape for what is divine which, if still bound down to the sensuous, is incapable of concentration into the simple unity of *one* god and therefore can only be interpreted as a *group* of divine figures. Nevertheless, conversely, what is human, alike in content and form still remains in the context of human individuality as such, although this is brought into association and unification now with the Divine and now with the animal.

In this way sculpture acquires the following spheres from which it can draw its configurations. As their essential centre I have more than once mentioned the group of the particular gods. Their difference from human figures consists above all in the fact that in their expression they appear as raised above the finitude of concern and baneful passion and as collected in themselves into blissful tranquillity and eternal youth, while their bodily forms are not only purified from the finite particular characteristics of a man but also, without any loss of vitality, are stripped of everything hinting at the exigency and poverty of physical life. An interesting subject for art is, for example, a mother pacifying her child; but the Greek goddesses are always represented as childless. Juno, according to the myth, casts her child, Hercules, away, and the Milky Way is the result. To associate the majestic spouse of Zeus with a son was *infra dig.* in the eyes of the Greeks. Aphrodite herself does not appear in sculpture as a mother; Eros is indeed in her train but his relation to her is not that of a child. Similarly Jupiter is given a goat for a nurse, and Romulus and Remus were suckled by a wolf. Whereas in Egyptian and Indian images there are many in which gods receive their mother's milk from goddesses. In the case of the Greek goddesses what predominates is the maiden form which least of all permits the appearance of a woman's natural vocation.

This constitutes an important contrast between classical art and the romantic art in which a mother's love provides a principal topic.

From the gods as such sculpture then goes on to heroes and those figures which, like fauns, centaurs, and satyrs, are a mixture of the human with the animal.

Heroes are distinguished from gods by very subtle differences and are thus superhuman, raised above ordinary human existence. Of a certain Battus[1] on coins of Cyrene, for example, Winckelmann says (iv. 105): 'a single look of a lover's joy might make us take him for a Bacchus, his trait of divine grandeur for an Apollo'.[2] But here, where it is a matter of making the power of the will and bodily strength visible, the human forms are larger, especially in certain parts; the artists impart to the muscles an impression of quickness and movement and in violent actions they set in motion all the natural springs of action. Nevertheless, since in the same

[1] The Battiadae were kings of Cyrene in the fifth-century B.C.
[2] i.e. *K.d.A.*, bk. 5, ch. i, § 39.

hero a whole series of different, indeed opposed, situations occur, the masculine forms approach the feminine here again. For example, when Achilles first appeared amongst the maiden daughters of Lycomedes[1] he did not come on the scene in that heroic strength which he displayed before Troy but in women's clothes and with such attractive features that his sex is almost doubtful. Even Hercules is not always depicted in the seriousness and force that accomplished those toilsome labours, but just as often in his form as Omphale's servant, in the repose of his deification, and, in short, in the greatest variety of situations. In other connections the heroes again have often the greatest kinship with the figures of the gods themselves, Achilles, for instance, with Ares, and it is therefore only the most profound study that can recognize the precise meaning of a statue solely from the character given to it and without any additional attribute. Nevertheless practised art-scholars can infer from single bits the character and form of the whole figure and can fill in what is missing, and in this way we have once again learnt to admire the fine judgement and logical individualization in Greek art. Its masters understood how to keep and carry out a harmony between every smallest detail and the character of the whole.

As for satyrs and fauns, there is introduced into their sphere what remains excluded from the lofty ideal figures of the gods, namely human need, delight in life, sensuous enjoyment, satisfaction of desire, and other things of the same kind. Yet especially the young satyrs and fauns are presented by the Greeks as a rule in such beauty of form that, as Winckelmann asserts (iv, 78),[2] 'every single part of them, the head excepted, could be exchanged for an Apollo, above all with Apollo the lizard-killer,[3] the position of whose legs is precisely that of the fauns'. Fauns and satyrs are recognizable on their heads by pointed ears, their unkempt hair, and tiny horns.

A second sphere comprises the human as such. What especially belongs here is the beauty of the human form as it is developed in

---

[1] His mother dressed him as a girl in the hope of thus keeping him away from the battle before Troy where it had been prophesied he would perish (e.g. Apollodorus, III. xiii. 8).

[2] i.e. *K.d.A.*, bk. 5, ch. i, § 8.

[3] Apollo Sauroctonos is illustrated, for instance, in K. Clark, *The Nude*, p. 43. The description by Pliny, xxxiv. 70, identifies this as a work of Praxiteles (see Richter, op. cit., pp. 262–3).

THE IDEAL OF SCULPTURE 761

its force and skill in contests at the games: consequently a chief topic is wrestlers, discus-throwers, etc. In such productions sculpture already approaches portraiture in which, nevertheless, the Greeks, even when displaying actual individuals, always understood how to preserve that principle of sculpture which we have already come to know.

The final sphere which sculpture embraces is the portrayal of animal forms as such, especially lions, dogs, etc. Even in this sphere the Greeks could keep in view the principle of sculpture, the underlying substance of form, and give it individual life, and achieve that perfection which has become famous, e.g. in Myron's cow[1] and his other works. Goethe in his *Art and Antiquity*[2] has described them with remarkable grace; and has especially drawn our attention to the fact that, as we have already seen above, an animal function like giving suck occurs [in sculpture] only in the animal field. Goethe repudiates all the conceits of poets in Greek epigrams and with his artistic sense confines himself wholly to the naïveté of the conception which is productive of the most familiar image.

(c) *Portrayal of the Individual Gods*

To conclude this chapter we have now to say something in more detail, especially in connection with the portrayal of the gods, about the single individuals into whose character and liveliness the differences already mentioned have been worked out.

(α) In general, and particularly in respect of the spiritual gods of sculpture, there may be a prevalent opinion that spirit is precisely liberation from individuality and that therefore the ideal figures, the more ideal and excellent they are, must remain all the less distinguished from one another as individuals; but in this matter the amazing way in which the Greeks have solved this problem in sculpture consisted precisely in their having, despite the universality and ideality of their gods, still preserved their individuality and distinction from one another, no matter how far, it is true, there was a struggle in some specific cases to cancel fixed boundaries and display particular forms in their transition.

[1] This bronze figure stood on the Acropolis at Athens. It was very highly praised in antiquity but exists no longer. Myron fl. fifth-century B.C.
[2] Hegel cites vol. ii, second part, of this periodical.

Moreover, if we take individuality in the sense that specific traits were appropriate to certain gods, as they are in a portrait, then it looks as if a fixed type were coming on the scene instead of a living product, and this is to the detriment of art. But [in Greek sculpture] this is not the case at all. On the contrary, invention in individualizing and vitalizing the figures was all the more subtle the more their substantive type remained their basis.

(β) In further considering the individual gods it quickly occurs to us that *one* individual stands above all these ideal figures as their lord. This dignity and supremacy Phidias above all has reserved for the figure and expression of Zeus, but at the same time the father of gods and men is presented with a cheerful and gracious appearance, enthroned with benignity, of mature years without the full cheeks of youth, yet, on the other hand, with no hint of any harshness of form or indication of decrepitude or age. Most akin to Zeus in figure and expression are his brothers, Neptune and Pluto; in their interesting statues [which in September 1824 Hegel saw] in Dresden, despite all that they have in common with Zeus, their difference is nevertheless maintained—Zeus benign in his majesty, Neptune more savage, Pluto, who corresponds with the Egyptain Serapis, darker and gloomier.

More essentially different from Zeus are Bacchus, Apollo, Mars, and Mercury—Bacchus has more youthful beauty and delicacy of form; Apollo is more manly but has no beard; Mercury is more agile, taller, with exceptionally fine facial features; Mars is not in the least like Hercules in the strength of his muscles, etc., but a young and beautiful hero, ideally formed.

Of the goddesses I will mention only Juno, Pallas, Diana, and Venus.

Amongst the female figures Juno has the greatest majesty in form and expression, just as Zeus has amongst the male figures. Her large rounded eyes are proud and commanding; her mouth is similar and it at once makes her recognizable, especially when seen in profile. On the whole she gives the impression of 'a queen who intends to rule, and must be worshipped and awaken love' (Winckelmann, iv. 116).[1]

Pallas by contrast has an expression of more severe maidenhood and chastity; tenderness, love, and every kind of feminine weakness are far removed from her; her eye is less open than Juno's,

---

[1] i.e. *K.d.A.*, bk. 5, ch. ii, § 8.

moderately curved, and somewhat sunk in calm meditation, while her head, though armed with a helmet, is not so proudly carried as Zeus' consort's is.

Diana is presented with a similar maidenly form, but she is endowed with greater attraction; she is lighter and slimmer yet without any self-consciousness or delight in her grace. She does not stand, absorbed in peaceful contemplation, but is usually displayed as moving, pressing forward, with her eye gazing straight in front of her into the distance.

Finally, Venus, the goddess of beauty as such, is alone, except the Graces and the Hours, portrayed by the Greeks, even if not by all artists, in the nude. Nudity in her case has a very important reason, however, because she has as her chief expression sensuous beauty and its victory, in short, grace, delicacy, amorousness, all moderated and elevated by the spirit. Even where her eye is meant to be more serious and sublime, it is smaller than Pallas' or Juno's, not in length but narrower because the lower eyelid is slightly raised, and it is in this way that the languishing lover's ogling is most beautifully expressed. Yet she differs in expression and figure, now she is more serious and powerful, now more graceful and delicate, now younger and now of riper years. For example, Winckelmann (iv. 112)[1] compares the Medici Venus with a rose which after a beautiful dawn opens out at sunset; whereas Venus Urania is indicated by a diadem like Juno's and Venus Victrix wears it too.

(γ) The discovery of this plastic individuality, the whole expression of which is completely effected by means of the bare abstraction of form, was indigenous to the Greeks alone in a like degree of unsurpassable perfection, and it has its basis in Greek religion. A more spiritual religion can be content with *inner* contemplation and worship so that sculptures count for it as merely a luxury or a superfluity; whereas a religion like the Greek which is so concentrated on contemplating what it *sees*, must continually go on producing [objects for contemplation], because for it this artistic creation and invention is itself a religious activity and satisfaction, and for the people the sight of such works is not contemplation merely but something itself intrinsic to religion and life. In general, the Greeks did everything for the public, for the life of everybody, in which every individual found his pleasure, his pride, and his

[1] i.e. *K.d.A.*, bk. 5, ch. ii, § 3.

honour. Now in this public life the art of the Greeks is not just a decoration but a living need, necessarily to be satisfied, just as painting was to the Venetians in the days of their splendour. It is only for this reason that we can explain, given the difficulties of sculpture, the enormous mass of statues, these forests of statues of every kind, which existed by the thousand or two thousand in a single city, in Elis, Athens, Corinth, and even in considerable numbers in every smaller city, as well as in Magna Graecia and the Aegean Islands.

Chapter III

THE DIFFERENT KINDS OF PORTRAYAL AND MATERIAL, AND THE HISTORICAL STAGES OF SCULPTURE'S DEVELOPMENT

Up to this point in our treatment of sculpture, we have looked first for the *universal* categories from which we could develop the most appropriate content for sculpture and the corresponding form. We found this content in the classical ideal, so that in the second place we had to determine how sculpture, amongst the particular arts, was best adapted to give shape to the ideal. Since the ideal is to be understood essentially as individuality, not only does the inner artistic vision broaden out into a group of ideal and separate gods, but the external mode of portrayal and its execution in existing works of art fell apart into the different sorts of sculpture. Yet in this matter the following points remain over for discussion:

first, the mode of portrayal which, in actual execution, forms either single statues or groups until finally, in reliefs, it makes the transition to the principle of painting;

secondly, the external material in which these differences are realized;

thirdly, the stages of historical development in which works of art are executed in their different kinds and material.

1. *Modes of Portrayal*

Just as in the case of architecture we made an essential distinction between buildings that were independent on their own account and those that served some purpose, so now here we can establish a similar difference between sculptures that are independent of anything else and those which serve rather as a mere decoration of spaces in or on buildings. For the former the surroundings are no more than a place prepared already by art, while in the case of the latter the essential thing is always their relation to the building that they decorate, and this determines not only the form of the sculpture but also, for the most part, its content too. In this connection we may say, on the whole and in the main, that single statues exist on their own account, whereas groups, and *a fortiori* reliefs, begin to give up this independence and are employed by architecture for its own artistic ends.

(a) The Single Statue

The original function of single statues is the real function of sculpture as such, i.e. to furnish images in temples; they are erected in temple interiors where the whole surroundings have a bearing on them.

(α) Here sculpture retains its most perfect purity because in executing the figure of the gods it sets them in beautiful, simple, inactive repose in no specific situation, or free, unaffected, in naïve [or harmless] situations without any specific action or complication, as I have more than once indicated already.

(β) The first departure of the figure from this severe loftiness or blissful self-absorption consists in the fact that in the whole position the beginning or the end of an action is now indicated without any disturbance of the divine repose and any representation of the figure in conflict or struggle. Of this kind are the famous Medici Venus and the Apollo Belvedere. At the time of Lessing and Winckelmann boundless admiration was paid to these statues as the supreme ideals of art; nowadays, when we have come to know works deeper in expression and more vital and more mature in form,[1] these have become depressed in value, and they are ascribed to a later period in which the smoothness of treatment had in view what pleased and was agreeable to the eye and did not adhere any longer to the severe and genuine style. An English traveller (*Morning Chronicle*, 26 July 1825) goes so far as to call the Apollo in plain terms 'a theatrical coxcomb', and he allows to the Venus great sweetness, softness, symmetry, and modest grace, but only a faultless lack of intellect, a negative perfection, and 'a good deal of insipidity'.[2] This movement away from that more severe repose and sanctity we may understand in a general way as follows: Sculpture is of course the art of high seriousness, but this

---

[1] Hegel's view of these two famous figures is borne out by the discussion of them in Sir Kenneth Clark, *The Nude* (ed. cit., pp. 44–5, 79–80), where Winckelmann is also mentioned.

[2] This is an extract from 'Notes of a Journey through France and Italy', but the newspaper gives no indication of authorship.

lofty seriousness of the gods, since they are no abstractions but [in sculpture] formed individually, brings with it at the same time absolute cheerfulness and therefore a reflection of the real and finite world in which the cheerfulness and serenity of the gods expresses not a sense of being immersed in such finite matters but the sense of reconciliation, of spiritual freedom and self-content.

(γ) Therefore Greek art has spread itself into the whole cheerfulness of the Greek spirit and found a pleasure, a joy in occupying itself with an endless number of extremely delightful situations. For every time that it won its way from the more severe abstract modes of portrayal to reverence for the living individuality which unifies everything in itself, it became fond of the living and the cheerful, and the artists launched out into a variety of representations which do not rove away into the painful, horrible, distorted, and agonizing, but keep within the limits of innocent humanity. On these lines the Greeks have transmitted to us many sculptures of supreme excellence. Here of the numerous mythological subjects of a playful but entirely pure and cheerful nature I will cite only the sports of Eros which already come nearer to ordinary human life, as well as others in which the vivacity of the portrayal gives it its chief interest; and the grasp of and preoccupation with such subjects is just what constitutes their cheerfulness and innocence. In this sphere the dice-player and Doryphorus of Polyclitus, for example, were as highly valued[1] as his statue of Hera at Argos; similar fame was enjoyed by the Discobolus and the Ladas the runner[2] of Myron. Further, how charming is the boy plucking a thorn from his foot,[3] and other sculptures of a similar kind of which in the main we know only the name. These are moments when nature has been listened to; they pass fleetingly but they appear now made permanent by the sculptor.

(b) Groups

From such beginnings of a tendency outwards sculpture now proceeds to the presentation of situations in movement, to conflicts and actions, and therefore to groups. For what comes into

---

[1] e.g. by Pliny, *N.H.* xxxiv. 55.
[2] This is now altogether lost (see Richter, op. cit., pp. 210–11).
[3] In the British Museum. A Hellenistic work illustrated in Richter, op. cit., p. 369.

appearance with a more defined action is a more concrete liveliness which is expanded into oppositions and reactions and therefore into essential relations between several figures and their interlacing.

(α) Yet the first thing [to mention] here too are the mere peaceful juxtapositions like, for instance, the two colossal horse-tamers in Rome on Monte Cavallo, which are meant for Castor and Pollux.[1] One statue is ascribed to Phidias, the other to Praxiteles, without any sure proof, although the great excellence of the conception and the graceful thoroughness of the execution justifies names so important. These are only free groups not expressive of any real action or its consequence, and they are entirely fitted for representation in sculpture and for public exhibition in front of the Parthenon where they are supposed to have stood originally.

(β) In the group, however, sculpture proceeds, secondly, to display situations which have as their content conflicts, discordant actions, grief, etc. Here once again we may praise the Greek genuinely artistic sense which did not place such groups in independent positions; on the contrary, since sculpture here is beginning to depart from its own proper and therefore independent sphere, these groups were brought into closer connection with architecture so that they served to decorate spaces in or on buildings. The temple image as a single statue stood peaceful, calm, and sacred in the inner shrine, which was there for the sake of this statue; whereas the pediment outside the building was decorated with groups displaying specific actions of the god and therefore could be elaborated into a more animated movement. An instance is the famous group of Niobe and her children.[2] Here the general form for the arrangement is given by the space for which it was designed. The chief figure stands in the centre and could be the largest and most prominent of them all; the rest needed different postures down to a recumbent one at the acute angles where the pediment ends.

---

[1] 'The Dioscuri with their steeds gave to the Quirinal the modern name of Monte Cavallo. They must be dated about 330 A.D.' An inscription describes one as *Opus Fidiae* and the other as *Opus Praxitelis*. This can only mean that they are copies of works by these sculptors, for their date is proved by details of their sculpture (A. Rumpf, *Stilphasen der spätantiken Kunst*, Cologne, 1955).

[2] The pediment of the temple of Apollo Sosianus in Rome, described by Pliny (*N.H.* xxxvi. 28). Hegel would have seen somewhere a reproduction of the copy in Florence.

KINDS OF PORTRAYAL AND MATERIAL 769

Of other well-known works I will mention only the Laocoon group. For the last forty or fifty years it has been the subject of many investigations and prolonged discussions. In particular it has been thought of real importance to decide whether Virgil took his description of the scene from the sculpture or whether the artist worked from Virgil's description;[1] further, whether Laocoon is actually crying out and whether it is appropriate for sculpture in general to attempt to express a cry; and so on. Previously there was much preoccupation with such matters of psychological importance because Winckelmann's enthusiasm and genuine artistic sense had not yet sunk in, and, besides, such bookworms were the more disposed to indulge in such discussions because frequently they had neither the opportunity to see actual works of art nor the ability to understand them if they had seen them. The most essential thing to consider in the case of this group is that despite the profound grief and profound truth it conveys, despite the convulsive contraction of the body and the tension of all the muscles, still nobility and beauty are preserved, and not in the remotest degree is there any approach to grimaces, distortion, or dislocation. Nevertheless, in the spirit of the subject-matter, the artificiality of the arrangement, the mathematical character of the pose, and the manner of its execution, the whole work undoubtedly belongs to a later age[2] which aims at outstripping simple beauty and life by a deliberate display of its knowledge in the build and musculature of the human body, and tries to please by an all too subtle delicacy in its workmanship. The step from the innocence and greatness of art to a mannerism has here already been taken.

(γ) Sculptures are set up in the most various places, e.g. before entrances to galleries, on esplanades, staircase-landings, in alcoves, etc.; and along with this variety of position and the

[1] The date of the Laocoon is still a matter of controversy, but the various dates now advanced all pre-date the *Aeneid* (see ii. 201 ff.). Of the literary remains of antiquity the *Aeneid* is the first to involve the priest, as well as the boys, in the coils of the serpents. Lessing, whose interesting discussion in his *Laocoon* Hegel must have read, was inclined to think that this was decisive and that the *Aeneid* inspired the Greek sculptors who otherwise would have followed Greek writers. But there may have been literary originals, now perished, available to the sculptors and Virgil as well; or alternatively, in order to produce a pyramidal effect, the sculptors may have had the idea of involving the priest too. As Hegel apparently felt, the problem may be as unprofitable an exercise as asking about the priority of the hen and the egg, but he deserves credit for being one of the first in Germany to see that this famous sculpture was not a work of classical Greek art.

[2] i.e. some centuries later than the age of classical Greek art.

architectural purpose which on its side has many relations to human situations and affairs, there is an alteration, in infinite ways, of the content and subject-matter of works of art and this, occurring in groups, may approach human life still more nearly. Yet it is always a mistake to set up such more animated and elaborate groups on the tops of buildings against the sky with no background, even if their subject is devoid of conflict. This is because the sky is at one time grey, at another blue and dazzlingly clear, so that the outlines of the figures cannot be clearly seen. But in most cases everything depends on these outlines, on the silhouette, since they are really the chief thing that we recognize and that alone makes the rest intelligible. For in the case of a group many parts of the figures stand one in front of the others, e.g. the arms before the trunk, or one leg of a figure in front of the other. At a certain distance the outline of such parts is obscure and unintelligible or at least much less clear than that of the parts which stand out quite freely. We only need to imagine a group drawn on paper where some limbs of a figure are strongly and sharply outlined whereas others are only dim and indicated vaguely. A statue and, to a greater extent, a group has this same effect if it has no other background but the sky; in that case we see only a sharply outlined silhouette where there remain recognizable only some weaker indications of what lies within.

This is the reason why, for instance, the Victory on the Brandenburg Gate in Berlin[1] has such a beautiful effect, not only because of its simplicity and repose but because we are enabled to see the individual figures with precision. The horses stand well apart from one another, and do not hide one another, and all the same the figure of Victory rises high enough above them. Whereas Tieck's[2] Apollo, drawn in his car by griffins, on the top of the Opera House, appears less excellent, no matter how artistically correct otherwise the whole conception and execution may be. By the courtesy of a friend I saw these figures in Tieck's workshop. They gave the promise of a splendid effect, but, now that they stand aloft, too much of the outline of one figure falls on another which forms its background, and the result is a silhouette which is all the less free and clear because the figures as a group lack simplicity. Apart from the fact that the griffins on account of their

---

[1] Bronze by J. G. Schadow, 1793.
[2] C. F., sculptor, 1776–1851.

shorter legs do not stand so high and freely as the horses [on the Victory], they have wings besides, and Apollo has his crest of hair and his lyre on his arm. All this is too much for the position of the group and contributes to the blurring of the outlines.

(c) *Reliefs*

The last mode of presentation whereby sculpture takes an important step towards the principle of painting is the relief, first the high relief and later the bas-relief. Here what conditions the work is the surface, so that the figures stand on one and the same plane, and the three-dimensional character, from which sculpture starts, begins more and more to disappear. But the ancient relief does not yet come so near to painting as to proceed to perspective differences between foreground and background; on the contrary it keeps rigidly to the surface without making the different subjects appear in their different spatial positions to be either in front or behind, as the skill of foreshortening could do. Consequently the favourite practice is to adhere to figures in profile, set beside one another on the same surface. But in that event, owing to this simplicity, very complicated actions cannot be adopted as the subject-matter but only actions which proceed in real life along one and the same line, e.g. processions, sacrificial trains, and the like, trains of Olympic victors, etc.

Still, reliefs have the greatest variety. Not only do they fill and adorn temple walls and friezes; they surround utensils, sacrificial bowls, votive offerings, cups, tankards, urns, lamps, etc.; they decorate seats and tripods, and are allied with associated handicrafts. Here above all it is the wit of invention which launches out into the greatest variety of figures and their combination and can no longer keep in view the proper aim of sculpture.

2. *Materials for Sculpture*

We have been driven by the individuality which serves as the fundamental principle of sculpture to particularize not only the spheres of gods, men, and nature from which plastic art derives its subjects, but also the modes of presentation in single statues, groups, and reliefs. So now we have to examine the same variety of particularization in the material of which the artist can avail himself for his statuary. For different kinds of subject-matter and mode of treatment are closely connected with different kinds of physical material and have a secret sympathy and harmony with them.

As a general remark I will here only observe that just as the Greeks were unsurpassed in invention, so too they amaze us by the astounding elaboration and skill of their technical execution. Both of these things are equally difficult in sculpture because its media cannot present the many-sidedness of the inner life in the way that the other arts have at their command. Architecture, to be sure, is still poorer, but [unlike sculpture] it has not the task of using plainly inorganic material to make the living spirit itself, or the life of nature, actually present to us. Yet this developed skill in the completely perfect handling of the material is inherent in the very nature of the ideal itself, because the ideal has, as its principle, entire entry into the sensuous field and the fusion of the inner life with its external existence. The same principle is therefore asserted where the ideal is achieved in the real world. In this connection we ought not to be surprised when it is maintained that in the days of great artistic dexterity artists either worked their marble without having models in clay or, if they did have such, went to work far more freely and unconstrainedly 'than happens in our day when, to speak the strict truth, the artist provides only copies in marble of originals, called models, previously worked in clay' (Winckelmann, v. 389, note).[1] The ancient artists therefore acquired the living inspiration which is always more or less lost by repetitions and copies; although it cannot be denied that now and again even in famous works of art, single defective parts occur, as, for example, eyes that are not equal in size, ears one of which is higher or lower than the other, feet of somewhat unequal length, and so on. The Greeks did not keep every time to the strictest accuracy in such things as the ordinary run of mediocre artists do. Such accuracy is the sole merit of mediocre artists, no matter how highly they may plume themselves on their productions and artistic judgement.

(a) Wood

Amongst the various kinds of material in which sculptors fabricated images of the gods, one of the oldest is wood. A stick, a post on the top of which a head was placed—that was the beginning.

---

[1] This note, which is by the editor of Winckelmann's works, is note 456 to K.d.A., bk. 7, ch. i, § 4.

Many of the earliest temple images are wooden but even in the time of Phidias this material was still used. So, for instance, the colossal statue of Athene at Plataea by Phidias consisted of gilded wood, though head, hands, and feet were marble (Meyer, *Gesch. d. bild. Künste*, i. 60), and Myron constructed a wooden image of Hecate, with only one face and one body,[1] at Aegina where Hecate was particularly honoured and where her festival is celebrated every year; the Aeginetans maintain that Orpheus of Thrace instituted it (Pausanias, ii. 30).

But on the whole, unless wood is gilded or otherwise overlaid, it seems on account of its own grain, and the way the grain runs, to be unsuited for grand works and more adapted to smaller ones for which it was commonly used in the Middle Ages and is still employed even today.

(b) Ivory, Gold, Bronze, and Marble

Other materials of the first importance are ivory associated with gold, cast bronze, and marble.

(α) It is well known that Phidias used ivory and gold for his masterpieces, e.g. for his Zeus at Olympia and for the famous colossal statue of Athene on the Acropolis at Athens; she carried on her hand a Victory, itself above man's height.[2] The nude parts of the body were made of laminated ivory, her robe and mantle of gold-plates which could be removed. The method of working in yellowish ivory and gold dates from the time when statues were coloured, a sort of presentation which gave way more and more to monochromatic bronze or marble.[3] Ivory is a very clean material, smooth without the granular character of marble, and moreover costly; for the costliness of their statues of the gods was also a great matter for the Athenians. The Athene at Plataea was only superficially gilt, but the one at Athens had solid plates of gold. At the same time these chryselephantine statues should be big and rich. Quatremère de Quincy[4] has written a masterpiece on these works,

---

[1] Later, Hecate is represented with three heads and three bodies.
[2] Eight feet high, according to Pausanias, i. 24.
[3] If Hegel had seen the Acropolis, this sentence might have been expressed otherwise. The difference was between laying on colour and leaving the material in its natural colour, but the Greeks seem to have preferred the former.
[4] A. C. Q. de Quincy (1755–1849): *Le Jupiter Olympien . . . ouvrage qui comprend . . . l'explication de la toreutique* (Paris, 1815). Toreutics = the art of carving, chasing, and embossing metal (*O.E.D.*).

i.e. on the toreutics of the ancients. 'Toreutics'—τορεύειν, τόρευμα—should properly be used of engraving on metal, chasing, cutting deep figures, e.g. on precious stones; but τόρευμα is also used to mean embossed figures on metal worked in half or full relief by means of moulds and castings and not by engraving or chasing, and then further, also improperly, to mean raised figures on earthenware vessels, and finally any sculpture in bronze. Quatremère has especially investigated the technical side of their execution and calculated how large the sheets cut from elephant tusks could be and how much ivory was used, having regard to the colossal dimensions of chryselephantine figures. But he has gone to no less trouble, on the other hand, on the basis of accounts given by classical authors,[1] to reproduce for us a sketch of the seated figure of Zeus and particularly of his great throne with its superb bas-reliefs, and so in both these ways to give us an idea of the magnificence and perfection of the work.[2]

In the Middle Ages ivory was used especially for smaller works of the most varied kinds, crucifixes, the Virgin, etc., but also for drinking vessels with pictures of hunts and similar scenes where ivory had the great advantage of wood on account of its smoothness and hardness.

(β) But in antiquity the most widespread and favourite material was bronze, and the Greeks brought the casting of it up to supreme mastery. At the time of Myron and Polyclitus especially [fifth-century B.C.] it was used universally for statues of the gods and other works of sculpture. The darker vaguer colour, the sheen, the smoothness of bronze lacks in general the abstractness of white marble but it is, as it were, warmer. The bronze used by the Greeks was a mixture, sometimes of gold and silver, sometimes of copper with various metals.[3] So, for instance, the so-called Corinthian bronze is a special mixture from which, as a result of the fire of Corinth, its unexampled wealth of statues and other things in bronze was formed. Mummius[4] shipped away a number of statues and this excellent man attached such a high value to this treasure and was

---

[1] e.g. Callimachus, Pausanias, and Strabo.
[2] It was nearly sixty feet high and the throne was ornamented with gold and precious stones as well as with sculptured and painted figures. Theodosius I removed it to Constantinople where it was destroyed in A.D. 475.
[3] Tin only is mentioned, one part of tin to nine of copper.
[4] L. Mummius, praetor 154 B.C., and later conqueror of Achaea and responsible for the conflagration of Corinth in 146 B.C.

KINDS OF PORTRAYAL AND MATERIAL 775

so full of anxiety to get it to Rome that he commended them to the sailors, with the threat that if these were lost they would have to create others the same in their place.[1]

In bronze casting the Greeks acquired an incredible mastery which enabled them to cast it thinly but no less firmly. This may be regarded as something purely technical, having nothing to do with art proper, but every artist works in a physical material and it is the peculiar capacity of genius to become a complete master of his material, so that one aspect of genius is skill and dexterity in technique and handicraft. Given this virtuosity in casting, such a sculpture can be finished more cheaply and could be produced more quickly than by chiselling in marble. A second advantage which the Greeks were able to achieve by their mastery in casting was the purity of the cast which they pushed so far that their bronze statues did not need to be chiselled at all, and therefore in their finer traits there was nothing of the loss which can never be wholly avoided with chiselling. If we consider the enormous mass of works of art which arose from this lightness and mastery of technique, we must betray the greatest astonishment, and grant that the artistic sense of sculpture is an impulse and instinct belonging to the spirit which could exist precisely in such a measure and so widespread at only a single period in a single nation. In the whole of Prussia today (1829) we can very easily count up the bronze statuary: there are the unique bronze church-doors in Gnesen, only a few bronze statues in Königsberg and Düsseldorf, and statues of Blücher in Berlin and Breslau and of Luther at Wittenberg.[2]

[1] Velleius Paterculus, i. 13, says only 'bring back' instead of 'create'. But the implication is that what Mummius shipped in 146 B.C. included Corinthian bronzes, while Hegel has just said that Corinthian bronze was a result of the fire in that year. This follows Pliny, *N.H.* xxxiv. 3: 'Of the bronze that was renowned in early days, the Corinthian was the most highly praised. This is a compound produced by accident when Corinth was burned.' Strabo (17. xii) says that this bronze was an alloy of gold and silver, and (8. vi. 23) that, a century after the conflagration, when Corinth was being rebuilt in 44 B.C., bronze vessels found in graves were sold at high prices in Rome.

[2] Raising bronze statues to public figures did not become fashionable anywhere in Europe until Hegel's day. From his list he excludes Schadow's bronze *Victory*, mentioned above, and he omits the same sculptor's statue of Blücher in Rostock (1819). The bronze doors in Gnesen cathedral (*c.* 1200) are indeed a rarity. The statue of Frederick I in Königsberg was cast in bronze by Jakobi at the end of the seventeenth century after a model by Schlüter. The equestrian bronze in Düsseldorf of Count J. Wilhelm is by Grupello of Innsbruck, 1703. Luther's monument at Wittenberg was completed by Schadow in 1821. The bronze statues of Blücher are both by C. D. Rauch, Berlin 1826, Breslau 1827.

The very different tone and infinite malleability and, as it were, fluidity of this material, which can be compatible with all sorts of portrayal, permits sculpture to pass into every conceivable variety of productions and adapt this so flexible and visible material to a host of conceits, compliments, vessels, decorations, and graceful trivialities, whereas marble has a limited use in the portrayal of objects and in their size; e.g. it can provide, on a certain scale, urns and vases with bas-reliefs, but for smaller objects it is unsuitable. Whereas bronze, which can not only be cast in certain forms but beaten and engraved, excludes hardly any size or manner of portrayal.

As an example on a smaller scale we may make appropriate mention here of the art of numismatics. Even in this art the classical artists have transmitted to us perfect masterpieces of beauty, although in the technical matter of die-stamping they are far behind our modern development of machine techniques. The coins were not really stamped but beaten out from almost circular pieces of metal. This branch of art reached its apex in the age of Alexander; in the Roman Empire coins were already poorer; in our own day it was Napoleon especially who tried in his coins and medallions to revive the beauty of the classics, and they are of great excellence. But in other states the chief consideration in striking the coinage has been the value of the metal and its correct weight.

(γ) The final material for sculpture, the one above all most appropriate to it, is stone which has in itself the objective character of consistency and permanence. Already in their time the Egyptians chiselled their colossal sculptures with painful labour in the hardest granite, syenite, basalt etc., but marble in its soft purity, whiteness, absence of colour, and the delicacy of its sheen harmonizes in the most direct way with the aim of sculpture, and especially through its granular character and the gentle infusion of light has a great advantage over the chalk-like dead appearance of gypsum[1] which is too clear and its glare easily kills the finer shadow-effects. We find the use of marble in Greece above all in the later period,[2] i.e. that of Praxiteles and Scopas who achieved the most acknowledged mastery in marble statues. Phidias did work in marble, but for the most part only in heads, feet, and hands;

---

[1] i.e. selenite, alabaster, or even plaster of Paris.
[2] i.e. fourth century B.C. Phidias belonged to the fifth.

Myron and Polyclitus generally used bronze; but Praxiteles and Scopas tried to eschew colour, this character heterogeneous to abstract sculpture. Of course we cannot deny that the pure beauty of ideal sculpture can be executed just as completely in bronze as in marble, but when, as happened in the case of Praxiteles and Scopas, art begins to pass over into softer grace and attractiveness of form, then marble is the more appropriate material. For marble (Meyer, op. cit., i. 279)

because of its translucency encourages softness of outlines, their gentle blending and tender conjunction; in marble a delicate and artistic perfection appears much more clearly in the mild whiteness of the stone than is ever possible in the noblest bronze: the more beautifully bronze goes greenish all the more disturbing are the shafts of light and reflections which it causes.

Moreover, a further reason for preferring to use this stone instead of metal was the care taken at this time about light and shade, even in sculpture; their nuances and finer differences were made more visible in marble than they could be in bronze.

(c) *Precious Stones and Glass*

To these most important sorts of material we have to add, in conclusion, precious stones and glass.[1] The Greek gems, cameos, and pastes are beyond price because, although in the smallest compass, they repeat in supreme perfection the whole range of sculpture from the simple figure of a god, through the most varied kinds of grouping, to all possible conceits, cheerful and graceful. Yet, in connection with the Stosch[2] collection, Winckelmann remarks (III. xxvii) that

Here for the first time I lighted on a truth which was of great use to me later in the explanation of the most difficult monuments, and this consisted in the principle that on cut stones as well as on sublime works the images were very seldom drawn from events occurring later than the Trojan war or after the return of Odysseus to Ithaca, if we except e.g. stories of the Heraclidae or descendants of Heracles; for stories about

---

[1] i.e. glass paste, a vitreous composition used for making imitation stones. Glass-blowing was not invented until the first-century B.C.

[2] P. Baron von Stosch, 1691–1757. Winckelmann's *Description des pierres gravées du feu Baron von S.* appeared in 1766.

them border on fable, a proper subject-matter for artists. Nevertheless I am acquainted with only a single portrayal of the story of the Heraclidae.

As for gems, the genuine and more perfect figures display supreme beauty like the organic works of nature and they can be examined with a magnifying glass without losing the purity of their delineation. I mention this only because here the technique of art approaches a technique of feeling, since the artist, unlike the sculptor who can examine his work all round and direct it with his eye, must have it almost in his touch. For he holds the stone, stuck to wax, against small sharp little wheels turned by a flywheel and in this way the design is scratched. In this way it is the sense of touch which is in possession of the conception, of the intention of the strokes and marks, and it directs them so perfectly that when we see these stones lit up we think we have before us a relief work.

Secondly, of an opposite kind are cameos which display figures cut from stone and embossed. For these use was made especially of onyx in which the Greeks could ingeniously emphasize with taste and sensitivity the differently coloured layers, especially white and tawny ones. Aemilius Paulus[1] had a great number of such stones and small vases shipped with him to Rome.

For productions in these varied kinds of material the Greek artists did not take as a basis situations fabricated by themselves but drew their topics every time, except for Bacchanalia and dances, from myths about the gods and traditions, and even on urns and portrayals of funeral processions they had in view specific things related to the individual in whose honour the procession had been designed. On the other hand what is specifically allegorical does not belong to the genuine ideal but occurs only in more modern art.

3. *Historical Stages in the Development of Sculpture*

Up to this point we have treated sculpture throughout as the most adequate expression of the classical ideal. But the ideal not only has a progressive inner development in the course of which it

---

[1] L. Aemilius Paulus Macedonicus, d. 160 B.C. Plutarch, in his life of him, refers to the size and solidity of the embossed work on the goblets, etc., displayed at his triumph after his Macedonian victories.

becomes explicitly what it is in accordance with its implicit character, and even so begins to transcend this harmony with its own essential nature; on the contrary, as we saw above in Part II in the discussion of the particular forms of art, it also has behind it in the symbolic mode of artistic presentation a presupposition which, in order to be ideal, it must surmount, as well as, in advance of it, a further art, the romantic, by which it must be superseded in turn.

Both the symbolic and the romantic forms of art likewise take the human form as the medium of their portrayals; they cling to its spatial outline and therefore display it visibly in the manner of sculpture. Consequently when our business is with the historical development of sculpture we have to discuss not merely Greek and Roman sculpture, but oriental and Christian sculpture as well. Yet amongst the peoples for whom the symbolic was the basic type for artistic productions, it was above all the Egyptians who began to apply, for their images of the gods, the human form as it struggled to escape from a purely natural existence, so that it is especially in their case that we meet with sculpture because they give to their insights in general an artistic existence in material things. Whereas Christian sculpture is far more widespread and far richer in development, both in its strictly romantic medieval character and also in its further development where it endeavoured to approximate further to the principle of the classical ideal again and so to produce what was specifically sculptural.

Granted these considerations, I will conclude this whole Section *first* by making a few observations about Egyptian sculpture in distinction from Greek and as the preamble to the genuine ideal.

Next a *second* stage is formed by the proper development of Greek sculpture, to which the Roman is allied. But here we have mainly to glance at the stages which precede the really ideal mode of representation, because we have already considered ideal sculpture itself at length in the second chapter.

Thirdly, therefore, it only remains for us to indicate in brief the principle governing Christian sculpture, although in this matter I can only embark on pure generalities.

(a) Egyptian Sculpture

When we are on the point of studying the classical art of sculpture in Greece historically, we are met at once, before achieving our aim, by Egyptian art as sculpture too; as sculpture, that is to say, not in connection with enormous works produced in an entirely individual artistic style by supreme technique and elaboration, but as a starting-point and source for the forms of Greek plastic art. The fact that the latter is the case, that it is actually historically true that Greek artists did learn from the Egyptians and adopt shapes from them—all this must be made out, so far as the meaning of the divine figures portrayed is concerned, on the field of mythology, and in respect of the manner of artistic treatment, by the history of art. That there was a connection between Egyptian and Greek ideas of the gods was believed and proved by Herodotus [ii. 41 ff.]; an external connection in works of art Creuzer thinks he can find most obviously in coins especially, and he rests his case above all on old Attic ones. In Heidelberg [in 1821] he showed me one in his possession, on which the face indeed, in profile, had exactly the cut of faces on Egyptian pictures. Here, however, we can leave this purely historical question alone[1] and have only to see if, instead of this, an inner and necessary connection can be exhibited. This necessity I have touched on already. The ideal, and art in its perfection, must be preceded by imperfect art, and it is only through the negation of this, i.e. through getting rid of the defects still clinging to it, that the ideal becomes the ideal. In the instance before us, classical art of course *comes into being*, but that from which it develops must have an independent existence of its own outside it, because classical art, as classical, must leave behind it all inadequacy, all becoming, and must be perfect in itself. Now this [pre-classical] process of becoming classical consists in the fact that the content of the presentation begins to meet the ideal, yet remains incapable of an ideal treatment because it still belongs to the symbolic outlook which cannot form into one the universality of the meaning and the individual visible shape. The one thing that I will briefly indicate here is that Egyptian sculpture has such a fundamental character.

---

[1] Nothing is more striking in Hegel than his dismissal of 'purely' historical questions, although history is the guiding thread through all his major works, indeed including these Lectures. The reason is that he distinguishes between a philosopher's study of history and a historian's. It is the business of the latter to find the facts, to deal with 'purely' historical questions; once these are found, the philosopher can get to work to find their meaning, or the spiritual purpose which they are working out. He would probably have preferred, e.g., Toynbee to Ranke.

KINDS OF PORTRAYAL AND MATERIAL 781

(α) The first thing to mention is the lack of inner and creative freedom, despite all perfection of technique. Greek sculptures proceed from the vitality and freedom of imagination which reshapes existing religious ideas into individual figures, and in the individuality of these productions makes objective to itself its own vision of ideal and classical perfection. But the Egyptian images of the gods retain a stationary type, as Plato says as long ago as his day (*Laws*, ii. 656, *d–e*) [in Egypt] the representations of the gods were settled from antiquity by the priests and

neither painters nor practitioners of other arts of design were allowed to innovate on these models or to invent any but native and traditional standards, and this prohibition still exists. You will therefore find that what was produced ten thousand years ago (and I mean 'ten thousand' literally) is neither better nor worse than what is produced to-day.

The corollary of this stationary fidelity was that in Egypt, as is implied by Herodotus (ii. 167), craftsmen enjoyed less respect, and they and their children had to be lower in repute than all the other citizens who did not ply any craft.[1] Besides here a craft or art was not practised of one's own accord but, owing to the domination of caste, son followed father, not only in his calling but in the manner of his exercising his profession and art; one trod in the footsteps of the other so that, as Winckelmann puts it (III. 2, p. 74),[2] 'no one seems to have left a footprint which he could call his own'. Therefore art maintained itself in this rigorous servitude[3] of the spirit, where the liveliness of the free artistic genius is banned along with (not the urge for honour or reward from others but) the higher honour of being an *artist*; i.e. one who does not work as a craftsman from mechanical forms and rules available and settled abstractly in a general way, but who sees his own individuality in his work as specifically his own creation.

(β) Secondly, as for the works of art themselves, Winckelmann, whose descriptions here once again attest his great acuteness and subtlety of observation, characterizes the chief features of Egyptian

[1] Art, skill, handicraft are as little differentiated by the Greek word as artists and craftsmen. But Herodotus is actually *saying* that this depreciation of the artist or craftsman is Greek, *implying* that it was Egyptian, and speculating on whether the Greeks borrowed it from that source.
[2] i.e. *K.d.A.*, bk. 2, ch. i, § 11.
[3] Reading *Gebundenheit* with Hotho's first edition. The second edition has *Ungebundenheit*, but this seems inappropriate in the context. See below, p. 786.

sculpture in the following way (III. 2, pp. 77–84)[1]: In general, there are lacking in the whole shape and its forms the grace and vivacity which result from the properly organic sweep of the lines; the outlines are straight and in scarcely swerving lines, the posture seems forced and stiff, the feet pressed closely together, and if in erect figures one foot is placed in front of the other they still keep the same direction and are not turned outwards; on male figures the arms hang straight down pressed firmly against the body. The hands, Winckelmann goes on [§ 8], have the shape of those of a man who has hands originally not ill-formed but now spoiled and neglected; but the feet are flatter and more spread out, the toes are of equal length and the little toe is neither bent nor curved inwards. Nevertheless, hands, nails, and toes are shaped not badly, even if the joints of fingers and toes are not indicated, as after all on all the other unclothed parts muscles and bones are little marked, and nerves and veins not at all. The result is that in detail, despite the laborious and skilled execution, there is lacking that sort of workmanship which alone imparts real animation and life to the figure. On the other hand, the knees, ankles and elbows are prominent, as they are in reality. Masculine figures are distinguished especially by an unusually slender waist above the hips, but their back is not visible because the statues lean against columns and were worked in one piece with them.

This immobility has nothing at all to do with any lack of skill on the part of the artist but must be regarded as due to an original conception of what images of the gods and their deeply secret repose should be. Along with this immobility there is directly connected an absence of situation[2] and the lack of any sort of the action which is displayed in sculpture by the position and movement of hands, by gesture and the expression of the features. It is true that we do find amongst what the Egyptians present on obelisks and walls many figures in movement, but only as reliefs and usually painted.

To cite a few more details, the eyes do not lie deep at all, as they do in Greek ideal figures, but stand on the contrary almost level with the forehead, drawn out flatly and slanting;[3] the eyebrows,

[1] i.e. bk. 2, ch. ii, §§ 1–9.
[2] Cf. above in Vol. I, p. 200.
[3] It is difficult to see what was meant by *schief*. We expect 'with narrow slits', or the like. See below on the Aeginetan sculptures. Reproductions of long-slitted or narrow-slitted eyes do not show any slant.

eyelids, and rims of the lips are generally presented by engraved lines, or the brows are indicated by a more emphasized stroke which extends to the temples and is cut short there at an angle. What is missing here above all is the prominence of the forehead, and along with this lack there are correspondingly unusually high ears and curved-in noses, and these bring with them a strong emphasis and indication of cheek-bones which ordinarily are not prominent, whereas the chin is always drawn back and small, the firmly closed mouth has its corners drawn rather upwards than downwards, and the lips appear separated from one another only by a simple incision. On the whole these figures are not merely lacking in freedom and life; on the contrary the head above all has no expression of spirituality, because animalism prevails and does not allow the spirit to emerge in independent appearance.

Animals, on the other hand, according to Winckelmann,[1] are treated with full understanding and a graceful variety of softly deviating outlines and parts flowing evenly from one to another. In human figures spiritual life is not yet freed from the animal model and not made ideal by a fusion in a new and free way with what is physical and natural. Nevertheless the specifically symbolical meaning of both human and animal forms is explicitly displayed in those figures presented even in sculpture in which human and animal forms appear in an enigmatic association with one another.[2]

(γ) Works of art which still bear this character remain therefore at a stage which has not yet overcome the breach between meaning and shape, because for it the chief thing is still the meaning, and what matters is (a) rather the *universal* idea of that meaning than its incorporation in an *individual* shape and (b) the enjoyment springing from artistic contemplation.

Here sculpture still proceeds from the spirit of a people of whom on the one hand we may say that they have advanced only so far as the need for pictorial ideas, because they are satisfied to find *indicated* in a work of art what is implicit in ideas and here indeed in *religious* ideas. Therefore, whatever their achievement in diligence and the perfection of technical execution, still so far as sculpture goes we ought to call the Egyptians children because they do not require for their figures the truth, life, and beauty whereby alone the free work of art becomes ensouled. Of course, on the other hand, the Egyptians do go beyond mere ideas and the need

[1] § 5 of the last reference to *K.d.A.*   [2] e.g. in the Sphinx.

for them; they advance to the vision and illustration of human and animal shapes, and indeed they can even grasp and present clearly, without distortion, and in correct proportions the forms that they reproduce. But they do not breathe into them either the life that the human form otherwise has in reality, or the higher life which can be the vehicle for expressing what the spirit effects or weaves in these forms now made adequate to it. On the contrary, their works reveal only a rather lifeless seriousness, an undisclosed secret, so that the shape is to give an inkling not of its own individual inner being but of a further meaning still alien to it. To quote only one example, there is a frequently recurring figure of Isis holding Horus on her knee. Here, looked at from the outside, we have the same subject as a Mary and child in Christian art. But in the Egyptian symmetrical, rectilinear, and unmoved pose there is (to quote a recent description in *Cours d'Archéologie* par [D.] Raoul-Rochette, i–xii, Paris, 1828)

neither a mother nor a child; no trace of affection, of smiling or cuddling; in short not the least expression of any kind. Tranquil, imperturbable, unshaken is this divine mother who suckles her divine child, or rather there is neither goddess, nor mother, nor son, nor god—there is only a physical sign of a thought incapable of emotion or passion, and no true presentation of an actual event, still less the correct expression of natural feeling.

This does precisely mark the breach between meaning and object and the inadequate development of artistic intuition in the Egyptians. Their inner spiritual sense is so dulled that it does not encourage the need for the precision of a true and lively presentation, made really definite, to which the spectator has nothing to add but needs only to have an attitude of reception and reproduction because the artist has given everything already. A higher sense of one's own individuality than the Egyptians possessed had to be awakened before there could be dissatisfaction with vagueness and superficiality in art and before the claim in works of art for intellect, reason, movement, expression, soul, and beauty could be made good.

(b) Greek and Roman Sculpture

This sense of self we see completely made alive for the first time, so far as sculpture is concerned, in the Greeks, and therefore we

KINDS OF PORTRAYAL AND MATERIAL 785

find all the deficiencies of this Egyptian preamble expunged. Still, in this development we have not to make any violent leap from the imperfections of a still symbolic sculpture to the perfection of the classical ideal; on the contrary, as I have said more than once, in its own sphere, even if lifted now to a higher stage, the ideal has to proceed to strip off that defectiveness which at first was in the way of its perfection.

(α) As such beginnings within classical sculpture itself I will mention very briefly the so-called Aeginetan and ancient Etruscan works of art.

Both these stages or styles transcend the point at which, as in the case of the Egyptians, the artist is content simply to repeat the not unnatural but still lifeless forms just as they have been transmitted to him by others, and is satisfied to present to imagination a figure, from which imagination can abstract and be reminded of its own religious content, though without his producing anything for contemplation in a way that reveals the work as the artist's own conception and life.

But all the same this stage, really preliminary to ideal art, does not extend all the way right into what is actually classical because on the one hand it is obviously preoccupied with what is typical and therefore without life, and on the other, while approaching life and movement, it can reach at first only the life of nature; not the life of that spiritually animated beauty which displays the life of the spirit unseparated from the life of its natural shape and derives the individual forms of this really accomplished unification equally from a vision of what is presently existent and from the free creation of genius.

With the Aeginetan works of art we have become more closely acquainted only in recent times[1] and there is a dispute as to whether they are in the category of Greek art or not. In examining them we must at once make an essential distinction in respect of artistic presentation between the head and the rest of the body. The whole body, except the head, witnesses to the truest treatment and imitation of nature. Even the accidental features of the skin are imitated and carried out excellently with a marvellous handling of the marble; the muscles are strongly emphasized, the bone

[1] Sculptures from the pediment of the temple of Zeus at Aegina were discovered in 1811. They were transferred to Munich into the possession of the Crown Prince of Bavaria and described in Wagner's book cited on p. 786 below.

structure of the body is indicated, the shapes are constrained by the severity of the design, yet reproduced with such knowledge of the human organism that the figures almost deceive us into thinking that they are alive, why! even that we are almost scared by them and shrink from touching them (according to [J. M. von] Wagner in his *Über die ägin. Bildwerke*, Tübingen, 1817).

On the other hand, a true presentation of nature was entirely sacrificed in the workmanship of the heads; a uniform cut of the faces was preserved in all the heads, whatever all their difference of action, character, and situation: the noses are sharp, the forehead still lies back without rising freely and straight; the ears stand high, the long-slitted eyes are set flat and slanting; the closed mouth ends in angles drawn upwards, the cheeks are kept flat but the chin is strong and angular. Equally repetitive are the form of the hair and the folds of the robes in which what predominates is symmetry, asserted above all in the posing and grouping of the figures and the peculiar kind of decoration. In part the blame for this uniformity has been put on a non-beautiful treatment of national characteristics; in part it has led people to infer from it that the hands of the artists were tied by a reverence for an ancient tradition of imperfect art. But the artist who is alive in himself and in what he produces does not allow his hands to be tied in this way, and this adherence to a type, along with great skill in other respects, must therefore be indicative simply of a bondage of the spirit which cannot yet be free and independent in its artistic creations.

Finally, the postures are just as uniform; yet they are not exactly stiff but rough, and cold, and in the case of combatants they are like those that craftsmen commonly take in the course of their business, e.g. that joiners take in planing.

We may say that the general conclusion to be drawn from these illustrations is that *spiritual* animation is what is missing in them, though they are so extremely interesting for the history of art and display a clear division between tradition and the imitation of nature. For, as I have explained already above in Chapter II, the spirit can be expressed [in sculpture] only in features and posture. The other parts of the body do indicate spirit's *natural* differences, e.g. those of sex and age, but what is entirely spiritual the posture alone can reproduce. But in the Aeginetan sculptures facial expressions and the posture are precisely what is relatively spiritless.

The Etruscan works of art which are testified as genuine by inscriptions show just the same imitation of nature, though in a still higher degree, but the posture and facial expressions are free, and some of these works are very nearly portraits. So, for instance, Winckelmann speaks (iii, ch. 2, p. 189)[1] of a male statue which seems to be wholly a portrait, though emanating from the art of a later period. It is a life-size figure of a man, apparently a sort of orator, a magisterial and dignified person, presented with great and unforced naturalness and with no vagueness of posture or expression. It would be noticeable and significant if what was at home on Roman soil from the start was not the ideal but nature in its prosaic actuality.

(β) Now, *secondly*, in order to attain the summit of the classical ideal, really ideal sculpture has to abandon the typical and a reverence for tradition and make room for artistic freedom of production. This freedom alone succeeds, on the one hand, in entirely working the universality of the meaning into the individuality of the shape, and, on the other, in raising the physical forms to the height of being a genuine expression of their spiritual meaning. In this way we see freed into vitality both the stiffness and bondage intrinsic to the outlook of the older art, and also the predominance of the meaning over the individuality through which that meaning should be expressed. In this vitality the bodily forms on their side lose both the abstract uniformity of a traditional character and also a deceptive naturalness, and proceed on the other hand to the classical individuality which animates the universality of the forms by particularizing them and at the same time makes their sensuous reality throughout a perfect expression of animation by the spirit. This sort of vitality affects not only the shape as such but also the posture, movement, drapery, grouping, in short all the aspects which I have distinguished in detail and discussed above.

The union achieved here is that of universality and individuality which, in respect alike of the spiritual content as such and the sensuous form, must first be harmonized before they can enter one with another into the indissoluble bond which is genuinely classical. But, once more, this identity has its series of stages. That is to say, at one end, the ideal inclines still to the loftiness and severity which does not begrudge the individual his living stir and movement but yet keeps him still firmly under the domination of the

[1] i.e. *K.d.A.*, bk. 3, ch. ii, § 10.

universal: while at the other end the universal is gradually more and more lost in the individual, with the result that it is deprived of its depth, and this loss can be repaired only by substituting the development of the individual and sensuous aspect of the object, so that the ideal passes over from loftiness to what is pleasing and delicate, to cheerfulness and a coaxing gracefulness. Between these extremes there is a second stage which carries the severity of the first forward into fuller individuality, yet without finding its main aim achieved by mere gracefulness.

(γ) *Thirdly*, in Roman art we see the dissolution of classical sculpture beginning. Here, that is to say, it is no longer on the ideal proper that the whole conception and execution of the work of art depends. The poetry of spiritual animation, the inner breath and nobility of a representation perfect in itself, these excellences peculiar to Greek plastic art, disappear and give place on the whole to a preference for something more like a portrait. This developing artistic 'truth to nature' permeates every aspect of Roman sculpture. Nevertheless in this its own sphere, it is always at such a high stage that essentially it is only inferior to Greek because it lacks what is really perfect in a work of art, the poetry of the ideal in the strict sense of the word.

(c) *Christian Sculpture*

As for Christian sculpture, on the other hand, from the very beginning it has a principle of treatment and mode of portrayal which does not so directly cohere with the material and forms of sculpture as is the case in the classical ideal portrayed by Greek imagination and art. For romantic art, as we saw in Part II, is essentially concerned with the inner life that has withdrawn into itself out of the external world, with spiritual self-related subjective life; this does appear outwardly but it leaves this external manifestation alone in its own particular character without forcing its fusion with the inner and spiritual life, as the ideal of sculpture requires. Grief, agony both physical and mental, torture and penance, death and resurrection, spiritual and subjective personality, deep feeling, heart, love, and emotion, this proper content of the religious and romantic imagination is no topic for which the abstract external shape as such in its three spatial dimensions and the material in its physical, not idealized, existence could provide the really adequate form and the equally congruent material. Therefore in the romantic field sculpture does not afford, as it does in Greece, the distinctive characteristic of the other arts and indeed of the whole of existence. On the contrary it yields to painting and music as the arts more appropriate to portraying the inner life and, in the particularity of an external object, its free permeation by that life. In the Christian period we do find sculpture practised in wood, marble, bronze, silver, and gold, and often brought to the height of mastery, but it is not the art which presents, as Greek sculpture does, a truly adequate picture of God. On the contrary the religious sculpture of romantic art remains, to a greater extent than Greek, an adornment of architecture. The saints stand mostly in niches of turrets and buttresses, or on entrance doors; while the birth, baptism, Passion, Resurrection, and so many other events in the life of Christ, as well as the great visions of the Last Judgement, etc., are at once concentrated, because of their varied content, in reliefs on doors and walls of churches, on fonts, choir stalls, etc., and they readily approximate to arabesques. In short, because what prevails here is the expression of the inner life of the spirit, the whole of this sculpture acquires a pictorial principle in a higher degree than is allowed to ideal plastic art. On the other hand, sculpture seizes rather on common life and therefore on the portraiture which, like painting too, it does not regard as alien to religious portrayals. For example, the goose-seller on the market-place in Nürnberg,[1] so highly praised by Goethe and Meyer, is a country peasant holding a goose for sale on each arm and presented in an extremely lively way in bronze (impossible in marble). So too the many sculptures on the church of St. Sebald and so many churches and buildings [in Nürnberg], produced especially in the time of Peter Vischer [1455–1529], which exhibit religious subjects drawn from the history of the Passion, etc., give a clear sight of this sort of particularization in shape, expression, mien, and gestures, especially in gradations of grief.

On the whole, therefore, though romantic sculpture has deviated all too often into the greatest aberrations, it remains faithful to the proper principle of plastic art when it sticks more closely to the Greeks again and now struggles to approach antiquity and to treat ancient subjects in the sense that the Greeks did or to treat

[1] The artist is unknown but he may have been a pupil of P. Vischer.

sculpturally both portraits and standing figures of heroes and kings. This is especially the case nowadays. But even in the field of religious subjects sculpture has been able to produce excellent work. In this connection I will only refer to Michelangelo. We cannot sufficiently admire his figure of the dead Christ[1] of which there is a plaster cast in the Royal collection here in Berlin. Some claim that the figure of Mary in St. Mary's church in Bruges is not authentic, though it is an excellent work. But I have been attracted above all by the tomb of the Count of Nassau at Breda.[2] The Count lies beside his Countess in white alabaster, life-size on a black marble base. At the corners Regulus, Hannibal, Caesar, and a Roman warrior stand, bent down, carrying on their shoulders a black marble slab similar to the one below. Nothing is more interesting than to see a character, like Caesar, depicted by Michelangelo. Yet for religious subjects there are required the spirit, imaginative power, force, profundity, audacity, and capability of an artist like him in order to make possible by such productive originality a combination of the plastic principle of the Greeks with the sort of animation intrinsic to romantic art. For the whole drift of the Christian mind, where religious vision and ideas are at their peak, is, as I said, not towards the classical form of the ideal which is the first and highest vocation of sculpture.

From this point we can make the transition from sculpture to another principle of artistic treatment and portrayal, a principle needing for its realization a different physical material. In classical sculpture it was objective, substantial, and human individuality that was central, and the human form as such was given such a lofty position that it was maintained abstractly as pure beauty of *form* and reserved for representing the Divine. But, for this reason, the man who enters the portrayal here as both its form and its content is not the full and wholly concrete man; the anthropomorphism of art remains incomplete in ancient sculpture. For what it lacks is (*a*) humanity in its objective universality which at the same time is identified with the principle of absolute personality, and (*b*) what is so commonly called 'human', i.e. the factor of subjective individuality, human weakness, particular and contingent

---

[1] The *Pietà* in St. Peter's.
[2] Hegel described this in a letter to his wife from Breda, 9 October 1822, and from The Hague on 10 October. Hegel's attribution of the work to Michelangelo seems to be a mistake on the part of his informant in Holland.

character, caprice, passion, natural needs, etc. This factor must be introduced into that universality so that the entire individual, the person in his total range and in the endless sphere of his actual life may appear as the principle for both the content and the mode of portrayal in works of art.

In classical sculpture one of these factors, namely man in his purely natural aspect, comes into view only in animals and figures that are half man and half animal, such as fauns, etc.; here this [animal] aspect [of man] is not recalled into subjective consciousness and negatived there. On the other hand this sculpture itself passes over into the factor of particularization and an outward tendency only in the pleasing style, in the thousands of pleasantries and conceits in which even ancient plastic art indulged. Whereas throughout it lacks the principle of the depth and infinity of subjective consciousness, of the *inner* reconciliation of the spirit with the Absolute and the ideal unification of man and mankind with God. The subject-matter which enters art in accordance with this principle is brought to our eyes by Christian sculpture; but the very presentation of Christian art shows that sculpture is insufficient for giving actuality to this material, so that other arts had to appear in order to realize what sculpture is never able to achieve. These new arts we may group together under the name of 'the romantic arts' because they are most in correspondence with the romantic form of art.

SECTION III

THE ROMANTIC ARTS

INTRODUCTION

The general transition from sculpture to the other arts is produced, as we saw, by the principle of subjectivity which was breaking into the subject-matter and the artistic mode of its portrayal. Subjectivity is the essential nature of the spirit which is explicitly ideal in its own eyes and withdraws out of the external world into an existence within; and consequently it no longer coincides in indissoluble unity with its body.

What therefore follows at once from this transition is the dissolution of unity, i.e. the separation of the two sides contained and involved with one another in the substantive and objective unity of sculpture at the focal point of its peace, stillness, and rounded self-perfection. We can consider this cleavage in two aspects. (i) Sculpture, in its content, intertwined the substantive character of the spirit with that individuality which is not yet reflected into itself as an individual person, and therefore constituted an *objective* unity in the sense that 'objectivity' as such means what is eternal, immovable and true, substantive with no part in caprice or singularity. (ii) On the other hand, sculpture did not get beyond pouring this spiritual content into the corporeal form as its animation and significance and therefore forming a new objective unification in that meaning of the word 'objective' which signifies external real existence, i.e. 'objective' contrasted with what is purely inner and 'subjective'.

Now if these two sides, made adequate to one another for the first time by sculpture, are separated, then the spirit which has withdrawn into itself stands opposed to externality as such, to nature and also to the inner life's own body; moreover, in the sphere of the spiritual itself, so far as the substantive and objective aspect of the spirit is no longer confined to simple and substantive individuality, it is cut apart from the living and individual subject. The result is that all these factors hitherto fused into a unity become free from one another and independent, so that now in this very freedom they can be fashioned and worked out by art.

1. For subject-matter, therefore, we acquire, on the one side, the substantiality of the spiritual sphere, the world of truth and eternity, the *Divine* which here, however, conformably with the principle of subjectivity, is grasped and actualized by art as itself subject, personality, as the Absolute conscious of itself in its infinite spirituality, as God in spirit and in truth. On the other side there enters the mundane and *human* subject [or person] who, no longer immediately one with the substantive aspect of the spirit, can unfold himself in the entirety of his human particular character, so that the whole of the human heart and the entire wealth of human manifestations are made accessible to art.

But both sides here have their point of reunification in the principle of subjectivity which is common to both. On this account the Absolute is manifest as a living, actual, and therefore human subject, just as the human and finite subject in virtue of his being spiritual, makes the absolute substance and truth, the Spirit of God, living and actual in himself. But the new unity thus won no longer bears the character of that first immediacy presented by sculpture, but of a unification and reconciliation displayed essentially as the mediation of the two different sides, and capable of being completely manifested, adequately to its nature, in the inner and ideal life alone.

In the general Introduction to our whole study of art [Vol. I, p. 85] I have described this by saying that when sculpture displays present and visible the inherently compact individuality of the god in the bodily shape entirely adequate to him, there emerges, confronting this object, the community as the spirit's reflection into itself. But the spirit which has drawn back into itself can present the substance of the spiritual world to itself only as spirit and therefore as subject, and in that presentation it acquires at the same time the principle of the spiritual reconciliation of the individual subject with God. Yet as an individual subject a man has also a contingent existence in nature and a wider or more restricted range of finite interests, needs, aims, and passions in which he can gain independence and satisfaction or which he can equally well submerge in his ideas of God and his reconciliation with God.

2. Secondly, as for the external side of the representation, it likewise becomes independent in all its details and acquires a right

to come on the stage in this independence, because the principle of subjectivity forbids that immediate correspondence between, and perfect interpenetration of, inner and outer in all their parts and relations. For here subjectivity is precisely the inner life, explicit to itself, turned back out of its embodiment in externality into feeling, heart, mind, and meditation. This ideal sphere does manifest itself in its external shape, but in such a way that that shape itself reveals that it is *only* the external shape of a subject with an independent inner life *of his own*. The firm connection of body and spirit in classical sculpture is not on this account dissolved into the lack of any connection at all, but it is made so slack and loose that, although neither side is there without the other, both sides preserve in this loose connection their individual and mutual independence; or at least, if a deeper unification is actually achieved, the spirit becomes a centre essentially shining out as the inner life transcending its fusion with what is objective and external. Thus, on account of this relatively increased independence of what is objective and real, the result in most cases is the portrayal of external nature and its separate and most particularized objects, but, in this event, despite all the fidelity of their treatment, there is made obvious in them a reflection of the spirit, because in the manner of their artistic realization they make visible the liveliness of their treatment, the participation of the spirit, the mind's very indwelling in this uttermost extreme of externality, and therefore an inner and ideal life.

Therefore on the whole the principle of subjectivity necessarily implies on the one hand the sacrifice of the naïve unity of the spirit and its body and also the positing of the body more or less as negative in order to lift the inner life out of externality, and on the other hand the grant of free play to the details of the variety, disunion, and movement of spirit and sense alike.

3. Thirdly, this new principle has also to be made to prevail in the material which art uses for its new productions.

(*a*) Up to this point the material was something material as such, heavy mass in all three spatial dimensions, while the shape was simply abstracted as mere shape. When this material is now entered by the subjective inner life, full and particularized in itself, this life, in order to be able to appear outwardly *as* inner, will extinguish the spatial dimensions of the material and change it out of their immediate existence into something opposite, namely a pure appearance produced by the spirit; but, on the other hand, in respect of the shape and its external sensuousness and visibility, it will have to introduce the entire particularity of the appearance which the new content requires. But here art has still to move at first in the sensuous and visible sphere because, consequentially on the process described hitherto, the inner life must of course be understood as a reflection into self, but at the same time as a return into itself out of externality and corporeality, and therefore has to appear as a coming to itself which, to begin with, can once again be displayed only in the objective reality of nature and the existence of spirit in the body.

The *first* of the romantic arts will therefore still exhibit its content visibly, in the manner indicated, in the forms of the external human figure and the whole of nature's productions in general, though yet going beyond the visible and abstract character of sculpture. To do this is the task to which *painting* is called.

(*b*) But painting does not afford, as sculpture does, the fully accomplished coalescence of spirit and body as its fundamental type, but instead the outward appearance of the self-concentrated inner life; and it follows that in general the spatial external form is clearly no truly adequate mode of expression for the subjectivity of spirit. Consequently art abandons its previous mode of configuration and adopts, in place of spatial figuration, figurations of notes in their temporal rising and falling of sound; for a note wins its more ideal existence in time by reason of the negativing of spatial matter,[1] and therefore it corresponds with the inner life which apprehends itself in its subjective inwardness as feeling, and which expresses in the movement of notes every content asserting itself in the inner movement of heart and mind. The second art which follows this principle of portrayal is *music*.

(*c*) Therefore music puts itself again on the opposite side, and, in contrast to the visual arts both in its content and its sensuous material and mode of expression, keeps firmly to the inner life without giving it any outward shape or figure. But, if it is to be adequate to the *whole* of its essential nature, art has to bring to our contemplation not only the inner life but also, and equally, the appearance and actuality of that life in its external reality. But if art has given up incorporating the inner life in the actual and

---

[1] For Hegel, time is the negativing of space. See e.g. *Philosophy of Nature*, § 257.

therefore visible form of objectivity and turned over exclusively into the element of the inner life, then the objectivity to which it recurs can no longer be a *real* objectivity but only a purely intellectual one, one formed and shaped for inner contemplation, ideas, and feelings. The presentation of this, as the communication to spirit of the spirit which is creative in its own sphere, must use the sensuous material of its disclosure as simply a means of communication and therefore must degrade it to being a sign which has no significance by and in itself. *Poetry*, the art of speech, is in this position. Just as the spirit makes intelligible to spirit in language what is already implicit in the spirit itself, so now poetry embodies its productions in language developed into being an instrument of art. At the same time, because in its element it can unfold the totality of the spirit, it is the universal art which belongs equally to all the art-forms and it fails to appear only where the spirit, not yet having made its highest content clear to itself, can become conscious of its own presentiments only in the form of a content external to and other than itself.

Chapter I

PAINTING

INTRODUCTION

The most suitable subject for sculpture is the peaceful and substantive immersion of character in itself. The character's spiritual individuality emerges into and completely masters the body in which it has its real existence, and the sensuous material, in which this incorporation of the spirit is displayed, is made adequate to the spirit only in its external shape as such. A person's own subjective inwardness, the life of his heart, the soul of his most personal feelings are not revealed in the sightless figure nor can such a figure convey a concentrated expression of the inner life, or of spiritual movement, distinction from the external world or differentiation within. This is the reason why the sculptures of antiquity leave us somewhat cold. We do not linger over them long, or our lingering is rather a scholarly study of the fine shades of difference in their shape and in the forms given to a single individual. We cannot take it amiss if people do not show that profound interest in profound sculptures which they deserve. For we have to study them before we can appreciate them. At a first glance we are either not attracted or the general character of the whole is quickly revealed, and only afterwards have we to examine details and see what further interest the work supplies. But a pleasure that can only be produced after study, reflection, scholarship, and examination often repeated, is not the direct aim of art. And, even in the case of a pleasure gained by this circuitous route, what remains unsatisfied in the sculpture of antiquity is the demand that a character should develop and proceed outwardly to deeds and actions, and inwardly to a deepening of the soul. For this reason we are at once more at home in painting. Painting, that is to say, opens the way for the first time to the principle of finite and inherently infinite subjectivity, the principle of our own life and existence, and in paintings we see what is effective and active in ourselves.

In sculpture the god confronts our vision as a mere object; but in painting, on the other hand, God appears in himself as a spiritual and living person who enters the Church and gives to every individual the possibility of placing himself in spiritual community and reconciliation with him. The Divine is therefore not, as in sculpture, an individual inherently fixed and immobile, but the Spirit who has drawn into the Church and become particularized there.

The same principle distinguishes the subject from his own body, and his surroundings in general, while at the same time it brings the inner life into harmony with them. The sphere of this subjective particularization involves (*a*) the individual man's achievement of independence against God, nature, and other individuals whether in their mental or physical life, and (*b*), conversely, the most intimate connection and firm relation between God and the Church and between the individual and his God, his natural environment, and the endlessly varied needs, aims, passions, actions, and deeds of human existence. Within this sphere there falls the whole movement and life which have to be missing in sculpture's content as well as in its means of expression, and thus there is introduced into art afresh an immeasurable richness of material and a vast variety in the mode of portrayal which hitherto had been lacking. So the principle of subjectivity is on the one hand the basis of particularization and, nevertheless, on the other hand, the principle of mediation and synthesis, so that painting now unites in one and the same work of art what hitherto devolved on two different arts; the *external* environment which architecture treated artistically, and the shape which sculpture worked out as an embodiment of the *spirit*. Painting places its figures in nature or an architectural environment which is external to them and which it has invented in the same sense as it has invented the figures; and by the heart and soul of its treatment it can make this external background at the same time a reflection of what is subjective, and no less can it set the background in relation and harmony with the spirit of the figures that are moving against it.

This we may take as the principle of the new mode of representation which painting adds to those considered hitherto.

Asked about the route to be followed in our more detailed consideration of painting, I propose to divide the subject as follows:

First, as before, we must look for the *general* character which painting, in view of its essential nature, must assume as regards its specific content, the material corresponding to this content, and the artistic treatment conditioned thereby.

Secondly, we must next expound the *particular* characteristics which are implicit in the principle of the content and its portrayal and which place fixed limits on painting's corresponding subject-matter as well as on its modes of treatment, composition, and colouring.

Thirdly, owing to these particular characteristics painting is *individualized* in different schools which, as is the case in the other arts, are here too developed in historical stages.

1. *General Character of Painting*

I have specified as the essential principle of painting the subjectivity of mind which in the life of its feelings, ideas, and actions embraces the whole of heaven and earth and is present in a variety of situations and external modes of appearance in the body; and therefore I have placed the centre of painting in romantic and Christian art. Consequently it can occur at once to any critic that not only in Greece and Rome were there excellent painters who reached as high a level in this art as others then did in sculpture, i.e. the highest level, but that other peoples too, the Chinese, the Indians, the Egyptians acquired fame on the score of their paintings. Of course owing to the variety of subjects it adopts and the manner in which it can portray them, painting is less restricted than sculpture in the range of its spread amongst different peoples. But this is not the point really at issue. If we look only at empirical facts, then this or that has been produced at the most different periods in this or that manner in this, that, or the other nation. But the deeper question is about the *principle* of painting, i.e. to examine its means of portrayal, and therefore to determine what that subject-matter is which by its very nature so precisely harmonizes with the form and mode of portrayal employed by painting that this form corresponds exactly with that content.

Of the paintings of antiquity we have only few remains, pictures that clearly are neither amongst the most excellent ones produced in antiquity nor are the work of the most famous masters of their time. At any rate, this is true of what has been found in excavations of Roman villas. Nevertheless, we must admire in these survivals, the delicacy of taste, the suitability of the subjects, the clarity of the grouping, the lightness of touch in the execution, and the freshness of colouring, excellences which surely were possessed in a far higher degree by the original models after which, for instance, the murals in the so-called 'House of the Tragic Poet' at Pompeii were produced.[1] Unfortunately nothing by masters known to us by name has come down to us.[2] But however excellent even these original paintings may have been, we still have to say that, compared with the unsurpassable beauty of their sculptures, the Greeks and Romans could not bring painting to that degree of proper development which was achieved in the Christian Middle Ages and then especially in the sixteenth and seventeenth centuries. This backwardness of painting in comparison with sculpture in antiquity is quite naturally to be expected, because the inmost heart of the Greek outlook corresponds, more than is the case with any other art, precisely with the principle of what sculpture, and sculpture alone, can achieve. But in art the spiritual content is not separated from the mode of presentation. If, this granted, we ask for a reason why painting has been brought to its own proper height through the content of romantic art alone, the answer is that the spiritual depth of feeling, the bliss and grief of the heart is precisely this deeper content which demands spiritual animation and which has paved the way to the higher artistic perfection of painting and made that necessary.

As an example in this connection I will refer again only to what Raoul-Rochette says about the treatment of Isis holding Horus on her knees. In a general way the subject here is the same as it is in Christian pictures of the Madonna: a divine mother with her child. But the difference in the treatment and portrayal of this subject is enormous. In this pose the Egyptian Isis occurs in bas-reliefs: there is nothing maternal in her, no tenderness, no trait of that soul and feeling which is not entirely missing even in the stiffer Byzantine pictures of the Madonna. What has Raphael or indeed any other of the great Italian masters not made of the Madonna and the Christ-child! What depth of feeling, what spiritual life, what inner wealth of profound emotion, what sublimity and charm, what a human heart, though one wholly penetrated by the divine Spirit, does not speak to us out of every line of these pictures! And

---

[1] For coloured reproductions of some paintings in Roman villas and of one from Pompeii, see T. B. L. Webster, *Hellenistic Art* (London, 1967).

[1] This is not now true, e.g. of Polygnotus.

how endlessly various are the forms and situations in which this subject has been portrayed, often by the same master, but still more by different artists! The mother, the young Virgin, the beauty of form and spirit, the sublimity and charm—all this and far more is emphasized in turn as the chief characteristic expressed. But above all it is not the visible beauty of the figures but the spiritual animation whereby mastery is displayed and which leads to the mastery of the presentation.

It is true that Greek art far outsoared Egyptian and even took as a subject the expression of man's inner life, but it could not yet attain the spiritual inwardness and depth of feeling characteristic of the Christian mode of expression and, owing to its entire character, it did not strive at all for this kind of animation. The faun who holds the young Bacchus in his arms, which I have mentioned already, is extremely attractive and lovable; the same is true of the nymphs who attend on Bacchus, a most beautiful group displayed on a small gem. Here we have the like feeling of naïve love for the child, a love without desire or longing, but, let alone maternal love, there is here no expression at all of the inner soul, the depth of heart which we do meet with in Christian paintings. In antiquity many excellent portraits may have been painted but neither the classical treatment of natural objects nor its vision of human or divine affairs was of such a kind as to make possible in painting the expression of such a depth of spirituality as was presented in Christian painting.

But the fact that painting demands this more subjective sort of animation is already implicit in its material. The sensuous element in which it moves, that is to say, is extension on a surface and the formation of a picture by means of particular colours whereby the form of the object as our vision sees it is transformed from the shape of something real into a pure appearance artistically created by the spirit [of the artist]. It is implicit in the principle of this material that the external existent is no longer to have validity in the last resort on its own account in its actual, even if spiritually animated, existence, but in this reality it must precisely be degraded to being merely a pure appearance of the inner spirit which wants to contemplate itself there on its own account. When we look at the thing more deeply we can see that the advance from the totality of the sculptural figure has no other meaning but this. It is the inner life of the spirit which undertakes to express itself as *inner* in the mirror of externality. Then, secondly, the surface on which painting makes its subjects appear, leads on by itself to surroundings, connections, and relations; and colour, as the particularization of the *appearance* in the picture, demands also a particularization of the inner life, which itself can become clear only by definite expressions, situations, and actions, and therefore requires a direct variety, a movement, and a detailed inner and outer life. But this principle of that inwardness as such which in its actual appearance is linked at the same time with the varied forms of external existence, and is recognized as collected together in itself out of its detailed existence, we have seen as the principle of the romantic form of art; and therefore it is the sphere of painting, and that one sphere alone, which has its entirely correspondent *object* in the content and mode of presentation of that form. But on the other hand we may say likewise that when romantic art wishes actually to produce works of art, it must look for a material correspondent with its content and find it first of all in painting which in all objects and modes of treatment other than those of romantic art remains more or less formal. Therefore, although there is oriental, Greek, and Roman painting outside Christian painting, nevertheless the real heart of painting remains the development which this art has attained within the confines of the romantic sphere. And we can only speak of oriental and Greek painting in the sense in which we referred to Christian sculpture in comparison with the sculpture that was rooted in the classical ideal and reached its true peak in portraying that ideal. In other words, everyone must admit that only in the material available in the romantic art-form does painting acquire topics completely meeting its means and forms, and therefore only in treating those topics has it used its means and exhausted them to the full.

When we pursue this matter purely in general terms, the following are the points that arise in connection with the subject-matter, the material, and the artistic mode of treatment in painting.

(a) The Chief Determinant of the Subject-matter

The chief determinant of the subject-matter of painting is, as we saw, subjectivity aware of itself.

(α) Therefore, if we consider it on its *inner* side, individuality may not pass over entirely into what is substantive [and universal] but must on the contrary display how it contains in itself, as this individual, every content, and has and expresses in that content its inner being, its very own life of idea and feeling; nor can its *outer* shape appear, as in sculpture, purely and simply dominated by the individual's inner life. For the subject masters the external thing as the object belonging to itself, yet at the same time it is that identity, returning into itself, which owing to this self-enclosure is indifferent to the external and lets it go its own way. For this reason, so far as the *spiritual* side of the content is concerned, the individual person is not directly made one with what is substantive and universal but is reflected into himself up to the extreme pinnacle of personal independence. So too the particularity and universality of the external shape departs from that plastic unification into a predominance of the individual and therefore of what is rather accidental and indifferent in the same way that in empirical reality too this [contingency] is already the dominant character of all phenomena.

(β) A second point concerns the enlargement which painting receives, owing to its principle, in the subjects which it is to portray.

The free subjective individual allows independent existence to the entire range of things in nature and all spheres of human activity but, on the other hand, he can enter into every particular thing and make it into material for inner contemplation; indeed, only in this involvement with concrete reality does he prove himself in his own eyes to be concrete and living. Therefore it is possible for the painter to bring within the sphere of his productions a wealth of things that remain inaccessible to sculpture. The whole range of religious topics, ideas of Heaven and Hell, the story of Christ, the Apostles, the saints, etc., the realm of nature outside us, human life down to the most fleeting aspects of situations and characters—each and everything of this can win a place in painting. For to subjectivity there also belongs what is particular, arbitrary, and contingent in human interests and needs, and these therefore equally press for treatment in art.

(γ) A third thing is a corollary of this, namely that painting takes the heart as a content of its productions. What lives in the heart is present in a subjective way, even if the objective and the absolute are the burden of it. For the heart's feeling may have the universal as what it feels, and yet, as feeling, the universal does not retain the form of this universality but appears in the way that I, this specific individual, know and feel myself in it. If I am to set forth an objective content of feeling in its objectivity, I must forget myself. Thus painting does of course bring to our vision the inner life in the form of an external object, but the real content which it expresses is the feeling of the individual subject; consequently it cannot after all provide, so far as form goes, such specific visions of the Divine, for example, as sculpture can, but only those more indefinite ideas which feeling can provide. This may seem a contradiction, for we see the greatest masters often preferring to choose as subjects for painting our external environment, hills, valleys, forests, burns, trees, shrubs, ships, clouds, sky, the sea, buildings, rooms, etc., and yet it seems contradictory to say that the heart of these pictures is not the subjects themselves but the liveliness and soul of the subjective treatment and execution, the mind of the artist which is mirrored in his work and provides not only a mere copy of these external things but at the same time himself and his inner soul. Precisely for this reason the subjects painted, even so regarded, are indifferent to us because the manifestation of the individual artist in them begins to become prominent as the chief thing. It is by this orientation to the heart, [the expression of] which, in the case of natural objects, can often be no more than a general echo of the mood they produce, that painting is most clearly distinguished from architecture and sculpture, because it more nearly approaches music and makes the transition from the plastic arts to the art of sound.

(b) The Sensuous Material of Painting

More than once already I have described the most general chief features of the sensuous material used by painting as distinct from sculpture; here therefore I will only touch on the closer connection between this material and the spiritual content which it is its principal business to portray.

(α) The first point to be considered in this connection is that painting contracts the spatial totality of *three* dimensions. Their complete contraction would be their concentration into a point which implies cancelling all juxtaposition and, in this cancellation, a restlessness like that belonging to a point of time. But only music goes to the length of carrying out this negation completely and

PAINTING

logically. Painting, however, does allow space to persist and extinguishes only *one* of the three dimensions, so that a *surface* becomes the medium of its representations. This reduction of the three dimensions to a level surface is implicit in the principle of interiorization which can be asserted, as inwardness, in space only by reason of the fact that it restricts and does not permit the subsistence of the totality of the external dimensions.

People are commonly inclined to suppose that this reduction is a caprice on the part of painting and that for this reason painting has an inescapable defect. For it is supposed to want to make visible to us even natural objects in their whole reality and, by the medium of the human body and its deportment, spiritual ideas and feelings, but, it is held, the surface is insufficient for this purpose and always inferior to nature which confronts us in a totally different sort of completeness.

(αα) Of course, so far as matter in space is concerned, painting is more abstract than sculpture, but this abstraction, far from being a purely capricious restriction or a lack of human skill in contrast to nature and its productions, is precisely the necessary advance beyond sculpture. Even sculpture was not a bare imitation of what was existent in nature or corporeally; on the contrary, it was a reproduction issuing from the spirit and therefore it stripped away from the figure all those features in ordinary natural existence which did not correspond with the specific matter to be portrayed. In sculpture this included the detail of the colouring, so that all that remained was the abstraction of the visible *shape*. In painting, however, the opposite is the case, for its content is the spiritual inner life which can come into appearance in the external only as retiring into itself out of it. So painting does indeed work for our vision, but in such a way that the object which it presents does not remain an actual total spatial natural existent but becomes a reflection of the spirit in which the spirit only reveals its spiritual quality by cancelling the real existent and transforming it into a pure appearance in the domain of spirit for apprehension by spirit.

(ββ) Therefore painting *has to* renounce the totality of space and it is not required by any lack of human skill to sacrifice this completeness. Since the subject-matter of painting in its spatial existence is only a pure appearance of the spiritual inner life which art presents for the spirit's apprehension, the independence of the actual spatially present existent is dissolved and it acquires a far closer relation to the spectator than is the case with a work of sculpture. The statue is predominantly independent on its own account, unconcerned about the spectator who can place himself wherever he likes: where he stands, how he moves, how he walks round it, all this is a matter of indifference to this work of art. If this independence is to be preserved, the statue must give something to the spectator wherever he stands. But this independence the work of sculpture has to retain because its content is what is, within and without, self-reposing, self-complete, and objective. Whereas in painting the content is subjectivity, more precisely the inner life inwardly particularized, and for this very reason the separation in the work of art between its subject and the spectator must emerge and yet must immediately be dissipated because, by displaying what is subjective, the work, in its whole mode of presentation, reveals its purpose as existing not independently on its own account but for subjective apprehension, for the spectator. The spectator is as it were in it from the beginning, is counted in with it, and the work exists only for this fixed point, i.e. for the individual apprehending it. Yet for this relation to vision and its spiritual reflection the pure *appearance* of reality is enough, and the actual totality of spatial dimensions is really disturbing because in that case the objects perceived retain an existence of their own and do not simply appear as configurated artificially by spirit for its own contemplation. For this reason nature cannot reduce its productions to a level surface since they have, and at the same time are meant to have, a real independence of their own. In painting, however, satisfaction does not lie in the objects as they exist in reality but in the purely contemplative interest in the external reflection of the inner life, and consequently painting dispenses with all need and provision for a reality and an organization totally spatial in all dimensions.

(γγ) With this reduction to a surface there is associated, thirdly, the fact that painting is at a still further remove from architecture than sculpture is. For even if sculptures are set up independently on their own account in public squares or gardens, they always need an architecturally treated pedestal, while in rooms, forecourts, halls, etc., architecture serves purely as an environment for the statues or, alternatively, sculptures are used as a decoration of buildings, and therefore there is a closer connection between the two arts. Whereas painting, whether in the confines of a room or in open galleries or in the open air, is confined to a wall. Originally it has only the purpose of filling empty wall-surfaces. This function it fulfilled, especially in antiquity where the walls of temples, and later of private houses, were decorated in this way. The chief task of Gothic architecture was to provide an enclosure of the most grandiose proportions, and it affords still larger surfaces, indeed the most immense surfaces conceivable, yet in its case, whether for the outside or inside of the buildings, painting occurs only in earlier mosaics as a decoration of empty surfaces. The later architecture of the fourteenth century, on the contrary, fills its tremendous walls in a purely architectural way; of this the main façade of Strasbourg Cathedral provides the most magnificent example. In this case, apart from the entrance doors, the rose window and other windows, the empty surfaces are adorned with much grace and variety by window-like decorations traced on the walls and by statuesque figures, so that no paintings are required at all over and above. Therefore in religious architecture painting enters again only in buildings which begin to approach the model of classical architecture. Nevertheless, on the whole, Christian religious painting is separated from architecture, and its works become independent as, for instance, in large altar-pieces or in chapels or on high altars. Even here the painting must remain related to the place for which it is intended, but in other respects its function is not merely filling surfaces on a wall; on the contrary, it is there on its own account, as a sculpture is. Finally, painting is used to decorate halls and rooms in public buildings, town-halls, palaces, private houses, etc., and this links it again more closely with architecture, although in this link it ought not to lose its independence as a free art.

(β) But the further necessity which makes painting reduce the spatial dimensions to a surface depends on the fact that painting is called on to express the inner life particularized in itself and therefore possessed of a wealth of varied specifications. The pure restriction to the spatial forms of the figure, with which sculpture can be satisfied, is therefore dissipated in the richer art, for the spatial forms are the most abstract thing in nature, and now, when a more inherently varied material is required, particular differences must be grasped. The principle of representation in space therefore carries with it here a *physically* specified definite material; if its differentiations are to appear as the essential ones in the work of art, then they display this themselves at the expense of that totality of space which no longer remains the ultimate mode of representation. In order to make prominent the appearance of the *physical* element[1] there must be a departure from the totality of the spatial dimensions. For in painting the dimensions are not present on their own account in their proper reality but are only made apparent and visible by means of this physical element.

(αα) Now if we ask about the character of the physical element which painting uses, the answer is that it is *light* as what makes visible universally the whole world of objects.

The sensuous concrete material of architecture, considered above, was resistant heavy matter which, especially in architecture, presented precisely this character of heavy matter as compressing, burdening, carrying, and being carried, etc., and this same character was not lost in sculpture. Heavy matter presses because it has its material point of unity not in itself but in something else; it seeks and strives for this point but it remains where it is owing to the resistance offered by other bodies which therefore serve as its support. The principle of light is the opposite of the heavy matter which has not yet achieved its unity. Whatever else may be said about light, we cannot deny that it is absolutely weightless, not offering resistance but *pure identity with itself* and therefore purely self-reposing, the earliest ideality, the original self of nature.[2] With light, nature begins for the first time to become subjective and it is now the universal physical self which, it is true, has neither advanced to particularization nor become concentrated into individuality or the self-perfection of a point, but still it does cancel the pure objectivity and externality of heavy matter and can abstract from the sensuous and spatial totality of matter. From this point of view of the more *ideal* quality of light, light becomes the physical principle of painting.

(ββ) But light as such exists only as *one* side of what is implicit in the principle of subjectivity, i.e. as this more ideal [self-]identity. In this respect light only manifests, in the sense that it proves in nature to be simply what makes things *in general* visible; but the

---

[1] The four physical elements were earth, air, water, and fire. Hegel, however, is alluding to his philosophy of nature where *physics*, which begins with light, supervenes on *mechanics*, which deals with space, matter, gravity, weight, etc. In this whole passage 'physical' is a reference to that treatment of physics.

[2] A reader perplexed by this must be referred to the relevant passage in Hegel's *Philosophy of Nature*, §§ 275–8.

particular character of what it reveals remains outside it as an object which is not light but the opposite of light and so is dark. Now light makes these objects known in their differences of shape, distance from one another, etc., and it does this by irradiating them; i.e. it lightens to a greater or lesser extent their darkness and invisibility. It makes single parts more visible the more nearly they come before the spectator's eye while others it keeps in the background as darker, i.e. further removed from the spectator. For when the specific colour of an object is not in question, bright and dark as such are related in general to the distance of the irradiated objects from us, i.e. to the way in which they are specifically lit. In this relation to objects, light does not now present itself as light pure and simple but produces that already inherently particularized brightness and darkness, light and shadow, the varied figurations of which reveal the shape of the objects and their distance from one another and from the spectator. This is the principle which painting uses because particularization is implicit in its very nature from the start. If we compare painting in this respect with architecture and sculpture, these arts do actually present the real differences in the spatial form and they produce the effect of light and shadow both by the illumination provided by natural light and also by the position of the spectator. In this case the roundness of the forms is there already on its own account, and the light and shadow which makes them visible is only a consequence of what was actually there already independently of this being made visible. In painting, on the other hand, light and darkness with all their gradations and finest nuances belong themselves to the principle of the material used in painting and they produce only the intended pure *appearance* of what sculpture and architecture shape in *reality*. Light and shadow, the appearance of objects in their illumination, are produced by art and not by natural light which therefore only makes visible that brightness and darkness and the illumination which had already been produced by the painter's art. This is the positive reason, drawn from the very material itself, why painting does not need the three dimensions. The painted shape is made by light and shadow, and the shape of a real [three-dimensional] object is in itself superfluous.

($\gamma\gamma$) Bright and dark, light and shadow, and their interplay are, however, only an abstraction which does not exist as this abstraction in nature and therefore cannot be used as a sensuous material either.

Light, as we have seen already, is related to its opposite, darkness. But yet in this relation these two opposites do not remain independent at all but are set in unity, in an interplay of light and dark. Light darkened, made in this way murky in itself, which at the same time penetrates and illumines the dark,[1] provides the principle of *colour* as the real material for painting. Light as such remains colourless, the pure indeterminacy of identity with itself. Colour, which in contrast to light is something relatively dark, entails something different from light, a murkiness with which the principle of light is united, and it is therefore a bad and false idea to suppose that light is compounded out of different colours,[2] i.e. out of different darkenings.

Shape, distance, boundaries, contours, in short all the spatial relations and differences of objects appearing in space, are produced in painting only by colour. Its more ideal principle is capable of representing too a more ideal content, and by its profound contrasts, infinitely varied modulations, transitions, and delicacies of arrangement it affords the widest possible scope for the softest nuances in presenting the wealth and particular characteristics of the objects to be selected for painting. It is incredible what colour can really achieve in this way. Two men, for example, are altogether different; each of them in his personality and bodily organism is a perfect totality in mind and body, and yet in a painting this entire difference is reduced to a difference of colours. At one point a colour stops and another begins, and by this means everything is there, form, distance, play of features, expression, the entire visible and spiritual character. And this reduction, as I have said, we may not regard as a makeshift and a deficiency, but the very contrary. Painting does not at all feel the lack of the third dimension; it discards it deliberately in order to substitute for what is simply a real object in space the higher and richer principle of colour.

(γ) This richness enables painting to develop in its productions the entirety of appearance. Sculpture is more or less restricted to the fixed self-enclosedness of the individual; but in painting the individual is not firmly kept to the like limitation within, and

---

[1] Goethe's theory of colour as a synthesis of light and dark is never far from Hegel's mind.
[2] Newton, *Opticks*, i, pt. 2: 'The whiteness of the sun's light is compounded of all the primary colours mixed in a due proportion.'

against what is without, but enters into relations of the greatest possible variety. For on the one hand, as I have mentioned already, the individual [in a painting] is put into a far closer relation with the spectator, while on the other hand he acquires a more varied connection with other individuals and the external natural environment. The simple fact of presenting only the *appearance* of objects makes possible in one and the same work of art the presentation of the furthest distances and widest spaces as well as the objects of the most various kinds occurring in them. Yet the work of art must nevertheless be a self-enclosed whole, and in this self-enclosure must show that its limits and boundaries are not arbitrary but that it is an entirety of particular details belonging to one another as the topic in hand requires.

(c) *Principle of the Artistic Treatment*

Thirdly, after this general consideration of the subject-matter and material of painting we have to indicate briefly the general principle of the artist's mode of treatment.

More than architecture and sculpture, painting admits of two extremes: what is made the chief thing is (a) the depth of the subject-matter, i.e. religious and moral seriousness in the treatment and presentation of the ideal beauty of form, and (b), in the case of insignificant subjects chosen by the artist, the details of them as they actually are and the subjective skill of the artist in his work. For this reason we can often hear two extreme judgements: on the one hand, the exclamation 'what a magnificent subject, how deep the conception, how attractive, how marvellous, what sublimity of expression, what boldness of design!' And then the opposite: 'how magnificently and incomparably painted!' This separation of judgements is implicit in the very nature of painting itself; indeed we could even say that both these aspects are not to be unified or uniformly developed but that each must be independent on its own account. For painting has as its means of portrayal both the shape as such, the forms of objects delimited in space, and also colour. Owing to this character that it has it lies in the middle between what is ideal and plastic and, at the other extreme, the immediate particular character of what is actual. For this reason two kinds of painting come before us: (i) the ideal kind with the *universal* as its essence, and (ii) the other which presents what is individual in its closeness of *particular* detail.

(α) In this respect, painting, in the first place, like sculpture, has to accept [for presentation] what is substantive, i.e. the objects of religious faith, great historical events, the most pre-eminent individuals, although it brings this substantive material before our contemplation in the form of inner subjectivity. Here what is important is the magnificence, the seriousness of the action represented, the profundity of the mind expressed there, and the result is that full justice cannot be done to the development and application of all the rich artistic means which painting can use or to the skill required for perfect virtuosity in the use of those means. It is the power of the subject-matter to be represented, and immersion into its essential and substantive character, which push into the background, as something less essential, that overwhelming skill in the painter's art. So, for example, Raphael's cartoons are of inestimable value and they display every excellence of conception, but, even in his completed pictures, whatever mastery he may have achieved in design, composition, and colouring, and in the purity of his ideal yet always living and individual figures, he is nevertheless certainly outclassed by the Dutch painters in colour, landscape, etc. Still more true is this sort of thing in the case of the earlier Ialtian masters; in depth, power, and deep feeling of expression Raphael is just as inferior to them as he soars above them in a painter's skill, in the beauty of vivid grouping, in design, etc.

(β) Conversely, however, as we saw, painting must go beyond this immersion in the rich content of subjectivity and its infinity. On the contrary it must free, and release into independence, particular detail, i.e. what constitutes as it were something otherwise incidental, i.e. the environment and the background. In this progress from the most profound seriousness to external details, painting must press on to the extreme of pure appearance, i.e. to the point where the content does not matter and where the chief interest is the artistic creation of that appearance. In supreme art we see fixed the most fleeting appearance of the sky, the time of day, the lighting of the trees; the appearances and reflections of clouds, waves, lochs, streams; the shimmering and glittering of wine in a glass, a flash of the eye, a momentary look or smile, etc. Here painting leaves the ideal for the reality of life; the effect of appearance it achieves here especially by the exactitude with which every tiniest individual part is executed. Yet this is achieved by no mere assiduity of composition but by a spiritually rich industry which perfects each detail independently and yet retains the whole connected and flowing together; to achieve this, supreme skill is required. Here the thus achieved liveliness in creating an appearance of reality seems to have a higher specific character than the ideal and therefore in no art has there been more dispute about ideal and nature, as I have already explained at greater length on another occasion.[1] We could of course blame the application of all artistic means to such a trivial subject-matter, on the ground of extravagance, yet painting may not spurn this subject-matter which on its side and alone is fitted to be treated with such art and to provide this infinite subtlety and delicacy of pure appearance.

(γ) But, in painting, artistic treatment does not remain in this more general opposition [between ideal and nature], but, since painting in general rests on the principle of the subjective and the particular, it proceeds to still closer particularization and individualization. Architecture and sculpture do display national differences, and sculpture especially makes us aware of a more detailed individuality of schools and single masters. But, in painting, this variation and subjectivity in the mode of treatment expands widely and to an incalculable extent, just as the subjects selected for portrayal cannot be delimited in advance. Here above all we find asserted the particular spirit of nations, provinces, epochs, and individuals, and this affects not only the choice of subjects and the spirit of the artist's conception, but also the sort of design, grouping, shading, handling of the brush, treatment of specific colours, etc., right down to individual mannerisms and habits.

Since painting has the function of engaging so unrestrictedly in the sphere of particulars and the inner life, few precise generalizations can be made about it, just as there are few specific facts about it which could be cited as universally true. Yet we ought not to be content with the explanation I have so far given of the principle of painting's subject-matter, material, and mode of artistic treatment. On the contrary, even if we leave on one side the vast variety of empirical detail, we must give closer consideration to some particular aspects of painting which appear to be decisive.

[1] See Vol. I, pp. 41–6.

2. *Particular Characteristics of Painting*

The different considerations governing this firmer characterization which we now have to undertake are prescribed to us in advance by our previous discussion. Once again they concern the subject-matter, the material, and the artistic treatment of both of these.

(i) The subject-matter, as we have seen, corresponds with the content of the romantic form of art; but we must raise the further question of what specific spheres of the wealth of this art-form are pre-eminently fitted and appropriate to portrayal in painting.

(ii) We are already acquainted with the sensuous material *in principle*, but we must specify in more detail the forms which can be expressed on a plane surface by colour, because the human form and other things in nature are to be made visible in order to make manifest the inner life of the spirit.

(iii) Similarly, there is a question about the specific nature of the artistic treatment and portrayal which corresponds in different ways with the differing character of the subject-matter and therefore introduces particular *genres* of painting.

(a) *The Romantic Subject-matter*

Earlier on I referred to the fact that there were excellent painters in antiquity, but at the same time I remarked that the mission of painting could only be really fulfilled by means of that sort of outlook and feeling which is in evidence and active in the romantic form of art. But if we consider this in relation to the subject-matter it seems to contradict the fact that precisely at the zenith of Christian painting, at the time of Raphael, Correggio, Rubens,[1] etc., mythological subjects were used and portrayed partly on their own account, partly decoratively and allegorically in connection with great exploits, triumphs, royal marriages, etc. A similar thing has been mentioned in various ways in most recent times. Goethe, for example, has taken up again the descriptions of the paintings of Polygnotus by Philostratus, and with his poetic treatment has freshened up these subjects and renewed them for painters. But if with these suggestions there is bound up a demand that the topics of Greek mythology and the stories in the Greek sagas, as well as scenes from the Roman world (for which the French at

---

[1] His inclusion here may seem odd since he is nearly a century later than the other two: 1483–1520; 1489–1534; 1577–1640.

a certain period of their painting showed a great preference) be treated and portrayed in exactly the sense and spirit of antiquity, it must at once be retorted that this past cannot be recalled to life and that what is specifically characteristic of antiquity cannot be made perfectly conformable with the principle of painting. Therefore the painter must make of these materials something totally different, and insert into them a totally different spirit, a different mode of feeling and illustration, from that of antiquity itself, if such subject-matter is to be brought into harmony with the proper tasks and aims of painting. So after all the range of these classical materials and situations is on the whole not that which painting has developed in a consistent way; on the contrary it has abandoned them as at the same time a heterogeneous matter which has first to be transformed. For, as I have already indicated more than once, painting has primarily to grasp that material which, in contrast to sculpture, music, and poetry, it is especially able to represent in an external form. This is the concentration of the spirit in itself, the expression of which sculpture must ever renounce, while music in its turn cannot pass over into an external perceptible manifestation of the inner life, and poetry itself can only provide an imperfect vision of what is corporeal. Whereas painting can link both sides together; in the external itself it can express the full range of deep feeling; it can take as its essential subject-matter the deeply stamped particularity of character and characteristics, and the spiritual depth of feeling in general as well as in particular; as an expression of that depth of feeling, specific events, relations, or situations must not appear as simply the unfolding of an individual character; on the contrary, what is specifically particular in that character must appear as deeply engraved or rooted in the soul and facial expression and as entirely assumed by the external shape.

But what is required for the expression of spiritual depth as such is not that original and ideal independence and magnificence of the classical figures in which individuality remains in immediate harmony with the substance of its spiritual being and with the visible aspect of its appearance in the body; neither is the representation of the heart satisfied by the Greek natural serenity, cheerfulness in enjoyment, and bliss of self-absorption. On the contrary the depth and profound feeling of the spirit presupposes that the soul has worked its way through its feelings and powers and the whole of its inner life, i.e. that it has overcome much, suffered grief, endured anguish and pain of soul, and yet in this disunion has preserved its integrity and withdrawn out of it into itself. In the myth of Hercules the Greeks have presented us with a hero who after many labours was placed amongst the gods and enjoyed blissful peace there. But what Hercules achieved was only something outside him, the bliss given him as a reward was only peaceful repose. The ancient prophecy that he would put an end to the reign of Zeus, he did not fulfil, supreme hero of the Greeks though he was. The end of that rule only began when man conquered not dragons outside him or Lernaean hydras, but the dragons and hydras of his own heart, the inner obstinacy and inflexibility of his own self. Only in this way does natural serenity become that higher serenity of the spirit which completely traverses the negative moment of disunion and by this labour has won infinite satisfaction. The feeling of cheerfulness and happiness must be transfigured and purified into bliss. For good fortune and happiness still involve an accidental and natural correspondence between the individual and his external circumstances; but in bliss the good fortune still attendant on a man's existence as he is in nature falls away and the whole thing is transferred into the inner life of the spirit. Bliss is an acquired satisfaction and justified only on that account; it is a serenity in victory, the soul's feeling when it has expunged from itself everything sensuous and finite and therefore has cast aside the care that always lies in wait for us. The soul is blissful when, after experiencing conflict and agony, it has triumphed over its sufferings.

(α) If we now ask what can be strictly *ideal* in this subject-matter, the answer is: the reconciliation of the individual heart with God who in his appearance as man has traversed this way of sorrows. The substance of spiritual depth of feeling is religion alone, the peace of the individual who has a sense of himself but who finds true satisfaction only when, self-collected, his mundane heart is broken so that he is raised above his mere natural existence and its finitude, and in this elevation has won a universal depth of feeling, a spiritual depth and oneness in and with God. The soul wills *itself*, but it wills itself in something other than what it is in its individuality and therefore it gives itself up in face of God in order to find and enjoy itself in him. This is characteristic of *love*, spiritual depth in its truth, that religious love without desire which gives to the human spirit reconciliation, peace, and bliss. It is not the pleasure and joy of actual love as we know it in ordinary life, but a love without passion, indeed without physical inclination but with only an inclination of soul. Looked at physically, this is a love which is death, a death to the world, so that there hovers there as something past the actual relationship of one person to another; as a real mundane bond and connection this relationship has not come essentially to its perfection; for, on the contrary, it bears in itself the deficiency of time and the finite, and therefore it leads on to that elevation into a beyond which remains a consciousness and enjoyment of love devoid of longing and desire.

This is the trait constituting the soulful, inner, higher ideal which enters here in place of the quiet grandeur and independence of the figures of antiquity. The gods of the classical ideal too do not lack a trait of mourning, of a fateful negative, present in the cold necessity imprinted on these serene figures, but still, in their independent divinity and freedom, they retain an assurance of their simple grandeur and power. But their freedom is not the freedom of that love which is soulful and deeply felt because this depends on a relation of soul to soul, spirit to spirit. This depth of feeling kindles the ray of bliss present in the heart, that ray of a love which in sorrow and its supreme loss does not feel sang-froid or any sort of comfort, but the deeper it suffers yet in suffering still finds the sense and certainty of love and shows in grief that it has overcome itself within and by itself. In the ideal figures of antiquity, on the other hand, we do see, apart from the above-mentioned trait of quiet mourning, the expression of the grief of noble beings, e.g. in Niobe and the Laocoon. They do not lapse into grief and despair but still keep their grandeur and large-heartedness. But this preservation of their character remains empty; grief and pain is as it were final, and in place of reconciliation and satisfaction there can only enter a cold resignation in which the individual, without altogether collapsing, still sacrifices what he had clung to. It is not a matter of suppressing what is beneath him; he does not display any wrath, contempt, or vexation, and yet the loftiness of his individuality is only a persistent self-consistency, an empty endurance of fate in which the nobility and grief of his soul still appear as not balanced. It is only the religious love of romanticism which has an expression of bliss and freedom.

This oneness and satisfaction is in its nature spiritually concrete because it is what is felt by the spirit which knows itself in another as at one with itself. Here therefore if the subject-matter portrayed is to be complete, it must have two aspects because love necessarily implies a double character in the spiritual personality. It rests on two independent persons who yet have a sense of their *unity*; but there is always linked with this unity at the same time the factor of the *negative*. Love is a matter of subjective feeling, but the subject which feels is *this* self-subsistent heart which, in order to love, must desist from itself, abandon itself, and sacrifice the inflexible focus of its own private personality. This sacrifice is what is *moving* in the love that lives and feels only in this self-surrender. Yet on this account a person in this sacrifice still retains his own self and in the very cancelling of his independence acquires a precisely affirmative independence. Nevertheless, in the sense of this oneness and its supreme happiness there still remains left the negative factor, the moving sense not so much of sacrifice as rather of the undeserved bliss of feeling independent and at unity with self in spite of all the self-surrender. The moving emotion is the sense of the dialectical contradiction of having sacrificed one's personality and yet of being independent at the same time; this contradiction is ever present in love and ever resolved in it.

So far as concerns the particular *human* individual personality in this depth of feeling, the unique love which affords bliss and an enjoyment of heaven rises above time and the particular individuality of that character which becomes a matter of indifference. The ideal figures of the gods in sculpture do pass over into one another, as has been noticed already, but although they are not without the content and range of original and immediate individuality, this individuality does still remain the essential form of their sculptural portrayal. Whereas in the pure ray of bliss which has just been described, particular individuality is superseded: in the sight of God all men are equal, or piety, rather, makes them all actually equal so that the only thing of importance is the expression of that concentration of love which needs neither happiness nor any particular single object. It is true that religious love too cannot exist without specific individuals who have some other sphere of existence apart from this feeling. But here the strictly ideal content is provided by the soulful depth of spiritual feeling which does not have its expression and actuality in the particular difference of a character with its talent, relationships, and fates, but is rather raised above these. Therefore, when we hear nowadays that the chief thing in education, and in what a man should require of himself, is concern for differences of personal character (which implies the fundamental principle that everyone should be treated, and that an individual should treat himself, differently from everyone else), this way of thinking is entirely opposed to religious love in which such individual differences fall into the background. Conversely, however, just because individual characterization is the non-essential element which is not absolutely fused with love's spiritual kingdom of heaven, it acquires here a greater determinacy. This is because, in conformity with the principle of the romantic form of art, it becomes liberated, and it becomes all the more characteristic in that it does not have for its supreme law classical beauty, i.e. the permeation of immediate life and finite particularity by the spiritual and religious content. Nevertheless this individual characterization cannot and should not disturb that spiritual depth of love which on its side is likewise not tied down to individual character as such but has become free and is in itself the truly independent and spiritual ideal.

The ideal centre and chief topic of the religious sphere, as has been explained in our consideration of the romantic form of art, is love *reconciled* and at peace with itself. Painting has to portray spiritual subject-matter in the form of actual and bodily human beings, and therefore the object of this love must not be painted as a purely spiritual 'beyond' but as actual and present. Here we may specify the Holy Family, and above all the Madonna's love for her child, as the absolutely suitable ideal subject for this sphere. But on either side of this centre there extends a still wider material, even if in one respect or another it is in itself less perfect for painting. This whole subject-matter we may articulate in the following way:

(αα) The first topic is the object of love itself in its simple universality and undisturbed unity with itself—i.e. God in his essence, devoid of any appearance, i.e. God the Father. Here, where painting intends to present God the Father as he is conceived in Christian ideas, it has great difficulties to surmount. The father of gods and men as a particular individual is exhaustively represented in art in the figure of Zeus. Whereas what God the Father lacks at once in Christianity is the human individuality in which alone art can reproduce the spirit. For, taken in himself, God the Father is certainly spiritual personality, supreme power, wisdom, etc., but he is always kept shapeless and as an abstract *ens rationis*. But art cannot renounce anthropomorphism and must therefore give him a human shape. Now, however universal this shape may be, however lofty, profound, and powerful it may be kept, nevertheless what emerges from it is only a masculine, more or less serious, individual who cannot completely correspond with our idea of God the Father. Amongst the older Dutch painters van Eyck has achieved the summit of excellence possible in this sphere in his presentation of God the Father in the altar picture at Ghent.[1] This is a work which can be set beside the Olympian Zeus. Nevertheless, however perfect it may be in its expression of eternal peace, sublimity, power, and dignity, etc.—and in conception and execution its depth and grandeur are unsurpassable—it still has in it something unsatisfying according to our ideas. For God the Father is presented here as at the same time a human individual, and this can only be Christ the Son. In him alone have we a vision of this factor of individuality and humanity as a factor in the Divine, and we see it in such a way that it is not a naïve imaginative shape, as in the case of the Greek gods, but proves to be an essential revelation, as what is most important and significant.

(ββ) The more important object of love presented in paintings is therefore Christ. With this topic art passes over at the same time into the *human* sphere which expands beyond Christ into a further province, to the portrayal of Mary, Joseph, John the Baptist, the Disciples, etc., and finally the people, partly those who follow the Saviour, partly those who demand Christ's Crucifixion and mock at his sufferings.

But here the difficulty already mentioned returns when Christ is to be conceived and portrayed in his *universality*, as has been attempted in busts and portraits. I must confess that to me at least the satisfaction they are intended to afford is not given by the heads of Christ that I have seen, e.g. by Carracci,[2] and above all the famous head painted by van Eyck, once in the Solly[3] collection,

---

[1] This altar-piece in twelve parts is regarded as the masterpiece of J. van Eyck (1390–1441). It may have been begun by his elder brother Hubert. Hegel saw it in 1827.

[2] A. Carracci, 1560–1609, probably, but his brother and his uncle were also painters.

[3] An English picture-dealer who sold a remarkable collection of fourteenth-

now in the Berlin Gallery, and that head by Hemling once belonging to the brothers Boisserée,[1] now in Munich. Van Eyck's head is in shape, in the forehead, and in its colour and whole conception magnificent, but at the same time the eye and the mouth do not express anything superhuman. The impression given is rather of a fixed seriousness which is intensified by the typical character of the form, parting of the hair, etc. Whereas if such heads incline in expression and form to that of an individual man, and therefore to something gentle, rather soft and weak, they quickly lose depth and powerfulness of effect. But, as I have already observed, what is least of all suited to them is the beauty of the Greek form.

Therefore Christ may be more appropriately taken in the situations of his earthly life as a subject for paintings. Yet in this matter an essential difference is not to be overlooked. In the life-story of Christ the human subjective manifestation of God is a chief feature; Christ is one of the Trinity and, as one of its Persons, comes into the midst of men, and therefore he can be portrayed also in his appearance as a man, in so far as that appearance expresses the inner life of the spirit. But, on the other hand, he is not only an individual man but very God. Now in situations where his Divinity should break out from his human personality, painting comes up against new difficulties. The depth of all that this implies begins to become all too powerful. For in most cases where Christ teaches, for instance, art can get no further than portraying him as the noblest, worthiest, wisest man, like Pythagoras, for example, or one of the other philosophers in Raphael's School of Athens. Accordingly, one very favourite expedient painting finds, and is only able to find, by bringing the Divinity of Christ before our eyes, in the main, through placing him in his surroundings, particularly in contrast to sin, remorse, and penitence, or to human baseness and wickedness, or alternatively through his worshippers who, by their worship, deprive him of his immediate existence as man, as man like themselves, a man who appears and exists, so that we see him raised to the spiritual heaven, and at the same time we have a sight of his appearance not

and fifteenth-century Italian pictures, as well as others, to Frederick William III in 1821. They were transferred to the Berlin Gallery when it opened in 1830, so 'now' is Hotho's word, not Hegel's.

[1] In 1804 Melchior (1786–1851) and Sulpiz (1783–1854) Boisserée founded a collection of pictures in Heidelberg. It was transferred into the possession of the King of Bavaria in 1827. For Hemling read Memling.

only as God but as an ordinary and natural, not ideal, man; we see too that as Spirit he exists essentially in humanity, in the Church, and expresses his Divinity as reflected there. Yet we must not interpret this spiritual reflection by supposing that God is present in humanity only accidentally or in an *external* form and mode of expression; on the contrary, we must regard the existence of the Spirit in the consciousness of man as the essential spiritual existence of God. Such a mode of portrayal will have to appear especially where Christ is to be put before our eyes as man, teacher, risen, or transfigured and ascended into heaven. But the means at the disposal of painting, the human figure and its colour, the flash and glance of the eye, are insufficient in themselves to give perfect expression to what is implicit in Christ in situations like these. Least of all can the forms of classical beauty suffice. In particular, the Resurrection, Transfiguration, and Ascension, and in general all the scenes in the life of Christ when, after the Crucifixion and his death, he has withdrawn from immediate existence as simply this individual man and is on the way to return to his Father, demand in Christ himself a higher expression of Divinity than painting is completely able to give to him; for its proper means for portraying him, namely human individuality and its external form, it should expunge here and glorify him in a purer light.

More advantageous for art and more in correspondence with its aim are therefore those situations out of the life-story of Christ where he appears not yet spiritually perfect or where his Divinity is restricted and abased, i.e. at the moment of his self-negation. This is the case in the childhood of Christ and the story of the Passion.

The fact that Christ is a child does in one way definitely express the meaning he has in our religion: he is God who becomes man and therefore goes through the stages of human life. But at the same time the fact that he is portrayed as a child implies the obvious impossibility of clearly already exhibiting everything that is implicit in him. Now here painting has the incalculable advantage that from the naïveté and innocence of the child it can make shine out a loftiness and sublimity of spirit which gains in power by this contrast; though just because it belongs to a child it is asked to display this depth and glory in an infinitely lower degree than it would be in Christ the man, the teacher, the judge of the world, etc. So Raphael's pictures of the Christ-child, especially the one in the Sistine Madonna in Dresden, have the most beautiful expression of childhood, and yet we can see in them something beyond purely childlike innocence, something which makes visible the Divine behind the veil of youth and gives us an inkling of the expansion of this Divinity into an infinite revelation; and at the same time the picture of a *child* has justification in the fact that in him the revelation is not yet perfect. On the other hand, in van Eyck's pictures of the Madonna the child is every time the least successful part: he is usually stiff and in the immature shape of a new-born infant. Some people propose to see something intentional and allegorical in this, on the ground that the reason why the child is not beautiful in these pictures is that it is not the beauty of the Christ-child that is the object of worship, but Christ as Christ. But in art such reflections are out of place, and Raphael's pictures of the Christ-child stand in this respect far above van Eyck's as works of art.

Equally appropriate is the portrayal of the Passion story—the mockery, the crown of thorns, the *Ecce Homo*, the carrying of the cross, the Crucifixion, the Descent from the Cross, the Entombment, etc. For here the subject is provided precisely by God in the opposite of his triumph, in the abasement of his limitless power and wisdom. Not only does it remain possible for art to portray this material in a general way, but originality of conception has at the same time great scope here without deviating into the fantastic. It is God who suffers in so far as he is man, confined within this specific limitation, and so his grief does not appear as merely human grief over a human fate; on the contrary, this is an awesome suffering, the feeling of an infinite negativity, but in a human person as his personal feeling. And yet, since it is God who suffers, there enters again an alleviation, a lowering of his suffering which cannot come to an outburst of despair, to grimaces and horror. This expression of suffering of *soul* is an entirely original creation especially by several Italian masters. In the lower parts of the face grief is just seriousness, not, as in the Laocoon, a contraction of the muscles which could be taken to indicate an outcry, but in the eyes and on the forehead there are waves and storms of the soul's suffering which, as it were, roll over one another. Drops of sweat break out, indicating inner agony, on the forehead, just where the chief determinant is the immovable bone. And precisely at this point where nose, eyes, and forehead meet, and where inner thinking and the nature of spirit are concentrated and emergent, there are only a few muscles and folds of skin which, being incapable of any great play, can therefore exhibit this suffering as restrained and at the same time as infinitely concentrated. I have in mind in particular a head in the Schleissheim gallery[1] in which the master (Guido Reni, I think) has discovered, as other masters too have done in similar pictures, an entirely peculiar tone of colour which is not found in the human face. They had to disclose the night of the spirit,[2] and for this purpose fashioned a type of colour which corresponds in the most splendid way to this storm, to these black clouds of the spirit that at the same time are firmly controlled and kept in place by the brazen brow of the divine nature.

As the most perfect subject for painting I have already specified inwardly *satisfied* [reconciled and peaceful] love, the object of which is not a purely spiritual 'beyond' but is present, so that we can see love itself before us in what is loved. The supreme and unique form of this love is Mary's love for the Christ-child, the love of the one mother who has borne the Saviour of the world and carries him in her arms. This is the most beautiful subject to which Christian art in general, and especially painting in its religious sphere, has risen.

The love of God, and in particular the love of Christ who sits at the right hand of God, is of a purely spiritual kind. The object of this love is visible only to the eye of the soul, so that here there is strictly no question of that duality which love implies, nor is there any natural bond established between the lovers or any chain linking them together from the start. On the other hand, any other love is accidental in the inclination of one lover for another, or, alternatively, the lovers, e.g. brothers and sisters or a father in his love for his children, have outside this relation other concerns with an essential claim on them. Fathers or brothers have to apply themselves to the world, to the state, business, war, or, in short, to general purposes, while sisters become wives, mothers, and so forth. But in the case of maternal love it is generally true that a mother's love for her child is neither something accidental nor

---

[1] In a fine palace north of Munich. G. Reni, 1575–1642.
[2] This is the Second Night in the Dark Night of St. John of the Cross, from whom Hegel's metaphor seems to be drawn.

just a single feature in her life, but, on the contrary, it is her supreme vocation on earth, and her natural character and most sacred calling directly coincide. But while other loving mothers see and feel in their child their husband and their inmost union with him, in Mary's relation to her child this aspect is always absent. For her feeling has nothing in common with a wife's love for her husband; on the contrary, her relation to Joseph is more like a sister's to a brother, while on Joseph's side there is a secret awe of the child who is God's and Mary's. Thus religious love in its fullest and most intimate human form we contemplate not in the suffering and risen Christ or in his lingering amongst his friends but in the person of Mary with her womanly feeling. Her whole heart and being is human love for the child that she calls her own, and at the same time adoration, worship, and love of God with whom she feels herself at one. She is humble in God's sight and yet has an infinite sense of being the one woman who is blessed above all other virgins. She is not self-subsistent on her own account, but is perfect only in her child, in God, but in him she is satisfied and blessed, whether at the manger or as the Queen of Heaven, without passion or longing, without any further need, without any aim other than to have and to hold what she has.

In its religious subject-matter the portrayal of this love has a wide series of events, including, for example, the Annunciation, the Visitation, the Birth, the Flight into Egypt, etc. And then there are, added to this, other subjects from the later life of Christ, i.e. the Disciples and the women who follow him and in whom the love of God becomes more or less a personal relation of love for a living and present Saviour who walks amongst them as an actual man; there is also the love of the angels who hover over the birth of Christ and many other scenes in his life, in serious worship or innocent joy. In all these subjects it is painting especially which presents the peace and full satisfaction of love.

But nevertheless this peace is followed by the deepest suffering. Mary sees Christ carry his cross, she sees him suffer and die on the cross, taken down from the cross and buried, and no grief of others is so profound as hers. Yet, even in such suffering, its real burden is not the unyieldingness of grief or of loss only, nor the weight of a necessary imposition, nor complaint about the injustice of fate, and so a comparison with the characteristic grief of Niobe is especially appropriate. Niobe too has lost all her children and now confronts us in pure sublimity and unimpaired beauty. What is kept here is the aspect of her existence as an unfortunate woman, the beauty that has become her nature and makes up the whole of her existence in reality; her actual individuality remains what it is in her beauty. But her inner life, her heart, has lost the whole burden of its love and its soul; her individuality and beauty can only turn into stone.[1] Mary's grief is of a totally different kind. She is emotional, she feels the thrust of the dagger into the centre of her soul, her heart breaks, but she does not turn into stone. She did not only *have* love; on the contrary, her whole inner life *is* love, the free concrete spiritual depth of feeling which preserves the absolute essence of what she has lost, and even in the loss of the loved one she ever retains the peace of love. Her heart breaks; but the very substance and burden of her heart and mind which shines through her soul's suffering with a vividness never to be lost is something infinitely higher. This is the living beauty of *soul* in contrast to the abstract *substance* which, when its ideal existence in the body perishes, remains imperishable, but in stone.

Lastly, a final subject for painting in connection with Mary is her death and her Assumption.[2] The death of Mary in which she recovers the attraction of youth has been beautifully painted by Scorel especially. Here this master has given to the Virgin the expression of walking in her sleep, of the presence of death, of rigidity, and of blindness to everything external, along with the expression of her spirit which, though still peeping through her features, exists and is blissful elsewhere.

(γγ) But, thirdly, there enters into the sphere of this actual presence of God in his and his friends' life, in his sufferings and glory, *humanity*, the *subjective* consciousness which makes God, or in particular his acts in his historical life, into an object of its love and so is related to the Absolute and not to some temporal state of affairs. Here too there are three aspects to emphasize: (i) tranquil worship, (ii) repentance and conversion which internally and externally repeat the Passion story of God in man, and (iii) the soul's inner transfiguration and bliss of purification.

(i) Worship as such especially provides the subject-matter of

---

[1] Hegel has in mind again the story that, after the death of her children, Niobe went to Mt. Sipylon and, at her own request, was turned into a stone by Zeus.

[2] The doctrine of the Bodily Assumption had not been defined in Hegel's day, but it was believed in many places.

prayer. This is indeed a situation of humility, of the sacrifice of self and the quest for peace in another, but still it is not so much begging (*Bitten*) as praying (*Beten*). Of course begging and praying are closely related because a prayer may also be a begging. Yet begging proper wants something for itself; it is addressed to someone who possesses something essential to me, in the hope that my begging will incline his heart to me, weaken his heart, and stimulate his love for me and so arouse in him a sense of identity with me. But what I feel in begging him is the desire for something that he is to lose when I get it; he is to love me so that my own selfishness can be satisfied and my interest and welfare furthered. But I give nothing in return except perhaps an implicit avowal that he can ask the same things of me. This is not the kind of thing that prayer is. Prayer is an elevation of the heart to God who is absolute love and asks nothing for himself. Worship itself is the prayer answered; the petition itself is bliss. For although prayer may also contain a petition for some particular thing, this particular request is not what should really be expressed; on the contrary, the essential thing is the assurance of simply being heard, not of being heard in respect of this particular request, but absolute confidence that God will give me what is best for me. Even in this respect, prayer is itself satisfaction, enjoyment, the express feeling and consciousness of eternal love which is not only a ray of transfiguration shining through the worshipper's figure and situation, but is in itself the situation and what exists and is to be portrayed. This is the prayerful situation of e.g. Pope Sixtus in the Raphael picture that is called after him,[1] and of St. Barbara in the same picture; the same is true of the innumerable prayerful situations of Apostles and saints (e.g. St. Francis) at the foot of the Cross, where what is now chosen as the subject is, not Christ's grief or the timorousness, doubt, and despair of the Disciples, but the love and adoration of God, the prayer that loses itself in him.

Especially in the earlier ages of painting there are faces of this kind, usually of old men who have gone through much in life and

[1] The Sistine Madonna is so called because it came from the church of San Sisto in Piacenza. The St. Sixtus to whom the church is dedicated was a saint who became Pope Sixtus III (d. 440). In the picture Raphael gave him the features of Pope Julius II who died in 1513, i.e. at about the time when the picture was painted. It has no connection with the Sistine Chapel or, despite what Bénard thinks, with Pope Sixtus V who was not born until a year after Raphael died.

suffering. The faces have been treated as if they were portraits, yet they are those of worshipful souls. The result is that this worship is not their occupation at this moment only, but on the contrary they become priests, as it were, or saints whose whole life, thought, desire, and will is worship, and their expression, despite all portraiture, has in it nothing but this assurance and this peace of love. Yet things are different already in the case of the older German and Flemish masters. The subject of the picture in Cologne Cathedral, for instance, is the patron saints of Cologne and the adoration of the Magi, and this topic is much favoured too in the school of van Eyck. Here those in prayer are often well-known people, princes, etc., as e.g. it has been proposed to recognize in the famous prayer picture (in the Boisserée collection), *said* to be by van Eyck,[1] as two of the Magi, Philip of Burgundy and Charles the Bold. In these figures we see that they are something else beyond praying and that they have other business. It is as if they go to Mass only on Sundays or early in the morning, while in the rest of the week, or the day, they pursue their other concerns. Especially in Flemish or German pictures those who commissioned them appear as pious knights, or God-fearing housewives, with their sons and daughters. They are like Martha who goes about the house, careful and troubled about many things external and mundane, and not like Mary who chose the better part.[2] Their piety does not lack heart and spiritual depth, but what constitutes their whole nature is not the song of love which should have been their whole life, as it is the nightingale's, and not merely an elevation, a prayer or thanks for a mercy received.

The general distinction to be made in such pictures between saints and worshippers on the one hand, and, on the other, pious members of the Christian church in their actual daily life may be indicated by the fact that, especially in Italian pictures, the worshippers display in the expression of their piety a perfect correspondence between their inner self and their outward behaviour. The soulful mind appears also as the soulfulness especially of the cast of features which expresses nothing opposed to the feelings of the heart or different from them. Yet this correspondence does not always exist in real life. A child in tears, for example, especially

---

[1] The picture was catalogued as by van Eyck, but it is actually by Rogier van der Weyden (1400–64).
[2] Luke 10: 41–2.

when it is just beginning to cry, often leads us to laugh at its grimaces, quite apart from the fact that we know that its suffering is not worth tears. Similarly, older people screw up their faces when they want to laugh, because their features are too fixed, cold, and stiff for them to be accommodated to a natural unrestrained laugh or friendly smile. This lack of correspondence between the feeling and the visible forms in which piety is expressed must be avoided by painting which, so far as possible, must produce a harmony between inner and outer; and this, after all, the Italian painters have done in the fullest measure, while the Flemish and German ones, because of their portraiture, have been less successful.

I will add, as a further comment, that this soulful worship must not be a call of anguish in distress, whether in soul or in outward circumstances, like that in the Psalms and many Lutheran hymns —e.g. [Psalm xlii] 'as the hart panteth after the water brooks, so panteth my soul after thee, O God'—but on the contrary a fusion with the Divine (even if not so sweet as it is in the case of nuns), a surrender of the soul, and a delight in this surrender, a sense of satisfaction and completion. For the beauty of the romantic ideal has nothing to do with the distress of faith, the anguished pining of the soul, the doubt and despair which gets no further than struggle and disunion, with hypochondriacal piety like this, which never knows whether it is not still sunk in sin, whether its repentance is genuine, whether its pardon is assured, or with such a surrender in which the individual cannot relinquish himself and shows this precisely by his anguish. Rather may worship direct the eye longingly to heaven, although it is more artistic and satisfying if the eye is directed to a present and this-world object of prayer, e.g. to Mary, Jesus, a saint, etc. It is easy, far too easy, to give a higher interest to a picture by making the chief figure raise his eyes to heaven, to something beyond this world; after all, nowadays this easy means has often been used to make God and religion the foundation of the state or to prove anything and everything by biblical quotations instead of from the rational heart of actuality. In Guido Reni, for instance, it has become a mannerism of his to give his figures this look and raising of the eyes. His Assumption of Mary, in the Munich gallery, for example, has won the highest fame from friends and connoisseurs of art, and certainly it has a supreme effect in the lofty glory of the transfiguration, the immersion and dissolving of the soul in heaven, and in the entire attitude of a figure hovering aloft in heaven, as well as in the clarity and beauty of the colour. Nevertheless I find it less satisfactory for Mary than when she is portrayed in her present love and bliss as she has her eye on her child. The longing and striving in her look towards heaven borders too nearly on modern sentimentalism.

(ii) The second point concerns the entry of the *negative* into this spiritual worship and love. The Disciples, saints, and martyrs have to traverse the road of grief (whether within or imposed on them from without) which Jesus walked before them in the events of the Passion.

This grief lies in a way at the boundaries of art which painting may readily be inclined to cross by taking as subjects the cruelty and horror of *physical* suffering—flaying, burning at the stake, the torment and agony of crucifixion. But, if painting is not to depart from the spiritual ideal, this it cannot be allowed to do, and not simply because there is no beauty in bringing martyrdoms of this sort clearly before our eyes or because we have weak nerves nowadays, but for a deeper reason, namely that the ideal has nothing to do with this physical aspect of suffering. The real topic to be felt and presented is the history of the spirit, the *soul* in its sufferings of love (not the immediate physical suffering of an individual in himself), grief at the sufferings of someone else, or grief of heart at personal unworthiness. The steadfastness of the martyrs in their physical horrors is a steadfastness which does endure purely physical suffering, but in the spiritual ideal the soul has to do with itself, its pain, the wounding of its love, with inner repentance, sorrow, regret, and remorse.

But even in this inner agony the *positive* element is not missing. The soul must be assured of the *objective* absolutely complete reconciliation of man with God and be anxious only about whether this eternal salvation is purely *subjective* within it. Thus we commonly see penitents, martyrs, monks who in their certainty of an objective reconciliation are still plunged in mourning for a heart which should have been surrendered, or who have actually accomplished this self-surrender and yet still want to know this reconciliation achieved ever anew and so have ever again and again imposed penances on themselves.

Here two different starting-points can be taken. If artists take as a basis an original and natural cheerfulness, freedom, serenity, and a decisiveness which can take life easily with its actual ties and quickly make its account with them, then there can still more readily be associated with it a natural nobility, grace, cheerfulness, freedom, and beauty of *form*. If on the other hand the presupposition is a stiff-necked, arrogant, crude, and narrow mentality, then for overcoming it a harsh power is required to extricate the spirit from sense and the world, and win the religion of salvation. Therefore in the case of this refractoriness harsher forms of force and firmness enter; the scars of the wounds which have to be inflicted on this obstinacy are more visible and permanent, and beauty of form disappears.

(iii) The positive aspect of reconciliation, transfiguration out of grief, bliss won as a result of repentance, may be made an independent topic for painting, a subject, it is true, which may easily lead the artist astray.

These are the chief differences in the absolute spiritual ideal as the essential subject-matter of romantic painting. This is the burden of its most successful, most celebrated works—works that are immortal because of the depth of their thought. And when their burden is truthfully portrayed, they are the supreme elevation of mind to its blessedness, the most soulful thing, the greatest spiritual depth that any artist can ever provide.

After this religious sphere we have now to mention two other different areas of romantic painting.

(β) The opposite of the religious sphere is, taken in itself, altogether lacking in spiritual depth or the Divine, i.e. it is nature, and, more precisely in the case of painting, *landscape*. The character of religious subjects we have so interpreted as expressing in them the substantive spiritual depth of the soul, love's abiding in itself in God. But spiritual depth of feeling has still another content. In what is plainly external it can find an echo of the heart, and in the objective world as such can recognize traits akin to the spirit. In their direct appearance, hills, mountains, woods, glens, rivers, meadows, sunshine, the moon, the starry heavens, etc., are perceived as simply mountains, rivers, sunshine, etc., but *first*, these objects are of interest in themselves because it is the free life of nature which appears in them and produces a correspondence with the spectator who is a living being too, and *secondly*, these particular natural and objective things produce moods in our heart which correspond to the moods of nature. We can identify our life with this life of nature that re-echoes in our soul and heart, and in this way possess in nature a spiritual depth of our own. Just as Arcadians spoke of a Pan who made them shuddering and terror-struck in the gloom of the woods,[1] so the different features of the natural landscape in their calm serenity, their fragrant peace, their freshness in spring and deadness in winter, their morning wakening and their evening repose, etc., correspond to specific states of the soul. The peaceful depths of the sea, the possibility that these depths may burst forth with infinite power, have a relation to the soul, while, conversely, a storm, the roaring, swelling, foaming, and breaking of storm-tossed waves move the soul to a sympathetic voice. This depth of spiritual feeling painting also takes as a subject. But on this account these natural objects as such in their purely external form and juxtaposition should not be the real subject-matter of painting, because, if they were, painting would become mere imitation; on the contrary, the life of nature, which extends through everything, and the characteristic sympathy between objects thus animated and specific moods of the soul, is what painting has to emphasize and portray in a lively way in its landscapes. This profound sympathy is alone the spiritual and deeply emotional factor which can make nature not a mere environment [or background] but a subject for painting on its own account.

(γ) A third and last kind of spiritual depth of feeling is what we find partly in wholly insignificant objects torn from their living environment, and partly in scenes of human life which may appear to us as purely accidental or even base and vulgar. Elsewhere[2] I have tried already to justify the artistic appropriateness of such subjects. Here I will add to the previous discussion only the following remarks with reference to painting.

Painting is concerned not only with the subjective inner life as such but at the same time with the inner life as *particularized* within. Precisely because it is the particular which is the principle of this inner life, this life cannot stay with the absolute subject-matter of religion, nor can it take as its content from the external world the life of nature only and its specific character as landscape; on the contrary, it must proceed to anything and everything in which a man as an individual subject can take an interest or find satisfaction. Even in pictures drawn from the sphere of religion,

---

[1] 'Barbarians were seized by the Panic terror. It is said that terror without a reason comes from Pan' (Pausanias, x. 23. 5).

[2] See above in Vol. I, pp. 168–171 and 597–600.

the higher art rises the more does it carry its subject-matter into mundane and present reality, and thereby give to it the perfection of worldly existence, with the result that the chief thing is the sensuous existent created by art, while the interest of worship decreases. For here, after all, art has the task of working out these ideal subjects into actuality, of making visible to sense what is withdrawn from sense, and bringing into the present, and humanizing, topics drawn from scenes that are far off and past.

At the stage we have now reached it is a deep sense of oneness with what is immediately present, with our everyday surroundings, with the commonest and tiniest details, that becomes the subject-matter of painting.

(αα) If we ask what the really artistically appropriate subject-matter is in what otherwise is the poverty and accidental character of such material, the answer is that the *substance* maintained and emphasized in these things is the *life* and joy of independent existence in general which persists amid the greatest variety of individual aims and interests. Man always lives in the immediate present; what he does at every moment is something particular, and the right thing is simply to fulfil every task, no matter how trivial, with heart and soul. In that event the man is at one with such an individual matter for which alone he seems to exist, because he has put his whole self and all his energy into it. This cohesion [between the man and his work] produces that harmony between the subject and the particular character of his activity in his nearest circumstances which is also a spiritual depth and which is the attractiveness of the independence of an explicitly total, rounded, and perfect existence. Consequently, the interest we may take in pictures of objects like those mentioned does not lie in the objects themselves but in this soul of life which in itself, apart altogether from the thing in which it proves to be living, speaks to every uncorrupt mind and free heart and is to it an object in which it participates and takes joy. We therefore must not allow our pleasure to be diminished by listening to the demand that we are to admire these works of art on the ground of their so-called 'naturalness' and their deceptive imitation of nature. This demand which such works seem to make obvious is itself only a deception which misses the real point. For it implies that our admiration results from an external comparison between a work of art and a work of nature and is based only on a correspondence between the painting and something that exists there already, while here the real subject-matter and the artistic thing in the treatment and execution is the correspondence of the portrayed object with *itself*, for this is reality explicitly ensouled. On the principle of deception, Denner's portraits may be praised: they are indeed imitations of nature, but for the most part they do not hit that life as such which is the important thing here; on the contrary, they go on in detail to portray hairs and wrinkles, and in general what is not exactly something abstract and dead, though neither is it the life of the human face.

Further, if we allow our pleasure to be trivialized by accepting the supercilious intellectual reflection that we should regard such objects as vulgar and unworthy of our loftier consideration, we are taking the subject-matter of painting in a way quite different from that in which art really presents it to us. For in that case we are bringing with us only the relation we take up to such objects when we need them or take pleasure in them or regard them from the point of view of the rest of our culture and our other aims; i.e. we are treating them only according to their external purpose, with the result that it is our needs which become the chief thing, a living end in itself, while the life of the object is killed because the object appears as destined essentially to serve as a mere means or to remain wholly indifferent to us because we cannot use it. For example, a ray of sunshine falling through the open door of a room we are entering, a neighbourhood we travel through, a sempstress, a maid we see busy at her work, all these may be something wholly indifferent to us because we are giving free rein to thoughts and interests far remote from them. Consequently, in our soliloquy or conversation with others, the existing situation confronting us is too weak, in comparison with our thoughts or talk, to be put into words, or it arrests an entirely fleeting attention which goes no further than the bare judgement: 'How beautiful, or pleasing, or ugly'. Thus we enjoy even the jollity of a ceilidh because we are just lookers-on in a casual way, or we get out of the road and despise it because we 'are enemies of everything uncivilized'.[1] Our attitude is the same to the human faces that we meet in company every day or encounter by accident. Here our personality and our varied preoccupations always have their part to play. We are impelled to say this or that to this or that man; we have business

---

[1] Goethe, *Faust*, line 944 (pt. i, sc. 2).

to transact, things to consider; we have this or that to think about him, we see him in this or that situation of his that we know, and we direct our conversation accordingly, for we say nothing about this or that in order not to wound him, we do not touch on a subject because he might take it ill of us if we did. In short, we always keep in view his life-story, his rank and class, our attitude to him and our business with him, so that either we preserve a *practical* relation to him or else we are indifferent to him and absent-mindedly fail to attend to him.

But, in portraying such living realities, art entirely alters our attitude to them because it cuts away all the *practical* ramifications, which otherwise connect us with things in the world, and brings them to us in an entirely *contemplative* way; and it also cancels all our indifference to them and leads our notice, preoccupied otherwise, entirely to the situation portrayed, on which, if we are to enjoy it, we must pull ourselves together and concentrate. By its mode of portraying the ideal, sculpture in particular suppresses from the start a practical relation to its subject, because a sculpture shows at once that it does not belong to this practical and real sphere. Whereas painting conducts us at once, on the one hand, into the present and its more closely related world of every day, but, on the other hand, in that present-day world it cuts all the threads of attractiveness or distress, of sympathy or antipathy, which draw us to it or the reverse, and it brings these present objects nearer to us as ends in themselves in their own particular liveliness. What happens here is the opposite of what [A. W.] Schlegel, in the story of *Pygmalion*, describes so wholly prosaically as the return of the perfect work of art to common life, where what matters is subjective inclination and enjoyment in the real. This return is the opposite of that removal of objects from any relation to our needs which art affords and precisely in this way puts before our eyes their own independent life and appearance.

($\beta\beta$) Just as art in this sphere revindicates the lost independence of a subject-matter to which we otherwise do not allow full liberty in its own special character, so, secondly, it can immobilize those objects which in reality do not stay long enough for us to notice them explicitly. The greater the height that nature reaches in its organisms and their mobile appearance, the more it resembles an actor who works for a momentary effect. In this connection I have already earlier eulogized art for its ability to triumph over reality and give permanence to what is most fleeting. In painting this making the momentary permanent is evident in the momentary life that is concentrated in specific situations and also in the magic of their pure appearance in their varying momentary colour. For example, a troop of calvary can alter at every minute in its grouping and in the position of its every member. If we ourselves belonged to it we would have plenty of other things to do than to notice the living spectacle of these changes: we would have to mount, dismount, fill our knapsack, eat, drink, rest, unharness the horses, water them, fodder them, etc.; or if in our ordinary practical life we were spectators, we would look on with a totally different interest: we would want to know what the troop was doing, where its members came from, why they were drawn up, etc. The painter, on the other hand, espies the most ephemeral movements, the most fleeting facial expressions, the most momentary appearances of colour in this kaleidoscope, and brings them before our eyes in the interest of this vivacity of appearance which, but for him, would vanish. It is especially the play of colour's appearance, not just colour as such, but its light and shadow, the way that objects appear in the foreground or the background, that provides the reason why the picture seems life-like. This is something which art alone brings to our awareness, but it is an aspect of works of art to which we commonly give less attention than it deserves. Moreover, in these matters the artist borrows from nature its privilege of entering into the smallest detail, of being individualized concretely and definitely, because he confers on his subjects the like individuality of living appearance in its quickest flashes, and yet he does not provide immediate and slavishly imitated details for mere perception but produces for imagination something quite specific in which at the same time the universal remains effective.

(γγ) The more trivial are the topics which painting takes as its subjects at this stage, in comparison with those of religion, the more does the chief interest and importance become the artist's skill in production, his way of seeing, his manner of treatment and elaboration, his living absorption in the entire range of his chosen tasks, and the soul and vital love of his execution itself. But whatever his subject becomes under his hand, it must not be different from what it is or can be in fact. We think that we are looking at something quite different and new only because in the real world we have not attended in such detail to similar situations and their colour. Of course, on the other hand, something new is indeed added to these commonplace subjects, namely the love, the mind and spirit, the soul, with which the artist seizes on them, makes them his own, and so breathes his own inspiration of production as a new life into what he creates.

These are the most essential points for notice in connection with the subject-matter of painting.

(b) *More detailed Characterization of the Sensuous Material of Painting*

The aspect next to be discussed concerns the more detailed characteristics to which the sensuous material must prove to be amenable if it is to lend itself to the subject-matter indicated above.

(α) The first thing of importance in this connection is linear perspective. It comes in of necessity because painting has at its disposal only a suface; it can no longer spread out its figures alongside one another on one and the same plane, as the bas-relief of Greek sculpture could, but must proceed to a mode of presentation which has to make apparent to us the distance between objects in all three spatial dimensions. For painting has to develop its chosen subject-matter, to put it before our eyes in its manifold movement, and to bring figures into a varied connection with their external natural landscape, or with buildings, the rooms they are in, etc., to an extent quite beyond what sculpture can achieve in any way, even in reliefs. Instead of what painting in this connection cannot place before us in its actual distance, as sculpture can in a *real* way, it must substitute the pure *appearance* of the reality. In this matter its first recourse is to divide the *one* surface confronting it into different planes *apparently* lying distant from one another. In this way it acquires the opposition of a near foreground and a distant background, and they are connected together again by the middle distance. It sets down its subjects on these different planes. Now the further that objects lie from the eye, the more do they diminish proportionately, and this decrease in size follows in the very nature of optical laws determinable mathematically. Consequently painting has to accept and follow these rules which have a specific sort of application owing to the transfer of objects to a single surface. This is the necessity for the so-called linear or mathematical perspective in painting; but the detailed rules for it we do not have to discuss here.

(β) Secondly, however, the subjects painted are not only at a specific distance from one another, but they are also different in form. This particular spatial delimitation by which each object is made visible in its specific shape is a matter of *draughtsmanship*. It is the drawing alone which provides the distance of objects from one another and also their individual shape. Its principal law is exactitude in [delineating] form and distance. It is true that this is primarily related not to the expression of spirit but only to what appears externally, and therefore it constitutes only a purely external fundamental principle. Nevertheless, it is of great difficulty, especially in the case of organic forms and their manifold movements owing to the foreshortenings which these necessitate. Since these two aspects relate purely to the shape and its spatial totality, they constitute the plastic or sculptural element in painting. Since this art also expresses the inmost life in an external shape, it can neither give up this element, nor, from another point of view, fail to go beyond it. For its proper task is colouring, so that, in genuine painting, distance and shape win their proper presentation and their real appearance only in differences of colour.

(γ) Consequently, it is *colour*, colouring, which makes a painter a painter. It is true that we linger over draughtsmanship and especially over sketches as over something clearly indicative of genius; but no matter with what richness of invention and wealth of imagination the inner spirit may directly emerge in sketches from the, as it were, more transparent and thinner veil of form, still painting must *paint* if it intends to portray its subjects in their living individuality and particular detail and not to stop, in its visible aspect, at presenting only an abstraction. Nevertheless, this is not to imply that significant value is to be denied to the drawings, and especially the free-hand drawings, of great masters like Raphael and Albrecht Dürer. On the contrary, from one point of view it is precisely these free-hand drawings which have the greatest interest because we see in them the miracle that the whole spirit of the artist passes over immediately into the manual dexterity which with the greatest ease, without groping, sets before us in the production of a moment everything that the artist's spirit contains. For example, Dürer's marginal drawings in the Prayer Book in the Munich Library have an indescribable spirituality and freedom: conception and execution appear as one and the same, whereas in paintings we cannot get rid of the idea that perfection has been achieved in them only after several over-paintings and a continuous process of advance and improvement.

Despite this, it is only by the use of colour that painting gives to the life of the soul its really living external appearance. But not all schools of painting have reached the same height in the art of colouring. Indeed it is a peculiar phenomenon that hardly any painters, except the Venetian and especially the Flemish, have become perfect masters of colour: both these groups lived near the sea in a low-lying country intersected by fens, streams, and canals. In the case of the Dutch, their mastery may be explained by the fact that, owing to their always misty horizon, they had before them the persistent idea of a grey background and then, owing to this murkiness, they were all the more induced to study and emphasize colour in all its effects and varieties of lighting, reflection, brilliance, etc., and to find precisely in this the chief task of their art. Compared with the Venetians and the Dutch, the rest of Italian painting, with the exception of Correggio and a few others, seems dry, sapless, cold, and lifeless.[1]

In connection with colour, the following more detailed points of the greatest importance may be emphasized.

(αα) *First*, the abstract foundation of all colour, namely the light and the dark. If effect is given to this opposition and its mediations independently of colour differences, what then comes into view are only the oppositions of white, as light, to black, as shadow, and their transitions and nuances; these integrate the drawing because they belong to the strictly plastic character of the shape, and produce the prominence, the lowering, the contours, and the distance of the objects portrayed. In this connection we may mention here, in passing, the art of etching which is solely concerned with the light and the dark as such. Apart from the endless industry and most careful workmanship demanded by this art, which is to be valued highly when it reaches its zenith, there are linked together in it, as in the art of printing too, both intelligence and the utility of multiplying copies. Yet, unlike drawing as such, it is not confined purely to light and shade but, especially in its recent development, it struggles to rival painting and, over and above the light and the

---

[1] If the 'others' had been specified, this judgement might have seemed less sweeping.

dark effect produced by the lighting, to express also those differences of greater light and darkness which arise from local colour itself;[1] as, for instance, in an etching the difference between light and dark hair can be made visible with the same lighting.

But although in painting, as I said, light and dark provide only what is fundamental, this foundation is of the highest importance. For this alone determines the foreground and background, the contours, in general the proper appearance of the shape as a visible shape, and, in short, what is called 'modelling'.[2] Those who are masters in colour have pursued this, in this respect, into the most extreme opposition between the clearest light and the darkest shadows, and only in this way do they produce their supreme effects. Yet they are allowed this opposition only in so far as it does not remain rigid, i.e. in so far as it does not remain devoid of a wealthy play of transitions and mediations which put everything into a flow and interconnection and proceed to the most delicate nuances. But if such oppositions are missing, the whole thing becomes flat, because it is only the difference of light and dark which can emphasize some specific parts and put others in the background. Especially in rich compositions with wide distances between the subjects to be represented is it necessary to go into the darkest detail in order to have a broad scale of light and shadow.

The closer determinacy of light and shadow depends principally on the sort of illumination chosen by the artist. All the most varied differences arise from daylight, morning, midday, and evening light, sunshine or moonshine, clear or cloudy skies, light in storms, candlelight, a protected light, one falling on one spot or spread equally through a room, in short all the most varied modes of illumination. In the case of a public and complicated affair, a situation clear in itself to which we are wide awake, artificial lighting is rather an accessory, and the artist does best to use ordinary daylight, so long as the demands of dramatic vivacity, the desired emphasis on specific figures and groups and the soft-pedalling of others, do not necessitate an unusual mode of lighting which is more favourable for such differences. For this reason the great painters in the older schools made little use of contrasts in lighting

---

[1] Any black and white representation of a scene can, like a photograph, differentiate (*a*) the varying intensity of illumination falling on various objects, and (*b*) the varying brightness of the local colour of objects under the same illumination.

[2] i.e. glazing, to bring out in relief through light and shade, or to produce chiaroscuro effects.

or, in general, of entirely specific situations demanding, as it were, unusual lighting. And they were right, because they made straight for the spirit as such rather than for the effect of a visible mode of appearance, and with their emphasis on the inwardness and importance of their subject they could dispense with this always more or less external aspect. Whereas in the case of landscapes and the insignificant objects in our daily life, the lighting has a quite different importance. Here the great artistic, but also often contrived, and magical effects have their place. For example, in landscape bold contrasts of great masses of light and strong parts in shadow make their best effect, and yet they may become only a mannerism. Conversely, in this range of subjects, there are reflections, pure appearance and the mirror of it, this marvellous echo of light which produces an especially living play of light and dark, demanding from the spectator, no less than from the artist, serious and constant study. Next, in this matter, the lighting which the painter has seized upon in the external world, or in his inner conception of a subject, can only be a quickly passing and altering appearance. But however sudden or unusual the lighting so grasped may be, the artist must still take care, even in the case of the most animated action, to make sure that the whole picture, despite its variety, shall not be restless, swithering, or confused but remain clear and co-ordinated.

($\beta\beta$) The implication of this, however, as I have said already above, is that painting must not express the light and the dark in their bare abstraction but through difference of colour itself. Light and shadow must be coloured. Therefore we must proceed, *secondly*, to discuss colour as such.

The *first* point here again primarily affects the lightness and darkness of colours in relation to one another, because they win their effect in their reciprocal relation to one another as light and dark and emphasize one another or repress and interfere with one another. For example, red, and, still more, yellow is in itself brighter than blue, given the same intensity. This is connected with the nature of the different colours themselves which in recent times Goethe alone has seen correctly. For example, in blue the predominant thing is darkness which appears as blue only by working through a clearer but not completely transparent medium. The sky, for example, is dark; on the highest mountains it always becomes blacker; through a transparent but murky medium, like the atmosphere at lower levels, it appears blue and all the more clearly so the less transparent the atmosphere is. In the case of yellow, conversely, pure clarity works through a murky medium which still enables clarity to shine through it. Smoke, for instance, is such a murky medium: seen in front of something black which is effective through it, it appears bluish, while in front of something bright it appears yellowish and reddish. Pure red is the effective regal and concrete colour in which blue and yellow, contraries again themselves, are fused together. Green can also be regarded as such a unification, not however as a concrete unity but as purely expunged difference, as saturated and calm neutrality. These colours are the purest, simplest, and original fundamental colours. For this reason it is possible to look for a symbolical meaning in the manner in which the older masters used them, especially in the employment of blue and red. Blue corresponds to softness, sensuousness, stillness, to inward-looking depth of feeling, because it has as its principle the darkness which offers no resistance, while the light is rather what resists, produces, lives, and is cheerful. Red is masculine, dominant, regal; green indifferent and neutral. In accordance with this symbolism, when the Virgin Mary is portrayed enthroned as Queen of Heaven she usually has a red mantle, but when she appears as a mother, a blue one.

All the other colours in their endless variety must be regarded as mere modifications in which one or other of the shades of those fundamental colours is to be recognized. In this sense, no painter would call violet, for example, a colour. In their reciprocal relationship all these colours become lighter or darker in their effect on one another. This is a fact to which the painter must give essential consideration if he is not to fail to give the right tone necessary at each point for the relief and distance of objects. Here a quite exceptional difficulty arises. For example, in the face the lips are red, the eyebrows dark, black, or brown, or even if they are fair, still whatever their colour they are darker than the lips. Similarly, owing to their redness the cheeks are brighter than the nose where the main colour is yellowish, brownish, or greenish. In virtue of their local colour these parts of the face may be more brilliantly and intensively coloured than is consonant with their modelling.[1] In sculpture, and indeed even in a drawing, such

[1] i.e. there may be a conflict between truth to local colour and the require-

parts are kept light and dark purely and simply in accordance with the relation of their shape and the way they are lit. The painter, however, must adopt them in their local colouring and this disrupts that relation. The same thing is still more the case with objects at a greater distance from one another. When we look at things in an ordinary way, our intellectual judgement about the distance and form etc. of objects is not based merely on the colour of their appearance but on totally different grounds too. But in painting it is colour alone that is available and this may impair what demands light and darkness on its own account. Now at this point the skill of the painter consists in his wiping out such a contradiction and putting colours together in such a way that they do not interfere with one another either in their local tints in the modelling or in any other respect of their relationship. Only by attention to both points can the actual shape and colouring of objects come into appearance in perfection. For example, with what skill have the Dutch painted the lustre of satin gowns with all the manifold reflections and degrees of shadow in the folds, etc., and the sheen of silver, gold, copper, glass vessels, velvet, etc., and, by van Eyck, the lighting of precious stones, jewels, and goldbraid! The colours whereby the flash of gold, for instance, is produced have nothing metallic about them in themselves; looked at closely there is nothing in them but pure yellow which, considered by itself, has little brightness; the whole effect depends partly on an emphasis of the form and partly on the proximity into which every single nuance of colour is brought.

Secondly, a further aspect is the *harmony* of colours.

I have already observed that colours form an ensemble articulated by the very nature of colour itself. They must now appear in this completeness: no fundamental colour should be missing altogether, because otherwise our sense of this ensemble is to some extent lost. It is especially the older Italian and Flemish painters who give us complete satisfaction in relation to this system of colour: in their paintings we find blue, yellow, red, and green. This completeness constitutes the basis of harmony. Further,

---

ments of tonal gradations to achieve relief. In a black and white picture, the nose, projecting more than the cheeks, would be brighter than the cheeks in order to make it stand out. But in colour the red cheeks would be brighter than the yellowish-green nose, and the painter must therefore tone down the red from the properly observed local colour in order to bring the nose into relief.

however, the colours must be so assembled that what we are given for our eye is both their pictorial opposition and also the mediation and dissolution of this opposition, so that peace and reconciliation are achieved. It is partly the manner of their assembly, partly the degree of the intensity of each colour which produces such power of contrast and the peace of reconciliation. Amongst the older painters it was especially the Flemish who used the fundamental colours in their purity and their simple lustre; the sharpness of their contrast makes harmony more difficult, but, when it is achieved, the eye is satisfied. But in that case, along with this decision and power of colour the character too of the objects and the power of expression must also be decisive and simple. This implies at the same time a higher harmony between the colouring and the subject-matter. For example, the chief people must have the most salient colour, and in their character and their bearing and expression they must appear grander than their entourage to whom only mixed colours are assigned. In landscape painting such contrasts of the pure fundamental colours occur to a lesser extent; on the other hand, those simpler colours have their place in scenes where persons are the chief thing, and especially where robes take up the largest parts of the whole canvas. Here the scene is drawn from the world of the spirit where the inorganic, the natural surroundings, must appear more abstractly, i.e. not in their natural completeness and isolated effect, and the various tints of landscape in their variegated wealth of shades are less suitable.

In general, landscape as an environment for scenes of human life is not so completely suitable as a room or something architectural, since situations that take place in the open air are on the whole not as a rule those actions that reveal as the essential thing the fulness of the inner life. But if a man is placed out of doors, then nature must have its value only as an environment. In pictures like these, as has been said, the decisive colours principally have their right place. Yet their use requires boldness and power. Faces that are sweet, blurred, or doting are unsuited for decisive colours; a weak expression like that, or a mistiness of expression, like what has commonly been regarded as ideal since Mengs, would be entirely wiped out by such colours. In most recent times in Germany the faces that have principally become the fashion are insignificant and weak with affected airs, especially graceful or simple and pretending to be grandiose. Then this unimportance of inner spiritual character also carries with it unimportance in colour and the tone of colour, so that all the colours are kept in unclarity and enervated feebleness and they are damped down, with the result that nothing really emerges; it is true that one colour does not suppress another but at the same time no colour is emphasized. Yes, this is a harmony of colours and often of great sweetness and a flattering loveliness, but it is all insignificant and unimportant. In the same connection Goethe says in the notes to his translation of Diderot's *Essay on Painting*:

It cannot be admitted that it is easier to harmonize a weak colouring than a strong one; but it is true that if the colouring is strong, if colours appear vivid, then the eye senses harmony or disharmony much more vividly. Yet if the colours are weakened, if in a picture some are used pure, others mixed, others smudged, then it is true that no one knows whether he is looking at an harmonious or an inharmonious picture. All the same, he can say in any case: 'That is ineffective and meaningless.'

But in the matter of colouring not everything is achieved by a harmony of colours, for, *thirdly*, other aspects must be added if perfection is to be attained. In this connection I will mention here only the so-called atmospheric perspective, carnation [i.e. flesh-tints], and, finally, the magic of colour's pure appearance.

Linear perspective primarily concerns only the differences of size made by the lines of the objects in their greater or lesser distance from the eye. But this alteration and diminution of the *form* of the object is not the only thing that painting has to copy. For in reality everything undergoes a different sort of colouring owing to the atmosphere which pervades and differentiates objects and indeed their different parts. This tone of colour, diminishing with distance, is what constitutes atmospheric perspective, because in this way objects are modified in the manner of their outlines as well as in their dark or light appearance and their other colouring. People usually suppose that what lies nearest to the eye in the foreground is always the brightest while the background is darker, but in fact things are different. The foreground is at once the darkest and the lightest, i.e. the contrast of light and shadow is at its strongest in what is near at hand, and the outlines are at their maximum clarity of definition; but the further the objects are removed from the eye all the more do they become colourless, vague in their shape, because the opposition of light and shadow is more and more lost and the whole thing disappears into a clear grey. Yet the different kind of illumination produces in this matter the most varied sorts of deviation in colour.—Especially in landscape painting, but also in all other pictures which portray wide spaces, atmospheric perspective is of supreme importance, and the greatest masters of colouring have achieved magical effects here too.

But, secondly, the most difficult thing in the matter of colour, the ideal or, as it were, the summit of colouring, is 'carnation', the colour tone of human flesh which unites all other colours marvellously in itself without giving independent emphasis to either one or another. The youthful and healthy red of the cheeks is pure carmine without any dash of blue, violet, or yellow; but this red is itself only a gloss, or rather a shimmer, which seems to press outwards from within and then shades off unnoticeably into the rest of the flesh-colour, although this latter is an ideal inter-association of all the fundamental colours. Through the transparent yellow of the skin there shines the red of the arteries and the blue of the veins, and into the light and the dark and other manifold brightnesses and reflections there come tones as well of grey, brownish, and even greenish which at a first glance look extremely unnatural to us and yet they may be correct and have their true effect. Still, this combination of appearances is wholly lustreless, i.e. the appearance of one colour does not shine in another; on the contrary, the whole appearance is animated and ensouled from within. This way that the inner shines through is what especially presents the greatest difficulty for portrayal in a picture. We might compare this to a lake in the light of the evening where we can see both the things mirrored in it and at the same time the clear depth and special character of the water. On the other hand the lustre of metal is shining and reflecting, and precious stones are transparent and flashing; but in these cases there is no shining of one colour through another as there is in flesh; the same is true of satin, lustrous silks, etc. The skin of animals, whether hair, feathers, wool, etc., has similarly the most varied sorts of colouring, but has one direct and independent colour in specific parts, so that the variety is rather a result of different surfaces and planes, small points and lines of different colouring, than of an interpenetration of different colours as occurs in human flesh. The nearest approach to the latter is the interplay of colour on a bunch of grapes and the marvellous, delicate, and transparent shades of colour in a rose. But even these do not reach the pure appearance of inner animation which flesh colour must have, and to produce this pure appearance and its lustreless emanation of the soul is amongst the most difficult things known to painting. For this inwardness and the subjective side of life should not appear on a surface as laid on, as material colour in strokes and points etc., but as itself a living whole—transparent, profound, like the blue of the sky which should not be in our eyes a resistant surface, but something in which we must be able to immerse ourselves. In this connection Diderot says in the *Essay on Painting* translated by Goethe: 'The man who has got the feel of flesh has already gone far. Everything else is nothing in comparison. Thousands of painters have died without having had this feeling, and thousands more will die without having had it.'[1]

As for the material to be used for producing this lustreless vitality of flesh, the short answer is that oils alone have proved perfectly suitable for this purpose. Treatment in mosaic is least of all fitted for producing this effect of fusion of colours; its permanence is a recommendation but it has to express shades of colour by juxtaposing differently coloured glass studs or small stones and therefore it can never produce the flowing fusion of the ideal shining of one colour through another. An improvement on this is painting frescoes or in tempera.[2] But in fresco painting the colours laid on wet plaster were absorbed too quickly, so that, for one thing, the greatest facility and sureness of brushwork was necessary, and, for another thing, the work had to be executed in great strokes alongside one another, and these dried too quickly to permit of any finer shading. A similar thing is true of painting in tempera colours; they can be given inner clarity and beautiful illumination, yet owing to their drying quickly they likewise lend themselves less to harmony and shading and necessitate a treatment dashed off with strokes of the brush. On the other hand, oil

---

[1] *Essai sur la peinture. Œuvres complètes* (Paris, 1876), vol. x, p. 471.

[2] *Frescoes* are wall-paintings, so-called because they must be painted on the wall while the plaster is still fresh, i.e. wet (E. H. Gombrich, *The Story of Art*, London 1970, p. 144). In the Middle Ages painters prepared their own colours by grinding coloured plants or minerals to powder and then using egg as a liquid to bind the powder into a paste. Painting in tempera is painting with this kind of colour-preparation (ibid., p. 172). Hegel mentions other sizes below in dealing with the history of Italian art.

colour not only permits the most delicate and soft fusion and shading of colours, with the result that the transitions are so unnoticeable that we cannot say where a colour begins and ends, but it also acquires, given correct mixing and the right way of applying the paint, a brilliance like that of precious stones, and by means of the difference between opaque pigments and glazes it can produce, in a far higher degree than painting in tempera can, a translucency of different layers of colour.[1]

The third point, finally, which we must mention concerns *sfumato*, the magical effect of colouring. This magic of the pure appearance of colour has in the main only appeared when the substance and spirit of objects has evaporated and what now enters is spirit in the treatment and handling of colour. In general, it may be said that the magic consists in so handling all the colours that what is produced is an inherently objectless play of pure appearance which forms the extreme soaring pinnacle of colouring, a fusion of colours, a shining of reflections upon one another which become so fine, so fleeting, so expressive of the soul that they begin to pass over into the sphere of music. What is relevant here, in connection with *modelling*, is mastery of chiaroscuro where, amongst the Italians, Leonardo da Vinci and, above all, Correggio, were supreme. They proceeded to portray the deepest shadows, but light nevertheless breaks through these again and, by unnoticed transitions, they rise to the clearest light. In this way there is evident a supreme rounding; nowhere is there any harsh or sharp line, transition is everywhere; light and shadow are not effective as purely direct light and shadow, but they both shine into one another, just as an inner force works throughout an external thing. This is true similarly about the *handling* of colour in which the Dutch too were the greatest masters. Owing to this ideality, this fusion, this hither and thither of reflections and sheens of colour, this mutability and fluidity of transitions, there is spread over the whole, with the clarity, the brilliance, the depth, the smooth and luscious lighting of colours, a pure appearance of animation; and this is what constitutes the magic of colouring and is properly due to the spirit of the artist who is the magician.

[1] In oil-painting, layers of opaque colours and glazes (transparent colours) can be superimposed to produce varying effects of translucence. In tempera only opaque colours are available, so that light could not penetrate superimposed layers of colour.

PAINTING

(γγ) This leads to a final point and I will discuss it briefly.

We began with linear perspective and then proceeded to draughtsmanship, and finally colour, and there with (i) light and shade in connection with modelling, (ii) colour itself and in particular with the relative lightness and darkness of colours in their relation to one another, as well as with harmony, atmospheric perspective, carnation, and their magic. Now (iii) we consider the subjective activity of the artist in the production of colouring.

It is commonly supposed that in this matter the artist can proceed in accordance with entirely definite rules. But, first, this is true only in the case of linear perspective as a purely geometrical science, although even here the rule as an abstract rule should not shine through, or otherwise it would destroy what is really pictorial. Secondly, a drawing cannot be entirely reduced to the general laws of perspective, and least of all can colouring. The sense of colour must be a property of the artist, an individual way of looking at and conceiving tones of colour as they really exist; it must as well be an essential feature of reproductive imagination and invention. On account of this personal way in which the artist sees colour-tone in his world and which at the same time he continually produces in his work, the great difference in pictorial colouring is no mere caprice or a favourite way of adopting a colour that does not exist *in rerum natura*, but on the contrary it lies in the nature of the case. For example, Goethe in his *Poetry and Truth*[1] relates the following incident that is relevant here:

After a visit to the Dresden Gallery when 'I went again to my shoemaker's' (where he had a whim to lodge)

to have my lunch, I could hardly believe my eyes, for I thought I was looking at one of Ostade's pictures, so perfect that it should have been hung only in a gallery. The position of the objects, the light and shade, the brownish tint of the whole, everything that we admire in these pictures I saw here in real life. This was the first time that I became aware, in such a high degree, of the gift that I later exercised with clearer consciousness, namely that of seeing nature with the eyes of this or that artist to whose works I had actually given special attention. This faculty has given me much pleasure, but has also increased the desire to indulge vigorously from time to time a talent which nature seemed to have denied me.

[1] His autobiography, Book viii (Eng. tr. London 1932, pp. 278–9).

On the one hand this difference of colouring is prominent above all in the portrayal of human flesh as such, apart altogether from all externally effective modifications of lighting, age, sex, situation, nationality, passion, etc. On the other hand, whether it is a matter of portraying a natural landscape or ordinary daily life out of doors or inside houses, inns, churches, etc., the wealth of objects and colours here leads every painter more or less to his own attempt to treat, reproduce, and invent from his own insight, experience, and imagination this manifold play of pure appearance.

(c) The Artist's Conception, Composition, and Characterization

Up to now we have spoken, in respect of the particular points to be made about painting, first of the subject-matter, and secondly of the material in which the subject-matter can be pictured. Thirdly, and finally, it still remains to us to establish the manner in which the artist, as a painter, is to conceive and execute his subject-matter in conformity with this specific sensuous material. The huge subject thus offered for our consideration may be divided as follows:

First, it is the more general modes of conception which we must distinguish and follow in their advance to an ever richer liveliness.

Secondly, we must concern ourselves with the more specific aspects which within these kinds of treatment affect the strictly pictorial composition, the artistic motifs of the selected situation and grouping.

Thirdly, we will cast a glance at the characterization which proceeds from differences in both the objects portrayed and the conception of them.

(α) The most general modes of pictorial treatment have their origin partly in the subject-matter itself which is to be portrayed, and partly in the course of the evolution of painting which does not at its start work out the whole wealth implicit in a subject but achieves perfect vitality only after various stages and transitions.

(αα) In this matter the first form that painting can adopt shows its descent from sculpture and architecture, because in the general character of its entire mode of conception it is still closely connected with these arts. This may principally be the case when the artist restricts himself to individual figures which he puts before us not in the living distinctness of a situation with all its variety but in their simple independent self-repose. Out of the different ranges of the subject-matter which I have described as appropriate to painting, what are especially suitable in this sphere are religious topics, Christ, individual Apostles, and saints. For such [independent] figures must be able to have sufficient meaning, by themselves in their individuality, to be a whole in themselves, and to be a substantive object of our conscious worship and love. This is the sort of thing that we find principally in the earlier painting, where Christ and the saints are portrayed as isolated, without any specific situation or natural environment. If an environment is added, it chiefly consists in architectural (especially Gothic) decor, as occurs, for instance, frequently in the older Flemish or north German painters. In this relation to architecture where many such figures, the twelve Apostles, etc., are set alongside one another between pillars and arches, painting does not yet proceed to the liveliness of later art, and even the figures themselves still retain the stiff statuesque character of sculpture or they do not yet get beyond a rigid type like that borne in, for example, Byzantine painting. For such individual figures without any environment, or with a purely architectural enclosure, a severer simplicity and cruder decision of colour is suitable after all. For this reason the oldest painters kept, instead of an elaborate natural environment, a uniform background of gold which the colours of the robes must make head against and parry, as it were; and therefore these colours are more decisive, more crude, than is the case in the times of painting's most beautiful development—not to speak of the fact that barbarians in general take their pleasure in simple and vivid colours like red and blue, etc.

Miracle-working pictures belong in the main to this first sort of treatment. A man's attitude to them as to something stupendous is stupid, indifferent to their character as art; and therefore they are not brought nearer to his mind in a friendly way by their possessing human vivification and beauty; and those that are given the greatest religious veneration are, from the point of view of art, the very worst of all.

But if such isolated figures cannot be an object of veneration and interest on the score of their having the independent and perfect wholeness of a complete personality, then their portrayal, carried out on the principle of a sculptural treatment, has no sense. For example, portraits, to those who know the sitter, are interesting because of the man himself and his whole personality. But if the subjects are forgotten or unknown, then their portrayal in an action or a situation with a definite character arouses a totally different interest from the one we could gain from such an entirely simple [statuesque] mode of conception. If great portraits confront us through all the means at the disposal of art, in their full vitality, we already have in this *amplitude* of their existence this advance and emergence from their frames. For example, in Van Dyck's portraits, especially when the position of the sitter is not entirely *en face* but slightly turned away, the frame has looked to me like the door into the world that the sitter is entering. For this reason, if individuals, unlike saints, angels, etc., are not something perfect and complete in themselves and so can be interesting only on account of some specific situation, some single circumstance or action, it is inappropriate to portray them as figures independently of that situation. So, for example, there is the last work of Kügelgen,[1] in Dresden, a picture with four heads, half-length figures of Christ, John the Baptist, John the Evangelist, and the Prodigal Son. When I saw it [in 1824] I found the treatment of Christ and John the Evangelist entirely appropriate. But in the Baptist and above all in the Prodigal Son I did not see at all that independent individuality which might have enabled me to recognize them in a half-length picture. To make them recognizable it is necessary to put these figures into movement and action, or at least to bring them into situations in which they could acquire, in living connection with their external surroundings, the characteristic individuality of a whole and inherently perfect personality. Kügelgen's head of the Prodigal Son does express very finely his grief, deep penitence, and remorse, but the fact that what is meant to be portrayed is the penitence precisely of the *Prodigal* is only indicated by a very tiny herd of swine in the background. Instead of this symbolic hint, we should have seen him in the midst of the herd, or in some other scene of his life. For he has no existence or complete and general personality for us, if he is not to become purely allegorical, except in the familiar series of situations in which he is sketched in the story. He should have been brought before us in concrete and actual life as he is leaving his father's house, or in his misery, repentance, and return. But those swine in the background are not much better than a label with his name on it.

[1] G. von, 1772–1820.

(ββ) Painting in general has to take for its subject-matter the full details of subjective depth of feeling; and therefore less than sculpture can it keep to a situationless self-repose and the treatment of the mere substance of a character. On the contrary, it must surrender this independence and struggle to display its subject-matter in a specific situation, in the variety and difference of characters and shapes in relation to one another and their environment. The advance which enables painting at last to reach its own particular point of view consists in this abandonment of purely traditional and static types, and of the architectural placing and surrounding of figures and the sculptural way of treating them; in this liberation from repose and inactivity; in this search for a living and human expression and a characteristic individuality; and in investing its every subject with detail both in the person himself and in his variegated external surroundings. For this reason painting, more than the other visual arts, is not merely allowed, but a demand must even be made on it, to advance to *dramatic* liveliness, so that the grouping of its figures indicates their activity in a specific situation.

(γγ) Then, thirdly, this entry into the perfect life of the existence and dramatic movement of situations and characters carries with it the ever greater and greater importance placed, in the conception and execution of the work, on individuality and on the complete vitality of the coloured appearance of all objects, because, in painting, the highest degree of liveliness can be expressed only in colour. Yet this magic of pure appearance may ultimately be asserted so preponderantly that the subject of the painting becomes in comparison a matter of indifference. In this way, just precisely as sculpture in the further development of reliefs begins to approach painting, so painting in the pure *sfumato* and magic of its tones of colour and their contrast, and the fusion and play of their harmony, begins to swing over to music.

(β) The next point for consideration now concerns the specific rules which must be followed in the production of paintings owing to the mode of composition required to portray a specific situation, and the more detailed motifs involved, by means of juxtaposing and grouping different figures or natural objects into a whole perfect in itself.

(αα) The chief requirement which we may place at the top is the happy choice of a situation suitable for painting.

Here above all the imagination of the painter has an unlimited field: from the simplest situation consisting of an insignificant object, a bunch of flowers, or a wine-glass with plates, bread, and some fruit round it, up to the richest compositions of great public events, important or state occasions, coronations, battles, and the Last Judgement where God the Father, Christ, the Apostles, the Heavenly Host, the whole of mankind, Heaven, earth, and Hell all meet.

On this matter it may be said, in particular, that what is strictly paintable is clearly distinct from what is sculptural on the one hand, and poetic on the other, for it is poetry alone which can give perfect expression to what is poetic.

The essential difference between a sculptural situation and a paintable one lies, as we have seen already, in the fact that sculpture's principal vocation is to portray both what is independently self-reposing and also an absence of conflict in harmless situations where definiteness is not the decisive thing, and only in reliefs does it begin to advance to grouping, to an epic spread of heroic figures, and to the presentation of actions with more movement and with a collision as their basis; painting on the other hand only begins on its proper task when it departs from the relationless independence of its figures and from lack of definiteness in the situation, in order to be able to enter the living movement of human circumstances, passions, conflicts, and actions, in steady relation to their environment, and, even in the treatment of landscape, to keep to the same definiteness of a specific situation and its most living individuality. For this reason we demanded of painting at the very beginning that it should provide a portrayal of character, the soul, the inner life, not however in such a way that this inner life shall afford a recognition of itself directly in its external figure but only as it develops and expresses what it is through *actions*.

It is chiefly this latter point which brings painting into closer connection with poetry. In this matter both arts have an advantage and a disadvantage as well. Painting, unlike poetry and music, cannot portray the development of a situation, event, or action in a *succession* of changes but can only strive to seize on *one* moment. From this there follows the quite simple reflection that in this one moment the whole of the situation or action must be portrayed in its bloom, and that therefore painting must look for the instant in which what preceded and what followed is concentrated in *one* point. For example, in the case of a battle this would be the moment of victory: the fighting is still visible, but at the same time the outcome is already certain. The painter can therefore pick up a residue of the past which in its withdrawal and vanishing still asserts itself in the present, and at the same time he can hint at the future which must arise as a direct consequence of a specific situation. But I cannot go into further detail here.

Along with this disadvantage in comparison with the poet, the painter has over him the advantage of being able to paint a specific scene in its most perfect individuality because he brings it before our vision in the pure appearance of its actual reality. '*Ut pictura poesis*'[1] is a favourite saying often insisted on especially by theorists, and it is adopted literally and used by descriptive poetry in its sketches of seasons, times of the day, flowers, and landscapes. But the description of such objects and situations in words is on the one hand very dry and tedious, and even so, when it goes into detail, can never be complete; and on the other hand it remains confusing because it must provide in a succession of ideas what painting sets simultaneously before our eyes. The result is that we always forget what preceded and lose the thread, whereas what preceded should always be in essential connection with what follows, because both belong to the same space and have value only in this simultaneity and connection. On the other hand it is precisely in these simultaneous details that the painter can compensate for what escapes him in the matter of the continuing succession of past and future events.

Yet in another connection painting is left behind again by poetry and music, namely in respect of what is lyrical. Poetry can develop feelings and ideas not only as such but also in their change, progress, and intensification. In relation to the concentration of the inner life, this is still more the case with music which has to do with the inner movement of the soul. But, for this purpose, painting has nothing but posture and facial expression, and it misconceives the means at its disposal if it launches out exclusively into what is lyrical. For however far it expresses the inner passion and feeling revealed by the play of countenance and movements of the body, this expression must not be the direct expression of feeling as such but the expression of feeling manifested in a *specific event or action*. The fact that painting portrays the inner life in an

[1] Horace, *Ars poetica*, 361: 'Poetry is like painting.'

external mode has not the abstract meaning of making the inner life visible through face and figure; on the contrary, the external medium in the form of which it expresses that life is precisely the individual situation of an action or the passion in a specific deed, whereby alone the feeling is explained and recognized. If therefore the poetic element in painting is supposed to lie in its expressing inner feeling in posture and facial expression directly without any precise motif and action, this only means thrusting painting back into an abstraction which is exactly what it must be rid of, and requiring it to master the special character of poetry; but if it ventures on an attempt at such mastery, it merely falls into aridity or insipidity.

I emphasize this point here because in the Berlin Art Exhibition last year (1828) several pictures from the so-called Düsseldorf school became very famous. These artists with great intelligence and technical skill have adopted this tendency to pure inwardness, i.e. to what can be presented by poetry alone and exclusively. Their subjects were for the most part poems by Goethe or were drawn from Shakespeare, Ariosto, and Tasso, and were especially made up of the inner feeling of love. Each of the best pictures generally portrayed a pair of lovers, e.g. Romeo and Juliet, Rinaldo and Armida,[1] without any more definite situation, so that the two do nothing and express nothing except being in love with one another and so, having an inclination for one another, regard each other as true lovers and look one another in the eye as true lovers. Naturally in these cases the chief expression is concentrated on the mouth and the eye, and Rinaldo in particular is so placed that he really does not know what to do with his long legs as they lie. They stretch so far as to become wholly meaningless. Sculpture, as we have seen, dispenses with the glance of the eye and the soul, whereas painting seizes on this richly expressive feature. But it must not concentrate on this one point or endeavour to make the chief aim of the expression, without any motive, the fire or the overflowing langour and longing of the eye or the sweet friendliness of the mouth.

Of a similar kind was Hübner's[2] *Fisherman*. This subject was taken from the familiar poem of Goethe which describes with such wonderful depth and grace of feeling the vague longing for the peace, cooling, and purity of the water. The youthful fisherman

---

[1] In Tasso's *Jerusalem Delivered*.   [2] J., 1806–82.

who in the picture is attracted into the water naked has, like the masculine figures in the other pictures, very prosaic features, and if his face were in repose it would not occur to us that he could be capable of deep and fine feelings [like those of the youth in the poem]. In general we cannot say of all these male and female figures that they were endowed with healthy beauty. On the contrary they display nothing but the nervous excitement, languishing, and sickliness of love, and of feeling generally, which we do not want to see reproduced and which we would rather be always spared in life, and still more in art.

In the same category is the manner in which Schadow, the Master of this School, has portrayed Goethe's Mignon.[1] Her character is wholly poetic. What makes her interesting is her past, the harshness of her inner and outer fate, the conflict of an Italian strongly aroused passion in a heart which is not clear to itself about it, which lacks any purpose and decision, and which, a mystery in itself, intentionally mysterious, cannot now help itself. This self-expression, introverted and incoherent, which lets us see only in isolated and disconnected outbursts what passes in her mind is the awfulness of the interest which we have to take in her. Such a wealth of complexity may well be posed to our imagination, but painting cannot do what Schadow intended, namely display it simply by Mignon's figure and expression without any definiteness of situation and action.

On the whole, therefore, we may assert that these pictures that I have named are conceived without any imagination of situations, motives, or expression. For what is implicit in a painting which is to be a genuine work of art is that the whole subject portrayed shall be imaginatively grasped and brought before our vision in figures expressing themselves, displaying their inner life through a succession of feelings, through an action so indicative of them that each and every feature in the work of art appears to have been completely used by imagination for the expression of the chosen subject-matter.

The older Italian painters especially have certainly also, like

---

[1] The fairy-like girl in *Wilhelm Meister's Apprenticeship*. She pines for her Italian home and dies from unrequited love. In the Preface to his translation of this work, Carlyle says: 'The history of Mignon runs like a thread of gold through the tissue of the narrative ... This is poetry in the highest meaning of the word.'

these modern ones, portrayed love-scenes and to some extent have taken their material from poems, but they have understood how to shape it with imagination and healthy cheerfulness. Cupid and Psyche, Cupid with Venus, Pluto's rape of Proserpine, the Rape of the Sabine Women, Hercules with the distaff in the halls of Omphale who has clad herself in his lion's skin, all these are subjects portrayed by the older masters in living and specific situations, in scenes motivated and not merely, without any imagination, as a simple feeling not involved in any action. Love-scenes are borrowed from the Old Testament too. For example, in Dresden there is a picture by Giorgione:[1] Jacob, arriving from a distance, greets Rachel, presses her hand, and kisses her; in the background a few labourers are busy drawing water from a well for their large herd grazing in the valley.[2] Another picture portrays Jacob and Rebecca: Rebecca gives a drink to Abraham's servants whereby she is recognized.[3] Scenes are also taken from Ariosto: e.g. Medoro is writing Angelica's name at the edge of a spring.[4]

When so much has been said in recent times about the poetry in painting, this ought to mean only conceiving a subject with imagination, making feelings explicable by an action, and not proposing to adhere to a feeling in the abstract and expressing it like that. Even poetry, which can express a feeling in its inner depth, spreads itself in ideas, images, and descriptions. For example, if it is proposed to go no further in expressing love than saying 'I love you', and always just repeating 'I love you', this indeed might be agreeable to those gentlemen who have had much to say about the 'poetry of poetry'[5], but it would be the flattest prose. For art in general consists, as regards feeling, in the grasp and enjoyment of feeling by imagination which, in poetry, translates passion into images and gives us satisfaction by their expression whether in lyric, the events of epic, or the actions of drama. In painting, however, mouth, eye, and posture are insufficient for expressing the inner life; only a total and concrete object can have value as the external existence of the inner life.

In a painting, then, the chief thing is the portrayal of a situation,

---

[1] 1478–1510. [2] Genesis 29.
[3] If, as it seems to be, this is a reference to Genesis 24, then 'Jacob' is an error for 'Isaac'. [4] In *Orlando Furioso*, canto xxi. 36.
[5] F. von Schlegel, and others of his school, thought that a man's ordinary self may achieve poetry, but only his transcendental self (a conception they drew from the philosophy of Fichte) could achieve the 'poetry of poetry'.

the scene of an action. In this connection the first law is intelligibility. Here religious subjects have the great advantage that everyone knows them. The Annunciation by the angel, the Adoration of the Shepherds or the Three Kings, the repose during the Flight into Egypt, the Crucifixion, the Entombment, the Resurrection, as well as the legends of the saints, were not strange to the public for which the canvases were painted, even if nowadays the stories of the martyrs are further from our ken. For example, what was usually portrayed for a church was the story of a patron-saint, either of the church or of the town. Therefore it was not by their choice that the painters themselves kept to such subjects, but the subjects were needed for altars, chapels, religious houses, etc., with the result that the very place of exhibition contributed to the intelligibility of the picture. This is in a way necessary because painting lacks the language, words, and names which poetry can call in aid, quite apart from its other means of designation. For example, in a royal castle, in a town-hall, in a House of Parliament, scenes of great events, important features in the history of this state, this town, this House, have their place and are known everywhere in the locality for which the pictures are destined. For a royal castle in this country, for instance, no one would readily select a subject drawn from English or Chinese history or from the life of King Mithridates. It is different in picture galleries where there is hung together everything that has been owned or could be bought up in the way of good works of art, and in that case it is true that the pictures lose their individual association with a specific place and the intelligibility afforded by that association. The same is the case in private houses: a private individual takes what he can get or collects as a gallery does, and besides he has his other preferences and whims.

Far below historical subjects in intelligibility are the so-called allegorical presentations which once had a considerable vogue and, apart from the fact that they must usually lack inner life and individuality of figure, they become vague, uninteresting, and cold. On the contrary, landscapes and situations drawn from daily human life are clear in what they are meant to indicate, and in individuality, dramatic variety, movement, and richness of detail they also afford an extremely favourable scope for invention and execution.

(ββ) It may be the painter's business to make a specific situation *intelligible*. To make it *recognizable* needs more than the mere place where the picture hangs and general acquaintance with its subject. For on the whole these are only external circumstances with little effect on the picture as such. The chief point of real importance consists, on the contrary, in the painter's having artistic sense and spirit enough to bring out and, with a wealth of invention, to give shape to the different motives involved in the specific situation. Every action in which the inner life is objectified has immediate external characteristics, visible consequences, and relations which, by being in fact effects of the inner life, betray and mirror feeling, and therefore they can be used in the happiest way for the purpose of making the subject of the picture intelligible and individual. For example, it is a familiar and often repeated reproach against Raphael's Transfiguration that it falls apart into two actions entirely devoid of any connection with one another, and in fact this is true if the picture is considered *externally*: above on the hill we see the Transfiguration, below is the scene with the child possessed of an unclean spirit. But if we look at the *spirit* of the composition, a supreme connection is not to be missed. For, on the one hand, Christ's visible Transfiguration is precisely his actual elevation above the earth, and his departure from the Disciples, and this must be made visible too as a separation and a departure; on the other hand, the sublimity of Christ is here especially transfigured in an actual simple case, namely in the fact that the Disciples could not heal the possessed child without the help of the Lord. Thus here the double action is motivated throughout and the connection is displayed within and without in the fact that one Disciple expressly points to Christ who has departed from them, and thereby he hints at the true destiny of the Son of God to be at the same time on earth, so that the saying will be true: Where two or three are gathered in my name, there am I in the midst of them.[1]

To cite another example, Goethe once prescribed as a subject for a prize competition the portrayal of Achilles in girl's clothes being discovered by Odysseus.[2] In one sketch Achilles looks at the helmet of the hero in arms, his heart glows at the sight and, following on his inner agitation, he breaks the pearl necklace he

---

[1] Matthew 18: 20. Luke 9: 28–42.
[2] There are different versions in ancient authors of the way that Odysseus penetrated the disguise (note 1 on p. 760 above). See Sir James Frazer's notes to Apollodorus III. xiii. 8.

is wearing on his neck; a boy looks for the pearls and picks them up from the ground. These are motives of a happy kind.

Moreover, the artist has spaces more or less large to fill: he needs landscape as a background, lighting, architectural surroundings, incidental figures, furnishings, etc. This whole visible mass of material he must, so far as is feasible, use for presenting the motives implicit in the situation, and so he must be able to bring what is external into relation with these motives so that it no longer remains insignificant. For example, two princes or patriarchs shake hands: if this is to be a sign of peace or setting the seal on a treaty, then the appropriate environment for the pact is made up of soldiers, weapons, and the like, or preparations for a sacrifice to consecrate the oath. If on the other hand the same persons happen to meet on a journey and shake hands to say good-day or au revoir, then totally different motifs are necessary. To invent such things in such a way that significance emerges for the scene, and individualization for the entire presentation, is above all the thing to which in this respect the spiritual and artistic sense of the painter has to address itself. For this reason, after all, many artists have proceeded to introduce symbolical features into the surroundings and the action. For example, in a picture of the Adoration of the Three Kings we often see Christ lying in a crib under a dilapidated roof with old walls in decay and, round about, the ruins of an ancient building, while in the background is the beginning of a cathedral. This crumbling masonry and the rising cathedral have a bearing on the destruction of heathenism by the Christian Church. In a similar way, especially in the school of van Eyck,[1] in pictures of the Annunciation, Mary often has at her side flowering lilies without anthers, and these thus hint at the virginity of the Mother of God.

(γγ) Now, thirdly, owing to the principle of the inner and outer variety within which painting has to bring out the specific character of situations, occurrences, conflicts, and actions, it has to proceed to manifold differences and oppositions in its subjects, whether these be natural objects or human figures; and at the same time there is imposed on it the task of articulating this variety of separate parts, and bringing them together into an harmonious whole. The result is that one of the most important demands on it is the necessity of placing and grouping its figures artistically. Granted the great

---

[1] The lilies appear in Italian painting a century earlier.

mass of separate principles and rules that are applicable here, the most general thing that can be said about them can only be formal, and I will cite briefly only a few chief points.

The primary sort of arrangement remains still entirely architectonic, i.e. an homogeneous juxtaposition of the figures or a regular opposition and symmetrical conjunction both of the figures themselves and also of their bearing and movements. Of this kind it is especially the pyramidal form of the group which is the chief favourite. In a Crucifixion, for instance, the pyramid is formed as it were automatically, because Christ hangs on the Cross above and then the Disciples, Mary, or saints stand at the sides. The same is the case in Madonna pictures where Mary with the child sits on a raised throne and below her at both sides has Apostles, martyrs, etc. as her worshippers. In the Sistine Madonna too this sort of grouping is still retained as decisive. In general this shape is soothing for the eye, because by its apex the pyramid grips together what otherwise would be separated and dispersed and gives to the group an external unity.

Within such a general and rather abstract symmetrical arrangement, there can be, in particulars and details, great liveliness and individuality of placing, expression, and movement. By using together all the means that his art possesses, the painter has several planes enabling him to give greater emphasis to the chief figures than to the others, and moreover for the same purpose he has lighting and colour at his command. Thus it is obvious how, with this in view, he will place his group: the chief figures will not be put at the side nor will incidental things be given a place where they will attract the maximum of attention. Similarly he will cast the most brilliant light on the things constituting the main subject of the picture; he will not put them in the shade or use the most important colours to put subsidiary figures in the clearest light.

Given a less symmetrical and therefore more lively grouping, the painter must take special care not to press the figures against one another or, as we sometimes see in pictures, so confuse them that we first have to seek out the limbs and have trouble in distinguishing which legs belong to which head or how the different arms, hands, borders of clothes, weapons, etc., are to be allotted. On the contrary, in the case of larger canvases the best thing will be to keep the whole in separate and clearly surveyable parts, but not to isolate them from one another, or disperse them, altogether.

This is especially so in the case of scenes and situations which are already by their very nature a dispersed medley, as for instance the collection of manna in the wilderness, annual fairs, and others of the same kind.

On this occasion I will limit myself to these general suggestions on this subject.

(γ) After having dealt, first, with the general sorts of pictorial treatment, and, *secondly*, with composition in relation to the choice of situations, ferretting out motifs, and grouping, I must, in the *third* place, add something about the mode of characterization by which painting is distinguished from sculpture and its ideal plasticity.

(αα) As has been said on various occasions already, free scope is allowed in painting to the mental and physical particularity of personality which on this account does not need to be that beauty of the individual which is elevated into being an ideal beauty, but on the contrary may proceed to that specialization whereby there first emerges what in our modern sense is called *characteristic*. In this connection, what is characteristic has commonly been made the distinguishing mark of modern art as opposed to that of antiquity; and, in the meaning we propose to give to the word 'characteristic' here, this notion of course has its justification. Measured by modern standards, Zeus, Apollo, Diana, etc., are strictly not characters at all, although we must admire them as these eternal, lofty, plastic, and ideal individuals. In Homer's Achilles, in Agamemnon and Clytemnestra in Aeschylus, in Odysseus, Antigone, Ismene, etc., in Sophocles (who makes them expose their inner life by their words and deeds), there does enter a more specific individualization on which these figures are founded as on something belonging to their own essence and in which they maintain themselves. Thus, it is true, we do find characters portrayed in antiquity, if we like to call those just mentioned 'characters'. But in Agamemnon, Ajax, Odysseus, etc., the individuality always remains of a universal kind, the character of a prince, of an insane mood, of cunning, in only a rather abstract, specific way; the individual element is combined and closely interlaced with the universal, and the character is raised to an *ideal* individuality. Painting, on the other hand, does not confine particularity of character to that ideal but develops precisely the whole variety of even accidental particulars, so that now we see confronting us not those plastic ideals of gods and men but particular persons in all the accidents of their particular character. Therefore the physical perfection of the figure and the complete adaptation of the mentality to its healthy and free existence—in a word, what we called the ideal beauty of sculpture—is something that we should not require in painting to the same extent, nor may we make it the chief thing, because what is central now is the deep feeling of the soul and its living subjective character. This more ideal or subjective region is not so deeply penetrated by the realm of nature:[1] the piety of the heart, the religion of the mind, can dwell even in the external form of a body which, considered in itself, is ugly, just as a moral disposition and activity can dwell in the Silenus features of Socrates. Of course for the expression of spiritual beauty the artist will avoid what is absolutely ugly in external forms, or he can subdue and transfigure it through the power of the soul that breaks through it, but nevertheless he cannot entirely dispense with the ugly. For the subject-matter of painting, described at length above, has in it an aspect to which what strictly corresponds consists of the abnormal and of misshapen human figures and faces. This aspect is the sphere of the bad and the evil which comes into appearance in religious subjects especially in the soldiers who play their part in the Passion story, or in the devils and sinners in Hell. Michelangelo especially could paint devils who, in their fantastic shape, exceed the proportions of human figures and yet at the same time still remain human.

But however far the individuals portrayed in painting must be in themselves a complete ensemble of particular characteristics, this is not at all to say that there cannot appear in them something analogous to what constitutes the plastic ideal. In religious paintings the chief thing is the fundamental trait of pure love, especially in Mary whose whole being lies in this love, but also in the women who accompany Christ and, amongst the Disciples, John, the loving Disciple. But with the expression of this there can also be closely associated the sensuous beauty of the figures, as in Raphael's pictures for example; only there may not be any

[1] In Greek art there is a sort of natural harmony between beauty of form and the mentality expressed within it. We have a plastic figure which is universal rather than a real individual. Individuality implies an emphasis on a man's own convictions, and their spiritual character can persist even in an external expression which is ugly. The natural ugliness does not dominate or penetrate or interfere with moral conviction which can find expression even in an ugly face.

attempt to assert this beauty as mere beauty of form; on the contrary, it must be spiritually animated and transfigured by the inmost soul of the expression, and this spiritual inmost depth of feeling must be made to evince itself as the real aim and subject of the painting. In pictures of the childhood of Christ and John the Baptist, beauty has free scope too. In the case of the other figures, Apostles, saints, Disciples, sages of antiquity, etc., that expression of intensified depth of feeling is as it were rather a matter of specific and more fleeting situations. This apart, these men appear as more independent, as characters present in the world, equipped with the power and constancy of courage, faith, and action, so that here the fundamental trait, despite all differences of character, is serious and dignified manliness. These are not ideal divinities but entirely human ideals, not simply men as they should be, but ideal men as they actually live and exist, men lacking neither particularity of character nor a connection between particularity and that universal which fills their individual lives. Figures of this kind have been transmitted to us by Michelangelo and Raphael, and by Leonardo da Vinci in his famous Last Supper, and they possess a dignity, grandeur, and nobility totally different from that in the figures of other painters. This is the point at which painting meets antiquity on the same ground, without abandoning the character of its own sphere.

(ββ) Now since among the visual arts painting is the one which most of all allows to the particular figure and its special character the right to emerge independently, the transition to portraiture proper lies especially near to its nature. It would therefore be very wrong to condemn portrait painting as incompatible with the lofty aim of art. Who would want to dispense with the huge number of excellent portraits by the great masters? Who is not curious, apart altogether from the artistic worth of such pictures, to have not merely an idea of famous individuals, their spirit and their deeds, but to have brought before him this idea completely portrayed in specific detail for contemplation? After all, the greatest, most highly placed man was or is an actual individual, and this individuality, spirituality in its most actual particularization and life, we want to bring before our vision. Yet apart from such aims which fall outside art, it may in a certain sense be maintained that the advances made by painting from its unsuccessful attempts onwards have consisted precisely in its working its way to the portrait. At first it was the sense of piety and worship which produced the *inner* life; higher art animated this sense by adding to it truth of expression and particular existence, and, with this deeper entry into external appearance, the inner life was deepened also, and it was with this that art had to do.

Yet, even so, if the portrait is to be a genuine work of art, it must, as has been mentioned already, have stamped on it the unity of the spiritual personality, and the spiritual character must be emphasized and made predominant. The principal contribution to this end is made by all parts of the face, and the painter's keen sense of physiognomy enables him to bring the special character of the individual before our eyes by treating and emphasizing precisely those traits and parts in which this spiritual special character is expressed most clearly, pregnantly, and vividly. In this respect a portrait may be very faithful to nature and most industriously executed, and yet be spiritless, whereas a sketch thrown off by a master hand with a few strokes may have infinitely more life and be strikingly true. But in that case such a sketch must present in the really significant and expressive strokes the character's simple but entire fundamental image which less spiritual execution and more fidelity to nature glosses over and makes invisible. In this matter the most advisable course will once again be to keep to the happy mean between such sketching and a faithful imitation of nature. One example of this kind is afforded by Titian's masterly portraits. They meet us so individually and they give us a conception of spiritual vitality unlike what a face actually confronting us gives. This is like what happens with a description of great deeds and events provided by a truly artistic historian who sketches for us a picture that is far higher and truer than any we could gain by ourselves as eye-witnesses. Reality is overburdened with appearance as such, with accidental and incidental things, so that often we cannot see the wood for the trees and often the greatest matter slips past us like an ordinary daily occurrence. It is their indwelling sense and spirit which alone makes events into great actions, and these are given to us by a genuinely historical portrayal which does not accept what is purely external and reveals only that in which the inner spirit is vividly unfolded. In this way too the painter must set before us by means of his art the spiritual sense and character of his subject. If this is done with perfect success, then we can say that such a portrait hits the mark better as it were, is more like the individual than the actual individual himself.

Portraits like this have been painted by Albrecht Dürer too. With few means at his disposal he has emphasized the features so simply, definitely, and splendidly that we think we have before us the entirety of a spiritual life. The longer one looks at such a picture, the more deeply one immerses oneself in it, all the more does one see emerging from it. It remains like a clear-cut, spiritually full sketch which contains the character perfectly, and it executes everything else in colours and forms only to make the picture more intelligible, clearer, more of an ensemble, but without entering, like nature, into the detail of life's mere poverty. For example, in a landscape too, nature paints the most complete outline and colouring of every leaf, bough, blade of grass, etc., but a landscape painting may not propose to imitate nature in this comprehensiveness but should present details only in so far as they conform to the mood which the whole expresses; while, even if it must remain characteristic and individual in essentials, it may not make a portrait of the details, faithful in itself to nature in every little fibre and indentation, etc.

In the human face *nature's* drawing is the bone structure or the hard parts around which the softer ones are laid, developed into a variety of accidental detail; but however important those hard parts are for the character drawing of *portraiture*, it consists in other fixed traits, i.e. the countenance transformed by the spirit. In this sense we may say of a portrait that it not only may but must flatter, because it renounces what belongs to the mere chance of nature and accepts only what makes a contribution to characterizing the individual himself in his most personal inmost being. Nowadays it is the fashion, with a view to making them friendly, to give to all faces a smiling air; this is very hazardous and difficult to keep within limits. Charming it may be, but the mere polite friendliness of social intercourse is not a fundamental trait of any character, and in the hands of many painters it all too easily lapses into mawkish insipidity.

(γγ) Yet however portrait-like its procedure may be in all its presentations, painting must still always make individual features, figures, postures, groupings, and kinds of colouring conform to the specific situation in which it places its figures and natural objects with a view to expressing some subject-matter or other.

For it is this subject-matter in this situation which is to be portrayed.

I will touch briefly on only one principal point out of the infinitely varied detail which could come under consideration here. Either the situation is by its nature transient and the feeling expressed in it is momentary, so that one and the same individual could express many other similar feelings or even opposite ones, or alternatively, the situation and the feeling pervade the whole soul of the character who therefore manifests in these the fulness of his inmost nature. These latter situations are the true decisive moments for characterization. In the Madonna's situations which I mentioned above there is nothing which does not belong to the Mother of God, to the whole range of her soul and character, no matter how distinctly she may also be envisaged as an individual complete in herself. Here she must also be so characterized that it is clear that she is nothing other than what she can express in this specific situation. So the greatest masters have painted the Madonna in such eternal situations and crises of maternity. Other masters have given to her character an expression of a different life in the world and another sort of existence. This latter expression can be very beautiful and alive, but the same figure, the same traits, the like expression would nevertheless be suitable for other interests and circumstances of *conjugal* love etc., and therefore we are inclined to look at such a figure from a point of view different from that appropriate to a Madonna, whereas in supreme pictures we cannot find room for any thought except the one which the situation is meant to arouse. This is the reason why Correggio's Mary Magdalene in Dresden seems to me to be so worthy of admiration and it will ever be admired. She is the repentant sinner, yet we see in her that sin is not the serious thing for her, but that from the start she was noble and cannot have been capable of bad passions and actions. So her profound but reserved withdrawal into herself is but a return to herself and this is no momentary situation but her whole nature. In the whole presentation, in the figure, facial traits, dress, pose, surroundings, etc., the artist has therefore left no trace of reflection on one of the circumstances which could hint back to sin and guilt; she is unconscious of those times, absorbed only in her present situation, and this faith, this sensitiveness, this absorption seems to be her entire and real character.

Such perfect accord between inner and outer, between specific character and its situation, has been reached above all by the Italians in the most beautiful way. In Kügelgen's half-length picture of the Prodigal Son, mentioned above, on the other hand, the remorse of his repentance and his grief is indeed expressed vividly, but the artist has not achieved the unity of the whole character, which the Prodigal would have had outside this situation, with the situation itself in which he is portrayed to us. If we study his features quietly, they give us only the face of any man whom we might meet on the bridge at Dresden. In the case of a genuine correspondence between a character and the expression of a concrete situation, that sort of thing would never occur to us. After all, in genuine genre-painting the liveliness, even in the case of the most fleeting moments, is too great to leave any room for the idea that these figures would ever adopt a different position, other features, and a changed expression.

These are the chief points relative to the subject-matter and its artistic treatment in the sensuous material of painting, namely canvas and colour.

3. *Historical Development of Painting*

But, thirdly, we cannot stop, as we have done up to now, at a purely general indication and discussion of the subject-matter appropriate to painting and the mode of configuration arising from the principle of painting. For, since this art rests entirely on the individuality of characters and their situation, on the figure and its position, colouring, etc., we must have before us and discuss the actual reality of its particular productions. The study of painting is only perfect when you know the pictures themselves in which the points made above have their validity and when you can enjoy and judge them.[1] This is the case with every art, but, amongst the arts so far considered, with painting most of all. For architecture and sculpture you can make do, at first, with copies, descriptions, and casts, because in these arts the range of the subject-matter is more restricted, the forms and means of representation are less plentiful and varied, and their particular specific characteristics are simpler and more decisive. Painting demands a sight of the individual works of art themselves; in its case especially mere descriptions

---

[1] A reprint of Hegel's lectures on painting with coloured illustrations is much to be desired.

are inadequate, however often you have to content yourself with them. Owing to the infinite variety of ways in which painting is deployed and aspects of which occur separately in particular works, these works appear at first sight as only a variously coloured medley which, neither organized nor classified for examination, makes even the special character of individual paintings scarcely visible. For example, unless we bring with us in the case of each picture a knowledge of the country, period, and school to which it belongs and of the master who painted it, most galleries seem to be a senseless confusion out of which we cannot find our way. Thus the greatest aid to study and intelligent enjoyment is an *historical* arrangement. Such a collection, historically ordered, unique and invaluable of its kind, we shall soon have an opportunity to admire in the picture gallery of the Royal Museum constructed here in Berlin.[1] In this collection there will be clearly recognizable not only the external history of painting, i.e. the development of technique, but the essential progress of the inner history of painting, i.e. its different schools and subjects, as well as the conception of these and their mode of treatment. It is only such a living spectacle that can give us an idea of painting's beginning in traditional and static types, of its becoming more living, of its search for expression and individual character, of its liberation from the inactive and reposeful existence of the figures, of the progress to dramatically moved action and grouping and the full magic of colouring, as well as of the difference of the schools, some of which treat the same subjects in their own peculiar way, while others are marked out from one another by the difference of the subject-matter which they adopt.

The historical development of painting is of great importance not only for its ordinary study but also for its philosophical treatment and exposition. The subject-matter that I indicated, the development of the material, the principal different features of the treatment, all these things acquire their concrete existence in a factually consistent sequence and variety only in painting's history, and I must cast a glance at this and emphasize its most prominent features.

In general terms, the essence of painting's progress is this: a start is made with *religious* subjects, still *typically* treated, arranged

[1] Hotho adds in a note that this statement was made in a lecture on 17 February 1829. The gallery was opened on 3 August 1830.

PAINTING 871

simply and architectonically with elementary colouring. Next there enter more and more into the religious situations the present, the individual, the living beauty of the figures, depth of inner feeling, alluring and magical colouring, until painting turns towards the world; it takes possession of nature, the everyday experiences of human life, or historically important national events, whether past or present, portraits and the like, all down to the tiniest and most insignificant detail, and it does this with the same love that had been lavished on the ideal content of religion. And in this sphere above all it attains not only the supreme perfection of painting but also the greatest liveliness of conception and the greatest individuality in the mode of execution. This progress can be followed in sharpest outline in the general course of Byzantine, Italian, Flemish, and German painting,[1] and after characterizing these briefly we will, at the end, make the transition to music.

(a) Byzantine Painting

The Greeks had always kept exercising the art of painting to a certain extent, and the Greek examples were beneficial for this better technique of Byzantine painting as well as for the portrayal of postures, robes, etc. On the other hand, this art entirely forsook nature and life; in facial expressions it remained traditional, in figures and modes of expression typical and stiff, in the arrangement more or less architectonic: the natural environment and the background of landscape were missing, the modelling by light and shade, clear and dark, and their fusion, like perspective and the art of live grouping, attained no development at all or only a very trifling one. Given an adherence to one and the same type already settled earlier, independent artistic production had very little scope. The art of painting and mosaic often sank into a mere craft and therefore became more lifeless and spiritless, even if these craftsmen, like the workers who made Greek vases, had before them excellent models which they could follow in postures, folds of drapery, etc.

[1] The omission of Spain was not unnatural in Hegel's lifetime. The omission of England may seem less excusable until we reflect that in what he says of modern (i.e. post-Byzantine) painting, Hegel relies almost entirely, and not improperly, on what he had seen for himself in Paris, the Low Countries, Austria, and Germany (where, unlike Italian works, English paintings may not have been on view at his date).

A similar type of painting covered the ravaged West also with its sombre art and spread to Italy above all. Here, however, even if in weak beginnings at first, there already appeared in early times the urge to go beyond completely finished forms and ways of expression and to advance towards a higher, even if originally crude, development, whereas in the Byzantine pictures, as von Rumohr (op. cit. i, p. 279) says of the Greek Madonnas and pictures of Christ, 'we see even in the most favourable examples that they had their direct origin in mummies and that artistic development had been renounced in advance'. Confronted by a similar type of art, the Italians, in contrast to the Byzantines, strove for a more spiritual treatment of Christian subjects even before the times of their independent artistic development in painting. So, for example, the scholar just mentioned cites (i, p. 280) as a remarkable proof of this difference the manner in which the Byzantine Greeks and the Italians present the body of Christ on pictures of the Crucifixion. 'The Greeks', he says,

accustomed to the sight of gruesome physical punishments, pictured the Saviour on the Cross hanging down with the whole weight of his body, the lower part swollen, knees slackened and bent to the left, the bowed head struggling with the agony of a gruesome death. Thus what they had in view as their subject was physical suffering as such. On the other hand, in the older Italian memorials (where we must not overlook the fact that the Virgin with the Child, and the Crucified [Christ] too are portrayed extremely seldom) the Italians were accustomed to give a comforting appearance to the face of the Saviour on the Cross, and so, as it seems, followed the idea of the victory of the spirit and not, as the Byzantines did, the succumbing of the body. This undeniably nobler sort of treatment came early to light in the far more favourable climate of the West.

This suggestion may suffice for this subject here.

(b) *Italian Painting*

But in the freer development of Italian painting we have to look for a different character of this art. Apart from the religious subject-matter of the Old and the New Testament and the life-stories of martyrs and saints, Italian painting takes its other subjects for the most part from Greek mythology, seldom from events in national history, or, portraits excepted, from the present day and contemporary life, and equally seldom, and only in late and isolated pictures, from natural landscapes. But what above all it introduces for the treatment and artistic elaboration of the religious sphere is the *living* actuality of the spiritual and corporeal existence into which now all the figures are materialized and animated. The fundamental principle for this life is, on the side of the spirit, that natural serenity, on the side of the body, that beautiful correspondence with the visible form which in itself, as beautiful form, proclaims innocence, cheerfulness, virginity, natural grace of disposition, nobility, imagination, and a richly loving soul. Now if there is added to this natural endowment the elevation and adornment of the inner life by the deep feeling of religion, by that spiritual trait of a more profound piety which soulfully animates the originally more decided assurance and complete acceptance of existence in this sphere of salvation, then we have before us an original harmony between a figure and its expression which, when it reaches perfection, gives us a vivid reminder, in this sphere of romantic and Christian art, of the pure ideal of art.

It is true that even within such a new harmony the deep feeling of the heart must preponderate, but the inner feeling is a happier and purer heaven of the soul, the way to which, by reversion from the sensuous and the finite and by return to God, still remains easy and unburdensome,[1] even if it lies through immersion in the deep grief of repentance and death; for the grief is concentrated in the region of the soul, ideas, and faith, without rising to the field of powerful desires, refractory barbarism, harsh self-seeking and sin, and without fighting these enemies of bliss in order to gain a hard-won victory. It is a transition remaining ideal, a grief that in its suffering is more ecstatic than harmful, a rather abstract, richly soulful suffering which proceeds in the inner life; it does not reveal physical agony, nor are the traits of stubbornness, crudity, and ruggedness, or those of trivial and vulgar people, visible in the character of the faces and bodily forms, for, if they were, a persistent battle would be needed before they could be susceptible of an expression of piety and religious feeling. This more peaceful deep feeling of the soul and more original adaptation of the forms to this inner life constitutes the attractive clarity and unclouded enjoyment which the truly beautiful works of Italian painting must give us. Just as we say of instrumental music that there is

[1] Matthew 11: 30. 'My yoke is easy, and my burden is light.'

timbre and song in it, so here the pure song of the soul, a penetrating melody, sings over the whole figure and all its forms. And just as in Italian music and the notes of its song, when voices ring out in their purity without any associated screeching, it is the pleasure of the voice itself which resounds in every part and modulation of the sound and the melody, so such self-enjoyment of the loving soul is the keynote of Italian painting too.

It is the same depth of feeling, clarity, and freedom that we find again in the great Italian poets. The skilful echo of rhymes in terza-rima, canzone, sonnets, and stanzas, this sound which not only satisfies the need for uniformity in a single repetition but preserves uniformity in a triple one, is a free melodious sound which flows along for its own sake, for the sake of its own enjoyment. The like freedom is shown in the spiritual subject-matter. In Petrarch's sonnets, sestets, canzone, it is not for the actual possession of its object that the longing of the heart struggles; there is no thought or feeling seriously concerned with the actual object or the thing at issue or expressing a need for possession; on the contrary, the expression itself is the satisfaction. It is the self-enjoyment of love which seeks its happiness in its mourning, its laments, descriptions, memories, and fancies; it is a longing satisfied as longing, and with the picture and the spirit of the loved one it is already in full possession of the soul with which it longs to be at one. Dante too, led by his master, Virgil, through Hell and Purgatory, sees the most frightful horrors, he is uneasy and is often in floods of tears, but he strides on, tranquil and consoled, without fear and anxiety, without the ill-humour and exasperation that says 'things should not be thus'. Indeed even his damned souls in Hell still have the bliss of eternity—*io eterno duro*[1] stands over the gate of Hell—they are what they are, without repentance or desire; they say nothing of their torments—these affect neither us nor them, as it were, at all, for they endure for ever—they keep in mind only their disposition and deeds, firm and constant to themselves in their same interests, without lamentation and longing.

When you have grasped this trait of blissful independence and freedom of soul in love, you understand the character of Italy's greatest painters. In this freedom they are masters of the details of expression and situation; on the wings of this inner freedom they have at their command figure, beauty, and colour; since they have

---

[1] *Inferno*, canto iii, 8. 'Eternal I endure.'

their feet entirely on the ground and often give us, or seem to give us, portraits, the pictures they produce in the most exact portrayal of reality and character are pictures of another sun, another spring; they are roses blossoming at the same time in heaven. So in beauty itself their concern is not with beauty of form alone, not with that sensuous unity of the soul with its body which is effused over the sensuous corporeal forms, but instead with this trait of love and reconciliation in each figure, form, and individuality of character. It is the butterfly, the Psyche, which in the sunlight of its heaven hovers even over withered flowers.[1] Only through this rich, free, perfect beauty were the Italians enabled to produce the ideals of antiquity amid those of the modern world.

Yet such a level of perfection Italian painting did not achieve all at once from the beginning; on the contrary, before it could reach it, it first travelled the whole length of a long road. But purely innocent piety, the magnificent artistic sense of the whole conception, naïve beauty of form, and deep feeling of soul are often most strikingly present in the old Italian masters, despite all imperfection in the development of technique. In the eighteenth century, however, the older masters were little valued but were rejected as being clumsy, dry, and paltry. Only in recent times have they been rescued from oblivion by scholars and artists; but now they have been admired and imitated with a preference that is excessive, that has induced people to deny a further development in the mode of treatment and portrayal, and that therefore was bound to lead to the opposite wrong road.

In connection with the details of the chief phases in the history of the development of Italian painting up to the stage of its perfection, I will briefly emphasize only the following points that are of importance in the characterization of the most essential aspects of painting and its manner of expression.

(α) After earlier crudity and barbarity the Italians departed with a new impetus from the mainly mechanical type propagated by the Byzantines. But the range of subjects portrayed was not great and the chief thing remained severe dignity, solemnity, and religious majesty. As is testified by von Rumohr (op. cit. ii, p. 4), an important connoisseur of these earlier epochs, Duccio of Siena and

---

[1] In Greek mythology Cupid is an emblem of the heart, as Psyche is of the soul. She was represented with the wings of a butterfly, itself another symbol of the soul.

Cimabue of Florence[1] already tried to adopt and as far as possible to rejuvenate in their own spirit the miserable relics of the classical draughtsmanship, founded on perspective and anatomy, which, mechanically imitated, had been accepted in old Christian works of art, especially by the later Byzantine painting. They 'sensed the value of such designs but they strove to soften the crudity of their ossification because they compared these half-understood traits with life—or so we may conjecture or assume from seeing their productions'. These are only the first beginnings of the art, lying between what was typical and stiff and what had life and full individual expression.

(β) But the second step consisted in emancipation from those late Byzantine models, in entry to humanity and individuality in both the whole conception and execution, and in the developed and deeper adaptation of human characters and forms to the religious material which was to be expressed.

(αα) Here the first thing to mention is the great influence exercised by Giotto[2] and his pupils. Giotto changed the former way of preparing colours, just as he altered the mode of treatment and the aim of the composition. The Byzantines, as chemical investigations have shown, probably used wax either as a means of binding colour or as a varnish, and from this there resulted 'the yellowish-green, darkish tone which cannot always be explained as a result of lamp-light' (op. cit. i, p. 312). This viscous binding-material of the Byzantine painters Giotto entirely rejected and on this account went over to the grinding of colours with the clarified sap of young plant-shoots, unripe figs, and other less oily sizes which, possibly, had been used by Italian painters in the earlier Middle Ages before they turned again to the stricter imitation of the Byzantines (ibid. ii, p. 312). These binding-materials had no darkening influence on the colours, but left them brilliant and clear. More important, however, is the change introduced by Giotto into Italian painting by the choice of subjects and the manner of their portrayal. Ghiberti,[3] as long ago as that, praised Giotto for abandoning the crude manner of the Byzantine Greeks and for introducing nature and grace without exceeding the bounds of proportion (ibid. ii, p. 42). And Boccaccio too (*Decameron*, Sixth Day, fifth story) says of him that 'nature produces nothing

---

[1] 1255–1319 and *c.* 1240–1302.   [2] *c.* 1266–1327.
[3] L., 1378–1455, sculptor and art-historian.

which Giotto cannot imitate to the point of deception'. In Byzantine painting we can scarcely descry a trace of a vision of nature; it was only Giotto who directed his attention outwards to the present and real world and compared the forms and sentiments, which he undertook to portray, with life itself as it moved around him. With this drift outwards there is connected the fact that at Giotto's time not only did morals become freer and life more cheerful as a general rule, but nearer to his date lay the veneration of many new saints.[1] These were especially selected as subjects of his art by Giotto in view of the direction of his attention to the actual present, with the result that now once again the subject-matter itself demanded the naturalness of the way the body appeared, and also the portrayal of specific characters, actions, passions, situations, postures, and movements. But what was relatively lost in Giotto's attempts was that splendid holy seriousness which had been the basis of the previous stage of art. The world wins a place and development, as after all, Giotto, true to the sense of his age, gave a place to the burlesque as well as to the pathetic, so that von Rumohr justly says (ibid. ii, p. 73) 'in these circumstances I cannot understand how some people who have given the whole strength of their attention to the subject, praise the aim and achievement of Giotto as the most sublime thing in modern art'. To have given us once again the right point of view for estimating Giotto is the great merit of this profound scholar who also drew attention to the fact that Giotto, while aiming at humanizing his figures and at naturalness, still always remained on the whole at a lower stage of painting's development.

(ββ) Within this mode of conception awakened by Giotto Italian painting developed further. The typical portrayal of Christ, the Apostles, and the more important events reported in the Gospels, were put more and more into the background; but on the other side, the range of subjects is extended (ibid. ii, p. 213)

because all hands were busy painting the transition of modern saints into life: their previous worldliness, the sudden awakening of their consciousness of sanctity, their entry into the life of piety and asceticism, the miracles they wrought in life and especially after their death, all these enter into the portrayal where (as is implied by the external conditions of art) the expression of the feeling of the living prevails over an indication of their invisible power of miracle-working.

[1] e.g. St. Francis of Assisi (c. 1182–1226), canonized in 1228.

Along with this, however, the events in the Passion story of Christ are not neglected. In particular, the birth and upbringing of Christ, and the Madonna and the Child, rise to being favourite subjects and were invested rather with more living family affection, with tenderness and intimacy, with something human and rich in feeling, while too

in themes taken from the Passion story, what is emphasized is no longer the sublimity and the triumph but rather the emotion—the immediate consequence of that enthusiastic outpouring of sympathy with the earthly sufferings of the Redeemer, an outpouring to which by example and teaching St. Francis gave a new and hitherto unexampled impulse.[1]

In connection with a further progress towards the middle of the fifteenth century there are especially two names to mention, Masaccio and Fra Angelico.[2] In them the essentially important thing in connection with the progressive incorporation of the religious material into the living forms of the human figure and the soulful expression of human traits was, on the one hand, as von Rumohr puts it (op. cit. ii, p. 243), an increased rotundity of all the forms; on the other hand 'a deeper penetration into the distribution, co-ordination, and varied degrees of attraction and significance in human facial expressions'. The first solution of this artistic problem, the difficulty of which might at that time have been beyond the powers of a *single* artist, was shared by Masaccio and Fra Angelico. 'Masaccio took over the exploration of chiaroscuro, the roundness and separation of figures set together; Fra Angelico, on the other hand, the investigation of inner co-ordination, the indwelling meaning of human facial expressions, the rich sources of which he was the first to open up for painting' —Masaccio not, as you might think, in an effort after grace, but with grand treatment, manliness, and in the need for a more decisive unity; Angelico with the fervour of a religious love remote from the world, with a conventual purity of disposition, elevation and sanctity of soul, so that Vasari tells of him that he never painted anything without first praying from the depths of his heart and

---

[1] 'Modern' saints presumably means those canonized in the fifteenth century or later. If Hegel was no stylist, von Rumohr may not be one either. Hegel has said that sometimes we have to put up with mere descriptions of pictures, and here he seems to rely on von Rumohr, possibly not altogether a blind guide.
[2] 1401–28 and 1387–1455.

never painted his Redeemer's Passion without bursting into tears (ibid. ii, p. 252).

The result is that what was of importance on the one side in this advance of painting was intensified liveliness and naturalness, but on the other side, although the depth of the pious heart and the simple deep feeling of the soul in faith were not absent, what still preponderated was the freedom, skill, natural truth, and beauty of the composition, posture, colour, and clothing. If the later development could attain a still far loftier and more complete expression of spiritual inwardness, nevertheless the epoch with which we are dealing at present has not been surpassed in its purity and innocence of religious disposition and serious depth of conception. Many pictures of this time do have about them something repellent for us in their colouring, grouping, and drawing, because the vivid forms required for the portrayal of inner religious feeling do not yet appear perfectly elaborated for expressing this. However, if we consider the spiritual artistic sense which produced these works of art, we should not miss their naïve purity, their familiarity with the inmost depths of truly religious convictions, the certainty of a believing love even in affliction and pain, and often too the gracefulness of innocence and bliss. We have all the less reason to miss these things when we reflect that even if later epochs made advances in other aspects of artistic perfection, they never again attained these original merits after they had been lost.

($\gamma\gamma$) In painting's further progress a third point in addition to those mentioned concerns the greater spread of subjects which a new artistic sense adopted for portrayal. Just as, in Italian painting, sanctity approached reality from the very beginning by reason of the fact that men nearly contemporaneous with the painters themselves were canonized, so art now drew into its own sphere other parts of the real and contemporary world. From that stage of pure deep feeling and piety which aimed only at the expression of this religious animation itself, painting proceeded more and more to associate life in the external world with religious subjects. The cheerful and powerful self-reliance of the citizens with their industriousness, their trade and commerce, their freedom, their manly courage and patriotism, their well-being in enjoying life in the present, this reawakening gusto of man in his virtue and witty cheerfulness, this reconciliation with reality both in his inner spirit and its external form—all this is what entered artistic treatment and portrayal and asserted itself there. In this artistic sense we see coming to life a love for landscape backgrounds, for views of cities, for the surroundings of churches and palaces; contemporary portraits of famous scholars, friends, statesmen, artists, and other persons who in their day had won favour on the strength of their wit or their cheerfulness, gain a place in religious situations; traits of domestic or civil life are used with more or less freedom and skill; and even if the spiritual character of the religious material remained fundamental, still the expression of piety was no longer isolated on its own account but was linked with the fuller life of reality and the spheres of mundane life (cf. op. cit. ii, p. 282). Of course, owing to this trend, the expression of religious concentration and its inner piety is weakened, but in order to reach its peak painting needed this mundane element too.

(γ) Out of this fusion of living and fuller reality with the inner religious feeling of the heart there sprang a new spiritual problem, and its perfect solution was reserved for the great artists of the sixteenth century. For it was now a matter of harmonizing soulful depths of feeling, the seriousness and profundity of religion, with that sense for the liveliness of the physical and spiritual present of characters and forms, so that the physical figure in its posture, movement, and colouring should not remain merely an external scaffolding but become itself full of soul and life and, thanks to the perfect expression of all the parts, appear at the same time beautiful alike physically and spiritually.

Amongst the most excellent masters who had this goal in view, special mention is to be made of Leonardo da Vinci. He it was who, with almost subtle profundity and delicacy of intellect and feeling, not only accepted more deeply than any of his predecessors the forms of the human body and the soul of their expression, but, with equal mastery of the technique of painting, also acquired great assurance in applying the means which his study had put into his hands. In this way he could at the same time preserve a fully reverential seriousness for the conception of his religious themes, so that, however much his figures tend to acquire the pure appearance of a fuller and rounded actual existence and in their mien and graceful movement display the expression of sweet and smiling joy, they still do not lack the sublimity which reverence for the dignity and truth of religion demands (cf. ibid. ii, p. 308).

But in this sphere the purest perfection is achieved by Raphael alone. Von Rumohr ascribes especially to the Umbrian school of painters from the middle of the fifteenth century a secret charm to which every heart is open, and he tries to explain this attraction by the depth and delicacy of feeling as well as by the wonderful union into which those painters could bring dim recollections of the oldest Christian artistic strivings and the softer ideas of the modern and contemporary world; and in this respect he thinks that they outclassed their Tuscan, Lombard, and Venetian contemporaries (ibid. ii, p. 310).[1] This expression of 'spotless purity of soul and total surrender to bitter-sweet and ecstatic tender feelings' Perugino,[2] Raphael's master, could make his own and therefore could fuse together the objectivity and the life of external figures, compliance with the real and the individual, as this had been developed principally by the Florentines.[3] From Perugino, to whose taste and style Raphael seems to have been still addicted in his early works, Raphael proceeded to the most complete fulfilment of the demand mentioned above. In him, that is to say, there were united (a) the supreme spiritual feeling for religious subjects, as well as the full knowledge of and affectionate attention to natural phenomena in the whole liveliness of their colour and form, and (b) the like sense for the beauty of antiquity. Yet this great admiration for the ideal beauty of antiquity did not lead him at all to the imitation, adoption, and use of the forms which Greek sculpture had so perfectly developed; on the contrary, he only took up in a general way the principle of their free beauty which in his case was penetrated through and through by pictorial and individual liveliness and by deeper soul of expression as well as by what was hitherto unknown to the Italians, an open and cheerful clarity and thoroughness of portrayal. In the development of these elements and equally in their harmonious combination he reached the summit of perfection in his art.

Still greater were Correggio in the magical wizardry of chiaroscuro, in the soulful delicacy and gracefulness of heart, forms, movement, and grouping, and Titian in the wealth of natural life, and the illuminating shading, glow, warmth, and power of

[1] Umbria—Raphael, 1483–1520. Tuscany—Michelangelo, 1475–1564. Lombardy—Correggio, 1489–1564. Venice—Giorgione, 1478–1510, and Titian, ?1477–1576.
[2] c. 1450–1523.
[3] Fra Angelico (of Fiesole), Uccello, 1396–1475, B. Gozzoli, 1420–98, etc.

colouring. There is nothing more attractive than the naïveté, in Correggio, of a grace not natural but religious and spiritual, nothing sweeter than his smiling unselfconscious beauty and innocence.

The perfection of painting in these great masters is a peak of art which can be ascended only once by one people in the course of history's development.

(c) *Flemish and German Painting*

As for German painting we may affiliate what is strictly German to that of the Low Countries.

The general difference from the Italians consists here in the fact that the German and the Flemish painters neither could nor wished to attain from their own resources those free ideal forms and modes of expression that corresponded with a transition to spiritual and transfigured beauty. For this reason they develop, on the one hand, an expression for depth of feeling and subjective self-sufficiency of mind; on the other hand, they add to this deep feeling of faith a more extended specification of the individual character which now does not manifest an exclusive inner preoccupation with the interests of faith and the salvation of the soul, but also shows how the individuals portrayed are troubled by mundane affairs, enwrapped in the cares of life, and through this hard effort have acquired mundane virtues, fidelity, steadfastness, integrity, chivalrous tenacity, and civil efficiency. Along with this artistic sense, immersed more or less in limited affairs, we find at the same time, in contrast with the always purer forms and characters of the Italians, the expression rather of a formal obstinacy of refractory characters who either set themselves against God with the energy of defiance and brutal self-will or else are compelled to do violence to themselves in order to be able to extricate themselves, by painful labour, from their limitations and crudity and to battle their way to religious reconciliation; the result is that the deep wounds which they had to inflict on their inner life still appear in the expression of their piety.

In detail I will only draw attention to a few of the main points of importance concerning the older Flemish school in distinction from the North-German and later Dutch painters of the seventeenth century.

(α) Amongst the older Flemish painters the brothers Hubert and Jan van Eyck were especially prominent at the beginning of the fifteenth century; their mastery we have only now in recent times learnt to value again. As is well known, they are named as the inventors of oil-painting, or at least as really the first men to bring it to perfection. Their step forward was so great that we might suppose that it must be possible to demonstrate a series of stages from earlier beginnings along the route to perfection. But of such a gradual progress history has preserved no artistic memorials. Beginning and perfection confront us, so far as our knowledge goes, simultaneously. For hardly anything can be more excellent than what these brothers painted. Moreover, their surviving works, in which the typical is already discarded and overcome, not only give proof of great mastery in drawing, in placing and grouping subjects, in mental and physical characterization, in the warmth, clarity, harmony, and delicacy of colouring, in the grandeur and finish of composition, but in addition in them the whole wealth of painting in relation to natural environment, architectural accessories, backgrounds, horizon, magnificence and variety of cloth etc., robes, sort of weapons and decoration etc., is treated already with such fidelity, with so much feeling for the pictorial, and with such virtuosity, that even later centuries have nothing to show which is more perfect, at least in respect of profundity and truth. Nevertheless, when we compare these Flemish pictures with the masterpieces of Italian painting, we are more attracted by the latter, because the Italians with all their depth of religious feeling give prominence to spiritual freedom and imaginative beauty. The Flemish figures do delight us by their innocence, naïveté, and piety; indeed in depth of heart they surpass the best Italian ones to some extent. But the Flemish masters could not rise to the same beauty of form and freedom of soul; and their pictures of the Christ-child especially are ill-formed; and however far their other characters, men and women, display within their religious expression a soundness, sanctified by depth of faith, in mundane interests as well, they would seem beyond this piety, or rather below it, to be insignificant and as it were incapable of being free in themselves, imaginative, and particularly bright.

(β) A second aspect which deserves notice is the transition from a more peaceful and reverential piety to the portrayal of torments and the ugliness of the world generally. This is the sphere in which especially the masters of North Germany excel when, in scenes from the Passion story, it is the crudity of the soldiers, the malignity of the mockery, the barbarity of their hatred of Christ in his suffering and death, that they reveal with great energy in characterizing the greatest uglinesses and deformities which are external forms corresponding to an inner corruption of heart. The quiet and beautiful effect of peaceful and deeply felt piety is disdained and, in the case of the movement prescribed by the situations just mentioned, portrayal goes on to horrible grimaces and gestures expressive of ferocious and unbridled passions. Owing to the crowd of figures pressing on one another in confusion and the preponderating barbarity of the characters, there is easily visible in these pictures a lack of inner harmony whether in composition or colour, so that, especially when a taste for the older German painting was reborn, its far from perfect technique gave rise to many blunders in assessing the date of these works. They were regarded as older than the more perfect paintings of the period of van Eyck, whereas most of them belong to a later time. Yet the North German masters did not stick exclusively to such portrayals of the Passion at all; they have also treated various religious subjects, and, like Albrecht Dürer for example, have been able, even in situations from the Passion story, to tear themselves free in triumph from the extreme of plain barbarity, because they preserved for such subjects too an inner nobility and an external finish and freedom.

(γ) The final achievement of German and Flemish art is its utterly living absorption in the world and its daily life, and consequently the differentiation of painting into the most varied kinds of portrayal which are distinguished from one another, and one-sidedly developed, in respect of both subject-matter and treatment. Even in Italian painting there is noticeable a progress from the simple splendour of worship to an ever increasingly evident worldliness, but here, as, for example, in Raphael, this remains in part penetrated by religious feeling and in part limited and concentrated by the principle of the beauty of antiquity; while the later history is less a dispersal into the portrayal of subjects of every kind under the guidance of colouring than a rather superficial confusion or eclectic imitation of forms and styles. On the other hand, German and Flemish painting ran through, in the clearest and most striking way, the whole range of subject-matter and modes of treating it: from the purely traditional ecclesiastical pictures, individual figures, and half-lengths, to sensitive, pious, and reverential portrayals, and then from these up to the animation and extension of these in huge compositions and scenes in which, however, the free characterization of the figures, the intensified life in processions, servants, persons accidentally in the entourage, decoration of robes and vessels, as well as the wealth of portraits, architectural works, natural environment, vistas of churches, streets, cities, rivers, forests, mountain formations, etc., in short the entirety of life and reality is still collected together and carried by the religious foundation. It is this central foundation which is absent now, so that the range of subjects, hitherto kept in unity, is dispersed, and particular things in their specific individuality and the accidents of their alteration and change are subject to the most varied sorts of treatment and pictorial execution.

To frame a complete judgement on this last phase in our consideration of painting's history, we must, as we have done before, visualize again the national situation in which it had its origin. What was responsible here was movement away from the Catholic Church, and its outlook and sort of piety, to joy in the world as such, to natural objects and their detailed appearance, to domestic life in its decency, cheerfulness, and quiet seclusion, as well as to national celebrations, festivals, and processions, to country dances and the jollities and boisterousness of wakes-weeks; and we have to defend this as follows: the Reformation was completely accepted in Holland; the Dutch had become Protestants and had overcome the Spanish despotism of church and crown. And what we find here in political matters is neither a superior nobility expelling its prince and tyrant or imposing laws on him, nor a people of farmers, oppressed peasants, who broke free, like the Swiss; on the contrary by far the greater part, except the courageous warriors on land and the bold heroes on the sea, consisted of townspeople, burghers active in trade and well-off, who, comfortable in their business, had no high pretensions, but when it was a question of fighting for the freedom of their well-earned rights, of the special privileges of their provinces, cities, and corporations, they revolted with bold trust in God and in their courage and intelligence, without any fear of exposing themselves to all sorts of danger in face of the tremendous repute of the Spanish domination of half the world; courageously they shed their blood and by this righteous boldness and endurance triumphantly won for themselves both civil and religious independence. If we can call any particular trend of mind '*deutsch*' [i.e. Dutch or German], it is this loyal, comfortable, homely bourgeois type: this remains in house and surroundings simple, attractive, and neat, in a self-respect without pride, in a piety without the mere enthusiasm of a devotee, but instead concretely pious in mundane affairs and unassuming and content in its wealth; and it can preserve unimpaired an ancestral soundness in thorough carefulness and contentedness in all its circumstances along with independence and advancing freedom, while still being true to its traditional morality.

This sensitive and artistically endowed people wishes now in painting too to delight in this existence which is as powerful as just, satisfying, and comfortable; in its pictures it wishes to enjoy once again in every possible situation the neatness of its cities, houses, and furnishings, as well as its domestic peace, its wealth, the respectable dress of wives and children, the brilliance of its civil and political festivals, the boldness of its seamen, the fame of its commerce and the ships that ride the oceans of the world. And it is just this sense for an honest and cheerful existence that the Dutch painters bring with them to objects in nature too; and now in all their paintings they link supreme freedom of artistic composition, fine feeling for incidentals, and perfect carefulness in execution, with freedom and fidelity of treatment, love for what is evidently momentary and trifling, the freshness of open vision, and the undivided concentration of the whole soul on the tiniest and most limited things. This painting has developed unsurpassably, on the one hand, a through and through living characterization in the greatest truth of which art is capable; and, on the other hand, the magic and enchantment of light, illumination, and colouring in general, in pictures of battle and military life, in scenes in the tavern, in weddings and other merry-making of peasants, in portraying domestic affairs, in portraits and objects in nature such as landscapes, animals, flowers, etc. And when it proceeds from the insignificant and accidental to peasant life, even to crudity and vulgarity, these scenes appear so completely penetrated by a naïve cheerfulness and jollity that the real subject-matter is not vulgarity, which is just vulgar and vicious, but this cheerfulness and naïveté. For this reason we have before us no vulgar feelings and passions but peasant life and the down-to-earth life of the lower classes which is cheerful, roguish, and comic. In this very heedless boisterousness there lies the ideal feature: it is the Sunday of life which equalizes everything and removes all evil; people who are so whole-heartedly cheerful cannot be altogether evil and base. In this matter it is not all one whether evil enters a character momentarily or is its basic trait. In the Dutch painters the comical aspect of the situation cancels what is bad in it, and it is at once clear to us that the characters can still be something different from what they are as they confront us in this moment. Such cheerfulness and comicality is intrinsic to the inestimable worth of these pictures. When on the other hand in modern pictures a painter tries to be piquant in the same way, what he usually presents to us is something inherently vulgar, bad, and evil without any reconciling comicality. For example, a bad wife scolds her drunken husband in the tavern and really snarls at him; but then there is nothing to see, as I have said once before,[1] except that he is a dissolute chap and his wife a drivelling old woman.

If we look at the Dutch masters with these eyes, we will no longer suppose that they should have avoided such subjects and portrayed only Greek gods, myths, and fables, or the Madonna, the Crucifixion, martyrs, Popes, saints male or female. What is an ingredient in any work of art is one in painting too: the vision of what man is as man, what the human spirit and character is, what man and *this* man is. The poetical fundamental trait permeating most of the Dutch painters at this period consists of this treatment of man's inner nature and its external and living forms and its modes of appearance, this naïve delight and artistic freedom, this freshness and cheerfulness of imagination, and this assured boldness of execution. In their paintings we can study and get to know men and human nature. Today however, we have all too often to put up with portraits and historical paintings which, despite all likeness to men and actual individuals, show us at the very first glance that the artist knows neither what man and human colour is nor what the forms are in which man expresses that he is man in fact.

[1] In Vol. I, p. 169.

Chapter II

MUSIC

INTRODUCTION AND DIVISION OF THE SUBJECT

To take a glance back at the road we have travelled up to now in the development of the several arts, we began with architecture. It was the most incomplete art because we found it incapable, in the mere heavy matter which it took as its sensuous element and treated in accordance with the laws of gravity, of portraying the spirit in a presence adequate to it, and we had to restrict it, from its own spiritual resources, to preparing for the spirit in its living and actual existence an artistically appropriate *external* environment.

Sculpture, secondly, did make the spirit itself its subject, but neither as a particular character nor as subjective inwardness of heart, but as free individuality separated neither from the substantive content nor from the corporeal appearance of the spirit; on the contrary, as an individual, the spirit enters the portrayal only in so far as is required for the individual vivification of a content inherently substantial, and it penetrates the bodily forms as an inner spiritual life only in so far as the inherently inseparable unity of spirit and its corresponding shape in nature permits. This identity, necessary for sculpture, of the spirit that is self-confronting only in its *bodily* organism and not in the element of its own *inner* life, imposes on this art the task of still retaining heavy matter as its material; but the shape of this material it has not to form, as architecture does, into a purely inorganic environment constructed according to the laws of bearing and loading; on the contrary, it has to transform it into a classical beauty adequate to the spirit and its ideal plasticity.

In this respect sculpture appeared especially adapted to vivify in works of art the content and mode of expression of the *classical* form of art, while architecture, which could also prove serviceable for that subject-matter, did not get beyond the fundamental model of a *symbolic* indication in its mode of portrayal. This being so, with painting, thirdly, we entered the sphere of the *romantic*. For in painting, the *external* shape is indeed still the means by which the inner life is revealed, but this inner life is ideal and *particular* personality, the mind turned into itself out of its corporeal existence, the subjective passion and feeling of character and heart, which are no longer totally effused in the external shape, but precisely in that shape mirror spirit's inner self-apprehension and its preoccupation with the sphere of its own circumstances, aims, and actions. On account of this inwardness of its content, painting cannot be satisfied with a material which can only be shaped with difficulty or which is unparticularized and can only be treated externally, but has to choose as a means of sensuous expression pure appearance and the pure appearance of colour. Yet colour is available to make spatial forms and figures visible as they exist in actual life only when the art of painting has developed to the magic of colour in which what is objective begins as it were to vanish into thin air, and the effect scarcely comes about any longer by means of something material. For this reason, however far painting develops to a more ideal liberation, i.e. to that pure appearance which is no longer tied to the figure as such but which has liberty to expatiate independently in its own element, in the play of appearance and reflection, in the enchantments of chiaroscuro, still this magic of colour is always of a spatial kind, and a pure appearance of *separated* things, which therefore *persists*.

1. But if the inner life, as is already the case in the principle of painting, is in fact to be manifested as a *subjective* inwardness, the genuinely correspondent material cannot be of such a kind that it *persists* on its own account. Consequently we get a different mode of expression and communication where objectivity does not enter into its sensuous element as a spatial figure in order to have stability there, and we need a material which for our apprehension is without stability and even as it arises and exists vanishes once more. This obliteration not of *one* dimension only [as in painting] but of the whole of space, purely and simply, this complete withdrawal, of both the inner life and its expression, into subjectivity, brings completely into being the *second* romantic art—music. Thus viewed, it forms the real centre of that presentation which takes the subjective as such for both form and content, because as art it communicates the inner life and yet even in its objectivity remains subjective, i.e., unlike the visual arts, it does not permit the manifestation in which it flourishes to become free and independent and reach an existence self-reposing and persistent but, on the contrary, cancels

it as objective and does not allow the external to assume in our eyes a fixed existence as something external.

Yet since the cancellation of spatial objectivity as a means of portrayal is a renunciation beginning within the sensuous spatiality of the visual arts themselves, this negation must be actively applied to the previously peaceful and independently persistent material, just as painting in its own field reduced the spatial dimensions of sculpture to a flat surface.[1] The cancellation of space therefore consists here only in the fact that a specific sensuous material sacrifices its peaceful separatedness, turns to movement, yet so vibrates in itself that every part of the cohering body not only changes its place but also struggles to replace itself in its former position. The result of this oscillating vibration is sound or a note, the material of music.

Now, with sound, music relinquishes the element of an external form and a perceptible visibility and therefore needs for the treatment of its productions another subjective organ, namely hearing which, like sight, is one of the theoretical and not practical senses, and it is still more ideal than sight. For the peaceful and undesiring contemplation of [spatial] works of art lets them remain in peace and independence as they are, and there is no wish to consume or destroy them; yet what it apprehends is not something inherently posited ideally but on the contrary something persisting in its visible existence. The ear, on the contrary, without itself turning to a practical relation to objects, listens to the result of the inner vibration of the body through which what comes before us is no longer the peaceful and material shape but the first and more ideal breath of the soul. Further, since the negativity into which the vibrating material enters here is on one side the cancelling of the spatial situation, a cancellation cancelled again by the reaction of the body, therefore the expression of this double negation, i.e. sound, is an externality which in its coming-to-be is annihilated again by its very existence, and it vanishes of itself. Owing to this double negation of externality, implicit in the principle of sound,

---

[1] Sculpture is still three-dimensional, but it is less purely objective spatially than architecture because it portrays the subjective spirit more adequately. Thus within these arts the abandonment of purely objective spatiality begins. It goes further in painting which is only two-dimensional. And music now goes further still in the same negative direction by negating the 'peaceful' or motionless material of painting, its canvas and colour, and adopting sound which results from the 'vibration' of matter.

inner subjectivity corresponds to it because the resounding, which in and by itself is something more ideal than independently really subsistent corporeality, gives up this more ideal existence also and therefore becomes a mode of expression adequate to the inner life.[1]

2. If now we ask, conversely, of what kind the inner life must be to prove itself adequate again on its part to this sounding and resounding, we have already seen that, taken by itself as real objectivity, sound in contrast to the material of the visual arts is wholly abstract. Stone and colouring receive the forms of a broad and variegated world of objects and portray them as they actually exist; sounds cannot do this. On this account what alone is fitted for expression in music is the object-free inner life, abstract subjectivity as such. This is our entirely empty self, the self without any further content. Consequently the chief task of music consists in making resound, not the objective world itself, but, on the contrary, the manner in which the inmost self is moved to the depths of its personality and conscious soul.

3. The same is true of the effect of music. What it claims as its own is the depth of a person's inner life as such; it is the art of the soul and is directly addressed to the soul. Painting too, for example, as we saw, can also express the inner life and movement, the moods and passions, of the heart, the situations, conflicts, and destinies of the soul, but it does so in faces and figures, and what confronts us in pictures consists of objective appearances from which the perceiving and inner self remains distinct. No matter how far we plunge or immerse ourselves in the subject-matter, in a situation, a character, the forms of a statue or a picture, no matter how much we may admire such a work of art, may be taken out of ourselves by it, may be satisfied by it—it is all in vain: these works of art are and remain independently persistent objects and our relation to them can never get beyond a vision of them. But in music this distinction disappears. Its content is what is subjective in itself, and its expression likewise does not produce an object *persisting* in space but shows through its free unstable soaring that it is a communication which, instead of having stability on its own account, is carried by the inner subjective life, and is to exist for

---

[1] For clarification of Hegel's view of sound, obscurely expressed here, see his Philosophy of Nature (*Enc.*, §§ 299 ff.). Sound is said to be a double negation because vibration momentarily *breaks* up, e.g. a string, into its parts but at once *unifies* them again in a sound.

that life alone.¹ Hence the note is an expression and something external, but an expression which, precisely because it is something external, is made to vanish again forthwith. The ear has scarcely grasped it before it is mute; the impression to be made here is at once made within; the notes re-echo only in the depths of the soul which is gripped and moved in its subjective consciousness.

This object-free inwardness in respect of music's content and mode of expression constitutes its formal aspect. It does have a content too but not in the sense that the visual arts and poetry have one; for what it lacks is giving to itself an objective configuration whether in the forms of actual external phenomena or in the objectivity of spiritual views and ideas.²

As for the course we intend to follow in our further discussions, we have

(1) to bring out more specifically the general character of music and its effect, in distinction from the other arts, in respect both of its material and of the form which the spiritual content assumes.

(2) Next we must explain the particular differences in which the musical notes and their figurations are developed and mediated, in respect of their temporal duration and the qualitative differences in their real resonance.

(3) Finally, music acquires a relation to the content it expresses in that, either it is associated as an accompaniment with feelings, ideas, and thoughts already expressed on their own account in words, or launches out freely within its own domain in unfettered independence.

But if after this general indication of the principle of music and the division of the subject we propose to go on to distinguish its particular aspects, we are met in the nature of the case with a peculiar difficulty. Since the musical element of sound and the inner life, in which the content proceeds, is so abstract and formal, we cannot go on to particularize without at once running into

---

¹ i.e. in the memory. The notes of a tune vanish successively and the tune exists as a tune in memory alone and for subjective apprehension alone.

² Hegel might have said that music has a meaning, but that the meaning cannot be stated otherwise than in the notes. But he thinks that the meaning or message of the other arts can be translated, and he is not wholly consistent. See pp. 933 ff. He seems to think that music ought to have a meaning but that this can only be detected when it is associated with words in opera and songs. This is perhaps why he may be at sea when he comes to deal with instrumental music.

MUSIC

technical matters such as numerical relations between notes, differences between instruments, keys, concords, etc. But I am little versed in this sphere, and must therefore excuse myself in advance for restricting myself simply to the more general points and to single remarks.[1]

1. *General Character of Music*

The essential points of importance in relation to music in general may be brought before our consideration in the following order:

(*a*) We have to compare music with the visual arts on the one hand and with poetry on the other.

(*b*) Next, therefore, we must expound the manner in which music can apprehend a subject-matter and portray it.

(*c*) In the light of this manner of treatment we can explain more specifically the special effect which music, in distinction from the other arts, produces on our minds.

(*a*) *Comparison with the Visual Arts and Poetry*

In connection with the first point, when we propose to set out clearly the specific and particular character of music, we must compare it with the other arts in three respects.

(α) First, although it stands in contrast to architecture, it still has an affinity with it.

($\alpha\alpha$) In architecture the subject-matter to be impressed on architectonic forms does not go wholly into the shape as it does in sculpture and painting but remains distinct from it as merely an external environment for it; so too in music, as a properly romantic art, the classical identity between the inner life and its external existence is dissolved again in a similar, even if opposite, way to what was the case in architecture which, as a symbolic mode of portrayal, could not attain that unity. For the spiritual inner life proceeds from pure concentration of mind to views and ideas and to forms for these developed by imagination; but music remains

---

[1] This confession of limited knowledge comes as a relief. It might have been more comprehensive. Hegel studied and loved painting, but in music he was less at home. His predilection for opera (especially Rossini and Mozart) and his lack of enthusiasm for instrumental music may explain or be explained by his views on the human voice. The fact that he never mentions Beethoven, his exact contemporary, is not surprising, because he is by no means the only person to have a distaste for contemporary music. If he ever heard Beethoven's music, he probably regarded it, as I regard e.g. Prokofiev's, as restless and incoherent.

capable rather of expressing only the element of feeling, and it accompanies explicitly enunciated spiritual ideas with the melodious sounds expressive of feeling, just as architecture in its own sphere surrounds the statues of the god (true, in a rigid way) with the mathematical forms of its pillars, walls, and entablatures.

(ββ) In this way sound and its figuration becomes an element artificially moulded by art and by purely artistic expression, and this is quite different from the way that painting and sculpture proceed with the human body and its posture and facial expression. In this respect too music may be compared more closely with architecture which derives its forms, not from what exists, but from the spirit's invention in order to mould them according to the laws of gravity and the rules of symmetry and eurhythmy. Music does the same in its sphere, since, on the one hand, independently of the expression of feeling, it follows the harmonic laws of sound which rest on quantitative proportions, and, on the other, in relation both to the repetition of the beat and the rhythm and to the further development of the notes it is itself subject in many ways to the forms of regularity and symmetry. Consequently what dominates in music is at once the soul and profoundest feeling and the most rigorous mathematical laws so that it unites in itself two extremes which easily become independent of one another. When they do, music acquires an especially architectonic character because, freed from expressing emotion, it constructs on its own account, with a wealth of invention, a musically regular building of sound.

(γγ) In spite of all this similarity, the art of sound moves in a realm totally opposed to architecture. It is true that in both arts the foundation is relations of quantity, or more precisely proportion, but the material shaped in accordance with these relations is directly opposite in the two arts. Architecture takes heavy visible masses in their peaceful juxtaposition and external spatial shape, whereas music takes the soul of tone, working itself free from spatial matter, in the qualitative differences of sound and in the movement of the ever-rolling stream of time. Thus the works of the two arts belong to two quite different spheres of the spirit, for architecture erects its colossal buildings to endure in symbolic forms to be looked at from outside; but the world of sounds, quickly rustling away, is directly drawn by the ear into the inner life of the heart and harmonizes the soul with emotions in sympathy with it.

(β) Secondly, as for the closer relation of music to the other two visual arts, the similarity and difference that can be cited is partly grounded in what I have just indicated.

(αα) Music is furthest away from sculpture in respect both of the material and the manner of its configuration and also of the perfect fusion of inner and outer which sculpture attains. With painting, on the other hand, music has a closer relationship partly on account of the preponderating inwardness of expression, partly in relation to the treatment of the material in which, as we saw, painting may undertake to touch on the territory of music very nearly. But painting always has as its aim, in common with sculpture, the portrayal of an objective spatial figure, and it is tied down by that form of the figure which is actual and present already outside art. Of course neither the painter nor the sculptor takes every time a human face, a bodily posture, the contours of a mountain, the branches and leaves of a tree, exactly as he sees these external phenomena in nature here and there; on the contrary, his task is to adjust what is given to him in advance and make it conform to a specific situation and to the expression which follows necessarily from the nature of that situation. Thus in this case there is on one side an explicitly ready-made subject-matter which is to be individualized artistically, and on the other side natural forms equally existent independently on their own account; and when the artist, in accordance with his vocation, proposes to fuse these two elements into one another, he has in both of them fixed points for the conception and execution of his work. Since he starts from these firm specific terms he has to give a concrete body to the universal element in the idea and also to generalize and spiritualize the human figure or other natural forms which can serve him individually as models. The musician on the other hand does not abstract from each and every topic but finds a topic in a text which he sets to music or, independently of any text, he clothes a mood in the form of a musical theme which he then elaborates further; but the real region of his compositions remains a rather formal inwardness, pure sound; and his immersion in the topic becomes not the formation of something external but rather a retreat into the inner life's own freedom, a self-enjoyment, and, in many departments of music, even an assurance that as artist he is free from subject-matter altogether.

Now if in general we may regard activity in the realm of the beautiful as a liberation of the soul, as freedom from oppression and restrictedness (since, by presenting figures for contemplation, art itself alleviates the most powerful and tragic fates and makes them become satisfying), music carries this liberation to the most extreme heights. Music must achieve in a totally different way what the visual arts attain by their objective and plastic beauty which sets forth in the particularity of the individual the totality of man, human nature as such, the universal and the ideal, without losing the inner harmony of particular and universal. The visual artist needs only to bring out, i.e. to produce, what is veiled in an idea, what is there in it from the beginning, so that every individual feature, in its essential definiteness, is only a further unfolding of the totality which floats before the spirit on the strength of the subject-matter to be portrayed. For example, a figure in a plastic work of art demands in this or that situation a body, hands, feet, trunk, head, with such and such an expression, pose, and other figures, other associations, etc., and each of these things demands the others in order to close with them into a whole founded in itself. Here the development of the theme is a more exact analysis of what the theme already contains in itself, and the more elaborated the image is which confronts us in this way, the more concentrated is the unity and the stronger the definite connection of the parts. If the work of art is of a genuine kind, the most perfect expression of the individual must at the same time be the production of supreme unity. Now of course a work in music too may not lack an inner articulation and a rounding of the parts into a whole in which one part makes the others necessary; but in the case of music the execution is of a totally different kind and we have to take the unity in a more restricted sense.

(ββ) The meaning to be expressed in a musical theme is already exhausted in the theme; if the theme is repeated or if it goes on to further contrasts and modulations, then the repetitions, modulations, transformations in different keys, etc. readily prove superfluous for an understanding of the work and belong rather to a purely musical elaboration and an assimilation into the manifold realm of harmonic differences etc. which are neither demanded by the subject-matter nor remain carried by it; while in the visual arts, on the other hand, the execution of individual parts down to individual details is solely an ever more exact mode of bringing the subject-matter itself into relief and an analysis of it in a living way.

Yet we cannot deny, it is true, that in a musical composition a topic can be unfolded in its more specific relations, oppositions, conflicts, transitions, complications, and resolutions owing to the way in which a theme is first developed and then another enters, and now both of them in their alternation or their interfusion advance and change, one becoming subordinate here and then more prominent again there, now seeming defeated and then entering again victorious. But, even so, such elaboration does not, as in sculpture and painting it does, make the unity more profound and concentrated; it is rather an enlargement, an extension, a separation of elements, a flight and a return, for which the content to be expressed does form the more general centre; but the content does not hold the entire work so closely together as is possible in the figures of visual art, especially where that art is restricted to the human organism.

(γγ) In this respect, music, in distinction from the other arts, lies too near the essence of that formal freedom of the inner life to be denied the right of turning more or less away above the content, above what is given.[1] Recollection [*Erinnerung*] of the theme adopted is at the same time the artist's inner collection [*Er-innerung*] of *himself*, i.e. an inner conviction that *he* is the artist and can expatiate in the theme at will and move hither and thither in it. And yet the free exercise of imagination in this way is expressly to be distinguished from a perfectly finished piece of music which should essentially be an articulated whole. In the free exercise of imagination,[2] liberation from restriction is an end in itself, so that now the artist can display, amongst other things, freedom to interweave familiar melodies and passages into what he is producing at present, to give them a new aspect, to transform them by nuances of various kinds, to make transitions from them, and so to advance from them to something totally heterogeneous.

On the whole, however, the composer of a piece of music has liberty generally either to execute it within strict limits and to observe, so to say, a plastic unity or, with subjective liveliness, to let himself go at will in greater or lesser digressions from every point, or similarly to rock to and fro, stop capriciously, make this or

---

[1] This is Hegel's defence, perhaps reluctant, of instrumental music. If he had not said what he does below about 'characterization' in music, he might have been thought to welcome 'programme music'.

[2] i.e. in instrumental music, when the composer has no libretto or words to set to music.

that interrupt his course or rustle forward again in a flooding stream. While therefore we must recommend the painter and the sculptor to study natural forms, music does not possess a natural sphere outside its existing forms, with which it is compelled to comply. The range of its compliance with law and the necessity of its forms fall principally in the sphere of the notes themselves which do not enter into so close a connection with the specific character of the content placed in them, and in their use mostly leave a wide scope for the subjective freedom of the execution.

This is the chief point from which a comparison can be made between music and the objective and visual arts.

(γ) Thirdly, in another way music has the greatest affinity with poetry because they both make use of the same perceptible material, i.e. sound. And yet there is the greatest difference between the two arts both in their way of treating sounds and in their mode of expression.

($\alpha\alpha$) In poetry, as we have seen already in our general division of the arts, the sound as such is not elicited from various instruments invented by art and richly modified artistically, but the articulate tone of the human organ of speech is degraded to being a mere token of a word and acquires therefore only the value of being an indication, meaningless in itself, of ideas. Consequently the sound in general remains an independent audible existent which, as a mere sign of feelings, ideas, and thoughts, has its *immanent* externality and objectivity in the fact that it is only this *sign*. For the proper objectivity of the inner life as inner does not consist in the voices and words but in the fact that I am made aware of a thought, a feeling, etc., that I objectify them and so have them before me in my ideas or that I develop the implications of a thought or an idea, distinguish the inner and outer relations of my thought's content or its different features in their bearing on one another. Of course we always think in words but without needing actual speech for that reason.

Since the speech-sounds, as perceptible, are in this way accidental to the spiritual content of our ideas which they are used to communicate, sound here again acquires independence. In painting, colours and their juxtaposition, regarded as colours simply, are likewise meaningless in themselves and are a sensuous medium wholly independent in face of the spirit; but colour as such does not make a painting, since a figure and its expression must be added. In that event colour's connection with these spiritually animated forms is far closer than that which speech-sounds and their assembly into words have with ideas.

If we look now at the difference between the poetic and the musical *use* of sound, music does not make sound subservient to speech but takes sound independently as its medium, so that sound, just as sound, is treated as an end in itself. In this way, since the range of sound is not to serve as a sign, it can enter in this liberation into a mode of configuration in which its own form, i.e. artistic note-formation, can become its essential end. Especially in recent times music has torn itself free from a content already clear on its own account and retreated in this way into its own medium;[1] but for this reason it has lost its power over the whole inner life, all the more so as the pleasure it can give relates to only one side of the art, namely bare interest in the purely musical element in the composition and its skilfulness, a side of music which is for connoisseurs only and scarcely appeals to the general human interest in art [!].

(ββ) But what poetry loses in external objectivity by being able to set aside its sensuous medium (so far as that may be permitted to any art), it gains in the inner objectivity of the views and ideas which poetic language sets before our apprehension. For these views, feelings, and thoughts have to be shaped by imagination into a self-complete world of events, actions, moods, and outbursts of passion, and in this way imagination fashions works into which the entirety of reality, alike in its external appearance and in its inner content, enters for apprehension by our spiritual feelings, vision, and ideas. This sort of objectivity music must renounce in so far as it means to remain independent [e.g. of words] in its own field. The realm of sound, as I have indicated already, has a relation to the heart and a harmony with its spiritual emotions, but it gets no further than an always vague sympathy, although in this respect a musical composition, so long as it has sprung from the heart itself and is penetrated by a richness of soul and feeling, may even so be amply impressive.

Elsewhere, our feelings do proceed further out of their element of vague immersion in their object and subjective implication with it to a more concrete vision and more general idea of the object. This can happen in a musical composition too, so soon as the feelings which it arouses in us on the strength of its own nature and

---

[1] Is this an allusion to, for instance, Schubert and Beethoven?

artistic animation develop new ideas and insights in us and so bring to our minds the definiteness of mental impressions in firmer views and more general ideas. But in that case this is only *our* idea and our vision, aroused indeed by the musical composition, but not having been produced directly by the musical treatment of notes.[1] Poetry on the other hand expresses the feelings, views, and ideas themselves and can sketch a picture of external objects for us, although it cannot approach the clear plasticity of sculpture and painting or the depth of soul of music. It must therefore summon in supplementation our other sensuous perceptions and our wordless apprehension of our emotions.

(γγ) Thirdly, however, music does not remain in this independence of poetry and the spiritual content of consciousness but closely allies itself with a subject-matter already completely developed by poetry and clearly expressed in a series of feelings, thoughts, events, and actions. Yet if the musical side of such an artistic composition remains its essential and prominent feature, then poetry, as poem, drama, etc., may not come forward with a claim to validity of its own. In general, within this link between music and poetry the preponderance of one art damages the other. Therefore, if the text, as a poetic work of art, has throughout independent worth on its own account, it may only have a weak support from music, as, for example, the choruses in Greek tragedy were only a subordinate accompaniment. But if on the other hand the musical side gets the place of a greater and more special independence of its own, then the text in its poetic execution can only be more or less something superficial and can get no further than expressing general feelings and generally held ideas. Poetical elaborations of profound thoughts are as little able to provide a good musical text as sketches of things in nature or descriptive poetry in general. Songs, operatic arias, the texts of oratorios, etc., can therefore, so far as the *details* of poetic execution go, be meagre and of a certain mediocrity; if the musician is to have free scope, the poet must not try to be admired as a poet. In this respect it is the Italians, like Metastasio[2] e.g. and others, who have displayed great

[1] Hegel's diction here is evidence of his perplexity about instrumental music. It is curious that a lover of Mozart's operas did not have more appreciation, e.g. of Mozart's symphonies, than his remarks below suggest. Mozart died when Hegel was twenty-one.

[2] P. A. D. B., 1698–1782, author of libretti used again and again by eighteenth-century composers including Handel, Haydn, Mozart, and especially Gluck.

skill, while Schiller's poems, certainly not written at all for this purpose, prove very awkward and useless for musical composition.[1] Where music reaches an artistically adequate development, we understand little or nothing of the text, especially in the case of our German language and its pronunciation. Therefore it is after all an unmusical trend to put the main emphasis of interest on the text. For example, an Italian public chatters during the less important scenes of an opera, eats, plays cards, and so on, but when a striking aria begins or an important piece of music, everyone is all attention. We Germans, on the contrary, take the greatest interest in the fate of princes and princesses in opera and in their speeches with their servants, esquires, confidants, and chamber-maids, and even now there are perhaps many of us who groan as soon as a song begins because the interest is interrupted and who then take refuge in conversation.

Even in sacred music the text is for the most part a familiar Credo or is put together out of some passages in the Psalms, so that the words are only to be regarded as an opportunity for a musical commentary which is an independent construction of its own; it is not meant in any way merely to emphasize the text but rather derives from it only the universal element in its meaning in much the same way that painting may select its subject-matter from sacred history.

(b) *Musical Treatment of the Subject-matter*

If, secondly, we examine the mode of treatment, in the form of which, in distinction from the other arts, music, whether guided by or independent of a specific text, can grasp and express a specific subject-matter, I have said already that amongst all the arts music has the maximum possibility of freeing itself from any actual text as well as from the expression of any specific subject-matter, with a view to finding satisfaction solely in a self-enclosed series of the conjunctions, changes, oppositions, and modulations falling within

---

[1] This might be taken as a criticism (perhaps unfortunate) of the Ninth Symphony and many of Schubert's songs. But although this symphony was first performed in 1824 in Vienna, it was not performed in Berlin until after Hegel's death, and it is a fair inference that he never heard it. Whether he knew Schubert's songs and disliked them or whether he was ignorant of them it is not possible to say. Schubert was 27 years Hegel's junior and died in 1828 at the age of thirty-one.

the purely musical sphere of sounds. But in that event music remains empty and meaningless, and because the one chief thing in all art, namely spiritual content and expression, is missing from it, it is not yet strictly to be called art. Only if music becomes a spiritually adequate expression in the sensuous medium of sounds and their varied counterpoint does music rise to being a genuine art, no matter whether this content has its more detailed significance independently expressed in a libretto or must be sensed more vaguely from the notes and their harmonic relations and melodic animation.

(α) In this respect the proper task of music is to vivify some content or other in the sphere of the subjective inner life, not however for spiritual apprehension in the way that happens when this content is present in our consciousness as a general *idea*, or when, as a specific external *shape*, it is already present for our apprehension or acquires through art its appropriate appearance. The difficult task assigned to music is to make this inwardly veiled life and energy echo on its own account in notes, or to add to the words and ideas expressed, and to immerse ideas into this element of sound, in order to produce them anew for feeling and sympathy.

(αα) Inwardness as such is therefore the form in which music can conceive its subject-matter and therefore it can adopt everything which can enter the inner life as such and which above all can be clothed in the form of feeling. But in that case this implies that music's purpose cannot be an attempt to work for visual apprehension but must be limited to making the inner life intelligible to itself, whether by making the substantial inner depth of a subject-matter as such penetrate the depths of the heart or whether by preferring to display the life and energy of a subject-matter in a single subjective inner life so that this subjective deep feeling itself becomes music's own proper subject-matter.

(ββ) The inner life in its abstraction from the world has as its first differentiation the one that music is connected with, namely feeling, i.e. the widening subjectivity of the self which does proceed to have an objective content but still leaves this content remaining in this immediate self-sufficiency of the self and the self's relation to itself without any externality at all.[1] Therefore feeling remains

---

[1] Religious feeling has religion as an 'objective content', but as *feeling* it is purely subjective, a state of consciousness suffusing the self without any reference to any kind of externality (Hegel's *Philosophy of Mind, Enc.* § 400). Thinking

the shrouding of the content, and it is to this sphere that music has laid claim.

(γγ) Here then all particular feelings spread out from one another for expression, and all nuances of cheerfulness and serenity, the sallies, moods, and jubilations of the soul, the degrees of anxiety, misery, mourning, lament, sorrow, grief, longing, etc., and lastly, of awe, worship, love, etc., become the peculiar sphere of musical expression.

(β) Outside art a sound as an interjection, as the cry of pain, as a sigh or a laugh, is already the direct and most living expression of states of soul and feelings, is the 'och' and 'oh' of the heart. What lies in it is a self-production and objectification of the soul as soul, an expression midway between (a) the unconscious immersion, and reversion into self, in inward specific thoughts, and (b) a production, not practical but contemplative, just as the bird has in its song this delight and this production of itself.

But the purely natural expression in the form of interjections is still not music, for these outcries are not articulate and arbitrary signs of ideas, like language-sounds, and therefore do not utter something envisaged in its universality as an idea; on the contrary, in and on the sound itself they manifest a mood and a feeling which express themselves directly in such sounds and give relief to the heart by their utterance; but this liberation is not a liberation by art. Music must, on the contrary, bring feelings into specific tone-relationships, deprive the natural expression of its wildness and crude deliverance, and mitigate it.

(γ) Interjections do form the starting-point of music, but music is itself art only by being a cadenced interjection, and in this matter has to dress up its perceptible material artistically to a greater extent than is the case in painting and poetry; not until then can the material express a spiritual content in an artistically adequate way. The manner in which the range of sounds is transformed into this adequacy we have to consider in more detail later; meanwhile I will only repeat the remark that the notes in themselves are an ensemble of differences and may be separated and combined in the most varied sorts of direct harmonies, essential oppositions, contradictions, and modulations. To these unifications and oppositions,

---

distinguishes between itself and what is thought, but in *feeling* this distinction is only implicit. 'The thing felt is interwoven with the feeling itself' (see p. 904, final paragraph of this section, *b*).

to the variety of their movements and transitions, to their entry, progress, struggle, dissolution and disappearance there corresponds more closely or more distantly the inner nature of this or that subject-matter, as well as of the feelings in the form of which the heart and mind master a subject-matter, so that now such note-relationships, treated and formed in this correspondence, provide the animated expression of what is present in the spirit as a specific content.

But therefore the medium of sound proves to be more akin to the inner simple essence of a subject-matter than the sensuous material hitherto considered, because instead of being fixed in spatial figures and acquiring stability as the variety of things separated or juxtaposed in space it has rather assigned to it the ideal sphere of *time*, and therefore it does not reach the difference between what is simply inner and its corporeal concrete appearance and shape. The same is true of the form of the *feeling* of a subject-matter which it is principally the business of music to express. As in self-conscious thinking, so here too there already enters into our vision and ideas the necessary distinction between (*a*) the self that sees, has ideas, and thinks, and (*b*) the object of sight, ideas, and thought. But, in feeling, this distinction is expunged, or rather is not yet explicit, since there the thing felt is interwoven with the inner feeling as such, without any separation between them. When therefore music is linked with poetry as an art accompanying it, or, conversely, when poetry as the elucidating interpreter is linked with music, music cannot propose to give an external illustration to ideas and thoughts as these are consciously apprehended by us, or to reproduce them, but, on the contrary, as I said, must bring home to our feelings the simple essence of some subject-matter in such note-relationships as are akin to the inner nature of that subject; or, more particularly, it must try to express that very feeling which the object of views and ideas may arouse in the spirit (itself just as capable of having sympathetic feelings as of having ideas), and to do this by means of its notes that accompany and inwardize the poetry.

(*c*) *Effect of Music*

From this trend of music we can derive the power with which it works especially on the heart as such; for the heart neither proceeds to intellectual considerations nor distracts our conscious attention to separate points of view, but is accustomed to live in deep feeling and its undisclosed depth. For it is precisely this sphere of inner sensibility, abstract self-comprehension, which music takes for its own and therefore brings movement into the seat of inner changes, into the heart and mind as this simple concentrated centre of the whole of human life.

(α) Sculpture in particular gives to its works of art an entirely self-subsistent existence, a self-enclosed objectivity alike in content and in external appearance. Its content is the individually animated but independently self-reposing substance of the spirit, while its form is a three-dimensional figure. For this reason, by being a perceptible object, a sculpture has the maximum of independence. As we have already seen in considering painting (pp. 805–6), a picture comes into a closer relation with the spectator, partly on account of the inherently more subjective content which it portrays, partly because of the pure appearance of reality which it provides; and it proves therefore that it is not meant to be something independent on its own account, but on the contrary to be something essentially for apprehension by the person who has both vision and feeling. Yet, confronted by a picture, we are still left with a more independent freedom, since in its case we always have to do with an object present externally which comes to us only through our vision and only thereby affects our feelings and ideas. Consequently the spectator can look at a picture from this angle or that, notice this or that about it, analyse the whole (because it stays in front of him), make all sorts of reflections about it, and in this way preserve complete freedom for his own independent consideration of it.

(αα) A piece of music, on the other hand, does also proceed, like any work of art, to a beginning of the distinction between subjective enjoyment and the objective work, because in its notes as they actually sound it acquires a perceptible existence different from inner appreciation; but, for one thing, this contrast is not intensified, as it is in visual art, into a permanent external existent in space and the perceptibility of an object existing independently, but conversely volatilizes its real or objective existence into an immediate temporal disappearance; for another thing, unlike poetry, music does not separate its external medium from its spiritual content. In poetry the idea is more independent of the sound of the language, and it is further separated from this external expression than is the case in the other arts, and it is developed in a special course of images mentally and imaginatively formed as such. It is true that it might be objected that music, as I have said previously, may conversely free its notes from its content and so give them independence, but this liberation is not really compatible with art. Compatibility here consists in using the harmonic and melodious movement entirely as an expression of the content once chosen and of the feelings which that content is capable of arousing. Expression in music has, as its *content*, the inner life itself, the inner sense of feeling and for the matter in hand, and, as its *form*, sound, which, in an art that least of all proceeds to spatial figures, is purely evanescent in its perceptible existence; the result is that music with its movements penetrates the arcanum of all the movements of the soul. Therefore it captivates the consciousness which is no longer confronted by an object and which in the loss of this freedom [of contemplation] is carried away itself by the ever-flowing stream of sounds.

Yet, even here, given the varied directions in which music can develop, a varied kind of effect is possible. For when music lacks a deeper content or, in general, does not express fullness of soul, it may happen that, on the one hand, we take delight, without any movement of emotion, in the purely sensuous sound and its melodiousness or, on the other hand, follow with purely intellectual consideration the course of the harmony and melody by which the heart itself is no further touched or led. Indeed in the case of music above all it is possible to indulge in such a purely intellectual analysis for which there is nothing in the work of art except skill and virtuosity in compilation. But if we take no account of this intellectualistic attitude and approach a musical work of art naïvely instead, then it draws us into itself and carries us along with it, quite apart from the power which art, by being art, generally exercises over us. The peculiar power of music is an elemental one, i.e. it lies in the element of sound in which art moves here.

($\beta\beta$) The self is not only gripped by this element in some particular part of its being or simply through a specific content; on the contrary in its simple self, in the centre of its spiritual existence, it is elevated by the musical work and activated by it. So for example, in the case of prominent and easily flowing rhythms we at once desire to beat time with them and to join in singing the melody; and dance music even gets into our feet; in short, music gets hold of the individual as *this* man. Conversely, in the case of a purely regular action which, falling into time, conforms with the beat

MUSIC 907

owing to this uniformity and has no further content at all, on the one hand we demand an expression of this regularity as such so that this action can come to the individual's apprehension in a way itself subjective, and on the other hand we desire an interest less empty than this uniformity. Both are afforded by a musical accompaniment. It is thus that music accompanies the march of troops; this attunes the mind to the regularity of the step, immerses the individual in the business of marching, and concentrates his mind on what he has to do. For the same sort of reason, the disorderly restlessness of a lot of people in a restaurant and the unsatisfying excitement it causes is burdensome; this walking to and fro, this clattering and chattering should be regulated, and since in the intervals of eating and drinking we have to do with empty time, this emptiness should be filled. This is an occasion, like so many others, when music comes to the rescue and in addition wards off other thoughts, distractions, and ideas.

($\gamma\gamma$) Here there is also in evidence the connection between (a) subjective feeling and (b) time as such which is the universal element in music. The inner life in virtue of its subjective unity is the active negation of accidental juxtaposition in space, and therefore a negative unity. But at first this self-identity remains wholly abstract and empty and it consists only in making *itself* its object and yet in cancelling this objectivity (itself only ideal and identical with what the self is) in order to make *itself* in this way a subjective unity. The similarly ideal negative activity in its sphere of externality is *time*. For (i) it extinguishes the accidental juxtaposition of things in space and draws their continuity together into a point of time, into a 'now'. But (ii) the point of time proves at once to be its own negation, since, as soon as *this* 'now' is, it supersedes itself by passing into another 'now' and therefore reveals its negative activity. (iii) On account of externality, the element in which time moves, no truly *subjective* unity is established between the first point of time and the second by which it has been superseded; on the contrary, the 'now' still remains always the *same* in its alteration; for each point of time is a 'now' just as little distinguished from the other, regarded as merely a point of time, as the abstract self is from the object in which it cancels itself and, since this object is only the empty self itself, in which it closes with itself.

Furthermore the actual self itself belongs to time, with which, if we abstract from the concrete content of consciousness and self-consciousness, it coincides, since it is nothing but this empty movement of positing itself as 'other' and then cancelling this alteration, i.e. maintaining itself in its other as the self and only the self as such. The self is in time, and time is the being of the subject himself. Now since time, and not space as such, provides the essential element in which sound gains existence in respect of its musical value, and since the time of the sound is that of the subject too, sound on this principle penetrates the self, grips it in its simplest being, and by means of the temporal movement and its rhythm sets the self in motion; while the further figuration of the notes, as an expression of feelings, introduces besides a still more definite enrichment for the subject by which he is likewise touched and drawn on.

This is what can be advanced as the essential reason for the elemental might of music.

(β) If music is to exercise its full effect, more is required than purely abstract sound in a temporal movement. The second thing to be added is a *content*, i.e. a spiritual feeling felt by the heart, and the soul of this content expressed in notes.

Therefore we may not cherish a tasteless opinion about the all-powerfulness of music as such, a topic on which ancient writers, profane and sacred alike, have told so many fabulous stories. In the case of the civilizing miracles of Orpheus, his notes and their movement sufficed for wild beasts which lay around him tame, but not for men who demanded the contents of a higher doctrine. After all the Hymns called Orphic which have come down to us, whether in their original form or not, contain mythological and other ideas. Similarly the war-songs of Tyrtaeus are famous; by their means, so it is said, the Spartans, after a long series of unsuccessful battles, were fired with irresistible enthusiasm and were victorious over the Messenians. In this case too the content of the ideas stimulated by these elegies was the chief thing, although the worth and effect of their musical side too is not to be denied, especially at a period of deeply stirred passions and amongst barbarian peoples. The pipes of the Highlanders made an essential contribution to inflaming their courage, and the power of the Marseillaise, the *ça ira* of the French Revolution, is not to be gainsaid. But enthusiasm proper has its ground in the specific Idea, in the true spiritual interest which has filled the nation and which can be raised by music into a momentarily more lively feeling because the notes, the rhythm, and the melody can carry the man away who gives himself up to them. Nowadays, however, we will not regard music as capable of producing by itself such a courageous mood and a contempt for death. Today nearly all armies have really good regimental music which engrosses the troops, diverts them, spurs on their march, and incites them to attack; but we do not suppose that all this is to defeat the enemy. Mere bugle-blowing and drum-beating does not produce courage, and it would take a lot of trumpets before a fortress would tumble at their sound as the walls of Jericho did.[1] It is enthusiastic ideas, cannon, the genius of generals which achieve this now, and not music, for music can only count as a support for those powers which in other ways have already filled and captured the mind.

(γ) A final aspect of the effect of the notes on the mind con sists of the manner in which a musical work, as distinguished from other works of art, comes home to us. Unlike buildings, statues, and paintings, the notes have in themselves no permanent subsistence as objects; on the contrary, with their fleeting passage they vanish again and therefore the musical composition needs a continually repeated reproduction, just because of this purely momentary existence of its notes. Yet the necessity of such renewed vivication has still another and a deeper significance. For music takes as its subject-matter the subjective inner life itself, with the aim of presenting itself, not as an external shape or as an objectively existing work, but as that inner life; consequently its expression must be the direct communication of a living individual who has put into it the entirety of his own inner life. This is most clearly the case in the song of the human voice, but it is relatively true also of instrumental music which can be performed only by practising artists with their living skill both spiritual and technical.

It is only this subjective aspect in the actual production of a musical work that completes in music the significance of the subjective; but the performance may go so far in this subjective direction that the subjective side may be isolated as a one-sided extreme, with the result that subjective virtuosity in the production may as such be made the sole centre and content of the enjoyment.

I will let these remarks suffice in relation to the general character of music.

[1] Joshua, 6.

2. *Particular Characteristics of Music's Means of Expression*

Up to this point we have considered music only on the side of its having to shape and animate notes into the tones of the subjective inner life; the next question is about the means that make it possible and necessary for the notes not to be a purely natural *shriek* of feeling but the developed and artistic *expression* of it. For feeling as such has a content [it is a feeling of something], while a mere note has none [it is not the sound of anything]. Therefore the note must first be made capable, by artistic treatment, of assimilating the expression of an inner life. On this point the following conclusions may be formulated in most general terms.

Each note is an independent existent, complete in itself, but one which is not articulated and subjectively comprehended as a living unity as is the case with the animal or human form; and, on the other hand, it is unlike a particular limb of a corporeal organism or some single trait of a spiritually or physically animated body, which shows on the surface that this particular detail can exist at all and win significance, meaning, and expressiveness only in animated connection with the other limbs and traits. So far as the external material goes, a picture consists of single strokes and colours which may exist on their own account also; but the real matter which alone makes those strokes and colours into a work of art, i.e. the lines, surfaces, etc. of the figure, have a meaning only as a concrete whole. On the other hand, the *single* note is more independent in itself and can also up to a certain point be animated by feeling and become a definite expression of it.

Conversely, however, the note is not a merely vague rustling and sounding but can only have any musical worth on the strength of its definiteness and consequent purity. Therefore, owing to this definiteness in its real sound and its temporal duration, it is in direct connection with other notes. Indeed it is this relation alone which imparts to it its own proper and actual definiteness and, along with that, its difference from other notes whether in opposition to them or in harmony with them.

Owing to their relative independence this relation remains something external to the notes, so that the connections into which they are brought do not belong to the single notes themselves, do not belong to them by their nature as they do to the members of an animal or a human organism, or even to the forms of a natural landscape. Bringing different notes together in specific relations is therefore something, if not contradicting the essence of the note, still only artificial and not otherwise already present naturally. Consequently such a relation proceeds from a third party [the composer] and exists only for a third party, i.e. the man who apprehends it [i.e. either the executant or the listener].

On account of this externality of the relation, the specific character of the notes and their assembly rests on *quantity*, on numerical proportions which of course have their basis in the nature of sound itself, but they are used by music in a way first discovered by art and most variously modified.

From this point of view, what constitutes the basis of music is not life in itself, as an organic unity, but equality, inequality, etc., in short the mathematical form dominant in the quantitative sphere. Therefore if musical notes are to be discussed with precision, our statements must be made solely in terms of numerical proportions and the arbitrary letters by which we are accustomed to designate the notes according to these proportions.

In this reduction to pure *quanta* and their mathematical and external character music has its principal affinity with architecture, because, like architecture, it constructs its inventions on the firm basis and the frame of proportions; but there is no expansion into an organic and living articulation where with one detail the rest are given, and no closure of detail into a living unity. On the contrary, music, like architecture, begins to become a free art only in the further developments which it can produce out of those proportions. Now while architecture gets no further in this process of liberation than producing a harmony of forms and the animation characteristic of a secret eurhythmy, music *per contra*, having as its content the inmost subjective free life and movement of the soul, breaks up into the profoundest opposition between this free inner life and those fundamental quantitative proportions. Yet it cannot rest in this opposition but acquires the difficult task of both adopting and overcoming it, because through those necessary proportions it gives to those free movements of the heart, which it expresses, a more secure ground and basis on which the inner life then moves and develops in a freedom made concrete only through that necessity.

In this connection we must distinguish in the note two aspects in accordance with which it can be used in an artistic way: (i) the abstract foundation, the universal but not yet specifically physical[1] element, namely *time*, within the sphere of which the note falls. (ii) The sounding itself, the difference in reality between notes both in respect of differences in the sensuous sounding material and in respect of the notes themselves in their relation to one another as single notes and as an ensemble. Then (iii) there is the soul which animates the notes, rounds them off into a free whole, and gives to them, in their temporal movement and their real sounding, an expression of the spirit. These three aspects provide us with the following series of stages for the more specific articulation of our subject.

(i) First, we have to concern ourselves with the purely temporal duration and movement which the art of music may not leave to chance but must determine in fixed measures; it has to diversify them by introducing differences, and yet restore unity amid these differences. This provides the necessity for time, bar or beat, and rhythm.

(ii) But, secondly, music is not only concerned with time as such and relations of longer or shorter duration, pauses, emphases, etc., but with the concrete time of specific notes in their resonance which therefore do not differ from one another solely in their duration. This difference rests, on the one hand, on the specific quality of the sensuous material from the vibrations of which the note proceeds, and, on the other hand, on the different number of vibrations in which the resonant bodies tremble during the same length of time. Thirdly, these differences afford the essential aspects for the relationship of notes in their harmony, opposition, and modulation. We may indicate this part of our subject by giving it the general name of the theory of harmony.

(iii) Thirdly and lastly, it is melody whereby, on these foundations of the rhythmically animated beat and the harmonic differences and movements, the realm of notes closes into one spiritually free expression; and this thus leads us on to the following, and final, chief section which has to consider music in its concrete unification with the spiritual content it is to express in beat, harmony, and melody.

[1] In Hegel's Philosphy of Nature mechanics precedes physics. Time belongs to the former, sound to the latter. Nevertheless, in § 330, *Zusatz*, Hegel says that 'sound belongs to the mechanical sphere.... It is a free physical expression of the ideal realm which yet is linked with mechanism—it is freedom *in* heavy matter and at the same time freedom *from* it.'

(a) *Time, Bar,*[1] *Rhythm*

If we take in the first place the purely temporal aspect of musical sound, we have to discuss (a) the necessity of time's being in general the dominant thing in music; (b) the bar as the purely mathematically regulated measure of time; (c) rhythm which begins to animate this abstract rule by emphasizing some specific beats and subordinating others.

(α) The figures of sculpture and painting are juxtaposed in space and this extension in space is presented as an actual or apparent whole. But music can produce notes only by making a body existing in space tremble and setting it in vibratory motion. These vibrations belong to art only in the sense of following one another, and so the sensuous material enters music not with its spatial form but only with the temporal duration of its movement. Now it is true that any movement of a body is also always present in space, so that although the figures of sculpture and painting are actually at rest they still have the right to portray the appearance of movement; music however does not adopt movement as it occurs in space, and therefore there is left for its configuration *only* the time in which the vibration of the body occurs.

(αα) But it follows, as we have seen already, that time, unlike space, is not a positive juxtaposition but, on the contrary, a negative sort of externality, i.e. as a point, external juxtaposition being cancelled, and as a negativing activity, cancelling *this* point of time to give place to another which likewise is cancelled to give place to another, and so on and on. In the succession of these points of time each note can be fixed independently as a single note or it can be brought into a quantitative connection with others, and in this way time becomes countable. Conversely, however, time is the unbroken series of the coming to be and the passing away of these points of time, which, taken purely as such and in their unparticularized abstraction, have no difference from one another; consequently time proves to be both a uniform stream and also an inherently undifferentiated duration.

(ββ) Yet music cannot leave time in this indeterminacy; it must

---

[1] *Takt.* The word also means 'beat' in the sense of any 'measured sequence of sounds' (*O.E.D.*), but 'bar' is less misleading in many contexts, especially where Hegel discusses the divisions of the bar in 2/4, 6/8 time etc. 'Beat', in the sense of a conductor's beat, is also used in the translation.

on the contrary determine it more closely, give it a measure, and order its flow by the rule of such a measure. It is owing to this regulating treatment that time enters for notes. Then the question arises at once why music requires such a measure at all. The necessity for specific periods of time may be developed from the fact that time stands in the closest connection with the simple self which perceives and is meant to perceive in the notes its own inner life; this is because time as externality has in itself the same principle which is active in the self as the abstract foundation of everything inner and spiritual. If it is the simple self which as inner is to become objective to itself in music, then the universal element in this objectivity must be treated in conformity with that principle of the inner life. But the self is not an indeterminate continuity and unpunctuated duration, but only becomes a self by concentrating its momentary experiences and returning into itself from them. The process of self-cancellation whereby it becomes an object to itself it turns into self-awareness and now only through this self-relation does it come to have a sense and consciousness, etc., of itself. But this concentration of experiences essentially implies an *interruption* of the purely indefinite process of changes which is what time was as we envisaged it just now, because the coming to be and passing away, the vanishing and renewal of points of time, was nothing but an entirely formal transition beyond this 'now' to another 'now' of the same kind, and therefore only an uninterrupted movement forward. Contrasted with this empty progress, the self is what persists in and by itself, and its self-concentration interrupts the indefinite series of points of time and makes gaps in their abstract continuity; and in its awareness of its discrete experiences, the self recalls itself and finds itself again and thus is freed from mere self-externalization and change.

(γγ) Accordingly, the duration of a note does not go on indefinitely but, by its start and finish, which thereby become a specific beginning and ending, the note cancels the series of moments of time which in itself contains no differences. But if many notes follow one another and acquire a different duration from one another, then in place of that first empty indefiniteness there is substituted anew only an arbitrary and therefore equally indefinite *variety* of particular quantities. This unregulated running riot contradicts the unity of the self just as much as the abstract forward movement does, and the self can find itself again and be satisfied in

MUSIC

this diversified definiteness of duration only if single *quanta* are brought into one unity. Since this unity subsumes particulars under itself, it must be a definite unity, although as a mere identity in the external sphere, it can at first remain only of an external kind.

(β) This leads us to the further regulation produced by the *bar* (or beat).

($\alpha\alpha$) The first point for consideration here consists in the fact, already mentioned, that different divisions of time are bound together into a unity in which the self makes itself aware of its self-identity. Since the self in the first place affords the foundation here only as an *abstract* self, this equality of the onward flow of time and its notes can also itself prove to be effective only as an *abstract* equality, i.e. as the uniform repetition of the same temporal unit. Accordingly the simple purpose of the bar is (*a*) to establish a specific temporal unit as the measure and rule both for the marked interruption of the previously undifferentiated temporal succession and also for the equally arbitrary duration of single notes which now are brought together into a definite unity, and (*b*) to bring about the continual renewal of this time-measure in an abstractly uniform way. In this respect the bar has the same function as regularity in architecture where, for example, columns of the same height and thickness are placed alongside one another at equal intervals, or a row of windows of a specific size is regulated by the principle of equality. Here too a fixed definiteness and a wholly uniform repetition of it is present. In this uniformity self-consciousness finds itself again as a unity, because for one thing it recognizes its own equality as the ordering of an arbitrary manifold, and, for another thing, the repetition of the same unity calls to mind the fact that this unity was already there and precisely through its repetition shows itself as the dominating rule. But the satisfaction which the self acquires, owing to the bar, in this rediscovery of itself is all the more complete because the unity and uniformity does not pertain either to time or the notes in themselves; it is something which belongs solely to the self and is inserted into time by the self for its own self-satisfaction. For in nature this abstract identity does not exist. Even the heavenly bodies have no uniform beat or bar in their motion; on the contrary, they accelerate or retard their course so that in the same time they do not traverse the same space. The case is similar with falling bodies, the projection of a missile, etc., and still less do animals reduce their running, jumping, snatching, etc. to the precise repetition of a measure of time. In this matter, the beat proceeds from the spirit alone far more than do the regular fixed magnitudes of architecture, analogies for which may more easily be found in nature.

($\beta\beta$) But the individual always perceives the like identity which proceeds from and is himself, and if in the midst of the multitude of notes and their duration he is to revert into himself as a result of the bar, this implies in addition the presence of what is unregulated and not uniform, if the definite unity is to be felt as rule. For only if the definiteness of the measure conquers and regulates what is arbitrarily unlike, is that definiteness proved to be the unity of the accidental variety and the rule for it. For this reason this definiteness must therefore absorb the variety into itself and make uniformity appear in what is not uniform. This it is which first gives to the beat its own definite character in itself and also therefore distinguishes this character from that of other measures of time which can be repeated in conformity with a beat.

($\gamma\gamma$) Accordingly, the multiplicity of notes enclosed in a bar has its specific norm by which it is divided and regulated, and from this, thirdly, the different sorts of bar arise. The first thing to be noticed in this context is the internal division of the bar in accordance with either the even or odd number of the repeated equal parts. Of the first kind examples are two–four and four–four time. Here the even number is clearly predominant. A three–four time is a different kind; in it the parts, of course equal to one another, still form a unity in an uneven number. Both characteristics are united, for example in a six–eight time, which seems numerically the same as a three–four one; but in fact it falls not into three but into two parts, although both of these in their further division take three, i.e. the odd number, for their principle.

A specification like this is the steadily repeating rule for every particular sort of bar. But however strictly the specific beat has to govern the *variety* of duration and its longer or shorter sections, nevertheless its domination is not to extend so far that it dominates the variety quite abstractly in such a way that in a four–four bar, for instance, only four entirely equal minims can occur, in a three–four one only three, in a six–eight one only six crotchets etc.; on the contrary, regularity is restricted here in such a way that in a four–four bar the *sum* of the single notes amounts only to four equal minims which, however, not only may divide besides into crotchets and quavers, but conversely may just as readily contract again and also are capable of great variations in other ways.

(γ) Yet the further this abundant variation goes, the more necessary it is for the essential sections of the bar to be asserted in it and actually marked out as the principal rule to be emphasized. This is brought about by means of *rhythm* which alone brings proper animation to the time and the bar. In relation to this vivification too, different aspects can be distinguished.

(αα) The first is the *accent* which can be laid more or less audibly on specific parts of the bar while others flit by unaccented. Through such stress or absence of stress, once more varied, each individual kind of bar receives its peculiar rhythm which is exactly connected with the specific way in which this kind is divided. A four–four bar, for example, in which the even number dominates, has a double arsis, first on the first minim and next, though weaker, on the third. The more strongly accentuated parts are called 'strong' parts of the bar, others the 'weak' ones. In a three–four bar the accent falls wholly on the first minim, but in six–eight on the first and fourth, so that here the double accent emphasizes the precise division into two halves.

(ββ) When music is an accompaniment, its rhythm has an essential relation to that of the poetry. On this matter I will only remark, in the most general terms, that the accent of the bar must not directly conflict with that of the metre. If, for example, a syllable not accented in the rhythm of the verse falls into a strong part of the bar while the arsis or even the caesura falls into a weak part, the result is a false contradiction, better avoided, between the rhythm of the poetry and that of the music. The same is true of long and short syllables; these too must in general so correspond with the duration of the notes that longer syllables fall on longer notes and shorter on shorter, even if this correspondence cannot be carried through to the last degree of exactitude, since music may often be allowed greater scope for the duration of long notes as well as for the more abundant division of them.

(γγ) Thirdly, to make a preliminary remark at once about melody, its animated rhythm is to be distinguished from the abstractness and regular and strict return of the rhythm of the beat. In this connection music has a freedom similar to poetry's and an even greater one. In poetry, as we all know, the beginning and ending of words need not correspond with the beginning and ending of the feet of a line, for on the contrary such a coincidence of the two produces a lame line with no caesura. Similarly the beginning and ending of sentences and periods must not always be the beginning and ending of a line. On the contrary, a period ends better at the beginning or even in the middle and towards the later feet of the line; and there a new period begins which carries one line over to the next one. It is the same in music with bar and rhythm. The melody and its different periods need not begin strictly with the beginning of a bar and end with the closing of another; indeed they can be emancipated in the sense that the chief arsis of the melody falls in that part of a bar which, so far as its ordinary rhythm goes, has no such emphasis, while conversely a note which in the natural course of the melody should have had no marked emphasis may stand in the strong part of the bar which requires arsis. Thus the value of a note in the rhythm of a bar differs from that which this note may claim for itself in the melody. But the counter-thrust between the rhythm of the bar and that of the melody comes out at its sharpest in what are called syncopations.

If on the other hand the melody keeps strictly in its rhythm and parts to the rhythm of the beat, then it readily sounds humdrum, bare, and lacking in invention. What may be demanded in this connection is, in brief, freedom from the pedantry of metre and the barbarism of a uniform rhythm. For deficiency in greater freedom of movement, along with dullness and carelessness, readily leads to what is gloomy and melancholy, and thus many of our popular tunes[1] have about them something lugubrious, drawling, and lumbering because the soul has available only a rather monotonous movement as a medium of expression and is led consequently to put into that medium the plaintive feelings of a broken heart.

The southern languages, on the contrary, especially Italian, leave open a rich field for a varied and more lively rhythm and an outpouring of melody. In this there already lies an essential difference between German and Italian music. The uniform and flat iambic scansion which recurs in so many German songs kills any free and joyous *abandon* of melody and inhibits any higher flight and variety. In modern times Reichardt[2] and others seem to me to have brought a new rhythmic life into song-composition precisely by

---

[1] i.e. folk-songs.

[2] J. F., 1752–1814. Master of Music to Frederick the Great. Of his numerous compositions only his *Singspiele* and *Lieder* are remembered.

abandoning this iambic sing-song, although in some of their songs it does still predominate. Yet the influence of the iambic rhythm occurs not only in songs but in many of our greatest musical compositions. Even in Handel's *Messiah* the composition in many arias and choruses follows with declamatory truth not only the sense of the words, but also the fall of the iambic rhythm, partly in the mere difference between longs and shorts, partly in the fact that the long syllable of the iambus is given a higher note than the short one. This character is indeed one of the features which make us Germans so completely at home in Handel's music, along with its other excellences, its majestic swing, its impetuous movement, and its wealth of feelings, as profoundly religious as they are idyllically simple. This rhythmical ingredient in melody falls on our ear much more easily than on an Italian one. The Italians may find in it something unfree and strange and uncongenial to their ear.

(b) Harmony

The other content which alone fills in music's abstract foundation in bar and rhythm, and, therefore makes it possible for that foundation to become really concrete music, is the realm of notes as such. This more essential province of music comprises the laws of *harmony*. Here a new element comes on the scene because by its vibration not only does a body cease to be portrayable by art in its *spatial* form and move over instead to the development of, as it were, its *temporal* form, but, depending on its physical character, its varying length or shortness, and the number of vibrations it makes during a specific time, it sounds differently. Therefore this is something which art must seize upon and mould to its artistic purposes.

In this second element there are three main points to emphasize in more detail.

(α) The first point that demands our consideration is the difference between the particular instruments. It has been necessary for music to invent and construct them in order to produce an ensemble which even in relation to the audible sound, independently of all difference in the reciprocal relation of treble and bass or high and low pitch, constitutes a compact range of different notes.

(β) Yet, secondly, the sound of music, apart from variations in instruments and the human voice, is in itself an articulated ensemble of different notes, scales, and keys which depend primarily on quantitative relations; determined by these relations, these are the notes which each instrument, and the human voice, has the task of producing in its own specific tonality with a greater or lesser degree of completeness.

(γ) Thirdly, music consists neither of single intervals[1] nor of purely abstract scales and separate keys; on the contrary, it is a concrete harmony, opposition, and modulation of notes which therefore necessitate a forward movement and a transition from one to the other. This juxtaposition and change does not rest on pure accident and caprice, but is subject to specific laws in which everything genuinely musical has its necessary foundation.

In now passing on to the more detailed consideration of these points I must particularly restrict myself here, as I said before, to the most general remarks.

(α) Sculpture and painting have their perceptible material, wood, stone, metal, etc., colours, etc., more or less at hand or, in order to make it fit for artistic use, they have to transform it to only a slight extent.

(αα) But music, which as such moves in an element first manufactured by and for art, must subject it to a significantly more difficult process of preparation before music achieves the production of notes. Apart from the mixture of metals for casting, the grinding of colours and fixing them with the sap of plants, oil, etc., and the mixture of them to form new shades, sculpture and painting need no further wealth of inventions. Except the human voice, which is provided directly by nature, music must itself first thoroughly fashion its usual media into actual notes before it can exist at all.

(ββ) So far as concerns these media as such, we have already considered sound as being the trembling of something existent in space, the first *inner* animation which asserts itself against purely objective juxtaposition in space, and, by the negation of this real spatiality, appears as an ideal unity of all the physical properties of a body, e.g. its specific gravity and sort of cohesion. If we go on to ask about the qualitative character of that material which is made to sound, it is extremely varied alike in its physical nature and in its construction for artistic purposes: e.g. (i) a straight or curved column of air enclosed in a fixed tube of wood or metal, (ii) a

---

[1] i.e. differences of pitch or harmony between notes.

surface of stretched parchment, (iii) a straightly stretched string of catgut or metal, or (iv) a metallic or glass bell.—In this matter the following chief differences may be noted.

First, the direction of a *line* is the dominating thing which produces instruments really and properly useful musically, whether the chief principle is provided by a non-cohesive column of air, as in wind instruments, or a column of matter which must be tightly stretched but preserve elasticity enough to enable it to vibrate, as in stringed instruments.

Secondly, there is the domination of a *surface* though this provides only subordinate instruments like the kettledrum, bell, and harmonica. For between the self-apprehending inner life and the 'linear' sounds there is a secret sympathy, and consequently the inherently simple self demands the resounding tremble of the simple length instead of that of broader and rounder surfaces. The inner life, that is to say, is as a self this spiritual point which apprehends itself in notes *qua* the expression of itself, but the first cancellation and expression of this point is not the surface but the simple direction of a line.[1] From this point of view, broad and round surfaces do not meet the needs or the power of our subjective apprehension.

In the case of the *kettledrum* a skin is stretched over a hemispherical basin and when it is struck at *one* point the whole surface is made to tremble into a hollow sound which can be made to harmonize but in itself, like the whole instrument, cannot be given sharper definition or any great variety. The opposite is the case with the *harmonica* and its lightly struck musical glasses. Here there is a concentrated and non-emergent intensity which is so fatiguing that many people cannot hear it without soon getting a nervous headache. Besides, in spite of its specific effect, this instrument has not been able to give permanent pleasure and it can be combined with other instruments only with difficulty because it is too little in accord with them. In the case of the *bell*, there is the same deficiency in different notes, and the same character of being struck at one point as occurs with the kettledrum, but the bell does not have such a hollow sound; it rings out freely although its reverberating boom is more like a mere echo of its being struck at one point.

---

[1] This is derived from Hegel's Philosophy of Nature. See, for instance, § 256: By cancelling itself the point constitutes a line which, cancelled in turn, produces a surface.

Thirdly, we may specify as the freest, and in its sound the most perfect instrument the human voice, which unites in itself the character of wind and string instruments because in this case it is a column of air which vibrates, while through the muscles there also comes into play the principle of tightly stretched strings. Just as we saw, in the case of the colour of the human skin, that, as an ideal unity, it contains the rest of the colours and therefore is the most perfect colour, so the human voice contains the ideal totality of sound, a totality only spread out amongst the other instruments in their particular differences. Consequently it is the perfection of sound and therefore marries most flexibly and beautifully with the other instruments. At the same time the human voice can apprehend itself as the sounding of the soul itself, as the sound which the inner life has in its own nature for the expression of itself, an expression which it regulates directly. On the other hand, in the case of the other instruments a vibration is set up in a body indifferent to the soul and its expression and, in virtue of its own character, more remote from these; but in song the soul rings out from its own body. Hence, like the heart and its own feelings, the human voice develops in a great variety of particular ways, a variety founded, so far as its more general differences are concerned, in national and other natural circumstances. So, for example, the Italians are a people of song and amongst them the most beautiful voices occur most frequently. A principal feature in this beauty is the material basis of the sound as sound, the pure metal of the voice which should not taper off to mere sharpness or glass-like thinness or remain dull and hollow; but, at the same time, without going so far as *tremolo*, it preserves within this as it were compact and concentrated sound an inner life and an inner vibration of the sound. In this matter the voice must above all be pure, i.e. along with the perfect note no noise of any kind should assert itself.

(γγ) Music can use this whole range of instruments singly or all together in complete harmony. It is especially in recent times that music has first developed this latter capacity. The difficulty of such an artistically satisfactory assembly is great, for each instrument has its own special character which does not immediately fit in with that of another. Consequently great knowledge, circumspection, experience, and gift for invention are required for harmonizing many instruments of different kinds, for the effective introduction of some particular species, e.g. wind or string instruments, or for the sudden thunder of trumpet-blasts, and the changing succession of the sounds emphasized out of the entire chorus, and for doing all this in such a way that, amidst such differences, changes, oppositions, transitions, and modulations, an inner significance, a soul and feeling cannot be missed. So, for instance, in the symphonies of Mozart who was a great master of instrumentation and its intelligent, living, and clear variety the change of the particular instruments has often presented itself to me as a dramatic concert, as a sort of dialogue in which the character of one sort of instrument proceeds to the point where the character of the others is indicated and prepared; one replies to another or brings in what the sound of the preceding instrument was denied the power to express adequately, so that by this means a dialogue arises in the most graceful way between sounding and echoing, between beginning, progress, and completion.

(β) The second element to be mentioned no longer concerns the physical quality of the sound but instead the specific character of the note in itself and its relation to other notes. This objective relation whereby sound first expands into a range of notes both as individual in themselves and firmly determinate, and also as continually in essential relation with one another, constitutes the properly harmonic element in music and rests, in what again is primarily its physical side, on quantitative relations and numerical proportions. At the present stage the following more detailed points about this system of harmony are of importance.

First, the individual notes in their specific measure and in its relation to other notes: the theory of individual intervals.

Secondly, the assembled series of notes in their simplest succession in which one note directly hints at another: the scale.

Thirdly, the difference of these scales which, since each of them takes its start from a different note as its keynote, become both particular keys different from each other and also a whole system of these keys.

($\alpha\alpha$) The individual notes acquire not merely their sound but its perfectly specific determinacy by the vibration of a body. If this determinacy is to be achieved, then the sort of vibration must not be accidental and arbitrary but fixedly determined in itself. A column of air or a stretched string or a surface etc., which sounds, has a certain length or extension. For example, if we take a string and fasten it at two points and vibrate the stretched part that lies between them, the first thing of importance is the thickness and tension of the string. If this is done with two identical strings, then, according to an observation first made by Pythagoras,[1] the principal matter is the length, because two strings similar in thickness but of different lengths give a different number of vibrations over the same period of time. The difference of this number from another number and its relation to another is the basis for the difference and relation between particular notes in relation to their pitch, whether high or low.

But when we hear such notes, our apprehension of them feels quite different from an apprehension of dry numerical relationships: we need not know anything of numbers and arithmetical proportions, and indeed if we see a string vibrating, then, for one thing, the trembling vanishes without our being able to count it, and, for another thing, we do not need to look at a body emitting a sound to get an impression of the sound it emits. Therefore the connection between the sound and these numerical relations may not merely strike us as incredible; on the contrary, we may get the impression that our hearing and inner understanding of the harmonies is actually degraded by referring their origin to something purely quantitative. Nevertheless, the numerical relation between vibrations occurring in the same length of time is and remains the basis for determining the notes. For the fact that our hearing is a feeling simple in itself provides no ground for a convincing objection. Even what gives us a simple impression may, alike in its nature and as it exists, be something inherently varied and essentially connected with something else. For example, if we see blue or yellow, green or red colours in their specific purity, they likewise have the appearance of being wholly and simply determinate, while violet is easily seen as a mixture of red and blue. Nevertheless even pure blue is not something simple, but a specific relation of interpenetration of light and dark.[2] Religious feelings and a sense of justice in this or that case seem equally simple, and yet everything religious, every legal relation contains a variety of particular features, and it is their unity which gives rise to the simple feeling. In the same way, however true it is that we hear and have a feeling for

---

[1] For references to ancient literature, see the action on Pythagoras in Hegel's lectures on the History of Philosophy. The numerical basis of harmony is discussed at some length in Hegel's *Philosophy of Nature*, Addition to § 301.

[2] If the example is unfortunate, Goethe's theory of colours is to blame.

a note as something purely simple in itself, the note still rests on a variety which, because the note arises from the trembling of a body and therefore falls with its vibrations within *time*, is to be derived from the specific character of this trembling in time, i.e. from the specific number of vibrations within a specific time. To further particulars of this derivation I will devote the following remarks.

The notes that harmonize directly and whose difference in sound is not perceptible as an opposition are those in which the numerical relation of their vibrations remains of the simplest kind, whereas those that do not harmonize naturally have more complex proportions. Octaves are an example of the first kind. If we tune a string whose specific vibrations give the keynote and then divide it equally, the second half has just as many vibrations as the first in the same period of time.[1] If the string giving the keynote vibrates twice and the shorter string thrice, the latter gives a fifth; the proportion of four to five produces a third. It is otherwise with a second and a seventh which are eight to nine and eight to fifteen respectively.

(ββ) Now we have seen already that these proportions cannot be selected by chance but must contain an inner necessity both for their particular characters and for their ensemble; consequently the single intervals determined by such numerical proportions cannot remain indifferent to one another but have to close together into a whole. But the first ensemble of sounds arising in this way is not a concrete harmony of different notes but a wholly abstract systematic succession of notes according to their simplest relations to one another and their position in their ensemble. This gives us the simple series of notes called a scale. The basic determinant of the scale is the keynote which is repeated in its octave, and the other six notes are spread within this double limit which, since the keynote harmonizes with itself directly in its octave, is a reversion into itself. The other notes of the scale either harmonize directly with the keynote as the third and fifth do, or have in contrast with it a more essential difference of sound, as the second and seventh have, and they are arranged in a specific order of succession, the details of which, however, I will not explain further here.

(γγ) From this [diatonic] scale, in the third place, the different keys

---

[1] Half the string produces the octave above the note of the whole string. If the string is divided in the proportion of two to three, then the vibrations are in the same proportion, and the shorter string gives the fifth sound in the octave, i.e. G if C is the keynote.

arise. Each note of the scale can itself be made again the key-note for a new particular series of notes arranged according to the same law as the first was. With the development of the scale[1] into a greater wealth of notes, the number of keys has been automatically increased; modern music, for example, moves in a greater multiplicity of keys than Greek music did. The different notes of the scale, as we saw, are related to one another either by immediate correspondence in harmony or by an essential deviation and difference, and it follows that the series of keynotes arising from these notes either display a closer affinity and therefore immediately permit a modulation from one to another or, alien to one another, are not susceptible of such an immediate transition. But, furthermore, the keys become separated into the differences between major and minor, and, finally, owing to the keynote on which they are based, they have a specific character which corresponds again on its side to a particular mode of feeling, e.g. to sorrow, joy, grief, incitation to courage, etc. In this sense the Greeks even in their day wrote much[2] about the difference of keys and used and developed them in various ways.

(γ) The third main point, with which we may conclude our brief suggestions on the theory of harmony, concerns the chiming together of the notes themselves, i.e. the system of chords.

($\alpha\alpha$) Up to this point we have seen that the intervals form a whole, yet in the first instance this totality unfolds, in the scales and keys, into mere rows of separate sounds where each note in succession appears individual on its own account. At this point the sound was still abstract because it was always only *one* determinant of it that was in evidence. But the notes were in fact what they were only in virtue of their relation to one another,[3] and thus the sound must itself also gain existence as this concrete sound, i.e. different notes have to close together into one and the same sound. This combination of sounds, in which the number of notes united is of no essential consequence so that even two notes may form such a unity, is the essential nature of the chord. The determinate character of the individual notes cannot be left to chance or caprice; they must be regulated by an inner conformity to law and be

---

[1] e.g. into a chromatic scale.

[2] The reference is primarily to Aristoxenus, fourth-century B.C. He distinguished thirteen keys.

[3] e.g. the third note in the diatonic scale is only third because it follows the second and precedes the fourth.

arranged in their order of succession. Consequently the like conformity to law will have to enter for the chords also in order to determine what sort of grouping of notes is permissible for musical use and what is not. These laws alone provide us with the theory of harmony in the strict sense, and it is in accordance with this theory that the chords once again unfold into an inherently necessary system.

(ββ) In this system particular and different chords are developed because it is always *specific* notes that chime in together. We are therefore concerned at once with a totality of particular chords. As for the most general division of this totality, the detailed points are valid here again which I touched on cursorily in dealing with intervals, scales, and keys.

The first kind of chords consists of those formed from notes which harmonize with one another immediately. In these notes no opposition or contradiction arises and their complete concord is unimpaired. This is the case with the so-called 'consonant' chords, the basis of which is the triad [or 'common chord']. Of course this consists of the keynote, the third or mediant, and fifth or dominant. In this case the conception of harmony, indeed the very nature of that conception, is expressed in its simplest form. For we have before us an ensemble of different notes which nevertheless display this difference as an undisturbed unity; this is an immediate identity which yet does not lack particularization and mediation, while at the same time the mediation transcends the independence of the different notes; it may not be content with the to and fro of a changing relationship [between the notes] but actually brings their unification about and in that way [the chord] reverts to immediacy in itself.

But, secondly, what is still lacking in the different sorts of triad, into the details of which I cannot enter here, is the actual appearance of a deeper opposition. But, as we saw earlier, the scale contains, over and above those notes that harmonize with one another without any opposition, other notes that cancel this harmony. Such notes are the diminished and the augmented seventh. Since these belong likewise to the ensemble of notes, they must also gain an entry into the triad. But, if this happens, that immediate unity and consonance is destroyed, because a note is added which sounds essentially different, and in this way alone does a specific *difference* really enter, and indeed an opposition. What constitutes the real depth of the note-series is the fact that it goes on even to essential oppositions and does not fight shy of their sharpness and discordance. For the true Concept is an inherent unity, though not a merely immediate one but one essentially split internally and falling apart into contradictions. On these lines, for example, in my *Logic*[1] I have expounded the Concept as subjectivity, but this subjectivity, as an ideal transparent unity, is lifted into its opposite, i.e. objectivity; indeed, as what is purely ideal, it is itself only one-sided and particular, retaining contrasted with itself something different and opposed to it, namely objectivity; and it is only genuine subjectivity if it enters this opposition and then overcomes and dissolves it. In the actual world too there are higher natures who are given power to endure the grief of inner opposition and to conquer it. If music is to express artistically both the inner meaning and the subjective feeling of the deepest things, e.g. of religion and in particular the Christian religion in which the abysses of grief form a principal part, it must possess in the sphere of its notes the means capable of representing the battle of opposites. These means it gains in the so-called dissonant chords of the seventh and ninth, but what these indicate more specifically is a matter on which I cannot enter further here.

If on the other hand we look, in the third place, at the general nature of these chords, the further important point is that they keep opposites, even in this form of contradiction, within one and the same unity. But to say that opposites, just as opposites, should be in unity is plainly contradictory and invalid. Opposites as such have, owing to their nature, no firm support either in themselves or in their opposition. On the contrary, in their opposition they perish themselves. Harmony therefore must go beyond such chords as present to the ear nothing but a contradiction which must be resolved if satisfaction is to be given to the ear and the heart. Consequently along with the contradiction there is immediately given the necessity for a resolution of the discords and a return to the triad. Only this movement, as the return of the identity into itself, is what is simply true. But in music this complete identity itself is only possible as a dispersal of its essential features in *time* and they therefore become a succession; yet they prove

---

[1] e.g. Section 1 of the Subjective Logic (Eng. tr. by A. V. Miller: *The Science of Logic*, pp. 599 ff.). Or, more briefly, in the first edition of the *Encyclopaedia*, §§ 109-39.

their intimate connection by displaying themselves as the necessary movement of a progress founded upon itself and as an essential course of change.

(γγ) This brings us to a third point to which we have to give our attention. We saw that the scale is a series of successive sounds which is fixed in itself although primarily still abstract; so now the chords too do not remain separate and independent but acquire an inner bearing on one another and the need of change and progress. Although this progress may acquire a more significant area of change than is possible for scales, yet in it there must be no ingredient of mere caprice; on the contrary, the movement from chord to chord must rest on the nature partly of the chords themselves, partly of the keys into which they pass. In this matter the theory of music has laid down a multitude of prohibitions; but to explain and establish these might involve us in all too difficult and extensive discussions. Therefore I will let these few very general remarks suffice.

(c) Melody

To recapitulate what we were concerned with in relation to the particular media of musical expression, we treated first the way of dealing with the temporal duration of notes in respect of time, beat, bar, and rhythm. We then proceeded to the actual notes, and there, first, to the sound of instruments and the human voice; secondly, to the fixed proportions determining the intervals and their abstract serial succession in the scales and different keys; thirdly, to the laws of the particular chords and their modulation into one another. The final sphere in which the earlier ones form into a unity, and in this identity provide the basis for the first genuinely free development and unification of the notes, is melody.

Harmony comprises only the essential proportions constituting the necessary law for the world of notes; yet, as little as the beat, bar and rhythm, are they already in themselves music proper, for, on the contrary, they are only the substantive basis, the ground and soil which conforms to law and on which the soul expatiates in its freedom. The poetic element in music, the language of the soul, which pours out into the notes the inner joy and sorrow of the heart, and in this outpouring mitigates and rises above the *natural* force of feeling by turning the inner life's present transports into an apprehension of itself, into a free tarrying with itself, and by liberating the heart in this way from the pressure of joys and sorrows—this free sounding of the soul in the field of music—this is alone melody. This final domain is the higher poetic element in music, the sphere of its properly artistic inventions in the use of the elements considered hitherto, and this is now above all what we would have to discuss. Yet here precisely those difficulties that were mentioned earlier stand in our way. On the one hand, a spacious and well-founded treatment of the subject would require a more exact knowledge of the rules of composition and a far wider acquaintance with the masterpieces of music than I possess or have been able to acquire, because from real scholars and practising musicians—least of all from the latter who are frequently the most unintelligent of men—we seldom hear anything definite and detailed on these matters. On the other hand, it is implicit in the nature of music itself that it is and should be less permissible in it than it is in the other arts to take account of and to emphasize specific and particular points in a more general way. For however far music too adopts a spiritual subject-matter and makes it its business to express the inner meaning of this topic or the inner movements of feeling, still just because this subject-matter is apprehended on its inner side or reverberates as subjective feeling, it remains indefinite and vague; and the musical changes do not always correspond at the same time to changes in a feeling or an idea, a thought or an individual person, but are a purely musical development where the artist plays with himself and into which he introduces method. For these reasons I will confine myself to the following general observations which have struck me and which seem interesting.

(α) In its free deployment of notes the melody does float independently above the bar, rhythm, and harmony, and yet on the other hand it has no other means of actualization except the rhythmical measured movement of the notes in their essential and inherently necessary relations. The movement of the melody is therefore confined to these media of its existence and it may not seek to win an existence in them which conflicts with their inherently necessary conformity to law. But in this close link with harmony the melody does not forgo its freedom at all; it only liberates itself from the subjectivity of arbitrary caprice in fanciful developments and bizarre changes and only acquires its true independence precisely in this way. For genuine freedom does not stand opposed to necessity as an alien and therefore pressing and suppressing might; on the contrary, it has this substantive might as its own indwelling essence, identical with itself, and in its demands it is therefore so far following its own laws and satisfying its own nature that to depart from these prescriptions would be to turn away from itself and be untrue to itself. Conversely, however, it is obvious that the bar, rhythm, and harmony are, taken by themselves, only abstractions which in their isolation have no musical worth, but can acquire a genuinely musical existence only through and within the melody as the essential features and aspects of the melody itself. In thus bringing into an accord the difference between harmony and melody there lies the chief secret of the greatest compositions.

(β) Secondly, the following points seem to me to be of importance in connection with the *particular* character of melody.

(αα) First, in relation to its harmonic course, a melody can be restricted to a quite simple range of chords and keys by moving within the limits of the notes which harmonize with one another without any opposition and which it then uses purely as a basis in order to find there more general points of support for its further figuration and movement. For example, song melodies, which need not on this account be superficial at all but may express depth of soul, are commonly allowed to move within the simplest harmonic proportions. They do not, as it were, make a problem of the more difficult complications of chords and keys, but are content with such progressions and modulations as, in order to produce a harmony, do not push further on to sharp oppositions, and require no manifold mediations before the satisfying unity is established. Of course this sort of treatment may lead to shallowness too, as in many modern French and Italian melodies where the harmonic succession is of a wholly superficial kind, while the composer tries to substitute for what he lacks in this respect only a piquant charm of rhythm or other seasonings. In general, however, the emptiness of a melody is not a necessary effect of the simplicity of a harmonic basis.

(ββ) Secondly, a further difference consists in the fact that a melody is no longer developed, as in the first case, simply in a succession of simple notes on the basis of a relatively independent forward-moving harmonic series; on the contrary each single note of the melody is filled out as a concrete whole into a chord and thereby acquires a wealth of sound and is so closely interwoven with the course of the melody that no such clear distinction can any longer be made between an independent and self-explanatory melody and a harmony providing only the accompanying points of support and a firm ground and basis. In that case harmony and melody form one and the same compact whole, and a change in the one is at the same time necessarily a change in the other. This is especially the case, for example, in chorales set for four voices. Similarly one and the same melody may so weave through several voices that this interlacing may form a progression of harmonies, or in the same way there may even be different melodies worked harmonically into one another so that the concurrence of specific notes in these melodies affords a harmony, as e.g. occurs often in Bach's compositions. In that case development is split into progressions deviating from one another in numerous ways; they seem to draw along beside one another independently or to be interwoven with one another, and yet they retain an essential harmonic relation to one another and this then introduces again in this way a necessary match between them.

($\gamma\gamma$) In such a mode of treatment more profound music not only *may* push its movements up to the very limits of immediate consonance, indeed may even first transgress them in order then to return into itself, but, on the contrary, it *must* tear apart the simple first harmony into dissonances. For such oppositions alone are the basis of the deeper relations and secrets of harmony which have a necessity of their own, and thus the deeply impressive movements of the melody also have their basis solely in these deep harmonic relations. Boldness in musical composition therefore abandons a purely consonant progression, goes on to oppositions, summons all the starkest contradictions and dissonances and gives proof of its own power by stirring up all the powers of harmony; it has the certainty nevertheless of being able to allay the battles of these powers and thereby to celebrate the satisfying triumph of melodic tranquillity. We have here a battle between freedom and necessity: a battle between imagination's freedom to give itself up to its soaring and the necessity of those harmonic relations which imagination needs for its expression and in which its own significance lies. But if the chief thing is harmony, the use of all its means, and the boldness of the battle in this use and against these means, then the composition easily becomes awkward and pedantic, because either it actually lacks freedom in its movements or at least it does not let the triumph of that freedom emerge in its completeness.

(γ) In every melody, thirdly, the properly melodic element, i.e, what can be sung, must appear, no matter in what kind of music, as the dominant and independent element which in all the wealth of its expression is neither forgotten nor lost. Accordingly, melody is the infinite determinability and possibility of the advance of the notes, but it must be so regulated that what we apprehend is always an inherently total and perfect whole. This whole does contain variety and it has an inner progress, but, being a whole, it must be firmly rounded in itself, and thus needs a definite beginning and end, so that the middle is only the mediation between the beginning and the termination. Only as this movement, which never runs off into vagueness but is articulated in itself and returns into itself, does melody correspond to that free self-subsistence of subjective life which it is its task to express. In this way alone does music in its own element of inwardness perfect the immediate expression of the inner life, and it imparts to that expression, immediately becoming inner, the ideality and liberation which, while being obedient to the necessity of harmonic laws, yet at the same time lift the soul to the apprehension of a higher sphere.

3. *Relation between Music's Means of Expression and their Content*

After indicating the general character of music we have considered the particular guides necessary for fashioning the notes and their temporal duration. But with melody we have entered the sphere of free artistic invention and actual musical creation and so the question arises at once of a subject-matter which is to gain an artistically adequate expression in rhythm, harmony, and melody. The establishment of the general sorts of this expression gives us the final point of view from which we now still have to cast a glance at the different provinces of music. In this matter the first thing is to emphasize the following difference.

(i) As we saw earlier, music may be an *accompaniment*, if its spiritual content is not simply seized in the sense of its abstract inwardness or as subjective feeling but enters into the musical movement exactly as it has been already formulated by the imagination and put into words. (ii) On the other hand, music tears itself free from such a previously ready-made content and makes itself *independent* in its own field so that *either*, if it still makes some specific content its general concern, it immerses that content directly in melodies and their harmonic elaboration, *or* it can rest satisfied with the entirely independent sounds and notes as such and their harmonic and melodic figuration. Although in a totally different field, there recurs here a difference similar to what we have seen in architecture as that between independent architecture and architecture that serves a purpose. But music as an accompaniment is essentially freer and it enters into a much closer unity with its content than can always be the case in architecture.

In music as it exists, this difference is marked by the difference in kind between vocal and instrumental music. But we must not take this difference in a purely external way as if it were simply that what is used in vocal music is only the *sound* of the human voice and in instrumental music the various sounds of the other instruments; on the contrary, in singing, the voice speaks words which give us the idea of a specific subject-matter. The result is that if both sides, the notes and the words, are not to fall apart unrelated and indifferent to one another, music by being a *sung* word can only have the task, so far as music can execute it, of making the musical expression adequate to this subject-matter which, by being contained in words, is brought before our minds in its clearer definition and no longer remains a property of vaguer feeling. But despite this unification, the topic envisaged can be apprehended and read by itself in a libretto and therefore our minds distinguish it from the musical expression. Consequently the music added to a libretto is an accompaniment, whereas in sculpture and painting the content represented does not come before our minds independently and outside its artistic form. On the other hand, neither must we take the nature of such accompaniment in the sense of its being the servant of a purpose, for the truth is precisely the reverse: the text is the servant of the music and it has no worth other than creating for our minds a better idea of what the artist has chosen as the subject of his work. That being so, music preserves this freedom principally by the fact that it does not apprehend this content at all in the way that a libretto makes it intelligible, but on the contrary it masters a medium other than that of perception and ideas. In this connection I have indicated, in dealing with the general character of music, that music must express the inner life as such, but this life can be of two kinds. To get at the heart of an object may mean on the one hand grasping it not as it appears in external *reality* but in its *ideal significance*; on the other hand, it can also mean expressing it just as it is living in the sphere of subjective feeling. Both modes of apprehension are possible for music. I will try to make this more nearly intelligible.

In old church-music, e.g. in a *Crucifixus*, the deep elements lying in the nature of Christ's Passion, e.g. this divine suffering, death, and entombment, are often so treated that what is expressed is not a *subjective* feeling or emotion of sympathy or individual human grief at these events, but as it were the thing itself, i.e. the profundity of its meaning moves through the harmonies and their melodic course. Of course even in this case the work is meant to appeal to the listener's feeling; he should not *contemplate* the grief of the Crucifixion and the entombment, should not merely form a general idea of it. On the contrary, in his inmost self he should live through the inmost meaning of this death and this divine suffering, immerse himself in it with his whole heart so that now the thing becomes in him something apprehended which extinguishes everything else and fills him with this one thing. Similarly, if his work of art is to have the power of producing this impression, the composer must immerse his heart entirely in the thing and in it alone and not have familiarized himself with only a subjective feeling of it and tried to make that alone alive in notes addressed to 'inner sense'.[1]

Conversely, I can read a book or a libretto which relates an event, presents an action, or puts feelings into words, and as a result my most heartfelt feeling may be most vigorously stimulated so that I shed tears, etc. This subjective feature, feeling namely, may accompany every human deed and action, every expression of the inner life, and it may be aroused even by the perception of every action and the apprehension of any occurrence. This feature music is equally entirely able to organize, and in that event, by its impression on the listener, softens, pacifies, and idealizes the sympathetic feeling to which he finds himself disposed. Thus in both cases the topic resounds for the inner self, and, just because music masters the self in its simple self-concentration, it can for that self set limits to the roving freedom of thinking, ideas, and contemplation and to a passage beyond the specific

---

[1] Kant, *K.d.r.V.*, A. 98.

topic at issue, because it keeps the heart firmly to one particular thing, engages it in that topic, and, within this sphere, moves and occupies the feelings.

This is the sense in which we have to discuss music here as an accompaniment, namely that, in the way indicated, it develops the inward side of a topic already set before our minds by the libretto. But because music can discharge this task in vocal music especially and then besides links instruments with the human voice, it is customary to describe the instrumental music itself preferably as an accompaniment. Of course it does accompany the voice and in that case should not try to be absolutely independent or the chief thing; yet in this alliance vocal music comes more directly under the above-mentioned category of an accompanying sound because the voice utters articulate words for *intellectual* apprehension and the song is only a further modification of the burden of these words, namely an elaboration of them for the heart's inner *feeling*, while, in the case of really and purely instrumental music, utterance for the intellect disappears and this music must be restrcted to its own means of a purely musical mode of expression.

Finally to these differences a third is added, and it must not be overlooked. Earlier on I drew attention to the fact that the living actuality of a musical work must always be reproduced anew. In this respect sculpture and painting amongst the visual arts have the advantage. The sculptor or the painter conceives his work and executes it completely; the whole of the artistic activity of creation is concentrated in one and the same individual, and in this way the inner correspondence between invention and actual execution wins easily. The architect, however, is worse off because he needs the many activities of numerous branches of craftsmanship and these he has to entrust to other hands. The composer likewise has to give his work over to other hands and throats, but with the difference that in this case the technical execution and the expression of his work's inner animating spirit requires the activity of an artist over again, not that of a mere craftsman. Especially in this connection, while in the other arts no new discoveries have been made, nowadays again, as happened long ago in the older Italian opera, two miracles have occurred in music: one in the conception, the other in the genius of virtuosi in the execution. The result is that, in regard to the latter, the notion of what music is and what it can do has been more and more widened, even for greater experts.

This gives us the following main points for the division of these final considerations about music:

First, we have to concern ourselves with music as an accompaniment and to ask of what ways of expressing a content it is generally capable.

Secondly, we must raise the same question about the precise character of independent music.

Thirdly, we will end with a few remarks about the execution of musical works of art.

(*a*) *Music as an Accompaniment*

A direct consequence of what I have already said about the respective positions of libretto and music is the demand that in this first sphere of music the musical expression must be far more strictly associated with a specific topic than is the case when music may surrender itself to its movements and inspirations independently. For from the very start the libretto gives us distinct ideas and tears our minds away from that more dreamlike element of feeling which is without ideas and in which we need not abandon either wandering to and fro undisturbed or the freedom to derive this or that feeling from the music or to feel ourselves moved in this that or the other way. But in this interweaving of music and words music must not sink to such servitude that, in order to reproduce the words of the libretto in their really entire character, it forgets the free flow of its own movements and thereby, instead of creating a self-complete work of art, produces merely the intellectual trick of using musical means of expression for the truest possible indication of a subject-matter outside them and already cut and dried without them. Every perceptible compulsion, every cramping of free production, breaks up the impression [to be made by music]. Yet, on the other hand, music must avoid what has become the fashion now with most modern Italian composers, i.e. it must not emancipate itself almost entirely from the contents of the libretto, which in that case seem to be a chain because of their definiteness, and then seek to approach the character of independent music throughout. This art consists, on the contrary, in being filled with the sense of the spoken words, the situation, the action, etc., and then, out of this inner animation, finding and musically developing a soul-laden expression. This is what all the great composers have done. They produce nothing alien to the words but neither do they let go a-missing either the free outpouring of notes or the undisturbed march and course of the composition which is therefore there on its own account and not on account of the words only.

Within this genuine freedom three different sorts of expression may be distinguished.

(α) I will start with what may be described as the strictly melodic element in the expression. Here it is feeling, the resounding soul, which is to become explicit and to enjoy itself in its expression.

(αα) The human breast, the mood of the heart, i.e., in general, the sphere in which the composer has to move, and melody, this pure resounding of the inner life, is music's own inmost soul. For a note only acquires a soul-laden expression by having a feeling introduced into it and resounding out of it. In this respect there are already extremely expressive the natural cry of feeling, e.g. the scream of horror, the sobbing of grief, the triumphal shout and thrills of exultant pleasure and joyfulness, etc., and I have already described this sort of expression as the starting-point of music, but I have added at the same time that music must go beyond merely natural interjections. This is where the special difference between music and painting lies. Painting can often produce the most beautiful and artistic effect when the painter familiarizes himself with the actual form, colouring, and soul-laden expression of the sitter confronting him in a specific situation and environment, and he now reproduces entirely true to life what has so impressed him and what he has absorbed. In this instance truth to nature is entirely in place when it coincides with artistic truth. Music, on the other hand, must not reproduce as a natural outburst of passion the expression of feelings as they existed but must animate the sound with a wealth of feeling and develop it into specific notes and their relations. In this way it has to elevate the expression into an element created by and for art alone, in which the simple cry is analysed into a series of notes, into a movement, the change and course of which is supported by harmony and rounded into a whole by melody.

(ββ) This melodic element acquires a more precise meaning and function in relation to the entirety of the human spirit. Sculpture and painting, as fine arts, portray the spiritual inner life in an externally existent object, and they liberate the spirit again from this external object of contemplation, because in that object, produced by the spirit, the spirit finds itself again and its inner life, while nothing is left over for individual caprice, for arbitrary ideas, opinions, and reflections, because the content [the inner life] is set forth in the object in its entirely specific individuality. Music, on the contrary, as we have seen more than once, has for such an object only the element of the subjective itself, whereby the inner life therefore coincides with itself and it reverts into itself in its expression which is feeling's song. Music is spirit, or the soul which resounds directly on its own account and feels satisfaction in its perception of itself. But as a fine art it at once acquires, from the spirit's point of view, a summons to bridle the emotions themselves as well as their expression, so that there is no being carried away into a bacchanalian rage or whirling tumult of passions, or a resting in the distraction of despair, but on the contrary an abiding peace and freedom in the outpouring of emotion whether in jubilant delight or the deepest grief. The truly ideal music is of this kind, the melodic expression of Palestrina, Durante, Lotti, Pergolesi, Gluck, Haydn, Mozart.[1] Tranquillity of soul is never missing in the compositions of these masters; grief is expressed there too, but it is assuaged at once; the clear rhythm inhibits extremes; everything is kept firmly together in a restrained form so that jubilation does not degenerate into a repulsive uproar, and even a lament gives us the most blissful tranquillity. In connection with Italian painting I have said already that, even in the deepest grief and the most extreme distraction of soul, that reconciliation with self which even in tears and sorrows preserves the traits of peace and happy assurance is not allowed to be missing. In a profound soul grief remains beautiful, just as what dominates in Harlequin[2] is gracefulness and charm. In the same way, nature has bestowed on the Italians above all the gift of melodic expression. In their older church-music we find at the same time along with the deepest religious worship the pure sense of reconciliation, and, even if grief stirs the depths of the soul, we still find beauty and bliss, the simple grandeur and expatiation of imagination in its variously expressed self-enjoyment. This is a beauty of sensuousness and this melodic satisfaction is often taken to be a purely sensuous enjoyment but it is precisely in the element of sense that art has to

---

[1] Their selection is of interest and so are their dates: 1525–94; 1684–1755; 1667–1740; 1710–36; 1714–87; 1732–1809; 1756–91.

[2] i.e. as he appears in Italian comedy, rather than in English pantomime.

move and to lead the spirit on into a sphere in which, as in nature, the keynote remains the satisfaction of the self with and in itself.

(γγ) While therefore melody must be the expression of a *particular* feeling, music makes passion and imagination issue in a stream of notes and therefore should lift the soul above this feeling in which it is immersed, make it hover above its content, and in this way form for it a region where a return out of this immersion can occur unhindered, along with a pure sense of self. This properly constitutes what is really singable, the genuine song of a musical piece. In that case it is not the progress of the *specific* feeling itself (love, longing, cheerfulness, etc.) which is the principal thing, but the inner life which dominates it, which develops and enjoys its own self alike in grief and joy. The bird on the bough or the lark in the air sings cheerfully and touchingly just in order to sing, just as a natural production without any other aim and without any specific subject-matter, and it is the same with human song and melodious expression. Therefore Italian music, where in particular this principle prevails, often passes over, like poetry, into melodious sound as such and may easily seem to sacrifice, or may actually sacrifice, feeling and its definite expression because it looks only to the enjoyment of art as art, to the melodious sound of the soul in its inner satisfaction. But this is more or less the character of what in general is really properly melodious. Although the pure definiteness of what is expressed is not missing, it is at the same time cancelled because the heart is immersed not in something different or definite but in its self-apprehension, and only so does it, like pure light's vision of itself, give us the supreme idea of blissful deep feeling and reconciliation.

(β) Now just as in sculpture ideal beauty and self-repose must prevail, while painting already advances to characterizing the particular and fulfils a chief task in the energy of its expression of something specific, so music cannot be content with melody as described above. The soul's pure feeling of itself and the resonant play of its self-apprehension is in the last resort merely a mood and so too general and abstract, and it runs the risk of not merely abandoning a closer indication of the content expressed in the libretto but of becoming purely empty and trivial. But if grief, joy, longing, etc. are to resound in the melody, the actual concrete soul in the seriousness of actual life has such moods only in an actual context, in specific circumstances, particular situations, events, and actions, etc. If, for instance, a song awakens in us a feeling of mourning or a lament for a loss, the question arises at once: 'What loss? Is it loss of life with its wealth of interests, or loss of youth, happiness, spouse, or beloved, or loss of children, parents, or friends?' In this way a further task is imposed on music in relation to the specific subject-matter and the *particular* relations and situations with which the heart is familiar and in the midst of which it makes its inner life resound in notes, namely the further task of giving to its expression the like particular detail. For music is concerned not with the inner life in the abstract, but with a concrete inner life, the specific content of which is most intimately linked with the specific character of the feeling, so that *pari passu* with the difference in the content there must essentially enter a difference in the expression. Consequently, the more the heart flings itself with all its might into some particular experience, the more are its emotions intensified; instead of keeping that blissful self-enjoyment of the soul, it becomes distracted and subject to internal struggles and the mutual conflict of passions, and, in a word, it descends to a depth of particularization to which the expression previously considered no longer corresponds. The details of the content are precisely what the *libretto* provides. In the case of a melody proper, which is less concerned with this specific subject-matter, the finer points of the libretto are only accessories. A song, for example, may have as its words a poem which is a whole containing a variety of shades of moods, perceptions, and ideas, and yet it usually has at bottom the ring of one and the same feeling pervading the whole, and therefore it strikes above all *one* chord of the heart. To hit this chord and to reproduce it in notes is the chief function of such song-melodies. Such a melody may therefore remain the same throughout the poem and all its lines no matter how variously their meaning is modified, and this repetition so far from impairing the effect may intensify it. The same is true of a landscape where also objects of the most varied kinds are placed before our eyes and yet one and the same fundamental mood and situation of nature animates the whole. Even if such a tune fits some lines of the poem and not others, it must dominate in the song because here the specific sense of the words must not be the prevailing thing; on the contrary, the melody floats simply and on its own account above all the variety. On the other hand, in the case of many compositions which begin every new verse with a new tune, often different from its predecessor in beat, rhythm, and even key, we cannot see why, if such essential changes were really necessary, the poem too did not have to change at every verse in metre, rhythm, and arrangement of rhyme.

(αα) But what proves suitable for the song, which is a genuinely musical voice of the soul, is not adequate for every sort of musical expression. We have therefore to emphasize in contrast to melody a second aspect which is of the same importance and which alone makes the song a genuinely musical accompaniment. This is the case in that mode of expression which dominates in recitative. Here there is no self-enclosed melody which comprises as it were the keynote of that content, in whose development the soul apprehends itself as a subject at one with itself; on the contrary, the meaning of the words in its precise specific character is stamped on the notes and it determines whether they are high or low, emphasized or not. In this way music becomes, in distinction from expression in a tune, a *declamation* in sound, closely tied to the words alike in their meaning and their syntactical connection. What it adds to them as a new element is only a more exalted feeling, and so it stands between melody as such and the speech of poetry. This position thus introduces a freer accentuation which keeps strictly to the specific sense of the individual words; the libretto itself does not need any fixedly determinate metre, and the musical recital, unlike melody, does not require to follow the beat and the rhythm similarly or to be tied down to them; on the contrary this aspect, in connection with accelerando and rallentando, pausing on certain notes and quickly passing over others, can be freely left to the feeling which is moved entirely by the meaning of the words. So too the modulation is not so restricted as it is in melody: start, progression, pause, breaking off, starting again, conclusion—all of this is allowed a more unlimited freedom according to what the libretto to be expressed requires. Unexpected accentuation, less mediated transitions, sudden changes and conclusions are all allowed; and in distinction from the flowing stream of melody, even a mode of expression which is fragmented, broken off, and passionately torn asunder, when this is what the words require, is not disturbing.

(ββ) In this connection, expression in declamation and recitative is evidently equally fitted both for the tranquil consideration and peaceful record of events and also for that feeling-burdened description of the soul which displays the inner life torn into the midst of some situation and awakens the heart, by living tones of the soul, to sympathy with all that moves in that situation. Recitative therefore has its chief application (i) in oratorio, partly as the recitation of a narrative, partly a more lively introduction to a momentary event, (ii) in dramatic song,[1] where, whether it is expressed in abrupt changes, briefly, fragmentarily, or in a storm of aphorisms, it is competent to break up all the nuances of a fleeting communication and every sort of passion in a dialogue with rapid flashes and counter-flashes of expression or alternatively to make them all stream connectedly together. Moreover, in both spheres, epic and dramatic, instrumental music may be added, either quite simply to indicate pauses for the harmonies, or else to interrupt the song with intermezzi which in a similarly characteristic way paint in music other aspects and progressive movements of the situation.

(γγ) Yet what this recitative kind of declamation lacks is precisely the advantage which melody as such has, namely specific articulation and rounding off: the expression of that deep feeling and unity of soul which is indeed inserted into a particular content but in that content manifests precisely the soul's unity with itself, because it is not distracted by individual features, torn and split hither and thither, but asserts in them only their subjective collocation. Therefore, in relation to such more definite characterization of the topic given to it by the libretto, music cannot be content with recitative and declamation nor can it remain satisfied with the mere difference between melody, which floats in a relative way over the individual words and their details, and recitative which tries to cling as closely as possible to them. On the contrary, it must try to find a middle way, combining these two elements. We may compare this new unification with what we saw coming on the scene earlier in relation to the difference between harmony and melody. Melody adopted harmony as not only its general foundation but its inherently specific and particularized foundation, and therefore instead of losing the freedom of its movements won for them a power and definiteness similar to that acquired by the human organism through its skeleton which hinders inappropriate postures and movements only and gives support and security to

[1] Hegel has in mind not only opera but especially the place of music in Greek drama.

appropriate ones. This leads us to a final point of view for considering music as an accompaniment.

(γ) The third mode of expression consists in this, that the melodic song which accompanies a libretto turns towards particular characterization and therefore it refuses to be confronted by the principle of recitative as if that were purely indifferent to it; on the contrary, it makes that principle its own so that there can be bestowed (*a*) on itself the definiteness which it lacked, and (*b*) on the characterizing declamation the organic articulation and fully unified completeness [which it had lacked on its side]. For even melody, as was observed above, could not remain altogether empty and vague. Above, I gave special emphasis to one point only about melody, namely that in each and every content what is expressed is a mood of the soul, preoccupied with itself and its deep feelings, and blissful in this unity with itself, and that this mood corresponds to melody as such because the latter, regarded musically, is the like unity and circular return into itself. But I said this only because this point indicates the specific character of melody in the abstract and differentiates it from recitative and declamation. But the further task of melody consists, we may say, in its making into its own property what at first seems necessarily to move outside it and in its acquiring a truly concrete expression by means of this plenishing which makes it as much declamatory as melodious. On the other side, therefore, the declamation is no longer there separate and independent but has its own one-sidedness supplemented by being drawn into the melodic expression. This constitutes the necessity of this concrete unity.

In order to go into further detail, the following distinctions must be made:

First, we must cast a glance at the character of the *libretto* which is suited to musical composition, because the specific meaning of the words has now proved to be of essential importance for music and its expression.

Secondly, a new element has entered the *composition* itself, namely the characterizing declamation, which we must therefore consider in its relation to the principle that we originally found in melody.

Thirdly, we will review the *genres* of music within which this sort of musical expression has its principal place.

(αα) At the stage with which we are concerned now, music does not merely accompany the text in general but, as we saw, has to comply with its more detailed character. It is therefore a disastrous prejudice to suppose that the character of the text is a matter of indifference so far as composition goes. On the contrary, great music [when an accompaniment] has as its basis an excellent text which the composers have selected with true seriousness or have written themselves. For the material treated by an artist can never be a matter of indifference to him, and this is all the more true of a musician the more that poetry has worked out and settled for him in advance the precise epic, lyric, or dramatic form of the subject-matter.

The chief thing to be demanded of a good libretto is that its content shall have an inherent and true solidity. Nothing musically excellent and profound can be conjured out of what is inherently flat, trivial, trumpery, and absurd; the composer can add what seasoning and spices he likes, but a roasted cat will never make a hare-pie.[1] It is true that in purely melodious pieces of music, the libretto is on the whole less decisive, but even these crave words with some real meaning. Still, on the other hand, what the words convey must not be all too difficult thoughts or profound philosophy, as, for example, the grand sweep of the 'pathos' in Schiller's lyrics soars above any musical expression of lyrical feelings. It is similar with the choruses of Aeschylus and Sophocles, which, with all their depth of insight, are worked out in detail so imaginatively, sensitively, and profoundly, and are so perfect already in their poetic form, that there is nothing left for music to add; it is as if the inner life is left with no scope for playing with this content and developing it in new variations. The newer materials and modes of treatment in the so-called 'romantic' poetry are of an opposite kind. They are supposed to be for the most part naïve and popular, but this is all too often a precious, artificial, and screwed up naïveté which instead of being genuine feeling amounts only to forced feelings elaborated by reflection, miserable wistfulness, and self-flattery; it glories in banality, silliness, and vulgarity just as much as, on the other hand, it loses itself in absolutely empty passions, envy, debauchery, devilish wickedness, and more of the like, and it has a self-satisfied delight in its own excellence in the one case as well as in this distraction and worthlessness in the other. Original, simple, serious, impressive feeling is totally

[1] See Index, s.v. Newton.

lacking here, and when music produces the same in its sphere, nothing does it greater damage.

Thus a genuine content for a libretto is not afforded either by profundity of thought or by self-complacent or worthless feelings. What therefore is most suitable for music is a certain intermediate kind of poetry which we Germans scarcely allow to be poetry at all, whereas the French and Italians have had a real sense for it and skill in it: a poetry which in lyrics is true, extremely simple, indicating the situation and the feeling in few words, and in drama without all too ramified complications, clear and lively, not working out details but concerned as a rule to provide sketches rather than to produce works completely elaborated poetically. In this case, and this is what is necessary, the composer is given only a general foundation on which he can erect his building on the lines of his own invention, exhausting every motive, and moving in a living way in every direction. For since music is to be associated with the words, these must not paint the matter in hand down to the last detail because otherwise the musical declamation becomes petty, dispersed, and drawn too much in different directions so that unity is lost and the total effect weakened. In this matter errors of judgement are all too often made about the excellence or inadmissibility of a libretto. How often, for example, have we not heard chatter to the effect that the libretto of *The Magic Flute* is really lamentable, and yet this 'bungling compilation' is amongst the finest opera libretti. On this occasion, after many mad, fantastic, and trivial productions, Schikaneder[1] has hit the nail on the head. The realm of night, the queen, the realm of the sun, the mysteries, initiations, wisdom, love, tests, and along with these a sort of commonplace morality excellent in its general principles—all this combined with the depth, the bewitching loveliness and soul, of the music broadens and fills the imagination and warms the heart.

To cite still further examples, for religious music the old Latin words for High Mass, etc., are unsurpassed because they set forth in the greatest simplicity and brevity the most general doctrines of the faith and the corresponding essential stages in the feelings and minds of the congregation of the faithful, and they allow the musician the greatest scope for composition. The Requiem and

---

[1] E., 1748–1812. He also wrote (as Hegel indicates) the libretto for numerous popular operas, now forgotten.

passages from the Psalms, etc., are equally serviceable. In a similar way Handel has assembled, into a rounded whole, texts drawn from religious doctrines themselves and above all from the Bible and situations with a symbolic connection, etc.

As for lyric, particularly suitable for composition are deeply felt shorter poems, especially those that are simple, laconic, profound in sentiment which express with force and soul some mood and condition of the heart, or even those that are lighter and merrier. Hardly any nation lacks poems of this kind.

For the dramatic field I will mention only Metastasio and Marmontel, this Frenchman with his wealth, of feeling, his exquisite culture, and his lovableness, who taught Piccinni[1] French, and who could link grace and cheerfulness in drama with skill in developing an action and making it interesting. Above all, however, preference must be given to the texts[2] of the more famous operas of Gluck. They are concerned with simple motives and keep within the sphere of the most sterling objects of feeling; they sketch love of mother, spouse, brother, or sister, as well as friendship, honour, etc., and these simple motives and their essential collisions are developed peacefully. In this way passion remains throughout pure, great, noble, and of plastic simplicity.

($\beta\beta$) A correspondence must be established by music between such a content and music which is both melodious and characteristic in its expression. If this is to be possible, the text must contain the seriousness of the heart, the comedy and tragic greatness of passions, the depths of religious ideas and feeling, and the powers and fates of the human breast; moreover, the composer too on his side must identify himself with these with his whole mind and must have lived through this content and felt it all with his whole heart.

Further, equally important is the relation into which the two sides, the characteristic and the melodic, must be brought. In this matter the chief demand seems to me to be that the victory shall always be given to the melody as the all-embracing unity and not to the disunion of characteristic passages scattered and separated individually from one another. For example, today's dramatic music often looks for its effect in violent contrasts by forcing into one and the same musical movement opposite passions which are artistically at variance. So, for instance, it expresses cheerfulness,

[1] N., 1728–1800. Used Marmontel's French libretti.   [2] By Metastasio.

a wedding, festivities, and then shoves in at the same time hate, revenge, and enmity, so that in the midst of pleasure, joy, and dance-music there is a storm of violent quarrels and most repugnant discord. Such contrasts between things rent from one another toss us from one side to another without giving us any unity and they are all the more opposed to the harmony of beauty the more sharply characterized are the opposites in their direct contact with one another; and in that case there can be no question of pleasure and the return of the inner life into itself in a melody. In general the union of melody with characterization involves the risk that the more specific sketching of the content may overstep the delicately drawn limits of musical beauty, especially when it is a question of expressing violence, selfishness, wickedness, impetuosity, and other extremes of one-sided passions. So soon as music commits itself to the abstraction of characterization in detail, it is inevitably led almost astray into sharpness and harshness, into what is thoroughly unmelodious and unmusical, and is reduced even to the misuse of discords.

The like is the case in respect of the *particular* characterizing passages. If these are kept fixedly in view and strongly pronounced, they quickly become loosened from one another and become as it were immobile and independent, whereas in the musical development, which must be an essential advance and a firm relationship between the parts of this progress, isolation of them at once disturbs the flow and the unity in a disastrous way.

From these points of view, truly musical beauty lies in the fact that, while an advance is made from pure melody to characterization, still within this particularization melody is always preserved as the carrying and unifying soul just as, for example, within the characteristic detail of a Raphael painting the note of beauty is always still retained. Further, melody is meaningful, but in all definition of its meaning it is the animation which permeates and holds together the whole, and the characteristic particulars appear only as an emergence of specific aspects which are always led back by the inner life to this unity and animation. But in this matter to hit the happy medium is of greater difficulty in music than in the other arts because music more easily breaks up into these opposed modes of expression. After all, judgement of musical works has in almost every period been divided: some give the preponderance to melody, others prefer characteristic detail. For example, even in his operas Handel often demanded a strictness of expression for every single lyrical feature and already in his day had to encounter battles enough with his Italian singers, until at last when the public sided with the Italians he turned over entirely to the composition of oratorios in which his productive gift found its richest field. Further, the long and lively dispute between the Gluckists and the Piccinnists in Gluck's time became famous. Again, Rousseau for his part has given preference to the richly melodic music of the Italians over the older French music with its absence of melody. Finally people have disputed in a similar way for or against Rossini[1] and the newer Italian school. Rossini's opponents decry his music as a mere empty tickling of the ear; but when we become more accustomed to its melodies, we find this music on the contrary full of feeling and genius, piercing the mind and heart, even if it does not have to do with the sort of characterization beloved of our strict German musical intellect. For it is true that all too often Rossini is unfaithful to his text and with his free melodies soars over all the heights, and so the result is that we can only choose whether to stick to the subject-matter and grumble at the music that no longer harmonizes with it, or alternatively to abandon the subject-matter and take unhindered delight in the free inspirations of the composer and enjoy with fullness of soul the soul that they contain.

(γγ) In conclusion I will make the following brief remarks on the principal *genres* of music as an accompaniment.

The first chief kind we may call *church* music. It has to do not with the *individual's* subjective feeling but with the substantive content of all feeling or with the general feeling of the Church as a whole; it therefore remains for the most part solid, as an *epic* is, even if it does not acquaint us with events as such. But how an artistic treatment can still be epical without relating events is something that we have to explain later when we come to a detailed treatment of epic poetry. This serious religious music is amongst the deepest and most effective things that any art can produce. In

---

[1] 1792–1868, apparently the only composer younger than himself of whom Hegel approved. In the autumn of 1824 he spent some time in Vienna and wrote enthusiastically to his wife about the Italian opera there. At first he found Rossini's music 'occasionally wearisome' but after a further hearing of *The Barber of Seville* he thought Rossini's Figaro 'infinitely more pleasing than Mozart's'. He adds that the reason Rossini's music is not liked in Berlin is that it is 'made for Italian throats'.

so far as it is related to the priest's intercession for the congregation, it has its proper place within Roman Catholic worship as the Mass, and in general as a musical exaltation in connection with various ecclesiastical ceremonies and feasts. The Protestants too have given us similar music with the greatest depth of religious sense as well as of musical solidity and wealth of invention, as, above all, for example, Bach, a master whose grand, truly Protestant, robust, and yet as it were learned genius we have come only in recent times to admire completely.[1] But in distinction from the trend in Catholicism, what has principally been developed here is the form of the oratorio which has been perfected in Protestantism only, though it originates in commemorations of the Passion. It is true that in Protestantism nowadays, music is no longer so closely associated with actual worship and it does not intrude into divine service, and indeed it has become more of a scholarly exercise than a living production.

Secondly, *lyrical* music expresses in melody the mood of the individual soul, and must keep itself so far as possible free from the purely characteristic and declamatory, although it too may proceed to adopt into its expression the specific meaning of the words, whether the meaning is religious or of some other kind. But stormy passions, unassuaged and unending, the unresolved discord of the heart, and mere inner distraction are less fitted for independent expression in lyric and find their better place as part and parcel of particular sections of dramatic music.

Lastly, music develops likewise into *dramatic* music. Even Greek tragedy was musical, but in it music had no preponderance, for in strictly poetic works priority must always be given to an imaginative treatment of ideas and feelings, and since music's harmonic and melodic development had not risen in Greece to the level it reached later in Christian times, it could only serve in a rhythmical way to give a living enhancement to the musical sound of the words and make it more impressive for the feelings. However, after it had already come to perfection in church-music, and to a great extent in music's lyrical expression too, dramatic music has won an

---

[1] Interest in Bach, hitherto regarded as too arithmetical, was promoted by the publication of Forkel's book on him in 1802. But what made a sensation in Berlin was Mendelssohn's production of the St. Matthew Passion in 1829. Hegel was a visitor to Mendelssohn's home but he would also derive an appreciation of Bach from his colleague in the University of Berlin, C. F. Zelter, Mendelssohn's teacher.

independent position in modern opera, operetta, etc. Operetta, however, so far as song goes, is a rather trivial intermediate sort, which mixes up, quite disconnectedly, speech and song, the musical and the unmusical, prosaic words and melodious singing. It is commonly said that the singing in dramas is generally unnatural, but this reproach misses the mark and could have turned rather against opera where from beginning to end every idea, feeling, passion, and resolve is accompanied by and expressed through song. For this reason operetta is still to be justified, on the contrary, for making music enter, because in it feelings and passions are stirred in a living way and in general prove amenable to musical description; all the same its juxtaposition of prosaic chatter in the dialogue and artistically treated interludes of song always remains an impropriety, for in that case liberation by art is incomplete. In real opera, on the other hand, which treats one entire action musically throughout, we are once and for all transferred from prose to a higher artistic world. To the character of this world the entire work adheres, if the music takes for its chief content the inner side of feeling, the individual and universal moods aroused in different situations, and the conflicts and struggles of passions, in order to make these conspicuous for the first time as a result of the most complete expression of the way they affect us. In vaudeville, conversely, where separate, rather striking *jeux d'esprit* in rhyme are accompanied by favourite tunes already familiar in other contexts, the singing is as it were ironical about itself. The fact of singing is supposed to be a cheerful veneer or a sort of parody; the chief thing is an understanding of the words and the jokes, and when the singing stops we just have a laugh that there was any singing at all.

(b) Independent Music

Since melody is complete and perfectly finished and self-reposing, we were able to compare it with plastic sculpture, while in musical declamation we recognized again the model of painting which goes further into detail in its treatment. In such a more specific characterization [of the subject-matter] a wealth of traits is unfolded which the always simpler movement of the human voice cannot differentiate in all their richness, and therefore an instrumental accompaniment is added here, the more that music develops in variety and vitality.

Secondly, in addition to the melody which accompanies a libretto and to the characterizing expression of the words, we have to put forward the other side, namely liberation from a content communicated already on its own account outside the musical notes in the form of specific ideas. The principle of music is the inner life of the individual. But the inmost being of the concrete self is subjectivity as such, undetermined by any fixed content and therefore not compelled to move along one definite line or another but resting on itself in untrammelled freedom. Now if this subjective experience is to gain its full due in music likewise, then music must free itself from a given text and draw entirely out of itself its content, the progress and manner of expression, the unity and unfolding of its work, the development of a principal thought, the episodic intercalation and ramification of others, and so forth: and in doing all this it must limit itself to purely musical means, because the meaning of the whole is not expressed in words. This is the case in the sphere of what I have already called 'independent' music. What music as an accompaniment is to express is something outside itself and its expression is related not to itself as music but to another art, namely poetry. But if music is to be purely musical, then it must spurn this element which is not its own and, now that it has won complete freedom, it must be completely released from the determinate sphere of words. This is the point which we now have to discuss further.

Even in the sphere of music as an accompaniment we saw such an act of liberation already beginning. For while the poetic words did repress the music and make it subservient, music did also hover in blissful peace above the *details* of the precise words or cut itself free from the ideas they expressed in order to indulge itself as it liked, whether cheerfully or sorrowfully. We find a similar phenomenon again in the case of listeners too, i.e. the public, especially in relation to dramatic music. Opera, namely, has ingredients of many kinds: landscape or some other locality, march of the action, events, processions, costumes, etc., and, on the other side, passion and its expression. In this case the contents are double: the external action and the inner feeling. Now although the action is what holds all the individual parts together, its course is less musical and is for the most part elaborated in recitative. The listener easily frees himself from this subject-matter, he gives no special attention to the statements and repetitions of the recitative, and sticks simply to what is really musical and melodious. This is especially the case, as I said earlier, with the Italians; most of their more recent operas, after all, are so fashioned throughout that, instead of listening to the musical twaddle or other trivialities, people prefer to talk themselves, or amuse themselves otherwise, and only attend again with full pleasure to the strictly musical parts which in that case are enjoyed purely musically. It follows from this that the composer and the public are on the verge of liberating themselves altogether from the meaning of the words and treating and enjoying the music on its own account as independent music.

(α) But the proper sphere of this independence cannot be vocal music, an accompaniment always tied to a text, but instrumental music. For the voice, as I have already stated, is the sounding belonging to the entire subjective life which is not without ideas and words also and now in its own voice and song finds the adequate organ when it wishes to express and apprehend the inner world of its ideas, permeated as they are by an inner concentration of feeling. But the reason for an accompanying text disappears for instruments, so that here what may begin to dominate is music restricting itself to its own, its very own, sphere.

(β) Such music whether of single instruments or a whole orchestra proceeds, in quartets, quintets, sextets, symphonies, etc., without any libretto and without human voices and not in accordance with an independent run of ideas; and precisely on this account it is addressed to feeling generally and in the abstract, and this can be expressed in this medium in only a general way. But the chief thing remains the purely musical hither and thither, up and down, of the harmonious and tuneful movements, the progress of the music whether easy-flowing, or more hindered and difficult, deeply striking and incisive, as well as the elaboration of a melody by every musical means, the artistic harmony of the instruments in their sounding as an ensemble, in their succession, their alteration. and their seeking and finding themselves. It is especially in this region that an essential difference begins to arise between the dilettante and the expert. What the layman likes most in music is the intelligible expression of feelings and ideas, something tangible, a topic, and therefore turns in preference to music as an accompaniment: whereas the expert who has at his fingers' ends the inner musical relations between notes and instruments, loves instrumental music in its artistic use of harmonies and melodious interactings and changing forms: he is entirely satisfied by the music itself and he has the closer interest of comparing what he has heard with the rules and laws that are familiar to him so that he can fully criticize and enjoy the composition, although here the inventive genius of the artist may often perplex the expert who is not accustomed to precisely this or that development, modulation, etc. The mere amateur seldom has the benefit of such complete satisfaction, and at once the desire steals over him to supplement this apparently unsubstantial procession of sounds and to find some holds for the spirit to grasp and, in general, specific ideas and a more definite meaning for what rings in his soul. In these circumstances music for him becomes symbolical, but with his attempt at snatching a meaning he is confronted by mysterious enigmas which run swiftly past, cannot always be solved, and in general are capable of all sorts of interpretations.[1]

The composer for his part can of course put into his work a specific meaning, a content consisting of ideas and feelings and their articulated and complete succession, but, conversely, he can also not trouble himself with any such content and make the principal thing the purely musical structure of his work and the ingenuity of such architecture. But in that case the musical production may easily become something utterly devoid of thought and feeling, something needing for its apprehension no previous profound cultivation of mind or heart. On account of this lack of material not only do we see the gift for composition developed at the most tender age but very talented composers frequently remain throughout their life the most ignorant and empty-headed of men. Music is therefore more profound when the composer gives the same attention even in instrumental music to both sides, to the expression of a content (true, a rather vague one) and to the musical structure, and in that case he is free to give the preference now to melody, now to the depth and difficulty of harmony, now to characterization, or to interweave all these elements.

(γ) From the beginning of this section about independent music we have established as its general principle the composer's sub-

---

[1] We may think that these remarks have a measure of justification when we reflect that some 'amateurs' have given the name of 'Moonlight' to Beethoven's Sonata, op. 27 no. 2, even if Beethoven invited 'interpretation' by the title he prefixed to this work.

jective creation of music unhampered by any text. This freedom from a content already fixed on its own account will therefore always more or less carry on into caprice, and caprice must be allowed a scope not strictly definable. For although even this sort of composition has its specific rules and forms to which a mere whim must be made subject, still such laws affect only its more general aspects, and for its details an infinite sphere lies open in which, provided the composer keeps within the limits prescribed by the nature of note-relationships, he can do as he likes and exert his mastery in everything else. Indeed, in the series of the developments of the kinds of instrumental music the composer's own caprice becomes the untrammelled master along with, in contrast to the fixed course of melodic expression and the textual content of music as an accompaniment, its fancies, conceits, interruptions, ingenious freaks, deceptive agitations, surprising turns, leaps and flashes, eccentricities, and extraordinary effects.

(c) *The Execution of Musical Works of Art*

In sculpture and painting we have the work of art before us as the objectively and independently existent *result* of artistic activity, but not this activity itself as produced and alive. The musical work of art, on the other hand, as we saw, is presented to us only by the action of an executant artist, just as, in dramatic poetry, the whole man comes on the stage, fully alive, and is himself made into an animated work of art.

Just as we have seen music developing in two directions, either undertaking to be adequate to a specific subject-matter, or preferring to go its own way in freedom and independence, so we may now distinguish two chief ways in which a musical work of art is executed. The one immerses itself entirely in the given work of art and does not wish to render anything beyond what the work in hand already contains: whereas the other does not merely reproduce but draws expression, interpretation, the real animation in short, principally from its own resources and not only from the composition as it exists.

(α) Epic, in which the poet intends to unfold for us an objective world of events and ways of action, leaves no alternative for the rhapsodist in his recital but to make his individual personality retire in favour of the deeds and events which he is reporting. The more he effaces himself the better; indeed, without prejudice to his task, he may even be monotonous and soulless. What is to have an effect is not the actual tones of his voice, his speech and narrative, but the subject itself, its poetic treatment and narration. From this fact we can abstract a rule for the first kind of musical interpretation. If the composition has, as it were, objective solidity so that the composer himself has put into notes only the subject itself or the feeling which is entirely full of it, then the reproduction must be of a similar matter-of-fact kind. The executant artist not only need not, but must not, add anything of his own, or otherwise he will spoil the effect. He must submit himself entirely to the character of the work and intend to be only an obedient instrument. Yet, on the other hand, in this obedience he must not, as happens often enough, sink to being merely mechanical, which only barrel-organ players are allowed to be. If, on the contrary, art is still to be in question, the executant has a duty to give life and soul to the work in the same sense as the composer did, and not to give the impression of being a musical automaton who recites a mere lesson and repeats mechanically what has been dictated to him. The *virtuosity* of such animation, however, is limited to solving correctly the difficult problems of the composition on its technical side and in that process avoiding any appearance of struggling with a difficulty laboriously overcome but moving in this technical element with complete freedom. In the matter not of technique but of the spirit, *genius* can consist solely in actually reaching in the reproduction the spiritual height of the composer and then bringing it to life.

(β) Things are different in the case of works in which what preponderates is the composer's own freedom and caprice, and, in general, where we look less for thorough solidity in expression and in other ways of treating melody, harmony, characterization, etc. Here the bravura of the virtuoso is in its right place, while genius is not restricted to the mere execution of what is given but has a wider scope so that the executant artist himself composes in his interpretation, fills in gaps, deepens what is superficial, ensouls what is soulless and in this way appears as downright independent and productive. So, for example, in Italian opera much is always left to the singer: he has freer scope especially in cadenzas, and, since declamation here is freed from the strictest attachment to the particular meaning of the words, this more independent execution becomes a free melodic stream of the soul which rejoices to resound on its own account and lift itself on its own wings. Thus when it is said, for instance, that Rossini makes things easy for the singers, this is only partly correct. Indeed he makes it really difficult for them by so often referring them to the activity of their own musical genius. If this really is genius, the resulting work of art has a quite peculiar attraction, because we have present before us not merely a work of art but the actual production of one. In this completely living presence of art, all external conditions are forgotten—place, occasion, specific context in the act of divine service, the subject and sense of a dramatic situation; we no longer need or want any text; nothing at all is left beyond the universal note of feeling. In that element the self-reposing soul of the executant artist abandons itself to its outpouring and in it he displays his inventive genius, his heart's deep feeling, his mastery in execution and, so long as he proceeds with spirit, skill, and grace, he may even interrupt the melody with jokes, caprices, and virtuosity, and surrender to the moods and suggestions of the moment.

(γ) Thirdly, such vividness is still more wonderful if the instrument is not the human voice but one of the other instruments. These with their sound are more remote from the expression of the soul and remain, in general, an external matter, a dead thing, while music is inner movement and activity. If the externality of the instrument disappears altogether, i.e. if inner music penetrates this external reality through and through, then in this virtuosity the foreign instrument appears as a perfectly developed organ of the artistic soul and its very own property. I recall, for instance, that in my youth a virtuoso on the guitar had composed great battle music in a tasteless way for this trivial instrument. By trade he was, I think, a linen-weaver; if you addressed him, he was an ignorant man of few words. But when he started to play, you forgot the tastelessness of the composition, just as he forgot himself and produced marvellous effects because he put into his instrument his whole soul which, as it were, knew no higher execution than the one that made these notes resound on this instrument.

When virtuosity like this reaches its culminating point it not only evinces an astounding mastery over external material but displays its inner unbounded freedom by surpassing itself in playing with apparently insurmountable difficulties, running riot with ingenuity, making surprising jokes in a witty mood with interruptions and fancies, and making enjoyable in its original inventions even the grotesque itself. For a poor head cannot produce original works of art, but in the case of executants of genius their works reveal their incredible mastery of and in their instrument; the virtuoso can overcome the restrictions of his instrument and now and again, as an audacious proof of this victory, can go through the gamut of the different sorts of sound given by instruments other than his own. In this sort of execution we enjoy the topmost peak of musical vitality, the wonderful secret of an external tool's becoming a perfectly animated instrument, and we have before us at the same time, like a flash of lightning, the inner conception and the execution of the imagination of genius in their most momentary fusion and most quickly passing life.

These are the most essential things that I have heard and felt in music and the general points which I have abstracted and assembled for the consideration of our present subject.

Chapter III

POETRY

INTRODUCTION

1. The temple of classical architecture needed a god to live in it; sculpture places him before us in plastic beauty and gives to the material it uses for this purpose forms which by their very nature are not alien to the spirit but are the shape immanent in the selected content itself. But the body, sensuousness, and ideal universality of the sculptural figure has contrasted with it both the subjective inner life and the particular character of the individual; and the content alike of the religious and the mundane life must gain actuality in the subjective and particular by means of a new art. This subjective and particular characteristic mode of expression painting introduces within the principle of the visual arts themselves, because it reduces the real externality of the shape to a more ideal appearance in colour and makes the expression of the inner soul the centre of the representation. Yet the general sphere in which these arts move, the first symbolic in type, the second ideally plastic, the third romantic, is the sensuous *external* shape of the spirit and things in nature.

But the spiritual content, by essentially belonging to the inner life of consciousness, has at the same time an existence alien to that life in the pure element of external appearance and in the vision to which the external shape is offered. Art must withdraw from this foreign element in order to enshrine its conceptions in a sphere of an explicitly inner and ideal kind in respect alike of the material used and the manner of expression. This was the forward step which we saw music taking, in that it made the inner life as such, and subjective feeling, something for apprehension by the inner life, not in visible shapes, but in the figurations of inwardly reverberating sound. But in this way it went to the other extreme, to an undeveloped concentration of feeling, the content of which found once again only a purely symbolic expression in notes. For the note, taken by itself, is without content and has its determinate character only in virtue of numerical relations, so that although the qualitative character of the spiritual content does correspond in general to these quantitative relations which open out into essential differences, oppositions, and modulation, still it cannot be completely characterized qualitatively by a note. Therefore, if this qualitative side is not to be missing altogether, music must, on account of its one-sidedness, call on the help of the more exact meaning of words and, in order to become more firmly conjoined with the detail and characteristic expression of the subject-matter, it demands a text which alone gives a fuller content to the subjective life's outpouring in the notes. By means of this expression of ideas and feelings the abstract inwardness of music emerges into a clearer and firmer unfolding of them. Yet on the one hand what it develops in this unfolding is not ideas and their artistically adequate form but only their accompanying inner sentiment; on the other hand, music simply snaps its link with words in order to move at will and unhampered within its own sphere of sounds. Consequently, on its side too, the sphere of ideas, which transcend the rather *abstract* inner life of feeling as such and give to their world the shape of *concrete* actuality, cuts itself free from music and gives itself an artistically adequate existence in the art of poetry.

Poetry, the art of speech, is the third term, the totality, which unites in itself, within the province of the spiritual inner life and on a higher level, the two extremes, i.e. the visual arts and music. For, on the one hand, poetry, like music, contains that principle of the self-apprehension of the inner life as inner, which architecture, sculpture, and painting lack; while, on the other hand, in the very field of inner ideas, perceptions, and feelings it broadens out into an objective world which does not altogether lose the determinate character of sculpture and painting. Finally, poetry is more capable than any other art of completely unfolding the totality of an event, a successive series and the changes of the heart's movements, passions, ideas, and the complete course of an action.

2. But furthermore poetry is the third of the *romantic* arts, painting and music being the other two.

(*a*) Poetry (i) has as its general principle spirituality and therefore it no longer turns to heavy matter as such in order, like architecture, to form it symbolically into an analogous environment for the inner life, or, like sculpture, to shape into real matter the natural form, as a spatial external object, belonging to the spirit; on the contrary, it expresses directly for spirit's apprehension the spirit itself with all its imaginative and artistic conceptions but without setting these out visibly and bodily for contemplation from the outside. (ii) Poetry, to a still ampler extent than painting and music, can comprise in the form of the inner life not only the inner consciousness but also the special and particular details of what exists externally, and at the same time it can portray them separately in the whole expanse of their individual traits and arbitrary peculiarities.

(b) Nevertheless poetry as a totality is on the other hand to be essentially distinguished from the specific arts whose characters it combines in itself.

(α) Painting, in this connection, has an over-all advantage when it is a matter of bringing a subject before our eyes in its external appearance. For, with manifold means at its command, poetry can indeed likewise illustrate, just as the principle of setting something out for contemplation is implicit in imagination generally, but since the element in which poetry principally moves, i.e. ideas, is of a spiritual kind and therefore enjoys the universality of thought, poetry is incapable of reaching the definiteness of sense-perception. On the other hand, the different traits which poetry introduces in order to make perceptible to us the concrete content of the subject in hand, do not fall together, as they do in painting, into one and the same whole which completely confronts us with all its details simultaneously; on the contrary, they occur separately because the manifold content of an idea can be expressed only as a succession. But this is a defect only from the sensuous point of view, one which the spirit can always rectify. Even where speech is concerned to evoke some concrete vision, it does not appeal to the sensuous perception of a present external object but always to the inner life, to *spiritual* vision, and consequently even if the individual traits only follow one another they are transferred into the element of the inwardly harmonious spirit which can extinguish a succession, pull together a varied series into *one* image and keep this image firmly in mind and enjoy it. Besides, this deficiency of sensuous reality and external definiteness in poetry as contrasted with painting is at once turned into an incalculable excess. For since poetry is exempt from painting's restriction to a specific space and still more to one specific feature of a situation or an action, it is given the possibility of presenting a subject in its whole inward depth and in the breadth of its temporal development. Truth is absolutely concrete in virtue of comprising in itself a unity of essential distinctions. But these develop in their appearance not only as juxtaposed in space, but in a temporal succession as a history, the course of which painting can only present graphically in an inappropriate way. Even every blade of grass, every tree has in this sense its history, alteration, process, and a complete totality of different situations. This is still more the case in the sphere of the spirit; as actual spirit in its appearance, it can only be portrayed exhaustively if it is brought before our minds as such a course of history.

(β) As we saw, poetry has sounds as an external material in common with music. The wholly external material (ordinarily, though not philosophically, called 'objective') slips away finally, in the progressive series of the particular arts, into the subjective element of sound which cannot be seen, with the result that the inner life is made aware of itself solely by its own activity.[1] But music's essential aim is to shape these sounds into notes. For although in the course and progress of the melody and its fundamental harmonic relations the soul presents to feeling the inner meaning of the subject-matter or its own inner self, nevertheless what gives music its own proper character is not the inner life as such but the soul, most intimately interweaved with its *sounding*, and the formation of this *musical* expression. This is so much the case that music becomes music and an independent art the more that what preponderates in it is the complete absorption of the inner life into the realm of *notes*, not of the spirit as such. But, for this reason, it is capable only to a relative extent of harbouring the variety of spiritual ideas and insights and the broad expanse of a richly filled conscious life, and in its expression it does not get beyond the more abstract and general character of what it takes as its subject or beyond vaguer deep feelings of the heart. Now in proportion as the spirit transforms this abstract generality into a concrete ensemble of ideas, aims, actions, and events and adds to this process their inspection seriatim, it deserts the inner world of pure feeling and works it out into a world of objective actuality developed likewise in the inner sphere of imagination. Consequently, simply on account of this transformation, any attempt to

---

[1] Sound is heard, not seen, but an activity of mind is required to interpret the sound as music and the meaning of the music as an expression of the inner life.

express this new-won wealth of the spirit wholly and exclusively through sounds and their harmony must be abandoned. Just as the material of sculpture is too poor to make possible the portrayal of the richer phenomena which it is painting's business to call to life, so now harmonious sounds and expression in melody cannot give full reality to the poet's imaginative creations. For these possess the precise and known definiteness of ideas and an external phenomenal form minted for inner contemplation. Therefore the spirit withdraws its content from sounds as such and is manifested by words which do not entirely forsake the element of sound but sink to being a merely external sign of what is being communicated. The musical note being thus replete with spiritual ideas becomes the sound of a word, and the word, instead of then being an end in itself, becomes in itself a dependent means of spiritual expression. This gives us, in accordance with what we established earlier, the essential difference between music and poetry. The subject-matter of the art of speech is the entire world of ideas developed with a wealth of imagination, i.e. the spirit abiding by itself in its own spiritual element and, when it moves out to the creation of something external, using that only as a sign, itself different from the subject-matter. With music, art abandons the immersion of the spirit in a tangible, visible, and directly present shape; in poetry it gives up the opposite element of sound and hearing, at least in so far as this sound is no longer formed into an adequate external object and the sole expression of the subject-matter. Therefore the inner life is expressed [in music] but it will not find its actual existence in the perceptibility (even if more ideal) of the notes, because it seeks this existence solely in itself in order to express the experience of the spirit as that is contained in the heart of imagination as such.

(c) If, thirdly and lastly, we look for the special character of poetry in its distinction from music, and from painting and the other visual arts, we find it simply in the above-mentioned subordination of the sensuous mode of presenting and elaborating all poetic subject-matter. Since sound, as in music (or colour, as in painting), is no longer able to harbour and present that entire subject-matter, the musical treatment of it by way of the beat, harmony, and melody necessarily disappears here, and what is left is, in general, only the tempo of words and syllables, rhythm, and euphony, etc. And even these remain not as the proper element for conveying the subject-matter but as a rather accidental externality which assumes an artistic form only because art cannot allow any external aspect to have free play purely by chance, arbitrarily, or capriciously.

(α) Granted the withdrawal of the spiritual content from sensuous material, the question arises at once: What, in default of musical notes, will now be the proper external object in the case of poetry? We can answer quite simply: It is the *inner* imagination and intuition itself. It is *spiritual* forms which take the place of perceptibility and provide the material to be given shape, just as marble, bronze, colour, and musical notes were the material earlier on. For here we must not be led astray by the statement that ideas and intuitions are in truth the subject-matter of poetry. This of course is true enough, as will be shown in detail later; but it is equally essential to maintain that ideas, intuitions, feelings, etc., are the specific forms in which every subject-matter is apprehended and presented by poetry, so that, since the sensuous side of the communication always has only a subordinate part to play, these forms provide the proper material which the poet has to treat artistically. The thing in hand, the subject-matter, is to be objectified in poetry for the spirit's apprehension, yet this objectivity exchanges its previously external reality for an internal one and it acquires an existence only within consciousness itself as something spiritually presented and intuited. Thus the spirit becomes objective to itself on its own ground and it has speech only as a means of communication or as an external reality out of which, as out of a mere sign, it has withdrawn into itself from the very start. Consequently in the case of poetry proper it is a matter of indifference whether we read it or hear it read; it can even be translated into other languages without essential detriment to its value, and turned from poetry into prose, and in these cases it is related to quite different sounds from those of the original.

(β) Further, the question arises: Granted that inner ideas constitute the material and form of poetry, for what is this material to be used? It is to be used for the absolute truth contained in spiritual interests in general, yet not merely for their substance in its universality of symbolical meaning [in architecture] or its classical differentiation [in sculpture] but also for everything detailed and particular within this substance, and so for almost everything which interests and occupies the spirit in any way. Consequently the art of speech, in respect of its subject-matter and its mode of expounding it, has an enormous field, a wider field than that open to the other arts. Any topic, all spiritual and natural things, events, histories, deeds, actions, subjective and objective situations, all these can be drawn into poetry and fashioned by it.

(γ) But this most variegated material is not made poetic simply by being harboured in our ideas, for after all a commonplace mind can shape exactly the same subject-matter into ideas and have separate intuitions of it without achieving anything poetic. In this connection we previously called ideas the *material* and element which is only given a poetically adequate form when art has shaped it afresh, just as colour and sound are not already, as mere colour and sound, painting and music. We can put this difference in general terms by saying that it is not ideas *as such* but the artistic imagination which makes some material poetic, when, that is to say, imagination so lays hold of it that, instead of confronting us as an architectural, sculptural, plastic, and painted shape or of sounding like musical notes, it can communicate with us in speech, in words and their beautiful spoken assembly.

The basic demand necessitated here is limited to this: (i) that the subject-matter shall not be conceived either in terms of scientific or speculative thinking or in the form of wordless feeling or with the clarity and precision with which we perceive external objects, and (ii) that it shall not enter our ideas with the accidents, fragmentation, and relativities of *finite* reality. In this regard the poetic imagination has, for one thing, to keep to the mean between the abstract universality of thought and the sensuously concrete corporeal objects that we have come to recognize in the productions of the visual arts; for another thing, it has on the whole to satisfy the demands we made in the First Part of these lectures in respect of any artistic creation, i.e. in its content it must be an end in itself and, with a purely contemplative interest, fashion everything that it conceives into an inherently independent and closed world. For only in this event does the content, as art requires, become by means of the manner of its presentation an organic whole which gives in its parts the appearance of close connection and coherence and, in contrast to the world of mutual dependence, stands there for its own sake and free on its own account.

3. The final point for discussion in connection with the difference between poetry and the other arts likewise concerns the

changed relation which the poetic imagination introduces between its productions and the external material of their presentation.

The arts considered hitherto were completely in earnest with the sensuous element in which they moved, because they gave to a subject-matter only a form which throughout could be adopted by and stamped on towering heavy masses, bronze, marble, wood, colours, and notes. Now in a certain sense it is true that poetry has a similar duty to fulfil. For in composing it must keep steadily in mind that its results are to be made known to the spirit only by communication in language. But this changes the whole relation to the material.

(*a*) The sensuous aspect acquires importance in the visual arts and in music. It follows that, owing to the specific determinacy of the material they use, it is only a *restricted* range of presentations that completely corresponds to particular real things existent in stone, colour, or sound, and the result is that the subject-matter and the artistic mode of treatment in the arts considered hitherto is fenced in within certain limits. This was the reason why we brought each of the specific arts into close connection with only *one* of the particular art-forms which this and no other art seemed best able to express adequately—architecture with the symbolic art-form, sculpture with the classical, painting and music with the romantic. It is true that the particular arts, below and above their proper sphere, encroached on the other art-forms too, and for this reason we could speak of classical and romantic architecture, and symbolic and Christian sculpture, and we also had to mention classical painting and music. But these deviations did not reach the real summit of art but either were the preparatory attempts of inferior beginnings or else displayed the start of a transition to an art which, in this transition, seized on a subject-matter, and a way of treating the material, of a type that only a further art was permitted to develop completely.

In the expression of its content on the whole, architecture is poorest, sculpture is richer, while the scope of painting and music can be extended most widely of all. For with the increasing ideality and more varied particularization of the external material, the variety of the subject-matter and of the forms it assumes is increased. Now poetry cuts itself free from this importance of the material, in the general sense that the specific character of its mode of sensuous expression affords no reason any longer for restriction to a specific subject-matter and a confined sphere of treatment and presentation. It is therefore not linked exclusively to any specific form of art; on the contrary, it is the *universal* art which can shape in any way and express any subject-matter capable at all of entering the imagination, because its proper material is the imagination itself, that universal foundation of all the particular art-forms and the individual arts.

This is the point that we reached at the close of our treatment of the particular art-forms. Their culmination we looked for in art's making itself independent of the mode of representation peculiar to *one* of the art-forms and in its standing above the whole of these particular forms. The possibility of such a development in every direction lies from the very beginning, amongst the specific arts, in the essence of poetry alone, and it is therefore actualized in the course of poetic production partly through the actual exploitation of every particular form, partly through liberation from imprisonment in any exclusive type and character of treatment and subject-matter, whether symbolic, classical, or romantic.

(*b*) From this point of view too the position we have assigned to poetry in our philosophical development of the arts can be justified. Since poetry is occupied with the universal element in art as such to a greater extent than is the case in any of the other ways of producing works of art, it might seem that a philosophical explanation had to begin with it and only thereafter proceed to particularize the ways in which the other arts are differentiated by their sensuous material. But, as we have seen already in connection with the particular art-forms, the process of development, regarded philosophically, consists on the one hand in a deepening of art's spiritual content, and on the other in showing that at first art only *seeks* its adequate content, then *finds* it, and finally *transcends* it. This conception of beauty and art must now be made good in the arts themselves too. We began therefore with architecture which only strove after the complete representation of spiritual material in a sensuous element, so that art achieved a genuine fusion of form and content only in sculpture; with painting and music, on account of the inwardness and subjectivity of their content, art began to dissolve again the accomplished unification of conception and execution in the field of sense. This latter character [of unification] poetry displays most strikingly because in its artistic materialization it is essentially to be interpreted as a withdrawal from the real world of sense-perception and a subordination of that world, yet not as a production that does not dare to embark yet on materialization and movement in the external world. But in order to expound this liberation philosophically it is first necessary to explain what it is from which art undertakes to free itself, and, similarly, how it is that poetry can harbour the entire content of art and all the forms of art. This too we have to regard as a struggle for a totality, a struggle that can be demonstrated philosophically only as the cancellation of a restriction to the particular, which in turn implies a previous treatment of the one-sided stages, the unique value possessed by each being negated in the totality.

Only as a result of considering the series of the arts in this way does poetry appear as that particular art in which art itself begins at the same time to dissolve and acquire in the eyes of philosophy its point of transition to religious pictorial thinking as such, as well as to the prose of scientific thought. The realm of the beautiful, as we saw earlier, is bordered on one side by the prose of finitude and commonplace thinking, out of which art struggles on its way to truth, and on the other side the higher spheres of religion and philosophy where there is a transition to that apprehension of the Absolute which is still further removed from the sensuous sphere.

(*c*) Therefore, however completely poetry produces the totality of beauty once and for all in a most spiritual way, nevertheless spirituality constitutes at the same time precisely the deficiency of this final sphere of art. In the system of the arts we can regard poetry as the polar opposite of architecture. Architecture cannot so subordinate the sensuous material to the spiritual content as to be able to form that material into an adequate shape of the spirit; poetry, on the other hand, goes so far in its negative treatment of its sensuous material that it reduces the opposite of heavy spatial matter, namely sound, to a meaningless sign instead of making it, as architecture makes its material, into a meaningful symbol. But in this way poetry destroys the fusion of spiritual inwardness with external existence to an extent that begins to be incompatible with the original conception of art, with the result that poetry runs the risk of losing itself in a transition from the region of sense into that of the spirit. The beautiful mean between these extremes of architecture and poetry is occupied by sculpture, painting, and music, because each of these arts works the spiritual content entirely into a natural medium and makes it intelligible alike to sense and spirit.

For although painting and music, as romantic arts, do adopt a material which is already more ideal, yet on the other hand for the immediacy of tangible objects, which begins to evaporate in this enhanced ideality of the medium, they substitute the wealth of detail and the more varied configuration which colour and sound are capable of providing in a richer way than is requirable from the material of sculpture.

Poetry for its part likewise looks for a substitute: it brings the objective world before our eyes in a breadth and variety which even painting cannot achieve, at least on a single canvas, and yet this always remains only a real existence in the *inner* consciousness; and even if poetry in its need for an artistic materialization makes straight for a strengthened sensuous impression, still it can produce this only by means foreign to itself and borrowed from painting and music, or else, in order to maintain itself as genuine poetry, it must always put these sister arts in the background, purely as its servants, and emphasize instead, as the really chief thing concerned, the spiritual idea, the imagination which speaks to inner imagination.

So much in general about the relation of the nature of poetry to the nature of the other arts. The more detailed consideration of the art of poetry must be arranged as follows:

We have seen that in poetry both content and material are provided by our inner ideas. Yet ideas, outside art, are already the commonest form of consciousness and therefore we must in the first place undertake the task of distinguishing poetic from prosaic ideas. But poetry should not abide by this inner poetical conception alone but must give its creations an expression in language. Here once again a double duty is to be undertaken. (i) Poetry must so organize its inner conceptions that they can be completely adapted to communication in language; (ii) it must not leave this linguistic medium in the state in which it is used every day, but must treat it poetically in order to distinguish it from expressions in prose by the choice, placing, and sound of words.

But despite its expression in language, poetry is free in the main from the restrictions and conditions laid on the other arts by the particular character of their medium, and consequently it has the widest possibility of completely developing all the different *genres* that a work of art can permit of, independently of the one-sidedness of any particular art. For this reason the most perfect articulation of the different *genres* of poetry comes into view.

Accordingly our further course is

First, to discuss poetry in general and the poetic work of art;
Secondly, poetic expression;
Thirdly, the division of this art into epic, lyric, and dramatic poetry.

A. THE POETIC WORK OF ART AS DISTINGUISHED FROM A PROSE WORK OF ART

To define the poetic as such or to give a description of what is poetic horrifies nearly all who have written about poetry. And in fact if a man begins to talk about poetry as an imaginative art without having previously examined what art's content and general mode of representation is, he will find it extremely difficult to know where to look for the proper essence of poetry. But the awkwardness of his problem especially increases if he starts from the individual character of single works and then proposes to assert some universal derived from this character and supposed to be valid for the most varied *genres* and sorts of poetry. Along these lines the most heterogeneous works count as poetry. If this assumption is presupposed and the question is then raised: By what right should such productions by recognized as poems? the difficulty just mentioned enters at once. Fortunately, at this point in our discussion we can evade this difficulty. In the first place, we have not reached the general conception of the matter in hand by deriving it from single examples; on the contrary, we have endeavoured to develop the real exemplifications of this conception from the conception itself and consequently we cannot be required, e.g. in the sphere we are dealing with now, to subsume under this conception whatever is commonly called a poem, because the decision on whether something actually is a poetical production or not is to be derived solely from the conception of poetry itself. Secondly, we need not now satisfy the demand that we should specify the conception of poetry, because to fulfil this task we would have to repeat everything already expounded in our First Part about beauty and the Ideal as such. For the nature of poetry coincides in general with the conception of the beauty of art and works of art as such, since the poetic imagination differs from the imagination in the visual arts and music where, owing to the kind of material in which it intends to work, it is restricted in its creation in many ways and driven in separate and one-sided directions. The poetic imagination, *per contra*, is subject only to the essential demands of an ideal and artistically adequate mode of representation. Therefore, of the numerous points which could be adduced here, I will emphasize only the most important, namely

1. The difference between poetic and prosaic treatment.
2. Poetic and prose works of art.
3. A few remarks in conclusion about the author of poems, namely the poet.

1. *Poetic and Prosaic Treatment*

(*a*) In the first place, externality as such, i.e. objects in nautre, can at once be excluded, relatively at least, from the subject-matter suitable for poetical conception. The proper subject-matter of poetry is spiritual interests, not the sun, mountains, woods, landscapes, or constituents of the human body like nerves, blood, muscles, etc. For however far poetry also involves an element of vision and illustration, it still remains even in this respect a spiritual activity and it works for *inner* intuition to which the spirit is nearer and more appropriate than *external* objects in their concrete visible and external appearance. Therefore this entire external sphere enters poetry only in so far as the spirit finds in it a stimulus or some material for its activity; in other words it enters as a *human* environment, as man's external world which has essential worth only in relation to man's inner consciousness and which may not claim the dignity of being, purely on its own account, the exclusive subject-matter of poetry. The subject-matter really corresponding to poetry is the infinite wealth of the spirit. For language, this most malleable material, the direct property of the spirit, of all media of expression the one most capable of seizing the interests and movements of the spirit in their inner vivacity, must be used, like stone, colour, and sound in the other arts, principally to express what it proves most fitted to express. Accordingly, the chief task of poetry is to bring before our minds the powers governing spiritual life, and, in short, all that surges to and fro in human passion and feeling or passes quietly through our meditations—the all-encompassing realm of human ideas, deeds, actions, and fates, the bustle of life in this world, and the divine rule of the universe. Thus poetry has been and is still the most universal and widespread teacher of the human race. For to teach and to learn is to know and experience what *is*. Stars, plants, and animals neither know nor experience what their law is; but man exists conformably to the law of his existence only when he knows what he is and what his surroundings are: he must know what the powers are which drive and direct him, and it is such a knowledge that poetry provides in its original and substantive form.

(b) But this same subject-matter is treated also by the prosaic mind which teaches the universal laws [of nature] and can classify, arrange, and explain the individual phenomena of our chequered world. The question therefore arises, as we have said, of the general difference between the prosaic and poetic modes of conception, granted a possible similarity of the subject-matter in both cases.

(α) Poetry is older than skilfully elaborated prosaic speech. It is the original presentation of the truth, a knowing which does not yet separate the universal from its living existence in the individual, which does not yet oppose law to appearance, end to means, and then relate them together again by abstract reasoning, but which grasps the one only in and through the other. Therefore it does not at all take something already known independently in its universality and merely express it in imagery. According to its immediate essential nature it abides by the substantive unity of outlook which has not yet separated opposites and then related them purely externally.

(αα) With this way of looking at things, poetry presents all its subject-matter as a totality complete in itself and therefore independent; this whole may be rich and may have a vast range of relations, individuals, actions, events, feelings, sorts of ideas, but poetry must display this vast complex as perfect in itself, as produced and animated by the single principle which is manifested externally in this or that individual detail. Consequently the universal and the rational are not expressed in poetry in abstract universality and *philosophically* proved interconnection, or with their aspects merely related together as in *scientific* thinking, but instead as animated, manifest, ensouled, determining the whole, and yet at the same time expressed in such a way that the all-comprising unity, the real animating soul, is made to work only in secret from within outwards.

(ββ) This apprehension, formation, and expression [of the subject-matter] remains purely contemplative in poetry. The aim of poetry is imagery and speech, not the thing talked about or its existence in practice. Poetry began when man undertook to express *himself*; for poetry, what is spoken is there only to be an expression. When once, in the midst of his practical activity and need, man proceeds to collect his thoughts and communicate himself to others, then he immediately produces a coined expression, a touch of poetry. To mention only one example, Herodotus[1] gives us one in that distich which he has preserved for us and which reports the death of the Greeks who fell at Thermopylae. The report is left entirely simple: the dry information that four thousand Peloponnesians fought a battle here against three myriads. But the interest lies in the preparation of an inscription to relate this event for contemporaries and posterity, purely for the sake of relating it, and so the expression becomes poetic, i.e. it is meant to be a ποιεῖν [a 'making'] which leaves the story in its simplicity but intentionally gives special form to its description. The Word enshrining the ideas is in itself of such a high dignity that it tries to distinguish itself from any other mode of speech, and makes itself into a distich.

(γγ) In this way, even on its linguistic side, poetry has the vocation of being a sphere of its own, and, in order to separate itself from ordinary speech, the formation of the expression becomes of more importance than mere enunciation. But in connection with this and with poetry's general outlook, we must make an essential distinction between a primitive poetry composed before ordinary prose had been skilfully developed and a poetic diction and mode of treatment developed within a period when prosaic expression had already been completely elaborated. The former is poetic in conception and speech unintentionally, whereas the latter knows the sphere from which it must liberate itself in order to stand on the free ground of art and therefore it develops in conscious distinction from prose.

(β) Secondly, the prosaic mind, which poetry must shun, requires a totally different kind of conception and speech.

(αα) On the one hand, the prosaic mind treats the vast field of actuality in accordance with the restricted thinking of the *Understanding* and its categories, such as cause and effect, means and end,

---

[1] vii. 228. 'Here four thousand from the Peloponnese fought against three myriads', an elegiac distich. Hegel follows Herodotus in taking the four thousand to be the number of the dead, whereas it is simply the number of those who fought. ('Poetry' in Greek originally means 'making'. Cf. Scots 'makar'.)

i.e., in general with relations in the field of externality and finitude. In this way of thinking, every particular either appears falsely as independent or is brought into a mere relation with another and therefore is apprehended only as relative and dependent; the result is that there is not established that free unity which still remains a total and free whole in itself within all its ramifications and separate particulars; for in such a whole its particular aspects are only the unfolding and appearance proper to the *one* content which is the centre and cohesive soul and which is actually manifested as this through and through animation. The sort of conception characteristic of the Understanding therefore gets no further than particular laws for phenomena; it persists in separating the particular existent from the universal law and in merely relating them together, and at the same time, in its eyes, the laws themselves fall apart into fixed particulars, while the relations between these are presented likewise under the categories of externality and finitude.

(ββ) On the other hand, *ordinary*[1] thinking has nothing to do with an inner connection, with the essence of things, with reasons, causes, aims, etc., but is content to take what is and happens as just this bare individual thing or event, i.e. as something accidental and meaningless. In this case there is none of the Understanding's dissection of that living unity in which the poetic vision keeps together the indwelling reason of things and their expression and existence; but what is missing is insight into this rationality and significance of things which therefore are without substance for this ordinary thinking and can make no further claim on a rational interest. In that event the Understanding's view of the world and its relations as connected by certain categories is exchanged for a mere view of a world of successive or juxtaposed accidents which may have a great range of external life but which is totally unable to satisfy the deeper need of reason. For genuine insight and a sound mind find satisfaction only when they glimpse and sense in phenomena the corresponding reality of what is genuinely substantial and true. For a deeper mind, what is alive in the outside world is dead unless through it there shines something inner and rich in significance as its own proper soul.

[1] i.e. the thinking of the man in the street as distinct from the scientific thinking of the Understanding and the philosophical (or 'speculative') thinking of Reason.

($\gamma\gamma$) Thirdly, these deficiencies of the Understanding's categories and the ordinary man's vision are extinguished by *speculative* thinking which therefore is from one point of view akin to the poetic imagination. Reason's knowing neither has to do with accidental details nor does it overlook the essence of the phenomena; neither is it content with those dissections and mere relations characteristic of the Understanding's outlook and reflections; on the contrary, it conjoins in a free totality what under a finite type of consideration falls to pieces into aspects that are either independent or put into relations with one another without any unification.

Thinking, however, results in thoughts alone; it evaporates the form of reality into the form of the pure Concept, and even if it grasps and apprehends real things in their particular character and real existence, it nevertheless lifts even this particular sphere into the element of the universal and ideal wherein alone thinking is at home with itself. Consequently, contrasted with the world of appearance, a new realm arises which is indeed the truth of reality, but this is a truth which is not made *manifest* again in the real world itself as its formative power and as its own soul. Thinking is only a reconciliation between reality and truth within thinking itself. But poetic creation and formation is a reconciliation in the form of a *real* phenomenon itself, even if this form be presented only spiritually.

(γ) In this way we acquire two different spheres of thought, poetry and prose. In primitive times poetry had an easier game to play: in those days a specific conception of the world, whether according with a religious faith or some other way of knowing, had not developed an intellectually organized set of ideas or knowledge, nor had it regulated the real world of human affairs in accordance with such knowledge. In those circumstances poetry was not confronted with prose as an independent field of internal and external existence, a field that it had first to overcome. Its task was restricted rather to merely deepening the meanings and clarifying the forms of other modes of consciousness. If, on the other hand, prose has already drawn into its mode of treatment the entire contents of the spirit and impressed the seal of that treatment on anything and everything, poetry has to undertake the work of completely recasting and remodelling and sees itself involved on every side in numerous difficulties because of the inflexibility of prose. For not only has it to tear itself free from adherence to the ordinary contemplation of indifferent and accidental things and either raise to rationality the Understanding's view of the connection of things or else take speculative thinking into the imagination and give it a body as it were within the spirit itself; but it must also in all these tasks transform the prosaic consciousness's ordinary mode of expression into a poetic one, and yet, despite all the deliberateness necessarily entailed by such an opposition, it must absolutely preserve the appearance of that lack of deliberation and that original freedom which art requires.

(c) We have now indicated very generally what the subject-matter of poetry is and we have distinguished its form from that of prose. The third point that must still be mentioned concerns the particularization to which poetry proceeds more than the other arts do, since their development has been less rich. It is true that we see architecture arising likewise amongst the most different nations and in the whole course of centuries, but sculpture reached its zenith in the ancient world, amongst the Greeks and Romans, just as painting and music have done in the modern world amongst Christian peoples. Poetry, however, enjoys its periods of brilliance and success in all nations and at practically every period which is productive of art at all. For it embraces the entire spirit of mankind, and mankind is particularized in many ways.

(α) The subject-matter of poetry is not the universal as it is abstracted in philosophy. What it has to represent is reason individualized. Throughout therefore it cannot dispense with the specific national character from which it proceeds; its subject-matter and mode of portrayal are made what they are by the ideas and ways of looking at things which are those of that character. This is why poetry has such a wealth of particularization and originality. Eastern, Italian, Spanish, English, Roman, Greek, German poetry, all are different throughout in spirit, feeling, outlook, expression, etc.

The same variety of differences is prominent also in the case of the historical periods in which poetry is composed. For example, what German poetry is now it could not be in the Middle Ages or at the time of the Thirty Years War. The things that arouse our deepest interest today belong to our own present period, and every age has its own mode of feeling, whether wider or more restricted, loftier and freer or more toned down, in short its own particular view of the world which is most clearly and completely brought before the artistic consciousness by poetry because the word can express the entirety of the human spirit.

(β) Further, amongst these national characters, tempers of the age, and views of the world, some are more poetic than others. For example, the Eastern mind is on the whole more poetic than the Western, Greece excluded. In the East the chief thing is always the One, undivided, fixed, substantive, and such an outlook is from start to finish the most sterling one, even if it does not press on to the freedom of the Ideal. The West, on the other hand, especially in recent times, starts from the endless dispersal and particularization of the infinite, and in this way, with the reduction of everything to atoms, the finite becomes something independent for our apprehension, and yet it becomes bent round again into something relative; whereas for the East nothing remains really independent; everything appears as only something accidental which is brought back to the One and the Absolute, where it is steadily concentrated, and where it finds its final deliverance.

(γ) This variety of national differences, however, and this course of development through centuries is permeated by something common to them all, and for this reason other nations and the tempers of different periods have in common something intelligible and enjoyable, namely universal human nature and art. For this double reason especially, Greek poetry is always admired and imitated anew by the most different peoples because human nature has reached its most beautiful development in it alike in its subject-matter and its artistic form. Yet even Indian poetry, despite all its distance from our view of the world and from our mode of portrayal, is not wholly strange to us, and we can laud it as a high privilege of our age to have begun more and more to unveil its sense for the whole richness of art and, in short, of the human spirit.

If now, granted this tendency to individualization which poetry has followed throughout its course in the ways described, we are to treat it in general terms, then this general character, which could be accepted as such, remains abstract and trite, and therefore, if we intend to speak of poetry proper, we must always take up the forms of the imagining spirit in their national and temporary particular character and not leave out of our notice even the subjective individuality of the poet.

These are the points that I wished to premise in dealing generally with poetry's treatment of its subject-matter.

2. The Poetic and the Prose Work of Art

But poetry must go beyond formulating inner ideas and must articulate and polish them into a poetic work of art.

The manifold considerations which this new topic invites may be brought together and arranged in such a way that

(*a*) first, we emphasize the most important point about the poetic work of art as such, and this poetic work of art we then

(*b*) secondly, distinguish from the chief kinds of prosaic portrayal in so far as this portrayal is also capable of being handled artistically. From this alone

(*c*) thirdly, can the conception of the *free* work of art be completely revealed.

(*a*) In connection with the poetic work of art in general, we need only repeat the demand that, like any other product of free imagination, it must be formed and rounded into an organic whole. This requirement can only be satisfied in the following way.

(α) First, the dominant subject-matter, whether it be a specific aim of an action or event, or a specific feeling and passion, must above all have unity in itself.

(αα) Everything must be related to this united whole and connected together with this whole concretely and freely. This is possible only if the chosen subject is not seized as an abstract universal but as human action and feeling, as aim and passion, which belong to the spirit, mind, and will of specific individuals and grow from the soil of this individual character itself.

(ββ) The universal, which is to be represented, and the individuals, in whose character, histories, and actions, it appears poetically, may therefore not fall apart from one another or be so related that the individuals become servants of purely abstract universals; on the contrary, both must always be vitally interwoven with one another. So, for example, in the Iliad the battle between the Greeks and the Trojans and the victory of the former are linked with the wrath of Achilles which therefore is the sustaining centre of the whole epic. Of course there are also poetic works in which the basic content is itself of a more general character or is treated in a more significantly general way, as for instance Dante's great epic poem which bestrides the entire divine world and portrays the most different sorts of individuals in relation to the punishments of Hell, to Purgatory, and to the blessings of Paradise. But even here there is no abstract separation of these two sides and no mere servitude of the individuals. For in the world of Christian thought the individual is not to be regarded as a mere accident of the Godhead but as an infinite end in himself, so that here the universal end, God's justice in pronouncing damnation or salvation, may appear at the same time as an immanent affair, the eternal interest and being of the individual himself. In this divine world, concern is purely for the individual: in the state he may indeed be sacrificed for the safety of the universal, i.e. the state, but in relation to God and in the Kingdom of God he is without qualification an end in himself.

(γγ) Yet, in the third place, the universal which provides the content of human feeling and action must appear as independent, complete and perfect in itself and constitute a closed world on its own account. For instance, if we hear nowadays of an officer, a general, an official, a professor, etc., and imagine what such figures and characters can will and accomplish in their circumstances and environment, we are confronted merely by a matter of interest and activity which *either* is not rounded off or independent in itself but is involved in infinitely varied external connections, relations, and subjections, *or* else, taken again as an abstract whole, may assume the form of a universal, like duty for example, violently abstracted from the rest of the individual's whole character.

Conversely, it is true that there is a subject-matter of a more solid kind which does form an enclosed whole but which is perfect and complete in a single sentence without any further development or advance. Of such a matter we cannot say with precision whether it is to be reckoned poetry or prose. For example, the great saying of the Old Testament [Genesis 1: 3]: 'God said, Let there be light: and there was light', is in its compactness and striking composure just as much supreme poetry as it is prose. The same is true of the Commandments [Exodus 20: 2–3, 12]: 'I am the Lord thy God . . . Thou shalt have no other gods before me . . . Honour thy father and thy mother'; in the same class are the 'Golden Verses' of Pythagoras,[1] the Book of Proverbs, and the Wisdom of Solomon, etc. These are pregnant sentences which precede, as it were, the difference between prose and poetry. But such collections, even if large, can scarcely be called a poetic work of art, for the perfect and

---

[1] A collection of hexameters, a series of old and well-known maxims, written or collected not by Pythagoras but by later Pythagoreans.

rounded whole that we found in poetry is at the same time to be regarded as a development, an articulation, and therefore as a unity which essentially proceeds to an actual particularization of its different aspects and parts. This demand for particularization, self-explanatory in visual art, at least in its figures, is of the highest importance for a poetic work of art.

(β) In this way we reach a second point in connection with the organic articulation of the work of art, namely the particularization of its individual parts which, to be able to enter an organic unity, must appear developed on their own account.

(αα) The first point that arises here is grounded in the fact that art in general loves to tarry in the particular. The Understanding hurries, because either it forthwith summarizes variety in a *theory* drawn from generalizations and so evaporates it into reflections and categories, or else it subordinates it to specific *practical* ends, so that the particular and the individual are not given their full rights.[1] To cling to what, given this position, can only have a relative value, seems therefore to the Understanding to be useless and wearisome. But, in a poetic treatment and formulation, every part, every feature must be interesting and living on its own account, and therefore poetry takes pleasure in lingering over what is individual, describes it with love, and treats it as a whole in itself. Consequently, however great the interest and the subject may be which poetry makes the centre of a work of art, poetry nevertheless articulates it in detail, just as in the human organism each limb, each finger is most delicately rounded off into a whole, and in real life, in short, every particular existent is enclosed into a world of its own. The advance of poetry is therefore slower than the judgements and syllogisms of the Understanding to which what is important, whether in its theorizing or in its practical aims and intentions, is above all the end result, while it is less concerned with the long route by which it reaches it.

But as for the extent to which poetry may indulge its inclination to linger on the details it depicts, we have seen already that it is not its function to describe at length the external world as such in the form in which it appears before our eyes. For this reason if it

[1] For Hegel, the physical and natural sciences are the province of the 'Understanding', but, in the sphere of practice, so is economics (see, for instance, *Philosophy of Right*, § 189). It has not exactly a practical aim, but seeks universal rules, disregarding individual activities, just as the individual apple is of no importance to the theory of gravitation.

makes such detailed descriptions its chief task, without mirroring spiritual relations and interests in them, it becomes ponderous and wearisome. Especially must it beware of competing in any exact details with the whole particularity of real existence. In this respect, even painting must be cautious and be able to remain within limits. In the case of poetry two points must be kept in view, namely that, on the one hand, it can make its effect only on our subjective contemplation, and, on the other hand, it can bring before our minds only in isolated traits one after another what we can see at one glance in the real world, and therefore in its treatment of an individual occurrence it cannot so far spread itself that the total view of it is necessarily disturbed, confused, or altogether lost. It has special difficulties above all to overcome when it is to set before our eyes an action or event of a varied kind which is carried out in the real world at its own moment and is in the closest connection with that contemporaneousness, while poetry can always present it only as a succession.

In connection with this point, as with the manner of lingering and advancing, etc., very different sorts of requirement arise besides from the different kinds of poetry. For example, epic poetry must linger on individual and external events to a greater extent than in the case with dramatic poetry which pushes forward in a more rapid course, or with lyric which is concerned with the inner life alone.

($\beta\beta$) Secondly, owing to such a development of the work of art, its particular parts become *independent*. This seems to be a direct contradiction of the unity which we laid down as the primary condition of a work of art, but in fact this contradiction is only apparent and deceptive. For this independence may not be so firmly established that each particular part is absolutely divorced from the others; on the contrary it must be asserted only to the extent of showing that the different aspects and members have come into the presentation on their own account in their own living reality and stand there freely on their own feet. But if the single parts lack life of their own, the work of art becomes cold and dead since, like art generally, it can give an existence to universal material only in the form of actual particulars.

($\gamma\gamma$) Yet despite this independence, these same single parts must still remain connected together, because the one fundamental subject, developed and presented in them, has to be manifested as the unity permeating all the particulars, holding them together as a totality, and drawing them all back into itself. If poetry is not at its height, it may easily founder on the reef of this demand, and the work of art will be transposed from the element of free imagination into the sphere of prose. The connection into which the parts are brought should not be a mere teleological one. For in a teleological relationship, the end is the independently envisaged and willed universal which can bring into conformity with itself the particulars through and in which it gains existence, but these particulars it uses merely as means and it robs them of all independently free existence and therefore of every sort of life. In that event the parts come only into an intended relation to the one end which alone is to be conspicuous as valid; everything else this end subjects to itself and takes abstractly into its service. This unfree relationship, characteristic of the Understanding, is the very contrary of the free beauty of art.

(γ) Thus the unity to be re-established in the particular parts of the work of art must be of another kind. The two points implicit in this we may put as follows:

(αα) We required each part to have a life of its own, and the first point is that this life shall be preserved. If we ask by what right the particular as such can be introduced into the work of art at all, our reply starts from the fact that a work of art is undertaken in order to present one fundamental idea. Therefore it must be from this idea that everything specific and individual derives its proper origin. In other words, the subject-matter of a poetic work must be concrete in nature, not inherently abstract, and lead automatically to a rich development of its different aspects. These differences may appear to fall apart from one another in the course of their actualization and become direct opposites, but if they are in fact grounded in that fully unified subject-matter, then this can be the case only if the subject-matter in its nature and essence contains in itself a closed and harmonious totality of particulars which are its own; and it is only by unfolding these seriatim that it really makes explicit what its own proper meaning is. For this reason it is only *these* particular parts, which belong to the subject-matter originally, that may be displayed in the work of art in the form of an actual, independently valid, and living existence. In this respect, however much in the realization of their own particular characters they may seem to become opposed to one another, they nevertheless have from the very beginning a secret harmony grounded in their own nature.

(ββ) Secondly, the work of art confronts us in the form of something that appears in the real world, and therefore if the living reflection of the *actual* in the real is not to be jeopardized, the unity itself must be only the *inner* bond which holds the parts together, apparently unintentionally, and includes them in an organic whole. It is this soul-laden unity of an organic whole which alone, as contrasted with the prosaic category of means and end, can produce genuine poetry. Where the particular appears only as a means to a specific end, it neither has nor should have any validity and life of its own, but on the contrary is to manifest in its entire existence that it is there only for the sake of something else, i.e. the specific end. The category of means and end makes obvious its dominion over the objective world in which the end is realized. But the work of art differentiates the fundamental topic that has been selected as its centre by developing its particular features, and to these it imparts the appearance of independent freedom; and this it must do because these particulars are nothing but that topic itself in the form of its actually corresponding realization. This may therefore remind us of the procedure of speculative thinking which likewise must develop the particular, out of the primarily undifferentiated universal, up to independence, but on the other hand has to show how, within this totality of particulars in which what is made explicit is only what was implicit in the universal, the unity is on this very account restored once more and is only now the actually concrete unity, proved to be such on the strength of its own differences and their harmonization. By means of this mode of treatment, speculative philosophy likewise produces works which, like poetical ones in this respect, have through their content itself perfect self-identity and articulated development; but when we compare these two activities, we must emphasize an essential difference over and above the difference between art's portrayal and the development of pure thought. Logical deduction does display the necessity and reality of the particular but, by dialectically superseding it, it expressly demonstrates in the particular itself that the particular has its truth and stability only in the concrete unity. Poetry, on the other hand, does not get so far as such a deliberate exposition: the harmonizing unity must indeed be completely present in every poetical work and be active in every part of it as the animating soul of the whole, but this presence is never expressly emphasized by art; on the contrary it remains something inner and implicit, just as the soul is directly living in all the members of the organism but without depriving them of their appearance of existing independently. The same is the case with colours and musical notes: yellow, blue, green, and red are different colours which may be brought into complete opposition to one another, and yet by being the totality implied in the very nature of colour, they can remain in harmony without their unity being expressly made explicit in them as such. Similarly the keynote, the third, and the fifth remain particular notes and yet provide the harmony of the chord: indeed they form this harmony only if each note is independently allowed its own free sound.

($\gamma\gamma$) But in respect of the organic unity and articulation of the work of art, essential differences are introduced both by the particular art-form in which the work of art originated, and also by the specific kind of poetry whose special character conditions the formation of the poem. For example, in the poetry of symbolic art the fundamental subject-matter involves meanings that are rather abstract and vague, and therefore this poetry cannot achieve a genuine organic accomplishment in the degree of purity possible in the case of works within the classical form of art. In symbolic art generally, as we saw above in Part I, the connection between the universal meaning and the actual appearance in which art embodies its subject-matter is of a looser kind, so that here at one time the particulars acquire a greater independence, and at another time again, as in sublimity, they are just superseded in order in this negation to make intelligible the *one* and only power and substance, or again there is only an enigmatic linkage of particular traits and aspects of natural and spiritual existence alike, and these in themselves are as often heterogeneous as akin. In the romantic art-form, conversely, the inner life, withdrawn into itself, reveals itself to the mind alone, and therefore this art-form gives to the particulars of external reality likewise a wider scope for independent development, so that here too, although the connection and unity of all the parts must indeed be present, it cannot be so clearly and firmly developed as it is in the products of the classical art-form.

In a similar way epic permits of a wider depiction of externals and a lingering over episodic events and deeds, with the result that, owing to the increased independence of the parts, the unity of the whole is less in evidence. Drama, on the other hand, demands a stricter concatenation, although even in drama romantic poetry allows a rich variety of episodes and a detailing of particulars in its characterization of both subjective and objective existence. Lyric poetry, proportionately to its different kinds, likewise adopts the most manifold modes of presentation: at one time it relates, at another it merely expresses feelings and reflections, at another again, moving along more quietly, it keeps to a more closely linking unity, or, in unrestrained passion, it can run riot in feelings and ideas apparently destitute of any unity.

This may suffice for the general character of the poetic work of art.

(b) Now, secondly, in order to bring out more definitely the difference between a poem organized in this way and a prose composition, we will turn to those kinds of prose which within their limits are best able to have their share of art. This is principally the case in the arts of historiography and oratory.

(α) Historiography of course leaves room enough for *one* aspect of artistic activity.

(αα) The development of human life in religion and the state, the affairs and fates of the most prominent individuals and nations who in these spheres have their vital activity, pursue great ends, or see their undertakings come to disaster—all this as the topic and subject-matter of historiography may be important on its own account, interesting, and of sterling worth, and, however much trouble the historian must take in recounting 'things as they actually happened',[1] he must absorb in his mind this varied material of events and characters and recreate it and present it out of his own genius for our minds to grasp. Further, in so reproducing it, he may not be content with mere exactitude in individual details; on the contrary, he must at the same time arrange and organize his material: he must so connect and group individual traits, occurrences, and facts, that on the one hand there leaps to our view a clear picture of the nation, the period, the external circumstances and the subjective greatness or weakness of the individual actors in their fully characteristic life, while, on the other hand, out of all

---

[1] This is not put as a quotation in the text, but it is clearly a reminiscence of Ranke's famous words in the preface to his *History of the Roman and Germanic Peoples* (1824). At that time Ranke was Hegel's colleague in Berlin.

the parts there proceeds their connection with the inner historical significance of a people, an event, etc. In this sense we speak even now of the 'art' of Herodotus, Thucydides, Xenophon, Tacitus, and a few others, and come to admire their narratives as classical works of the literary art.

(ββ) Nevertheless even these finest products of historiography do not belong to the sphere of free art; indeed even if we wanted to add to them an external poetic treatment of diction, versification, etc., no poetry would result. For it is not only the manner in which history is written, but the nature of its subject-matter which makes it prosaic. We will cast a further glance at this.

What is properly historical, whether in the nature of the case or in its subject-matter, takes its earliest beginning at the point when the heroic period, which poetry and art had originally to claim as its own, is ending, and when, in short, the definiteness and prose of life is present in the actual state of affairs as well as in its artistic treatment and presentation. So, for example, Herodotus describes not the expedition of the Greeks against Troy, but the Persian Wars and has struggled in many ways with laborious research and careful reflection to arrive at a precise knowledge of the events he intends to relate. Whereas the Indians, Orientals in general indeed, except perhaps the Chinese only, have not prosaic sense enough to give us an actual historical narrative because they run off into either purely religious or else fantastic interpretations and transformations of the facts. The prosaic aspect of the historical period of a nation lies briefly in what follows:

History requires in the first place a community, whether religious or political, with laws, institutions, etc., laid down on their own account already valid, or to be made valid, as universal laws.

Then, secondly, out of such a community there arise specific actions and changes necessary for maintaining and altering it; they may have a universal character and constitute the chief thing of importance, and they necessarily require corresponding individuals to decide on them and carry them out. These are great and outstanding individuals when in their individuality they prove equal to the common purpose implicit in the inner nature of the contemporary situation; they are small if they are not big enough to carry out that purpose; they are bad if, instead of fighting for the needs of the hour, they make their own individual interest prevail, an interest divorced from the common one and therefore arbitrary. If one or other of these things occurs, or if others do, then what we indicated above in our Part I as a requirement for a genuinely poetic subject-matter and world-situation is absent. Even in the case of great men, the substantive end to which they devote themselves is more or less given, prescribed, and compulsory, and in that case there is no establishing the individual unity in which a complete identity of the universal and the entire individual is to be an end in itself and a perfect whole. Then even if individuals have set a self-chosen aim before themselves, the subject-matter of history is not the freedom or unfreedom of their mind and heart, their individual living attitude, but the end that is pursued, and its effect on the actual world confronting them there, independent of themselves.

On the other hand in historical situations the play of chance is revealed, the breach between what is inherently substantive and the relativity of single events and occurrences as well as of the particular peculiarities of the characters in their own passions, intentions, and fates. These in this prose have far more things that are extraordinary and eccentric than those miracles of poetry which must always keep within the limits of what is universally valid.

Thirdly and lastly, there is introduced here again into the execution of historical actions, in distinction from what is strictly poetic, the prosaic cleavage between the individual's own personality and that consciousness of laws, principles, maxims, etc., which is necessary for the general weal; moreover, the realization of the prescribed ends itself requires many arrangements and preparations, and the external means for these are vast and dependent on and related to one another in many ways, and they have to be trimmed and used on purpose for the intended undertaking with intelligence, skill, and prosaic supervision. It is not a matter of directly putting the shoulder to the wheel; in the main enormous preliminary arrangements have to be made so that the single actions needed for accomplishing *one* end are either purely accidental in themselves, and always without any inner unity, or else, in the form of practical utility, they proceed from an intellectual concentration on ends but not from a life that is independent and directly free.

(γγ) The historian has no right to expunge these prosaic characteristics in his material or to transform them into poetical ones; he must relate what confronts him and as it confronts him without reinterpreting it or giving it a poetic form. Therefore no matter how much he may struggle to make the centre and single concatenating bond of his narrative the inner sense and spirit of the epoch, the people, or the specific event which he describes, he still has no freedom to subordinate to this purpose the circumstances, characters, and events confronting him, even if he shoves to one side what in itself is purely accidental and meaningless; to these circumstances etc. he must give free play in their external contingency, dependence on other things, and uncounselled arbitrariness. In a biography an individual vitality and independent unity does seem possible, because here what remains the centre of the work is the individual, together with what he effects and what reacts on this single figure, but an historical character is only a unity of two different extremes. For although on the one hand his character serves as a subjective unity, on the other hand numerous events, circumstances, etc., come to light and these are without any inner connection in themselves; they affect the individual without his contributing anything to them and so they draw him into this external sphere. Alexander, for example, is of course a single individual who stands on the summit of his age, and by his own individual decision, which harmonizes with external circumstances, embarks on his expedition against the Persian monarchy; but Asia, which he conquers, is only an accidental whole owing to the varied caprices of its individual populations and what happens there occurs simply in accordance with the direct superficial appearance of things.

Finally, if the historian carries his subjective inquiries so far as to probe the absolute reasons for what happens and even Divine providence, before which all accidents vanish and where a higher necessity is unveiled, nevertheless, in respect of events as they appear in reality, he may not allow himself the privilege of poetry for which this substantive basis of things must be the chief thing, because poetry alone is given freedom to dominate the available material without hindrance in order to make it adequate, even externally, to its inner truth.

(β) Secondly, oratory seems to approach the freedom of art more nearly.

($\alpha\alpha$) For although the orator likewise draws the occasion and the subject-matter for his work of art from things as they actually exist, from specific real circumstances and purposes, still, in the first place what he expresses is always his own free judgement, his own mood, and his subjective immanent end in which he can be vitally absorbed with his whole self. In the second place, he is given a completely free hand in the development of his subject and in his general way of treating it, so that we get the impression of being confronted in his speech with a thoroughly independent product of his mind. In the third place, he is not supposed to address our scientific or other logical thinking but to move us to adopt some conviction or other; and to achieve this result he should work on our whole man, on feeling, intuition, etc.

His topic is not the *abstract* side, i.e. the *conception*, of the thing in which he intends to interest us, or of the *end* that he intends to encourage us to achieve, but for the most part some specific fact or actuality. The result is that the speech must indeed comprise the substance of the thing at issue, but nevertheless it must seize on this universal element in the form of *appearance* and in this way bring it before our *concrete* thinking. Therefore, as we listen to him, he has not merely to satisfy our intelligence by the rigour of his deductions and conclusions, but he can also address our hearts, arouse our passions, carry us away along with him, absorb our attention, and in this way convince us and make an impression on every one of our faculties.

($\beta\beta$) Yet, seen in the right light, this apparent freedom in oratory is precisely subject, in the main, to the law of practical utility.

In the first place, what gives the speech its proper moving force does not depend on the particular end that the speaker had in view, but on something universal, i.e. laws, rules, principles, to which the individual case can be referred and which are already available in a universal form whether as the actual law of the land, or as moral, just, and religious maxims, feelings, dogmas, etc. The specific circumstances and purpose which afford the starting-point here are therefore separate from this universal from the beginning, and this cleavage is retained as their permanent relationship. It is true that the orator has the intention of setting the two sides together in one. This is something obviously achieved from the start in poetry that is poetic at all, but in oratory it is there only as a subjective aim of the orator, and its achievement lies outside the speech itself. The orator is left with no recourse but to proceed by *subsuming* the particular under the universal, with the result that the specific real manifestation of the universal (i.e. in this context the concrete case or end) is not fully developed from within in immediate unity with the universal but is given validity only by being brought under principles and related to laws, customs, usages, etc., and these on their side likewise exist independently. The fundamental type here is not the free life of the matter in hand in its concrete appearance, but the prosaic separation of concept from reality, a mere relation between the two, and a demand for their unification.

This is the way in which a preacher, for example, must often go to work because in his case it is the universal religious doctrines, and the moral, political, and other principles and rules of conduct derived from them, to which all sorts and kinds of cases have to be referred, because these doctrines are supposed to be experienced, believed, and known by the religious consciousness independently and essentially, as the substance of every act in life. In his sermon the preacher can of course appeal to our hearts, develop the divine laws from our minds as their source, and lead his hearers too to find them in that source, but they are not to be displayed and emphasized in any purely individual form; on the contrary, their dominating universality is to come before our minds precisely as commands, prescriptions, articles of faith, etc.

This is still more true in forensic oratory where a double feature enters: first, the principal thing at issue, i.e. a specific case, and, secondly, the subsumption of that case under general considerations and laws. As for the first point, the prosaic element lies in the necessary ascertainment of the actual facts and in the gleaning and adroit combining of every single circumstance affecting them and every accidental feature in them. This process, in contrast to the free creations of poetry, at once reveals to us the inadequacy of this knowledge of the actual case and the laboriousness of acquiring and communicating this knowledge. Then, further, the concrete fact has to be analysed, and not only must its individual aspects be set out separately, but every one of these aspects, like the entire case, has to be referred to laws fixed independently in advance. Yet even in this occupation scope is still always left for touching the heart and arousing feelings. For the rights or wrongs of the case expounded have to be made so vivid that the matter does not end with a mere understanding of the case and a general conviction of its merits: on the contrary, owing to the way the case is put every one of the listeners can come to regard the whole thing as subjective and so much his own that he cannot, as it were, stand back any longer, and everyone finds in the case his own interest and his own affair.

In the second place, in the art of oratory the final and supreme interest of the orator does not lie in the *artistic* presentation and perfection of his case; on the contrary, over and above art he has still another aim, namely to use the whole form and development of his speech as simply the most effective means of achieving an interest lying beyond the confines of art. From this point of view, even his hearers are not to be moved for their own sake; on the contrary, their being moved and their conviction are applied by him as likewise only a means towards carrying out the intention which, in his oratory, he has set himself to accomplish. Consequently the hearers do not regard the speech as an end in itself; they see that it proves to be only a means for convincing them of this or that or inciting them to specific decisions, activities, etc.

In the third place, for this reason oratory loses in this respect too its apparent freedom and it becomes something with an intended aim, something meant, but something that, so far as its success goes, does not find a final satisfactory outcome in the speech itself and its artistic treatment. The poetic work of art has no aim other than the production and enjoyment of beauty; in its case aim and achievement lie directly in the work itself, which is therefore independently self-complete and finished; and the artistic activity is not a means to a result falling outside itself but an end which in its accomplishment directly closes together with itself. But, in oratory, art acquires the position of being a mere accessory summoned by the orator as an aid to his purpose; his real purpose has nothing to do with art; it is practical, i.e. instruction, edification, decisions on legal questions or political affairs, etc. Consequently his intention is to serve the interest of something that has still to happen, or of some decision that is still to be reached, but that is not finalized and accomplished by the effect of oratory; on the contrary, accomplishment must be remitted to all sorts of other activities. For a speech may frequently end by producing a discord which the hearer, as judge, has to resolve, and then act in accordance with this resolution. For example, pulpit oratory often speaks to an unreconciled heart and finally makes the hearer a judge of himself and the character of his inner life. Here the aim of the preacher is the improvement of the religious life; but whether with all the edification and excellence of his eloquent admonitions the improvement follows and the preacher's aim succeeds is something which does not fall within the speech itself and must be left to other circumstances.

(γγ) In all these directions the essential nature of eloquence is to be sought not in the free poetic organization of a work of art, but rather in the mere purpose in view. The orator must make it his chief target to subject the whole of his speech and its single parts to the personal intention from which his work arises; in this way the independent freedom of his portrayal has been superseded and in its place there has been put service to a specific and no longer artistic end. But above all since he has his eye on a living practical effect, he has always to have regard to the place where he speaks, to his hearers' degree of education, their capability for understanding, and their character, if he is not to sacrifice the desired practical effect by striking precisely the wrong note for this hour, this locality, and these persons. Owing to this subjection to external circumstances and conditions the whole should not, and the single parts cannot, issue any longer from an artistically free mind, but there has to be evident in each and all of them a purely purposeful connection which remains dominated by cause and effect, ground and consequent, and other categories of the Understanding.

(c) Out of this difference between what is properly poetic and the productions of historiography and oratory, we can now establish the following points for the poetic work of art as such.

(α) In historiography the prosaic element lay especially in the fact that, even if its inner essence could be substantive and solidly effective, its actual form had to appear accompanied in many ways by relative circumstances, clustered with accidents, and sullied by arbitrariness, although the historian had no right to transform this form of reality which was precisely in conformity with what immediately and actually happened.[1]

(αα) The task of this transformation is one to which poetry is chiefly called if in its material it treads on the ground of historical

---

[1] In Hegel's view, historians must report the facts, but the philosopher penetrates below them to their underlying substance and moving force—i.e. the accomplishment of the will of God. In the sphere of art, the poet can do this too.

description. In this case it has to search out the inmost kernel and meaning of an event, an action, a national character, a prominent historical individual, but it has to strip away the accidents that play their part around them, and the indifferent accessories of what happened, the purely relative circumstances and traits of character, and put in their place things through which the inner substance of the thing at issue can clearly shine, so that this substance finds its adequate existence in this transformed external form to such an extent that only now is the absolutely rational developed and made manifest in an actuality absolutely in correspondence with itself. In this way alone can poetry, in respect of a specific work, concentrate its subject-matter into a more fixed centre; in that case the subject-matter can unfold into a rounded totality because it holds the particular parts together more rigorously, while, without jeopardizing the unity of the whole, it can grant to each individual part its appropriate right of being marked out independently.

($\beta\beta$) Poetry can go even further in this direction when it makes its chief subject-matter not the content and meaning of an historical fact that has actually occurred, but some fundamental thought more or less closely akin to it, in short a collision in human experience, and uses the historical facts or characters or locality, etc., rather as an individualizing covering. But in this case a double difficulty appears: either the known historical data, when taken into the poem, may not be wholly compatible with that fundamental thought, or, conversely, if the poet retains this familiar material but alters it in important points to suit his own ends, a contradiction arises between what is already firmly fixed in our minds and what the poet has newly introduced. It is difficult but necessary to resolve this contradiction and division and produce the right undisturbed harmony; after all, reality has an indisputable right to respect in its essential phenomena.

($\gamma\gamma$) A similar right is to be asserted for poetry in a wider sphere. For whatever poetry presents by way of external locality, characters, passions, situations, conflicts, events, actions, and fates, all this is already to be found, more than people may commonly believe, in actual life. So here too poetry treads as it were on an historical ground, and its departures and alterations in this field must likewise proceed from the indwelling reason of the thing at issue and the need to find for this inner rationality the most adequate living manifestation, and not from a lack of thorough knowledge and vital penetration of reality or from whims, caprices, and the search for the bizarre peculiarities of a wrong-headed originality.

(β) Secondly, oratory belongs to prose on account of the practical aim implicit in its intention, and for carrying out this aim in practice it has a duty to be guided by purpose throughout.

(αα) In this matter, if poetry is not likewise to relapse into prose, it must avoid every aim which lies outside art and the pure enjoyment of art. For if it gives essential importance to aims of that kind which in that case glint through the entire conception and mode of presentation, poetry is at once drawn down into the sphere of the relative out of those free heights on which it clearly lives for its own sake alone, and the result is either a breach between the requirements of art and the demands of other intentions, or else that art is used, contrary to its very conception, as a mere means and therefore is degraded to servitude to some aim. This is the sort of thing that occurs, for example, with the edification of many hymns in which specific ideas have a place solely for producing a religious effect and which are illustrative in a way opposed to the beauty of art. In general, poetry must not provide religious, or rather *purely* religious, edification, and endeavour by this means to transport us into a sphere which, although akin to poetry and art, is nevertheless different from them. The same is true of instruction, moral improvement, political agitation, or purely superficial pastimes and pleasures. For these are all objects which poetry, of all the arts, can of course best help us to attain, but if poetry, in giving this help incidentally, is still to move freely within its own sphere alone, it may not undertake explicitly to give help, because in poetry it is only the poetical, not something outside poetry, which must rule as the determining and executed end; and in fact these other ends are pursued and achieved still more effectively by other means.

(ββ) But, conversely, the art of poetry should not seek to maintain an absolutely isolated position in the real world, but must, as itself living, enter into the midst of life. We saw already in Part I how numerous are the connections which art has with the rest of existence, the substance and appearance of which it fashions into its own content and form. Poetry's living connection with the real world and its occurrences in public and private affairs is revealed most amply in the so-called *pièces d'occasion*. If this description were given a wider sense, we could use it as a name for nearly all poetic works: but if we take it in the proper and narrower sense we have to restrict it to productions owing their origin to some single present event and expressly devoted to its exaltation, embellishment, commemoration, etc. But by such entanglement with life poetry seems again to fall into a position of dependence, and for this reason it has often been proposed to assign to the whole sphere of *pièces d'occasion* an inferior value although to some extent, especially in lyric poetry, the most famous works belong to this class.

(γγ) Therefore the question arises: In what way can poetry still preserve its independence even when there is this conflict with its given subject-matter? Simply by not treating and presenting the external given occasion as an essential end, and itself only as a means to that, but instead by assimilating the essence of that actual fact and forming and shaping it by the freedom and the right of the imagination. In that event poetry is not the occasion and its accompaniment; but that essence is the *external* occasion; it is the stimulus which makes the poet abandon himself to his deeper penetration of the event and his clearer way of formulating it. In this way he creates from his own resources what without his aid we would not have become conscious of previously in this free way in the actual event directly presented to us.

(γ) It is now clear that every genuinely poetical work of art is an inherently infinite [i.e. self-bounded] organism: rich in matter and disclosing this matter in a correspondent appearance; a unity, yet not purposeful or in a form for which the particular is made abstract and subordinate, but where the same living independence is still preserved within what is individual; a whole, therefore, which closes with itself into a perfect circle without any apparent intention; filled with the material essence of actuality yet not dependent either on this content and its existence or on any sphere of life, but creating freely from its own resources in order to give shape to the essence of things in an appearance which is genuinely that of the essence, and so to bring what exists externally into reconciled harmony with its inmost being.

3. *The Poet's Creative Activity*

Of artistic talent and genius, of inspiration and originality, etc., I have spoken already at length in Part I and for this reason I will mention here only a few points of importance in relation to poetic activity as distinct from that in the sphere of the visual arts and music.

(a) An architect, or sculptor, or painter, or musician is tied to a quite concrete and perceptible material and he has to work his subject-matter into it completely. The restriction imposed by this material conditions the specific form of the entire mode of conception and artistic treatment. Consequently the more specific the task on which the artist must concentrate, the more specialized is (i) the talent required for precisely this and no other mode of portrayal, and (ii) the skill in technical execution that runs parallel with this. Poetry is exempt from the complete embodiment of its productions in a particular material, and therefore a talent for it is less subject to such specific conditions and so is more general and independent. All that it requires is a gift for richly imaginative formulations, and it is limited only by the fact that poetry, by being expressed in words, should not try to reach that complete perceptibility which the visual artist has to give to his subject-matter as its external form, nor can it remain satisfied with the wordless depth of feeling, the expression of which in soul-laden notes is the sphere of music. From this point of view, the task of the poet, in comparison with that of the other artists, may be regarded as both easier and more difficult. As easier, because, although the poetic treatment of language requires a developed skill, the poet is exempt from the relatively more complicated conquest of technical difficulties; as more difficult, because the less poetry has to create an external embodiment [that can be seen or heard], the more it has to seek a substitute for this lack of perceptibility in the inner proper kernel of art, i.e. in the depth of imagination and genuinely artistic treatment.

(b) In this way, secondly, the poet is able to penetrate all the depths of the contents of the spirit and can bring out into the daylight of consciousness whatever lies concealed there. For however far in other arts the inner life must, and does actually, shine through its corporeal form, still the word is the most intelligible means of communication, the most adequate to the spirit, the one able to grasp and declare whatever lies within consciousness or pervades its heights and depths. But in this connection the poet finds himself involved in difficulties; he has problems which the other arts are not required to face or solve to the same extent. Since poetry lives purely in the sphere of inner imagination and should not bethink itself of creating for its productions an external existence independent of this inner life, it remains in an element in which the religious, scientific, and other prosaic types of consciousness are also active, and it must take care not to trench on these spheres or modes of expression, or to make excursions into them. A similar proximity does exist in the case of every art, because all artistic production proceeds from the *one* spirit which comprises all spheres of self-conscious life in itself. But in the case of the other arts, the manner of conception remains, with its inner creative activity, in continual connection with the execution of its designs in a specific perceptible material and therefore is throughout distinct from the forms of religious imagery, scientific thinking, and the prosaic intellect. Poetry on the other hand, while availing itself of a means of external communication just as these spheres do, avails itself of language; and by the use of language it stands on a ground of conception and expression different from that of the visual arts and music.

(c) Thirdly, poetry is the art which can exhaust all the depths of the spirit's whole wealth, and therefore the poet is required to give the deepest and richest inner animation to the material that he brings into his work. The visual artists have likewise to apply themselves especially to the animation of spiritual expression in the external shape of the architectural, plastic, and pictorial figures, while the musician must apply himself to the inner soul of concentrated feeling and passion and its outpouring in melodies, although he like the others must be full of the inmost meaning and substance of his subject-matter. The range of what the poet has to experience in himself stretches further, because he has not only to polish an inner world of the heart and self-conscious ideas but to find for it a correspondent external appearance through which that ideal totality peeps in a fuller and more exhaustive way than is the case with the productions of the other arts. He must know both the inner and the external side of human existence and have absorbed the whole breadth of the world and its phenomena into his own mind, and there have felt it through and through, have penetrated, it, deepened and transfigured it.

In order to be able to create from his own resources, even when he is restricted to some quite narrow and particular sphere, a free whole which does not appear to be determined from without, he must have cut himself free from any practical or other preoccupation in his material and rise superior to it with an eye calmly and freely surveying all existence whether subjective or objective. From the point of view of *natural* capacity we may in this matter give special praise to the Mohammedan poets of the East. From the very start they enter upon this freedom which even in passion remains independent of passion, and amid all variety of interests always retains, as the real kernel of the work, the *one* substance alone, in face of which everything else then appears small and transitory, and passion and desire never have the last word. This is a contemplative view of the world, a relation of the spirit to the things of this world which lies nearer to the mind of age than of youth. For in age the interests of life are still present but not, as in youth, with the force of passion; they have the form of shadows rather, so that they lend themselves more easily to the contemplative considerations which art desires. Contrary to the usual opinion that the glow and warmth of youth is the finest age for poetic production, the precise opposite may therefore be maintained from this point of view, and we may assert that old age is the ripest period if it can preserve energy of insight and feeling. The wonderful poems transmitted to us under Homer's name were ascribed to the time when he was grey-haired and blind, and we may say even of Goethe that only in age did he reach his highest achievement when he had succeeded in freeing himself from all restricting trifles.

B. POETIC EXPRESSION

Owing to the infinite range of the previous section, we had to content ourselves with a few general points about it. It concerned poetry in general, its subject-matter and the treatment and organization of this into a poetic work of art. Following on this, the second aspect to deal with is (*a*) poetic expression, (*b*) ideas given inner objectivity in words as signs of ideas, and (*c*) the music of the words.

The relation of poetic expression in general to the mode of presentation in the other arts can be deduced from what has been explained above in relation to poetry as such. Words and their sounds are neither symbols of spiritual conceptions nor an adequate spatial and external embodiment of the inner life like the physical forms of sculpture and painting, nor the musical resounding of the entire soul: they are purely and simply *signs*. But as communications of *poetic* conceptions, these signs too must, in distinction from the prosaic mode of expression [where they are mere means], be made an *end* for contemplation and appear shaped accordingly.

In this matter three chief points can be more definitely distinguished.

First, poetic expression does seem to lie throughout in words alone and therefore to be related purely to language, but the words are only *signs* of ideas and therefore the real origin of poetic speech lies neither in the choice of single words and the manner of their collocation into sentences and elaborate paragraphs, nor in euphony, rhythm, rhyme, etc., but in the sort and kind of ideas [or of the way of imagining things]. Therefore we must look for the origin of the developed expression in the developed way of imagining things and concentrate our first question on the form which the way of imagining things must take in order to be expressed poetically.

But, secondly, the inherently poetic way of imagining things is objective only in words and therefore we have nevertheless to consider the *linguistic* expression on its purely linguistic side whereby poetic words are distinguished from prose ones, and poetic turns of phrase from those of ordinary life and prosaic thinking, even if at first we abstract from the way they sound in our ears.

Thirdly, poetry is actual *speaking*, i.e. audible words which in respect of their temporal duration as well as their real sound must be moulded by the poet, and this necessitates tempo, rhythm, euphony, rhyme, and so forth.

1. *The Poetic Way of Imagining Things*[1]

What in the visual arts is the perceptible shape expressed in stone or colour, in music the soul-laden harmony and melody, i.e. the external mode in which a subject *appears* artistically, this in poetry can only be the imaginative idea itself. This is a point to which we have to recur continually. The power of poetry's way of putting things consists therefore in the fact that poetry gives shape to a subject-matter within, without proceeding to express it in actual visible shapes or in series of melodies; and thereby it makes the external object produced by the other arts into an internal one which the spirit itself externalizes for the imagination in the form that this internal object has and is to keep within the spirit.

Here the same difference meets us once again which we have had to point out already in connection with poetry in general, namely the difference between what poetry was originally and what it became later by a reconstruction out of an established prose.

(*a*) In the ordinary consciousness there are two extremes: *either* it brings everything to mind in the form of immediate and therefore accidental particulars, without grasping their inner essence and the appearance of that essence, *or else* it differentiates concrete existence and endows the resulting differences with the form of abstract universality and then goes on to relate and synthesize these abstractions by means of the Understanding. The imagining of the original type of poetry is not divided into these extremes. On the contrary, a way of putting things is poetic only when these extremes are kept undivided and mediated with one another; and it is because

---

[1] Or conceiving things. *Vorstellen*. There is no single English word which will convey the range of meanings that Hegel packs into *Vorstellen* in this section. His point is quite simple and could have been put more briefly: In primitive times prose has not been developed and there is no clear distinction between poetry and prose; poetry describes the facts in language that can be called either poetic or prosaic. After prose has been developed, poetry is distinguished from it by not being literal but figurative or metaphorical. Its way of putting or looking at things is thus imaginative (*vorstellend*) rather than prosaic. The poetic idea (*Vorstellung*) is imaginative.

poetry does this that it can remain in the firm middle between the commonplace outlook and [scientific] thinking.

In general we may describe poetry's way of putting things as *figurative* because it brings before our eyes not the abstract essence but its concrete reality, not an accidental existent but an appearance such that in it we immediately recognize the essence through, and inseparably from, the external aspect and its individuality; and in this way we are confronted in the inner world of our ideas by the *conception* of the thing and its *existence* as one and the same whole. In this respect there is a great difference between what the figurative image gives us and what is made clear to us otherwise through some other mode of expression. We can compare this with what happens with reading. When we see the letters, which are signs representing the sounds of words, then we understand forthwith what we have read, merely by inspecting them without necessarily hearing the sounds of the words; and it is only someone without the knack of reading who has to enunciate the several sounds before he can understand the words.[1] But what in this case is lack of practice is in poetry beautiful and excellent, because poetry is not content with mere understanding or merely calling objects to our minds just as they exist in our memory in the form of thought and, in general, of their universally conceived and unimaged character; on the contrary it brings to us the concept *in* its existence, the species *in* its definite individualization. Using our ordinary intellectual mode of apprehension I understand the meaning of a word as soon as I hear or read it, without, that is to say, having an image of the meaning before my mind. If, for instance, we say 'the sun' or 'in the morning', the meaning is clear to us, although there is no illustration of the sun or dawn. But when the poet says: 'When in the dawn Aurora rises with rosy-fingers',[2] the same *thing* is expressed, but the poetic expression gives us *more*, because it adds to the understanding of the object a vision of it, or rather it repudiates bare abstract understanding and substitutes the real specific character of the thing. Similarly when it is said that 'Alexander conquered the Kingdom of Persia', this of

---

[1] In kindergarten schools children used to be taught reading by being first made to enunciate the sounds of the letters.

[2] Homer's usual description of the dawn.—Throughout this section Hegel is working with a usual eighteenth-century distinction between 'natural' and 'arbitrary' signs. Pictures and sculptures *are*, in a sense, what they represent, while words only convey meanings by arbitrary convention.

course is a picture with a concrete content, but its specification in detail—by being expressed as 'conquest'—is drawn together into a simple abstraction without any image and so our eyes are not led to see anything of the look and reality of Alexander the Great's achievement. The same is true of everything expressed in this way; we understand it, but it remains pale and grey, and, so far as any individual existent is concerned, vague and abstract. Consequently, in its imaginative way poetry assimilates the whole wealth of real appearance and can unite it into an original whole along with the inner meaning and essence of what is portrayed.

The first point that follows from this is that, because poetry expresses the full actuality of the thing at issue, it has an interest in lingering over what is external, in esteeming its consideration as worthwhile on its own account, and in laying emphasis on it. Poetry therefore is in general periphrastic in its expression: yet 'periphrasis' is not the right word; for when we compare poetic diction with the abstract characteristics familiar to us in our intellectual grasp of some subject, we are accustomed in poetry to take as periphrasis a great deal that the poet had not meant as such, with the result that from a prosaic standpoint the poetry may be regarded as circumlocution or a useless superfluity. But the poet must be concerned in his imagining to dwell with fondness on widening the real phenomenon which he wishes to describe. It is in this sense that Homer, for instance, gives each hero a descriptive adjective: 'the swift-footed Achilles; the well-greaved Achaeans; Hector of the gleaming helm; Agamemnon King of men', etc. The name of the hero does indicate an individual, but as a mere name it does not bring anything more concrete before our minds, so that for the specific illustration of this individual some further indication is required. Even in the case of objects that already are perceptible in themselves, like the sea, ships, swords, etc., Homer provides a similar epithet that seizes on and discloses some one essential quality of the specific object; he gives us a more definite picture and compels us in this way to set the thing before our minds in a more concrete guise.

Secondly, there is thus a distinction between an illustration which keeps close to reality and one which does not, and this latter kind introduces a further difference. The imitative or literal picture presents only the thing in the reality that belongs to it, whereas the non-imitative or metaphorical expression does not linger directly with the object itself but proceeds to the description of a second different one through which the meaning of the first is to become clear and perceptible to us. Metaphors, images, similes, etc., belong to this sort of poetical expression. In these cases the subject-matter in question has added to it a veil different from it which sometimes serves only as a decoration but sometimes cannot be used altogether as a clearer explanation of it because it is appropriate to only one of its aspects, as, for example, when Homer compares Ajax, when he was reluctant to take flight, to an obstinate ass.[1]

But it is Eastern poetry especially which has this magnificence and richness in images and similes, because its symbolic procedure necessitates a wide search for kinships, and to accompany its universal meanings it provides a great multitude of concrete and comparable phenomena, while the sublimity of its outlook leads it to use the whole vast variety of brilliant and magnificent superlatives to adorn the One being who alone is there for the mind to praise. In these circumstances these imaginative productions do not count at the same time as something which we know to be only the poet's work and the product of his comparisons and so not something independently real and present; on the contrary, the transformation of everything existent into the existence of an Idea grasped and moulded by the imagination is so regarded that nothing at all else is existent or can have any right to independent reality. Belief in the world, as *we* regard the world intellectually with a prosaic eye, becomes a belief in the imagination for which the sole world is that created for itself by the poetic consciousness.

The romantic imagination is the converse. It gladly expresses itself metaphorically, because in it what is external for the subjective life withdrawn into itself counts only as an accessory and not as adequate reality itself. This external field, in this way as it were a metaphorical one, configurated with deep feeling and detailed richness of insight or with humorous conjunctions, is the impetus which enables and stimulates romantic poetry to invent things always new. Consequently this poetry has nothing to do with merely presenting something definitely and visibly, for on the contrary the metaphorical use of these far-removed phenomena becomes in it an end on its own account: feeling is made the centre, it illuminates its rich environment, draws it to itself, uses it

[1] Iliad, xi. 558 ff.

ingeniously and wittily for its own adornment, animates it, and is delighted by this roving hither and thither, this involvement and expatiation in its self-portrayal.

(b) The poetic way of putting things stands in contrast to the prosaic one. In the latter there is no question of anything figurative but only of the meaning as such; this is the real heart of what is being expressed, while the manner of expression is only a means of bringing the subject-matter before our minds. Prose has no need of putting before our vision the details of its objects as they really appear nor has it to call up in us, as is the case with a metaphorical expression, another idea going beyond what was to be expressed. Certainly it may be necessary for prose too to indicate the exterior of objects firmly and sharply, but when this happens it is not for figurative purposes but for the sake of some particular practical end. Therefore we may prescribe, as a general rule for prose, literal accuracy, unmistakable definiteness, and clear intelligibility, while what is metaphorical and figurative is always relatively unclear and inaccurate. For in a literal expression, put figuratively by poetry, the simple thing at issue is carried over out of its immediate intelligibility into a phenomenal reality whence a knowledge of it is to arise; but in a metaphorical expression some related phenomenon—though far remote from the meaning—is used for illustrative purposes. The result is that prosaic commentators on poetry have a lot of trouble before they succeed by their intellectual analyses in separating meaning and image, extracting the abstract content from the living shape, and thereby disclosing to the prosaic consciousness an understanding of the poetic way of putting things. In poetry, on the other hand, the essential law is not merely accuracy and an immediate and adequate correspondence with the topic simply as it is. On the contrary, while prose has to keep with its ideas within the same sphere as its subject-matter and preserve abstract accuracy, poetry must conduct us into a different element, i.e. into the *appearance* of the subject-matter itself or into other analogous appearances. For it is precisely this real appearance which must come on the scene on its own account and, while portraying the subject-matter, is yet to be free from it as mere subject-matter, since attention is drawn precisely to the existent *appearance*; and the living shape is made the essential object of the contemplative interest.

(c) If these poetic requirements become prominent at a time

when the mere accuracy of the prosaic way of putting things has already become the ordinary rule, then poetry has a more difficult position even in respect of its figurativeness. At such a period the prevailing attitude of mind is the separation of feeling and vision from the intellectual thinking which makes feeling and seeing and what is felt and seen into either an incentive to knowing and willing or else a serviceable material for study and action. In these circumstances poetry needs a more deliberate energy in order to work its way out of the abstractions in the ordinary of putting things into the concrete life [of a new mode of expression]. But if it attains its aim, not only is it liberated from that separation between thinking, which is concentrated on the universal, and feeling and vision, which seize on the individual, but it also at the same time frees these latter forms of consciousness and their content and objects from their servitude to thinking and conducts them victoriously to reconciliation with the universality of thought. But now that the poetic and prosaic ways of putting things and looking at the world are bound together in the consciousness of one and the same individual, both these ways may possibly restrict and disturb and even fight one another—a dispute that it takes supreme genius to assuage, as witness our contemporary poetry. Apart from this, still other difficulties arise; of these, purely in relation to imagery, I will emphasize a few with greater precision.

When the prosaic intellect has taken the place of the original poetic way of conceiving and putting things, the revival of poetry, whether in its literal or metaphorical mode of expression, readily acquires a certain artificiality, and the result, even if it does not appear to be an actually intended one, is that poetry can scarcely be transposed into that original and direct way of hitting the truth. For many expressions that were still fresh in earlier times have themselves become familiar and domiciled in prose, through their repeated use and our consequential familiarity with them. If poetry is then to make its mark with new inventions, it is often driven willy-nilly, with its descriptive epithets, periphrases, etc., if not into exaggeration and floridity, still into artificiality, over-elegance, manufactured piquancy and preciosity, which does not proceed from simple and healthy feeling and insight, but sees objects in an artificial light contrived for an effect, and therefore does not leave them their natural colour and illumination. This is still more the case when the literal way of putting things is exchanged for the metaphorical which then finds itself compelled to outbid prose, and, in order to be unfamiliar, slips all too quickly into subtleties and snatching at effects that have not yet been outworn.

2. *Poetic Diction*

But since the poetic imagination is distinguished from the sort of invention in the other arts by the fact that it has to clothe its productions in words and communicate by means of language, it has a duty so to organize all its imaginative conceptions from the beginning that they can be completely exhibited by the means at language's command. In general, a poetic conception only becomes poetry in the narrower sense when it is actually embodied and cast in words.

The linguistic side of poetry could provide us with material for infinitely extensive and complex discussions; but these I must forgo in order to find room for the more important topics which still lie ahead of us. Therefore I intend only to touch quite briefly on the most important considerations.

(*a*) In every way art ought to place us on ground different from that adopted in our everyday life, as well as in our religious ideas and actions, and in the speculations of philosophy. Poetry can do this, so far as its diction is concerned, only if it uses a language different from the one we are already accustomed to in these other spheres. Therefore, on the one hand, it has to avoid in its diction what would drag us down into the commonplaces and trivialities of prose, while on the other hand it should not fall into the tone and manner of speech characteristic of religious edification or philosophical speculation. Above all it must hold far aloof from the clear-cut distinctions and relations of the Understanding, the categories of thought (when these have discarded all perceptible imagery), the philosophical forms of judgement and syllogism, etc., because all these forms transport us at once out of the province of imagination on to a different field. But in all these respects the boundary line where poetry ends and prose begins can only be drawn with difficulty and indeed cannot be generally indicated at all with assured accuracy.

(*b*) Therefore if we proceed at once to the particular means which poetic diction can use for the execution of its task, the following points may be emphasized.

(α) There are certain single words and expressions especially appropriate to poetry either for elevating the thought or for comically debasing and exaggerating it. The same is true of the combination of different words, specific sorts of inflection, and the like. In this matter poetry may sometimes cling to archaic words, little used therefore in everyday life, or at other times prove above all to be a progressive innovator in language, and in that case it displays great boldness of invention, provided that it does not merely run counter to the genius of the language.

(β) A further point concerns sentence-construction. To this field there belong the so-called 'figures of speech', so far, that is, as they are related to clothing thoughts in words. But their use easily leads to rhetoric and declamation (in the bad sense of these words). The individual vitality of a poem is destroyed if these word-forms substitute a universal mode of expression, constructed on rules, for the peculiar outpouring of feeling and passion. If they do, they form the very opposite of the deeply felt, fragmentary and laconic expression which the depths of the heart can utter despite its little command of eloquence, and which has such great efficacy, especially in romantic poetry, for the description of unV disburdened states of soul. But, in general, sentence-construction remains one of the richest external means available to poetry.

(γ) Finally, mention should be made of paragraph-construction which incorporates the two features just mentioned. It can make a great contribution to the expression of every situation, passion, and mode of feeling by the manner of its simple or more complex course, its restless disjointedness and dismemberment or its tranquil flow, or its surge and storm. For in all these ways the inner life must glint through the external linguistic expression and determine its character.

(c) In the application of the means just mentioned we may distinguish the same stages that we have brought to notice already in discussing the poetic imaginative idea.

(α) Poetic diction may become alive amongst a people at a time when language is still undeveloped, and only through poetry does it acquire its proper development. In that event the speech of the poet, as the expression of the inner life in general, is already something new which by itself arouses astonishment because it reveals by language what hitherto had been concealed. This new creation appears as a miracle wrought by a gift and a force not yet made familiar but, to men's amazement, freely unfolding for the first time what lay deeply enclosed within their own hearts. In this case the chief thing is the power of expression, the creation of language, though not yet its manifold formation and development, while on its side the diction remains entirely simple. For in these very early days there was neither any fluency of ideas nor manifold and varied turns of expression, but on the contrary what was to be said was made plain in an immediate and non-artistic expression which had not yet advanced to the fine shades of meaning, the transitions, mediations and other merits of a later artistic literary skill; for as a matter of fact at that time the poet was the first as it were to open the lips of a nation, to bring ideas into words, and by this means to help the nation to have ideas. It follows that language is not yet, so to say, common life, and poetry may avail itself, with a view to a fresh effect, of everything that later, by becoming the language of common life, is more and more separated from art. In this respect, Homer's mode of expression, for instance, may strike us nowadays as wholly ordinary: for every idea there is a literal expression; metaphorical expressions are few, and even if the narrative is very prolix, the language remains extremely simple. In a similar way Dante could likewise fashion for his people a living language of poetry and he manifested in this respect too the bold energy of his inventive genius.

(β) But when, with the growth of reflection, the range of ideas was widened, when the ways of connecting them multiplied, when there was increased readiness to follow such trains of thought, and when linguistic expression developed to complete fluency, then poetry acquired a totally different position *vis-à-vis* the kinds of diction. For in those circumstances a nation already possesses the marked prosaic speech of everyday life, and if poetic expression is to arouse any interest it must diverge from that ordinary speech and be made something fresh, elevated, and *spirituel*. In everyday life the reason for speaking arises from the accidents of the moment, but, if a work of art is to be produced, circumspection must enter instead of momentary feeling. Even the enthusiasm of inspiration should not be given free rein; on the contrary, a spiritual product must be developed out of an artist's tranquillity and take form in the mood of a seer with a clear vision of the world. In the days of poetry's youth this composure and tranquillity was already announced in the very speech and diction of poetry;

whereas, later on, the form and composition of poetry had to be in evidence in the difference acquired by poetic, as contrasted with prosaic, expression. In this respect there is an essential difference between the poems of times in which prose had already been developed and those of periods and peoples when, and amongst whom, poetry was only just originating.

But poetic production may go so far in this direction that it makes this composing of the expression the chief thing, and its eye is constantly directed less to inner truth than to the formation, smoothness, elegance, and effect of the language in which it is externally expressed. In that case this is the place where rhetoric and declamation, which I have mentioned already, are developed in a way destructive of poetry's inner life, because the circumspection which shapes the poem is revealed as *intentional*, and a self-conscious and regulated art impairs the true effect which must appear to be and be unintentional and artless. Whole nations have hardly been able to produce any poetical works except such rhetorical ones. The Latin language, for example, even in Cicero, sounds naïve and innocent enough. But in the case of the Roman poets, Virgil and Horace, for example, we feel at once that the art is something artificial, deliberately manufactured; we are aware of a prosaic subject-matter, with external decoration added, and we find a poet who, deficient in original genius, tries to find in the sphere of linguistic skill and rhetorical effects a substitute for what he lacks in real forcefulness and effectiveness of invention and achievement.[1] The French too in the so-called 'classical' period of their literature have a similar poetry, and in its case what are above all particularly suited to it are didactic poems and satires. In this rhetorical poetry the numerous rhetorical figures have their most pre-eminent place, but in spite of this the speech nevertheless remains prosaic on the whole, and the language becomes decorative and extremely rich in images just as, for example, the diction of Herder and Schiller does. But these two authors used such a mode of expression principally as an aid to expounding something prosaic, and they could make it permissible and tolerable owing to the importance of the thoughts and the happiness of their expression. The Spaniards too with their artificially elaborated

---

[1] On Horace at least this is an extraordinary judgement, but a failure to understand and appreciate his *Odes* has been shared even by more recent German scholars.

sort of diction cannot speak freely without pomposity. In general, the southern peoples, like the Spaniards and the Italians, and, earlier still, the Mohammedan Arabs and Persians have an enormous volume and wealth of images and comparisons. In antiquity, especially in Homer's case, expression always proceeds smoothly and peacefully, whereas in the case of these other peoples their vision of life bubbles over [like a spring], and, in a mind calm in other respects, struggles to increase the richness of its flood; this work of contemplation is still subject to an intellect that makes sharp distinctions, now making subtle classifications, now making connections wittily, ingeniously, and playfully.

(γ) Truly poetic expression refrains both from purely declamatory rhetoric and also from pompous and witty playing with words (although the free pleasure of composition may be manifested in a fine way even in these styles), because these jeopardize the inner truth of the topic, and the claims of the subject-matter are forgotten in the development of language and expression. For the diction should not become something independent on its own account or be made into the part of poetry which is really and exclusively important. In general, even in the matter of language, circumspect composition must never fail to give the impression of naïveté and should always have the appearance of having grown as if of itself out of the very heart of the subject in hand.

3. *Versification*

The third aspect of poetical expression is necessitated by the fact that a poetic idea is not only clothed in words but is actually *uttered*, and it therefore passes over into the perceptible element of sound, i.e. the sound of words and syllables. This takes us into the domain of versification. Versified prose does not give us any poetry, but only verse, just as a purely poetic expression in the middle of a composition otherwise prosaic produces only poetic prose; nevertheless, metre or rhyme is absolutely necessary for poetry, as its one and only sensuous fragrance, and indeed it is even more necessary than the rich imagery of a so-called 'beautiful' diction.

The fully artistic development of this perceptible element reveals to us at once, what poetry itself demands, a new domain, a new ground on which we can only tread after forsaking the prose of the theory and practice of our ordinary life and way of thinking. At the same time the poet is compelled to move beyond the limits of ordinary speech and to frame his compositions solely in accordance with the laws and demands of art. For this reason it is only a superficial theory which proposes to ban versification on the ground that it is unnatural. It is true that, in his opposition to the false bombast of the French alexandrine metre, Lessing tried to introduce prosaic speech into tragedy especially, as something more suitable, and Schiller and Goethe followed him in their early stormy works by a 'natural' pressure for imaginative writing with a richer subject-matter. But Lessing himself finally used iambics again in his *Nathan*; Schiller similarly forsook, with his *Don Carlos*, the path he had trodden before; and Goethe too was so little satisfied with his earlier prosaic treatment of his *Iphigenia* and his *Tasso* that he transferred them to the field of art itself, alike in expression and prosody, and recast them entirely into the purer form, which is the reason why our admiration of these works is ever excited anew.[1]

Of course the trick of metre and the interlacings of rhyme seem an irksome bond between the sensuous element and the inner ideas, more irksome than that forged in painting by colours. This is because things in nature, and the human form, are coloured naturally, and to portray them without colour is a forced abstraction; whereas an idea has only a very remote connection, or no inner connection at all, with the syllables used as purely arbitrary signs of a communication, with the result that the obstinate demands of the laws of prosody may easily seem to fetter the imagination and make it no longer possible for the poet to communicate his ideas precisely as they float before his inner consciousness. Consequently, while the flow of rhythm and the melodic sound of rhyme exercises on us an indisputable magic, it would be regrettable to find the best poetic feelings and ideas often sacrificed for the sake of this sensuous charm. But this objection is without force. In the first place it is obviously untrue that versification is a mere hindrance to the free outpouring of inspiration. A genuine

---

[1] Schiller's *Robbers, Fiesco, Intrigue and Love*, like Goethe's *Götz, Egmont, Tasso*, and *Iphigenia*, were written in prose. 'This was part of the mania for returning to Nature. Verse was pronounced unnatural' (G. H. Lewes, *Life of Goethe*, ed. cit., p. 263). Goethe later versified the two plays mentioned by Hegel.

artistic talent moves always in its sensuous element as in its very own, where it is at home; it neither hinders nor oppresses, but on the contrary it uplifts and carries. So as a matter of fact we see all the great poets moving freely and assuredly in the field of their own self-created metre, rhythm, and rhyme, and only in translations is following the same metres, assonances, etc., a frequent constraint for the translator and a torture for his skill. But in free poetry, apart from the necessity of giving new turns to the expression of ideas, drawing them together, and elaborating them, the poet is also given what without this impetus would never have occurred to him, namely *new* ideas, fancies, and inventions. Yet, apart from this relative advantage, sensuous existence is essential to art from the very beginning, and in poetry the sound of words must not remain so formless and vague as it immediately is in our casual speech, but must be given a living form, and, even if in poetry it merely chimes in as an external medium, it still must be treated as an end in itself and shaped therefore within harmonious limits. This attention devoted to the sensuous aspect adds, as happens in all art, to the seriousness of the subject-matter another aspect which removes this seriousness, frees the poet and his audience from it and lifts them into a sphere of brighter charm and grace. In painting and sculpture a perceptible and spatial limitation of form is imposed on the artist for the design and colouring of human limbs, rocks, trees, flowers, or clouds; and in architecture too for the needs and purposes of a building there is prescribed a more or less specific rule for walls, partitions, roofs, etc.; similarly, music is fixedly bound by the absolutely necessary fundamental rules of harmony. But in poetry the perceptible sound of words in their juxtaposition is at first free from restriction, and the poet gets the task of putting order into this lack of rule and making something perceptually delimited, and therefore of sketching, as it were, for his conceptions, for their structure and sensuous beauty, a sort of firmer contour and resounding framework.

Just as in musical declamation the rhythm and melody must take on the character of the subject-matter and be made appropriate to it, so versification too is a music which, though in a remoter way, makes re-echo in itself that dim, yet specific, direction of the course and character of the ideas in question. To this end the metre must announce the general tone and spiritual touch of a whole poem; and it is not a matter of indifference whether iambics, trochees, stanzas, alcaic or other strophes are adopted as external forms for the poem.

For the more detailed division of the subject, there are principally two systems and we have to cast light on their distinction from one another.

The first is rhythmic versification, which depends on the specific length and shortness of syllables, their manifold ways of figured conjunction and temporal progress.

The second consists in emphasizing sound as such, in respect both of single letters, consonants or vowels, and of whole syllables and words, ordered and figured either according to the law of the uniform repetition of the same or a similar sound, or to the rule of symmetrical interchange. This is the sphere of alliteration, assonance, and rhyme.

Both systems are closely connected with linguistic prosody whether this is chiefly grounded in the original length and shortness of syllables or whether it rests on the logical accent produced by the significance of the syllables.

Thirdly, the rhythmical progress and the independently arranged sound can be *linked* together; but since the concentration and emphasized echoing sound of the rhyme falls strongly on the ear, and therefore is asserted predominantly over the purely temporal feature of duration and forward movement, the rhythmical side in such a linkage must recede and occupy the attention less.

(a) Rhythmic Versification

The following are the most important points connected with the rhythmical system where there is no rhyme:

First, the fixed tempo of the syllables in their simple difference between long and short and the numerous ways of fitting them together in specific relations and metres.

Secondly, the enlivenment of rhythm by accent, caesura, and the opposition between verbal and verse-accentuation.

Thirdly, the euphony of word-sounds that can be produced within this movement of verse, without their being drawn together into rhymes.

(α) The chief thing in rhythm is not sound picked out and isolated as such but temporal duration and movement. Its simple starting-point is (αα) the natural length and shortness of syllables. The basis of their simple difference is provided by the speech-sounds themselves, by the letters to be pronounced, i.e. by consonants and vowels.

Diphthongs, pre-eminently, are long by nature, e.g. ai, oi, ae, because, whatever modern schoolmasters may say, they are in themselves a concrete and double sound brought together into a unity, like green amongst the colours. Long-sounding vowels are similar. To these we can add a third principle, peculiar to [languages] as ancient as Sanskrit, as well as to Greek, and Latin, namely position;[1] i.e., if two vowels are separated by two or more consonants, the latter obviously make transition more difficult for pronunciation: in order to get over the consonants the tongue requires a longer time for articulation, and a delay is produced which, despite the shortness of the vowel preceding the consonants, makes the syllable rhythmically long even if it is not naturally so. For example, if I say '*mentem, nec secus*',[2] the progress from one vowel to another in *mentem* and *nec* is not so simple or easy as in *secus*. Modern languages do not retain this latter difference but apply other criteria for determining longs and shorts. However, syllables used as short despite their position are in consequence felt to be harsh, often enough at least, because they obstruct the more rapid movement required.

In distinction from the lengthening produced by diphthongs, long vowels, and position, syllables are clearly short by nature if they are formed by short vowels, without two or more consonants being placed between one vowel and the following one.

(ββ) Since polysyllabic words have in themselves a variety of longs and shorts, while monosyllables are put into connection with other words, the result is the emergence of an interchange of different sorts of syllables and words which at first is accidental and subject to no fixed measure. To regulate this accidental character is just as much the duty of poetry as it was the task of music to determine with precision, by means of the unity of tempo, the unordered duration of single notes. Poetry therefore lays down for itself particular combinations of longs and shorts as the law according to which the temporal duration of the succession of the syllables

---

[1] In scansion, a vowel, even if normally short, becomes long if it is succeeded by two or more consonants.
[2] Horace, *Odes*, II. iii. 2.

has to be governed. The first thing we derive from this is various temporal relations. The simplest of these is the relation of equals to one another, e.g. the dactyl and the anapaest, in which the short syllables may be brought together again, on specific rules, into a long one, so as to produce a spondee.¹ Secondly, a long syllable may be placed beside a short one, so that a more profound difference in duration is produced, even if in the simplest form, as in an iambus or a trochee. The combination is more complex still if a short syllable is inserted between two long ones, or a short one precedes two longs, as in a cretic and a bacchius.²

(γγ) But such *single* temporal relations would open the door wide again to unregulated chance if they were allowed to follow one another arbitrarily in their manifold differences. For if this happened in actual fact the whole aim of introducing law, i.e. a regulated succession of long and short syllables, into these relations would be destroyed, and on the other hand there would be no determining at all a beginning, a middle, and an end. The arbitrariness arising here again as a result would wholly run counter to what we laid down earlier, in our consideration of musical tempo and beat, about the relation of the perceiving mind to the temporal duration of notes. The mind requires self-concentration, a return to self out of the steady flux of time, and this it apprehends only through specific time-units, struck just as markedly [at the start] as they succeed one another and end according to a rule. This is the reason why, in the third place, poetry ranges the single time-relations into lines governed by a rule in relation to the sort and number of feet and to their beginning, middle, and end. For example an iambic trimeter consists of six iambic feet, each two of which form again an iambic dipody, and a hexameter consists of six dactyls which in certain positions can coalesce again into spondees. But since such lines may be continually repeated again and again in the same or a similar way, there enters once more in respect of their succession a monotony and a vagueness about their firm or ultimate conclusion, and therefore a perceptible deficiency in inwardly varied structure. To remedy this defect, poetry has finally proceeded to invent stanzas and their various modes of organization, especially for expression in lyrics. What is relevant in this connection are the elegiac couplets of the Greeks, the alcaic

---

[1] Dactyl, $-\cup\cup$ (i.e. two shorts = one long), anapaest, $\cup\cup-$, spondee, $--$.

[2] Iambus, $\cup-$; trochee, $-\cup$; cretic, $-\cup-$; bacchius, $\cup--$.

and sapphic stanzas, and what has been developed with a wealth of art by the genius of Pindar and by the famous dramatists in the lyrical outpourings and other observations of the choruses.

But however far music and poetry satisfy similar needs by their time-measures, we must not fail to mention the difference between the two. Their most important divergence is produced by the *beat*. For this reason there have been all sorts of disputes as to whether for the metres of antiquity we should or should not assume that there was a strictly regular beat repeated at equal time-intervals. In general it may be affirmed that poetry, which uses words purely as a means of communication, need not be subject, so abstractly as is the case with a musical beat, to an absolutely fixed measure of time for its communication and progress. In music the note is a fading sound without support which imperatively requires a stability like that introduced by the beat; but speech does not need this support, for it has this already in the idea that it expresses, and, furthermore, it does not enter completely and without qualification into the external sphere of sounding and fading but retains precisely the inner idea as its essential artistic medium. For this reason poetry actually finds directly in the ideas and feelings which it puts clearly into words the more substantive determinant for measuring retard, acceleration, lingering, dawdling, and so forth, just as, after all, music begins in recitative to liberate itself from the motionless sameness of the beat. Consequently, if metre were to bow altogether to the rule of the beat, the difference between poetry and music, in this respect at least, would be expunged altogether, and the element of time would be asserted more preponderantly than the whole nature of poetry allows. This may be given as a reason for the demand that while in poetry a time-measure, but not a beat, must remain the rule, this aspect shall be dominated to a relatively stronger extent by the sense and meaning of the words. If in this connection we look more closely at the metres of antiquity, then it is true that the hexameter above all follows a strict progress according to a beat, as old Voss[1] especially required, though in the way of this assumption there is the catalexis of the last foot.[2] When Voss

---

[1] J. H. Voss, the author of *Luise*, 'old' compared with his son, H. Voss (1779–1822), was regarded by himself and others as an authority on prosody. His translation of Homer into German hexameters (still respected, if not by Hegel) is much more important than *Luise*.

[2] i.e. the curtailment of the last foot which may be a trochee instead of a spondee.

wants to read even alcaic and sapphic stanzas in these abstractly uniform time-intervals, this is only a capricious fancy and means doing violence to the verse. This whole demand may on the whole be ascribed to our habit of seeing our German iambics treated with the same continual fall and tempo of the syllables. Yet the classical iambic trimeter acquires its beauty especially from its not consisting of six similarly timed iambic feet but on the contrary precisely in allowing spondees at the start of the dipody and dactyls and anapaests at the close, and in this way the continual repetition of the same time-measure and anything like the beat is avoided. Besides, the lyric stanzas are far more variable, so that it would have to be shown *a priori* that a beat is absolutely necessary in them, because *a posteriori* it is not to be found.

(β) But the really animating thing in rhythmical time-measure is introduced only by accent and caesura which run parallel with what we came to recognize in music as the rhythmical beat.

($\alpha\alpha$) In poetry too each specific time relation has in the first place its particular accent, i.e. specific positions are emphasized in accordance with a law, and these then attract the others and thus alone form with them a rounded whole. In this way a large field is opened up at once for variety in the value of syllables. For on the one hand the long syllables will generally be strongly marked in comparison with the short ones, so that, if the accent falls on them, they appear twice as important as the shorter ones and they are given prominence over the unaccented long ones. But on the other hand it can also happen that the accent falls on the shorter syllables so that now a similar but converse relation arises between the syllables.

Above all, however, as I have mentioned before, the start and finish of the single feet must not rigidly correspond with the beginning and end of single words; for, *first*, if a complete word runs over past the end of a foot, the effect is to link together rhythms that would otherwise fall apart; and, *secondly*, if the verse accent falls on the final syllable of a word running over from one foot to another, the further result is a noticeable time-interval, because a word-ending as such necessitates something of a pause; and consequently it is this pause, coming in unison with the accent, which becomes felt as a deliberate time interval occurring in the otherwise unbroken flow of time. Caesuras like this are required in every line. For although the specific accent[1] does give to the single feet

---

[1] e.g. on the last syllable of every foot in an iambic line.

an inner differentiation and so a certain variety, this sort of enlivenment, especially in lines where the same feet are uniformly repeated, as in our iambics, would still remain quite abstract and monotonous and the individual feet would be made to fall apart from one another without any connection. The caesura breaks this cold monotony and introduces a connection and more of a life into the flow of the verse, a flow that a line's undifferentiated regularity would make spiritless. Owing to the difference of the places where the caesura may occur, variety is given to this new liveliness, while it is prevented from lapsing into an unregulated arbitrariness by the specific rules for the caesura.

Thirdly, in addition to the verse-accent and the caesura, there is still a third accent which the words already possess in themselves quite apart from their metrical use, and this makes possible a once more increased variation in the kind and degree of emphasis, or the reverse, on single syllables. For, on the one hand, this word-accent may occur bound up with the verse-accent and the caesura, both of which it may strengthen in consequence; but, on the other hand, it may rest, quite independently of these, on syllables which are favoured by no other emphasis and now, as it were, because they still demand accentuation on account of their own value as syllables, produce a counter-thrust to the rhythm of the line, and this gives a new and appropriate life to the whole.

In all the respects mentioned, to make the beauty of the rhythm audible is a matter of great difficulty for our modern ear: for in our languages the elementary requisites which must be combined for producing metrical advantages of this kind are to some extent no longer available in the precision and firmness that they had in antiquity, but on the contrary different artistic means are now substituted for satisfying different artistic needs.

(ββ) Besides, however, in the second place, there hovers over all the validity that syllables and words have in their metrical position, the value that they have of signifying a poetical idea. Owing to this immanent sense of theirs they likewise become relatively emphasized or must be put in the background as insignificant, and in this way alone is the ultimate extreme of spiritual life breathed into the verse. But poetry must not yield to this to the extent of directly opposing the rhythmic rules of metre.

(γγ) The whole character of versification must have corresponding to it, especially in connection with rhythmical movement, a *specific* sort of subject-matter, above all a specific sort of movement in our feelings. Thus, for example, the hexameter in its tranquilly rolling stream is fitted to the uniform flow of epic narrative, whereas in combination with the pentameter and its symmetrically fixed intervals it becomes something of a strophe, but in the simple regularity of this combination is suitable for elegies. The iambic, again, rushes forward and is especially appropriate to dialogue in drama; the anapaest indicates something rushing along with a regular beat spiritedly and joyfully, and similar characteristic traits are easily recognizable in the other sorts of prosody.

(γ) But thirdly this first sphere of rhythmical versification is not exhausted by the mere figuration and enlivenment of temporal duration but is extended to the actual sound of syllables and words. But in this matter of sound there is clearly an essential difference between the classical languages, where rhythm is firmly retained as the chief thing, in the way described, and the modern languages which are chiefly apt for rhyme.

(αα) For example, in Greek and Latin, owing to the declensions and conjugations, the root syllable is developed into a wealth of variously sounding syllables which do have a meaning in themselves, but only as modifications of the root, so that the latter is asserted as the substantive meaning of those variously outspread sounds, and yet this meaning's *sound* does not come out as the principal or sole mistress of the whole. For example, if we hear 'amaverunt', three syllables are added to the root, and, owing to the number and extent of these syllables, even if none of them is naturally long, the accent is at once materially separated from the root syllable, with the result that the chief *meaning* and the sounding *accent* are separated. Therefore, because the accentuation does not fall on the *chief* syllable, but on another which expresses only an *accessory* feature, the ear can listen to the sound of the different syllables and follow their movement because it has full freedom to hear the natural prosody and now is encouraged to shape these natural longs and shorts rhythmically.

(ββ) It is quite otherwise with our modern German language, for example. What in Greek and Latin is expressed, in the way described, by prefixes and suffixes and other modifications, is cut adrift in modern languages from the root syllables, especially in verbs, so that there are split and separated into independent words what in classical languages were inflected syllables of one and the same word in the manifold related meanings. Thus, for example, we continually use auxiliary verbs, have special verbs for independently indicating the optative, etc., and separate the pronouns, etc. In the case cited previously the word was expanded into the manifold sounds of a polysyllable and amid these the accent on the root, on the main sense, was lost.[1] In the present case the word remains a simple whole, concentrated into itself, without appearing as a succession of notes which, by being as it were pure modifications, do not work so strongly through their *meaning* alone that the ear could not listen to their free *sound* and its temporal movement. On the other hand, owing to this self-concentration, the chief meaning acquires so much weight that it draws the impress of the accent entirely on to itself alone; and since the emphasis and the chief meaning are linked together, this coincidence of the two does not make conspicuous but drowns the natural length or shortness of the other syllables. The roots of most words are doubtless almost always short, terse, monosyllabic or disyllabic. If now, as is the case in full measure with our modern mother-tongue for example, these roots lay claim to the accent almost exclusively for themselves, this is throughout a preponderating accent on the meaning or sense; but it is not a feature which involves freedom of the material, i.e. sound, or could afford a relationship between long, short, and accented syllables independently of the idea contained in the words. For this reason in this language a rhythmic figuration of time-movement and accentuation, divorced from the root-syllable and its meaning, can no longer exist; and there is left, in distinction from the above-mentioned listening to the richness of sound and the duration of longs and shorts in their varied combinations, only a general hearing entirely captivated by the emphasized chief syllable which carries the weight of the meaning. For besides, as we saw, the modification or syllabic ramification of the stem grows on its own account into separate words which in this process are made important in their own right; and by acquiring their own meaning they now likewise make us hear the same coincidence of sense and accent which we have considered already in connection with the basic word round which they are grouped. This compels us, as if fettered, not to go beyond the sense of each word, and instead of our being preoccupied with the natural longs and shorts and their temporal movement and perceptible

---

[1] In *amaverunt*, the accent cannot fall on the stem, i.e. on *am*.

accentuation, to hear only the accent produced by the fundamental meaning.[1]

(γγ) In such [modern] languages there is little room for rhythm, or the soul has little freedom any longer to spread itself in it, because time, and the sound of syllables outpoured uniformly with the movement of time, is surpassed by something more ideal, i.e. by the sense and meaning of words, and in this way the power of a more independent rhythmical configuration is damped down.

In this respect we may compare the principle of rhythmical versification with plasticity. For here the spiritual meaning is not yet independently emphasized and does not determine the length of syllables or the accent; on the contrary, the sense of the words is entirely fused with the sensuous element of sound and temporal duration, so that this external element can be given its full rights in serenity and joy, and ideal form and movement can be made the sole concern.

But if this principle is sacrificed and if nevertheless, as art necessitates, the sensuous element is always to be a counterpoise to pure intellectuality, then in order to compel the ear's attention, with the destruction of that first plastic feature of natural longs and shorts and of sound not separated from rhythm and not emphasized independently, no other material can be adopted except the express, firmly isolated, figured sound of the linguistic syllables as such.

This leads us to the second chief kind of versification, namely rhyme.

(b) *Rhyme*

It is possible to try to give an external explanation of the need for a new treatment of language in its inner aspect by referring to the corruption suffered by the classical languages on the lips of barbarians; but this development lies in the very nature of the case. The first thing which poetry, on its external side, adapts to its

---

[1] What Hegel has in mind throughout this passage is the difference between Latin *amaverunt* (where modifying syllables ramify from the stem, *am*, to provide tense, *aver*, and number and person, *unt*), and German *Sie haben geliebt*. He argues that an accentual prosody, e.g. in modern German, involves a loss of rhythmical subtlety in comparison with Latin where the stress accent of natural speech forms a sort of counterpoint to a quantitative metrical scheme made possible by long inflected words.

inner message is the length or shortness of syllables independently of their meaning. For combining longs and shorts, for caesuras, etc., art frames laws which are supposed every time to harmonize in general with the character of the material to be presented, but in detail they preclude both longs and shorts and the accent from being solely determined by the spiritual meaning and from being rigorously subject to it. But the more inward and spiritual the artistic imagination becomes, the more does it withdraw from this natural aspect which it cannot any longer idealize in a plastic way; and it is so concentrated in itself that it strips away the, as it were, corporeal side of the language and in what remains emphasizes only that wherein the spiritual *meaning* lies for the purpose of communication, and leaves the rest alone as insignificant by-play. But romantic art in respect of its whole manner of treating and presenting its topics makes a similar transition into the self-concentrated composure of the spirit and tries [in music] to find in sound the material most correspondent to this subjective life. In this way, because romantic *poetry* as such strikes more strongly the soul-laden note of feeling, it is engrossed more deeply in playing with the now independent sounds and notes of letters, syllables, and words, and it proceeds to please itself in their sounds which, now with deep feeling, now with the architectonic and intellectual ingenuity of music, it can distinguish, relate to one another, and interlace with one another. Thus viewed, rhyme is not something accidentally elaborated in romantic poetry alone, but has become necessary in it. The need of the soul to apprehend itself is emphasized more fully, and it is satisfied by the assonance of rhyme which is indifferent to the firmly regulated time-measure and has the sole function of bringing us back to ourselves through the return of the same sounds. In this way the versification approaches what is as such musical, i.e. the notes of the soul, and it is freed from the stuffiness, so to say, of language, i.e. that natural measurement of longs and shorts.

As for the more detailed points of importance in this sphere, I will add only a few brief and general remarks on the following ones:

(α) on the origin of rhyme;

(β) on the more specific differences between this domain and rhythmic versification;

(γ) on the kinds into which this domain is divided.

(a) We have seen already that rhyme belongs to the form of romantic poetry which demands a stronger pronunciation of the independently formed sound because here our inner personality wishes to apprehend itself in the material medium of sound. When this need arises, romantic poetry either finds therefore available to it from the start a language of the kind indicated above in connection with the necessity of rhyme, or it uses an ancient but existing language, like Latin for example (which is differently constituted and requires a rhythmical versification), but adapted to conform to the character of the new principle, or it makes the ancient language into a new one of such a character that it loses rhythm altogether, and rhyme can be the chief thing as is the case in Italian and French, for example.

(αα) In this connection we find that in very early times Christianity forcibly introduced rhyme into Latin versification despite the fact that this versification rested on different principles. But these principles were themselves framed rather on the model of Greek; but instead of showing that that was their original source, they betray on the contrary, in the sort of modification they underwent, a tendency approaching the romantic character. On the one hand, in its earliest period Latin versification did not have its basis in natural longs and shorts but measured the value of syllables by the accent, so that it was only through the more exact knowledge and imitation of Greek poetry that the principle of Greek prosody was adopted and followed; on the other hand, the Romans hardened the lively and serene sensuousness of the Greek metres, especially by more fixed rules for inserting the caesura not only in the hexameter but also in the metres of sapphics and alcaics etc., and so they produced a more sharply pronounced structure and stricter regularity. Apart from this, rhymes enough occur in the most polished poets even at the zenith of Latin literature. So, for example, Horace writes in the *Ars Poetica* (ll. 99–100)

> Non satis est pulchra esse poemata: dulcia *sunto*,
> Et quocumque volent animum auditoris *agunto*.

Even if this came about quite unintentionally on the poet's part, it must still be regarded as an extraordinary chance that precisely where Horace is demanding '*dulcia* poemata', rhyme is encountered. Moreover Ovid avoids similar rhymes still less. Even if this, as I said, be accidental, rhymes do not seem to have been disagreeable to a cultivated Roman ear, or otherwise they could not have been inserted even in isolation and exceptionally. But in this playing with sounds there is missing the deeper significance of the romantic rhyme which emphasizes not the sound as such but what is within it, i.e. the meaning. It is precisely this characteristic which distinguishes the very old Indian rhymes from modern ones.

After the barbarian invasions the corruption of accentuation,[1] and the Christian emphasis on the personal inner life of feeling, there was produced in the classical languages a transition from the earlier rhythmical system of versification to one based on rhyme. In the Hymnal of St. Ambrose the prosody is already wholly governed by the accent of the pronunciation, and rhyme is allowed to break in; the first work of St. Augustine against the Donatists is likewise a rhymed song, and the so-called Leonine verses,[2] as expressly rhymed hexameters and pentameters, must of course also be clearly distinguished from the isolated rhymes mentioned above. These and similar phenomena are evidence of the emergence of rhyme out of the rhythmical system itself.

($\beta\beta$) On the other hand, of course the origin of this new principle of versification has been sought amongst the Arabs, but, for one thing, the culture of their great poets falls in a period later than the occurrence of rhyme in the Christian West, while the range of pre-Mohammedan art had no effective influence on the West; for another thing, there is inherent in Arabic poetry from its first beginnings an echo of the romantic principle, so that the knights of the West at the time of the Crusades were quick enough to find in Arabic poetry a mood that echoed their own. Consequently, just as the spiritual ground from which poetry arose in the Mohammedan East was akin to that from which it arose in the Christian West (although it was external to it and independent of it), so we may conjecture that a new sort of versification originally arose independently in both.

($\gamma\gamma$) The origin of rhyme and what is associated with it in poetry may be found, again without any influence from classical languages or Arabic, in the Germanic languages in their earliest development

---

[1] i.e. the classical quantities were not observed: e.g. 'salvator' came to be wrongly accented on the first syllable with the result that the long a of the second was shortened.

[2] Medieval Latin verse in hexameters or alternate hexameters and pentameters where the final word rhymed with the one immediately before the caesura.

amongst the Scandinavians. An example of this is provided by the songs of the old Edda,[1] to which an early origin cannot be denied, even if they were only collected and assembled later. In this instance, as we shall see, the truly harmonious sound of rhyme in its complete development is absent, but still there is an essential emphasis on single spoken sounds and a conformity to rule and law in their specific repetition.

(β) Secondly, more important than the origin of the new system is its characteristic difference from the old. The chief point of importance here I have already touched on above, and all that remains is to expound it in more detail.

Rhythmical versification reached its most beautiful and richest stage of development in Greek poetry, from which therefore we may draw the chief characteristics of this whole field. In brief, they are as follows:

First, this type of versification does not take for its material the sound as such of letters, syllables, or words, but the sound of syllables in their temporal duration, and so the result is that our attention is not to be exclusively directed to single syllables or letters or to the qualitative similarity or identity of their sound. On the contrary, the sound still remains in undivided unity with the fixed tempo of its specific duration, and as the two move forward the ear must follow equally the value of each single syllable and the law regulating the rhythmic progress of the ensemble. *Secondly*, the measurement of longs and shorts, of rhythmic emphasis and the reverse, and of the various sorts of enlivenment through sharper caesuras and pauses, rests on the *natural* element in language without being governed by that intonation whereby alone the *spiritual* meaning is impressed on a syllable or a word. In its assembly of feet, verse-accent, caesuras, etc., versification proves in this respect to be just as independent [of the sense] as language itself, which, outside poetry, likewise derives its accentuation from natural longs and shorts and their succession and not from the meaning of the root-syllables. *Thirdly*, therefore, for the purpose of an enlivening emphasis on specific syllables, we have on the one side the metrical accent and rhythm, and on the other side ordinary accentuation. Both of these means are intertwined with one another,

---

[1] Lays in Icelandic, collected possibly in the eleventh century, as distinct from the younger Edda of Sturluson, a thirteenth-century prose commentary on the former.

without mutual disturbance or suppression, to provide a double variety in the whole; and in the same way they also allow the poetic imagination's right so to arrange and move words as not to deprive of their due impression the words which for it are of greater importance than others in their spiritual meaning.

(αα) The first thing changed in this system by rhymed versification is the hitherto undisputed validity of natural quantities. Therefore, if some time-measure or other is still to remain, a basis for quantitative pausing or hurrying, no longer to be found in the natural length or shortness of syllables, must be sought in some different sphere. But, as we saw, this sphere can only be the element of the spirit, i.e. the sense of syllables and words. It is *meaning* which is the court of last instance in determining the quantitative measure of syllables if that is still to be respected at all as essential, and consequently the criterion passes over into the inner life out of the externally existent language and its character.

(ββ) Connected with this is a further consequence of still greater importance. For, as I have already indicated, this concentration of emphasis on the meaningful root-syllable destroys that independent expansion into a variety of inflected forms which the rhythmical system is not yet required to subordinate to the root, because it derives neither the measure of shorts and longs, nor the accent that is to be emphasized, from the spiritual meaning. But if such an expansion, and its naturally appropriate organization in metrical feet according to the fixed quantity of the syllables disappears, then the entire system falls to the ground of necessity because it rests on tempo and its rules. French and Italian lines, for example, are of this sort; they lack metre and rhythm in the classical sense altogether, so that everything depends solely on a specific number of syllables.

(γγ) The one possible compensation offered for this loss is rhyme. If, on the one hand, it is no longer temporal duration which enters the formation of lines and enables the sound of the syllables to pour forth with a uniform and natural force, while on the other hand the spiritual meaning dominates the root-syllables and forms with them a compact unity without further organic expansion, then the sound of the syllables alone is left as the final sensuous material, the only one that can be kept free from the measure of time and this accentuation on root-syllables.

But if this sound is to arouse attention on its own account, it must, in the *first* place, be of a much stronger kind than the alternation of different sounds that we find in the classical metres. It also has to appear with a far more preponderating force than the sound of the syllables dare claim in ordinary speech. The reason is that now not only is it to be a substitute for an articulated time-measure, but it also acquires the task of emphasizing the sensuous element in distinction from domination by the accentuating and overpowering meaning. For once an idea has gained access to that inwardness and depth of the spirit, for which the sensuous expression in speech is a matter of indifference, the sound of this inwardness must strike out more materially and be coarser, if only to get attention at all. Therefore, in contrast to the delicate movements of rhythmical harmony, rhyme is a thumping sound that does not need so finely cultivated an ear as Greek versification necessitates.

Secondly, while rhyme here is not divorced from the spiritual meaning alike of root-syllables as such and of ideas in general, it does nevertheless assist the perceptible sound to have a relatively independent force. This aim is only possible of realization if the sound of specific words is in itself discriminated from the ring of the other words and now gains in this isolation an independent existence in order by forceful material strokes to reinstate the perceptible element in its rights. Thus in contrast to the all-pervasive euphony of rhythm, rhyme is an isolated, emphasized, and exclusive sound.

Thirdly, we saw that it is the subjective inner life which in its ideal self-concentration is to expatiate and enjoy itself in these sounds. But if the previously discussed means of versification and its rich variety are discarded, there remains over for this self-apprehension, on the *perceptible* side, only the more formal principle of the repetition of wholly identical or similar sounds, with which, on the *spiritual* side, there can be linked an emphasis on and relation of associated meanings in the rhyming sound of the words indicative of them. In rhythmical versification metre appears as a variously articulated relation of different longs and shorts, whereas rhyme is on the one hand more material but, on the other hand, within this material existence is more abstract in itself, i.e. a mere drawing of the mind's and ear's memory to a recurrence of the same or associated sounds and meanings, a recurrence in which the percipient is made conscious of himself and in which he recognizes himself as the activity of creation and apprehension and is satisfied.

(γ) To conclude, this new system of versification, principally that of romantic poetry, is divided into certain particular kinds, and I will only touch quite briefly on the most important points about them in respect of alliteration, assonance, and rhyme proper.

(αα) Alliteration we find developed in the greatest thoroughness in the older Scandinavian poetry; there it is the principal basis, whereas assonance and end-rhyme, though playing a not insignificant part, occur only in certain types of verse. The principle of alliteration, or one-letter rhymes, is the most imperfect kind of rhyme because it does not demand the recurrence of whole syllables but only insists on the repetition of one and the same letter, and the initial letter at that. Owing to the weakness of this identity of sound, it is on the one hand necessary for such words only to be used for this purpose as already have on their own account an emphasizing accent on their first syllable, while on the other hand these words must not be set far apart from one another if the identity of their initial letters is still to be made really noticeable by the ear. For the rest, the alliterative letters may be a double or single consonant or even a vowel, but consonants are the chief thing owing to the nature of the language in which alliteration prevails. Observance of these conditions has made it an established fundamental rule in Icelandic poetry (R. K. Rask, *Die Verslehre der Isländer*, trans. by G. F. C. Mohnike, Berlin 1830, pp. 14–17)[1] that all rhyme letters require accented syllables, the first letter of which may not occur on the same lines in other principal words carrying an accent on the first syllable, while of three words whose first letter forms the rhyme two must stand in the first line, and the third, which provides the ruling letter, at the beginning of the second. While this identity of sound between initial letters merely is an abstract feature, it is principally words with a more important meaning that are used for alliterative purposes, so that even here a relation between the sound and the meaning of a word is not altogether lacking. But I cannot go further into detail.

(ββ) Assonance does not affect the initial letters but already approaches rhyme, because it is an identically sounding repetition

---

[1] Hotho provides this reference, but it cannot have been Hegel's (since his final lectures on aesthetics were in 1828–9) unless he inserted it in 1830 in his notes for his lectures, and Hotho drew it from there.

of the same letters in the middle or at the end of different words. These assonant words do not need to form the end of a line at all but can also occur in other positions, but the final syllables of the lines do especially, through the identity of single letters, enter into an assonant relation to one another, in contrast to alliteration which puts the chief letter at the beginning of the line. In its richest development this assonance appears amongst the Latin nations, especially the Spaniards whose sonorous language is especially fitted for the recurrence of the same vowels. In general, assonance is restricted to vowels; nevertheless it may allow the echoing of identical vowels, identical consonants, and even consonants in association with a vowel.

($\gamma\gamma$) What in this way alliteration and assonance are qualified to achieve only imperfectly, rhyme finally brings to life in full maturity. For in its case, there is produced a complete accord, of course with the exclusion of initial letters, between whole stems which, because of this accord, are brought into an express relation with their sound. In this connection the number of syllables does not matter; monosyllables, disyllables, and polysyllables can and may be rhymed, and this is why we have the masculine rhyme, restricted to monosyllables, the feminine rhyme, allowed two syllables, and the so-called 'gliding' rhyme [i.e. triple rhyme], stretching out over three syllables or more. The northern languages especially incline to the first, southern languages, like Italian and Spanish, to the second; German and French keep more or less to the middle between these extremes. Rhymes of more than three syllables occur in considerable numbers in only a few languages.

Rhyme has its place at the end of lines, the point at which the rhyming word draws attention to itself by its *sound*, although it is not at all necessary for it to concentrate in itself on every occasion the importance given to the spiritual *meaning*. Either the single lines follow one another according to the law of a purely abstract identical return of the same rhyme, or, by the more artistic form of regular interchange and various symmetrical interlacings of different rhymes, they are united, or separated, or brought into the most complex relations whether close or more distant. Consequently, it is as if the rhymes now find one another immediately, now fly from one another and yet look for one another, with the result that in this way the ear's attentive expectation is now satisfied without more ado, now teased, deceived, or kept in suspense owing to the longer delay between the rhymes, but always contented again by the regular ordering and return of the same sounds.

Amongst the particular sorts of poetry it is especially lyric which is fondest of using rhymes owing to its subjective character, i.e. its inner feeling and its mode of expressing it. Therefore its speech is made into a music of feeling and a melodic symmetry, not of time-measure and rhythmic movement, but of sound, which is clearly echoed in the inner life's own feeling. On this account, this way of using rhyme is developed into a simpler or more complex system of strophes, each of which is rounded into a complete and finished whole; as, for instance, sonnets and canzonets, madrigals and triolets are a playing with tones and sounds, which is both ingenious and richly felt. Epic poetry, on the other hand, when its character is less intermixed with a lyrical element, adheres rather in its complexities to a uniform progress without marking it out in strophes. An example is ready at hand in the distinction between Dante's lyric canzonets and sonnets and his *terza rima* in the *Divine Comedy*.[1] But I must not lose myself in further detail.

(c) *Unification of Rhythmical Versification and Rhyme*

But while in the way indicated we have distinguished and contrasted rhythmic versification and rhyme, the question arises whether a unification of the two is not conceivable and has not actually occurred. In this matter it is especially some modern languages that are important. We cannot absolutely deny that they have reintroduced the rhythmic system or combined it to some extent with rhyme. If we keep to German, for example, I need only refer, in connection with the first of these, to Klopstock who wanted little to do with rhyme and instead imitated the classics in both epic and lyric with deep seriousness and untiring industry. Voss[2] and others followed him and tried to find ever more rigid laws for this rhythmic treatment of our German language. Goethe, on the contrary, was not on firm ground in his classical syllabic measures, and he asked, not without reason: 'Do the wide folds [of classical metres] suit us as they did antiquity?'[3]

---

[1] The point appears to be that, while a sonnet can be complete in itself, the stanzas of the *Divine Comedy*, though often ending with a full-stop, are part of a continuous narrative and so not complete in themselves.

[2] i.e. J. H. Voss, 1751–1826. See above, p. 1017 n. 1.

[3] The motto prefixed to the section of Goethe's poems called *Antiker Form sich nähernd* ('Approaching the classical form').

(α) On this matter I will only reiterate what I have said already about the difference between classical and modern languages. Rhythmical versification rests on the *natural* length and shortness of syllables, and in this it has from the start a fixed measure which cannot be determined or altered or weakened by any *spiritual* emphasis. Modern languages, on the other hand, lack a natural measure like this because in them the verbal accent, given by the meaning, may itself make a syllable long in contrast to others which are without this significance. But this principle of accentuation provides no proper substitute for natural length and brevity because it makes the longs and shorts themselves uncertain. For greater emphasis on the significance of one word may degrade another by making it short even though taken by itself it has a verbal accent too, and so the proffered measure becomes simply relative. 'Thou lov'st', for example, may be a spondee, an iambus, or a trochee, depending on the difference in the emphasis which must be given to both words, or else to either one or the other. Of course attempts have been made to revert in German to the *natural* quantity of the syllables and to establish rules accordingly, but such prescriptions cannot be carried out because of the preponderance gained by the spiritual meaning and its more emphasized accent. And in fact this lies in the very nature of the case. For if the natural measure is to be the foundation, then the language must not have been already intellectualized in the world as it necessarily has been in the world of today. But if a language has won its way, in the course of its development, to such a domination of the sensuous material by the spiritual meaning, then the basis for determining the value of syllables must be derived not from the perceptible quantity itself but from what the words are the means of indicating. It is contrary to the spirit's freedom of feeling to allow the temporal element in speech to be established and fashioned independently in its objective reality.

(β) Yet this is not to say that we would have had to ban completely from our language the rhymeless and rhythmical treatment of syllabic measurement, but it is essential to indicate that, owing to the nature of modern linguistic development, it is not possible to achieve the plasticity of metre in the sterling way that classical antiquity did. Therefore, another element had to appear and be developed in compensation, one in itself of a more spiritual sort than the fixed natural quantity of the syllables. This element is the metrical accent and the caesura, which now instead of proceeding independently of the word-accent coincide with it. In this way they acquire a more significant, even if more abstract, emphasis, because the variety of that triple accentuation which we found in classical rhythm necessarily disappears owing to this coincidence. But, for the same reason, conspicuous success in the imitation of classical antiquity can be achieved only if it be confined to the rhythms that fall more sharply on the ear, because we lack the fixed quantitative basis for the finer differences and complex connections; and the as it were more ponderous accentuation, which now enters as the determinant, has no means in itself of being a substitute for what we lack.

(γ) As for the actual combination of rhythm and rhyme, it too is to be permitted, though to a still more restricted extent than the introduction of classical metres into modern versification.

($\alpha\alpha$) For the dominant distinction between longs and shorts by the word-accent is not throughout a sufficient *material* principle; and on the *sensuous* side it does not occupy the ear to an extent that would make it unnecessary for poetry, where the *spiritual* side predominates, to have recourse to a supplement in the sounding and resounding of syllables and words.

($\beta\beta$) Further, however, having regard to metre, there must be set over against the sound of rhyme and its strength an equally strong counterpoise. But since it is not the quantitative natural difference of syllables and its variety that is to be systematized and made dominant, in the matter of this time-relation recourse can be had only to the identical repetition of the same time-measure, with the result that here the beat begins to be asserted far more strongly than is permissible in the rhythmic system. Examples of this sort of thing are our German rhymed iambics and trochaics which, when recited, we are accustomed to scan more in accordance with a beat than is the case with the rhymeless iambics of classical antiquity. Nevertheless, halting at caesuras, the emphasis on single words to be markedly pronounced according to their sense, and stopping on them, may produce once more a counter-thrust to abstract sameness and therefore an enlivening variety. After all, in general, adherence to the beat in poetry cannot be preserved in practice so strictly as is usually necessary in music.

($\gamma\gamma$) But rhyme in general has to be combined only with such metres as, taken in themselves in rhythmically treated modern languages, cannot shape the sensuous element strongly enough, because of their simple alternation of longs and shorts and the firm repetition of similar feet. For this reason it would seem not only a superfluity but an unresolved contradiction to employ rhyme in the richer syllabic measures imitated from classical antiquity—in sapphics and alcaics, for instance, to quote but one example. For the two systems rest on opposite principles, and the attempt to unite them in the way indicated could only conjoin them in this very opposition itself; and this would produce nothing but an unresolved and therefore inadmissible contradiction. Thus viewed, the use of rhyme [combined with rhythm] is to be allowed only where the principle of classical versification is to prevail solely in more remote echoes and with the essential transformations necessitated by the system of rhyme.

These are the essential points to be established in connection with the general difference between poetical expression and prose.

C. THE DIFFERENT GENRES OF POETRY

INTRODUCTION AND DIVISION OF THE SUBJECT

1. The two chief lines on which we have treated the art of poetry up to this point have been (*a*) poetry as such, in particular poetry's way of looking at things, the organization of the poetic work of art, and the poet's subjective activity of composition: (*b*) the poetic expression, in regard both to the ideas that were to be put into words and also to their linguistic expression and versification.

What we had to contend above all in this conspectus was that poetry must take the spiritual life as its subject-matter, but that in working out this topic artistically it must not, like the visual arts, abide by what can be fashioned for sense-perception; nor can it take as its form either the purely inner life which resounds for the heart alone or the products and relations of reflective thinking. On the contrary it has to keep to the middle way between the extremes of what is directly visible or perceptible by the senses and the subjectivity of feeling and thinking. This central element of imagination [*Vorstellung*] therefore draws something from both spheres. From thinking it takes the aspect of spiritual universality which grips together into a simpler determinate unity things directly perceived as separate; from visual art it keeps things juxtaposed in space and indifferent to one another. For imagination is essentially distinguished from thinking by reason of the fact that, like sense-perception from which it takes its start, it allows particular ideas to subsist alongside one another without being related, whereas thinking demands and produces dependence of things on one another, reciprocal relations, logical judgements, syllogisms, etc. Therefore when the *poetic* way of looking at things makes necessary in its artistic productions an inner unity of everything particular, this unification may nevertheless remain hidden because of that lack of liaison which the medium of imagination cannot renounce at all; and it is precisely this which enables poetry to present a subject-matter in the *organically* living development of its single aspects and parts, while giving to all these the appearance of independence. In this way poetry is enabled to pursue its chosen topic by giving it a character now rather of thought, now rather of an external appearance. Therefore it can exclude neither the most sublime speculative thoughts of philosophy nor nature's external existence, provided only that it does not expound the former in the manner of ratiocination or scientific deduction or present the latter to us in its meaningless state. For poetry too has to give us a complete world, the substantive essence of which is spread out before us artistically with the greatest richness precisely in its external reality, i.e. in human actions, events, and outbursts of feeling.

2. But this unfolding acquires its perceptible existence, as we saw, not in wood, stone, or colour, but solely in language, where versification, accent, etc. are as it were the gestures of speech through which the spiritual subject-matter gains an external existence. Now if we ask where we are to look, so to say, for the *material* basis of this mode of expression, the answer is that, since speaking does not exist, like a work of visual art, on its own account apart from the artist, it is the living man himself, the individual speaker, who alone is the support for the perceptible presence and actuality of a poetic production. Poetic works must be spoken, sung, declaimed, presented by living persons themselves, just as musical works have to be performed. We are of course accustomed to read epic and lyric poetry, and it is only dramatic poetry that we are accustomed to hear spoken and to see accompanied by gestures; but poetry is by nature essentially musical, and if it is to emerge as fully art it must not lack this resonance, all the more because this is the one aspect in virtue of which it really comes into connection with external existence. For printed or written letters, it is true, are also existent externally but they are only arbitrary signs for sounds and words. Earlier we did regard words as likewise means for indicating ideas, but poetry imposes a form, at least on the timing and sound of these signs; in this way it gives them the higher status of a material penetrated by the spiritual life of what they signify. Print, on the other hand, transforms this animation into a mere visibility which, taken by itself, is a matter of indifference and has no longer any connection with the spiritual meaning; moreover, instead of actually giving us the sound and timing of the word, it leaves to our usual practice the transformation of what is seen into sound and temporal duration. Consequently, if we are satisfied with reading merely, this happens partly on account of the readiness with which we imagine as spoken what is seen, partly because poetry alone of all the arts is in its essential aspects already completely at home in the spiritual element and does not bring the

chief thing to our minds through either ear or eye. But, precisely on account of this spirituality, poetry as art must not entirely strip itself of this aspect of actual external expression, at any rate if it wants to avoid the imperfection of e.g. a black and white sketch substituted for a painting produced by a master of colour.

3. As a totality of art, not exclusively confined by any one-sidedness in its material to one particular sort of execution, poetry takes for its specific form the different modes of artistic production in general; and therefore the basis for dividing and articulating the different *sorts* of poetry must be derived from the *general* nature of artistic presentation.

A. In this connection, in the first place, what brings before our contemplation the objective thing at issue is the form of external reality in which poetry presents the developed totality of the spiritual world to our imagination. In doing so, poetry reproduces in itself the principle of visual art. On the other hand, poetry develops these sculptural pictures for our imagination by presenting them as determined by the action of gods and men, so that everything that happens either proceeds from morally self-subsistent divine or human powers or else is a reaction to external hindrances, and in its external mode of appearance becomes an *event* in which the thing at issue goes ahead on its own account while the poet retires. To describe such events in their wholeness is the task of *epic* poetry which reports poetically in the form of the broad flow of events an action complete in itself and the characters who produced it, either as one of substantive worth or as adventurously intermixed with external accidents. In this way it presents what is itself objective in its objectivity.

This world which is to be made objective for apprehension by spiritual vision and feeling is not presented by the bard in such a way that it could betoken his own thoughts and living passion; but the reciter, the rhapsode, speaks it mechanically and from memory, with a measurement of the syllables which is equally uniform, nearly approaching the mechanical, rolling and flowing on in tranquil independence. For what he tells should appear, in manner and matter, as an actual course of events complete in itself, and remote from him as an individual; and with it his mind should not be completely at one in respect of either the subject-matter or the delivery.

B. Secondly, *lyric*, as the converse of epic poetry, forms the second type of poetry. Its content is not the object but the subject, the inner world, the mind that considers and feels, that instead of proceeding to action, remains alone with itself as inwardness, and that therefore can take as its sole form and final aim the self-expression of the subjective life. Here therefore there is no substantive whole unfolded as external happenings; on the contrary, it is the intuition, feeling, and meditation of the introverted individual, apprehending everything singly and in isolation, which communicate even what is most substantive and material as their own, as *their* passion, mood, or reflection, and as the present product of these. The vocal delivery of this fullness and movement of soul should not be a mechanical speech like that which is sufficient and requisite for the recitation of epic. On the contrary, the singer must reveal the ideas and meditations of a lyrical work of art as something that fills his own soul and is felt by himself. And since it is the *inner* life which is to animate the delivery, the expression of that life will lean especially towards music and sometimes allow, sometimes necessitate, a varied modulation of voice, song, and musical accompaniment, etc.

c. The third and last mode of presentation conjoins the two previous ones into a new whole in which we see in front of us both an objective development and also its origin in the hearts of individuals. The result is that the object is displayed as belonging to the subject, while conversely the individual subject is brought before our eyes, now in his transition to an appearance in the real world, now in the fate which passion occasions as a necessary result of its own deed. Thus here, as in epic, an action is spread out before us with its conflict and the issue of it; spiritual powers express themselves and fight each other; complicated accidents occur; and human action depends on the action of an ineluctable fate or the guidance and universal rule of Providence. But the action is not presented to our vision in the purely external form of something that has really happened, i.e. as a past event brought to life by mere narrative; on the contrary, we see it actually present, issuing from the private will, from the morality or immorality, of the individual characters, who thus become the centre as they are in the principle of lyric. But at the same time it is not only the inner life of these characters that is exhibited as such; on the contrary they appear in the execution of purposes dictated by passion, and therefore, in the way that epic poetry emphasizes the material substance of things and its solid worth, they measure the value of those passions and purposes by the objective affairs and rational laws of concrete reality, in order to accept their fate in accordance with the measure of this value and the circumstances in which the individual remains determined to accomplish his aims. This objectivity which proceeds from the subject together with this subjectivity which gains portrayal in its objective realization and validity, is the spirit in its wholeness, and by being *action* provides the form and content of *dramatic* poetry.

This concrete whole is subjective but at the same time it is brought into appearance also in its *external* realization; consequently, in the matter of the actual presentation, apart from the painted scenery that makes the locality visible, poetry proper lays claim to the *entire* person of the actor, so that the living man himself is the material medium of expression. For in drama, as in lyric, the character, on the one hand, should express as his own the whole burden of his inner life, but on the other hand he reveals himself effectively in his actual existence as one entire person related to others; therein he directs action outwards and therefore immediately adds the gestures which, just as much as speech, are a language of the inner life, demanding artistic treatment. Even lyric poetry comes very near to assigning different feelings to different singers and distributing them to different scenes. In drama the subjective feeling issues at once in expression in action and therefore necessitates the visible play of gestures which concentrate the universality of speech into a nearer expression of personality and by means of posture, facial expression, gesticulation, etc., individualizes more specifically, and completes, what is said. If gestures are carried artistically to such a degree of expression that words can be dispensed with, then we have pantomime which, in that case, turns the rhythmic movement of *poetry* into a rhythmic and pictorial movement of *limbs*. In this plastic music of bodily posture and movement the peaceful and cold work of sculpture is ensouled and animated into a dance, and music and plastic art are in this way unified.

A. EPIC POETRY

The Greek ἔπος and the Scandinavian 'saga' both mean 'word', and what they state in general is what that thing is which has been transformed into the 'word'. This 'word' [ἔπος or epic] demands an inherently independent content in order to say *what* that content is and *how* it is. What is to be brought before our minds is the topic as such in all its relations and events, in the sweep of all the circumstances and their development, the topic in the entirety of its existence.

This premissed, we will first describe the *general* character of epic;

secondly, cite the *particular* points of principal importance in epic proper;

thirdly, mention certain particular modes of treatment which have actually occurred in individual epics within the historical development of this kind of poetry.

1. *General Character of Epic*

(*a*) That mode of exposition in epic which is the simplest, but which is still one-sided and imperfect because it is so abstractly condensed, consists in extracting from the concrete world and its wealth of changing phenomena something which is necessary and self-grounded and expressing that independently, concentrated into epic phraseology.

(α) We may begin our consideration of this type with what is most elementary, namely epigraph, so far, that is to say, as it remains literally an epigraph, i.e. an *inscription* on pillars, furnishings, memorials, oblations, etc. Such an inscription is as it were a spiritual hand pointing to something, because its words explain something existent apart from them, something otherwise merely having plastic or local character. In this case the epigraph simply says what *this* thing is. The author is not yet expressing his own concrete self; on the contrary, he looks around and attaches to the object or place which he sees confronting him, and which is claiming his interest, a compressed explanation concerned with the kernel of the thing itself.

(β) We find the next step taken when the duality of the externally real object and the inscription is expunged, i.e. when the poet expresses his idea of the object, without having the object present before his eyes. Examples of this are the classical γνῶμαι (maxims) or *sententiae* (moral and other apophthegms) which put together in a compressed form what is stronger than things we can see, more enduring and universal than the memorial of a specific deed, more lasting than votive offerings, temples, and pillars,— namely the duties of our human existence, worldly wisdom, the vision of what in the spiritual sphere forms the fixed foundations and stable bonds of human action and knowledge. The epic character in this mode of treatment consists in this, that maxims like these are not expressions of personal feeling or purely individual reflection, and neither is even the impression they make directed to our feelings with a view to touching us or promoting some interest of the heart, but instead they evoke an awareness that what is of intrinsic worth must be regarded as a human duty, as what is decent and honourable. The ancient Greek elegies have this epic tone in part, as, for instance, some things by Solon have been preserved of this sort which readily assume an hortatory tone and style, for they include exhortations and warnings about the life of the community in the state, about laws, morals, etc. The 'Golden Verses' attributed to Pythagoras may be included here too. Yet all these are hybrid kinds, arising because, while there is a general adherence to the tone of one specific kind (though it cannot be perfectly developed, since the subject-matter is incomplete), there is a risk of running into the tone of a different kind, the lyric in this case, for example.

(γ) Thirdly, as I have already indicated, such apophthegms may be lifted from their fragmentary character and independent separation, ranged together into a greater whole, and rounded off into a totality which is entirely of an epic sort. This is because in this totality the unity holding the parts together, and the real centre, is not provided by a purely lyrical mood or a dramatic action but by a specific and real sphere of life, the essential nature of which is to be brought home to our minds both in its general character and also in its particular trends, aspects, occurrences, duties, etc. Conformably with this whole stage of epic, which exhibits the permanent and the universal as such with the chiefly ethical aim of warning, teaching, and summoning to an inherently sterling moral life, productions of this kind acquire a didactic tone; but, owing to the novelty of their aphorisms, their fresh outlook on life, and the naïveté of their views, they are still far removed from the flatness of later didactic poetry; and, by allowing the descriptive element its necessary scope too, they prove completely that the whole of their doctrine and description is directly drawn from a reality that has been grasped in its substance and lived through. As a specific example I will cite only Hesiod's *Works and Days*. Its original manner of teaching and describing pleases us, from the point of view of poetry, in a way quite different from the colder elegance, erudition, and systematic consecutiveness of Virgil's *Georgics*.

(*b*) The *first* sorts of elementary epic, those previously considered, namely epigraph, apophthegm, and didactic poetry, take as their material *particular* spheres of nature or human existence, in order, whether piecemeal or comprehensively, to bring before our minds in concise language what is of eternal worth or really true in this or that object, situation, or field, and also to have a practical effect by using poetry as a tool and intertwining poetry and reality more closely. A *second* group digs deeper and aims less at teaching and improving. To this position we may assign cosmogonies and theogonies as well as those oldest productions of philosophy which had been unable to free themselves altogether from the poetic form.

(α) So, for example, the exposition of Eleatic philosophy remains poetical in Xenophanes and also in Parmenides, especially in the Proem to his philosophical work.[1] The topic here is the One which is imperishable and eternal in contrast to what is coming to be and what has been, i.e. to particular and individual phenomena. Nothing particular can any longer satisfy the spirit which strives for truth, and truth is brought to mind in the first place in its most abstract unity and solidity. Intensified by contemplating the greatness of this object and by struggling with its majesty, the soul's enthusiasm begins to become lyrical at the same time; but the

---

[1] So far as we know, Parmenides expounded his philosophy entirely in hexameters; Hegel means that more of the spirit of poetry is to be found in the Proem which describes the author's journey from night to daylight and the teaching of the goddess which Hegel summarized here. In dealing with Parmenides in his *History of Philosophy*, Hegel says: 'This allegorical preface is majestic. . . . Everywhere in it there is an energetic, impetuous soul which strives with Being in order to grasp and express it.'

entire exposition of the truths entering the poet's thinking has a purely matter-of-fact and therefore epic character.

(β) In the cosmogonies, secondly, the subject-matter is the coming-to-be of things, especially of nature, and the tumult and conflict of activities dominant in nature. Here the poetic imagination proceeds to present an occurrence more concretely and richly in the form of deeds and events, because it personifies more or less definitely the natural powers that work themselves out in different spheres and productions, and it clothes them symbolically with human events and actions. This sort of epic subject-matter and exposition belongs especially to the nature-religions of the East, and it is Indian poetry above all which has been extremely fruitful in inventing and blazoning such often wild and extravagant ways of conceiving the origin of the world and the powers continually working in it.

(γ) Thirdly, the like is found in theogonies, which are particularly in their right place when neither on the one hand are the numerous individual gods supposed to have the life of nature exclusively as the principal object of their power and productive activity, nor, conversely, on the other hand, is there *one* god who creates the world by his thought and spirit and who, in perfervid monotheism, suffers no other gods beside him. The Greek religious outlook alone keeps to this beautiful middle position, and it finds an imperishable material for theogonies in the extrication of Zeus' race of gods from the unruliness of the primitive powers of nature, as well as in the battle against these natural divinities— a coming-to-be and a strife which does indeed accord with the factual history of the origin of the eternal gods of poetry itself. The familiar example of such an epic way of putting things is the *Theogony* transmitted to us as by Hesiod. In this work, everything that happened takes the form of human events, and it remains all the less purely symbolic the more are the gods, with spiritual dominion as their vocation, free to take the shape of spiritual individuality which corresponds with their essential being, and for this reason they are justified in acting, and being portrayed, as human beings.

But what this sort of epic still lacks, for one thing, is a genuinely poetic finish. For although the deeds and events which such poems can sketch are an inherently necessary succession of incidents and occurrences, they are not an individual course of action proceeding from a single centre and looking to that for its unity and completeness. For another thing, the subject-matter here by its very nature does not afford the vision of a totality complete in itself, for in essence it lacks the strictly human reality which must alone provide the truly concrete material for the sway of the divine powers. Therefore if epic poetry is to attain its perfect form, it has still to free itself from this deficiency.

(*c*) This happens in that sphere which may be styled 'epic proper'. For in the previously treated preliminary sorts of epic, which are generally ignored, an epic tone is of course present, but their subject-matter is not yet concretely poetic. For particular moral maxims and apophthegms remain purely universal so far as their specific content goes, while what is genuinely poetic is concrete spirit in an individual form; and the epic, having *what is* as its topic, acquires as its object the occurrence of an action which in the whole breadth of its circumstances and relations must gain access to our contemplation as a rich event connected with the total world of a nation and epoch. Consequently the content and form of epic proper is the entire world-outlook and objective manifestation of a national spirit presented in its self-objectifying shape as an actual event. This whole comprises both the religious consciousness, springing from all the depths of the human spirit, and also concrete existence, political and domestic life right down to the details of external existence, human needs and means for their satisfaction; and epic animates this whole by developing it in close contact with individuals, because what is universal and substantive enters poetry only as the living presence of the spirit.

Further, such a total world, which nevertheless is concentrated into individual lives, must proceed tranquilly in the course of its realization, without hurrying on practically and dramatically towards some mark and the result of aiming at it, so that we can linger by what goes on, immerse ourselves in the individual pictures in the story and enjoy them in all their details. Therefore the entire course of the presentation in its objective reality acquires the form of a string of events external to one another which do have their ground, and their limitation, in the inner essence of the epic's specific subject-matter, although it is not expressly emphasized. If for this reason the epic poem becomes rather diffuse and, owing to the relatively greater independence of its parts, is rather loosely connected together, we still must not suppose that it may be composed bit by bit on and on, for on the contrary, like any other work of art, it must as poetry be finished off into an inherently organic whole; yet it moves forward in objective tranquillity so that we can take an interest in the detail itself and the pictures of living reality.

(α) As such an original whole the epic work is the Saga, the Book, the Bible of a people, and every great and important people has such absolutely earliest books which express for it its own original spirit. To this extent these memorials are nothing less than the proper foundations of a national consciousness, and it would be interesting to form a collection of such epic bibles. For the series of epics, excluding those which are later *tours de force*, would present us with a gallery of the spirits of peoples. Nevertheless, not all bibles have the poetic form of epics, nor are fundamental religious books possessed by all the peoples who have clothed in comprehensive epic works of art what has been most sacrosanct to them in religion and worldly life. For example, the Old Testament contains many sagas and actual histories as well as scattered poetic pieces, but the whole thing is not a work of art. Our New Testament too, like the Koran, is mainly confined to the religious sphere, on which the rest of the life of the peoples is consequential later. Conversely, while the Greeks have a poetic bible in the Homeric poems, they have no fundamental religious books like those which the Indians and the Parsis have. But where we meet with primitive epics, we must distinguish these poetical bibles from a people's later classical works of art which do not provide a total conspectus of the whole of the national spirit but only abstract from it certain specific tendencies and mirror it in these. For example, Indian dramatic poetry, or the tragedies of Sophocles, do not provide such a comprehensive picture as the *Ramayana* and *Mahabharata*, or the Iliad and the Odyssey, do.

(β) In epic proper the childlike consciousness of a people is expressed for the first time in poetic form. A genuine epic poem therefore falls into that middle period in which a people has awakened out of torpidity, and its spirit has been so far strengthened as to be able to produce its own world and feel itself at home in it, while conversely everything that later becomes firm religious dogma or civil and moral law still remains a living attitude of mind from which no individual separated himself, and as yet there is no separation between feeling and will.

($\alpha\alpha$) For (i) when the individual's spirit becomes disentangled from the nation's concrete whole and its situations, deeds, fates, and attitudes of mind, and (ii) when feeling and will become separated in the individual, then what reaches its ripest development is not epic, but in the first case dramatic poetry and, in the second, lyric. This comes about completely in the later days of a people's life when the universal principles which have to guide human action are no longer part and parcel of a whole people's *heart* and attitude of *mind* but already appear objectively and independently as a just and legal order, firmly established on its own account, as a prosaic arrangement of things, as a political constitution, and as moral and other prescriptions; the result is that man's substantive obligations enter as a necessity external to him, not immanent in himself, and compelling him to recognize their validity. It is then in contrast with such an already cut-and-dried and independent state of affairs that the mind develops into a likewise independent world of subjective vision, reflection, and feeling which does not proceed to action, and expresses *lyrically* its dwelling on self and its preoccupation with the inner life of the individual; alternatively, passion with a practical aim becomes the chief thing, and it tries in its action to make itself independent by robbing external circumstances, happenings, and events of the right to independence which they have in epic. When this firmness of individual character and aims in relation to action becomes intensified within, it then leads, conversely, to *dramatic* poetry. But epic still demands that immediate unity of feeling with action, of inner aims logically pursued along with external accidents and events, a unity which in its original and undisrupted character occurs only in the earliest periods of poetry and a nation's life.

($\beta\beta$) But we must not put the matter at all as if a people in its heroic age as such, the cradle of its epic, already had the skill to be able to describe itself poetically; for a nationality to be implicitly poetic in its actual life is one thing, but poetry as the imaginative consciousness of poetic material and as the artistic presentation of such a world is another thing altogether. The need to make play with *ideas* in such a presentation, i.e. the development of art, necessarily arises later than the life and the spirit which is naïvely at home in its immediate poetic existence.[1] Homer and the poems

---

[1] i.e. as distinct from the prosaic order mentioned in the preceding paragraph.

bearing his name are centuries later than the Trojan war which counts as an actual fact just as much as Homer is for me an historical individual. In a similar way, if the poems ascribed to Ossian are really his, he sings of an heroic past, the sunset splendour of which arouses in him the need for recalling it and giving it poetic form.

(γγ) In spite of this separation in time, a close connection must nevertheless still be left between the poet and his material. The poet must still be wholly absorbed in these old circumstances, ways of looking at things, and faith, and all he needs to do is to bring a poetic consciousness and artistic portrayal to his subject which is in fact the real basis of his actual life. If on the other hand there is no affinity between the events described in his epic and the actual faith, life, and customary way of looking at things impressed on the poet by his own present world, then his poem is necessarily split into disparate parts. For both sides—the subject-matter, i.e. the epic world which is to be described, and, what is independent of that, the other world of the poet's consciousness and way of looking at things—are of a spiritual kind and each has a specific principle giving it particular features of character. If, then, the spirit of the artist is different from that through which the actual life and deeds of the nation described acquired their existence, then this produces a cleavage which at once confronts us as inappropriate and disturbing. For in that case we see on the one side scenes of a past world, and, on the other, forms, attitudes of mind, modes of reflection belonging to a different present. The result is that the forms of the earlier faith now become, in the midst of this further developed reflective mentality, a cold affair, a superstition, and an empty decoration provided by poetic machinery, and they wholly lack their original soul and proper life.

(γ) This brings us to the general position which the poet has to take up in the case of epic proper.

(αα) However much the epic must be of a factual kind, i.e. the objective presentation of a self-grounded world, made real in virtue of its own necessity, a world to which the poet's own way of looking at things is akin and with which he can identify himself, still the work of art that portrays such a world is and remains the free production of an individual. In this connection, we may refer once more to the great remark of Herodotus: Homer and Hesiod gave the Greeks their gods. This free boldness of creation, which

Herodotus ascribes to the epics named, already gives us an example of the fact that epics must belong to an early period in a people's history and yet have not to describe its earliest period. Almost every people in its earliest beginnings has under its eyes a more or less foreign culture, a religious worship from abroad, and it lets these impose themselves on it; for it is precisely in this that the bondage, superstition, and barbarity of the spirit consists, namely not to have the Supreme Being as something indigenous, but to know it only as something alien not produced from its own national and individual consciousness. For example, before the time of their great epics, the Indians must certainly have gone through many a great revolution in their religious ideas and other circumstances. The Greeks too had to transform, as we saw earlier, material from Egypt, Phrygia, and Asia Minor. The Romans were confronted by Grecian elements, the barbarian invaders with Roman and Christian material, and so on. Only when the poet, with freedom of spirit, flings off such a yoke, scrutinizes his own powers, has a worthy estimate of his own spirit, and therefore has got rid of a beclouded consciousness, can the period of epic proper dawn. For, on the other hand, what is concretely indigenous is long superseded by periods of a culture that has become abstract, of dogmas that have been elaborated, of political and moral principles that have been securely established. The truly epic poet, despite the independence of his creation, remains entirely at home in his world, whether in respect of the passions, aims, and universal powers effective in the inner life of individuals, or in respect of all external circumstances. Homer, for example, has spoken as one at home in his world, and where others are at home, we are too, for there we contemplate truth, the spirit living and possessing *itself* in its world, and we are well and cheerfully disposed because the poet is there too with his whole mind and spirit. Such a world may stand at a lower stage of evolution and development but it remains at the stage of poetry and immediate beauty, so that we recognize and understand the substance of everything that our higher needs and real humanity demand—the honour, disposition, feeling, wisdom, and deeds of each and every hero; and we can enjoy these figures, throughout their detailed description, as being lofty and full of life.

(ββ) On account of the objectivity of the whole epic, the poet as *subject* must retire in face of his *object* and lose himself in it. Only the product, not the poet, appears, and yet what is expressed in the poem is *his*; he has framed it in his mind's eye and put his soul, his entire spirit, into it. But the fact that he has done this does not appear directly. In the Iliad, for example, we see now Calchas, now Nestor interpreting the events, and yet these are explanations which the poet provides. Indeed even what passes within the minds of the heroes he interprets objectively as an intervention of the gods as when Athene appears to the wrathful Achilles, trying to bring him to his senses.[1] This is the poet's invention, but because the epic presents not the poet's own inner world but the objective events, the subjective side of the production must be put into the background precisely as the poet completely immerses himself in the world which he unfolds before our eyes. This is why the great epic style consists in the work's seeming to be its own minstrel and appearing independently without having any author to conduct it or be at its head.

(γγ) Nevertheless, an epic poem as an actual work of art can spring from *one* individual only. Although an epic does express the affairs of an entire nation, it is only individuals who can write poetry, a nation collectively cannot. The spirit of an age or a nation is indeed the underlying efficient cause, but the effect, an actual work of art, is only produced when this cause is concentrated into the individual genius of a single poet; he then brings to our minds and particularizes this universal spirit, and all that it contains, as his own vision and his own work. For poetry is a spiritual production, and the spirit exists only as an actual individual consciousness and self-consciousness. If a work is already there with a distinctive note, then this, it is true, is something given, and others are then enabled to strike the same or a similar note, just as we now hear hundreds and hundreds of poems composed in Goethe's manner. But many pieces composed on and on in the same tone do not make up that unitary work which can be the product only of a single mind. This is a point of importance in connection with the Homeric poems and the *Nibelungenlied*, because we cannot prove the authorship of the latter with any historical certainty, while, in regard to the Iliad and the Odyssey we all know that some have advanced the opinion that Homer, supposedly the single author of both, never existed and that single pieces were produced by single hands and then assembled together to form these two great works. The

[1] Iliad, i. 194 ff.

fundamental question in relation to this contention is whether each of these poems forms an organic epic whole, or, according to widespread opinion today, has no necessary beginning or end and therefore could have been prolonged indefinitely. Of course the Homeric poems lack the close connection of a *dramatic* work of art and their unity is naturally less compact, so that, since each part may be and appear independent, they have been open to many interpolations and other changes. Nevertheless, they form throughout a genuine, inwardly organic, epic whole and such a whole can be composed only by *one* individual. The idea that these poems lack unity and are a mere juxtaposition of different sections composed in the same key is a barbaric idea at variance with the nature of art. But if this view is supposed only to mean that the poet, as subject, vanishes in face of his work, then this is the highest praise; for in that case nothing is said except that no subjective manner of thinking and feeling is recognizable in the work, and this is certainly true of the Homeric poems. What they reveal is solely the thing itself, the people's objective way of looking at things. But even folksong requires a singer who sings the song from a heart filled with the feelings of his folk, and still more does a work of art that is a unity in itself necessitate a *single* individual's spirit which also is a unity in itself.[1]

2. *Particular Characteristics of Epic Proper*

In dealing hitherto with the general character of epic poetry we began by citing the imperfect sorts of epic which have an epic tone but are not complete epics because they do not present either the whole situation of a people or a concrete event within such a whole. But it is only these latter topics which provide the adequate content of a perfect epic, the fundamental traits and conditions of which I have just indicated.

After these preliminary observations we must now survey the particular requirements which can be deduced from the nature of

---

[1] Hegel was in advance of his time when he repudiated the Homeric scholarship of his contemporaries. More recent scholars have abandoned the idea that Homer was a committee. For a summary of the arguments for unity, see, for example, C. M. Bowra in the *Oxford Classical Dictionary*, s.v. Homer. 'Perhaps the Homeric poems were not written by Homer, but by another poet of the same name' is an old saying, but even modern scholars would not regard Homer as the *sole* begetter of the two epics.

the epic work of art. In this connection we are at once met by the difficulty that little can be said in general terms on this more detailed topic, and consequently we would have to enter upon historical ground at once and consider the national epics singly; but in view of the difference of periods and nations this procedure would give us little hope of producing corresponding results. Yet this difficulty can be removed if we pick out from the many epic bibles *one* in which we acquire a proof of what can be established as the true fundamental character of epic proper. This *one* consists of the Homeric poems. From them above all I will therefore draw the traits which seem to me to be the chief characteristics naturally belonging to epic. These can be grouped together under the following heads:

(*a*) First, the question arises about what character the general world-situation must have if it is to provide a ground on which an epic event can be adequately portrayed.

(*b*) Secondly, we have to examine the quality of this individual event and consider of what sort it is.

(*c*) Thirdly, we must cast a glance at the form in which these two sides are intertwined and moulded into the unity of a work of art.

(*a*) *The General World-Situation of Epic*

We saw right at the beginning that what is accomplished in the genuinely epical event is not a single casual deed, and that consequently it is not a purely accidental happening which is related, but an action ramified into the whole of its age and national circumstances so that it can be brought before us only within an outspread world and demands the portrayal of this world in its entirety. The genuinely poetic form of this universal ground I can summarize briefly because I touched on the chief points when I was dealing in Part I of these lectures with the general world-situation of any ideal action. At this point, therefore, I will mention only what is important for epic.

(α) The state of human life most suitable as the background of an epic is that in which it exists for individuals *already* as a present reality but which remains most closely connected with them by the tie of a common primitive life. For if the heroes who are placed at the head of affairs have first to found an entire social order, the determination of what exists or is to come into existence devolves, to a greater extent than is suitable for epic, on their subjective character and cannot appear as an objective reality.

(αα) The relations of ethical life, the bond of the family, as well as the bond of the people—as an entire nation—in war and peace must all have been discovered, framed, and developed; but, on the other hand, not yet developed into the form of universal institutions, obligations, and laws valid in themselves without any ratification by the living subjective personality of individuals, and indeed possessed of the power of subsisting even against the will of individuals. On the contrary, the sole origin and support of these relations [in an epic world] must clearly be a *sense* of justice and equity, together with custom and the general mind and character, so that no intellectualism in the form of a prosaic reality can stand and be consolidated against the heart, individual attitudes of mind, and passion. We must dismiss out of hand the idea that a truly epic action can take place on the ground of a political situation developed into an organized constitution with elaborate laws, effective courts of law, well-organized administration in the hands of ministers, civil servants, police, etc. The relations of an objective ethical order must indeed have already been willed and developing, but they can acquire their existence only in and through the actions and character of individuals, and not yet otherwise in a universally valid and independently justified form. Thus in epic we find an underlying community of objective life and action, but nevertheless a freedom in this action and life which appear to proceed entirely from the subjective will of individuals.

(ββ) The same is true for man's relation to his natural environment whence he draws the means for satisfying his needs and for the manner of their satisfaction. In this matter too I must refer back to what I expounded earlier at length in dealing, in Part I, with the external determinacy of the Ideal. For his external life man needs house and garden, tents, seats, beds, swords and lances, ships for crossing the sea, chariots to take him to battle, kettles and roasting-tins, slaughter of animals, food and drink, but none of these and whatever else he may need, should have been only dead means of livelihood; on the contrary he must still feel himself alive in them with his whole mind and self, and therefore give a really human, animated, and individual stamp to what is inherently external by bringing it into close connection with the human individual. Our modern machines and factories with their products, as well as our general way of satisfying the needs of our external life, would from this point of view be just as unsuitable as our modern political organization is for the social background required by the primitive epic. For, just as the intellect with its universals and that dominion of theirs which prevails independently of any individual disposition must not yet have asserted itself in the circumstances envisaged in the whole outlook of the epic proper, so here man must not yet appear cut adrift from a living connection with nature and that link with it which is powerful and fresh, be it friendly or hostile.

(γγ) This is the world-situation which elsewhere [in Part I] I distinguished from the idyllic one and called 'heroic'. We find it sketched by Homer in the most beautiful poetry and with a wealth of human characteristics. Here we have before us in domestic and public life neither barbarism nor the purely intellectual prose of an ordered family and political life, but that originally poetic middle stage that I described above. But a chief point in it concerns the free individuality of all the figures. For example, in the Iliad Agamemnon is the King of Kings, the other Princes are under his sceptre, but his position as overlord does not become the dry connection of command and obedience, of a master and his servants. On the contrary, Agamemnon must be very circumspect and shrewd enough to give way, because the individual Princes are not his lieutenants and generals, summoned at his call, but are as independent as he is himself; they have assembled around him of their own free will or have been induced by some other means to join the expedition. He must take counsel with them, and if they are dissatisfied they stay away from the fight as Achilles did. This freely willed participation in the struggle, or the reverse, preserves the independence of the individual unimpaired, and this is what gives the whole relationship its poetic form. We find the same thing in the Ossianic poems as well as in the Cid's relation to the Princes served by this national hero of romantic chivalry. Even in Ariosto and Tasso this free relationship is still not jeopardized, and, in Ariosto especially, the individual heroes set off on adventures of their own in almost complete independence. The relation between Agamemnon and the Princes is repeated in the relation between the Princes and their people. The latter follow of their own will; there is no compelling law to which they are subject. The basis of their obedience is honour, respect, bashfulness in face of the more powerful Prince who could always use force, and the imposing nature of the heroic character, etc. Order prevails in the home as well, though it is not an organization of servants but a matter of disposition and *mores*. Everything looks as if it had grown up naturally. For example, Homer tells of the Greeks on the occasion of a battle with the Trojans that they had lost many vigorous warriors, but fewer than the Trojans because, Homer says, they always took thought for one another so as to avert cruel death in the mêlée.[1] They helped one another. If nowadays we wish to mark the difference between a well-disciplined and an uncivilized army, we would have to look for the essential difference of the civilized army in this bond and the mutual consciousness of counting only as a unity of one man with another. Barbarians are only a horde where no individual can rely on another. But what in our case appears as the result of a strict and laborious military discipline, training, and the command and domination of a fixed organization, is in Homer's case a spontaneous custom, inherent and living in individuals as individuals.

The same sort of thing is at the bottom of Homer's numerous descriptions of external things and situations. He does not dwell much on scenes in nature as our modern novels are fond of doing, whereas he is most circumstantial in his description of a staff, sceptre, bed, weapons, robes, door-posts, and he even does not forget to mention the hinges on which a door swings.[2] In our case such things would seem very external and indifferent; indeed in our civilization our attitude to a mass of objects, things, and words is one of an extremely inflexible gentility and we have an extensive hierarchy of grades of distinction in clothing, furnishings, etc. Moreover, nowadays the production and preparation of any and every means of satisfying our needs is split up between such a multitude of activities in factories and workshops that all the particular steps in this wide ramification are reduced to something subordinate which we need not notice or enumerate. But the world of the heroes was not like this; there was a more primitive simplicity of objects and contrivances, and it was possible to linger over their description because all these things rank alike and are counted as something in which a man may take pride on the score of his skill, his wealth, and his material interests, because he has

---

[1] Iliad, xvii. 360–5.   [2] e.g. Odyssey, vii. 88, xvii. 221, xxi. 42.

not been diverted from them by his whole course of life and led into a purely intellectual sphere. Slaughtering oxen and preparing them for food, pouring wine, etc. is an occupation of the heroes themselves, an occupation that they pursue with enjoyment for its own sake, whereas with us if a luncheon is not to be an ordinary everyday one, it must not only involve bringing rare delicacies to the table but require excellent talk besides. Therefore, Homer's circumstantial descriptions of things of this sort must not seem to us to be a poetic addition to rather dry material; on the contrary, this detailed attention is the very spirit of the men and situations described, just as in our case peasants, for example, talk at great length and in detail about external things, or as our horsemen can dilate with no less prolixity on their stables, steeds, boots, spurs, breeches, etc., all of which, it is true, is small beer in comparison with a more dignified and an intellectual life.

This heroic world should not comprise merely the restricted universal element in the particular event proceeding on such a presupposed ground, but must be extended to the *whole* of a national outlook. Of this we have the finest example in the Odyssey which not only introduces us to the domestic life of the Greek Princes and their servants and subjects, but also displays to us the manifold ideas of foreign peoples, sea voyages, the abode of the dead, etc. in the richest way. In the Iliad, owing to the nature of the subject-matter the theatre of the action had to be more restricted, and in the midst of battle and war little room could be found for scenes of peace; nevertheless, even here, with great art and marvellous insight, Homer has, for instance, brought together the whole sphere of the earth and human life, weddings, legal actions, agriculture, herds, etc., private wars between cities, and described all this[1] on the shield of Achilles, a description not to be regarded as an external parergon. On the other hand, in the poems called Ossian's the world is on the whole too restricted and vague and for this reason has a lyrical character already, while Dante's Paradise and Hell are not in themselves a world affecting us more nearly but serve only as a place for the reward or punishment of men. But the *Nibelungenlied* above all lacks the specific reality of a ground and soil, so that the narrative already approaches the tone of fairground entertainers. It is indeed prolix enough but it is as if apprentices had heard of the thing remotely and now proposed to tell the story

[1] Iliad, xviii.

in their own way. We do not manage to see the thing but only notice the incapacity and drudgery of the poet. It is true that this wearisome expanse of weakness is still worse in the *Heldenbuch* until finally it was outdistanced only by real apprentices, i.e. as the Mastersingers were.

(β) Yet since epic's artistic purpose is to give shape to a specific world, determinate in all its particular aspects, and since it must therefore be something individual in itself, the world mirrored in it must be that of one specific people.

(αα) All the truly primitive epics give us the vision of a national spirit in its ethical family life, in states of national war or peace, in its needs, arts, usages, interests, in short a picture of a whole way of thinking and a whole stage of civilization. To estimate epic poems, to examine them more closely, and to expound them therefore means, as we have seen already, nothing but to make the spirits of individual nations pass before our mind's eye. Together they present the history of the world in its most beautiful, free, specific life, achievements, and events. From no source but Homer, for example, do we learn in such a lively way or recognize in such a simple way the nature of the Greek spirit and Greek history, or at least the essence of what the Greeks were in their beginnings and what they achieved in order to overcome the conflict of their own history.

(ββ) But there are *two* sorts of a nation's reality. First, an entirely *positive* or *factual* world of the most specialized usages of precisely this individual people, at this specific period, in this geographical and climatic situation, with these rivers, mountains, and woods, in short with this natural environment. Secondly, the *substance* of the nation's *spiritual* consciousness in respect of religion, family, community, and so forth. Now if, as we required, a primitive epic is to be and remain the permanently valid Bible or Book of the people, the factual aspect of the reality that is past can only claim a continuing living interest if the factual characteristics have an inner connection with those really substantive aspects and tendencies of the nation's existence; for otherwise the factual becomes wholly fortuitous and indifferent. For example, nationality implies possession of a geographical home; but if its geography does not give a people its specific character, then provided that a remote and different natural environment does not contradict the nation's own special character, it may not be disturbing at all and may even have something attractive about it for the imagination. The immediate presence of our native hills and streams is linked with the visual memories of youth, but if the deeper bond with our whole way of thinking and looking at things is lacking, this link drops to being more or less an external one. Besides, in the case of military expeditions, as in the Iliad for example, it is not possible to keep to the native land; indeed in this instance there is something attractive and charming about the foreign natural environment.

But the enduring life of an epic suffers still more if in the course of centuries spiritual consciousness and life have been so transformed that the links between this more recent past and the original starting-point have been altogether snapped. This is what happened, in a different sphere of poetry, with Klopstock,[1] for example, when he set up a cult of national gods and brought Hermann and Thusnelda in their train. The same is to be said of the *Nibelungenlied*. The Burgundians, Chriemhild's revenge, Siegfried's deeds, the whole circumstances of life, the fate and downfall of an entire race, the Nordic character [of the poem], King Etzel, etc., all this has no longer any living connection whatever with our domestic, civil, legal life, with our institutions and constitutions. The story of Christ, Jerusalem, Bethlehem, Roman law, even the Trojan war have far more present reality for us than the affairs of the Nibelungs which for our national consciousness are simply a past history, swept clean away with a broom. To propose to make things of that sort into something national for us or even into the Book of the German people has been the most trivial and shallow notion. At a time when youthful enthusiasm seemed to be kindled anew, it was a sign of the grey hairs of a second childhood at the approach of death when an age reinvigorated itself on something dead and gone and could expect others to share its feeling of having its present reality in that.

(γγ) But if a national epic is to win the abiding interest of other peoples and times too, then the world it describes must not be only that of a *particular* nation; it must be such that what is *universally* human is firmly impressed at the same time on the particular

---

[1] i.e. his 'bardic' plays, plays interspersed with bardic songs and choruses. Three of these plays are about Hermann, i.e. Arminius, chief of the Cherusci, who destroyed Varus, A.D. 9, at the Teutoburg battle, and became the 'liberator of Germany' (Tacitus, *Ann.* ii. 88). Thusnelda was his wife.

nation described and on its heroes and their deeds. So, for example, we have in Homer's poems the undying and eternal presence of the immediate material of religion and ethics, splendour of character and the whole of existence, and the visible actuality in which the poet can bring before us things both supreme and trivial. In this matter a great difference prevails between different nations. For example, it cannot be denied that the *Ramayana* portrays in the most living way the spirit of the Indian people, especially in its religious aspect, but the whole character of Indian life is so preponderantly specialized, that the barrier presented by its peculiarity cannot be burst by what is really and truly human. It is quite otherwise, however, with the epic descriptions contained in the Old Testament, especially in the pictures of patriarchal conditions, because from early times the entire Christian world has found itself at home in them, and enjoyed ever anew this remarkably energetic illustration of the events set forth. Goethe, for example, even in childhood 'in the midst of his distracted life and miscellaneous learning brought his mind and feelings to tranquil effectiveness by concentrating them on this one point',[1] and in manhood he still says of the Old Testament, 'in all our wanderings through the East we still came back to these Scriptures as the springs of water which are the most refreshing, though here and there troubled, often disappearing under the ground, but then always bubbling up again, pure and fresh'.[2]

(γ) Thirdly, the general situation of a particular people must not be the proper subject-matter of an epic in this tranquil universality of its individual character as a people or be described simply on its own account; on the contrary it can appear only as a foundation on the basis of which a continually developing event occurs, touches all sides of the people's actual life, and incorporates them. Such a happening should not be a purely external accident but must be something carried out by the will in accordance with a substantial spiritual purpose. But if the two sides, the people's universal situation and the individual action, are not to fall apart, the specific event must find its occasion in the very ground and soil on which it moves. This simply means that the epic world presented to us must be seized in such a concrete and individual

---

[1] *Dichtung und Wahrheit*, part i, book iv.
[2] From the section entitled *Alttestamentliches* in the long notes and dissertations which Goethe appended to the *West-östliche Divan*.

situation that from it there necessarily proceed the specific aims whose realization the epic is to relate. Now we have already seen in Part I, in dealing with the ideal action in general, that this kind of action presupposes such situations and circumstances as lead to conflicts, i.e. injurious actions necessarily followed by reactions. The specific situation in which the epic state of the world is revealed to us must therefore be of a kind productive of collision. Therefore epic and dramatic poetry tread on the same ground and at this point we must therefore begin by establishing the difference between epic and dramatic collisions.

(αα) In the most general terms we can cite conflict in a state of war as the situation most suited to epic. For in war it is precisely the whole nation which is set in motion and which experiences a fresh stimulus and activity in its entire circumstances, because here the whole has an inducement to answer for itself. While this principle is confirmed in most of the great epics, it does seem to be contradicted not only by Homer's Odyssey but by much of the material in religious epics. The Odyssey recounts the history of a collision, but this collision had its origin likewise in the expedition against Troy, and although there is no actual description of the Trojan war, still in relation both to the domestic situation in Ithaca and to Odysseus' efforts to get home, the collision is an immediate consequence of the war; indeed, it is itself a kind of war, because many of the chief heroes had as it were to reconquer their home, since after ten years' absence they found a changed situation there. As for religious epics, it is chiefly Dante's *Divine Comedy* which confronts us. But here too the fundamental collision is derived from the Devil's original fall from God which leads in human affairs to the continual internal and external war between actions in conflict with God's will and those pleasing to him and which is perpetuated in damnation, purification, and beatification, i.e. in Hell, Purgatory, and Paradise. In [Klopstock's] *Messiah* too the central point can only be the direct war against the Son of God. Still, what is most lively and most appropriate will always be the description of an actual war as we find it already in the *Ramayana*, in the richest way in the Iliad, but later too in Ossian and the famous poems of Tasso, Ariosto, and Camoens. The reason is that in war bravery remains the chief interest, and bravery is a state of the soul,[1] and an activity, which is fitted not for expression in lyric,

[1] For Hegel's conception of the soul, see his *Encyclopaedia*, §§ 388 ff. Soul, as

nor for dramatic action, but above all for description in epic. For in drama the chief thing is inner *spiritual* strength or weakness, the ethically justified or unjustifiable 'pathos', whereas in epic it is the *natural* side of spirit, i.e. character. Consequently bravery is in its right place in national wars, because it is not a moral conviction adopted by the will itself as a will and a spiritual consciousness; on the contrary, its basis is natural, amalgamated with the spiritual side into a direct equipoise for the execution of practical purposes which are better described than comprised in lyrical feelings and reflections. What is true of bravery in war is true also of the actions themselves and their consequences. There is an equipoise likewise between the accidents of external happenings and what the will achieves. From drama, on the other hand, the mere happening with the purely external hindrances it involves is excluded, because in this case externality has no independent right of its own but must stem from the aims and inner purposes of individuals, so that if accidents do enter and seem to determine the issue they nevertheless have to have their true ground and their justification in the inner nature of the characters and their aims as well as of the conflicts and their necessary resolution.

(ββ) With such belligerent situations as the basis of the epic action it seems that a wide variety of material is open to epic; for it is possible to portray a mass of interesting deeds and events in which bravery plays a chief role, and likewise an undiminished right remains granted to the external power of circumstances and accidents. In spite of this we must not overlook that in this matter an essential restriction is placed on epic. For it is only the wars of nations foreign to one another that are of a genuinely epic kind, whereas dynastic battles, civil wars, and commotions are more suited to dramatic representation. Thus, for instance, Aristotle long ago recommended tragedians to select material with the war of brother against brother as its subject-matter (*Poetics*, 1453^b 19 ff.). The *Seven Against Thebes* [of Aeschylus] is an example of this. Polynices, a Theban, attacks the city, and its defender, Eteocles, his enemy, is his own brother. Here the enmity is not at all in the nature of things but depends, on the contrary, on the particular individuality of the two warring brothers. The funda-

---

feeling, disposition, and temperament, is natural, rather than spiritual; although it is the first, and therefore inadequate, form in which spirit rises above nature, it still has a natural basis.

mental tie between them would have been peace and harmony, and their necessary unity is severed only by their individual disposition and its supposed justification. A great number of similar examples could be cited, especially from Shakespeare's tragedies in which every time what would really be justified is the harmony of the individuals concerned, but inner motives of passion, and characters who want only their own way and have regard to nothing else, lead to wars and collisions. In respect of a similar action and one therefore defective for epic, I will refer only to Lucan's *Pharsalia*. However great in this poem are the purposes that are at variance, the combatants are too near one another, too closely related by their own country's soil, for their conflict not to seem a mere party-struggle instead of a war between whole nations. This struggle splits the people's underlying unity and leads, on the subjective side, to tragic guilt and corruption. Moreover, the objective events are not left clear and simple in the poem but are confusedly intermingled. The same thing is true of Voltaire's *Henriade*. On the other hand the enmity of nations foreign to one another is something substantial and fundamental. Every nation is on its own account a whole different from and opposed to another. If they become enemies, no ethical bond is snapped, nothing absolutely valid is impaired, no necessary whole is split up; on the contrary, it is a battle to maintain this whole intact, along with its right to exist. The occurrence of enmity like this is therefore absolutely fitted to the fundamental character of epic poetry.

($\gamma\gamma$) At the same time, however, once more it is not any ordinary war between nations hostilely disposed to one another that as such is to be peculiarly regarded as epical: a third aspect must be added, namely the justification claimed by a people at the bar of history, a claim which one people pursues against another. Only in such a case is the picture of a new higher undertaking unrolled before us. This cannot appear as something subjective, as a mere capricious attempt at subjection; on the contrary, by being grounded in a higher necessity it is something absolute in itself, even if the direct external occasion for it may assume the character of some single violation or of revenge. An analogue of this situation is to be found in the *Ramayana*, but it arises above all in the Iliad where the Greeks take the field against the Asiatics and thereby fight the first epic battles in the tremendous opposition that led to the wars which constitute in Greek history a turning-point in world-history.

In a similar way the Cid fights against the Moors; in Tasso and Ariosto the Christians fight against the Saracens, in Camoens the Portuguese against the Indians. And so in almost all the great epics we see peoples different in morals, religion, speech, in short in mind and surroundings, arrayed against one another; and we are made completely at peace by the world-historically justified victory of the higher principle over the lower which succumbs to a bravery that leaves nothing over for the defeated. In this sense, the epics of the past describe the triumph of the West over the East, of European moderation, and the individual beauty of a reason that sets limits to itself, over Asiatic brilliance and over the magnificence of a patriarchal unity still devoid of perfect articulation or bound together so abstractly that it collapses into parts separate from one another. If now in contrast to these epics we contemplate others that may perhaps be composed in the future, then these might have nothing to describe except the victory, some day or other, of living American rationality over imprisonment in particulars and measurements prolonged to infinity.[1] For in Europe nowadays each nation is bounded by another and may not of itself begin a war against another European nation; if we now want to look beyond Europe, we can only turn our eyes to America.

(b) *The Individual Epic Action*

Now it is on this ground, open to conflicts between whole nations, that, secondly, the epic event proceeds. Our task now is to look for the general characteristics of this event and our discussion will be divided into the following points:

(α) However firmly the aim of an epic action rests on a universal foundation, it must still be individually alive and definite.

(β) But since actions can only proceed from individuals, the question of the general nature of the epic characters arises.

(γ) Objectivity is portrayed in the epic event not merely in the sense of external appearance but at the same time in the sense of something necessary and fundamental. Therefore we must

---

[1] By America, as is clear from his Philosophy of History (*Ww.*² ix, pp. 100–8), Hegel means both North and South, and he envisages a possible war between the two. Hence here he may be contrasting the relatively rational order of the United States with the disorder, disconnection, and chaos of South America in his day.

establish the form in which this fundamental nature of the event appears effective either as an inner hidden necessity or as openly directed by eternal powers and Providence.

(α) Above we have postulated as the basis of the epic world a national undertaking in which the entirety of a national spirit could be strongly marked in the earliest freshness of its heroic situations. But on this foundation a *particular* aim must arise, the realization of which, being most intimately interwoven with the life of the whole nation, brings into view every aspect of the national character, faith, and action.

(αα) The whole nation proceeds to particularize this aim which is animated in individuals, and in this way, as we know already, the aim, thus animated and particularized, assumes in epic the form of an event. Consequently at this point we must above all refer in more detail to the manner in which willing and acting in general pass over into an event. Action and event both proceed from the inner life of the spirit, and the contents of that life are not only manifested by them subjectively and theoretically in the expression of feelings, reflections, thoughts, etc., but they are also carried out objectively and practically. To this realization there are two sides. First, the inner side, namely the intended and envisaged end, the general nature and consequences of which the individual must know, will, take responsibility for, and accept. Secondly, the external side, namely the reality of the environing spiritual and natural world within which alone a man can act. Its accidents he encounters as obstructions or encouragements, so that either he is fortunately led to his aim through their favour, or, if he refuses to submit to them forthwith, has to fight against them with all his individual energy. If the world of the will is conceived as the undivided unification of these two sides so that both are allowed the same justification, then the inmost life of the spirit itself at once acquires the form of a fact and this gives the shape of an event to all action because the inner will with its intentions, and subjective motives such as passion, principles, and aims, can no longer appear as the chief thing in action. In the case of *action* everything is referred back to the agent's inner character, his duty, disposition, purpose, etc.; whereas, in the case of *events* the external side too acquires its unimpaired right, because it is objective reality which provides both the form of the whole and also a principal part of the content itself. This is the sense in which I said earlier that the task of epic poetry is to present the *fact* of an action, and therefore not merely to cling to the external side as being the accomplishment of aims, but also to allow to the external circumstances, natural occurrences, and other accidental things the same right as that which the inner life claims exclusively for itself in an action as such.

(ββ) If we consider more closely the nature of the *particular* aim, the accomplishment of which is related in epic in the form of an event, all that I have already premissed implies that this aim must not be an abstract thing but must be concrete and definite, but without being a mere caprice since it is actualized within the substantive existence of the entire nation. For example, the state as such, our country, or the history of a state and country, is as such something universal which, taken in this universality, does not appear as something subjectively and individually existent, i.e. it is not inseparably coincident with a specific and living individual. Thus the history of a country, the development of its political life, its constitution, and its fate, may also be related as an event: but if what happens is not presented as the concrete act, the inner aim, the passion, life, and accomplishment of specific heroes whose individuality provides the *form* and the content of the whole actual occurrence, then the event exists only in the rigid independent advance of its *content* as the history of a nation or an empire. From this point of view the supreme action of the spirit may be world-history itself, and we might propose to work up this universal deed on the battlefield of the universal spirit into the absolute epic; the hero of such an epic would be the spirit of man, or humanity, which educates and lifts itself out of a dullness of consciousness into world-history; but precisely because of its universality this material could not be sufficiently individualized for art. For, in the first place, such an epic would lack from the start a fixed and specific background and world-situation in relation alike to locality and to morals, customs, etc. The one foundation that could be presupposed would be the universal world-spirit itself which cannot be visualized as a specific situation and which has the entire earth as its locality. Similarly the one aim accomplished in such an epic would be the aim of that world-spirit which can be grasped and clearly explained in its true meaning solely by thinking; but if it were to appear in poetic guise it would have to be emphasized every time as the agent acting independently from its own resources in order to give the whole story its proper sense and connection. This could only be done poetically if the inner architect of history, the eternal and absolute Idea, which realizes itself in humanity, either came into appearance as a directing, active, and executive individual, or else asserted itself as merely a hidden ever-operative necessity. But, in the first case, owing to the infinity of this subject-matter, the vessel of art, always limited in size to contain specific individuality alone, would be burst; or alternatively, to counter this drawback, would have to sink to a cold allegory consisting of general reflections on 'the vocation [of man]' and 'the education of the human race,'[1] on the aim of humanity or moral perfection, or however else the purpose of the world-spirit may be described. In the second case, the part of particular heroes would have to be played by the different national spirits, and their conflict would be the theatre in which the pageant of history would unfold and move forward in continuous development. But if the spirit of the nations in its actuality is to appear in poetry, this can only happen by bringing before us in their actions a succession of the really world-historical figures. But in that case we would only have a series of particular figures appearing and disappearing in a purely external succession; they would lack connection and would not form an individual unity because the ruling world-spirit, i.e. the inner nature and fate of the world, would not be placed at their head as itself an individual agent. And if an attempt were made to grasp the national spirits in their universality and make them act in that fundamental character, this too would only give us a similar series, and, besides, the individuals in it would only have, like Indian incarnations, a show of existence, a fiction that would have to grow pale in face of the truth of the world-spirit realized in the actual course of history.

(γγ) From this we can derive the general rule that the particular epic event can only be given vitality in poetry if it can be fused in the closest way with a single individual. Just as a single poet devises and carries out the whole epic, so at the head of the event there must be a single individual with whom the event is linked and by whose single figure it is conducted and ended. But in this matter there are additional and essentially more detailed postulates.

---

[1] These are titles of books by Fichte and Lessing, but Hegel may not be referring to them specifically.

For, as was the case previously with the poetic treatment of world-history, so now in the converse case of the individual it might seem that a biographical treatment of a specific life-history was the most perfect and proper epic material. But this is not the case. In a biography the individual does remain one and the same, but the events in which he is involved may fall apart from one another altogether independently, and their point of connection with him may be purely external and accidental. But if the epic is to be a unity in itself, the event in the form of which its subject-matter is presented must also have unity in itself. Both the unity of the individual and the unity of the occurrence must meet and be conjoined. In the life and deeds of the Cid on his native soil, the interest lies solely in the one great individual who remains true to himself throughout his development, heroism, and death; his exploits pass in front of him, as if he were a sculptured god, and in the end the whole thing has passed in front of us and him too. But as a chronicle in rhyme the poems of the Cid are not an epic proper, but something like later romances. These are a genus which requires something similar to what the Cid poems have, namely a splintering of the national heroic age into single situations which are under no necessity of closing together to form the unity of a particular event. On the other hand, what has been postulated is satisfied most beautifully in the Iliad and the Odyssey where Achilles and Odysseus stick out as the chief figures. The same is the case in the *Ramayana* too. In this matter Dante's *Divine Comedy* has an especially remarkable position. In it the epic poet himself is the one individual to whose wanderings through Hell, Purgatory, and Paradise each and every incident is linked, so that he can recount the productions of his imagination as his own experiences and therefore acquires the right, to a greater extent than is allowed to other epic poets, of interweaving his own feelings and reflections with the objective side of his work.

(β) It follows that however far epic poetry in general recounts what is and what happens and therefore has objectivity for its content and form, still, on the other hand, since it is the happening of an *action* which passes in front of us, it is precisely the individuals and their deeds and sufferings who really emerge. For only individuals, be they men or gods, can really act, and the more vitally they have to be interwoven with what is going on, all the more fully will they be justified in attracting the main interest. From this point of view, epic stands on the same ground with both lyric and dramatic poetry, and therefore it must be an important matter for us to emphasize more definitely the specifically *epic* way of presenting individuals.

(αα) The objectivity of an epic character, especially of the chief ones, implies that they are an entirety of characteristics, whole men, and therefore there must appear developed in them all aspects of the mind and heart, and in particular of the national disposition and manner of acting. In this connection I have already drawn attention, in Part I of these Lectures, to Homer's heroic figures, especially to the variety of purely human and national qualities vividly united in Achilles, to whom the hero of the Odyssey provides a most remarkable counterpart. The Cid is presented to us with a similar many-sidedness of character-traits and situations: as son, hero, lover, spouse, householder, father, and in his relation to his king, his friends, and his enemies. On the other hand, other medieval epics remain far more abstract in this sort of characterization, especially when their heroes only defend the interests of chivalry as such and are remote from the sphere of the strictly fundamental interests of their nation.

One chief aspect in the portrayal of epic characters is their self-disclosure as whole men in the greatest variety of scenes and situations. The tragic and comic figures of drama may also have a like wealth of inner life, but in their case the chief thing is the sharp conflict between an always one-sided 'pathos' and an opposing passion within quite limited spheres and aims; and consequently such many-sidedness of character is an incidental wealth if not a superfluous one or it is outweighed by the *one* passion and its grounds, ethical considerations, etc., and in the play is pressed into the background. But epic is a totality and all its aspects are entitled to development *in extenso* and independently. For in part this is implied in the principle of the epic form as such, and in part, the epic individual, in accordance with his entire world-situation, has a right to *be* and to assert what he is and what his nature is, because he lives in times to which precisely this *being*, this immediate individuality, belongs. Of course in relation to the wrath of Achilles moral pedants may very well ask us to consider what trouble this wrath produced and what damage it did, and then to draw an inference fatal to the excellence and greatness of Achilles on the ground that he could not be perfect either as hero or man when on the occasion of his wrath he had not self-mastery enough to modify the strength of his feeling. But Achilles is not to be blamed, and we need not excuse his wrath at all on the score of his other great qualities: the point is that Achilles is the man that he *is*, and with that, so far as epic goes, the matter is at an end. The same is to be said of his ambition and desire for fame. For the chief right of these great characters consists in the energy of their self-accomplishment, because in their particular character they still carry the universal, while, conversely, commonplace moralizing persists in not respecting the particular personality and in putting all its energy into this disrespect. Was it not a tremendous sense of self that raised Alexander above his friends and the life of so many thousands? Revenge, and even a trace of cruelty, are part of the same energy in heroic times, and even in this respect Achilles, as an epic character, should not be given moral lectures as if he were a schoolboy.

(ββ) Now precisely because these chief epic figures are whole and entire individuals who brilliantly concentrate in themselves those traits of national character which otherwise are separately dispersed, and who on this account remain great, free, and humanly beautiful characters, they acquire the right to be put at the head of affairs and to see the chief event conjoined with their individual selves. The nation is concentrated in them into a living individual person and so they fight for the national enterprise to its end, and suffer the fate that the events entail. For example, in Tasso's *Jerusalem Delivered*, although Godfrey of Bouillon is chosen to be commander of the whole army on the strength of his being the wisest, bravest, and most just of the Crusaders, he is no such outstanding figure as Odysseus or Achilles, this entire Greek spirit in its bloom of youth. The Achaeans cannot win when Achilles retires from the fight; by his defeat of Hector he alone conquers Troy. And in Odysseus' journey home there is mirrored the return of *all* the Greeks from Troy, with only this difference that in what *he* has to endure there is exhaustively portrayed the whole of the sufferings, circumstances, and views on life involved in this experience. On the other hand, characters in drama do not thus appear as in themselves the absolute head of the whole [national character] which is objectified in them; on the contrary, they are rather self-concentrated on the purpose they adopt either from their own character or from specific principles which have grown into their more solitary individual personality.

(γγ) A third aspect of epic individuals may be deduced from the fact that what epic has to describe is not an action as such, but an event. In drama what is all-important is that the individual shall actually be working for his end and shall be presented precisely in this activity and its consequences. Undisturbed concern for realizing one end disappears in epic. Here indeed the heroes may have wishes and ends of their own, but the chief thing is not the devotion of activity to their own end but what meets them in their pursuit of it. The circumstances are just as effective as their activity, and often more effective. For example, his return to Ithaca is the actual design of Odysseus. The Odyssey not only shows him to us in the actual achievement of his specific aim but relates, and develops in full detail, what he encounters in his wanderings, what he suffers, what hindrances are put in his way, what dangers he has to overcome, and how he is agitated. All these experiences are not, as would be necessary in drama, the result of one action, but occur as incidents in the journey mostly without the hero's contributing anything to them. After his adventures with the lotus-eaters, Polyphemus, and the Laestrygones, the divine Circe delays him with her for a year; next, after visiting the underworld and suffering shipwreck, he stays with Calypso until his homesickness makes him tired of the girl and with tearful eyes he looks out over the unharvested sea. At last Calypso herself gives him the materials for the boat he builds and equips him with food, wine, and clothes; she cares for him right well and bids him a friendly good-bye. In the end, after his stay with the Phaeacians, he is brought sleeping and unawares to the shores of his island. This way of achieving an aim would not be appropriate in drama.—In the Iliad again, the wrath of Achilles is the occasion for all that follows and is the particular subject-matter of the epic narrative, yet from the very start it is not a purpose or aim at all but a situation: Achilles is insulted and he flies into a passion; there is nothing of drama about this at all, for on the contrary he withdraws into inactivity and stays with Patroclus beside the ships on the shore, resenting the insult given him by the leader of the folk; then follow the consequences of this withdrawal, and not until his friend is slain by Hector is Achilles seen vigorously involved in the action. In a different way again, the end that Aeneas is to accomplish is prescribed to him, and Virgil then relates all the events which in so many ways delayed its achievement.

(γ) We have now still to mention a third important aspect of the form that an event takes in epic. Earlier I said that in drama the inner will, with its demands and intentions, is the essential determinant and permanent foundation of everything that goes on. The things that happen appear to be entirely the result of a character and his aims, and accordingly the chief interest turns principally on the justification, or the reverse, of the action performed within the presupposed situations and the resulting conflicts. Therefore even if in drama external circumstances are operative, they still can only count through what the will and the mind make of them and the manner in which a character reacts to them. But in epic, circumstances and external accidents count just as much as the character's will, and what he achieves passes before us just as what happens from without does, so that his deed must prove to be conditioned and brought about just as much by his entanglement in external circumstances. For in epic the individual does not act freely for himself and out of his own resources; on the contrary, he stands in the midst of a whole nation whose aim and existence in a widely correlated inner and outer world provides the immovable and actual foundation for every particular individual. This type of character with all its passions, decisions, and achievements must always be preserved in epic. Now when equal worth is given to external circumstances with their attendant accidents independent of the individual, it seems that indisputable playroom is given to that vein of accident, yet what epic should present to us is what is genuinely objective, i.e. the fundamental substance of existence. We can meet this contradiction at once by pointing out that *necessity* lies at the heart of events and happenings.

(αα) In this sense we can maintain that what rules in epic, though not, as is commonly supposed, in drama, is fate. In drama, owing to the sort of aim which a character is determined to carry out in given and known circumstances, with all the resulting collisions, he creates his fate *himself*, whereas an epic character has his fate made for him, and this power of circumstances, which gives his deed the imprint of an individual form, allocates his lot to him, and determines the outcome of his actions, is the proper dominion of fate. What happens, happens; it is so; it happens of necessity. In lyrics, feeling, reflection, personal interest, longing can be heard;

drama turns the inner right of the action inside out and presents it objectively; but epic poetry moves in the element of an inherently necessary total state of affairs, and nothing is left to the individual but to submit to this fundamental situation, i.e. to what *is*, be it adapted to him or not, and then suffer as he may or must. Fate determines what is to happen and what happens, and just as the individuals are clay in its hands, so too are the results, his success and failure, his life and his death. For what is really presented to us is a great universal situation in which the actions and fates of men appear as something transient, merely belonging to them as individuals. This destiny is the great justice and it becomes tragic not in the dramatic sense of the word in which the individual is judged as a *person*, but in the epic sense in which the individual is judged in his whole situation; and the tragic nemesis is that the greatness of the situation is too great for the individuals. Consequently an air of mourning is wafted over the whole epic; we see excellence pass early away; even in his life Achilles laments over his death, and in the Odyssey we see him and Agamemnon as no longer living, as shades with the awareness of being shades. Troy perishes too; old Priam is murdered at the altar in his house, his wives and daughters are enslaved; Aeneas withdraws, commanded by the gods to found a new realm in Latium; and the conquering heroes return, only after manifold sufferings, to a happy or bitter end in their own homeland.

(ββ) But the ways in which this necessity underlying events is presented in epic may be very different.

The first and most undeveloped way is the mere statement of events. Here the poet does not introduce a world of gods directing affairs in order to explain more clearly the necessity implicit in individual occurrences and their general outcome by referring it to the decree, intervention, and co-operation of eternal powers. But in this case, the whole tone of the exposition must impress on us the feeling that in the narrative of events and the great destinies of the lives of single individuals and whole families we have not to do with what is only mutable and transient in human existence but with fates having their *raison d'être* in themselves; yet their necessity remains the dark working of a power which is not itself specifically individualized as *this* power in its divine dominion or presented poetically in its activity. This is throughout the tone of the *Nibelungenlied*, for example, since it ascribes the ultimate bloody issue of all deeds neither to Christian Providence nor to a heathen world of gods. For in relation to Christianity nothing at all is said except about church-going and the Mass, and what the Bishop of Spires says to the beautiful Ute when the heroes intend to move into King Etzel's country: 'May God preserve them there.' In addition, warning dreams occur, the prediction of the Danube women to Hagen, and the like, but no real direction or interference by the gods.[1] This gives the work a stiff and undeveloped appearance, a tone of mourning, objective as it were and therefore extremely epical. The Ossianic poems are a complete contrast; in them likewise no gods appear, but the lament over the death and downfall of the whole race of heroes is manifestly the subjective grief of the veteran poet and the ecstasy of melancholy recollection.

This kind of treatment is essentially different from the complete interweaving of all human fates and natural occurrences with the decree, will, and action of a world of manifold gods as we find it in, for example, the great Indian epics, in Homer, Virgil, etc. The poet's varied interpretation of apparently accidental events as the co-operation and manifestation of the gods I have already noticed and tried to illustrate by examples from the Iliad and the Odyssey.[2] Here what is especially required is that in the actions of gods and men the poetic relation of their mutual independence shall be preserved, so that neither can the gods be degraded to lifeless abstractions nor human individuals to being obedient servants. How this danger is to be averted I have also already explained at length elsewhere.[3] In this respect the Indian epic has not been able to force its way to the properly ideal relation between gods and men, because at this stage when the imagination is symbolic the human element in its free and beautiful actuality still remains repressed, and the action of human individuals either appears as an incarnation of the gods or disappears as merely something accessory or is described as an ascetic elevation into the life and power of the gods. Conversely again, in Christianity the particular personified powers, passions, and genii of men, i.e. angels etc., have for the most part too little individual independence and therefore they readily become something cold and abstract. The same is the

---

[1] The Mass, §§ 2, 13, 17. Bishop of Spires, § 25 (Eng. tr. has 'preserve their honour there'). Danube women (i.e. 'water fairies'), § 25.
[2] In Vol. I, pp. 480–1.
[3] In Vol. I, pp. 225 ff.

case in Mohammedanism. When the gods have flown from the world of nature and men, and men's minds are full of a consciousness of the prosaic order of things, then within this outlook, especially when it becomes addicted to the fabulous, it is more difficult to avoid the danger of giving a miraculous interpretation to what is absolutely accidental and indifferent in external circumstances which are only there, without an inner support and basis, as an occasion for human action and the preservation and development of the individual character. In this way the endless chain of causes and effects is broken, and the numerous links in this prosaic chain of circumstances, which cannot all be interpreted, collapse immediately into one; if this happens without necessity or inner rationality, this method of explanation, frequent for example in the Arabian Nights, is manifestly a mere play of imagination which by such inventions explains what is otherwise incredible and presents it as something possible or as having really happened.

On the other hand, in this respect too Greek poetry adheres to the most beautiful middle course, because on the lines of its whole fundamental outlook it can give to its gods, its heroes, and its men a mutually undisturbed force and freedom of independent individuality.

($\gamma\gamma$) But, especially in relation to the entire world of gods, an aspect of epic comes into view which I have indicated already, namely the contrast between primitive epics and those composed artificially in later times. This difference is most pronounced in the cases of Homer and Virgil. The stage of civilization which gave rise to the Homeric poems remains in beautiful harmony with their subject-matter, whereas in Virgil every hexameter reminds us that the poet's way of looking at things is entirely different from the world he intends to present to us, and the gods above all lack the freshness of individual life. Instead of being alive themselves and generating a belief in their existence, they are evidently *mere* inventions and external means, not capable of being taken very seriously by the poet or his hearers, although they are given a show of being taken very seriously indeed. Throughout the whole Virgilian epic we see the life of every day; and the ancient tradition, the Saga, the fairyland of poetry enters with prosaic clarity into the frame of the scientific intellect. What goes on in the *Aeneid* is similar to Livy's Roman History where ancient kings and consuls speak just as an orator in Livy's day would do in the

Roman Forum or a school of rhetoric, whereas what is retained from tradition, as oratory of ancient times, presents a violent contrast, e.g. Menenius Agrippa's fable of the belly and the members (Livy, ii. 32). But in Homer the gods hover in a magic light between poetry and actuality; they are not brought so closely to our minds that their appearance could strike us as an entirely everyday affair, and yet neither are they left so vague that they could have no living reality in our eyes. What they do can equally well be explained from the inner life of the human agents, and what compels us to believe in them is the substantive reality which is the basis of their character. This is the aspect which makes the poet take them seriously, and yet he does himself treat their form and external reality ironically. Accordingly, it seems, antiquity too believed in this external form of manifestation as only a work of art acquiring from the poet its sense and authenticity. This cheerful and human freshness of illustration whereby the gods themselves appear human and natural is a chief merit of the Homeric poems, while Virgil's divinities wander up and down within the actual course of events as coldly invented marvels and artificial machinery. In spite of his solemnity, or indeed precisely because of this solemn mien, Virgil has not escaped travesty, and Blumauer's[1] Mercury as a courier, booted and spurred, with a whip in his hand, is well enough justified. The Homeric gods do not need someone else to make them laughable: Homer's own description makes them laughable enough. For in Homer himself the gods have to laugh at the limping Hephaestus and at the ingenious net in which Mars and Venus are caught,[2] and where Venus gets a box on the ear and Mars cries out and trembles. By this naturally cheerful gaiety the poet liberates us from the external figure that he exhibits; and yet on another occasion he cancels and abandons this purely human existence while maintaining the fundamental self-necessitating power of the gods and a belief in it. I will cite one or two closer examples. The tragic episode of Dido[3] has so much modern colouring that it could fire Tasso to imitate it, even to translate some of it word for word, and nowadays it still makes the French almost ecstatic.[4] And yet how different, human, naïve,

---

[1] A. Blumauer, Austrian poet, 1755–98; *Virgils Aeneis travestirt*, 1783
[2] Odyssey, viii. 266–366 (but this denouement is not there).
[3] *Aeneid*, iv. Cf. canto xvi of *Jerusalem Delivered*.
[4] Hegel apparently knew nothing of Marlowe or Purcell.

natural, and true everything is in the stories of Circe and Calypso.[1] The same is the case with Homer's account of Odysseus' descent into the underworld[2]. This dark twilight abode of the shades appears as in a murky cloud, as a mixture of fancy and reality which grips us with marvellous magic. Homer does not make his hero descend into an actual underworld, for Odysseus himself digs a trench and pours into it the blood of the goat he has slaughtered; then he calls on the shades who have to crowd on him and tells some to drink the living blood so that they can speak to him and give him information, while others, pressing on him in their thirst for the life in the blood, he fends off with his sword. All this happens in a living way, the work of the hero himself who has none of the humility that Aeneas and Dante have. In Virgil, for example, Aeneas goes down in an ordinary way, and the steps, Cerberus, Tantalus, and the rest, acquire the look of a specifically arranged household, like items in a pedantic compendium of mythology.

This poetically manufactured material confronts us all the more as something not drawn from the subject naturally but as an artificially contrived compilation if the events narrated are already known and familiar to us from elsewhere in their own fresh form or historical reality. Examples of this are Milton's *Paradise Lost*, Bodmer's *Noachide*, Klopstock's *Messiah*, Voltaire's *Henriade*, and many others. In all these poems we cannot miss the cleft between the subject-matter and the personal reflections on which the poet draws when he describes events, persons, and situations. In Milton, for example, we always find feelings and considerations drawn from a modern imagination and the moral ideas of his day. Similarly in Klopstock we have on one side God the Father, the story of Christ, patriarchs, and angels, and, on the other side, German eighteenth-century culture and the concepts of Wolff's metaphysics. And this duality is visible in every line. Of course here the subject-matter puts many difficulties in the way. For God the Father, heaven, the heavenly host, are not so fitted for individualization by free imagination, as the Homeric gods were. Like the partly fantastic inventions in Ariosto, these Homeric gods in their external appearance are, if not essential elements in human

---

[1] Odyssey, x and v.
[2] Ibid., xi. Hegel's memory of Odysseus' first encounter with the shades is a little at fault. For Virgil, see *Aeneid*, vi.

actions, real individuals independent of one another, and yet at the same time they can make a joke of this appearance.

So far as religion is concerned, Klopstock gets into a world with no foundation which he invests with the brilliant products of a wide-roaming imagination and then he requires us to take seriously what *he* seriously means. This is at its worst with his angels and devils. Such fictions may have something solid, individual, and indigenous about them if, like the Homeric gods, the material of their actions has its basis in the human mind and sentiment or some other reality, if, for instance, they get worth as the personal genii and guardian angels of specific individuals, as patron saints of cities, etc.; but without such a concrete meaning they are signalized as mere empty imaginings, all the more so if existence is seriously ascribed to them. Abbadona, for example, the repentant devil in *The Messiah* (canto II, 627–850), is not an inherently concrete figure nor has he a strictly allegorical meaning, for in that fixed abstraction called the devil there is none of the illogicality of vice converted to virtue. If Abbadona were a man, then turning to God would clearly be justified, but in the case of the evil one, who is not an individual evil man, it remains only a sentimental moral triviality. Klopstock above all delights in such unreal inventions of persons, circumstances, and events which are not drawn from the existing world and its poetic contents. For he fares no better with his moral judgement on the licence of courts, etc.; he is a great contrast to Dante who condemns to Hell, with a quite different degree of reality, individuals well known in his day. But in Klopstock there is the same poetical unreality in the resurrection joy felt by souls assembled in God's presence, Adam, Noah, Shem, Japhet, etc., who at Gabriel's command visit their own grave again (ibid., canto XI). There is nothing rational about this and it is inherently untenable. The souls have lived in the sight of God; they now see the earth but enter into no new relation with it. The best thing would be that they should appear to men, but even this does not happen at all. In this passage there is no lack of fine feelings and delightful situations, and the description of the moment when the soul is re-embodied is attractive, but at bottom the whole thing is for us only an invention in which we do not believe. Contrasted with such abstract ideas, the blood-drinking phantoms in Homer, their return to the life of memory and speech, have infinitely more poetic truth and reality. As imaginations, these pictures of Klopstock's are richly decorated, but the most essential thing always remains the lyrical rhetoric of the angels who only appear as mere tools and servants, or the patriarchs and other biblical figures whose speeches and explosive utterances harmonize ill enough with the historical form in which we know them already from another source. Mars and Apollo, War and Wisdom, etc., these powers in their substance are neither something purely invented, like the angels, nor purely historical persons with an historical background, like the patriarchs, but abiding powers whose form and appearance is constructed by the poet alone. But *The Messiah*—whatever excellence it may contain, a pure heart and a brilliant imagination—has in it, precisely because of its sort of fancy, an endless amount that is hollow, governed by abstract categories, and dragged in for some ulterior purpose; this along with the manner of conceiving the subject and the absence of continuity, has resulted only too soon in making the whole poem obsolete. For an epic lives and is always new only if it continuously presents primitive life and work in a primitive way. Therefore we must keep to the primitive epics and disentangle ourselves not only from views antagonistic to them and current in our actual present but also, and above all, from false aesthetic theories and claims, if we wish to study and enjoy the original outlook of peoples, this great natural history of the spirit. We may congratulate recent times, and our German nation in particular, on attaining this end by breaking down the old limitations of the scientific intellect, and, by freeing the spirit from restricted views, making it receptive of such outlooks. These we must receive as those of individuals, entitled to be what they were, as the justified spirits of peoples whose mind and deeds confront us as revealed in their epics.

(c) The Epic as a Fully Unified Whole

In connection with the particular requirements for epic proper, we have discussed (i) the general world-background, (ii) the individual event proceeding on this ground, and the individuals acting under the direction of the gods or fate. These two chief features must now (iii) be closed together into one and the same epic whole, and in this connection I will touch in more detail on the following points only:

(α) the whole of the *objects* which should come into the narrative on account of the connection between the particular action and its fundamental ground;

(β) the difference between epic's way of *developing* the subject and the ways of lyric and dramatic poetry;

(γ) the concrete unity into which an epic work has to be rounded, despite the wide dispersal of its parts.

(α) The contents of the epic, as we saw, are the entirety of a world in which an individual action happens. Consequently this involves the greatest variety of topics belonging to the views, deeds, and situations of such a world.

(αα) Lyric poetry does envisage specific situations within which the lyric poet is permitted to draw a great variety of matters into his feeling and reflection; but in this kind of poetry it is always the form of the inner life which is the fundamental model and this at once excludes the detailed illustration of external reality. Conversely, the dramatic work of art presents characters to us, and the occurrence of the action itself, in actual life, so that in this case a description of the locality and the externals of the agents and the event as such is excluded from the start, and what has to come into the speeches is rather inner motives and aims than the broad connection between the agents and their world or their real situation in it. But in epic, over and above the encompassing national life on which the action is based, both inner life and outer reality have their place, and thus here there is spread out before us all the detail of what can be regarded as the poetry of human existence. In this we may include the natural environment, and, at that, not at all only as the specific place where the action proceeds from time to time but as it is viewed in its entirety, as for example, what I have already quoted, namely that from the Odyssey we can get to know how the Greeks in Homer's day visualized the earth, the encircling sea, etc. Yet these natural features are not the chief topic but the mere foundation on which the events take place. On the contrary, what is unfolded for us as more essential is the Greek idea of the entire world of gods in their existence, effectiveness, and activity and, then, in between nature and the gods, humanity enters in the entirety of its domestic and public, pacific and bellicose situations, its morals, customs, characters, and events. And the poet always directs his attention both to the individual event and also to a universal situation within national or foreign life.

Finally, within this spiritual content what is presented is not at all only the external happening; on the contrary, there should be brought before our minds the inner feelings, aims and intentions of the agents, and the exposition of the justified or unjustified individual action. Thus the proper material of lyric and dramatic poetry is likewise not absent, although in epic such matters should not provide the fundamental form of the whole narrative; they should be asserted only as occasional features, and should not strip epic of its peculiar character. Therefore it cannot be regarded as truly epical when lyrical expressions, as in Ossian for example, determine the tone and colour of the whole, or when, as happens to some extent in Tasso, but above all in Milton and Klopstock, they are pre-eminently that part in which the poet has reached the height of his actual and possible achievement. On the contrary, feelings and reflections, like external reality, must be recounted as something that has happened, been said, been thought, and must not interrupt the smoothly flowing epic tone. There is therefore no scope in epic for the heart-rending cry of passion, or the outburst of the inner soul pouring forth in song for the sake of *self-revelation* alone. Epic poetry spurns no less the life of dramatic dialogue where individuals converse on the basis of their present situation, and the chief aspect is always the characteristic interchange between the dramatis personae who try to convince, command, impress, or, as it were, run one another down with the violence of their reasoning.

(ββ) But, in the second place, the task of epic is not limited to putting before our eyes in its purely independently existing objectivity the many-sided subject-matter to which I have just referred. On the contrary, it is made an epic proper in virtue of its form, and, this, as I have said more than once already, is an *individual* event. If this necessarily limited action is to remain bound up with the material that comes in additionally from elsewhere, then this latter wider sphere must be brought into relation with the occurrence of the individual event and should not fall outside it independently. Of interweaving like this the Odyssey gives us the finest example. The domestic arrangements of the Greeks in peacetime, for instance, the pictures of foreign and barbarian peoples and countries, of the realm of the shades, etc., are so closely interwoven with the individual wanderings of Odysseus on his homeward journey and with the expedition of Telemachus in search of his father, that none of these aspects is abstracted and detached from the real event and made separately independent; nor can any of them withdraw into ineffectiveness, like the chorus in Greek tragedy which does nothing and has only universal considerations in view, but on the contrary every one of them influences the advance of events. In the same way nature and the world of gods acquire an individual and fully lively presentation, not on their own account, but only on the strength of their relation to the particular action which the gods have an obligation to direct. In this case alone can the narrative avoid appearing as a mere description of independent objects, because it recounts throughout the continuous happenings of the event which the poet has chosen as the material to unify the whole. But, on the other hand, the substantive national foundation and entirety on which the particular event moves must not be deprived of all independent existence and shown to be a servant of the event by being completely assimilated and consumed by it. Thus viewed, Alexander's expedition against the East would not be good material for a genuine epic. For this heroic deed, alike in the decision to undertake it and in its execution, rests so completely on *him*, this single individual, and is so completely borne solely by his spirit and character, that the independent position and existence, which we indicated above as necessary, is altogether denied to the national basis and to the army and its commanders. Alexander's army is his people, absolutely bound to him and at his command, purely subservient to him, not following him of its own free will. But the vitality of epic proper lies in the fact that the two chief sides, (i) the particular action and its agents, and (ii) the general world-situation, are always conciliated, and yet in this mutual relation they each preserve at the same time the independence necessary for the assertion of an existence of their own which on its own account wins and has reality.

(γγ) We have already postulated that the fundamental ground on which the subject of an epic takes place must be fruitful of collisions if an individual action is to be made to arise out of it, and we saw that this universal foundation should not come into view on its own account but only in the form of a specific event and in relation to that. It follows from this that the starting-point of the whole epic poem must be sought in this individual event. This is especially important for the situations at the beginning of the poem. Here too we may take the Iliad and the Odyssey as examples. In the former the Trojan war is the general and living accompanying background, but it comes before us only within the specific event linked with the wrath of Achilles, and so the poem begins in most beautiful clarity with the situations which stimulate the passion of the chief hero against Agamemnon. In the Odyssey there are two different situations which can provide the material for the beginning: the wanderings of Odysseus and the domestic happenings at Ithaca. Homer draws both close together because at first he relates, briefly only, that the returning hero is detained by Calypso, and then at once he passes on to Penelope's sufferings and the voyage of Telemachus. We see at one glance both what makes possible a hindrance to the return and also what this necessitates for those left at home.

(β) Secondly, from such a beginning the epic work has to proceed in a way quite different from lyric and dramatic poetry.

($\alpha\alpha$) The first thing to notice here is the breadth of separated incidents in which the epic is told. This breadth is grounded in both the content and form of the epic. We have already seen what a variety of topics there is in the completely developed epic world, whether these are connected with the inner powers, impulses, and desires of the spirit or with the external situation and environment. Since all these aspects assume the form of objectivity and a real appearance, each of them develops an independent shape, whether inner or outer, within which the poet may linger in description or portrayal, and the external development of which he may allow; whereas everything comprised in lyric is concentrated into the depths of feeling or assembled and evaporated in the universals of reflection. Along with objectivity separation is immediately given, as well as a varied wealth of diverse traits. Even in this respect in no other kind of poetry but epic is an episode given so much right to freedom almost up to the point of a seemingly unfettered independence. Yet pleasure in what is *there* objectively and in the form of actual reality may not go so far, as I have said already, as to assemble in the poem situations and phenomena which have no connection whatever with the particular action or its basis; on the contrary, even the episodes must be shown to be effective in relation to the progress of the event, even if as a hindrance to it or as an intercalary event delaying the progress of the action. Nevertheless, owing to the form of objectivity, the connection of the individual parts in the epic may be of rather a loose kind, for in the objective world the conciliation of parts (or objects) is inner and implicit, while what appears on the face of things is the independent existence of particulars. The fact that the individual parts of an epic poem lack strict unification and an emphatic bearing of one on another, and, in addition, the fact that the epic arose in its original form at an early period, provide the reason why epic lends itself, more easily than lyric and dramatic poetry do, to later additions or omissions, while on the other hand it itself takes single sagas previously polished up to a certain artistic height and ranges them as particular aspects into a new comprehensive whole.

($\beta\beta$) We turn now, secondly, to the manner in which epic poetry can be entitled to motivate the progress and course of the events. It cannot draw the reason for what happens either from a subjective mood alone or from mere individuality of character, for if it did so it would be treading on the ground proper to lyric and dramatic poetry. On the contrary, even in this respect it must keep to the form of objectivity which is what is fundamentally typical of epic. We have seen more than once already that, for the presentation of the narrative, external situations were of no less importance than the inner determinants of the individual's character. For, in epic, character and external necessity stand alongside one another with equal strength, and for this reason the epic individual can seem to yield to external circumstances without detriment to his poetic individuality. His action may seem to be the result of circumstances and these therefore appear as dominant, whereas in drama it is exclusively the individual character who produces results. In the Odyssey above all, the progress of events is almost throughout motivated in this way. The same is true of the adventures in Ariosto and in other epics which chant medieval material. The command of the gods too which destines Aeneas to be the founder of Rome, as well as the manifold accidents which defer the fulfilment of this destiny for a long time, are motivated in a way that would be wholly undramatic. The same is the case in Tasso's *Jerusalem Delivered* where, apart from the courageous resistance of the Saracens, numerous natural phenomena obstruct the aim of the Christian army. Similar examples could be drawn from almost every famous epic, because such materials for which this epic mode of presentation is possible and necessary are precisely those that the poet has to choose.

The same thing is true where the result is supposed to issue from the actual decision of individuals. Here too there must not be picked out and expressed what a character in a drama, pursuing his aim and animated exclusively by a single passion, makes of his situation and circumstances in order to assert himself against these and in the face of other individuals. On the contrary a character in epic bars this pure acting according to his subjective character as well as the outpouring of subjective moods and casual feelings, and clings conversely to circumstances and their reality, while at the same time what he is moved by must be what has absolute validity and is universally moral, etc. Homer, in particular, occasions inexhaustible reflections on this matter. For example, Hecuba's lament for Hector's death, and Achilles' for Patroclus', which, so far as the subject-matter goes, could be treated entirely lyrically, never sound other than an epic note; neither does Homer ever lapse into a dramatic style in situations that would be fit for dramatic representation, for example, the quarrel between Agamemnon and Achilles in the council of the Princes, or Hector's parting from Andromache.[1] This latter scene, to take it for an example, is one of the most beautiful things that epic poetry can ever provide. Even in Schiller's *Robbers* [act IV, sc. iv] the dialogue between Amalia and Karl, meant to be a purely lyrical treatment of the same subject, has echoes of the epic note of the Iliad. But with what marvellous epic effect in the sixth book of the Iliad does Homer describe how Hector looks for Andromache in vain in the house and only finds her on the road at the Scaean Gate, how she rushes to him, meets him, and says to him as he looks with a quiet smile at his baby boy in the nurse's arms:

You are possessed. This courage of yours will be your death. You have no pity for your little boy or for me, your unhappy wife, soon to be your widow. For soon the Achaeans will kill you as they attack *en masse*. But for me, should I lose you, death would be better. When you have met your fate, no comfort remains to me but grief. Now I have neither father nor my mother, the queen.

And now she tells in detail how the deaths of her father and her seven brothers came about—they were all slain by Achilles, and speaks of her mother's capture, release, and death. Only after this does she turn again to Hector with pressing entreaty; he is now

[1] Iliad, xxii. 431 ff.; xviii. 79 ff.; i. 59 ff.; vi. 369 ff.

her father and her mother, her brother, and her vigorous spouse; and she implores him to remain on the tower and not make his boy an orphan or her, his wife, a widow. In the same strain Hector answers her:

All this is my concern too, my wife; but I fear the ill opinion of the Trojans too much to stay here like a coward and avoid the battle. It is not the excitement of the moment that drives me, because I have learnt always to be brave, and to fight along with the Trojans in the front line, defending the great honour of my father, and my own too. Well I know in my mind and heart that the day will come when Ilium will perish and Priam too and the people of Priam of the skilful spear. But not for the Trojans do I care so much, or for Hecuba herself and King Priam, or for my noble brothers who will bite the dust at the hands of the enemy, as for you if you are dragged away in tears by one of the brazen-tuniced Achaeans, reft of your day of freedom; if in Argos you spin at another's wheel and draw water laboriously and against your will. But the might of necessity impends, and then someone may well say, seeing you in tears: 'She is the wife of Hector. He was the best of all the horse-taming Trojans when Ilium was besieged.' Thus perhaps someone will speak, and then you will lament the loss of a man who might have averted your slavery. But may the earth cover me or ever I hear you scream as you are carried away.

What Hector says here is deeply felt and touching, but the manner is that of epic, not of lyric or drama, because the picture he sketches of his sufferings, and which gives pain to himself, in the first place portrays the purely objective circumstances, while in the second place what drives and moves him appears not as his own will or personal decision but as a necessity which is as it were *not* his own intention and will. Equally epically touching are the pleas with which the vanquished beg their lives from the conquering heroes, citing various circumstances and reasons. For a movement of the heart, proceeding from circumstances alone, and trying to move others by merely alleging circumstances and situations, is not dramatic, although modern tragedians have also now and again used this way of producing an effect. For example, the scene on the battlefield in Schiller's *Maid of Orleans* between the English knight, Montgomery, and Joan of Arc (act II, sc. vi [–vii]) is, as others have justly remarked already, rather epic than dramatic. In the hour of danger the knight loses all his courage, and yet, pressed by the exasperated Talbot who punishes cowardice with death and by the Maid who conquers even the bravest, he cannot embark on flight and cries out:

Would that I had never taken ship over the sea, miserable man that I am! An empty fancy deluded me into seeking cheap fame in the French war. And now a baleful fate leads me to this bloody battlefield. Would I were far from here, at home beside the flowery banks of Severn, safe in my father's house where my mother stayed behind in sorrow, with my tender sweet betrothed.

These are unmanly expressions which make the whole figure of the knight unsuitable for either epic proper or tragedy; they are more indicative of comedy. When Joan cries out to him: 'Thou art to die! A British mother bore thee!', he flings away his sword and shield, falls at her feet and begs for his life. To move her, he cites reasons at some length: he is defenceless; his father is rich and will give gold for his ransom; the gentleness of the sex to which Joan belongs; the love of his sweet betrothed who in tears at home awaits the return of her beloved; the grief-stricken parents whom he left at home; the hard fate of dying unwept in a foreign land. On the one hand, all these reasons concern inherently objective matters which have their worth and validity; on the other hand, their calm exposition is epical in character. In the same way the poet accounts for the fact that Joan has to listen to him by an external consideration, namely that the suppliant is defenceless, whereas if the incident had been taken in a dramatic way she would have had to kill him on the spot without hesitation because she appears as the relentless enemy of all Englishmen; this hatred, fraught with disaster, she expresses with a great deal of rhetoric, and she justifies it by claiming that she is morally bound to the spiritual realm by a frightfully stringent compact 'to slay with the sword everyone whom the God of battles dooms and sends to her for execution'. If the only thing of importance to her were that Montgomery should not die unarmed, then since she had listened to him for so long he had in his hands the best means of remaining alive: all he needed to do was not to take up his arms again. Yet when she summons him to fight with her, mortal herself, for the sweet prize of life, he grasps his sword again and falls by her arm. The progress of this scene would have been better fitted for drama if the lengthy epic explanations had been omitted.

($\gamma\gamma$) Thirdly, the sort of course which events take in epic poetry, in relation both to the breadth of external material necessary for more detailed illustration and also to the steps preceding the final result of the action, may be characterized in general, especially in contrast to dramatic poetry, as follows. Epic poetry not only lingers over the portrayal of external reality and inner situations but in addition puts *hindrances* in the way of the final denouement. Therefore it especially turns aside in many ways from the execution of the main purpose, of which with its logically developing conflict the dramatic poet may never lose sight, and this gives it an opportunity to bring to our view the entirety of a world of situations which could not otherwise be brought on the tapis. For example, with such a general hindrance the Iliad begins: Homer at once tells of the deadly plague which has broken out in the Greek camp by Apollo's influence, and then joins with it the quarrel between Achilles and Agamemnon. This wrath is the second hindrance. More strikingly still, in the Odyssey every adventure that Odysseus has to endure is a postponement of his return home. But it is especially *episodes* which serve to interrupt the direct progress of affairs, and these are for the most part of the character of hindrances: take, for example, in Virgil, the shipwreck of Aeneas and his love for Dido, and in Tasso the appearance of Armida; and, in the romantic epic in general, the many independent love-affairs of the individual heroes, which in Ariosto are piled up and interwoven in such variety and profusion that the battle between the Christians and the Saracens is wholly hidden under them. In Dante's *Divine Comedy* there are no express hindrances to the proceedings, but the slow advance of the story, as in epic, is present partly in the halt of the description at every step throughout, and partly in many small episodic stories and conversations with individuals damned or otherwise, of which the poet makes a more detailed report.

In this matter it is above all important that such hindrances obstructing a hurried approach to the final goal must not be made to seem merely means used to attain some end external to them. For, just as the general situation, the ground on which the epic world lives, is only truly poetic if it seems to be self-made, so the whole course of events, in virtue of the circumstances and the original fate, must arise as it were out of itself, without our being able to detect in it any subjective intentions of the poet. This is all the more the case because the very form of objectivity in respect alike of what really appears and of the substantive character of the content, assigns to the whole and to the individual parts a title to exist spontaneously in and by themselves. But if a world of gods is at the apex of everything, directing affairs and with the control of events in their hands, then in this case the poet himself must have a fresh and lively belief in the gods, because it is usually the gods who introduce such hindrances. Consequently, if these powers are treated only as lifeless machinery, what they effect must also be degraded to an intentional and merely artificial creation of the poet.

(γ) After briefly touching on the entirety of the subject-matter which epic can unfold by interweaving a particular event with a universal national situation, we next proceeded to the manner in which the course of events was developed. We have now still to ask, in the third place, about the unity and rounded whole of an epic work.

(αα) This is a point which, as I have indicated already, is all the more important today because currency has recently been given to the idea that an epic can be made to end anywhere or may be continued at will. Although this view has been defended by able and learned men like F. A. Wolf,[1] for example, it nevertheless remains excessively crude because in fact it means nothing but denying to the most beautiful epic poems the proper status of works of art. For an epic is only a work of free art at all by describing a whole world perfect in itself and only for this reason independent, a world distinct from dispersed actuality trailing along in an endless course of dependent causes, effects, and consequences. It is true that this much may be granted, i.e. that, in the case of epic proper (an original one), a purely aesthetic criticism of the plan, the organization of the parts, the placing and wealth of episodes, the sort of similes, etc., is not the chief thing, because here, to a greater extent than in later lyrics and the later skilful development of drama, the preponderating aspect must be claimed by the general outlook, the religious faith, and, in short, the wealth of content in these national bibles. Nevertheless, however, national bibles like the *Ramayana*, the Iliad and Odyssey, and even the *Nibelungenlied*, are not to be denied the possession of what, from the point of view of beauty and art, can alone confer on them the dignity and

[1] 1759–1824. His *Prolegomena ad Homerum* was published in 1795, his commentary on the Iliad later.

freedom of works of art, namely the fact that they bring before our contemplation a rounded entirety of action. It is therefore alone necessary to discover what form this finished character takes in conformity with the nature of art.

(ββ) 'Unity' taken in an entirely general sense of the word has become trivial, even in its application to tragedy, and it can lead people astray into its frequent misuse. For every event is prolonged *ad inf.* backwards in its causes and forwards in its consequences, and it extends into both past and future in a chain of particular circumstances and actions so innumerable that there is no determining which of all the situations and other details are part and parcel of the event or are to be regarded as connected with it. If all that we have in mind is this *sequence*, then it is true that an epic can always be continued backwards or forwards and in addition it affords an ever open opportunity for interpolation. But such a succession is simply prosaic. To quote an example, the Greek cyclic poets sang the entire compass of the Trojan war and therefore continued from where Homer left off and began from Leda's egg; but precisely for this reason they were a contrast to the Homeric poems and became rather prosy. Neither, as I said above, can one individual as such provide the sole centre because he may be the agent of all sorts of occurrences, or he may encounter them, without their being brought into connection with one another as a single event. Therefore we must look for another kind of unity.

In this regard we must settle briefly the difference between a mere happening and a specific action which is narrated in epic in the form of an event. What is to be called a mere happening is the external and objectively real aspect of any human deed (without its needing to be in itself the execution of some particular purpose), or, in short, any external alteration in the form and appearance of what exists objectively. If lightning kills a man, this is a mere happening, an external accident; but in the conquest of an enemy's city there is something else, namely the fulfilment of an intended aim. An inherently determinate aim, such as the liberation of the Holy Land from the yoke of the heathen and the Saracens, or, better still, the satisfaction of a particular passion like the wrath of Achilles, must, in the shape of an epic event, form the cohering unity of the epic, because the poet relates only what is the proper effect of this self-conscious aim or this specific passion and what therefore together with the aim or purpose is rounded into a perfectly enclosed unity. But man alone can act and carry out his purpose, and therefore at the summit there is an individual united with his aim and passion. Moreover, the action and the satisfaction of the heroic character, from whom the aim and the passion spring, occur only in quite specific situations and causes which run backwards as links in a wide chain of connection, while, again, the execution of the aim has all sorts of subsequent consequences. If all this be so, then of course it follows that for the specific action there are numerous presuppositions and numerous after-effects, but these have no closer poetic connection with the specific character of just this aim that is portrayed.

In this sense the wrath of Achilles, for example, is as little related to the rape of Helen or the judgement of Paris, although each of these presupposes its predecessor, as it is to the actual taking of Troy. Therefore, when it is maintained that the Iliad has no necessary beginning or appropriate end, this is only evidence of an absence of any clear insight into the fact that it is the wrath of Achilles which is to be sung in the Iliad and to provide the unifying point. If the figure of Achilles is kept firmly in view and adduced, in respect of the wrath aroused by Agamemnon, as the support that holds the whole narrative together, then we see that no finer beginning and end could be invented. For, as I said before, it is the immediate occasion for the wrath that is the beginning, while its consequences are contained in the further course of the narrative. But, if so, it is then urged by those who have tried to make a contrary view prevail that the final books are useless and might as well have been omitted. But in face of the whole poem this view is wholly untenable: for when Achilles stays by the ships and abstains from the battle, this is a consequence of his indignant wrath; with this inactivity there is linked the quickly won success of the Trojans over the Greek army, as well as the fight and death of Patroclus: closely bound up with this fall of his courageous friend there follow the noble Achilles' lament and revenge and his victory over Hector. If someone supposes that all is at an end with Hector's death and that now everyone can go home, this is only evidence of how crude his ideas are. With death nature is at an end, but not man, not moral principle and the ethical order which demands the honour of burial for the fallen heroes. Accordingly there are added to all the foregoing the games at the grave of Patroclus, the harrowing pleas of Priam, Achilles' reconciliation with him, his returning to him the corpse of his son [Hector] so that Hector too may not lack the honour given to the dead—all this provides a most beautiful and satisfying ending.

(γγ) But while, in the way mentioned, we propose to make a specific and individual action proceeding from known aims or heroic passions the thing in which the entire epic is to find support for its connection and finished character, it may seem that we are shifting the unity of an epic too nearly to that of a drama. For in drama too *one* particular action springing from a man's character and his self-conscious aim and involving conflict is central. In order that the two kinds of poetry, epic and dramatic, may not be confused, even only seemingly, I may refer expressly once again to what I have said already about the difference between an action and an event. Apart from this, the interest in epic is not merely restricted to these characters, aims, and situations founded in the particular action narrated as such in the epic; on the contrary this action finds the further occasion for conflict and its resolution, as well as its entire progress, only within a national whole and its fundamental entirety which on its side fully justifies the introduction of a variety of characters, situations, and occurrences into the narrative. Thus viewed, the rounding off and the finished shape of the epic lies not only in the particular content of the specific action but just as much in the entirety of the world-view, the objective realization of which the epic undertakes to describe; and the unity of the epic is in fact only perfect when there is brought before us in all their entirety not only the particular action as a closed whole in itself but also, in the course of the action, the total world within the entire circumference of which it moves; and when nevertheless both these principal spheres remain in a living conciliation and undisturbed unity.

These are the most essential points which can be briefly established in connection with epic proper.

But the same form of objectivity is applied to other things, the substance of which lacks genuine objectivity in the true meaning of the word. Such collateral kinds [of composition] may plunge the philosopher into perplexity if he is required to produce classifications into which all poems are to be fitted without any overlap—and everything included in these mixed kinds is supposed to be poetry. However, in a true classification a place can only be given to what accords with an essential category of the nature of the thing being classified; but anything imperfect in form or content or both is not what it ought to be and precisely for this reason cannot readily be brought under the essential nature of its field, i.e. under the specific category defining what a thing ought to be and, in truth, actually is. As an appendix, in conclusion, I will add a little about such subordinate collateral branches of epic proper.

The chief of these is the idyll, in the modern sense of the word. In this sense it disregards all the deeper general interests of the spiritual and moral life and portrays mankind in its state of innocence. But in this context to live 'innocently' only means to know of nothing except eating and drinking, and indeed of none but very simple foods and drinks, e.g. the milk of goats and sheep, and, at a pinch, cows; vegetables, roots, acorns, fruit, cheese made from milk; bread, I suppose, is really post-idyllic, but meat must be allowed earlier because shepherds and shepherdesses will not have wished to sacrifice their sheep whole to the gods. Their occupation consists in tending their beloved flock the whole livelong day with their faithful dog, providing their food and drink, and all the time nursing and cherishing, with as much sentimentality as possible, such feelings as do not disturb this peaceful and contented life; i.e. in being pious and gentle in their own way, blowing on their shawms, scrannel-pipes, etc., singing in chorus, and especially in making love to one another with the greatest tenderness and innocence. On the other hand, the Greeks in their plastic productions had a merrier world, Bacchus and his train, satyrs, fauns who, harmlessly courting a god's favour, raised animal nature to human joviality with a life and truth quite different from that pretentious idyllic innocence, piety, and vacuity. The same essence of an animated outlook on the world, illustrated in lively examples of national life, may be recognized in the Greek bucolic poets too, for example in Theocritus, whether he lingers over contemporary situations in the life of herdsmen and fishermen or carries over to other subjects his mode of expressing that life or another like it and now either describes such pictures of life epically or treats them in a lyric or dramatic way. Virgil in his Eclogues is colder, but the most wearisome of all is Gessner. Hardly anyone reads him nowadays and it is only remarkable that he was at any time so much to the taste of the French that they could regard him as the supreme German poet. But their French sensibility, which fled from the tumult and complications of life while nevertheless desiring movement of some kind, and also the fact that they were perfectly void of all true interests, so that the other disturbing concerns of our culture have had no impact on them, may both have made their contribution to this preference.

Amongst these hybrid kinds we can include, from a different sphere, those half-descriptive, half-lyrical poems beloved of the English, and taking nature, the seasons, etc. especially as their subject. To this group of hybrids there also belong various didactic poems, compendiums of physics, astronomy, medicine, chess, fishing, and the art of love. The prosaic subject-matter is given a decorative border of poetry, as was already done in later Greek poetry and later still in Roman; and this sort of thing has been most ingeniously elaborated in modern times especially by the French. Despite their generally epic tone they may equally easily succumb to a lyrical treatment.

More poetic, it is true, though without constituting a fixed and different species, are the Romaunts and ballads produced in medieval and modern times: their subject-matter is partly epic, but the treatment is mainly lyrical, so that some could be classed as epic and others as lyric.

But it is quite different with romance, the modern popular epic. Here we have completely before us again the wealth and many-sidedness of interests, situations, characters, relations involved in life, the wide background of a whole world, as well as the epic portrayal of events. But what is missing is the *primitive* poetic general situation out of which the epic proper proceeds. A romance in the modern sense of the word presupposes a world already prosaically ordered; then, on this ground and within its own sphere whether in connection with the liveliness of events or with individuals and their fate, it regains for poetry the right it had lost, so far as this is possible in view of that presupposition. Consequently one of the commonest, and, for romance, most appropriate, collisions is the conflict between the poetry of the heart and the opposing prose of circumstances and the accidents of external situations; this is a conflict resolved whether comically or tragically, or alternatively it is settled either (i) when the characters originally opposed to the usual order of things learn to recognize in it what is substantive and really genuine, when they are reconciled with their circumstances and effective in them, or (ii) when the prosaic shape of what they do and achieve is stripped away, and therefore what they had before them as prose has its place taken by a reality akin and friendly to beauty and art. So far as presentation goes, the romance proper, like the epic, requires the entirety of an outlook on the world and life, the manifold materials and contents of which come into appearance within the individual event that is the centre of the whole. But in the more detailed treatment and execution here all the more scope may be given to the poet the less he can avoid bringing into his descriptions the prose of real life, though without for that reason remaining himself on the ground of the prosaic and the commonplace.

3. *The Historical Development of Epic Poetry*

If now we look back over the manner in which we have considered the other arts, we viewed the different stages of the artistic spirit in *architecture* all the time in their historical development in symbolic, classical, and romantic architecture. But we maintained for *sculpture* that Greek sculpture, which coincides absolutely with the whole conception of this *classical* art, is the real centre from which we developed its particular characteristics, so that a detailed historical treatment did not need to be very extensive. The same sort of thing, so far as its character as a *romantic* art goes, is true of *painting* which yet, owing to the nature of its subject and the mode of its presentation, expands into an equally important development in different countries and schools, so that here a greater wealth of historical notes was necessary. This requirement could after all be made in the case of *music*, but since I have no detailed acquaintance of my own with the history of this art and have not had the ground prepared for me in a useful way by others, I had no alternative but to insert a few historical indications as opportunity offered. So far as epic poetry, our present topic, is concerned, it is in more or less the same case as sculpture. Epic's mode of presentation ramifies into numerous species and collateral species and occurs extensively in many epochs and amongst many peoples, but we have come to know it in its perfect form as epic proper and found epic proper actualized in the most artistically adequate way by the Greeks. For epic in general is inwardly most akin to the plasticity of sculpture, and its objectivity, in virtue of both its substantial content and the fact that what it portrays has the form of objective appearance. Consequently we should not regard it as a matter of accident that epic poetry and sculpture both appeared in Greece in this original and unsurpassed perfection. But both before and after this culminating point there are stages of development not at all subordinate in kind or negligible, but necessary for epic, because the sphere of poetry includes every nation, and epic brings to our view precisely the substantial kernel of a nation's life. It follows that the development of world-history is of more importance here than it is in the case of sculpture.

Therefore for the entirety of epic poetry and more particularly of individual epics we can distinguish the three chief stages constitutive of the development of art as a whole:

(*a*) the oriental epic with the symbolic type as its centre;

(*b*) the classical epic of the Greeks, and its imitation by the Romans;

(*c*) the rich and many-sided development of romantically-epic poetry amongst the Christian peoples who yet first came on the scene in their Germanic heathenism. Nevertheless, apart from the properly medieval poems of chivalry, antiquity returned in a different sphere partly as generally promoting culture by purifying taste and the manner of portrayal, partly more directly by being used as a model. Finally, the romance takes the place of epic proper.

Now that I am passing on to mention individual epic works of art, I can only emphasize what is of most importance and, in general, I will not give to this whole section more space than is enough for a fleeting and sketchy survey, whatever that may be worth.

(*a*) *The Oriental Epic*

In the East, as we have seen, poetry generally is rather primitive because it always keeps closer to viewing things in terms of the substantive whole and to the absorption of the individual consciousness in this one whole; the result is that, so far as the particular species of poetry are concerned, the individual cannot work his way through to that independence of personal character and its aims (with the collisions that these involve) which the genuine development of dramatic poetry imperatively demands. Therefore, in essence, what we encounter here is limited to poems that have to be included in the epic class, apart from lyrics that are either charming, delicate, and perfumed, or aspirations to the *one* ineffable god. Nevertheless epics proper are to be found only in India and Persia, but then in colossal proportions.

(α) The Chinese, on the contrary, have no national epic. For insuperable obstacles are put in the way of the highest class of epic from the very start by the fundamentally prosaic outlook of the Chinese, which gives to the earliest beginnings of history the matter-of-fact form of a prosaically ordered historical life, as well as religious ideas incompatible with any really artistic formulation. What in substitution we find elaborated in plenty are later tiny stories and long spun-out novels which must astonish us by their vivid illustration of all sorts of situations, by their precise revelation of private and public affairs, by the variety, delicacy, often indeed the attractive tenderness, of characters, especially female ones, as well as by the whole art of these finished works.

(β) An utterly opposite world is opened up for us in the Indian epics. To judge from the little so far made known to us from the Vedas, the earliest religious views of the Indians already contained the fruitful germ of a mythology describable in epic; this then ramifies after all into heroic human deeds (many centuries B.C.— the chronological details are still very much in the balance) and it is worked into actual epics which yet still stand half on religious ground and only half at the level of poetry and art. Above all, the two most famous of these poems, the *Ramayana* and the *Mahabharata*, explain to us the entire outlook of the Indians in its whole splendour and magnificence, its confusion, fantastic flabbiness and lack of real truth, and yet, on the other hand, its overwhelming delightfulness and also the individual fine traits of the feeling and heart of these spiritual but plant-like beings. These saga-like human deeds are expanded into the actions of incarnate gods, whose action hovers vaguely between divine and human nature, and individual figures and deeds are no longer limited but enlarged and expanded immeasurably. The substantive foundations of the whole thing are of such a kind that our Western outlook can neither be really at home there nor sympathize with it because we cannot resolve to abandon the higher demands of freedom and ethical life. The unity of the particular parts [of these Indian epics] is very loose, and extremely extensive episodes come on the scene with histories of the gods, stories of ascetic penances and the power thence won, spun out expositions of philosophic doctrines and systems, and all sorts of other things so unconnected with the whole that we are bound to suppose that there have been later additions here and there; but the spirit which has produced these enormous poems gives evidence throughout of an imagination which not only preceded a prosaic social organization but is absolutely incapable of the prosaic circumspection of the intellect. It could give shape only in primitive poetry to the fundamental tendencies of the Indian mind collected together as an inherently total conception of the world. On the other hand, the later epics, called *Puranas*[1] in the stricter sense of the word Purana, i.e. poems of bygone times, seem to be the same sort of thing that we find in the post-Homeric or cyclic poets. Everything concerned with the cycle of myths about a specific god is arranged seriatim prosaically and dryly in these epics and they start from the origin of the world and the gods, and, as they proceed, come down to genealogies of human heroes and princes. In the end, on the one hand, the epic kernel of the old myths is dissolved into thin air and into the artificial adornment of an external poetic form and diction, while on the other hand the imagination that dreamily indulges in miracles becomes a sapient fabulism with the principal task of teaching morality and worldly wisdom.

(γ) We may put together in a third group of oriental epic poets, the Hebrews, Arabs, and Persians.

(αα) The sublimity of the Jewish imagination contains many elements of primitive epic poetry in its idea of the creation, in the stories of the patriarchs, the wanderings in the wilderness, the conquest of Canaan, and in the further course of national events, along with vigorous illustration and a treatment that is true to nature. Yet in all this the religious interest prevails so strongly that what we have, instead of epic proper, are sagas and histories told in religious poetry, or only narratives meant to teach religion.

(ββ) But from the very beginning the Arabs have been naturally poetic and from early times onwards have had real poets. The lyrically told songs of the heroes, the Mu'allaqat,[2] which

---

[1] These belong to the Christian era and might be as late as *c.* A.D. 800. In any case, they are apparently some centuries later than the two great epics.

[2] *Collections*, i.e. the earliest collection of pre-Islamic poems, compiled by Hammad al Rawiya in the eighth-century A.D.

partly stem from the last century before Mohammed, describe now with brusque and striking boldness and conspicuous impetuosity, now with calm reflection and gentle tenderness, the primitive situation of the still heathen Arabs: the honour of the clan, the fervour of revenge, hospitality, love, thirst for adventures, benevolence, sorrow, melancholy—all this is described with undiminished force and with traits that may recall the romantic character of Spanish chivalry. Here, for the first time in the East, we have real poetry, without either prose or fantasticalness, without mythology, without gods, devils, genii, fairies and other Eastern beings, but instead with solid and independent individuals; and the whole is humanly real and firmly self-contained, even if play is made with images and comparisons that are queer and eccentric. A view of a similar heathen world is given to us also by the later collection of poems called the *Hamasa* as well as by the so far unpublished Divan of the Hudsilites.[1] But after the wide and successful conquests of the Mohammedan Arabs, this original heroic character is gradually effaced and in the course of centuries was replaced in the sphere of epic poetry partly by instructive fables and cheerful proverbs, partly by those fairy-tale narratives that we find in the Arabian Nights, or by those adventures of which Rückert has given us a picture, deserving of the highest applause, in his translation of the Mu'allaqat of Hariri [1054–1121], where the poet plays equally wittily and ingeniously with assonance, rhyme, sense, and meaning.

(γγ) The flower of Persian poetry, on the other hand, falls into the period of the new civilization introduced when Mohammedanism transformed the Persian language and the nation. But just at the beginning of this most beautiful blossoming we encounter an epic poem which at least in its subject-matter takes us back to the remotest past of the ancient Persian sagas and myths, and presents us with a narrative proceeding all through the heroic ages right down to the last days of the Sassanids. This comprehensive work, derived from the Bastanama, is the *Shahnama* of Firdausi, the gardener's[1] son from Tus. Yet we cannot call even this poem an epic proper because it does not have as its centre an individually

---

[1] Hegel is relying here on F. Rückert's translation of the *Hamasa* and on information from him about the poems now transliterated 'Hudhaylites'.

[2] Landowner, not gardener (A. J. Arberry, *Classical Persian Literature*, London 1958, p. 43. Arberry adds that Firdausi's chief source was the prose Shahnama of Abu Mansur. 'Bastanama' may therefore be a doubtful transliteration.)

self-enclosed action. With the lapse of centuries there is no fixed costume in either period or locality and, in particular, the oldest mythical figures and murkily confused traditions hover in a fantastic world, and they are so vaguely expressed that we often do not know whether we have to do with individuals or whole clans, while on the other hand actual historical figures appear again. As a Mohammedan, the poet had more freedom in the treatment of his material, yet precisely on account of this freedom he lacked that firmness in individual pictures which distinguished the original Arabian songs of the heroes, and owing to his distance from the long disappeared world of the sagas he lacks that fresh air of immediate life which is absolutely indispensable in a national epic. In its further sequel the epic art of Persia went on into love-epics of great tenderness and a lot of sweetness, in which Nisami [1141–1202] especially became famous. Alternatively, with a rich experience of life, it turned to being didactic, where the far-travelled Saadi [1184–1291] was a master, and eventually was buried in the pantheistic mysticism which Jalal-ed-Din Rumi taught and recommended in stories and legendary narrations.

These brief indications must suffice here.

(b) *The Classical Epic of Greece and Rome*

Greek and Roman poetry now takes us for the first time into the truly epic world of art.

(α) Amongst these epics there belong those that I have already put at the top—the Homeric ones.

(αα) Whatever may be said to the contrary, each of these poems is such a perfect, definite, and finely conceived whole that the view that they were both composed and continued by a series of rhapsodists, seems to me to be merely giving these works their due praise for being absolutely national and factual in their whole tone of presentation and so finished in all their individual parts that each part might appear to be a whole in itself.

While in the East the substantive and universal character of the outlook absorbs, symbolically or didactically, individual characters and their aims and histories and therefore leaves the articulation and unity of the whole both vague and loose, we find in the Homeric poems for the first time a world hovering beautifully between the universal foundations of life in the ethical order of family, state, and religious belief, and the individual personal character; between spirit and nature in their beautiful equipoise; between intended action and external outcome; between the national ground of undertakings and the intentions and deeds of individuals; and even if individual heroes appear predominant on the score of their free and living movement, this is so modified again by the specific character of their aims and the seriousness of their fate that the whole presentation must count for us as the supreme achievement of what we can enjoy and love in the sphere of epic. For even the gods who oppose or aid these primitive human, brave, upright, and noble heroes we must recognize in their proper significance, and in the shape of their appearance we are bound to be satisfied by the utter naïveté of an art which smiles cheerfully at their humanly shaped divine figures.

($\beta\beta$) The cyclic poets who followed Homer deserted this genuinely epic portrayal more and more; on the one hand, they split up the entirety of the national outlook into its particular spheres and tendencies; and on the other hand, instead of keeping to the poetic unity and completeness of one individual action, they clung rather to the completeness of the occurrences from the beginning to the end of the event, or to the unity of a person. The result was that epic poetry was given an historical tendency and became assimilated to the work of the pre-Herodotean chroniclers.

($\gamma\gamma$) Later epic poetry, after Alexander the Great's time, turns in part to the narrower sphere of bucolic poetry, and in part produced both epics that were not so much really poetic as pedantic and artificial and also didactic poems. These, like everything else in this sphere, lack in an increasing degree the naïve freshness and animation of the original epics.

(β) This characteristic with which the Greek epic ends is dominant in Rome from the beginning. Therefore we look in vain here for an epic bible like the Homeric poems, despite recent attempts to resolve the beginnings of Roman history into national epics.[1] On the contrary, alongside the artistic epic proper, of which the *Aeneid* remains the finest example, the historical epic and the didactic poem were there from early times as a proof that the

---

[1] The first volume of Niebuhr's Roman History was published in 1811 and Hegel is probably referring to this. In Niebuhr's hands 'the tale which our fathers had believed on the authority of Livy sank to the level of a myth, the invention of a poet' (E. A. Freeman's review of Mommsen's History).

Romans were especially suited to the development of that sphere of poetry which was already half prosaic, as after all it was satire that they brought to perfection as the kind of poetry native to them.

(c) *The Romantic Epic*

Consequently a new breath and spirit could enter epic poetry only through the outlook, religious faith, deeds, and fates of *new* peoples. This is the case with the Germanic peoples, both in their origin when they were still heathen and also later after their conversion to Christianity, as well as with the Latin ones. This new epic poetry became all the richer the further these national groups ramified and the more manifold were the stages through which the principle of Christendom and its outlook developed. But this spreading in so many directions, and its intricacy, place great difficulties in the way of a brief review and therefore I will confine myself here to mentioning only the following points about the main tendencies.

(α) In a first group we may include all the poetic remains which have survived from the pre-Christian days of these new peoples, for the most part in oral tradition and therefore not unimpaired.

In this group it is principally the poems commonly ascribed to Ossian that are to be numbered. Although famous English critics like Dr. Johnson and Shaw[1] have been blind enough to pretend that these poems are a bungled work of Macpherson himself, it is nevertheless absolutely impossible for any modern poet to have created such ancient national situations and events out of his own head. In this case, therefore, primitive poems must necessarily lie at the basis of 'Ossian', even if their whole tone and the manner of conception and feeling expressed in them has often been altered in the course of many centuries and given a modern look. It is true that the age of the Ossianic poems has not been settled, but they may well have remained alive on the lips of the people for a thousand or fifteen-hundred years. In their ensemble they appear to be predominantly lyric: it is Ossian, the old blind singer and hero, who in his melancholy recollections makes the days of glory rise before him. Yet although his songs are born of grief and mourning, in

[1] William Shaw, 1749–1831. Author of a Gaelic–English Dictionary, 1780. See Boswell's *Johnson*, December 1783. Nethertheless Hegel seems to have been right. See D. S. Thomson, *The Gaelic Sources of Macpherson's 'Ossian'* (1952).

their contents they still remain epic, for even these laments are concerned with what has been. The world that has only just perished, its heroes, love-affairs, deeds, expeditions over land and sea, love, fortunes of war, fate, and death, are described in a factual and epic way, even with lyrical interruptions, very much as in Homer heroes like Achilles, Odysseus, or Diomedes speak of their deeds, exploits, and fates. Yet although heart and mind play a deeper part, the spiritual development of feeling and the whole national life has not progressed so far as it has done in Homer; what is particularly lacking is the firm plasticity of the figures and an illustration clear as daylight. For, so far as locality goes, we are referred to a northern land of storm and mist, with a murky sky and heavy clouds on which the spirits ride, or else, clad in the form of clouds, they appear to the heroes on desolate moors.— Moreover, still other old Gaelic [Celtic] bard-songs have been discovered only recently; these point not merely to Scotland and Ireland but also to Wales where bards continued to sing in unbroken succession and a great deal was registered in writing at an early date. In these poems we hear, amongst other things, of voyages to America; and Caesar's invasion is mentioned too, but the reason for it is ascribed to love for a king's daughter who returned home to England after he had seen her in Gaul. As a remarkable form of this poetry I will mention only the triads, a native construction which puts together in three parts three similar events, though they are separated in time.[1]

More famous than these poems are (i) the songs of the heroes in the older Edda, (ii) the myths with which, for the first time in this sphere, we encounter, along with the narrative of the fates of human beings, all sorts of stories about the origin, deeds, and downfall of the gods. But I have been unable to acquire a taste for these hollow longueurs, these fundamental natural symbols which yet come into the narrative with a particular human form and face,

[1] In 1801 there appeared *The Myvyrian Archaiology of Wales*, a vast compendium of early Welsh poetry and prose, mostly printed for the first time from manuscript sources. However, in additon to the medieval Welsh Triads in the volume, which are genuine and ancient, there is the so-called 'Third Series' of triads, which are spurious. At Hegel's date this series was the only one which had been translated into English, and presumably the only one of which he had information. His references to its contents are both drawn from that translation, but his version of the second is very garbled. This note I owe to Dr. Rachel Bromwich, the authority on the Welsh Triads. Hegel's knowledge of them may have been derived from an article in an English newspaper or periodical.

Thor with his hammer, the Werewolf, the terrible mead-drinker,[1] in short the wildness and murky confusion of this mythology. It is true that this whole Nordic sort of nationality is nearer to us than, for example, the poetry of the Persians or of Mohammedans generally, but to try to impress on our civilization today that this is something which should claim our own deep native sympathy and must be something national for *us*, is an attempt, however often ventured, which means overvaluing these partly misshapen and barbaric ideas and completely misconceiving the sense and spirit of our own present.

(β) When we cast a glance at the epic poetry of the Christian Middle Ages, we have above all to consider first those works which, without being directly and decisively influenced by the literature and civilization of antiquity, issued from the fresh spirit of the Middle Ages and their established Catholicism. In this we find the most varied elements providing the subject-matter of epic poems and the impetus to their production.

(αα) What I will mention briefly at first are those genuinely epic materials comprising in their subject-matter still purely *national* medieval interests, deeds, and characters. Here first mention must be made of the Cid. What this blossoming of national medieval heroism meant for the Spaniards, they have in epic form in the poem of the Cid and then they exhibited it later in more charming excellence in a succession of narrative romances with which Herder has made us acquainted in Germany.[2] It is a string of pearls, each single picture is a rounded whole in itself, and yet each is so fitted in to the other that they are ranged together into a single whole—throughout in the sense and spirit of chivalry but at the same time of Spanish nationality; rich in content and full of all sorts of interests: love, marriage, family pride, honour, and regal rule in the fight of the Christians against the Moors. This is all so epic, so plastic, that the thing itself alone is brought before us in its pure and lofty content, and yet with a wealth of the noblest human scenes in an exposition of the most magnificent deeds and at the same time in such a beautiful and

---

[1] Presumably Hymir, the frost-giant, the mead-, or beer-, drinker, of the Hymiskvitha (see, for instance, *The Poetic Edda*, tr. H. A. Bellows, New York, 1923).

[2] Late in his life Herder produced in German verse a number of the Romances of the Cid, based on a French version of the Spanish original.

attractive bouquet, that we moderns may set this alongside the most beautiful productions of antiquity.

The *Nibelungenlied* is not to be compared with the Iliad and the Odyssey, but neither does it come into comparison with this [Spanish] world which, though fragmentary, still is in its fundamental character an epic world of romance. For although in this valuable genuinely Germanic and German work there is not lacking an inner vigour and a national substantive content in relation to family, matrimonial love, vassalage, loyalty in service to a superior, and heroism, still, despite all epic breadth, the whole collision is rather tragic and dramatic than completely epic, and, despite its prolixity, the narrative never provides a wealth of individuals nor does it attain truly living vividness, and it is often lost in what is harsh, wild, and gruesome. Even if the characters appear strong and taut in their action, still in their abstract roughness they are too like crude woodcuts to be comparable with the humanly elaborated and spiritual individuality of the Homeric women and heroes.

(ββ) A second chief group consists of the medieval religious poems which take for their subject-matter the story of Christ, Mary, the Apostles, Saints, and Martyrs, the Last Judgement, etc. But the most solid and richest work in this sphere, the artistic epic proper of the Christian Catholic Middle Ages, the greatest poem and the one with the greatest material is Dante's *Divine Comedy*. We could indeed refuse to call this strictly regulated, even almost systematic, poem an epic in the ordinary sense of the word, because it has no individual rounded action proceeding on the broad basis of the whole, and yet it is precisely this epic which is least lacking in the firmest articulation and rounded completeness. Instead of a particular event it has for its subject-matter the eternal action, the absolute end and aim, the love of God in its imperishable activity and unalterable sphere, and for its locality Hell, Purgatory, and Paradise; into this changeless existent it plunges the living world of human action and suffering and, more particularly, the deeds and fates of individuals. Here, in the face of the absolute grandeur of the ultimate end and aim of all things, everything individual and particular in human interests and aims vanishes, and yet there stands there, completely epically, everything otherwise most fleeting and transient in the living world, fathomed objectively in its inmost being, judged in its worth or worthlessness by the supreme Concept, i.e. by God. For as individuals *were* in their passions and sufferings, in their intentions and their accomplishments, so now here they are presented for ever, solidified into images of bronze. In this way the poem comprises the entirety of objective life: the eternal condition of Hell, Purgatory, and Paradise; and on this indestructible foundation the figures of the real world move in their particular character, or rather they *have* moved and now in their being and action are frozen and are eternal themselves in the arms of eternal justice. While the Homeric heroes have been made permanent in *our* memories by the muse, these characters have produced their situation for *themselves*, as individuals, and are eternal in themselves, not in our ideas. The immortality created by the poet's muse[1] counts here objectively as the very judgement of God in whose name the boldest spirit of his time has pronounced damnation or salvation for the entire present and the past.—This character of the subject-matter, already independently finished, must be followed by the manner of its portrayal. This can only be a journey through realms fixed once and for all, and although they are invented, equipped, and peopled by the same freedom of imagination with which Homer and Hesiod formed their gods, still they are meant to provide a picture and a report of what has really happened: in Hell the movement is energetic but the figures are plastic and stiff in their agony, lit terrifyingly, though the picture is modified by Dante's own mournful sympathy; in Purgatory things are milder but all fully worked out and rounded off; finally, in Paradise all is clear as crystal, a region of eternal thought where external shapes are no more. There are glimpses of antiquity in the world of this Catholic poet, but antiquity is only a guiding star and a companion of human wisdom and culture, for, when it is a matter of doctrine and dogma, it is only the scholasticism of Christian theology and love which speaks.

(γγ) As a third main sphere in which medieval epic poetry moves we may cite chivalry, both in its mundane content of love-affairs and struggles for honour and also in its ramification, with religious aims, into the mysticism of Christian knighthood. The actions achieved here, and the events, do not affect any national interests; on the contrary, they are the actions of individuals with the individual himself as such as their substance; this I have described already in dealing with romantic chivalry. It is true, consequently, that the individuals stand there on their own feet, free

---

[1] *Mnemosyne*, Hegel writes, i.e. Memory, the mother of the Muses.

and fully independent, and thus, within a surrounding world not yet consolidated into a prosaic organization, they form a new group of heroes who nevertheless in their interests, whether fantastically religious or, in mundane matters, purely subjective and imaginary, lack that fundamental realism which is the basis on which the Greek heroes fight either alone or in company, and conquer or perish. No matter how various are the epic productions occasioned by this subject-matter, still the adventurous character of the situations, conflicts, and complications which can arise out of such material leads, on the one hand, to a sort of ballad treatment so that the numerous single adventures are not bound together into any strict unity; and on the other hand to something like a novel, though here the incidents do not move on the foundation of a fixedly regulated civil organization and prosaic march of events. Nevertheless the imagination is not content to invent chivalric hero-figures and adventures altogether apart from the rest of the real world, but links their deeds to great saga-centres, outstanding historical persons, and decisive battles of the period, and in this way acquires, in the most general way at least, some basis, as is indispensable for epic. But even these foundations are transferred again for the most part into the sphere of the fantastic and therefore they are not given that clearly executed objective illustration which marks out the Homeric epic above all others. Besides, the similar way in which the French, English, Germans, and, to some extent, the Spanish work out the same material lacks, relatively at least, that properly national character which is the abiding kernel of epic, both in its subject-matter and portrayal, in the case of the Indians, Persians, Greeks, Celts, etc.—But, when it comes to detail, I cannot let myself go on this subject so far as to characterize and criticize single works, and therefore I will only indicate the larger spheres in which, so far as their material goes, the most important of these epics of chivalry move.

The first chief sort is provided by Charlemagne and his Paladins [or twelve Peers] in the fight against the Saracens and the heathen. In this Frankish saga-cycle, feudal chivalry is a chief foundation, and this cycle ramifies in all sorts of ways into poems where the principal material is made up of the deeds of one or other of the twelve heroes, e.g. of Roland or Doolin of Mainz,[1] and others. Many of these epics were composed in France especially in Philip

[1] Both of these were Paladins of Charlemagne.

Augustus's reign.[1]—Another cycle of sagas has its origin in England, and its subject-matter consists of the deeds of King Arthur and the Knights of the Round Table. Saga-stories, Anglo-Norman knighthood, uxoriousness, fidelity of vassals, are mingled here obscurely and fantastically with Christian allegorical mysticism. One chief aim of all the knightly exploits is the search for the Holy Grail, a vessel containing the blood of Christ, around which a most varied web of adventures is woven until at last the whole brotherhood skedaddles to Prester John in Abyssinia.—These two sets of material have their richest development in, especially, Northern France, England, and Germany.—More capricious, more trivial in contents, and with more exaggerations of chivalrous heroism, with fairyland and fabulous ideas from the East, is a further cycle of poems of chivalry which point to Portugal and Spain as their ultimate origin and have as their heroes Amadis and his numerous relatives.[2]

Secondly, a kind that is more prosaic and abstract consists of the long allegorical poems that were favourites especially in northern France in the thirteenth century. As an example I may mention the well-known *Roman de la Rose*. We may set beside these, though as a contrast, the numerous anecdotes and longer narratives called *contes* and *fabliaux*. These drew their material instead from the life of the day and tell of knights, priests, burghers, and especially provide tales of love and adultery, sometimes comically, sometimes tragically, now in prose, now in verse. This genre was perfected by Boccaccio[3] with his more cultivated mind and in the purest style.

A final group, with a rough knowledge of the Homeric and Virgilian epic and the sagas and stories of antiquity, turned to Greece and Rome and in the style of the epics of chivalry, without altering it in any way, sang the deeds of the Trojan heroes, the founding of Rome by Aeneas, Alexander the Great's adventures[4] and lots more of the same.

This may suffice about medieval epic poetry.

[1] 1165–1223. But the *Chanson de Roland*, for example, is earlier.
[2] *Amadis of Gaul*, a Spanish or Portuguese romance, partly compiled from French materials, was produced early in the sixteenth century by G. de Montalvo. There are continuations, relating the adventures of the son, nephews, and grandson of Amadis.
[3] The *Decameron* was published in 1349–58.
[4] e.g. the French *Roman d'Alexandre* of the twelfth century.

(γ) In the third chief group which I still have to discuss, the thorough and pregnant study of classical literature opened the way for the start of the purer artistic taste of a new civilization. But in its learning, its ability to assimilate the old and fuse it with the new, we can frequently miss that original creativity which we may well admire in the Indians and Arabs as well as in Homer and the Middle Ages. From this period of the renaissance of learning and its influence on national literature there began a many-sided and progressive development of actual life in respect of religion, politics, morals, social relations, etc. Consequently epic poetry too adopts the most varied sorts of subject-matter and the greatest variety of form, but I can trace only, and in brief, the most essential characteristics of its historical development. The following chief differences are to be emphasized.

(αα) First it is still the Middle Ages, which, as before, provide the materials for epic although these are grasped and portrayed in a new spirit permeated by the culture of antiquity. Here epic poetry proves to be active in two directions above all.

In the *first* place, the advancing spirit of the age necessarily leads to making fun of the capriciousness of the medieval adventures, the fantastic exaggerations of chivalry, the purely formal independence of the heroes and their individual separation within a real world which was already disclosing a greater wealth of national situations and interests. The result is that this whole world is brought before our eyes in the light of comedy, however far what is genuine in it is still brought out with seriousness and predilection. At the top of those who treated the whole essence of chivalry in this brilliant way I have already placed Ariosto and Cervantes. Here therefore I will only draw attention to the brilliant adroitness, the attraction and wit, the charm and racy naïveté with which Ariosto (whose poem[1] still moves within the poetic aims of the Middle Ages) in a purely hidden way makes the fantastic merrily destroy itself within by incredible buffooneries. The deeper novel of Cervantes has chivalry already behind it as something past which therefore can enter the real prose of present-day life only as an isolated illusion and a fantastic madness, and yet in its great and noble aspects it nevertheless overtowers again what is clumsy and silly, senseless and trivial, in this prosaic reality and brings its deficiences vividly before our eyes.

[1] *Orlando Furioso* was published in 1532; *Don Quixote* in 1605–15.

As an equally famous representative of the *second* direction I will cite only Tasso. In his *Jerusalem Delivered*[1] we see, in contrast to Ariosto, the great common aim of Christian chivalry, the liberation of the Holy Sepulchre, this conquering pilgrimage of the Crusades; and it has been chosen as central without any addition at all of a comic mood. Following the examples of Homer and Virgil, and with enthusiasm, industry, and study, Tasso has brought into being an epic which as a work of art is possibly to be placed alongside these examples themselves. And of course we find here, over and above a real and sacred interest, national too in part, a kind of unity, development, and rounded completion of the whole which we laid down above as requisite for epic. Moreover, there is a coaxing euphony in the stanzas; their melodious words still live on the lips of the people. And yet this poem is lacking most of all precisely in the primitiveness which alone could make it the bible of a whole nation. For an epic proper, as is the case with Homer, is a work which finds language for all that a nation is in its deeds, and expresses it with direct simplicity once and for all, whereas Tasso's epic appears as a poem, i.e. a poetically manufactured event, and it finds pleasure and satisfaction chiefly in the artistic development of form in general, and, in particular, of a fine language now lyrically now epically descriptive. Tasso may therefore have taken Homer for his model in the arrangement of the epic material, but in the entire conception and presentation of his work what we recognize is principally the influence of Virgil, and this is not exactly to the advantage of the poem.

In addition to the cited epics with a classical education as their basis, we may add the *Lusiads*[2] of Camoens. With this work, wholly national in its contents because it sings the bold sea-voyages of the Portuguese, we have already left what is properly medieval, and it takes us over into interests proclaiming a new era. Here, however, despite the fire of patriotism, the liveliness of the descriptions drawn for the most part from the poet's own vision and experience of life, and the epically rounded unity of the whole, we cannot but feel the cleavage between the national subject-matter and the artistic formation derived partly from antiquity and partly from the Italians, and this destroys the impression of the primitive originality of epic.

(ββ) But the essentially new phenomena in the sphere of religious

---

[1] Published in 1581.   [2] Published in 1572.

belief and in the reality of modern life have their origin in the principle of the Reformation; but the whole tendency arising from this transformed outlook on life is more favourable to lyric and dramatic poetry than to epic proper. Yet even in this field the religious epic, as a work of art, enjoyed a late efflorescence especially in Milton's *Paradise Lost* and Klopstock's *Messiah*. In virtue of a culture acquired by the study of the classics, and a correct elegance of expression, Milton does stand out as a praiseworthy example in his times, but in depth of matter, in energy, in original invention and execution, and especially in epic objectivity, he is clearly inferior to Dante. For on the one hand the conflict and catastrophe of *Paradise Lost* tends towards drama, while on the other hand, as I have already had occasion to remark, lyrical vigour and a morally didactic tendency form a characteristic fundamental trait lying far enough away from the original form of the subject-matter.—Of a similar cleavage between the subject and the way that the culture of the age mirrors it in epic I have already spoken with reference to Klopstock. Apart from this there is visible in his case a continual effort by means of a forced rhetorical sublimity of expression to create for the reader the same recognition of his topic's inspiring dignity and sanctity to which he has risen himself.—In a totally different way this is also essentially true to a certain extent of Voltaire's *Henriade*. At any rate the poetry here remains all the more something manufactured, as the subject, to repeat what I have said already, is clearly unsuitable for the primitive type of epic.

(γγ) If we try to find truly epic productions in the most recent times, we have to look around for some sphere different from that of epic proper. For the whole state of the world today has assumed a form diametrically opposed in its prosaic organization to the requirements which we found irremissible for genuine epic, and the revolutions to which the recent circumstances of states and peoples have been subject are still too fixed in our memory as actual experiences to be compatible with the epic form of art. Consequently epic poetry has fled from great national events into the restrictedness of private domestic situations in the countryside or a small town in order to find there situations which might be fit for presentation in epic. Therefore, especially in Germany, epic has become idyllic, after the idyll proper with its sweet and wishy-washy sentimentality had had its day. As the handiest example of an idyllic epic, I will refer only to Voss's *Luise* and, above all, to Goethe's masterpiece *Hermann and Dorothea*. In the latter our eyes are opened to a background consisting of the greatest world-event of our time, and then there are directly linked with this the affairs of the innkeeper and his family, the pastor, and the apothecary. Consequently, since the village is not shown to us in its political circumstances, we may find ourselves taking a leap that is unjustified and we may regret the absence of a middle term connecting the background and foreground together. But it is precisely by leaving out the middle term that the whole poem preserves its own special character. For although Goethe has been able to use the French Revolution in the happiest way in the development of the poem, he has been able, master as he is, to keep it far away in the background and to weave into the action only those features of it which in virtue of their simple humanity are throughout linked unconstrainedly with those domestic and village concerns and situations. But what is of the most importance is that for this work Goethe has been able to find and present out of our modern world today characteristics, descriptions, situations, and complications which in their own sphere bring alive again what is undyingly attractive in the primitive human circumstances of the Odyssey and the pictures of patriarchal life in the Old Testament.

In the other spheres of our present national and social life there is opened up in the domain of epic an unlimited field for romances, tales, and novels; yet I am unable here to pursue any further, even in the most general outline, the vast history of their development from their origin up to the present day.

B. LYRIC POETRY

The poetic imagination, as the activity of a poet, does not, as plastic art does, set before our eyes the thing itself in its external reality (even if that reality be produced by art) but gives us on the contrary an *inner* vision and feeling of it. Even from the point of view of this general mode of production, it is the *subjective* side of the poet's spiritual work of creating and forming his material which is clearly the predominant element in his illustrative production, and this is a contrast to the visual arts. Since epic poetry brings its subject-matter before our contemplation as something obviously alive, whether in its underlying universality or in the manner of a sculpture or a painting, then, at least when it reaches its height, the poet who imagines and feels disappears in his poetic activity before the objectivity of his creation. This alienation of himself can only be completely avoided by the artist on his subjective side if on the one hand he absorbs into *himself* the entire world of objects and circumstances, and stamps them with his own inner consciousness, and if, on the other hand, he discloses his self-concentrated heart, opens his eyes and ears, raises purely dull feeling into vision and ideas, and gives words and language to this enriched inner life so that as inner life it may find expression. The more this mode of communication remains excluded from the matter-of-factness of the art of epic, the more—and precisely on account of this exclusion—has the subjective form of poetry to be developed in a sphere of its own, independent of epic. Out of the objectivity of the subject-matter the spirit descends into itself, looks into its own consciousness, and satisfies the need to display, not the external reality of the matter, but its presence and actuality in the spirit's own *subjective* disposition, in the experience of the heart and the reflections of imagination, and at the same time to display the contents and activity of the inner life itself. But in order that this expression may not remain a merely casual expression of an individual's own immediate feelings and ideas, it becomes the language of the *poetic* inner life, and therefore however intimately the insights and feelings which the poet describes as his own belong to him as a single individual, they must nevertheless possess a universal validity, i.e. they must be genuine feelings and meditations for which the poet invents or finds the adequate and lively expression. If therefore the heart can find relief when its grief or pleasure is put, described, and expressed in words of any sort, a poetic outburst can certainly perform the like service; but it is not confined to its use as an old wife's medicine. Indeed it has on the contrary a higher vocation: its task, namely, is to liberate the spirit not *from* but *in* feeling. The blind dominion of passion lies in an unconscious and dull unity between itself and the entirety of a heart that cannot rise out of itself into ideas and self-expression. Poetry does deliver the heart from this slavery to passion by making it see itself, but it does not stop at merely extricating this felt passion from its immediate unity with the heart but makes of it an object purified from all accidental moods, an object in which the inner life, liberated and with its self-consciousness satisfied, reverts freely at the same time into itself and is at home with itself. Conversely, however, this first objectification must not be so far continued as to display the subject's heart and passion in practical activity and *action*, i.e. in the subject's return into himself in his actual deed [as in drama]. For the primary realization of the inner life is itself still inwardness, so that this emergence from self means only liberation from that immediate, dumb, void of ideas, concentration of the heart which now opens out to self-expression and therefore grasps and expresses in the form of self-conscious insights and ideas what formerly was only felt.—This in essence establishes the sphere and task of lyric poetry in distinction from epic and dramatic.

To come forthwith to the more detailed consideration of this new sphere, I can follow for its division the same route that I traced earlier for epic poetry. So

1. the question is about the general character of lyric;
2. we must survey the particular characteristics to be considered in relation to the lyric poet, the lyrical work of art and the sorts of it; and
3. we end with a few remarks on the historical development of this kind of poetry.

But here on the whole I will deal with the subject briefly for two reasons: (i) we must [in a course of lectures] leave the room necessary for the discussion of the dramatic field; (ii) I must restrict myself entirely to general points, because here, more than is the case in epic, the detail comprises minutiae and their incalculable variety and so could be treated completely and at greater length only historically, and that is not our business here.

1. *General Character of Lyric*

What leads to epic poetry is the need to listen to something which is unfolded as an independent and self-complete totality, objective over against the subject; whereas in lyric what is satisfied is the opposite need, namely that for self-expression and for the apprehension of the mind in its own self-expression. The following are the most important points at issue in connection with this outpouring:

(*a*) what that is in which the inner self has a sense of itself and which it brings into its ideas, i.e. the *content* [of lyric poetry];

(*b*) the *form* which makes the expression of this content into lyric poetry;

(*c*) the stage of consciousness and culture at which the lyric poet is when he discloses his feelings and ideas.

(*a*) The content of a lyric work of art cannot be the development of an objective action extending through all its connections into the whole wealth of a world; on the contrary, it must be the individual person and therefore with all the details of his situation and concerns, as well as the way in which his mind with its subjective judgement, its joy, admiration, grief, and, in short, its feeling comes to consciousness of itself in and through such experiences. Owing to this principle of detailing, particularization, and individuality, which is inherent in lyric, its contents may be of extreme variety and touch national life in every direction, but with this essential difference, that while in one and the same work an epic unfolds the entirety of the national spirit in its actual deeds and situation, the more specific content of a lyric is restricted to one or other particular aspect, or at least it cannot attain that explicit completion and development which an epic must have if it is to fulfil its function. The entirety of a nation's lyric poetry may therefore run through the entirety of the nation's interests, ideas, and aims, but a single lyric cannot. Of poetic bibles like those we found in the sphere of epic poetry, lyric has none to show. On the other hand it has the advantage of being producible at almost any date in a nation's history, while epic proper is always bound up with specific primitive epochs, and in later periods, when nations have developed a prosaic organization, it falls short of success.

(α) Within this field of individualization there falls in the first place the universal as such, i.e. the height and depth of human faith, ideas, and knowledge: the essential content of religion and art and, indeed, even philosophical thoughts so far as these are accommodated to the form of imagination and intuition and enabled to enter the sphere of feeling. General views, the fundamental basis of an outlook on the world, deeper conceptions of the decisive relations of life are therefore not excluded from lyric, and a great part of the subject-matter, which I mentioned in dealing with the more imperfect sorts of epic, is equally within the province of this new species of poetry.

(β) Within the sphere of what is inherently universal, there consequently enters, in the second place, the aspect of particularity which on the one hand can be so interwoven with what is fundamental that any single situation, feeling, idea, etc. is seized in its deeper essential character and therefore is itself expressed in a fundamental guise. This is almost always the case in Schiller, for example, both in his strictly lyrical poems and also in his ballads, in connection with which I will refer only to the magnificent words of the chorus of the Furies in *Die Kraniche des Ibycus*;[1] it is neither epic nor dramatic but lyric. On the other hand, the connection [of universal and particular] may be brought about if a variety of particular traits, situations, moods, accidents, etc. is ranged as an actual proof of comprehensive views and maxims and is intertwined in a living way with the universal. This kind of connection is frequently used in elegies and epistles, for example, and, in general, in the case of a reflective consideration of life.

(γ) Since in lyric it is the poet who expresses himself, the most inherently trivial matter may satisfy him in the first place for this purpose. In that event, his heart itself, his individual subjective life as such is the proper content of the poem, so that what matters is only the soul of feeling and not what the object of the feeling is. The momentary and most fleeting mood, the heart's jubilant cry, the quickly passing flashes of carefree happiness and merriment,

---

[1] *The Cranes of Ibycus*: Ibycus sees in a flight of them his avengers as he lies dying at the hands of robbers, who are in fact discovered, as a result of that flight, by the Furies, i.e. by the 'Eumenides' as Schiller and Hegel write.

the outbursts of melancholy, dejection, and lament—in short the whole gamut of feeling is seized here in its momentary movements, or in its single fancies about all sorts of things, and made permanent by its expression. Here there comes into poetry something like what I mentioned earlier in connection with genre painting. The content of what is said, the topics, are wholly accidental, and the important thing is only the poet's treatment and presentation of them. The attractiveness of treatment and presentation in lyric poetry may lie either in the sweetness that the heart exhales or in the novelty of striking ways of looking at things and in the wit of surprising points or turns of phrase.

(*b*) Secondly, as for the *form* in which such a content becomes a lyric work of art, we may say in general terms that the central thing is the individual in his inner ideas and feelings. The whole thing therefore starts from his heart and mind, in particular from the poet's special mood and situation. Consequently the content and connection of the particular aspects developed within the subject-matter itself are supported not objectively and automatically by being a matter of substance nor by their external appearance as a closed and individual event, but by the poet himself. But on this account he must be clearly in himself poetic, rich in imagination and feeling, or splendid, with profound meditations and thoughts, and above all independent by being in himself an enclosed inner world from which all the dependence and mere caprice of prose has been stripped away.

A lyric poem therefore has a unity of a totally different kind from epic, namely the inwardness of mood or reflection which expatiates on itself, mirrors itself in the external world, sketches and describes itself, or is preoccupied otherwise with one or other object and, in virtue of this subjective interest, acquires the right of starting or breaking off more or less when it likes. For example, Horace often comes to an end just where, given our usual way of thinking and the manner of its expression, we might suppose that the thing would only just have to have its beginning, i.e. he describes, for instance, only his feelings, commands, and arrangements for a feast and we have no idea at all of how the thing went cheerfully on or of its outcome.[1] Moreover norms of the most

---

[1] Since the numerous Odes (e.g. i. 20, iii. 28, iv. 12, etc.) to which Hegel refers are invitations to a future feast, we ought not to be surprised at not being told the outcome. But Hegel seems to be.

varied kinds for the inner progress and connection of the whole poem are supplied by the sort of mood, the individual mental disposition, the degree of passion, its impetuosity, its gushing and springing from one thing to another, or, alternatively, the peace of the soul and the tranquillity of meditation and its slow progress. The mutability of the inner life can be determined in so many different ways that in relation to all these points hardly anything can be firmly and thoroughly laid down in general terms. Consequently I will only emphasize the following clearer differences.

(α) Just as we found several kinds of epic which tended to have a lyric tone of expression, so now lyric may adopt in subject-matter and form an event which is epic in matter and external appearance, and therefore touches on epic. Songs about heroes, romaunts, ballads, etc. belong to this class. In these sorts of lyric the form of the whole is, on the one hand, narrative, because what is reported is the origin and progress of a situation and event, a turning-point in the fate of a nation etc. But, on the other hand, the fundamental tone is wholly lyric, because the chief thing is not the non-subjective description and painting of a real occurrence, but on the contrary the poet's mode of apprehending and feeling it, the mood resounding through the whole, whether it be a mood of joy or lament, courage or submission, and consequently the effect which such a poem was meant to produce belongs entirely to the sphere of lyric. This is the case because what the poet aims at producing in his hearer is the same mood which has been created in him by the event related and which he has therefore introduced entirely into his poem. He expresses his depression, his melancholy, his cheerfulness, his glow of patriotism, etc., in an analogous event in such a way that the centre of the thing is not the occurrence itself but the state of mind which is mirrored in it. For this reason, after all, he principally emphasizes, and describes with depth of feeling, only those traits which re-echo and harmonize with his inner emotion and which, by expressing that emotion in the most living way, are best able to arouse in the listener the same feeling. So the subject-matter is epic, but the treatment lyric.—In more detail, the following types are to be included:

($\alpha\alpha$) First, the epigram, when, that is to say, as an inscription it does not merely say quite briefly and objectively what the thing is, but adds a feeling to this expression, and in this way what is said is withdrawn from its factual reality and transferred into the inner life. In this event the writer does not sacrifice himself in favour of the object; on the contrary, the position is the very reverse because in the object he asserts *himself*, his wishes in relation to it, his subjective pleasantries, keen-witted associations, and unmeditated whims. The Greek Anthology even in its day contains many witty epigrams of this kind without any vestige of the tone of epic, and in modern times we find something of the kind belonging to this class in the piquant couplets so common in French vaudevilles, and, in Germany, in the *Sinndedichte* of Logau,[1] and the *Xenien* of Goethe and Schiller. Overpowering feeling may give this lyrical character to epitaphs too.

(ββ) Secondly, lyric expands similarly into descriptive narrative. As the first and simplest form in this sphere I will mention romances[2] only. Here the different scenes of an event are separated, and then each by itself is progressively treated quickly and compressedly in its chief traits with a description sympathetic throughout. This fixed and specific treatment of the characteristics proper to a situation and their sharp emphasis along with the author's complete participation in them occurs in a noble way especially in the Spaniards and makes their narrative romances very effective. Over these lyric pictures there is diffused a certain luminosity which is more akin to the precision of sight and its clear perception of distinctions than to the deep feeling of the heart.

(γγ) Most ballads, on the other hand, comprise, even if on a smaller scale than is the case in epic poetry proper, the entirety of a complete event. It is true that they can sketch a picture of this event in its most prominent features, but at the same time they can bring out everywhere more fully, yet more concentratedly and fervently, both the depth of the heart which is interwoven with the event throughout and also the emotional tone of lament, melancholy, mourning, joy, etc. The English possess many such poems, principally from earlier primitive epochs of their poetry;[3] and folk-poetry in general loves to relate such, usually sad, stories and conflicts in a tone of dreadful feeling that shuts in the heart with agony and smothers the voice. But in modern times too, in

---

[1] F. Baron von Logau, 1604–55; *Deutsche Sinngedichte drei tausend* (Three Thousand German Epigrams), 1654.

[2] e.g. the 'Romances' of the Cid, some of which Herder translated into German verse, mentioned already on p. 1102 above.

[3] This is doubtless a reference to Percy's *Reliques*, first published in 1765.

Germany, first Bürger,[1] and then above all Goethe and Schiller, have acquired a mastery in this field—Bürger by his homelike simplicity; Goethe, along with all his clarity of vision, by the deep feeling of the soul which is wafted lyrically through the whole; and Schiller again by his superb elevation of mind and his feeling for the fundamental thought which he yet intends to express, lyrically throughout, in the form of an event, in order thereby to stir in the hearer's heart and mind a similarly lyrical emotion and meditation.

(β) Secondly, the subjective element in lyric poetry emerges still more explicitly when some occurrence or actual situation provides the poet with a mere occasion for expressing himself in or about it. This is the case with so-called *poèmes d'occasion*. For example, so far back[2] as Callinus and Tyrtaeus their war-elegies originated in the actual circumstances of which they sang and for which they wished to make their hearers enthusiastic, although their own personality, their own heart and mind, is hardly in evidence. Pindar's prize odes too had their immediate occasion in specific competitions and victories and their special circumstances. Still more in many of Horace's odes we descry a special provocation and indeed a clear intention and the thought that 'as a cultured and famous man I will write a poem about this'. But Goethe above all has in recent times had an affection for this kind of poetry because in fact every occurrence in life became a poem for him.

(αα) But if a lyric work of art is not to fall into *dependence* on the external stimulus and the purposes implicit in it, but is to stand out by itself as an independent whole, then the essential thing is that the poet shall use the stimulus purely as an opportunity for giving expression to himself, to his mood of joy or sorrow, or to his way of thinking and his general view of life. The principal condition for the lyric poet is therefore that he shall entirely assimilate and make his own the objective subject-matter. For the truly lyrical poet lives in himself, treats circumstances in accordance with his own poetic individual outlook, and now, however variously his inner life may be fused with the world confronting him and with its situations, complexities, and fates, what he nevertheless manifests in his portrayal of this material is only the inherent and independent life of his feelings and meditations. For example, when Pindar

---

[1] G. A., 1747–94. His best-known ballad is *Lenore* (1773).
[2] i.e. seventh-century B.C.

was invited to sing the praises of a victor in the Games, or did so of his own volition, he still so mastered his topic that his work was not a poem *about* a victor at all, but was sung out of the depths of his own heart.

(ββ) The more particular mode of presentation used in such a poem *d'occasion* can of course, on the other hand, derive its specific material and character, as well as the inner organization of the work of art, from the real existence of the individual or the occurrence selected as a subject. For it is precisely by this subject that the poet's mind will evidently be moved. As the clearest example, even if an extreme one, I need only refer to Schiller's *Lied von der Glocke* [Song of the Bell][1] where the external stages in the business of bell-founding provide the essential supports for the steps in the development of the whole poem, and only after them are appended the corresponding castings of feeling as well as the most varied reflections on life and other sketches of human situations. In a different way Pindar too borrows from the birthplace of the victor, the deeds of his clan, or from other circumstances of life the immediate occasion for praising *these* gods and no others, mentioning only these deeds and fates, introducing only these specific meditations, inweaving these proverbs, etc. On the other hand, however, the lyric poet is entirely free here once again, because it is not the external stimulus as such that is the topic but he himself with his inner life, and therefore it depends on his particular personal insight and poetic attitude of mind alone what aspects of the topic are to be portrayed in the lyric and in what succession and association. There is no fixed *a priori* criterion for determining the extent to which the objective stimulus with its factual content or the poet's own subjective experience is to preponderate or whether both of these should interpenetrate one another.

(γγ) But the proper *unity* of the lyric is not provided by the occasion and its objective reality but by the poet's inner movement of soul and his way of treating his subject. For the single mood or general reflection aroused poetically by the external stimulus forms the centre determining not only the colour of the whole but also the whole range of particular aspects which may be developed, the manner of their exposition and linkage, and therefore the plan and

---

[1] In the poem, the stanzas alternate. The description of a stage in the casting of a bell is followed by an expression of the feelings or reflections to which that stage gives rise.

connection of the poem as a work of art. For example, Pindar has in the named objective circumstances of the lives of the victors whose praise he is singing a real kernel for the articulation and development of his work, but in the case of individual odes there are always other considerations, a different mood—admonition, consolation, exaltation, e.g.—which he makes prevalent throughout. Although these belong solely to the poet as the composer of his poems, they nevertheless provide him with the range of what within those objective circumstances he will touch upon, treat at length, or pass over, as well as with the sort of illumination and connection which he must use if he is to produce the intended lyric effect.

(γ) Yet, thirdly, the genuinely lyric poet does not need to start from the external events which he relates with such wealth of feeling, or from other objective circumstances and occasions which become a stimulus for his effusions; on the contrary, he is in himself a subjectively complete world so that he can look for inspiration and a topic within *himself* and therefore can remain within the sphere of subjective situations, states, and incidents and the passions of his own heart and spirit. Here in his subjective inner life the man becomes a work of art himself, while what serves as subject-matter for an epic poet is a stranger, i.e. a hero with his deeds and adventures.

(αα) Yet even in this field an element of narrative may still enter as is the case, for example, with many of the songs called Anacreon's which provide us with cheerful and charmingly finished miniatures of love-affairs, etc. But in that event such an incident must be only as it were a revelation of an inner attitude of mind. So Horace too, to mention him again in another way, uses in his *Integer vitae*[1] a chance meeting with a wolf, not so that we can call the whole ode a poem *d'occasion*, but as a proof of the proposition with which he begins and the imperturbability of the feeling of love with which he ends.

(ββ) The situation in which the poet depicts himself need not as a rule be restricted simply to the inner life as such. On the contrary, it should be evinced as a concrete and therefore also external entirety because the poet reveals himself as existent objectively as well as subjectively. For example, in the Anacreon songs

---

[1] *Odes*, i. 22. An upright man needs no weapons. So whatever dangers may come, wolves or other, I will go on loving Lalage undisturbed.

mentioned above the poet depicts himself amongst roses, lovely girls and youths, as drinking and dancing, in cheerful enjoyment, without desire or longing, without duty, and without neglecting higher ends, for of these there is no question here at all; in short, he depicts himself as a hero who, innocent and free and therefore without restriction or deficiency, is merely this one man who he is, a man of his own sort as a subjective work of art.

In the love-songs of Hafiz too we see the whole living individuality of the poet, so changing in content, situation, and expression that the whole thing almost approaches humour. Yet in his poems he has no special theme, no objective picture, no god, no mythology—indeed when we read these outpourings we feel that orientals generally could have had neither painting nor plastic art. The poet goes from one topic to another and marches over the whole field, but it is all a single scene in which the whole man is brought before us face to face, soul to soul, in his wine, his tavern, his girl, his court, etc. in beautiful frankness, in pure enjoyment without desire or self-seeking.—All sorts of examples could be given of experiments in this sort of way of portraying an inner situation which is an external one as well.

Yet if the poet goes far into detail about his subjective states of mind, we have no inclination at all to get to know his particular fancies, his amours, his domestic affairs, or the history of his uncles and aunts, like what we get even in the case of Klopstock's Cidli and Fanny;[1] on the contrary, we want to have in front of us something universally human so that we can feel in poetic sympathy with it. Consequently lyric may easily come to pretend, falsely, that what is subjective and particular must be of interest in and by itself. On the other hand, many of Goethe's songs may be called convivial although he has not issued them under that title. What I mean is that in society a man does not communicate his *self*; on the contrary, he puts his particular individuality in the background and amuses the company with a story or an anecdote or with traits of third parties which he then relates with a humour of his own and in a way suiting his own tone. In such a case the poet both is and is not himself; he does his best to communicate not himself but something else; he is, as it were, an

---

[1] Cidli is the name that Klopstock gave to Jairus's daughter in the *Messiah*, iv, 674. She is supposed to be a presentation of Fanny Schmidt, Klopstock's beloved in Langensalza.

actor who plays an endless number of parts, lingering now here now there, retaining now one scenic arrangement for a moment, now another, and yet, whatever he may portray, there is always vividly interwoven with it his own artistic inner life, his feelings and experiences.

(γγ) But since the inner subjective life is the proper source of lyric, the poet must retain the right to limit himself to expressing purely inner moods, reflections, etc., without spreading himself into portraying a concrete situation in its external features as well. In this respect, wholly senseless gibberish, tra-la-la, singing purely for the sake of singing, prove to be a genuinely lyric satisfaction of the heart for which words are more or less a purely arbitrary vehicle for the expression of joys and sorrows, although the aid of music is summoned at once to remedy their insufficiency. Folksongs especially seldom get beyond this mode of expression. Goethe's songs achieve a richer and less vague expression, but in their case too it is often only a matter of some single passing pleasantry, the tone of a fleeting mood, which the poet does not go beyond and out of which he makes a little song to be whistled for a moment. In other songs, however, he deals with similar moods at greater length, and even methodically, as for example in the song *Ich hab' mein Sach auf nichts gestellt*,[1] where money and property, then women, travel, fame and honour, and finally battle and war all appear transitory [and vanity] and what alone remains is the open and carefree cheerfulness of the ever-recurring refrain.

Conversely, however, in this connection, the subjective inner life may broaden and deepen as it were into states of mind where vision is grandest and ideas survey the whole world. A large proportion of Schiller's poems, for example, are of this kind. His heart is stimulated by what is rational and great; yet he does not give voice to a religious or fundamental topic in any sort of hymn, nor is he, like a bard, inspired from without by external occurrences; on the contrary, he starts with and from a mind which has as its highest interests the ideals of life and beauty and the imperishable rights and thoughts of mankind.

(*c*) A third and last point on which we have to touch in dealing with the general character of lyric poetry concerns the general

---

[1] 'My all I've set at nought', the first line of the poem headed *Vanitas! vanitatum vanitas!* The 'refrain' is *juchhe*, hurrah!

level of mind and culture from which the individual poem proceeds.

In this connection too lyric occupies a position opposed to that of epic poetry. We saw that the efflorescence of epic proper required a national state of affairs which was on the whole undeveloped, not yet matured into a prosaic type of reality, whereas the times most favourable to lyric are those which have achieved a more or less completed organization of human relationships, because only in those times has the individual person become self-reflective in contrast to the external world, and, reflected out of it, achieved in his inner life an independent entirety of feeling and thinking. For in lyric both form and content are provided precisely not by the whole external world or by individual action but by the poet himself in his own personal character. But this is not to be understood at all as if, in order to be able to express himself in lyrics, the individual must free himself from any and every connection with national interests and outlooks, and stand on his own feet in abstraction from these. On the contrary if he were thus abstractly independent, nothing would be left for the contents of his poem except a wholly accidental and particular passion, or a capricious appetite or passing pleasure, and unlimited scope would be given to bad and perverse notions and a bizarre originality of feeling. The genuine lyric, like all true poetry, has to express the true contents of the human heart. Yet, as contained in lyric, the most factual and fundamental matter must appear as subjectively felt, contemplated, portrayed, or thought.

Further, here it is not a matter of the bare expression of an individual's inner life, of the first word that comes directly to mind as an epic statement of what the thing is, but of a *poetic* mind's *artistic* expression, an expression different from an ordinary or casual one. Therefore, precisely because the mere self-concentration of the heart increasingly discloses itself in manifold feelings and more comprehensive meditations, and the individual becomes increasingly aware of his poetic inner life within a world already more prosaically stamped, lyric now demands [in the poet] a culture which has risen to art and which likewise must emerge in the excellence and the independent work of a subjective natural gift which has been developed to perfection. These are the reasons why lyric is not restricted to specific epochs in the spiritual development of a people but can flourish abundantly in the most different epochs and is especially opportune in modern times when every individual claims the right of having his own personal point of view and mode of feeling.

However, the following general points may be made as indicative of the most striking differences [in lyric expression]:

(*a*) The lyric mode of expression in folk-poetry.

(αα) This poetry above all brings to our view the manifold special characteristics of nationalities, and for this reason, now that today we take an interest in the whole world, people are not tired of collecting folk-songs of every kind with a view to getting to know the special character of every people and to share their feelings and their life. Herder did a great deal in this direction, and Goethe too has been able, in his freer imitations, to give us something of a feeling for extremely different sorts of products of this kind. But complete sympathy is possible only with the songs of one's own nation, and while we Germans can make ourselves at home with material from abroad also, still the final notes in the music of some other people's national inner life are always something strange, and before the domestic tone of our own feeling can echo in them they need the aid of a certain recasting. Yet Goethe could only give this aid, in the cleverest and most beautiful way, to the foreign folk-songs that he brought to us, by preserving throughout unimpaired the special and peculiar character of these poems, e.g. in the lament, from the Morlaccian, of Asan Aga's noble kinswomen.[1]

(ββ) The general character of lyrical folk-poetry is to be compared with the primitive epic in this respect, that the poet does not push himself forward but is lost in his subject-matter. Although, therefore, the most concentrated deep feeling of the heart can be expressed in folk-song, still what is made recognizable in such poetry is not a single individual poet with his own peculiar manner of portraying himself artistically, but a national feeling which the individual wholly and entirely bears in himself because his own inner ideas and feelings are not divorced from his people or its existence and interests. A necessary presupposition of such an undivided unity is a state of affairs in which independent individual

---

[1] The reference is to a Serbo-Croat folk-song which Goethe adapted (see the first of his *Vermischte Gedichte*) from Herder's collection of folk-songs. Asan Aga was a Serbian hero. Morlaccian is (or was) a dialect of Serbo-Croat spoken at Morlaccia on the Dalmatian coast.

reflection and culture has not yet come to birth, with the result that the poet becomes a mere tool, with his own person retreating into the background, by means of which the national life is expressed in its lyrical feeling and way of looking at things. This immediate and original character of course gives to folk-song a freshness, which is devoid of reflection, but has a solid compactness, and striking truth, which often has the greatest effect, but it therefore easily acquires at the same time a fragmentary and disordered character, a lack of development which leads to vagueness and unclarity. Feeling is deeply hidden and neither can nor will come to complete expression. Besides, although the form of this entire species is as a rule completely lyrical, i.e. subjective, in kind, what is missing is, as I have said, *the individual* who in the form and content of lyric expresses what is the property of precisely *his* own heart and spirit and is the product of *his* own artistic work.

(γγ) Peoples who have only got so far as poems of this kind and have not reached a higher stage of lyric or produced epic or dramatic works are therefore for the most part semi-barbaric, with an undeveloped organization and with transitory feuds and catastrophes. For amongst them, with their primitive poetry, really epic poets would have arisen if in these heroic times these peoples had made themselves into an inherently rich whole, the particular aspects of which had been already developed into independent yet harmonious realities and could have provided the ground for inherently concrete and individually perfected deeds. Therefore the situation out of which such folk-songs can issue as the one and final mode of expressing the national spirit is restricted to family life and clan-solidarity without the further organization characteristic of the states that have already matured into the age of heroes. If recollections of national events do occur, then these are mostly struggles against foreign oppressors or brigandage, reactions of savagery against savagery, or acts of one individual against another of the same folk, and then in the telling of these free scope is given to wailing and lament, or else to loud jubilation over a passing victory. The real but embryo life of the people, where independence has not yet been developed, is thrown back on the inner world of feeling, which then is, on the whole, equally undeveloped, and, even if it does thereby win an inner self-concentration, still is normally crude and barbaric in its contents. Therefore, whether folk-song is to interest us poetically or on the contrary, to some extent, to repel us, depends on the sort of situations and feelings which it portrays, for what seems excellent to the imagination of one people may be to another tasteless, sinister, and offensive. So, for example, there is a folk-song that tells of a woman who, at her husband's command, was immured, and only by her pleas were openings made for her breasts so that she could suckle her child, and she only lived long enough to reach a time when the child no longer needed its mother's milk. This is a barbaric and horrible situation. Similarly there are brigandages, individual deeds of bluster and mere savagery, nothing in themselves, with which different peoples of some other culture are supposed to have to sympathize. Therefore, folk-songs are usually trivial in the extreme, and there is no firm criterion of their excellence because they are too far removed from what is *universally* human. Therefore, our recently made acquaintance with the songs of the Iroquois, Eskimos, and other savage peoples has not always enlarged the sphere of our poetic enjoyment.

(*b*) But since lyric is the complete utterance of the inner spirit, it cannot rest with the mode of expression or the topics of actual folk-songs or with the similar and imitated tone in later poems.

(αα) For, on the one hand, as we have just seen, in what has just been described, there is present only imperfectly in lyric the essentially necessary thing, namely that the self-concentrated mind shall rise above this pure concentration and its immediate vision and press on to a free portrayal of itself. On the other hand, it must so expand as to absorb a rich world of ideas, passions, situations, and conflicts, in order that everything which the human heart can comprise may be transformed within the poet's mind and communicated by him as the progeny of his own spirit. For the whole of lyric poetry must give poetic expression to the entirety of the inner life, so far as that life can enter poetry at all, and therefore lyric belongs in common to every stage of spiritual development.

(ββ) Secondly, there is bound up with free self-consciousness the freedom of self-conscious *art*. Folk-song is sung from the heart as if spontaneously, like nature's song; but free *art* is conscious of itself, it desires to know and intend what it is producing; culture is needed for this knowledge, and perfection demands a practised virtuosity in production. Therefore while epic poetry, strictly so-called, must conceal the poet's own imaginative and creative activity, or while this cannot yet be made visible, given the whole character of the period when the epic is produced, this only happens because epic is concerned with the nation's existence, not as produced by the poet himself, but as it objectively is, and consequently this existence must appear in the poem not as something subjective but as a product developing independently on its own account; whereas in lyric the contents, no less than its creation, are subjective, and thus it is this subjectivity which has to be revealed precisely as what it is.

(γγ) In this respect the later, and *artistic*, lyric poetry is expressly differentiated from folk-song. There are indeed also folk-songs produced contemporaneously with really artistic lyrics, but in that case they belong to groups and individuals who have not participated in this development of art and who in their whole outlook have not dissociated themselves from the instinctive sense of their people. However, this difference between the lyrics of folk-poetry and those of artistic poetry is not to be understood as implying that lyric reaches its zenith only when reflection and an artistic intelligence, brilliantly and elegantly combined with deliberate skill, make their appearance as the most essential things. This would only mean that Horace, for example, and Latin lyric poets generally, would have to be counted amongst the most excellent of lyric poets or, in a different sphere, that the Mastersingers would have to be preferred to the preceding epoch of genuine Minnesong.[1] But our proposition is not to be taken in this extreme sense; it is correct only in the sense that subjective imagination and art, precisely because of the independent subjectivity which is its principle, must have as its presupposition and basis, for its real perfection, a free and developed self-consciousness of ideas and artistic activity.

(c) From these two earlier stages we may now distinguish a third, in the following way. Folk-song precedes the proper development and presence of a prosaic type of consciousness; whereas genuinely lyric poetry, as *art*, tears itself free from this already existent world of prose, and out of an imagination now become subjectively independent creates a new poetic world of subjective meditation and feeling whereby alone it generates in a living way the true contents of the inner life of man and the true way of expressing them. But, thirdly, there is a form of the spirit

[1] The chief of the Minnesingers (courtly minstrels) was W. von der Vogelweide, *c.* 1200.

which, in one aspect, outsoars the imagination of heart and vision because it can bring its content into free self-consciousness in a more decisively universal way and in more necessary connectedness than is possible for any art at all. I mean philosophical thinking. Yet this form, conversely, is burdened with the abstraction of developing solely in the province of thinking, i.e. of purely ideal universality, so that man in the concrete may find himself forced to express the contents and results of his philosophical mind in a concrete way as penetrated by his heart and vision, his imagination and feeling, in order in this way to have and provide a total expression of his whole inner life.

Here two different modes of treatment prevail. (i) Imagination may exceed its own bounds in trying to rival the movement of thought but without being able to absorb the clarity and fixed precision of philosophical expositions. In that event lyric generally becomes the outpouring of a soul, fighting and struggling with itself, which in its ferment does violence to both art and thought because it oversteps one sphere without being, or being able to be, at home in the other. (ii) But a philosopher at peace with himself in his thinking may animate with his feeling his clearly grasped and systematically pursued thoughts, may give them visual illustration, and, as Schiller does in many of his poems, exchange the obviously necessary philosophical march and connection for the free play of particular aspects. To all appearance this free play of aspects is disconnected and behind it art must try all the more to conceal their inner unification, the less it means to fall into the prosaic tone of expounding them didactically seriatim.

2. *Particular Aspects of Lyric Poetry*

After considering the general character of the subject-matter of lyric poetry, the form in which it can express it, as well as the different stages of civilization which prove to be more or less in conformity with its principle, our next task is to examine in detail the particular chief aspects and bearings of these general points.

Here again, to start with, I will mention once more the difference between epic and lyric poetry. In considering the former we turned our attention chiefly to the primitive national epic and left aside both the inferior collateral types and also the poet himself. This we cannot do in our present sphere. On the contrary the most important topics for discussion here are the personality of the poet and the ramification of the different kinds into which lyric can expand, since it has as its principle the individualizing and particularizing of its subject-matter and its forms. What is to be said in more detail on this matter may therefore take the following course:

(*a*) We have to direct our attention to the lyric poet;
(*b*) then we must consider the lyric work of art as a product of his subjective imagination;
(*c*) and finally mention the kinds of lyrical portrayal which emanate from its essential nature.

(*a*) *The Lyric Poet*

(α) The contents of lyric, as we saw, consist of (i) meditations comprising the universal element in existence and its situations, and (ii) the variety of its particular aspects. But, by being pure generalities and particular views and feelings, both these constituents are mere abstractions which need a link if they are to acquire a living lyrical individuality, and this link must be of an inner and therefore subjective kind. Thus as the centre and proper content of lyric poetry there must be placed the poetic concrete person, the poet, but he must not proceed to actual deeds and actions or become involved in the movement of dramatic conflicts. His sole expression and act is limited, on the contrary, to lending to his inner life words which, whatever their objective meaning may be, reveal the spiritual sense of the person using them and are meant to arouse and keep alive in the hearer the same sense and spirit, the same attitude of mind, and the like direction of thought.

(β) This granted, however, although the expression is devised for apprehension by others, it may only be a free overflow of cheerfulness or of the grief that finds relief and reconciliation in song; alternatively, self-expression may be a deeper urge to *communicate* the heart's deepest feelings and most far-reaching meditations—for a man who is *able* to compose songs and poetry has a calling accordingly and *ought* to be a poet. Yet external stimuli, express invitations, and more of the like are not in any way excluded. But in such a case the great lyric poet soon digresses from the proper topic and portrays himself. So, to abide by an example cited often already, Pindar was frequently asked to celebrate this or that victor in the Games and indeed he made his living by taking money for his compositions; and yet, as bard, he puts himself in his hero's place and independently combines with his own imagination the praise of the deeds of his hero's ancestors, it may be; he recalls old myths, or he expresses his own profound view of life, wealth, dominion, whatever is great and honourable, the sublimity and charm of the Muses, but above all the dignity of the bard. Consequently in his poems he is not so much concerned to honour the hero whose fame he spreads in this way as to make himself, the poet, heard. He himself has not the honour of having sung the praises of victors, for it is they who have acquired honour by being made the subject of Pindar's verse. This pre-eminent greatness of soul is what constitutes the nobility of the lyric poet. As an individual, Homer is so far sacrificed in his epic that nowadays people will not allow that he ever existed at all, yet his heroes live on, immortal; whereas Pindar's heroes are only names to us while he himself, self-celebrated and self-honoured, confronts us unforgettably as poet. The fame which his heroes may claim is only an appendage to the fame of the lyric poet.

Amongst the Romans too the lyric poet acquires to some extent this same independent position. For example Suetonius reports [in his life of Horace] that Augustus wrote as follows to Horace: '*An vereris, ne apud posteros tibi infame sit, quod videaris familiaris nobis esse?*'[1] But except where Horace speaks of Augustus *ex officio*, and we can easily sense when this is so, he generally comes quickly enough back to himself. His Ode iii. 14, for example, begins with the return of Augustus from Spain after his victory over the Cantabrians; but Horace simply goes on to laud the fact that, owing to the peace that Augustus has restored to the world, he himself as a poet can peacefully enjoy his carefree leisure; and then he gives orders for garlands, perfumes, and old wine to be brought for a celebration, and for Neaera to be invited quickly—in short his concern is only with the preparations for his feast. Yet love-quarrels mean less to him now than they did in his youth when Plancus was consul, for he says expressly to the slave that he sends: '*Si per invisum mora ianitorem Fiet, abito.*'[2]

---

[1] It is after expressing wrath that he was not mentioned in some of Horace's *Epistles* that Augustus added: 'Are you afraid that it will go ill with your posthumous fame if you seem to be a friend of ours?' This prompted Horace to provide what Augustus wanted, i.e. an Epistle addressed to himself (see *Ep.* ii. 1).

[2] 'If a surly janitor makes difficulties, come away.'

To a still greater extent we may praise it as an honourable trait in Klopstock that in his day he felt once again the independent dignity of the bard, because he expressed it and bore and conducted himself in accordance with it: he extricated the poet from the position of being the poet of a court or anyone's servant, as well as from the tiresome and useless persiflage which ruins a man. Yet it happened to him at first that his publisher regarded him as *his* poet. His publisher in Halle paid him only one or two thalers a sheet for the *Messiah*, I think, but then over and above he got a waistcoat and breeches for him, brought him thus equipped into society, let him be seen in this guise, and made people notice that he had got these things for him. Whereas, according to later, even if not completely authenticated reports, the Athenians set up a statue of Pindar (Pausanias, I. viii. 5) because he had praised them in one of his songs, and in addition (according to Aeschines, *Ep.* iv) paid to him twice the fine which the Thebans imposed on him, and would not modify, for lavishing excessive praise on another city.[1] Indeed it is even reported that Apollo himself, through the mouth of the priestess at Delphi, declared that Pindar should receive half of the gifts that the whole of Greece used to bring to the Pythian games.

(γ) In the whole range of lyric poetry, thirdly, what is presented is the entirety of an individual in the movement of his poetic inner life. For the lyric poet is driven to express in song everything shaped poetically in his heart and mind. In this respect special mention must be made of Goethe who in all the variety of his full life was always a poet and who in this matter too is amongst the most remarkable of men. Seldom can an individual be found who was so actively interested in anything and everything and yet, despite this infinite spread of interest, lived throughout in *himself* and transformed into poetic vision whatever touched him. His outward life, the special character of his heart, rather closed than open in everyday affairs, his scientific tendencies and the issue of his continued research, the empirical principles of his accomplished practical sense, the impressions made on him by the variously complicated

---

[1] Pindar was born within the jurisdiction of Thebes but he does not seem to have shared the Theban non-intervention in the Persian War. The letter attributed to Aeschines is not now regarded as genuine. Isocrates (*On the Antidosis*, § 166) says that Athens gave Pindar 10,000 drachmae. Apollo's declaration is reported in the life of Pindar prefixed to editions of his works.

events of his time, the results he drew from these, the effervescent gusto and courage of his youth, the cultured force and inner beauty of his manhood, the comprehensive and joyful wisdom of his later years—all this in his case was poured out in lyrics in which he expressed both the lightest play of feeling and the hardest and most grievous conflicts of spirit and by this expression liberated himself from them.

(b) *The Lyrical Work of Art*

Little can be said, by way of generalization, about the lyric poem as a work of art, because here there is a fortuitous wealth of variety in the mode of treatment and the forms of the subject-matter which is just as incalculably varied itself. For although this whole sphere here too cannot propose to exempt itself from the general laws of beauty and art, its subjective character implies in the nature of the case that the scope of turns and tones of expression must remain absolutely unlimited. Therefore, for our purpose, we are concerned only with the question how the type of lyrical works of art differs from that of epic.

In this matter I will draw attention briefly to only the following points:

(α) the unity of the lyric work of art;
(β) the manner of its development;
(γ) the external matter of metre and presentation.

(α) The importance of epic for art, as I have said, already lies, especially in the case of primitive epics, less in the complete development of perfect artistic form than in the totality of a national spirit which one and the same work presents before us in its fullest development.

($\alpha\alpha$) To present such a totality to us in this graphic way is something which a properly lyric work of art must not undertake. The poet, as subjective spirit, may indeed proceed to comprehend the universe, but if he wishes truly to assert himself as a self-enclosed subject he must accept the principle of particularization and individualization. Yet this does not mean that from the start there are excluded a variety of insights drawn from the natural environment, memories of experiences, his own and those of others, of mythical and historical events, and the like. But in lyric this breadth of content should not arise by being implied by the entirety of a specific actual situation, as is the case in epic, but must look for its justification in the fact that it becomes alive in the poet's subjective memory and gift for agile combination.

(ββ) The central point of unity in a lyric must therefore be regarded as the inner life of the poet. But this inner life itself is partly the individual's pure unity with himself and partly it is fragmented and dispersed into the most diversified particularization and most variegated multiplicity of ideas, feelings, impressions, insights, etc.; and their linkage consists solely in the fact that one and the same self carries them, so to say, as their mere vessel. Therefore in order to be the centre which holds the whole lyric work of art together the poet must have achieved a *specific* mood or entered a specific situation, while at the same time he must identify *himself* with this particularization of himself as with himself, so that in it he feels and envisages *himself*. In this way alone does he then become a self-bounded subjective entirety and express only what issues from this determinate situation and stands in connection with it.

(γγ) What is most completely lyrical from this point of view is a mood of the heart concentrated on a concrete situation, because the sensitive heart is what is inmost in the subjective life, and most that life's own, while reflection and meditation on universal principles may easily slip into being didactic or may emphasize in an epic way what is substantive and factual in the subject-matter.

(β) Neither on the development of the lyric poem can anything specific be laid down in general terms and therefore here too I must confine myself to a few more important remarks.

(αα) The development of an epic is of a lingering kind and it expands in general into the portrayal of a widely ramified actual life. For in epic the poet, as subject, immerses himself in the objective sphere which proceeds and is formed on its own account in its independent reality. In lyric, on the other hand, it is feeling and reflection which, conversely, draw the objectively existent world into themselves and live it through in their own inner element, and only then, after that world has become something inward, is it grasped and expressed in words. In contrast to the spread of epic, lyric has *concentration* for its principle and must intend to make its effect principally by inner profundity of expression, and not by extended descriptions or explanations. Yet between an almost dumb conciseness and the eloquent clarity of an idea that has been fully worked out, there remains open to the lyric poet the greatest wealth of steps and nuances. Neither is the illustration of external objects banned. On the contrary, the really concrete lyric works display the poet in his external situation too and therefore incorporate the natural environment, locality, etc., likewise; indeed there are poems limited entirely to descriptions of these and the like. But in that case what is properly lyric is not objective fact and its plastic portrayal, but the echo of the external in the mind, the mood aroused by it, and the feelings of the heart in such surroundings. Consequently, by the traits brought before our eyes we are not to contemplate this or that object from the outside but to be inwardly conscious of the heart which has put itself into it and so to be moved by that consciousness to have the same mode of feeling or meditation. The clearest example of this is afforded by Romaunts and Ballads which, as I indicated above, are the more lyrical the more they emphasize in the event recounted only what corresponds to the inner state of soul in which the poet tells his story and give us the whole circumstances in such a way that the poet's mood itself has a living echo out of them in us. Therefore all exact painting of external objects, no matter how full of sentiment it may be, and even all detailed characterization of inner situations, always have less effect in lyric than tighter construction and richly significant concentrated expression.

($\beta\beta$) Episodes likewise are not forbidden to the lyric poet, but he should avail himself of them for a reason quite different from the one that an epic poet has. In the case of epic they are implied by the conception of a whole which gives objective independence to its parts, and in relation to the progress of the epic action they acquire the significance of delays and hindrances. But their justification in lyric is of a subjective kind; for the living individual runs through his inner world more rapidly; on the most varied occasions he recalls the most different things; he links together the most diverse things of all; and he lets himself be led hither and thither by his ideas and intuitions, though without thereby departing from his really basic feeling or the object on which he is reflecting. A similar vivacity belongs to the poet's inner life, although it is in most cases difficult to say whether this or that in a lyric poem is to be regarded as episodic or not. But, in general, precisely appropriate to lyric are digressions, so long as they do not disrupt the unity of the poem, and, above all, surprising turns of phrase, witty combinations, and sudden and almost violent transitions.

(γγ) Therefore in this sphere of poetry the sort of progress and connection may likewise be now different from and now wholly opposed to that of epic. As little as epic does lyric tolerate, in general, either the caprice of the ordinary man's thinking, or purely logical inferences, or the progress of philosophical thinking, expounded speculatively[1] in its necessity. On the contrary, it demands that the single parts shall be free and independent. But while for epic this relative isolation is derived from the form of the real phenomenon typical of all epic poetry's illustrations, the lyric poet gives to the particular feelings and ideas in which he expresses himself the character of free dispersal, because, although all of them are based on the same mood and the same manner of meditation, each of them in its particular character absorbs his mind, and his mind is concentrated on this one point all the time until it turns to other intuitions and modes of feeling. In this process the chain of connection may be smooth and little interrupted, but nevertheless there may be lyrical leaps producing transitions, with no intermediary, from one idea to another far removed from it, so that the poet is apparently unfettered and in a whirl, and in this flight of intoxicated enthusiasm—the very opposite of intellectual logic and circumspection—appears to be possessed by a power and a 'pathos' which rules him and carries him away against his will. The impetus and struggle of such a passion is so very proper to some kinds of lyric that Horace, for example, in many of his Odes, was at pains to use his calculated ingenuity to make leaps of this kind which apparently dissolve all connection of ideas.—For the rest, I must pass over the manifold stages of treatment that are intermediate between the extremes of (i) the clearest connection and tranquil course of ideas, and (ii) the untrammelled impetuosity of passion and enthusiasm.

(γ) The last point that still remains to be considered in this sphere concerns the external form and objective character of the lyrical work of art. The chief things here are metre and musical accompaniment.

[1] This is a term of approbation. In Hegel's vocabulary 'speculative' thinking is concrete in terms of 'reason' as opposed to the abstract categories of the 'understanding' (to use Kant's distinction). The neatest way of putting Hegel's point is Niels Bohr's remark to his son: 'You are just being logical, you are not thinking' (Professor N. Kemmer heard this said in Copenhagen in 1951–2).

(αα) It is easy to see that the finest measure for the syllables in epic is the hexameter as it streams ahead uniformly, firmly, and yet also vividly. But for lyric we have to require at once the greatest variety of different metres and their more many-sided inner structure. The material of a lyric poem is not an object in its own appropriate objective development but the subjective movement of the poet's own heart; and the uniformity or alteration of this movement, its restlessness or rest, its tranquil flow or foaming flood and fountains, must also be expressed as a temporal movement of word-sounds in which the poet's inner life is made manifest. The sort of mood and whole mode of treatment has to be announced in the metre. For the outpouring of lyric stands to time, as an external element of communication, in a much closer relation than epic narrative does. The latter places real phenomena in the past and juxtaposes them or interweaves them in rather a spatial extension, whereas lyric portrays the momentary emergence of feelings and ideas in the temporal succession of their origin and development and therefore has to give proper artistic shape to the varied kinds of temporal movement. This implies (i) a rather variegated ranging of longs and shorts in a broken inequality of rythmical feet, (ii) the varied kinds of caesura, and (iii) the rounding-off into strophes which in themselves and in their succession may have a wealth of variation both in the length and shortness of single lines and in their rhythmical figuration.

(ββ) More lyrical than this artistically adequate treatment of temporal duration and its rhythmical movement is the pure sound of words and syllables, and this is the place above all for alliteration, rhyme, and assonance. In this system of versification there preponderate what I have already distinguished above, (i) the spiritual significance of syllables, i.e. the accent on the sense, an accent exempt from the purely natural circumstance of independently fixed longs and shorts and now determining spiritually the duration and the loud or soft-pedalling of syllables, and (ii) the isolated sound expressly concentrated on specific letters, syllables, and words. This spiritualization of the language through the inner meaning of the words, as well as this emphasis on sound, is peculiarly appropriate to lyric, because, for one thing, what is *there* and in evidence it adopts and expresses only in the sense which this existent possesses for the inner life, and, for another thing, for the material of its communication it seizes mainly on sound and tone. Of course even in this sphere rhythm may be closely associated with rhyme, but in that case this happens in a way approximating once more to the musical beat. Therefore, strictly speaking, the poetic use of assonance, alliteration, and rhyme may be confined to the sphere of lyric; for although as a result of the nature of modern languages the medieval epic cannot abjure these forms, this is nevertheless for the most part only permissible because here from the start the lyrical element within epic poetry itself is operative to a greater extent and it makes its way still more vigorously in songs of the heroes, ballad-like and romance-like narratives, etc. The same thing occurs in dramatic poetry. But what belongs more peculiarly to lyric is a more ramified figuration of rhyme which, with the return of the same sounds of letters, syllables, and words, or the alternation of different ones, is developed and completed in variously articulated and interlaced rhyme-strophes. It is true that epic and dramatic poetry do likewise avail themselves of these divisions, but only for the same reason that they do not ban rhyme. The Spaniards, for example, at the time when the development of their drama was at its zenith, gave free room throughout to the subtle play of a passion little suited in expression to drama, and they incorporated *ottava rima*,[1] sonnets, etc. into their otherwise dramatic versification. At any rate they show in their continued assonances and rhymes their predilection for the musical element in language.

(γγ) Lastly, lyric poetry approaches music, to a greater extent than is possible by the use of rhyme alone, owing to the fact that its language becomes actual melody and song. This leaning to music is completely justified too. The material and subject-matter of lyric lacks an independence and objectivity of its own and is especially of a subjective kind, rooted solely in the poet himself; nevertheless its communication necessitates an external support. The more that all this is true, all the more does this subject-matter require for its presentation something external and decisive. Because it remains inner, it must provide an external stimulus. But this sensuous stimulation of our hearts can be produced by music alone.

After all, in the matter of external execution, we find lyric poetry almost always accompanied by music. Yet we must not

[1] An eight-line stanza, rhyming ab, ab, ab, cc, as, for example, in Byron's *Don Juan*.

overlook an essential series of stages in this union of poetry and music. For fusion with melodies in the strict sense is really only achieved in the case of romantic,[1] and, above all, modern lyrics; this is what we find especially in those songs where the mood and the heart preponderate, and music has then to struggle and develop this inner note of the soul into melody. Folk-song, for example, loves and calls for a musical accompaniment. On the other hand, canzonets, elegies, epistles, etc., and even sonnets will nowadays not easily find a composer [to set them to music]. Where ideas and reflections and even feelings are completely expounded in the poetry and thereby more and more liberated from being wholly concentrated within the mind and from the sensuous element in art, then lyric, as a communication in language, wins greater independence and does not lend itself so readily to close association with music. On the other hand, the less explicit is the inner life which seeks expression, the more it needs the help of melody. But we shall have an opportunity later to touch on the question why the Greeks, despite the transparent clarity of their diction, yet demanded the support of music when their verse was being recited, and to what extent they did so.

(c) *The Kinds of Lyric Proper*

Of the particular kinds into which lyric poetry develops I have already mentioned in detail some which form the transition from the narrative style of epic to a subjective manner of portrayal. I might equally look at the opposite aspect and exhibit the origin of drama in lyric; but this leaning of lyric towards the vivacity of drama is essentially restricted to the fact that, though without proceeding to describe an action that moves forward into conflicts, the lyric poem is a conversation and can therefore adopt the external form of a dialogue. However, these transitional stages and hybrid kinds we will leave on one side and only consider briefly those forms in which the proper principle of lyric is asserted unadulterated. The difference between them has its basis in the attitude which the poet consciously adopts to his subject-matter.

---

[1] 'Romantic', not in the sense of a nineteenth-century movement, but in Hegel's sense of the type of art which is post-classical. 'Modern' in the sense in which we speak of 'modern' languages. The argument of this paragraph apparently requires us to interpret 'romantic' as 'medieval', and 'modern' as sixteenth or seventeenth century, and this was normal usage in, for instance, F. Schlegel.

(α) In one aspect of lyric, the poet transcends the particular and private character of his ideas and feelings and immerses himself in the universal contemplation of God or the gods whose greatness and power pervades the entire inner life and makes the individuality of the poet disappear. Hymns, dithyrambs, paeans, psalms belong to this class which again is developed in different ways by different peoples. I will confine myself to drawing attention, in the most general terms, to the following difference.

(αα) The poet who rises above the restrictedness of his own inner and outer circumstances and situations and the ideas connected with these, and takes as his subject-matter what appears to him and his nation to be absolute and divine, may (i) concentrate the sphere of the divine into one objective picture, and then this picture, sketched and completed for his inner contemplation, he may place before others to the praise of the power and glory of the god so celebrated. The Hymns ascribed to Homer are, for example, of this kind. They contain situations and stories of the god for whose fame they have been composed. These stories are principally mythological, not treated merely symbolically at all, but given solid illustration, as in epic.

(ββ) A converse (ii) and more lyrical type is a dithyrambic soaring, a subjective elevation in worship. The poet, enraptured by the power of his object, shaken as it were and stunned in his inmost heart, and in a mood wholly without definition, is incapable of producing any single objective picture or shape and cannot get beyond an exultation of soul. In his ecstasy he is directly absorbed into the Absolute. Full of its essence and might, he jubilantly sings the praise of the infinity in which he immerses himself and of the magnificent phenomena in which the depths of the Godhead are revealed.

In their religious ceremonies the Greeks did not long acquiesce in such mere exclamations and invocations but proceeded to interrupt such outpourings by the relation of specific mythical situations and actions. These descriptions, intercalated between the lyrical outbursts, then gradually became the chief thing, and, by presenting a living and complete action explicitly in the form of an action, developed into drama which for its part incorporated the lyrics of the chorus again as an integral part of itself.

More impressive, on the other hand, we find in many of the sublime Psalms in the Old Testament this soaring flight of praise, this jubilation of the soul as it lifts its eye to heaven and cries out to the one God in whom the Psalmist finds the end and aim of his consciousness, the proper source of all might and truth, the proper object of all glory and praise. For example we read in Psalm 33 [1–6]:

Rejoice in the Lord, O ye righteous; for praise is comely for the upright. Praise the Lord with harp; sing unto him with the psaltery and an instrument of ten strings. Sing unto him a new song; play skilfully with a loud noise. For the word of the Lord is right; and all his works are done in truth. He loveth righteousness and judgment; the earth is full of the goodness of the Lord. By the word of the Lord were the heavens made; and all the host of them by the breath of his mouth . . .

Similarly in Psalm 29 [1–8]:

Give unto the Lord, O ye mighty, give unto the Lord glory and strength. Give unto the Lord the glory due unto his name: worship the Lord in the beauty of holiness. The voice of the Lord is upon the waters; the God of glory thundereth: the Lord is upon many waters. The voice of the Lord is powerful; the voice of the Lord is full of majesty. The voice of the Lord breaketh the cedars; yea, the Lord breaketh the cedars of Lebanon. He maketh them also to skip like a calf; Lebanon and Sirion like a young unicorn. The voice of the Lord divideth the flames of fire. The voice of the Lord shaketh the wilderness . . .

Such an elevation and lyrical sublimity contains ecstasy and therefore there is no such absorption in a concrete subject-matter as enables the imagination, satisfied and at peace, to let things be; on the contrary this ecstasy intensifies rather into a purely vague enthusiasm which struggles to bring to feeling and contemplation what cannot be consciously expressed in words. Caught in this vagueness, the subjective inner life cannot portray its unattainable object to itself in peaceful beauty or enjoy its self-expression in a work of art. Instead of a peaceful picture, imagination seizes on external phenomena and juxtaposes them fragmentarily and in disorder, and since in its inner life it does not achieve any firm articulation of its particular ideas, it avails itself in its external expression of only an arbitrary and irregular rhythm.

The Prophets, in their opposition to the multitude, usually have a fundamental tone of grief and lamentation for the situation of their people; they have a sense of their people's alienation and falling away from God, and at the same time they are animated by a sublime glow of zeal and political wrath. All this then leads them further in the direction of hortatory lyric.

But in later and imitative times this excessive heat is exchanged for a more artificial warmth which readily cools and becomes abstract. For example, many of Klopstock's poems in the manner of hymns and psalms neither have any depth of thought nor do they peacefully develop some religious topic. On the contrary, what is expressed in them is above all the quest for this elevation to the infinite, and, according to our modern 'enlightened' ideas, this infinite dissolves into the empty boundlessness and inconceivable power, greatness, and majesty of God in contrast to the therefore quite conceivable impotence and overwhelming finitude of the poet.

(β) There is a second aspect of lyric, namely those kinds of lyric poetry that may be called by the general name of 'Odes' in the newer sense of that word.[1] Here, in contrast to the preceding stage, it is at once the independently emphasized subjective personality of the poet which is the most important thing of all, and it may likewise be asserted in two different ways:

(αα) In the first place, within this new form and its manner of expression, the poet selects, as before, a topic important in itself, the fame and praise of gods, heroes, and chiefs, or love, beauty, art, friendship, etc.; and then he reveals his inner life as so captivated, engrossed, and pervaded by this topic and its concrete actuality that it looks as if, in his transports of enthusiasm, his subject has mastered his whole soul and rules in it as its sole determinant and master. If this were to be completely the case, then the topic could be shaped, developed, and concluded on its own account, objectively, and plastically, so as to become a sculptural image, like those in epic. On the other hand, however, it is precisely his own subjective personality and its grandeur that the poet has to express on its own account and make objective, so that on his side he masters his subject, transforms it within himself, brings himself to expression in it, and therefore, free and independent himself, interrupts the objective course of his topic's development with his own feelings and reflections, and illumines and alters it by his subjective activity. The result is that mastery belongs not to the topic but to his subjective enthusiasm, engrossed by the topic. Yet this brings into being two different, and even opposed, aspects: (i) the

[1] It is a Greek word, originally meaning 'song'.

captivating might of the topic, and (ii) the poet's own subjective freedom which flashes out in the struggle against the topic which is trying to master it. It is mainly the pressure of this opposition which necessitates the swing and boldness of language and images, the apparent absence of rule in the structure and course of the poem, the digressions, gaps, sudden transitions, etc.; and the loftiness of the poet's genius is preserved by the mastery displayed in his continual ability to resolve this discord by perfect art and to produce a whole completely united in itself, which, by being *his* work, raises him above the greatness of his subject-matter.

This sort of lyrical enthusiasm is the origin of many of Pindar's Odes, but all the same their victorious inner magnificence is disclosed by their rhythm which moves variously and yet is given a measure fixed by rule. On the contrary, especially where he wants to make the most of himself, Horace is very jejune and lacking in warmth, and he has an imitative artistry which seeks in vain to conceal the more or less calculated finesse of his composition. Even Klopstock's enthusiasm is not always genuine but often becomes something manufactured; many of his Odes, however, are full of true and real feeling and possess a captivating and masculine dignity and power of expression.

($\beta\beta$) But, secondly, the subject-matter need not be really important or of intrinsic value; on the contrary, the poet becomes of such importance to himself in his individuality that now, because he takes even rather insignificant things as his subject, he confers on them dignity and nobility, or, at the very least, a higher interest. Many things in Horace's Odes are like this and even Klopstock and others have adopted this attitude. In this case the poet has no struggle with the importance of his topic; on the contrary he elevates what is inherently unimportant in external occasions, trifling accidents, etc., to the height on which he senses and visualizes himself.

(γ) Lastly, the whole endless variety of lyric moods and reflections is spread out at the stage of the song.[1] Consequently it is in

---

[1] Nomenclature here is not easy in English. German can distinguish between *Gesang* (something actually sung, or essentially a tune) and *Lied* (a song with both words and music). But, as here, *Lied* may be a lyric, or lay, which indeed may, but need not, be set to music; and Mendelssohn's *Lieder* have no words. In English, many lyrics are called 'songs' but by no means all of those included in Hegel's category here. The French distinction between *chanson* and *chant* is similar to the German.

song that particular national differences and the special characteristics of individual poets are most completely in evidence. Every variety of sort and kind can be brought into this sphere and a precise classification is extremely difficult. In the most general terms the following differences may perhaps be distinguished.

(αα) First, the song proper, meant for warbling in private or for singing in company. This does not require much substance or inner grandeur and loftiness; on the contrary, dignity, nobility, gravity of thought would only hinder the pleasure of direct self-expression. Imposing reflections, profound thoughts, and sublime feelings simply force a man to escape from his immediate individuality and its interests and moods of soul. But this directness of joy or grief, whatever is deeply felt without hindrance, is just precisely what should find its expression in song. Therefore every people is most at home and comfortable in its songs.

No matter how far this domain may extend without limit in the range of its subject-matter and its differences of tone, each song is nevertheless distinguished at once from the previous sorts of lyric by its simplicity of material, movement, metre, language, images, etc. It begins automatically in the heart and does not proceed at all in a flight of enthusiasm from one topic to another, but clings fast to one and the same subject exclusively, whether that be an individual situation or some specific expression of joy or sorrow, the expression of a mood and ways of looking at things that tear at our hearts. In this feeling or situation the song persists tranquilly and simply without unevenness of flight or effect, without boldness of transitions or turns of phrase; and it makes this one theme into a rounded whole with an easy flow of thought, now broken off and concentrated, now more extended and consecutive, as well as with singable rhythms and recurring rhymes easily grasped and without great complexity. But the fact that a song generally has something rather fleeting in character for its subject-matter must not make us suppose that a nation had to sing the same songs for centuries and millennia. A nation that is developing at all is not so poor or so indigent as to have a writer of songs in its midst only once; the poetry of song, precisely unlike epic, does not die but awakens ever anew. This blossoming is renewed at every season, and old and most ancient songs are preserved only in the case of oppressed peoples, who have been cut off from every advance and have not attained the ever newly animated joy of making poetry. The single song, like the single mood, arises and passes away, stimulates, delights, and is forgotten. For example, who still knows and sings the songs that everyone knew and loved fifty years ago? Every age strikes its new note of song and the earlier one dies away until it is mute altogether. But all the same every song must not so much be a presentation of the personality of the poet himself as have a universal validity which makes it impress and please everyone and arouse the same feeling so that now it goes from mouth to mouth. Songs not universally sung in their own day are seldom of a genuine kind.

As for what essentially distinguishes song's mode of expression, I will emphasize only two chief points on which I have touched before: (i) The poet may express his inner life and its emotions quite openly and without reserve, especially his cheerful feelings and attitudes, so that he communicates in full everything that occurs within his consciousness. (ii) Alternatively he may go to the opposite extreme and, as it were by his approach to silence, make us only surmise what is concentrated in his undisclosed heart. The first kind of expression belongs mainly to the East and especially to the carefree cheerfulness and contented expansiveness of Mohammedan poetry which with its brilliant outlook loves to spread itself in all directions pensively and in ingenious combinations of images. The second kind, on the other hand, is more to the taste of the self-concentrated inner life of the Nordic heart which in repressed stillness can often seize only on purely external objects and indicate in them that the heart pressed in on itself cannot express or liberate itself but flickers and dies away like the child in the *Erl-King*,[1] who 'rides with his father through night and storm'. This difference, prominent in lyric generally as that between folk-poetry and artistic poetry, between the heart and comprehensive reflection, recurs here too in song with numerous shades and intermediate stages.

Of the individual kinds of song I will mention only the following.

First, *folk-songs* which on account of their immediacy generally remain at the level of song and are usually singable, indeed they demand a tuneful accompaniment [*Gesang*]. Their subject-matter consists of national deeds and events in which the nation has a sense of its very own life and which are alive in its memory. Alternatively they directly express the feelings and situations of the

[1] Goethe's poem, set to music by Schubert.

different classes, sympathy with nature, and the most intimate human relationships, and they strike most various notes of joy or of grief and melancholy.

In contrast to these there are, secondly, songs of a culture which has already been enriched in many ways and which delights in cheerful conviviality, so that the songs are full of the greatest variety of wit, graceful turns of phrase, little incidents, and other expressions of gallantry. Alternatively such a society turns more sentimentally to nature and to situations in a narrower sort of human life and describes these things and the feelings they involve or excite, while the poet retreats into himself and gloats over his own personality and emotions. If such poems do not go beyond mere description, especially the description of things in nature, they readily become trivial and show no evidence of any creative imagination. It is often no better either with descriptions of feelings about something. In the case of such descriptions of things and feelings, the poet must above all not be imprisoned in immediate wishes and desires but must have raised himself above them by his freedom of contemplation, so that what alone matters to him is the satisfaction afforded by imagination as such. This carefree freedom, this expansion of the heart and satisfaction of mind gives the loveliest charm of spiritual freedom and poetry to many of Anacreon's songs, for example, as well as to the poems of Hafiz and Goethe's *West-östliche Divan*.

But, thirdly, even at this stage a higher and universal subject-matter is not excluded at all. For example, most of the Protestant hymns [*Gesänge*] composed for the edification of the faithful belong to the class of songs [*Lieder*]. They express the longing for God, a prayer for his mercy, the repentance, hope, confidence, doubt, faith, etc., of the Protestant heart; in the first instance, no doubt, as the concern and situation of an *individual* heart, but they are expressed in a universal way so that these feelings and situations may or should be at the same time the concern of more or less everyone.

(ββ) Within this comprehensive stage, a second group consisting of sonnets, sestinas,[1] elegies, epistles, etc., may be included. These kinds are already rising beyond the previously considered sphere of song. The immediacy of feeling and expression is raised here to

---

[1] Poem with six stanzas of six lines and final triplet, each stanza having the same words as the others ending its lines but in different order (*O.E.D.*).

a communication of reflection and of a meditation that looks around in every direction and brings together under more general categories individual insights and emotional experiences: knowledge, scholarship, culture in general should prevail. And even if what remains conspicuous and dominant in all these respects is the individual who links together and conciliates the universal and the particular, still he takes a more general and wider view than he does in the song proper. For example, the Italians especially have given us in their sonnets and sestinas a brilliant example of an exquisitely reflective sensibility which in any given situation does not directly express with deeply felt concentration the mere moods of longing, grief, desire, etc., or perceptions of external objects, but allows itself many detours, looks far afield and circumspectly into mythology, history, the past and the present, and yet always returns into itself and remains coherent and self-restricted. Since neither the simplicity of the song nor the elevation of the ode is permissible in this kind of cultured poetry, singability disappears but, in compensation, as the opposite of a musical accompaniment, the language itself in its sounds and ingenious rhymes becomes the notes of a spoken melody. Elegy, on the other hand, may keep a more epic character in the measure of syllables, in reflections, apophthegms, and a descriptive portrayal of feelings.

(γγ) The third stage in this sphere is occupied by a mode of treatment, the character of which has recently emerged most clearly in Germany in Schiller. Most of his lyric poems like *Resignation, Ideals, The Kingdom of the Shades, Artists, The Ideal and Life*, are not, strictly speaking, songs, odes, hymns, epistles, sonnets, or elegies in the classical sense; on the contrary, their point of view is different from that of all these kinds of lyric. What is remarkable about them is especially the grand fundamental thought in them. But the poet is not driven by it into a dithyramb; nor, pressed by enthusiasm, has he to struggle with the greatness of his subject, since, on the contrary, his mastery of it is perfect. He fully develops its every aspect by his own poetic reflection, both with a feeling full of fire and also with a broad and comprehensive view expressed with captivating power in the most magnificent and harmonious words and images, and in rhythms and rhymes that are usually entirely simple, though striking. These great thoughts and serious interests, to which his whole life was devoted, appear therefore as the inmost property of his own spirit;

but he does not sing quietly to himself or in a convivial coterie, as Goethe does with his lips so full of song; on the contrary, he is a bard who recites a subject-matter dignified in itself to an assembly of all the best and most prominent people. So his songs sound, as he says of his Bell:

High above the life of earth below it shall swing, the neighbour of the thunder, in the azure band of heaven, and border on the world of stars. It shall be a voice from above like the clear host of the stars which in their wanderings praise their Creator and conduct the wreathèd year. Only to eternal and serious things may its metallic tongue be devoted and may time in its flight touch it hourly with its swift wings.

3. *Historical Development of Lyric*

From what I have said about the general character of lyric and then about the more detailed points which come under consideration in relation to the poet, the lyrical work of art, and the kinds of lyric, it is clear enough that especially in this domain of poetry a concrete treatment is possible only if it is historical at the same time. For any universal principle that can be established on its own account remains not only restricted in range but also abstract in its value, because in scarcely any other art is the determining factor for its form and content to the same extent a particular period and nationality and the individuality of the poet's genius. The more that this gives rise to the demand that we should not evade such an historical disquisition, the more must I precisely confine myself, because of this variety in which lyric poetry issues, exclusively to a short review of what I have come to know in this sphere and in which I have been able to take a livelier interest.

The basis for a general grouping of the manifold national and individual lyric poems must be found, as in the case of epic poetry, in the principal forms into which artistic production has developed and which we have come to know as the symbolic, the classical, and the romantic. In this sphere too, therefore, we must follow, for the main divisions of our subject, the series of stages by which we are led from oriental lyrics, to those of Greece and Rome, and from these to those of the Slavonic, Latin, and Germanic peoples.

(*a*) The oriental lyric is specially and essentially distinguished from the western one by the fact that, owing to its general nature, the East attains neither the independence and freedom of the individual nor the depth of the romantic heart which characteristically inwardizes its object without any limit. On the contrary, in respect of the *content*, the poet's mind, on the one hand, is sunk directly in what is external and single and he expresses himself in the situation and circumstances of this undivided unity, while, on the other hand, unable to find any firm support in himself he cancels himself in face of what counts for him in nature and human affairs as substance and power; related now negatively, now freely, to this substance, he strives, ever unsuccessfully, to attain an association with it in his feelings and ideas.—As for *form*, what we find here is not so much the poetic expression of independent ideas about objects or relations as rather the direct description of an unreflective assimilation of such objects, with the result that what is revealed to us is not the poet in his inner life and its reversion from externality but only his self-cancellation in face of external objects and situations. In this respect the oriental lyric, in distinction from the romantic especially, acquires as it were a more objective tone. For often enough the poet expresses things and situations not as they are in *him*, in his heart, but as they are in themselves, and he often confers on them on their own account an independent and animated life. Hafiz, for example, exclaims once: 'O come! the nightingale of the heart of Hafiz returns on the perfume of the roses of delight.'

In a different way, in the poet's liberation from himself and from anything and everything single and particular, this kind of lyric becomes a naïve expansion of the inner life which easily loses itself in the limitless and which cannot work its way through to a positive expression of what it makes its object, because this object is reality and substance itself to which no shape can be given. For this reason, in this latter respect, eastern lyric on the whole, especially with the Hebrews, the Arabs, and the Persians, has the character of a hymn-like exaltation. All the greatness, power, and magnificence of the creature the poet's imagination piles up extravagantly in order to make this splendour disappear nevertheless before the unspeakably higher majesty of God; alternatively the imagination never tires of at least arranging on a costly string everything lovable and beautiful as an offering to whom or to what the poet solely values, be it Sultan or mistress or tavern.

Lastly, the form of expression, to come down to detail, which is especially at home in this sort of poetry is metaphor, image, and simile. For, on the one hand, the poet, not free in himself in his own inner life, can express himself only by assimilating himself to something external and different from himself by way of comparison; while, on the other hand, what is universal and substantive remains abstract here, without any possibility of being fused with a specific content in order that something free and individual may emerge. Consequently the universal comes before contemplation only by its being compared with particular external phenomena, while these in the end get only the value of being able to serve as approximate comparisons with the One which alone has significance and is alone deserving of fame and praise. But these metaphors, images, and similes in which the inner life discloses itself, almost to the point of emerging into visibility, are not the actual feeling and reality itself but an expression purely subjectively manufactured by the poet. Therefore, what the lyrical heart lacks here in inner concrete freedom we find replaced by freedom of expression which starts from naïve simplicity in images and the language of simile, and then develops through the most varied intermediate stages until it reaches the most incredible boldness and most subtle wit of new and surprising combinations of ideas.

In conclusion, of the individual peoples who have made their mark in the oriental lyric I mention here the Chinese first, then the Indians, but above all the Hebrews, Arabs, and Persians, but I cannot go into their special characteristics here.

(*b*) The decisive characteristic at the second stage, namely Greek and Roman lyric, is classical individuality. In accordance with the principle of this, the poet, communicating his mind lyrically, does not give himself up to what is external and objective, neither does he rise beyond himself to the sublime call to all creatures: 'Let everything that hath breath praise the Lord',[1] nor, in joyful liberation from all the chains of finitude, does he immerse himself in the One who permeates and animates all things; on the contrary, he associates himself freely with the universal as the substance of his own spirit, and brings this unification within himself as an individual into consciousness of himself as a poet.

Just as the lyric of Greece and Rome is distinct from the oriental one, so it is in an opposite way from the romantic one. For instead of being engrossed in the deep feeling of particular moods and situations, it elaborates the inner life to the extent of the clearest

[1] Psalm 150: 6.

exposition of its individual passions, insights, and meditations. In this way, even when it expresses the inner spirit, it retains, so far as is permissible in lyric, the plastic type of the classical form of art. Whatever it enunciates in the way of views on life, wise saws, etc., does not lack, despite its transparent universality, the free individuality of an independent mood and mode of treatment, and it is expressed not so much in images and metaphors as directly and literally, while even subjective feeling becomes objective to itself, either in a universal way or else in some visualizable shape. Within this same individuality the particular kinds of lyric are distinguished by their conception, expression, idiom, and metre so that they may attain, in complete independence from one another, the culmination of their development. And, like the inner life and its ideas, their external presentation is also of a rather plastic kind, because, so far as music goes, what is emphasized is not so much the inner and soulful melody of feeling as the perceptible sound of words in the rhythmic measure of their movement, and at last permits the entry of the complications of the dance.

(α) In its original richest development, the Greek lyric affords the perfect example of this character of art, in the first instance as what still retains an epic flavour, i.e. hymns which in the metre of epic do not so much express an inner enthusiasm as a plastic picture of the gods set before our souls in fixed objective traits, as I have explained earlier. Then the next step in metre is the elegiac measure of syllables, i.e. the addition of a pentameter; here we have the first beginning of a rounding off into strophes, because the pentameter regularly recurs in succession to the hexameter and the caesura breaks are similar.[1] After all the whole tone of an elegy is already lyric, whether concerned with affairs of state or with love, although especially as a gnomic elegy it comes close to the epic emphasis on and expression of what is substantive as such, and therefore it belongs almost exclusively to the Ionians[2] with whom the sight of the objective is uppermost. On the musical side, it is especially rhythm which is developed.—Then lastly, with a new metre, the iambic poem is elaborated and it has already at this

---

[1] Elegiac couplets are a dactylic hexameter followed by a dactylic pentameter. The caesura is normally penthemimeral in both, i.e. comes at the end of two-and-a-half feet.

[2] e.g. Callinus of Ephesus, whom Hegel has already mentioned and may have in mind.

date a more subjective tendency owing to the sharpness of its invectives.[1]

But the really lyric reflection and passion was first developed in the lyric metres, sometimes called 'Melic' [or 'Lesbian']: here the metres become more varied in kind, with more changes, and the strophes richer; the elements of musical accompaniment are more complete owing to the added modulation: each poet makes his own syllabic measure to suit his own lyrical character; e.g. Sappho[2] hers for her feminine outpourings which nevertheless are effectively intensified in expression and inflamed by a glow of passion; Alcaeus his for his masculine and bolder odes. The scolia[3] especially, with their variety of subject and tone, permit of numerous shades of diction and metre.

In richness of ideas and reflections, in boldness of transitions, links, etc., as well as in their public recitations, it is lyrics in choruses which were most amply developed [in Greece]. The song of the chorus may be interchanged with single voices, and its inner movement is not satisfied by the mere rhythm of speech and musical modulations, but, as a plastic element [in the Greek drama], summons in aid the movements of a dance, so that here the subjective side of lyric acquires a complete counterpoise through being illustrated by means of an external mode of execution. The subject-matters of this kind of lyrical enthusiasm are those of the greatest importance and substantive worth, the glorification of the gods as well as of victors in those Games wherein the Greeks, so frequently at variance with one another politically, had an objective vision of their national unity; and then after all in the inner mode of treatment in these poems traces of an objective and epic treatment are not lacking. For example, Pindar who in this sphere attains the summit of perfection, easily turns, as I have said already, from the external stimuli given to him to profound utterances on the general nature of morality and religion, and then, along with this theme, on heroes, heroic deeds, the foundations of states, etc., and he has in his power not only their plastic illustration but also the subjective soaring of his own imagination. Consequently it is not the thing which goes ahead, as it does in epic, but subjective

---

[1] e.g. in the 'scorpion-tongued' Archilochus, still, like Callinus, of the seventh century B.C.

[2] She, like Alcaeus, may be slightly later than Archilochus.

[3] Drinking songs composed by Terpander, contemporary with these others, and by e.g. Alcaeus and Pindar.

inspiration, captivated by its object, so that this object seems on the other hand to be borne and produced by the poet's mind.

The later lyric poetry[1] of the Hellenistic age is hardly an independent further development but rather a pedantic imitation and a struggle for elegance and correctness of expression, until at last it is dissipated into tiny graces and pleasantries, or tries in epigrams to tie together anew, by the string of feeling and fancy, the already existent blossoms of art and life, and to freshen them by the wit of praise or satire.

(β) In Rome lyric poetry finds soil already frequently cultivated but less fruitful originally. Its brilliant epoch is therefore confined principally to the age of Augustus when it was pursued as an expression of contemplation and as a refined intellectual pleasure; or else it remains more a matter of skill in translating and copying, and the fruit of industry and taste, than of fresh feelings and original artistic conceptions. Nevertheless, despite the pedantry and alien mythology as well as the imitation of principally colder Hellenistic models, there emerges prominently and independently both what is peculiarly Roman and also the personal character and spirit of individual poets. This gives us, if we disregard the inmost soul of poetry and art, something complete and perfect throughout in the field of odes, epistles, satires, and elegies. But the later satire, which may be drawn into this class, with its bitterness against the corruption of the age, with its piercing indignation and declamatory virtue, fails to enter the proper sphere of untroubled poetic contemplation, all the more so because against its picture of a corrupt present it has nothing to set except this indignation and the abstract rhetoric of a virtuous zeal.

(c) Just as we saw in the case of epic poetry, so too it is the case with lyric that an original content and spirit enters it only with the appearance of new nations. This is true of the Germanic, Latin, and Slavonic peoples, who, even when they were still heathen, but especially after their conversion to Christianity both in the Middle Ages and since, have developed amply and variously a third main tendency of lyric in the general character of the romantic form of art.

In this third sphere lyric poetry is of such overwhelming importance that its principle is asserted, far more profoundly than was possible in the case of the Greeks and Romans, primarily in relation

[1] Hegel presumably has e.g. Callimachus and Theocritus in mind.

to epic but then, in its later development, in relation to drama too. Indeed some nations treated strictly epic matters entirely on the lines of lyrical narrative and thereby produced works of such a character that it seems doubtful whether they should be included in either the one class or the other. This inclination towards a lyrical treatment is essentially grounded in the fact that the entire life of these nations has been developed on the basis of the principle of the personality which is forced to produce out of its own resources as its own what is substantive and objective, and to give a shape to that, and this process of plumbing its own depths it pursues more and more consciously. This principle is effective in the most perfect and unclouded way in the case of the Germanic races, while the Slavonic ones, on the other hand, have first to struggle out of an oriental immersion in the universal substance of things. In the middle between these are the Latin peoples who found available to them in the conquered provinces of the Roman Empire not only the remains of Roman learning and civilization generally but a completely developed social and political situation, and in order to be assimilated to it they had to abandon part of their original nature.

As for the *subject-matter* of this lyric poetry, it is at almost all stages in the development of national and individual existence that peoples and centuries, now disclosing an ever greater wealth in the matter of their religious and secular life, come to express this life in the mirror of their inner consciousness as subjective states and situations. As for the *form* of this poetry, its fundamental type consists, in part, in the expression of a heart inwardly concentrated in depth of feeling, whether the heart immerses itself in national or other events, in nature and the external environment, or remains occupied purely with itself; and, in part, in a subjective reflection that becomes deeper in itself as it explores the depths of its own wider culture. On the external side, the plasticity of rhythmic versification changes into the music of alliteration, assonance, and the most varied interlacings of rhymes; and these new features are used, on the one hand, extremely simply and unpretentiously, and on the other hand with great skill and the invention of firmly marked forms, while the external delivery develops ever more completely the strictly musical accompaniment of melodic tune [*Gesang*] and instruments.

Finally, in dividing this comprehensive group we may follow in essence the route that I have indicated before in the case of epic poetry.

Accordingly we have first the lyric poetry of the new peoples in their original character when they were still heathen.

Secondly, lyric expands more richly in the Christian Middle Ages.

Thirdly, the essential influences are the reawakened study of classical art and the modern principle of Protestantism.

Yet I cannot go on here to expatiate on the more detailed characteristics of these chief stages in the development of lyric, and I will merely limit myself in conclusion to giving prominence to one German poet by whom our national lyric poetry has in recent times been given a great impetus and whose merit has not received sufficient recognition from our contemporaries: I mean the author of *The Messiah*. Klopstock is one of the great Germans who have helped to start a new artistic epoch amongst us; he is a great figure who by his spirited inspiration and inner pride has wrested poetry from the colossal insignificance of Gottsched's[1] period which with its own completely immovable insipidity took, in short, all the warmth out of whatever was still noble and dignified in the German spirit. Full of the sanctity of a poet's calling, Klopstock has given us poems, a great part of which remains classical, in a form of sterling even if severe worth.

His youthful odes are dedicated in part to a friendship which to him was something sublime, firm, and honourable, the pride of his soul, a temple of the spirit; and in part to a love profound and deeply felt. Nevertheless there belong precisely to this field many productions which must be regarded as wholly prosaic—for example *Selmar and Selma*, a miserable and tedious contest between lovers which, not without many tears, sadness, empty longing, and futile melancholy feelings, turns on the idle and lifeless speculation as to whether Selmar or Selma is to be the first to die. But what really does come to the fore above all in Klopstock in all sorts of connections is patriotism. The Christian mythology, legends of the saints etc. (angels perhaps excepted; for them he had a great poetic respect, although in a poetry of living actuality they remain abstract and dead) did not satisfy him, as a Protestant, either for the moral seriousness of art or the force of life and the spirit which is not purely melancholy and meek but which has

[1] 1700–66.

a sense of itself and is positively pious. But as a poet he was pressed by the need for a mythology and in particular for one that was at home here, the names and figures of which were already present as a firm footing for the imagination. For us in Germany a native imagery is not supplied by the Greek gods, and so Klopstock, from national pride we may say, tried to enliven again the old mythology of Wotan, Hertha, etc. Yet so far as objective effect and validity went he could achieve as little with these names of gods that *had been* Germanic but *are* so no longer as if he had tried to make the Diet at Ratisbon the ideal of our present-day political life. Therefore, however great was Klopstock's need to bring before himself in poetry and in fact and in our national dress a universal popular mythology, the truth of our nature and spirit, nevertheless those dead gods remained wholly and completely false and null, and there was a sort of silly hypocrisy in pretending to act as if reason and the national faith were supposed to take them seriously. But for pure imagination the figures of Greek mythology are infinitely more attractive and cheerful, moulded in a greater variety of ways and more like free human beings. In lyric, however, it is the bard who portrays himself: and in Klopstock we must honour the bard on account of his patriotic need and endeavour, an endeavour effective enough to produce late fruits and even in the field of poetry to direct scholarly attention to similar [pre-historic] subjects. Finally, Klopstock's patriotic sense emerges perfectly clear, beautiful, and very influentially in his enthusiasm for the honour and dignity of the German language and for historical figures in our earlier history, e.g. Hermann and above all some German Emperors who have done honour to themselves by the art of poetry.[1] Thus, with ever greater justification he enlivened the German muse's pride and its growing courage to measure itself, in cheerful consciousness of its power, against the Greeks, the Romans, and the English. No less modern and patriotic is the way that he directs his gaze on the German Princes and on the hopes that their character might arouse in respect of the national honour, art and science, public affairs, and great spiritual ends. Sometimes he expresses contempt for those of our Princes who 'in a cosy chair, surrounded by courtiers with their incense, are inglorious now and soon will be more inglorious still'; again he expresses his

---

[1] The Manesse Codex, a collection of German medieval lyrics, include poems by Emperor Henry IV and Conradin, both of the Staufen line.

grief that even Frederick the Great 'never saw that German poetry rose quickly from a firm root and enduring stem, and cast the shade of its branches far and wide'.[1] Equally grievous to him are the vain hopes that had made him see in the Emperor Joseph II the dawn of a new world of intellect and poetry. Finally what does honour to the heart of Klopstock in old age is his sympathy with the phenomenon[2] of a people's breaking chains of every kind, trampling underfoot the injustice of a thousand years, and intending to base its political life on reason and justice for the first time. He greets this new 'refreshing, yes undreamt-of, sun. Blessed be the gray hairs that cover my head and the power that remains with me after sixty years, for this power it was that brought me thus far to feel this dawn in my heart'. Indeed, he even addresses the French: 'Forgive me, ye Franks (the name of "Brothers" is the noble name) that once I called on Germany to flee from that in which now I beg it to imitate you.' But a still more bitter fury befell the poet when this beautiful dawn of freedom was transformed into a day of terror, blood, and the murder of freedom. Yet to this grief Klopstock could not give a poetic form, and he expressed it all the more prosaically, infirmly, and confusedly because he had nothing higher to set against his disappointed hope, for his heart could not visualize in what actually happened any higher demand of reason.[3]

Thus Klopstock remains great in virtue of his feeling for the nation, for freedom, friendship, love, and Protestant firmness; he is to be venerated for his nobility of soul and poetry, for his struggles and accomplishments; and even if in many respects he remained caught in the limitations of his age and composed many frigid Odes that were merely critical, grammatical, and metrical, nevertheless, with the exception of Schiller,[4] no figure has appeared since so independent, so noble, or with such a serious and manly disposition.

But Schiller and Goethe, on the other hand, have not lived merely as bards of their time, but as more universal poets. And, in

[1] This quotation, and the one which follows, are from Klopstock's poem *Die États Généraux*.   [2] i.e. the French Revolution.
[3] This remark rests on Hegel's philosophy of history. For him, history is not a tale told by an idiot but the work of Reason which, even in apparent disasters, is still pursuing its ends, cunningly if not overtly. If this view be correct, Klopstock's was too pessimistic.
[4] Klopstock died in 1803, Schiller in 1805. Goethe was still living when Hegel lectured, and this may be why he is not mentioned in this paragraph, but only in the next.

particular, Goethe's songs are the most excellent, profound, and effective things given to Germany in recent times, because they belong entirely to him and his nation, and since they have emerged on our own soil they also completely strike the fundamental note of our spirit.

C. DRAMATIC POETRY

Because drama has been developed into the most perfect totality of content and form, it must be regarded as the highest stage of poetry and of art generally. For in contrast to the other perceptible materials, stone, wood, colour, and notes, speech is alone the element worthy of the expression of spirit; and of the particular kinds of the art of speech dramatic poetry is the one which unites the objectivity of epic with the subjective character of lyric. It displays a complete action as actually taking place before our eyes; the action originates in the minds of the characters who bring it about, but at the same time its outcome is decided by the really substantive nature of the aims, individuals, and collisions involved. But this conciliation of epic with the inner life of the person who is acting in front of us does not permit drama to describe, as epic does, the *external* aspect of the locality and the environment, as well as of what happens and is done, and it therefore demands a complete scenic production in order to give real life to the whole work of art. Lastly, the action itself in the entirety of its mental and physical actuality is susceptible of two opposed modes of treatment, tragic and comic, and the predominant principle of these provides us with a distinction in kind as a third chief aspect of dramatic poetry.

From these general points we may derive the following course for our inquiries:

first, we have to consider the dramatic work of art in its general and special character as distinguished from epic and lyric;

secondly, we must direct attention to the scenic presentation and its necessity; and

thirdly, review the different sorts of dramatic poetry in their concrete historical development.

1. *The Drama as a Poetical Work of Art*

The first thing to be more specifically emphasized is the purely poetical side of a dramatic work, quite independently of the fact that it has to be presented scenically if we are to contemplate it directly. In this connection, the following are the more detailed points to consider:

first, the general principle of dramatic poetry;
secondly, the particular characteristics of the dramatic work of art;
thirdly, the relation of that work to the public.

(a) The Principle of Dramatic Poetry

What drama in general needs to be is the presentation, to our minds and imagination, of actual human actions and affairs and therefore of persons expressing their action in words. But a dramatic action is not confined to the simple and undisturbed accomplishment of a specific aim; on the contrary, it rests entirely on *collisions* of circumstances, passions, and characters, and leads therefore to actions and then to the reactions which in turn necessitate a resolution of the conflict and discord. Therefore what we see in front of us are certain ends individualized in living characters and very conflicting situations, and we see them in their self-assertion and display, in their reciprocal influence and design; and all this in the very moment of their mutual expression; and we see too the self-grounded final result of this whole human machinery in will and accomplishment, we see it in its criss-cross movement and yet in its final peaceful resolution.

The poetic treatment of this new subject-matter must be, as I have indicated, a conciliating union of the principles of epic and lyric.

(α) The first point to be made in this connection relates to the period in which dramatic poetry can assert itself as the pre-eminent kind of poetry. Drama is the product of a completely developed and organized national life. For in essence it presupposes as past both the primitive poetic days of the epic proper and the independent subjectivism of lyrical outpourings, because, comprising both of these, it is satisfied in neither of these spheres taken separately. For this poetic combination, the free self-consciousness of human aims, complications, and fates must have been already completely aroused and developed in a way possible only in epochs of the half-way or later development of a national life. Thus the earliest great deeds and events in a nation's life usually have an epic, rather than a dramatic, character: expeditions in common, usually abroad, like the Trojan war, the adventures of national migrations, the Crusades; or associations for defence at home against invaders, like the Persian wars; and only later do those single independent heroes appear who fasten on ends of their own and carry out exploits by their own resources.

(β) The following points are to be made about the *conciliation* of the epic and the lyric principles.

An epic does bring an action before our eyes, but it brings it as the substantive entirety of a national spirit in the form of objective and definite events and deeds in which there is an equipoise between (*a*) the agent's will and his individual aim, and (*b*) the external circumstances and the real hindrances that these impose on him. Whereas in lyric it is the individual who comes forward and expresses himself on his own account and in his own independent inner life.

Now if drama is to incorporate these two sides and keep them together

(αα) it must, in the first place, like epic, bring before us a happening, a deed, an action; but its first step must be, above all, to strip externals away and put in their place as the ground and cause of everything the self-conscious and active individual. For a drama does not fall apart into a lyrical inner life and an external sphere as its opposite, but displays an inner life and *its* external realization. It follows that in that case the happening does not proceed from external circumstances but out of an agent's inner will and character, and it acquires dramatic significance only by its relation to an individual's aims and passions. Nevertheless, it is equally true that the individual does not remain shut in to an independence of his own but finds himself brought into opposition and conflict with others owing to the nature of the circumstances (in which his character and his aim determine what he wills), as well as to the nature of this individual aim itself. In this way, action is at the mercy of complications and collisions which, against the will and intention of the agents, lead to an outcome in which the real inner essence of human aims, characters, and conflicts is revealed. This fundamental essence is asserted in individual agents acting independently and from their own resources, and this is the other aspect of epic which is evidently effective and vital in the principle of dramatic poetry.

(ββ) But however far the individual and his inner life is the centre of the drama, a dramatic presentation cannot be content with purely lyrical emotional situations or with letting the agent describe deeds that have been done without his participating in them or, in general, with sketching passive pleasures, views, and feelings; on the contrary, a drama must display situations, and the mood they arouse, as determined by the character of an individual who resolves on particular ends and makes these what he wills in practice. Therefore in drama a specific attitude of mind passes over into an impulse, next into its willed actualization, and then into an action; it externalizes and objectifies itself and so inclines towards the sort of reality that we find in epic. But the external phenomenon, instead of existing as a mere happening, contains, in the individual's view, his own intentions and aims. The action is the achievement of his will and is known as such as regards both its origin and beginning in himself and also its final result. The issue of his act proceeds from the individual himself and has its repercussion on his character and circumstances. The properly lyric principle in drama is this steady relation of the whole reality of the situation to the inner life of the self-determining individual who is the ground of it, while at the same time he absorbs it into himself.

(γγ) In this way alone does the action appear as an *action*, as the actual execution of inner intentions and aims. The individual identifies himself with their realization and in it finds his own will and his own satisfaction, and now with his whole being must take responsibility for what the issue is in the external world. The individual dramatic character himself picks the fruit of his own deeds.

But since interest is restricted to the inner aim, of which the individual agent is the hero, and since the only thing that the work of art need take from the external world is what has an essential relation to this consciously produced aim, drama is, in the first place, more abstract than epic. For, on the one hand, the action rests on the self-determination of the individual's character and must follow from this original inner source; it does not presuppose the epic ground of an entire world-view elaborated objectively in all its aspects and ramifications. On the contrary, it is concentrated into the simplicity of specific circumstances in which the individual decides on an aim and pursues it. On the other hand, it is not individuality which is to be unrolled before us in the *entire* complex of its national qualities (as in epic) but a character in respect of his *action* which has a *specific* end as its universal soul. This end, the thing on which everything depends, is beyond the particular scope of the individual who appears only as its living instrument and animating sustainer. A further development of the individual's character in its most varied aspects connected not at all, or only rather remotely, with his action, which is concentrated on one thing alone, would be superfluous, so that, so far as the individual agent is concerned, dramatic poetry must be more simply drawn together than epic. The same is true for the number and variety of the characters on the stage. For, as I have indicated, this tedious objective expatiation would be futile and disturbing [in a drama], because drama does not move forward on the soil of some total national life, which should bring before us the whole amazing variety of its different classes, with their varying age, sex, activities, etc.; on the contrary, drama has to fix our eye steadily on *one* aim and its accomplishment.

But, in the second place, the aim and object of an action is nevertheless only dramatic when it calls up in other individuals different and opposed aims and passions; this is because the aim is specific, and the individual agent can adopt it in its separate character only in circumstances that are specific likewise. This driving 'pathos' may indeed, in each of the actors, derive from spiritual, moral, and divine powers, such as law, patriotism, love of parents, relations, spouses, etc., but if this essential object of human feeling and activity is to appear dramatically, it must come on the scene separated into different and *opposed* ends, so that the action has to encounter hindrances from other agents and fall into complications and oppositions where both sides struggle for success and control. The real thing at bottom, the actually all-pervasive cause is therefore indeed the eternal powers, i.e. what is essentially moral, the gods of our actual life, in short what is divine and true; yet the Divine does not appear here in that tranquil might in which, instead of acting, the unmoved gods remain blessedly sunk in themselves like peaceful statuesque figures, but on the contrary it is the Divine here in its community, as the substance and aim of human individuality, brought into existence as something concrete, summoned into action and put in movement.

But if in this way the Divine is the inmost objective truth lying in the external objectivity of the action, then, in the third place, a decision on the course and outcome of the complications arising from the action cannot lie in the hands of the single individuals who oppose one another, but only in those of the Divine itself, as a totality in itself. Therefore the drama, no matter in what way, must display to us the vital working of a necessity which, itself self-reposing, resolves every conflict and contradiction.

(γ) Therefore the primary requirement for a dramatic poet as an author is that he shall have a full insight into the inner and universal element lying at the root of the aims, struggles, and fates of human beings. He must be fully aware of the oppositions and complications to which action may lead in the nature of the case, whether these arise from subjective passion and individuality of character, or from human schemes and decisions, or from concrete external affairs and circumstances. And at the same time he must be capable of recognizing what those powers are which apportion to man the destiny due to him as a result of what he has done. The right as well as the aberration of the passions that rage in the human heart and impel to action must be equally clear to the dramatist, so that where to the ordinary man's eye it is obscurity, chance, and confusion that prevail, there is clearly revealed to him the actual accomplishment of what is absolutely rational and true. Therefore he should go beyond both a mere vague exploration of the depths of the heart and also a one-sided adherence to some exclusive mood or to a restricted bias in outlook and way of thinking; what he must have is the greatest openness and most comprehensive breadth of mind. For in a mythological epic the spiritual powers are simply different, and their significance becomes vaguer owing to the many ways in which they are individualized in fact; but in a drama they enter in their simple and fundamental character and they *oppose* one another as 'pathos' in individuals. And the drama is the dissolution of the one-sidedness of these powers which are making themselves independent in the dramatic characters,[1] whether, as in tragedy, their attitude to one another is hostile, or whether, as in comedy, they are revealed directly as inwardly self-dissolving.

---

[1] e.g. in the *Antigone*, the 'spiritual power' of family piety is independently personified in her, while Creon is the independent personification of law and the state. The drama exposes the one-sidedness of both; and the tragedy is the result of the hostility arising from this one-sidedness, which is 'dissolved' in the sense that both powers are ultimately and truly seen to be complementary and not independent of one another (see below, p. 1195, n. 3).

(b) The Dramatic Work of Art

The chief points to be emphasized in relation to drama as a concrete work of art are, in brief, the following:

first, its unity as distinct from that of epic and lyric poetry;
secondly, the way the drama is divided up and unfolded;
thirdly, its external aspect, i.e. its diction, dialogue, and metre.

(α) The first and most general point to be made about the unity of a drama is connected with a remark I made earlier, namely that, in contrast to epic, dramatic poetry must be more strictly self-concentrated. For although epic too has a point of union in an individual event, the event proceeds on the variously extended field of a wide national life and it can be subdivided into numerous episodes and their objective independence. A similar appearance of a purely loose connection was allowed to some kinds of lyric, for an opposite reason. The necessity for a firmer unity of the whole drama arises because in drama the foundation that epic has disappears, as we have seen, and, on the other hand, the individuals do not simply express their own personality lyrically but, because they are opposed to one another in character and aim, enter so closely into relation with one another that it is precisely this individual interconnection which is the basis of their existence in the drama. This tighter consistency in a drama is both objective and subjective: objective in connection with the material ends which the individuals pursue in their struggle with one another; subjective, because this inherently substantive content in a drama appears as the passion of particular characters, so that individuals are essentially affected themselves, in the pursuit of their aim, by failure or success, fortune or misfortune, victory or defeat.

As more detailed rules for the unity of a drama we may refer to the familiar prescriptions for unity in respect of place, time, and action.

(αα) The unalterability of an exclusive locality for a specific action is one of those rigid rules which the French especially have drawn from Greek tragedy and the remarks of Aristotle. But Aristotle only says of tragedy (*Poetics* [1449^b 12 f.]) that the duration of the action should not normally exceed one day, and he does not touch at all on the unity of place which even the Greek poets did not abide by in the strict French sense; for example, the scene changes in the *Eumenides* of Aeschylus and the *Ajax* of Sophocles. Modern dramatic poetry is still less able to submit to the yoke of an abstract sameness of place if it is to present a wealth of collisions, characters, and persons and events in a secondary plot, in short an action whose inner complexity needs external diffusion also. So far as modern poetry is of the romantic type which may be more varied and capricious in external descriptions, it has therefore liberated itself from this demand for unity of place. But if the action is actually concentrated on a few important motifs so that it can be simple externally too, then there is no need for any varied change of scene. And this is an advantage; for, however false that conventional prescription may be, it does at least imply the right idea that a continual change of a purposeless hither and thither from one place to another must appear impermissible. For on the one hand the dramatic concentration of action has to be asserted in this external respect too, in contradistinction to an epic which may traverse space comfortably in the most varied way and with ample changes of scene. On the other hand, unlike epic which is addressed to imagination simply, a drama is composed to be actually and directly seen. In imagination we can readily transpose ourselves from one place to another; but, in the case of actual seeing, the imagination must not be overtaxed to the extent of contradicting what we see. For example, Shakespeare changes the scene very often in his tragedies and comedies, and he erected posts with labels stating where the action was taking place. But this is only a miserable expedient and it is always a distraction. Consequently unity of place recommends itself to us as being convenient and intelligible in itself, since by this means all obscurity is always avoided. Nevertheless, of course the imagination may be entrusted with much which runs counter to probability and to what we simply see with our eyes; and the most suitable procedure in this matter will always consist in the happy medium, i.e. neither in violating the claims of fact nor in demanding an all too precise adherence to them.

(ββ) It is exactly the same with the unity of time. For in imagination great spaces of time can be embraced without difficulty, but, when we are seeing something, a few years are not to be passed over so quickly. Therefore if the action is entirely simple in its entire range and in the conflict involved, the best thing will be simply to compress the time it takes for the conflict to reach a decision. Whereas if the action requires more richly endowed characters whose stages of development necessitate many situations separated in time, then the formal unity of a duration which is always only relative and wholly conventional becomes absolutely impossible; and therefore to propose to exclude such a portrayal from the sphere of dramatic poetry on the ground that it offends against that established unity of time would mean nothing but setting up the prose of realities we can see as the final judge of poetry's truth. But least of all is the law to be laid down on the strength of the purely empirical probability that, as spectators in a theatre for an hour or two, we could actually only envisage the passing of a *short* period of time. For it is precisely where the poet struggles to attain the maximum conformity with this rule that in other respects the worst and almost unavoidable improbabilities arise.

(γγ) On the other hand, the truly inviolable law is the unity of the action. But numerous disputes may arise about wherein this unity really consists, and I will therefore explain the meaning of it in more detail. In principle every action must have a specific end which the action is realizing; for with action a man steps actively into concrete reality where forthwith the most general matters are condensed and confined in a particular phenomenon. From this point of view unity would have to be sought in the realization of a purpose specific in itself and made a concrete aim in particular circumstances and conditions. But, as we saw, the circumstances for a dramatic action are of such a kind that one individual's aim encounters hindrances from other individuals, because an opposite aim, seeking commensurate realization, stands in the way, so that in this confrontation mutual conflicts and their complication result. The dramatic action therefore rests essentially on an action producing collisions, and the true unity can only be grounded in the total movement, i.e., given the determinate nature of the particular circumstances, the characters, and their ends, the collision is displayed as conforming with the characters and their ends, and finally their contradiction is annulled and unity is restored. In that case, the solution of the conflict, like the action itself, must be both objective and subjective. On the one hand the conflict of the opposing *ends* is assuaged; on the other hand, the *individuals* have more or less put their whole will and being into the undertaking they are pursuing, so that its success or failure, its complete or partial accomplishment, the inevitable disaster or the peaceful union with apparently opposed intentions, determine the fate of the individual also, since he was so completely involved with what he was driven to initiate. A genuine end is therefore only attained when the aim and interest of the action, on which the whole drama turns, is identical with the individuals and absolutely bound up with them.

Now the unity may be firmer or looser according to whether the difference and opposition of the characters in the play is kept simple or whether it ramifies into a variety of incidental actions and characters in a sub-plot. Comedy, for example, with its variously complicated intrigues does not need to be so firmly concentrated as a tragedy where the motives are generally of greater simplicity. Still, a romantic tragedy is even in this respect more varied and its unity is looser than is the case in Greek tragedy. Yet even here the relation of sub-plots and incidental characters to the whole must be recognizable, and at the denouement, every part of the whole thing must be closed and finished off. For example, in *Romeo and Juliet* the feud between the families lies outside the lovers, their aim, and their fate, but it is in fact the ground of the action though not the point of real importance, and at the close of the tragedy Shakespeare devotes rather slight but necessary attention to the ending of the feud. Similarly in *Hamlet* the fate of the Kingdom of Denmark is always a subordinate interest but it is noticed with the entry of Fortinbras, and its outcome at the end is satisfying.

It is true that the specific conclusion which resolves conflicts may involve the possibility of new interests and conflicts, but the *one* collision which is at issue [in a given play] must find its settlement in that one independently finished work. For example, the three tragedies of Sophocles about the Theban myth-cycle illustrate the point. The first discloses Oedipus as the murderer of Laius; the second his death in peace in the grove of the Eumenides; the third the fate of Antigone. Yet each of these three tragedies taken apart from the others is an independent whole in itself.

(β) In connection with the concrete way in which a dramatic work of art is developed, there are three points to be especially emphasized in which drama differs from epic and song: (i) its scope, (ii) the way it advances, (iii) its division into acts and scenes.

($\alpha\alpha$) We have already seen that a drama may not extend so widely as epic proper necessarily does. I have already mentioned that in drama the epic description of a world-situation in its entirety disappears and I have emphasized the simpler sort of collision which provides the essential subject of drama. Therefore, apart from these, I will cite only this further basis of difference, namely that, in drama, on the one hand most of what the epic poet must describe in a lingering and leisurely way for our contemplation is surrendered when it comes to actual performance on the stage, while on the other hand the chief thing is not an objective deed but the exposition of subjective passion. But in contrast to the breadth of the objective phenomenon, the subjective and personal life is concentrated in simple feelings, decisions, aphorisms, etc., and in this respect, in distinction from epic's use of the past and of things separated in space and time, it gives prominence to the lyric principle of concentration, to the present occurrence and expression of passions and ideas. But the presentation of a *single* situation does not suffice in dramatic poetry; on the contrary it portrays the invisible aspect of mind and spirit in action at the same time, i.e. as an entirety of the circumstances and aims of various characters who express all together what passes in their minds in relation to their actions, and the result is that, in comparison with a lyric poem, the drama has a far wider scope and is rounded off more completely. In general we may define the relation of drama to epic and lyric by saying that is stands more or less in the middle between the extensive spread of epic and the concentratedness of lyric.

(ββ) More important than this matter of external proportions is the way that a drama progresses in contrast with the way that an epic develops. The objective subject-matter of epic demands, as we saw, a form consisting of leisurely description which may then still set actual hindrances in a stronger light. At a first glance this might look as if, because in its presentation it opposes one aim and one character to other aims and other characters, dramatic poetry would really only have to take for its principle this checking and hindering. But in fact the truth is precisely the opposite. The progress of drama is strictly a steady movement forward to the final catastrophe. This is clear from the simple fact that *collision* is the prominent point on which the whole turns. At first the whole thing gravitates to the outbreak of this conflict, while it is precisely the discord and contradiction of opposing dispositions, aims, and activities which absolutely demands resolution and presses on towards this result. But this is not to mean that mere haste in the progress of the piece is in and by itself alone dramatically beautiful; on the contrary, the dramatic poet too must be allowed leisure to display every situation on its own account with all the motives it implies. But any incidental scenes that only hinder instead of advancing the progress of the action offend against the character of drama.

(γγ) The division of the course of a dramatic work is made most naturally when it follows the chief features that are grounded in the very nature of dramatic movement itself. In this connection, Aristotle said long ago (*Poetics* [1450^b 26 ff.])

a whole is that which has a beginning, a middle, and an end. A beginning is that which is not of necessity after something else but has or will have something else after it; an end on the contrary is naturally after something else, either necessarily or usually, but has nothing else after it; but a middle naturally has something else both before and after it.

Now in the world of our experience every action has numerous presuppositions, so that it is difficult to determine where the real beginning is to be found; but action in drama rests essentially on a definite collision, and therefore the appropriate starting-point will lie in that situation out of which that conflict must be developed as the action proceeds, even if it has not broken out already. The end will then be reached when the resolution of the dispute and its complication has been brought about in every respect. In between this beginning and this end there fall the feud between the colliding characters and the struggle of their conflicting aims. Now in a drama these different members or essential features of the action are themselves actions for which the name of 'acts' is appropriate. Nowadays they are sometimes called 'pauses', and once a Prince, who may have been in a hurry and did not want to be bothered with lack of continuity, scolded his man-in-waiting because there was still another 'pause'.

In every drama it suits the subject-matter best if the acts are three in number: in the first the emergence of the collision is explained; in the second, the collision comes to life as an encounter between interests, as struggle, difference, and complication; and then finally, in the third, when contradiction is at its peak it finds its necessary resolution. These sections of a drama are generally indistinct in Greek drama, but a corresponding analogy may be cited in the trilogies of Aeschylus in which, all the same, each part is rounded off into an independently complete whole. In modern dramatic poetry it is especially the Spanish who abide by a division into three acts; while the English, the French, and the Germans in the main generally divide the drama into five acts, where exposition falls into the first, the three intervening ones detail the quarrels and reactions, complications, and struggles of the opposing parties, and finally the fifth alone brings the collision to a complete conclusion.

(γ) The last thing we have to discuss is the means open for the use of dramatic poetry in its own domain, quite apart from its actual presentation on the stage. They are restricted to the specific kind of dramatically effective diction in general, and, in more detail, to a difference of monologue, dialogue, etc., and metre. As I have said often before, the chief thing in drama is not the objective action, but the exposition of the inner spirit of the action in respect of not only the general nature of the action and the conflict and fate involved, but also the dramatis personae and their passion, 'pathos', decision, mutual involvement and working on one another. This inner spirit, in so far as it is portrayed by poetry as poetry, therefore finds its adequate expression especially in poetic language as the most spiritual expression of feelings and ideas.

(αα) But just as drama comprises in itself the principles of epic and lyric, so dramatic diction has to contain and express both lyrical and epic elements. The lyric aspect has its place particularly in modern drama, and in general where the individual concentrates himself on himself and, in his decisions and actions, always means to retain his personal and inner life's sense of itself; yet, if the utterance of his own heart is to remain dramatic, it must not be a mere preoccupation with roving feelings, memories, and meditations, but must be kept steadily related to the action, and result in and accompany its different phases.

In contrast to this subjective 'pathos' there is an epic element, i.e. an objective 'pathos' consisting principally in addressing rather to the audience a development of the substance of affairs, aims, and characters.[1] Here again a partly lyrical tone may be adopted and the description remains dramatic only so long as it does not interrupt the progress of the action or cease to be related to it by appearing on its own account and independently.

In addition, narrated information, descriptions of battles, and

[1] This difference between subjective and objective 'pathos' is explained below, when Hegel discusses dramatic dialogue.

more of the like, as further relics of epic, can be woven into the drama, but there they must be more compressed and move more rapidly, and likewise must be clearly necessary for the progress of the action itself.

Lastly, what is properly dramatic is the speech of individuals in the conflict of their interests and the discord of their characters and passions. Here the first two elements [epic and lyric] can be present in their truly dramatic harmony. In addition there is the external aspect of what is happening which is likewise within the compass of linguistic description. For example, the exits and entrances of the chief dramatis personae are generally announced in advance and their external demeanour is often indicated by other individuals.

In all these respects there is an important difference between the mode of expression called 'natural' and a conventional language and rhetoric of the theatre. In modern times Diderot, Lessing, and even Goethe and Schiller in their youth, leaned principally to direct and natural expression—Lessing with well cultivated and subtle observation, Schiller and Goethe with a preference for the immediate life of unadorned strength and force. It was regarded as contrary to nature to suppose that men could speak to one another as they they do in Greek comedies and tragedies, but especially in French ones (and as regards French ones this is true enough). But with its superfluity of purely objective descriptions this sort of natural language may, on the other hand, readily lapse into dryness and prose, because the characters do not unfold the substance of their heart and their action but express only what they feel directly in their own living individuality without having any deeper consciousness of themselves or their circumstances. The more natural the individuals remain in their expressions, the more prosaic these expressions are. For 'natural' men behave in their conversations and quarrels preponderantly as purely *single* persons who, if they are to be described just as they directly are in their own *special* character, cannot come on the scene as men possessed of *substantial* significance. And in relation to the essence of the matter at issue [i.e. diction], crudity and polish[1] amount in the end to the same thing. For if crudity springs from a particular personality

---

[1] The contrast (and equivalence) which Hegel has in mind is that between the violent language of the German *Sturm und Drang* drama and the formal and stilted language of French classical drama.

which gives itself up to the immediate inspirations of an uneducated disposition and mode of feeling, polish looks, conversely, only on what is abstractly universal and formal in reverence, recognition of personality, love, honour, etc., without in the process expressing anything at all objective and concrete. Between this purely formal universality and the natural expression of uncouth personalities there stands the truly universal which is neither formal nor devoid of individuality but is given its twofold content by the determinacy of character and the objectivity of dispositions and aims. Consequently genuine poetry will consist in raising the character and individuality of immediate reality into the purifying element of universality and in making these two sides harmonize with one another. In that event we feel, in the matter of diction, that without leaving the ground of actuality and its real traits we are nevertheless in another sphere, i.e. in the ideal realm of art. This is the kind of language that we find in Greek dramatic poetry, in Goethe's later work and to some extent in Schiller's also. This is true also of Shakespeare's own manner although in conformity with the state of the stage in his day he must here and there have had to leave part of the speeches to the actor's gift of invention.

($\beta\beta$) Secondly, the dramatic mode of expression is divided into (*a*) outbursts of choral song, (*b*) monologues and dialogues. As everyone knows, the difference between chorus and dialogue was especially elaborated in Greek drama, whereas in modern drama this difference disappears because the material given to the chorus in Greek drama is now put into the mouths of the characters themselves. In contrast to the individual characters and their inner and outer strife, the *song of the chorus* expresses universal moods and feelings in language approaching now the solidity of the epic style, and now the impetuosity of lyric. In *monologues*, conversely, it is the inner life of an individual which becomes objective to itself in a specific situation. They therefore have their genuine dramatic place at those moments especially when the heart simply sums itself up after earlier experiences, gives itself an account of its difference with others or of its own inner discord, or brings to final decision resolves either slowly ripened or suddenly made. But the completely dramatic form is the *dialogue*. For in it alone can the individual agents express face to face their character and aim, both their personal character and the substance of their animating 'pathos'; in it alone can they come into conflict and so actually move the action forwards. In dialogue too we can distinguish once more between a subjective and an objective 'pathos'. The former belongs rather to a casual particular passion, whether it be self-concentrated and expressed only aphoristically or whether it can storm out and explain itself completely. Poets who intend to move our personal feelings by touching scenes make special use of this kind of 'pathos'. But however far in that case they may depict personal suffering and fierce passion or an unreconciled inner discord of the soul, still the truly human heart is less moved by this than by a 'pathos' in which something of objective worth is developed at the same time. For this reason, Goethe's earlier pieces make less of an impression on the whole, despite the depth of the subject-matter and the naturalism of the dialogue in his scenes. Similarly a healthy mind is touched only in a lesser degree by outbursts of unreconciled despair and unprincipled wrath, and horror in particular leaves us cold instead of warming us. It does not matter how movingly the poet may describe passion; this is no help; our hearts are only rent, and we turn away. For in such a description there is nothing positive, none of the reconciliation which art should never lack. The Greeks, on the other hand, made their effect in tragedy principally by the objective sort of 'pathos' in which human individuality was not lacking, so far as antiquity demanded it. Schiller's plays too have this 'pathos' of a great mind, a 'pathos' which is poignant and is exhibited and expressed everywhere as the basis of the action. It is to this fact especially that we must ascribe the enduring effect which Schiller's tragedies have retained even at the present day, especially on the stage. For what creates a universal, lasting, and profound dramatic effect is what is really substantive in action—i.e. morality as specific subject-matter, and greatness of spirit and character as form. And here too Shakespeare is supreme.

(γγ) I will add only a few remarks on metre. Dramatic metre does best to keep to the mean between the quiet and uniform flow of the hexameter and the rather jerky and metrically broken syllabic measures of lyric. What most of all commends itself as this mean is iambic metre. For iambics, which may be made more passionate and quicker by anapaests or more weighty by spondees,[1] accompany the forward movement of the action in the most

---

[1] In Greek dramatic dialogue, spondees and anapaests are allowed at certain points in an iambic trimeter.

fitting way with their advancing rhythm, and their six feet especially have the dignified tone of noble and moderated passion. In modern times, on the other hand, the Spanish make use of trochaic tetrameters, moving tranquilly and slowly. Whether these lines are without rhyme or have complicated rhymes and assonances, they seem extremely suitable for an imagination that revels in images and for the intellectually acute explanations which retard rather than forward the action. Besides this, for what are properly the sports of a lyrical ingenuity the Spanish intermix sonnets, *ottava rima*, etc., with the dialogue. In a similar way the French Alexandrine harmonizes formal dignity and rhetorical declamation with passions whether moderated or fiery, and the French drama has been at pains to develop their conventional expression artistically. The more realistic English, however, followed recently by Germans too, have clung again to the iambic metre which Aristotle (*Poetics* [1449ᵃ 25]) has called μάλιστα λεκτικὸν τῶν μέτρων [the most speakable of metres], but they have treated it not as a trimeter but with full freedom in a character less emotional.

(c) *Relation of the Dramatic Work of Art to the Public*

Although the merits or defects of diction and metre are of importance in epic and lyric poetry too, they must have a still more decisive effect ascribed to them in dramatic poetry because in this case we have to do with dispositions, characters, and actions which are to confront us on the stage in their living actuality. For example, a comedy by Calderón has a diction which is sometimes subtle, sometimes bombastic and packed with witty images; moreover there are alternations of varied lyrical metres. The result of this mode of expression is that only with difficulty would such a comedy win general sympathy from us nowadays. On the stage the play is so near to us and so present to our vision that it is the other aspects of its form and its content that have a far more direct relation to the public to which it is presented. We will cast a brief glance at this relation too.

Scientific works and epic or lyric poems have a public consisting as it were of specialists, or alternatively it is a matter of indifference and purely accidental into whose hands such poems and other writings fall. If a book does not please me, I can lay it aside, just as I can pass by pictures or statues that are not to my taste, and in that case the author always has available more or less the excuse that his book was not written for every Tom, Dick, or Harry. It is quite otherwise with dramatic productions. They are confronted by a specific public for which they are supposedly written, and the author is beholden to it. It has a right to bestow praise or blame because, as an assembled audience, it is in the presence of a work which is intended to arouse a lively sympathy and give pleasure in this place at this time. Now such a public, brought together haphazardly for the purpose of pronouncing judgement, is extremely mixed in character: its members differ in education, interests, habitual tastes, predilections, etc., so that now and again, in order to please everybody, the author may even need a talent for the bad as well as a certain shamelessness in disregarding the pure demands of genuine art. Of course the dramatist is always left with the expedient of despising the public, but, if he does, he misses his aim precisely in relation to his most proper mode of operation. Since Tieck's time this contempt for the public has become the fashion, especially in Germany. The German author insists on expressing himself according to his own private personality and not making his works agreeable to hearers or spectators. On the contrary, German self-will requires that everyone shall be something different from everyone else in order to display his originality. For example, Tieck and the brothers Schlegel with their premeditated irony could not master the mind and spirit of their nation and time; they declaimed against Schiller especially and maligned him for finding the right note for the German people and gaining the height of popularity. Our neighbours, the French, act altogether to the contrary: they write for immediate effect and keep their public constantly in view, and it for its part can be, and is, a keener and severer critic of the author because in France there is an established artistic taste, while in Germany anarchy reigns. Here everyone pronounces judgement out of his own head, and approves or condemns just as the accident of his own personal views, feelings, or caprices dictates.

But since the very nature of a dramatic work implies the possession of a vitality which creates for it a favourable reception in its own country, the dramatist must above all submit to the requirements which may secure this necessary success compatibly with art and independently of any accidental contemporary tendencies and circumstances. On this matter I will draw attention to the most general points.

(α) In the first place the aims, which are at variance in a dramatic action and have their conflict resolved there, must either have a universally human interest or at least have as their basis a 'pathos' which is a valid and substantive one for the nation for which the author is composing. But here what is universally human may lie wide apart, in respect of the substance of the conflicts, from what is specifically national. Consequently works which in one nation are at the very apex of dramatic art and its development cannot be enjoyed at all by another nation and at another period. For example, even today many Indian *lyrics* seem to us to be extremely graceful, tender, and of a charming sweetness without our feeling in them any repellent difference from us; but the collision on which the action turns in the *Shakuntala*, namely the angry curse of the sage on Shakuntala[1] because she does not see him and neglects to show her veneration of him, can only seem absurd to us. The result is that, despite all the other merits of this wonderfully attractive composition, we can take no interest in the central point of the action. The same is true of the manner in which the Spaniards treat the motive of personal honour again and again with an abstract and logical subtlety, and its horror does the deepest violence to our ways of thinking and feeling. For example, I recall an attempt to put on the stage one of Calderón's to us less familiar plays, 'Secret Vengeance for a Secret Injury',[2] an attempt that completely failed for this reason. Again, another tragedy of the same kind but portraying a deeper human conflict, 'The Physician of his own Honour',[3] has itself, with a few alterations, been more successful than 'The Steadfast Prince'[4] where a rigid and abstract Catholic principle stands in the way of our interest. On the other hand, in an opposite direction, Shakespeare's tragedies and comedies have attracted a larger and larger public because in them what preponderates by far, despite all purely national interests, is the universal interests of mankind. Consequently he has failed to find an entry only where national artistic conventions are of such a narrow and special kind that they altogether exclude, or at least diminish, the enjoyment of his works. The same merit that Shakespeare's dramas have would be shared by the Greek tragedians if, apart from the

---

[1] In the Prelude to Act IV of this play.
[2] *A secreto agravio, secreta venganza.*   [3] *El médico de su honra.*
[4] This play (*El príncipe constante*), among others, was translated by A. W. Schlegel.

change in what we are now accustomed to in scenic representations and in some aspects of our national outlook, we did not demand a greater depth of subjective inner life and a breadth of individual characterization. Nevertheless the actual *stuff* of Greek drama will never lose its effect at any time. In general, therefore, it may be maintained that whatever other excellence a dramatic work may have it will become all the more obsolescent the more, instead of dealing with fundamental human interests, it selects as subject-matter non-typical characters and passions, determined by the specific national tendencies of their own period.

(β) But, in the second place, these universally human aims and actions must be given living and actual individualization in poetry. For a drama has not only to speak to a living intelligence, which, to be sure, the public should not lack, but must exist on its own account as a living actuality of situations, circumstances, characters, and actions.

(αα) Elsewhere [in Vol. I, pp. 263–80] I have dealt at length with local environment, morals, customs, and other features external but relevant to the action produced before our eyes. The dramatic individualizing of these things either must be so through and through poetic, living, and rich in interests that we pass over what is foreign to us and, owing to this liveliness, feel ourselves even drawn into an interest in it, or instead it should be meant to be in evidence as merely an external form outbid by the spiritual and universal element implicit in it.

(ββ) More important than these external things is the vitality of the characters who should not be merely interests personified as, for example, is all too often the case with our present-day dramatists. These abstract presentations of specific passions and aims are always entirely ineffectual; even a purely superficial individualization is wholly unsatisfactory because content and form fall apart as they do in allegorical figures. For this defect no profound feelings and thoughts, no great dispositions or fine language can provide a remedy. On the contrary, an individual in a drama must be alive through and through in himself, whole and entire, his disposition and character being in harmony with his aim and action. In this connection the chief thing is not a mere wealth of particular traits of character but the all-pervasive individuality which collects everything together into the unity which is itself and which displays itself in speech as the one and the same source from which every particular word, every single trait of disposition, deed, and behaviour springs. A mere assembly of different qualities and activities, even if arrayed one by one into a whole, does not provide a living character, for that presupposes a living and richly imaginative creation by the author. Of this kind, for example, are the individuals in the tragedies of Sophocles, although they do not have the same wealth of particular traits that we meet with in Homer's epic heroes. Amongst modern dramatists it is Shakespeare and Goethe above all who have put before us characters most full of life, whereas the French, especially in their earlier dramatic poetry, have evidently been content with formal and abstract representatives of general types and passions rather than with truly living individuals.

(γγ) But, in the third place, the matter is not at an end with this liveliness of character. In this respect Goethe's *Iphigenia* and *Tasso*, for example, are excellent, and yet if we take the matter in the strictest sense, their characters neither live nor move dramatically. So Schiller already says[1] of the *Iphigenia* that in it the disposition, the ethical principle moving the heart, becomes action and thus as it were is brought before our eyes. And in fact the depiction and expression of the inner world of different characters in specific situations is still insufficient; what on the contrary has to be conspicuous and to be urged and pressed forward is the collision of their *aims*. For this reason Schiller finds in the *Iphigenia* too tranquil a march, too great a halting by the way, so that he goes so far as to say that, once judged by the strict concept of tragedy, it passes over into the field of epic. What after all is effective in drama is the action as action and not the exposure of the character as such independently of his specific aim and its achievement. In epic, space should be given to the breadth and variety of character, circumstances, accidents, and events, whereas in drama the greatest effect is produced by concentration on the specific collision and the conflict involved. In this sense Aristotle was right when he maintained (*Poetics* [1450^a 1–22]) that for action in tragedy there are two sources (αἴτια δύο), mind and character (διάνοια καὶ ἦθος), but the chief thing is the aim (τέλος) and that individuals did not act to display their own characters but that these were included for the sake of the action.

(γ) A final aspect for consideration here concerns the *dramatist*

---

[1] In his essay *Über die Iphigenie auf Tauris*.

in his relation to his public. Epic poetry in its genuine original character requires that the poet shall set aside his personality in the face of his objectively existent work and give us only the thing itself; whereas the singer of lyrics expresses his own heart and his personal outlook on life.

(αα) Now since drama produces an action in front of us so that we can see it going on, and individuals speak in their own name and act in their own person, it might seem that the author must withdraw to an altogether greater extent than he does in epic where he does at least appear as the narrator of the events. But this view of the matter is only partially correct. For, as I said at the start, drama owes its origin only to those epochs in which individual self-consciousness has reached a high stage of development both in its outlook on the world and in its artistic culture. Consequently a dramatic work need not give the impression of issuing, like an epic, from a national consciousness as such where the poet has been as it were an impersonal tool for its affairs; on the contrary what we want to find in a perfect drama is the product of self-conscious and original creative activity and therefore also the art and virtuosity of an individual author. It is only in this way that dramatic creations acquire their proper peak of artistic life and determinacy in distinction from the actions and events of every day. For this reason there has never been so much dispute about the authorship of dramas as there has been about the authorship of the original epics.

(ββ) On the other hand, however, if the public has itself retained the genuine sense and spirit of art, it will not be content at all to be confronted in a drama with the rather accidental whims and moods and the individual tendencies and one-sided outlooks of this or that character, for it is the lyric poet who remains more or less authorized to express these. On the contrary, it has the right to require that in the course and issue of the dramatic action, whether in tragedy or comedy, something absolutely rational and true shall be clearly realized and achieved. In this sense I have already earlier imposed on the dramatist the demand that he must acquire the most profound insight into the essence of human action and Divine Providence, as well as clearly and vividly revealing this eternal substance of all human characters, passions, and fates. Once actually possessed of this insight and armed with the might of art alive in him as an individual, the poet may, it is true, come into conflict, in certain circumstances, with the restricted and artistically tasteless ideas of his age and nation, but in that event the blame for this discord is to be imputed not to him but to the public. He himself has no other duty but to follow the truth and his impelling genius which, if only it be of the right sort, cannot fail to be victorious in the last instance, as is always the case when truth is at issue.

(γγ) Little can be laid down definitely about the extent to which the dramatist should present his personality and his own views to the public. On this matter I will therefore make only the general remark that at many periods dramatic poetry has been specially used to create a living entry for new contemporary ideas about politics, morals, poetry, religion, etc. Long ago Aristophanes conducted a polemic in his earlier comedies against the domestic affairs of Athens and the Peloponnesian war. Voltaire, again, tried to spread his 'enlightened' principles by means of his dramatic works too. But, above all, Lessing struggled in his *Nathan* to vindicate his moral faith against narrow religious orthodoxy; and, more recently, Goethe too in his earliest works tried to do battle against the prose of the German view of life and art, and in this matter he was followed in many ways by Tieck. If the poet's own outlook proves that he is standing on higher ground, and if it is not made intentionally so independent of the action portrayed that the latter appears to be degraded to being a mere means, then art is neither wronged nor prejudiced. But if the poetic freedom of the play is thereby impaired, the poet may well make a great impression on the public by this exhibition of his own inclinations which, however true, are relatively independent of his artistic production, yet the interest he arouses is in that event matter-of-fact, as it were, and has little to do with art itself. But the worst case of this kind occurs when the poet, purely for the sake of pleasing, no less deliberately intends to flatter a false tendency dominant in the public and thereby sins twice, once against truth and secondly against art.

Finally, to add a remark on a point of detail, of the different *genres* of dramatic poetry tragedy allows less scope for the free emergence of the poet's personal views than comedy does, because there from the very beginning the ruling principle is the contingency and caprice of subjective life. For example, Aristophanes in his *parabases* [choric digressions] puts himself in many ways into relation with the Athenian public because he does not fail to disclose his political views about the events and circumstances of the day and gives his fellow-citizens wise advice; moreover, he endeavours to snub his antagonists and rivals in art and sometimes goes so far as to disclose publicly his own personality and its peculiarities.

2. *The External Execution of a Dramatic Work of Art*

Of all the arts poetry alone does not appear outwardly in something completely real and also preceptible. Now drama does not relate bygone deeds at all for our spiritual contemplation, nor does it express an inner and subjective world with an appeal to our heart and imagination; its task, on the contrary, is to portray an action present before us in its present and actual character. Consequently it would fall into a contradiction with its own aim if it had to be restricted to the means which poetry as such has at its command. For the action confronting us is entirely the fruit of the inner life and, so viewed, can be completely expressed in words; on the other hand, however, action also moves outwards, into external reality, and therefore its portrayal requires the whole man in his body, in what he does and how he behaves in his bodily movement, and the facial expression of his feelings and passions, and all this not only as he is in himself but also in the way he works on others and in the reactions thence possibly arising. Then if an individual is to be portrayed as he actually is in the real world, a specific locality is necessary in which he moves and is active, and consequently dramatic poetry needs the aid of almost all the other arts if all these aspects are not to continue in their immediate accidental character but are to be given artistic shape as an essential feature of art itself. The surrounding scene is either an architectural one, like a temple, or else something in nature, but both of these are treated and carried out pictorially. Then the sculptural figures come on this scene animated and, having developed their willing and feeling artistically, they make them objective both by expressive recitation and also by a pictorial play of features and inwardly motivated positions and movements of the rest of the body.

In this matter I may emphasize a difference which recalls what I have indicated earlier in the field of music about a clash between declamation and melody. For just as in declamatory music words in their spiritual meaning are the chief thing and the musical side is throughout subordinate to their characteristic expression, while although melody may assimilate what the words mean, it proceeds and develops independently and freely in its own element, so dramatic poetry too, on the one hand, uses its sister arts only as a perceptible foundation and environment out of which poetic language rises in free dominion as the pre-eminent central feature which is strictly the thing concerned; but, on the other hand, what at first had worth only as an aid and an accompaniment becomes an end in itself and, in its own sphere, is shaped into having an inherently independent beauty—declamation becomes song, action becomes mimicry in dancing, and the scenery too makes a claim in itself to artistic perfection on the score of its splendour and pictorial attraction. If now, as has so often happened especially in more recent times, poetry as such has been placed in opposition to the externals of dramatic production that I have just mentioned, then further points have to be explained in connection with this matter:

first, dramatic poetry that means to restrict itself to itself and disregard the theatrical production of its works;

secondly, the properly theatrical art of the actor in so far as it is so limited in action, recitation, and play of features that poetic language may always remain the determining and dominant feature;

thirdly, that kind of execution which uses every means of scenery, music, and dance and makes them independent of the poet's words.

(a) *Reading Dramas and Reciting them*

The properly perceptible material of dramatic poetry, as we saw, is not merely the human voice and the spoken word but the whole man who does not merely express feelings, ideas, and thoughts, but is involved with his whole being in a concrete action and works on the ideas, purposes, acts, and behaviour of others, and experiences corresponding reactions or asserts himself against them.

(α) In defiance of this fundamental and basic characteristic of dramatic poetry, it has nowadays, especially in Germany, become one of our common ideas to regard organizing a drama for stage-production as an inessential superfluity, even though in fact, however indifferent or contemptuous all authors may be in this respect, they nourish the wish and the hope to put their piece on the stage. Indeed, after all, most of our recent dramas never see the stage for the simple reason that they are undramatic. True, it should not be maintained that a drama cannot be satisfying *poetically* on the score of its inner value alone, but this inner *dramatic* value is only to be provided by a treatment which makes a drama excellent on the stage. The best proof of this is the Greek tragedies which we see no longer in the theatre but which, when we consider them more closely, give us perfect satisfaction, to some extent precisely because they were in their own time written purely for the stage. What bans them from the theatre today depends less on their dramatic organization, so different from what we are accustomed to, especially because of its use of choruses, than on the national presuppositions and circumstances on which their subject-matter is frequently based and in which we cannot now feel at home because it is so foreign to our modern way of looking at things. For example, the sickness of Philoctetes, the festering ulcer on his foot, his groans and shrieks, we could as little hear and see as we could have our interest excited by the arrows of Hercules, which were what the whole thing was mainly about. Similarly the barbarity of human sacrifice in the *Iphigenia in Aulis* or *Iphigenia among the Tauri* may be comfortable to us in opera,[1] but in tragedy this must be turned altogether otherwise as Goethe has done [in his *Iphigenia*].

(β) But, unlike the Greeks, we are accustomed at times merely to *read* a drama as well as, at other times, to see it actually performed, and this fact has led dramatists themselves further astray by intending their work, to some extent, merely to be *read*, in the belief that this has no influence at all on the nature of the composition. Of course there are certain isolated matters comprised in the mere externals of what is called 'stagecraft', and infringement of these does not impair the value of a drama considered as poetry. For example, there is the calculation of how to set one scene in such a way that another, demanding considerable scenic preparations, may follow it conveniently, or how to give the actor time for rest or a necessary change of costume, etc. The knowledge and skill

[1] Gluck's *Iphigénie en Aulide* was first produced in 1774 and his *Iphigénie en Tauride* in 1779.

required in these matters provide no *poetic* advantage or disadvantage and depend more or less on theatrical arrangements which themselves are conventional and varying. But nevertheless there are other points in relation to which the poet, if he is to be really a dramatist, must keep essentially in view the live production of his piece, and he must make his characters speak and act with this in mind, i.e. with an actual and present performance in mind. In these matters, actual theatrical production is the touchstone. For in the eyes of the supreme tribunal—a healthy and artistically educated public—speeches and tirades in what is called 'flowery' language are in themselves futile if they lack dramatic truth. At certain epochs, indeed, the public may be corrupted by a highly praised 'culture', i.e. by having put into its head the perverse opinions and follies of critics and connoisseurs; but if it still has some genuine taste of its own, it is satisfied only when the characters so express themselves and act as the living actuality of nature, and of art too, demands and involves. If on the other hand the poet intends to write only for a reader alone in his study, he may easily come to the point of making his figures so speak and behave as if we were being told about them in a letter. If in a letter someone writes to us about the reasons for his purposes and actions, gives us assurances, or discloses his heart to us in some other way, then between receiving the letter and actually replying all sorts of reflections and ideas occur to us about what we do or do not want to say in reply. For thinking embraces a vast field of possibilities. But when a dialogue is actually going on in our *presence*, there is a valid presupposition that a man's will and heart, his decision and his emotion, are direct, and that, in general, without any detour of prolonged reflections, man speaks to man directly, heart to heart, eye to eye, and face to face and is taken so to speak and reply. In that event, actions and speech spring alive in every situation out of the character as such, and this no longer leaves time for choosing between all sorts of different possibilities. In this respect it is by no means unimportant for the dramatist to keep in view, in his composition, the stage which demands such dramatic liveliness. Indeed, in my opinion, no play should really be printed but should remain, more or less as the case was in antiquity, in manuscript for the theatre's repertory and get only an extremely insignificant circulation. If that happened, then at least we would not see so many dramas appearing which have indeed a cultivated style, fine feelings, excellent reflections, and profound thoughts, but which fail precisely in what makes a drama dramatic, namely action and its vital movement.

(γ) When it comes to reading dramas and reciting them, it is difficult to decide whether they are not of such a kind as to lose their effect even on the stage. Even Goethe, who in his later years had a long experience of the theatre at his command, had grave doubts about this, especially in view of the awful confusion of our taste which takes pleasure in anything and everything. If the character and aim of the dramatis personae are in themselves great and solid, then of course the understanding of them is easier; but by mere reading, without a theatrical production, it is difficult to make a firm judgement on the sway of interests, the steps in the action, the tension and complication of situations, the right extent to which characters work on one another, and the worth and truth of their behaviour and speech. Here even recitation provides only relative help. For in drama speech needs different individuals and not a single voice, no matter how artistically modulated and altered. Moreover, in recitation there is always the disturbing perplexity whether the speakers in the play are to be named every time or not, and in either case the thing is unsatisfactory. If the recitation is by one speaker, then the mention of the names is indispensable for intelligibility, but then the expression of the 'pathos' is always vitiated; if on the other hand the recitation is dramatically more lively so that we are drawn into the situation actually, then a new contradiction may be aroused, for it the ear is satisfied, the demands of the eye are not. For, if we listen to an action, we also want to see the agents, their demeanour and surroundings, etc. The eye wants completeness and is confronted by nothing but a reciter who sits or stands at his ease in a drawing-room. Thus recitation is always only an unsatisfying mean between an entire production in the theatre and the private reading which makes no claims and where the reality is left entirely to the imagination.

(b) *The Actor's Art*

Actual dramatic production involves not only music but the art of another executant, i.e. the actor, and this has been completely developed only in modern times. In principle it consists in calling on the aid of gestures, action, declamation, music, dancing, and scenery, but in giving overwhelming preponderance to speech and its poetic expression. This is the sole proper situation for poetry as such, because so soon as mimicry or singing and dancing begin to be developed on their own account and independently, poetry as an art is degraded to being a means and loses its dominion over these other arts which should be merely its accompaniment. In this connection the following points may be distinguished.

(α) At its first level we find the art of the actor in Greece. Here the art of speech is bound up with sculpture: the actor comes on the stage as a totally solid objective statue. But this statue is vitalized; it assimilates and expresses the subject-matter of the poetry; it is associated with every inner movement of passion and at the same time puts it into words and voices it. Consequently this presentation is more animated and is spiritually clearer than any statue or any picture. In this animation there are two aspects to distinguish.

(αα) First, declamation as artistic speech. This was little developed by the Greeks for whom intelligibility was the chief thing; whereas *we* want to recognize in the tone of voice, in the enunciation, and in the manner of recitation, the character's heart and personality totally objectified in its most delicate nuances and transitions, as well as in its sharper oppositions and conflicts. The Greeks, on the other hand, added a musical accompaniment to the declamation, partly to emphasize the rhythm, partly to gain a more richly modulated enunciation of the words, even if the words remained the principal thing. Yet the dialogue was probably spoken or only lightly accompanied, whereas the chorus recited in a lyrically musical way. It is possible that by its more pronounced accentuation the song made more intelligible the meaning of the words in the choral sprophes; without this assumption I at least can have no idea how it was possible for the Greeks to understand the choruses of Aeschylus and Sophocles. For even if the Greeks did not have to drudge away at them as we have to, I must still say that, although I understand German and can grasp a thing or two, a German lyric written in a like style would always remain obscure to me if it were spoken on the stage and even sung into the bargain.

(ββ) A second element [in the animation of a production] is provided by bodily gestures and movements. In this matter it is worth noting at once that in Greece the actors wore masks and therefore the play of features was altogether absent. The facial expressions of the masks presented an unalterable statuesque picture and its plasticity inhibited both the ever-shifting expression of particular emotional moods and also the revelation of the dramatis personae. These characters fought their way through the dramatic conflict, animated by a fixed and *universal* 'pathos', but the substance of this 'pathos' had not been developed into the deep feeling of the modern heart nor was it broadened by being *particularized* in the dramatis personae as it is today. The acting was equally simple, and this is why we know nothing of any famous Greek mimes.[1] Occasionally the poets acted themselves, as e.g. Sophocles and Aristophanes did, and occasionally ordinary citizens, whose *métier* was certainly not the art of acting, had parts in a tragedy. On the other hand, the choruses were accompanied with dancing, which we in Germany would consider frivolous in view of our contemporary style of dancing, while for the Greeks it was an essential feature in the whole spectacle of theatrical productions.

(γγ) In short, in Greece words and the spiritual expression of serious passions had full poetic rights, just as the external production was most completely elaborated by having an accompaniment of music and dancing. This concrete unity gives to the whole production a plastic character, because the spiritual element is not independently inwardized or expressed in the subjective experiences of these particular individuals; on the contrary, it is perfectly married and reconciled with the equally justified external aspect, i.e. with what is seen on the stage.

(β) Yet speech suffers under music and dancing because it should be the *spiritual* expression of spirit, and so, after all, in modern times the actor's art has been able to liberate itself from these things. For this reason the poet has only now a relation to the actor as such because the actor is to bring a poetic work to life perceptibly by his declamation, gestures, and play of features. But this relation of the author to external material is of an entirely special kind, not shared by the other arts. In painting and sculpture it is the artist himself who carries out his conceptions in

---

[1] The *Mimes* of Herodas were known only in a few fragments until some were discovered in a papyrus in 1891. The Greek mime was a kind of dramatic sketch, illustrating scenes from everyday life.

colour, bronze, or marble; and, even if musical performance requires other hands and throats, what prevails there is, more or less, virtuosity and a finished mechanical skill, although it is true that the performance must not lack soul. On the other hand, the actor enters the work of art as an entire individual with his figure, countenance, voice, etc., and he has the task of absolutely identifying himself with the character he is representing.

(αα) In this matter the author has the right to demand from the actor that he shall think himself entirely into his given part, without adding anything of his own, and act it exactly as the author has conceived it and given it poetic form. The actor should be, as it were, the instrument on which the author plays, or the sponge that can absorb any colour and give it back unchanged. In the case of the Greeks this was easier because, as I said, declamation was restricted in the main to clarity, and the matter of rhythm, etc., was looked after by music, while masks hid facial expressions, and even acting had little scope. Therefore the actor could easily adapt himself to a universal tragic 'pathos'; and even if, in comedy, figures of living people like Socrates, Nicias, Cleon, etc. were to be presented, the masks imitated their individual expression well enough, and, apart from that, further individualization was less necessary because Aristophanes used such characters only as representatives of general contemporary tendencies.

(ββ) It is all quite different in modern acting. Here there are neither masks nor musical accompaniment, and instead of them we have the play of feature, variety of gestures, and a wealth of shades in declamation. For, on the one hand, even when passions are characterized generally or typically by the poet, they are still expressed as alive in the character's heart, and, on the other hand, the characters have for the most part a far greater breadth of personality, and the appropriate expression of this should be made visible to us in similarly living actuality. Shakespeare's figures above all are whole people, entire and unique, so that we require of the actor that he shall for his part bring them before our eyes in this entire completeness. Tone of voice, manner of recitation, gestures, facial expression, in short all outward appearance, and inner attitude of mind too, must be adapted by the individual actor to his specific part. Therefore, quite apart from the words, the manifold nuances and plays of gesture have a quite different importance: indeed the poet leaves to the actor's gestures a great deal which the Greeks would have put into words. For example, consider the end of [Schiller's] *Wallenstein*: old Octavio had been an essential accomplice in Wallenstein's murder. He finds him traitorously murdered by Buttler's contrivance; and at the same moment when the Countess Terzky announces that she has taken poison, a letter from the Emperor is brought in. Gordon has read the address and, with a glance of reproach, he hands the letter to Octavio with the words of the address: 'To the *Prince* Piccolomini.' Octavio shrieks and, full of grief, gazes up to heaven. What he feels on receiving this reward for a service, knowing that he has to carry the greater share of the responsibility for its bloody outcome, is not expressed here in words but is left entirely for the actor to present in his mien and gestures.[1]—Owing to these demands on modern dramatic acting the poet may often, in connection with the material he uses in presenting his work, be thrown into an embarrassment unknown to the Greeks. The reason is that the actor, as a living man, has like every individual his own inborn peculiarities in his voice, figure, and facial expression; these he is compelled to suppress in favour of the expression of a *universal* 'pathos' and some *typical* character, or he has to harmonize them with the fuller figures of a poetry that individualizes them more fully.

(γγ) Nowadays actors are called artists and they are paid the whole honour of belonging to an artistic profession. According to our modern ideas, an actor is neither a moral nor a social blot. And rightly so, because this art demands a great deal of talent, intelligence, perseverance, industry, practice, and knowledge; indeed at its height it needs a richly endowed genius. For the actor has not only to penetrate profoundly into the spirit of the poet and of the part assigned to him and entirely adapt to it his mind and demeanour and his own personality, but he should also be productive on his own account by enlarging many points, filling gaps, and finding transitions; in short in playing his part by explaining the author through bringing out into something present and alive, and making

---

[1] Octavio Piccolomini is a Lieut.-General, raised to be a Prince for his share in Wallenstein's murder. Countess Terzky is Wallenstein's sister-in-law; she knows that Octavio is guilty and prefers a courageous death to a dishonoured life. Gordon is the Commandant at Eger where the murder takes place. Buttler commands a regiment of dragoons. 'It is to the *Prince* Piccolomini', i.e. the first notification of Octavio's elevation, are the final words of the play before the curtain falls.

intelligible, all his secret intentions and the profundity of his master-strokes.

(c) *The Art of the Theatre more Independently of Poetry*

Finally, the art of performance acquires a third shape when it is freed from its previous domination by poetry, and makes what was hitherto more or less a means and an accompaniment into an independent end in itself and gives it a development on its own account. In this emancipation during the course of the development of drama, it is music and dancing, as well as the special art of the actor, that have benefited.

(α) As for the last named there are on the whole two systems. The first of these, where the actor is meant more or less to be the spiritually and bodily living organ of the poet, we have already mentioned. The French, who keep so much to schools of acting, make the playing of a single type of part into a profession, and generally make theatrical productions the portrayal of types, have shown themselves especially true to this system in their tragedy and *haute comédie*. The opposite system of the actor's art is to be found where everything provided by the author is little more than an accessory and a frame for the natural character, skill, and art of the actor. We can often enough hear actors demanding that authors should write for *them*. In that event the composition is supposed to provide these artists solely with the opportunity to display and develop with the greatest brilliance their own soul and art, this final secret of their personality. An example of this kind of thing is the Italian *commedia dell' arte* in which the characters of Harlequin, doctors, etc., were fixed and the situations and succession of scenes were given, but the rest of the performance was left almost entirely to the actors. In our case some of Iffland's and Kotzebue's pieces, indeed a great number of them, are, considered as poetry, insignificant and in fact downright bad productions, but they provide an opportunity for free productivity by the actor who must now be the first to form and shape, out of these usually sketchily treated patchworks, something which on account of his living and independent achievement acquires an interest dependent on him and no other artist. Here after all it is especially the naturalness, so much favoured in Germany, that has its place, where now things have gone so far that droning and mumbling words, intelligible to nobody, is allowed to count as an excellent play. Goethe, altogether to the contrary, translated Voltaire's *Tancred* and *Mahomet* for the Weimar stage in order to chase its actors out of vulgar naturalness and accustom them to a higher tone. So too the French in general, even in the midst of the liveliness of their farces, always keep the public in view and look towards it. In fact nothing is achieved either by pure naturalness and its living routine or by pure intellectualism and skill in characterization; on the contrary, if the actor intends to create a really artistic effect in this sphere he must rise to that same virtuosity of genius which I have mentioned already in dealing with musical execution [i.e. in the section on music, *ad fin.*].

(β) The second department that may be included in this sphere is modern opera, granted the direction which it is beginning to take more and more. In opera generally, music is the chief thing, though its content is given to it by poetry and speech; but when it is used and treated for its own purposes alone as is happening especially with us today, then opera becomes a thing of luxury and it has given overwhelming independence to accessories, i.e. to magnificent décor, ostentatious costumes, and elaborate choruses and their arrangement. We often enough hear this display criticized now, but similar display was long ago the subject of Cicero's complaint about Roman tragedy.[1] In tragedy, where the poetry must always be fundamental, of course elaboration of these externals has no proper place, although Schiller has gone wrong in this with his *Maid of Orleans*. But in opera this prominent attractiveness of the external equipment and arrangements may well be allowed, in the case of the audible magnificence of arias and the resounding and rippling chorus of voices and instruments. For once the décor is splendid, then to vie with it, the costumes should not be less so, and everything else must be in harmony. To such visible magnificence (always a sign, it is true, of the already growing decadence of genuine art) there corresponds, as the most appropriate subject-matter, what is utterly devoid of any intelligible connection, namely what is miraculous, fantastic, and fabulous. Mozart has given us in *The Magic Flute* an example which is moderate and the best worked-out artistically. But when all the arts of scenery, costume, instrumentation, etc. are exhausted, the best thing left is to have no real seriousness about the proper

[1] The reference is to Cicero's letters. See *Epist. ad. Fam.*, VII. i. 2.

dramatic subject-matter, and to put us in the mood we have in reading one of the Arabian Nights.

(γ) The like is the case with our contemporary ballet to which likewise the miraculous and fabulous are agreeable. Here, apart from the pictorial beauty of arrangements and tableaux, what has become above all the chief thing is the changing magnificence and attraction of scenery, costume, and lighting, so that we at least find ourselves transported into a realm where we have left far behind us the logic of prose and the distress and pressure of everyday life. On the other hand, those who know about these things are captivated by the extraordinarily developed bravura and suppleness of the legs, and this always plays the chief part in dancing nowadays. But if some spiritual expression is to glint through this mere dexterity, which nowadays has wandered into an extreme of senselessness and intellectual poverty, what is required is not only a complete conquest of all the technical difficulties but measured movement in harmony with our emotions, and a freedom and grace that are extremely rare.

Here dancing enters instead of the choruses and solos of opera, but there is now added to it, as a real expression of action, the pantomime.[1] But the further that modern dancing has advanced in technical skill, the more has pantomime sunk in value and disappeared. The result is that we threaten to see more and more disappearing from modern ballet what alone could lift it into the free realm of art.

3. *The Genres of Dramatic Poetry and the Chief Features it has had in History*

If we glance back briefly on the course we have followed in our consideration of dramatic art up to now, we first established what its principle is in its general and particular characteristics as well as what it is in relation to the public. Then, secondly, we saw that a drama presents to us live the whole development of a complete and specific action, and therefore it imperatively needs a fully visible presentation, and this can only be given artistically by actual performance in the theatre. But if the action is thus to be made real objectively, it must itself be altogether determined and finished in itself in poetic conception and treatment. But this can

---

[1] i.e. dumb-show acting.

only be done if, thirdly, dramatic poetry is split into different *genres* which borrow their type, whether it involves oppositions or their reconciliation, from the difference between the ways in which the characters and their aims, their conflict and the outcome of the whole action are brought on the scene. The chief modes arising from this difference and having a varied historical development are tragedy and comedy, as well as the conciliation of these two modes of treatment, which only in dramatic poetry become of such essential importance that they may serve as the basis for the division of its different *genres*.

In explaining these points in more detail we have

(*a*) first to bring out the general principle of tragedy, comedy, and the so-called 'drama';

(*b*) secondly, to indicate the character of classical and modern dramatic poetry, their difference having been produced in the course of the historical development of tragedy and comedy;

(*c*) thirdly, to consider the concrete forms which comedy and tragedy especially have been able to take within this difference.

(*a*) *The Principle of Tragedy, Comedy, and Drama*

The essential principle for discriminating the kinds of epic poetry depended on whether the substantive material to be portrayed in an epic was expressed in its universality or related in the form of objective characters, deeds, and events.

Lyric, conversely, is divided into a series of different modes of expression by the degree and manner in which the subject-matter is more loosely or more tightly interwoven with the person whose inner life that subject-matter reveals.

Dramatic poetry, finally, makes central the collisions between characters and between their aims, as well as the necessary resolution of this battle. Consequently the principle for distinguishing its *genres* can only be derived from the relation of individuals to their aim and what it involves. The specific character of this relation is also what decides the particular manner of the dramatic conflict and outcome and so provides the essential type of the whole course of events in its living and artistic presentation.

As the principal points for consideration in this matter we must, in general, emphasize those features which in their harmony constitute the essence of every true action: (i) what is in *substance* good and great, the Divine actualized in the world, as the foundation of everything genuine and absolutely eternal in the make-up of an individual's character and aim; (ii) the *subject*, the individual himself in his unfettered self-determination and freedom. In whatever form dramatic poetry brings the action on the stage, what is really effective in it is absolute truth, but the specific way in which this effectiveness comes on the scene takes a different, and indeed an opposed, form according to whether what is kept dominant in the individuals and their actions and conflicts is their substantive basis or alternatively their subjective caprice, folly, and perversity.

In this connection we have to examine the principle for the following *genres*:

(α) for tragedy, taken in its substantive and original typical form;

(β) for comedy, in which the mastery of all relations and ends is given as much to the individual in his willing and action, as to external contingency;

(γ) for drama, i.e. for a play in the narrower sense of the word, as occupying a middle position between these first two kinds.

(α) At this point I will make brief mention of only the most general basic characteristics of tragedy; their concrete particularization can come into view only in the light of the stages in tragedy's historical development.

(αα) The true content of the tragic action is provided, so far as concerns the *aims* adopted by the tragic characters, by the range of the substantive and independently justified powers that influence the human will: family love between husband and wife, parents and children, brothers and sisters; political life also, the patriotism of the citizens, the will of the ruler; and religion existent, not as a piety that renounces action and not as a divine judgement in man's heart about the good or evil of his actions, but on the contrary, as an active grasp and furtherance of actual interests and circumstances. A similar excellence belongs to the genuinely tragic *characters*. Throughout they are what they can and must be in accordance with their essential nature, not an ensemble of qualities separately developed epically in various ways; on the contrary, even if they are living and individual themselves, they are simply the *one* power dominating their own specific character; for, in accordance with their own individuality, they have inseparably identified themselves with some single particular aspect of those solid interests we have enumerated above, and are prepared to answer for that identification. Standing on this height, where the mere accidents of the individual's purely personal life disappear, the tragic heroes of dramatic art have risen to become, as it were, works of sculpture, whether they be living representatives of the substantive spheres of life or individuals great and firm in other ways on the strength of their free self-reliance; and so in this respect the statues and images of the gods, rather abstract in themselves, explain the lofty tragic characters of the Greeks better than all other commentaries and notes.[1]

In general terms, therefore, we may say that the proper theme of the original type of tragedy is the Divine; not, however, the Divine as the object of the religious consciousness as such, but as it enters the world and individual action. Yet in this actual appearance it does not lose its substantive character, nor does it see itself there as inverted into the opposite of itself. In this form the spiritual substance of will and accomplishment is the concrete ethical order. For if we take the ethical order in its direct genuineness and do not interpret it from the point of view of subjective reflection as abstract morality,[2] then it is the Divine made real in the world and so the substantive basis which in all its aspects, whether particular or essential, provides the motive for truly human action, and it is in action itself that these aspects develop and actualize this their essence.

(ββ) Everything that forces its way into the objective and real world is subject to the principle of particularization; consequently the ethical powers, just like the agents, are differentiated in their domain and their individual appearance.[3] Now if, as dramatic

[1] The construction of Hegel's sentence has been interpreted differently. He has been taken to mean *either* that the tragic figures explain the rather abstract statues *or* that the latter cast light on the former better than commentators can. Like Bénard, and unlike others, I prefer the second interpretation. The mention of 'notes' seems to me to refer to the notes of commentators on Greek tragedies. This interpretation is confirmed by the final paragraph of the first chapter of the section on Sculpture.

[2] This distinction between 'ethical order' (*Sittlichkeit*) and 'abstract morality' (*Moralität*) is expounded at length in Hegel's *Philosophy of Right* (or *Law*), parts 2 and 3. See also in Vol. I, the Translator's Preface.

[3] For Hegel, the substantive basis of life is the Divine, and this is at least a moral order which ultimately rules. But this substantive basis is universal, and everything in the real world is particular. Consequently this order, or the

poetry requires, these thus differentiated powers are summoned into appearance as active and are actualized as the specific aim of a human 'pathos' which passes over into action, then their harmony is cancelled and they come on the scene in *opposition* to one another in reciprocal independence. In that event a single action will under certain circumstances realize an aim or a character which is one-sidedly isolated in its complete determinacy, and therefore, in the circumstances presupposed, will necessarily rouse against it the opposed 'pathos' and so lead to inevitable conflicts. The original essence of tragedy consists then in the fact that within such a conflict each of the opposed sides, if taken by itself, has *justification*; while each can establish the true and positive content of its own aim and character only by denying and infringing the equally justified power of the other. The consequence is that in its moral life, and because of it, each is nevertheless involved in *guilt*.

The general reason for the necessity of these conflicts I have touched upon already. The substance of ethical life, as a concrete unity, is an ensemble of *different* relations and powers which only in a situation of inactivity, like that of the blessed gods, accomplish the work of the spirit in the enjoyment of an undisturbed life. But the very nature of this ensemble implies its transfer from its at first purely abstract *ideality* into its actualization in *reality* and its appearance in the mundane sphere. Owing to the nature of the real world, the mere *difference* of the constituents of this ensemble becomes perverted into *opposition* and collision, once individual characters seize upon them on the territory of specific circumstances. Only from this point of view can we be really serious about those gods who dwell in their peaceful tranquillity and unity solely on Olympus and in the heaven of imagination and religious ideas, but who, when they now come actually to life as a specific 'pathos' in a human individual, lead, despite all their justification, to guilt and wrong owing to their particular specification and the opposition to which this leads.

Divine, must be particularized when it is effective in the real world. Thus the moral substance of Greek life is particularized in a group of gods, each (or some of them) with a part of the moral sphere as his (or her) own. Thus in tragedy the sphere of one god (or goddess) may conflict with that of another (e.g. in *Antigone*, see pp. 1217-8 below). When Hegel talks about the 'Divine' he does not always make clear whether it is Greek or Christian (or his own) ideas that are predominant, but, in dealing with tragedy, it is Greek ideas that are uppermost in his mind.

(γγ) In this way however, an unresolved contradiction is set up; it does appear in the real world but cannot maintain itself there as the substance of reality and what is genuinely true; its proper claim is satisfied only when it is annulled as a contradiction. However justified the tragic character and his aim, however necessary the tragic collision, the third thing required is the tragic resolution of this conflict. By this means eternal justice is exercised on individuals and their aims in the sense that it restores the substance and unity of ethical life with the downfall of the individual who has disturbed its peace. For although the characters have a purpose which is valid in itself, they can carry it out in tragedy only by pursuing it one-sidedly and so contradicting and infringing someone else's purpose. The truly substantial thing which has to be actualized, however, is not the battle between particular aims or characters, although this too has its essential ground in the nature of the real world and human action, but the reconciliation in which the specific individuals and their aims work together harmoniously without opposition and without infringing on one another. Therefore what is superseded in the tragic denouement is only the *one-sided* particular which had not been able to adapt itself to this harmony, and now (and this is the tragic thing in its action), unable to renounce itself and its intention, finds itself condemned to total destruction, or, at the very least, forced to abandon, if it can, the accomplishment of its aim.

In this connection Aristotle, as every one knows, laid it down [*Poetics*, 1449^b 26] that the true effect of tragedy should be to arouse pity and fear and accomplish the catharsis of these emotions. By 'emotions' Aristotle did not mean mere feeling, my subjective sense of something corresponding with me or not, the agreeable or disagreeable, the attractive or the repulsive—this most superficial of all criteria which only recently has been proposed as the principle of dramatic success or failure. For the only important thing for a work of art is to present what corresponds with reason and spiritual truth, and if we are to discover the principle of this, we must direct our attention to totally different considerations. Even in the case of Aristotle's dictum we must therefore fix our eyes not on the mere feelings of pity and fear but on the nature of the subject-matter which by its artistic appearance is to purify these feelings. A man can be frightened in face of, on the one hand, something finite and external to him, or, on the other hand, the power of the Absolute. What a man has really to fear is not an external power and oppression by it, but the might of the ethical order which is one determinant of his own free reason and is at the same time that eternal and inviolable something which he summons up against himself if once he turns against it. Like fear, pity too has two kinds of object. The first is the object of ordinary emotion, i.e. sympathy with someone else's misfortune and suffering which is felt as something finite and negative. Provincial females are always ready with compassion of this sort. For if it is only the negative aspect, the negative aspect of misfortune, that is emphasized, then the victim of misfortune is degraded. True pity, on the contrary, is sympathy at the same time with the sufferer's moral justification, with the affirmative aspect, the substantive thing that must be present in him. Beggars and rascals cannot inspire us with pity of this kind. Therefore if the tragic character has inspired in us a fear of the power of the ethical order that he has violated, then if in his misfortune he is to arouse a tragic sympathy he must be a man of worth and goodness himself. For it is only something of intrinsic worth which strikes the heart of a man of noble feelings and shakes it to its depths. After all, therefore, we should not confuse our interest in a tragic denouement with a naïve sense of satisfaction that our sympathy should be claimed by a sad story, by a misfortune as such. Such miseries may befall a man, without his contributing to them and without his fault, merely as a result of the conjuncture of external accidents and natural circumstances, as a result of illness, loss of property, death, etc., and the only interest in them by which we should properly be gripped is our eagerness to rush to the man's help. If we cannot help, then spectacles of wretchedness and distress are only harrowing. A truly tragic suffering, on the contrary, is only inflicted on the individual agents as a consequence of their own deed which is both legitimate and, owing to the resulting collision, blameworthy, and for which their whole self is answerable.

Above mere fear and tragic sympathy there therefore stands that sense of reconciliation which the tragedy affords by the glimpse of eternal justice. In its absolute sway this justice overrides the relative justification of one-sided aims and passions because it cannot suffer the conflict and contradiction of naturally harmonious ethical powers to be victorious and permanent in truth and actuality.

In virtue of this principle, tragedy rests primarily on the contemplation of such a conflict and its resolution. Consequently, owing to its whole manner of presentation, it is dramatic poetry alone which is capable of making the entire range and course of tragedy into the principle of a work of art and developing it completely. It is for this reason that I have only now taken the opportunity to speak of the tragic outlook, although it is at work extensively and variously, even if to a lesser extent, in the other arts also.

(β) In tragedy the eternal substance of things emerges victorious in a reconciling way, because it strips away from the conflicting individuals only their false one-sidedness, while the positive elements in what they willed it displays as what is to be retained, without discord but affirmatively harmonized. In comedy, conversely, it is subjectivity, or personality, which in its infinite assurance retains the upper hand. For, granted the cleavage of dramatic poetry into different *genres*, it is only these two fundamental features of action which can confront one another as the basis of such *genres*. In tragedy the individuals destroy themselves through the one-sidedness of their otherwise solid will and character, or they must resignedly accept what they had opposed even in a serious way. In comedy there comes before our contemplation, in the laughter in which the characters dissolve everything, including themselves, the victory of their own subjective personality which nevertheless persists self-assured.

(αα) The general ground for comedy is therefore a world in which man as subject or person has made himself completely master of everything that counts to him otherwise as the essence of what he wills and accomplishes, a world whose aims are therefore self-destructive because they are unsubstantial. Nothing can be done, for example, to help a democratic nation where the citizens are self-seeking, quarrelsome, frivolous, bumptious, without faith or knowledge, garrulous, boastful, and ineffectual: such a nation destroys itself by its own folly. But it does not follow at all that every unsubstantial action is comical on account of this nullity. In this matter the laughable is often confused with the comical. Every contrast between something substantive and its appearance, between an end and the means may be laughable; this is a contradiction in which the appearance cancels itself and the realization of an end is at the same time the end's own destruction. But for the comical we must make a deeper demand. For example, there is nothing comical about the vices of mankind. A proof of this is given us by satire, all the more tediously, the cruder are the colours in which it paints the contradiction between what actually exists in the world and what virtuous men ought to be. Neither need follies, senselessness, silliness, be comical, taken in and by themselves, although we laugh at them. In general, nowhere can more contradiction be found than in the things that people laugh at. The flattest and most tasteless things can move people to laughter, and they often laugh all the same at the most important and profound matters if they see in them only some wholly insignificant aspect which contradicts their habits and day-to-day outlook. In such a case their laughter is only an expression of a self-complacent wit, a sign that they are clever enough to recognize such a contrast and are aware of the fact. There is also the laughter of derision, scorn, despair, etc. On the other hand, the comical as such implies an infinite light-heartedness and confidence felt by someone raised altogether above his own inner contradiction and not bitter or miserable in it at all: this is the bliss and ease of a man who, being sure of himself, can bear the frustration of his aims and achievements. A narrow and pedantic mind is least of all capable of this when for others his behaviour is laughable in the extreme.

(ββ) I will touch generally on only the following more detailed points in connection with the sort of thing that can serve as the situation of a comical action.

In the first place, the characters and their aims are entirely without substance and contradictory and therefore they cannot accomplish anything. Avarice, for example, both in its aim and in the petty means it uses appears from beginning to end as inherently null. For the avaricious man takes the dead abstraction of wealth, money as such, as the ultimate reality beyond which he will not go; and he tries to attain this cold pleasure by depriving himself of every other concrete satisfaction, while nevertheless he cannot gain his chosen end because his aim and his means are helpless in face of cunning, betrayal, etc. But if an individual is *serious* in identifying himself with such an inherently false aim and making it the one real thing in his life, then, the more he still clings to it after he has been deprived of its realization, the more miserable he becomes. In such a picture there is none of the real essence of the comical, just as there is none anywhere when on one side there is the painfulness of the man's situation, and on the other side mere ridicule and malicious joy. Therefore there is more of the comic in a situation where petty and futile aims are to be brought about with a show of great seriousness and elaborate preparations, but where, precisely because what the individual willed was something inherently trivial, he is not ruined in fact when his purpose fails but can surmount this disaster with cheerfulness undisturbed.

In the second place, the converse situation occurs where individuals plume themselves on the *substantial* quality of their characters and aims, but as instruments for accomplishing something substantial their characters are the precise opposite of what is required. In this case the substantial quality is purely imaginary and has become in itself and in the eyes of onlookers an appearance giving itself the look and the value of something important; but this involves between aim and character, action and personality a contradiction whereby an achievement of the imagined character and aim is frustrated. An example of this kind of thing is the *Ecclesiazusae* of Aristophanes. There the women wish to decide on and to found a new political constitution, but they still retain all the whims and passions of women.

A third type, in addition to the first two, is based on the use of external contingencies. Through their various and peculiar complications situations arise in which aims and their accomplishment, inner character and external circumstances, are put in contrast with one another comically and then they lead to an equally comic solution.

(γγ) But the comical rests as such throughout on contradictory contrasts both between aims in themselves and also between their objects and the accidents of character and external circumstances, and therefore the comic action requires a solution almost more stringently than a tragic one does. In a comic action the contradiction between what is absolutely true and its realization in individuals is posed more profoundly.

Yet what is destroyed in this solution cannot be either fundamental principle or individual character.[1]

---

[1] In Hegel's terminology these alternatives are 'substance' and 'subject'. It is necessary to keep in mind the principle to which he always adhered and which he formulated in the Preface to his *Phenomenology* by saying that 'in my view everything depends on grasping and expressing the truth not only as substance but as subject as well'.

For, as genuine art, comedy too has to submit to the obligation of using its presentation to bring the absolutely rational into appearance, not at all as what is broken up and perverted in itself but on the contrary as what assigns neither the victory nor, in the last resort, permanence, in the real world to folly and unreason, to false oppositions and contradictions. Aristophanes, for example, did not make fun of what was truly moral in the life of the Athenians, or of their genuine philosophy, true religious faith, and serious art. On the contrary what he does put before our eyes in its self-destructive folly is what was real, i.e. the downright opposite of the genuine actuality of the state, religion, and art,[1] i.e. what he exhibits is sophistry, the deplorable and lamentable character of tragedy, flighty gossip, litigiousness, etc., and the aberrations of the democracy out of which the old faith and morals had vanished. Only in our day could a Kotzebue succeed in giving the palm to a moral excellence which is a form of baseness and in palliating and countenancing what can only exist in order to be destroyed.[2]

But neither should subjective personality as such come to grief in comedy. For even if what comes on the scene is only the show and imagination of what is substantive, or else mere downright perversity and pettiness, there still remains as a loftier principle the inherently firm personality which is raised in its freedom above the downfall of the whole finite sphere and is happy and assured in itself. The comic subjective personality has become the overlord of whatever appears in the real world. From that world the adequate objective presence of fundamental principle has disappeared. When what has no substance in itself has destroyed its show of existence by its own agency, the individual makes himself master of this dissolution too and remains undisturbed in himself and at ease.

(γ) In the centre between tragedy and comedy there is a third chief *genre* of dramatic poetry which yet is of less striking importance, despite the fact that it attempts to reconcile the difference between tragedy and comedy; or at least, instead of being isolated

---

[1] Hegel's distinction between reality and actuality has given rise to numerous misunderstandings. A man with an amputated limb is 'real', he exists, but he is not 'actual' because he is not what a man is meant to be; he does not conform to the concept or essential nature of man. Actuality is a complete correspondence of reality with its concept. Cf. the Translator's Preface to Vol. I.

[2] The moral value of Kotzebue's plays was questioned by Schiller as well as by Hegel. See references in the Index, *s.v.* Schiller's *Shakespeare's Ghost*.

in sheer opposition to one another, these two sides meet in it and form a concrete whole.

(αα) To this category there belong for example the Greek and Roman satyric dramas. In them the main action, even if not tragic, remains serious, while the chorus of satyrs is treated comically. Tragicomedy too may be included here. An example of it is provided by Plautus in the Prologue to the *Amphitruo* [ll. 52–5, 59] where this is announced through the mouth of Mercury addressing the audience as follows:

> Quid contraxistis frontem? quia Tragoediam
> Dixi futuram hanc? Deus sum: commutavero
> Eamden hanc, si voltis: faciam ex Tragoedia
> Comoedia ut sit omnibus iisdem versibus . . .
> Faciam ut conmista sit Tragicocomoedia.[1]

And as a reason for this mixture he adduces the fact that while on the one hand gods and kings appear as dramatis personae, there is also the comic figure of Sosia, the slave. In modern dramatic poetry, tragedy and comedy are still more intermingled, because even in modern tragedy the principle of subjectivity, free on its own account in comedy, becomes dominant from beginning to end and pushes into the background the substantive spheres of the ethical powers.

(ββ) But the deeper harmonization of tragic and comic treatment into a new whole does not consist in juxtaposing or upsetting these opposites [i.e. substance and subject] but in blunting both sides and reconciling their opposition. Instead of acting with comical perversity, the individual is filled with the seriousness characteristic of solid concerns and stable characters, while the tragic fixity of will is so far weakened, and the depth of the collisions involved so far reduced, that there can emerge a reconciliation of interests and a harmonious unification of individuals and their aims. It is in a conception like this that particularly our modern plays and dramas have the basis of their origin. The heart of this principle is the view that, despite all differences and conflicts of characters and their interests and passions, human action can nevertheless produce a really fully harmonious situation. As long

---

[1] 'Why have you screwed up your faces? Because I have said that this will be a tragedy? I am a god: I will change it if you like and make it a comedy, and with all the same lines too . . . I will make it a mixture, a tragicomedy.'

ago as their day the Greeks had tragedies which did have an outcome like this, in that individuals were not sacrificed but saved: for example, in the *Eumenides* of Aeschylus the Areopagus grants to both parties, Apollo and the avenging Furies, the right to be worshipped; and in the *Philoctetes* [of Sophocles] the divine appearance and advice of Heracles settles the fight between Neoptolemus and Philoctetes, and they go off to Troy together. But in these cases the reconciliation comes from outside by command of the gods, etc., and does not have its source within the parties themselves, while in modern plays it is the individuals themselves who are led in the course of their own action to this cessation of strife and to the mutual reconciliation of their aims or characters. In this respect Goethe's *Iphigenia* is a real poetic masterpiece of a play, more so than his *Tasso*. In the latter the reconciliation with Antonio is more or less only a matter of the heart and a subjective recognition that he possesses a sense for the realities of life which is missing from Tasso's character, while the right of the ideal life to which Tasso had clung in his conflict with reality, i.e. the life of propriety and decorum, is a right principally retained as such only subjectively in the minds of the spectators and appearing objectively [in Antonio] as, at best, consideration for Tasso and sympathy with his fate.

(γγ) But on the whole the boundary lines of this intermediate kind of dramatic poetry are less firm than those of tragedy and comedy. Moreover this kind almost runs the risk of departing from the genuine type of drama altogether or of lapsing into prose. Here the conflicts are meant to proceed via their own discord to a peaceful end and therefore from the start they are not such sharp oppositions as those in tragedy. The result is that the poet is easily induced to devote the whole force of his production to the inner life of the dramatis personae and to make the course of the situations a mere means to this sketching of character; or alternatively he allows preponderating scope to externals, i.e. to situations and customs of the period. If he finds both of these procedures too difficult, he restricts himself altogether to keeping attention alive merely through the interest of complicated and thrilling events. Consequently this sphere includes a mass of modern plays which make no claim to be poetry but only to have a theatrical effect. What they aim at producing is not a genuinely poetic emotion but only one that people ordinarily feel, or else they seek to reform the public or merely to entertain it. But, in any case, for the most part they manufacture all sorts of opportunities for the actor to give a brilliant display of his accomplished virtuosity.

(b) Difference between Ancient and Modern Dramatic Poetry

The same principle which gave us the basis for the division of dramatic art into tragedy and comedy provides us with the essential turning-points in the history of their development. For the lines of this development can only consist in setting out and elaborating the chief features implicit in the nature of dramatic action, where in tragedy the whole treatment and execution presents what is *substantial* and fundamental in the characters and their aims and conflicts, while in comedy the central thing is the character's *inner* life and his *private* personality.

(α) We are not concerned here to provide a complete history of art and therefore we may start by setting aside those beginnings of dramatic art which we encounter in the East. However far Eastern poetry advanced in epic and some sorts of lyric, the whole Eastern outlook inhibits *ab initio* an adequate development of dramatic art. The reason is that truly *tragic* action necessarily presupposes either a live conception of *individual* freedom and independence or at least an individual's determination and willingness to accept freely and on his own account the responsibility for his own act and its consequences; and for the emergence of *comedy* there must have asserted itself in a still higher degree the free right of the subjective personality and its self-assured dominion. In the East these conditions are not fulfilled. Mohammedan poetry, in particular, with its grandiose sublimity is throughout far away from any attempt at dramatic expression, because in such poetry, although the independence of the individual may be vigorously asserted, the One fundamental power still more persistently dominates its every creature and decides its lot irreversibly. Dramatic art demands the vindication of (*a*) a particular element in an individual's action, and (*b*) a personality probing its own depths, and it follows from what I have said that neither of these demands can be met in Mohammedan poetry. Indeed the individual's subjection to the will of God remains, precisely in Mohammedanism, all the more abstract the more abstractly universal is the One power which dominates the whole and which in the last resort inhibits anything particular. Consequently we find the beginnings of drama only in China and India; yet even here, to judge from the few samples so far known to us, there is no question of the accomplishment of a free individual action but merely of giving life to events and feelings in specific situations presented successively on the stage.

(β) Therefore the real beginning of dramatic poetry must be sought in Greece where the principle of free individuality makes the perfection of the classical form of art possible for the first time. Yet within this form of art the individual can enter in connection with action only so far as is directly required by the free vitalization of the *substantive* content of human aims. Therefore what principally counts in Greek drama, whether tragedy or comedy, is the universal and essential element in the aim which the characters are realizing: in tragedy, the moral justification of the agent's consciousness in respect of a specific action, the vindication of the act in and by itself; and, in comedy, at least in the old comedy, it is also the general public interests that are emphasized, statesmen and their way of steering the state, war and peace, the people and its moral situation, philosophy and its corruption, and so forth. Therefore neither the various descriptions of the human heart and personal character nor particular complications and intrigues can find their place completely in Greek drama; nor does the interest turn on the fates of individuals. Sympathy is claimed above all not for these particular and personal matters but simply for the battle between the essential powers that rule human life and between the gods that dominate the human heart, and for this battle's outcome. The *tragic* heroes come on the scene as the individual representatives of these powers in much the same way as the figures of *comedy* expose the general corruption into which the fundamental tendencies of public life have been actually perverted contemporaneously with the comedy.

(γ) In modern, or romantic, poetry, on the other hand, the principal topic is provided by an individual's passion, which is satisfied in the pursuit of a purely subjective end, and, in general, by the fate of a single individual and his character in special circumstances.

Accordingly the poetic interest here lies in the greatness of the characters who by their imagination or disposition and aptitude display the full wealth of their heart, and their elevation over their situations and actions, as a real possibility[1] (even if this be often impaired and destroyed solely by circumstances and complications), but at the same time they find a reconciliation in the very greatness of their nature. Therefore in this mode of treatment our interest is directed, so far as the particular matter at issue in an action is concerned, not on its moral justification and necessity but on the individual person and his affairs. This being so, a *leitmotiv* is thus provided by love, ambition, etc.; indeed, even crime is not excluded, though this easily becomes a rock difficult to circumnavigate. For after all if a criminal, especially one like the hero in Müllner's[2] *Guilt*, is weak and through and through base, he is only a disgusting sight. Here above all, therefore, we must demand formal greatness of character and a personality powerful enough to sustain everything negative and, without denying its acts or being inwardly wrecked, to accept its fate.—Nevertheless the substantive and fundamental ends, country, family, crown, and empire, are not to be held aloof at all, even if what matters to the individual character is not the substantial nature of these ends but his own individuality; but in that case they form on the whole the specific ground on which the individual stands with his own subjective character and where he gets into a conflict, instead of providing him with the proper ultimate object of his willing and acting.

Then, further, alongside this subjective element there may come on the scene a spread of particular details concerning both the inner life and also the external circumstances and relations within which the action proceeds. Therefore we find legitimately in place here, in distinction from the simple conflicts in Greek tragedy, a variety and wealth of dramatis personae, extraordinary and always newly involved complications, labyrinths of intrigue, accidental occurrences, in short all those features which, no longer fettered by the impressive and substantive character of an essential subject-matter, are indicative of what is typical in the romantic, as distinct from the classical, form of art.

Nevertheless despite this apparently unbounded mass of particulars, even here, if the whole play is to remain dramatic and poetic, the specific character of the collision which has to be fought out

---

[1] This is a term drawn from Hegel's *Logic* (e.g. *Enc.* § 147). What is 'really' possible is something possible in certain real circumstances, and, indeed, is really potent there. 'Pigs might fly' may be a possibility, but not a 'real' one.
[2] A., 1774–1829.

must be visibly emphasized, and, on the other hand, especially in tragedy, the authority of a higher world-governor, whether Providence or fate, must be made obvious in the course and outcome of the particular action.

(c) *The Concrete Development of Dramatic Poetry and its Genres*

The essential differences of conception and poetic execution [in drama] have now been considered. Along with them are the different *genres* of dramatic art and they acquire their truly real perfection only when they are developed at this or that stage [in history]. Therefore, in conclusion, our consideration must be directed to this concrete manner of their evolution.

(α) If for the reason given above we exclude oriental beginnings, the first main sphere confronting us at once is the dramatic poetry of the Greeks because that is the stage at which tragedy proper, and comedy too, had their highest intrinsic worth. It was in that poetry that for the first time there was a clear consciousness of what the real essence of tragedy and comedy is. After these opposed ways of looking at human action had been firmly separated and strictly distinguished from one another, tragedy and comedy developed organically, and first one, and then the other, attained the summit of perfection. Still later, Roman dramatic art gives us only a pale reflection of the Greek achievement, and here the Romans did not achieve even that measure of success which later came to them in their similar efforts in epic and lyric.—In order to touch briefly on only the points of greatest importance, I will limit a more detailed consideration of these stages to tragedy as viewed by Aeschylus and Sophocles and comedy by Aristophanes.

(αα) I have said of *tragedy* already that the basic form determining its organization and structure is to be found in emphasis on the substantial aspect of aims and their objects, as well as of individuals, their conflicts, and their fates.

The general background of a tragic action is provided in a tragedy, as it was in epic, by that world-situation which I have previously called the 'heroic' age. In that age the universal ethical powers have not been explicitly fixed as either the law of the land or as moral precepts and duties. Consequently, only in heroic times can these powers enter in original freshness as the gods who either oppose one another in their own activities or appear themselves as the living heart of free human individuals. But if the ethical order is to be exhibited from the outset as the substantive foundation and general background out of which the actions of individuals grow and develop into a conflict and then are tugged back out of it into unity again, we are confronted by two different forms of the ethical order in action.

First, the naïve consciousness which wills the substantial order as a *whole*, i.e. as an undivided identity of its different aspects. This consciousness therefore remains blameless and neutral, in undisturbed peace with itself and others. But this is a purely universal consciousness, undifferentiated in its worship, faith, and fortune. It therefore cannot attain to any specific action.[1] On the contrary, it has a sort of horror of the schism implicit there. Although, inactive itself, it reverences as higher that spiritual courage which, having selected its aim, proceeds to decide and act, it is still incapable of embarking on any such course. It knows that it is but the terrain or spectator of action. Therefore, there is nothing left for it to do with the agents, whom it venerates as higher than itself, and with the energy of their decisions and struggles, but to oppose to them the object of its own wisdom, i.e. the substantive ideality[2] of the ethical powers.

The *second* aspect is the individual 'pathos' which drives the dramatis personae, acting with an ethical justification, into opposition with others and thereby brings them into a conflict. The individuals animated by this 'pathos' are not what we call 'characters' in the modern sense of the word, but neither are they mere abstractions. They occupy a vital central position between both, because they are firm figures who simply are what they are, without any inner conflict, without any hesitating recognition of someone else's 'pathos', and therefore (the opposite of our contemporary

---

[1] Two aspects of the substantial or ethical order are the law of the land and family love. If these are not differentiated and the order is regarded as an harmonious whole, then action may be difficult, for in practice these aspects may conflict. And to sense this possible conflict may be to shrink from action.

[2] Ideally, or *sub specie aeternitatis*, these 'powers' are a unity. But, in the real and therefore finite world, the universal, or ideal, is necessarily differentiated, and some of these powers, in their realization, become opposed to others. The naïve consciousness is the undifferentiated basis and substratum of Greek ethical life from which the protagonist detaches himself, causes conflict, and has to suffer. In the ensuing struggle the naïve consciousness, half horrified and half admiring, can only oppose to the protagonist's energy its own knowledge of the moral substance of life.

'irony') lofty, absolutely determinate individuals, although this determinacy of theirs is based on and is representative of a particular ethical power. Since it is only the *opposition* of such individuals, justified in their action, which constitutes the essence of tragedy, it can come into view only on the territory of actual *human* life. For it is only in that life that a particular quality can be the substance of an individual in the sense that he puts himself with his entire being and interests into such a quality and makes it an overmastering passion. On the other hand, in the case of the *blessed gods* the undifferenced divine nature is the essential thing, and, if opposition arises, there is in the last resort no seriousness about it and, as I have already pointed out in dealing with the Homeric epic, it is ultimately dissolved again ironically.

Each of these two aspects is as important as the other for the whole drama. Both of them—the one and undivided consciousness of the Divine [or of the ethical powers], and the action which, resolving on ethical ends and achieving them, involves battle but comes on the scene with divine force and as a divine deed—provide the principal elements which in its works of art Greek tragedy displays as harmonized, i.e. in the chorus and the heroic agents.

In recent times the significance of the Greek *chorus* has been much discussed, and in the course of this discussion a question has been raised about whether it can or should be introduced into modern tragedy too. People have felt the need for such a substantial groundwork and yet at the same time have been unable to introduce or insert it because they have not understood or grasped deeply enough the nature of what is genuinely tragic or the necessity of the chorus in the Greek conception of tragedy. The chorus has indeed been understood to some extent by those who say that its business is tranquil reflection on the whole thing at issue while the dramatis personae remain caught in their own particular aims and situations and have now gained in the chorus and its meditations a criterion of the worth of their characters and actions, just as the public has found in the chorus an objective representative of its own judgement on what is going on in front of it in the work of art.

Upholders of this view have hit on part of the truth, because in fact the chorus confronts us as a higher moral consciousness, aware of the substantial issues, warning against false conflicts, and weighing the outcome. Nevertheless the chorus is not at all a moralist, disengaged like a spectator, a person reflecting on the thing purely from outside, in himself uninteresting and tedious, and introduced simply for the sake of his reflections. On the contrary, the chorus is the actual substance of the moral life and action of the heroes themselves; in contrast to these individuals it is the people as the fruitful soil out of which they grow (just as flowers and towering trees do from their own native soil) and by the existent character of which they are conditioned. Consequently the chorus is essentially appropriate in an age where moral complications cannot yet be met by specific valid and just laws and firm religious dogmas, but where the ethical order appears only in its direct and living actuality and remains only the equilibrium of a stable life secure against the fearful collisions to which the energies of individuals in their opposing actions must lead. But what the chorus gives us is the consciousness that such a secure refuge is actually present. Therefore the chorus does not in fact encroach on the action; it does not actively exercise any right against the warring heroes but pronounces judgement purely contemplatively; it warns and sympathizes, or it appeals to divine law and those inner powers which imagination portrays to itself objectively as the group of the gods who hold sway. In so expressing itself it is lyrical, as we saw; for it does nothing and has no events to relate epically. But what it says preserves at the same time the epic character of substantial universality and it does therefore move in one mode of lyric which may, in distinction from the proper form of odes, sometimes approach the paean and the dithyramb.

This position of the chorus in Greek tragedy needs essential emphasis. Just as the Greek theatre itself has its external terrain, its scene, and its surroundings, so the chorus, the people, is as it were the scene of the spirit; it may be compared, in architecture, with a temple surrounding the image of the gods, for here it is an environment for the heroes in the action. In our case, however, statues stand under the open sky without such a background, and modern tragedy does not need one either, because its actions do not rest on this substantial basis but on the individual's will and character as well as on the apparently external accidents of occurrences and circumstances.

This all implies that it is an utterly false view to regard the chorus as something casually dragged in and a mere relic of the time when Greek drama originated. No doubt its external origin is to be traced to the fact that at festivals of Dionysus the chief thing, in art at any rate, was choral song, until subsequently, as a break, a narrator came on the scene, and his message was finally transformed and elevated into the actual figures of a dramatic action. But in the age of tragedy's full bloom the chorus was not retained at all merely in honour of this feature of religious festivals and Dionysus worship; on the contrary it was developed ever more beautifully and in a more measured way simply because it belongs essentially to the dramatic action itself and is so necessary to it that the decay of tragedy is especially manifested in the deterioration of the choruses which no longer remain an integral part of the whole but sink down into being an unnecessary ornament. On the other hand, the chorus is plainly unsuitable for romantic tragedy which in any case did not originate in choral songs. On the contrary, the subject-matter here is of such a kind that any introduction of choruses in the Greek sense must inevitably have misfired. For even the oldest so-called mystery-plays, moralities, and other farces from which romantic drama arose, do not present any action in the original Greek sense or any emergence from that consciousness which is unaware of division in life or the Divine. Neither does the chorus fit in with chivalry or absolute monarchy, for there the people have to obey or become partisans involved in action only in the interests of their fortune or misfortune. In general it cannot find its proper place where it is individual passions, aims, and characters that are at issue or where the play of intrigue is being pursued.

The second chief feature, contrasted with the chorus, consists of the *individuals* who act and come continually into conflict. In Greek tragedy, as I have said more than once, the occasion for collisions is produced by the moral justification of a specific act, and not at all by an evil will, a crime, or infamy, or by mere misfortune, blindness, and the like. For evil in the abstract has no truth in itself and is of no interest. But, on the other hand, it must not look as if moral traits of character have been assigned to individuals merely by [the dramatist's] *intention*, for on the contrary their justification must be shown to lie in them *essentially*. Criminal types, like those of today, good-for-nothings, or even so-called 'morally noble' criminals with their empty chatter about fate, we therefore do not find in Greek tragedy any more than a decision or a deed resting on purely private interest and personal character, on thirst for power, lust, honour, or other passions, the right of which can be rooted only in an individual's private inclination and personality. But an individual's decision, justified by the object he aims at, is carried out in a one-sided and particular way, and therefore in specific circumstances, which already carry in themselves the real possibility of conflicts, he injures another and equally moral sphere of the human will. To this sphere another person clings as his own actual 'pathos' and in carrying out his aim opposes and reacts against the former individual. In this way the collision of equally justified powers and individuals is completely set afoot.

The range of the subject-matter here may be variously particularized but its essence is not very extensive. The chief conflict treated most beautifully by Sophocles, with Aeschylus as his predecessor, is that between the state, i.e. ethical life in its *spiritual* universality, and the family, i.e. *natural* ethical life. These are the clearest powers that are presented in tragedy, because the full reality of ethical existence consists in harmony between these two spheres and in absence of discord between what an agent has actually to do in one and what he has to do in the other. In this connection I need refer only to Aeschylus' *Seven against Thebes* and, still more appositely, Sophocles' *Antigone*. Antigone honours the bond of kinship, the gods of the underworld, while Creon honours Zeus alone, the dominating power over public life and social welfare. In [Euripides'] *Iphigenia in Aulis*, in Aeschlyus' *Agamemnon*, *Choephori*, and *Eumenides*, and in Sophocles' *Electra* we find a similar conflict. Agamemnon, as King and commander of the army, sacrifices his daughter in the interest of the Greeks and the Trojan expedition; thereby he snaps the bond of love for his daughter and his wife. This bond Clytemnestra, his wife and Iphigenia's mother, retains in the depths of her heart, and in revenge she prepares a shameful death for her home-coming husband. Orestes, her son and the King's son, honours his mother but he has to defend the right of his father, the King, and he slays the womb that bore him.

This is a subject valid for every epoch and therefore this presentation of it, despite all national differences, continues to excite our lively human and artistic sympathy.

A second main type of collision is less concrete. The Greek tragedians are fond of portraying it especially in the fate of Oedipus. The most perfect example of this has been left to us by

Sophocles in his *Oedipus Tyrannus* and *Oedipus Coloneus*. What is at issue here is the right of the wide awake consciousness, the justification of what the man has self-consciously willed and knowingly done, as contrasted with what he was fated by the gods to do and actually did unconsciously and without having willed it. Oedipus has killed his father; he has married his mother and begotten children in this incestuous alliance; and yet he has been involved in these most evil crimes without either knowing or willing them. The right of our deeper consciousness today would consist in recognizing that since he had neither intended nor known these crimes himself, they were not to be regarded as his own deeds. But the Greek, with his plasticity of consciousness, takes responsibility for what he has done as an individual and does not cut his purely subjective self-consciousness apart from what is objectively the case.

Lastly, there are other collisions depending partly on special circumstances and partly on the general relation between an individual's action and the Greek μοῖρα [fate]. For our purpose, these are of less importance.

But in considering all these tragic conflicts we must above all reject the false idea that they have anything to do with guilt or innocence. The tragic heroes are just as much innocent as guilty. On the presupposition that a man is only guilty if alternatives are open to him and he decides arbitrarily on what he does, the Greek plastic figures are innocent: they act out of this character of theirs, on *this* 'pathos', because this character, this 'pathos' is precisely what they are: their act is not preceded by either hesitation or choice. It is just the strength of the great characters that they do not choose but throughout, from start to finish, *are* what they will and accomplish. They are what they are, and never anything else, and this is their greatness. For weakness in action consists only in a cleavage between the individual and his object, in which case character, will, and aim do not appear as having grown into an absolute unity; and since no fixed aim is alive in the individual's soul as the substance of his own individuality, as the 'pathos' and power animating his whole will, he may swither irresolutely from this to that and let caprice decide. From this swithering the Greek plastic figures are exempt; for them the bond between the subject and what he wills as his object remains indissoluble. What drives them to act is precisely an ethically justified 'pathos' which they assert against one another with the eloquence of their 'pathos' not in sentimental and personal rhetoric or in the sophistries of passion, but in solid and cultivated objective language. (Sophocles above everyone else was a master in the depth, measure, and plastic and living beauty of language of this kind.) At the same time, however, their 'pathos' is pregnant with collisions and it leads them to injurious and guilty acts. But they do not claim to be innocent of these at all. On the contrary, what they did, and actually had to do, is their glory. No worse insult could be given to such a hero than to say that he had acted innocently. It is the honour of these great characters to be culpable. They do not want to arouse sympathy or pity, for what arouses pity is not anything substantive, but subjective grief, the subjective depth of personality. But their firm and strong character is one with its essential 'pathos', and what excites our admiration is this indestructible harmony and not the pity and emotion that Euripides alone has slipped into expressing.

The tragic complication leads finally to no other result or denouement but this: the two sides that are in conflict with one another preserve the justification which both have, but what each upholds is one-sided, and this one-sidedness is stripped away and the inner, undisturbed harmony returns in the attitude of the chorus which clearly assigns equal honour to all the gods. The true development of the action consists solely in the cancellation of conflicts *as conflicts*, in the reconciliation of the powers animating action which struggled to destroy one another in their mutual conflict. Only in that case does finality lie not in misfortune and suffering but in the satisfaction of the spirit, because only with such a conclusion can the necessity of what happens to the individuals appear as absolute rationality, and only then can our hearts be morally at peace: shattered by the fate of the heroes but reconciled fundamentally. Only by adherence to this view can Greek tragedy be understood.

Therefore we should not interpret such a conclusion as a purely moral outcome where evil is punished and virtue rewarded, i.e. 'when vice vomits, virtue sits at table'.[1] Here there is no question

---

[1] The last line of Schiller's *Shakespeares Schatten*. 'Is nothing great but only your own contemptible nature to be brought on the stage?', Shakespeare's ghost asks. Schiller sarcastically makes the reply that Kotzebue and others might make: 'After giving vice more than its fill in the earlier scenes, the poet

at all of an introverted personality's subjective reflection and its good and evil, but, when the collision was complete, of the vision of an affirmative reconciliation and the equal validity of both the powers that were in conflict. Neither is the necessity of the outcome a blind fate, a purely irrational and unintelligible destiny which many people call 'classical', but a rational one, although the rationality here does not appear as a self-conscious Providence whose divine end and aim becomes manifest to itself and others in the world and individuals. On the contrary, the rationality consists in the fact that the power supreme over individual gods and men cannot allow persistence either to one-sided powers that make themselves independent and thereby overstep the limits of their authority or to the conflicts that follow in consequence. Fate drives individuality back within its limits and destroys it if these are crossed. But an irrational compulsion and innocent suffering would inevitably produce in the soul of the spectator mere indignation instead of moral peace and satisfaction.

In another way, therefore, a tragic reconciliation is nevertheless different from an epic one. If we look at Achilles and Odysseus, for example, they reach their goal, and this is proper; but they are not steadily favoured by fortune; on the contrary, they have to taste the bitter wine of a sense of finitude and to fight their way through difficulty, loss, and sacrifice. For Truth demands that in the course of life and the objective sweep of events the nullity of the finite shall come into appearance too. The wrath of Achilles is appeased, he obtains from Agamemnon what he had been injured by losing, he wreaks his revenge on Hector, the funeral celebrations for Patroclus are completed, and Achilles is recognized as the most glorious of men. But his wrath and its appeasement has cost him his dearest friend, the noble Patroclus; in order to avenge his loss on Hector, he finds himself compelled to desist from his wrath and plunge once more into the battle against the Trojans, and when he is recognized as the most glorious of men he has at the same time a sense of his early death. Similarly, Odysseus does in the end arrive at Ithaca, the goal of his wishes, but asleep and alone after long years of delay and toil, after losing all his companions and all the booty from Troy. Thus both have paid their debt to finitude, and Nemesis has entered into its rights by

makes a bow to virtue at the end.' See Hegel's remarks on plays by Kotzebue and Iffland on p. 1233 below, where Schiller's poem is again in his mind.

the downfall of Troy and the fate of the Greek heroes. But Nemesis is simply the ancient justice which degrades what has risen too high only in order to restore by misfortune the mere equilibrium of good and ill fortune, and it touches and affects the realm of finitude without any further *moral* judgement. This is epic justice in the field of events, the comprehensive reconciliation which consists in mere equalization. The more profound tragic reconciliation, on the other hand, depends on the advance of specific ethical substantive powers out of their opposition to their true harmony. But the ways in which this harmony can be brought about are very different, and I will therefore bring to your notice only the chief features at issue in this connection.

First, it needs special emphasis that if the one-sidedness of a 'pathos' is the real ground of the collisions, this can only mean that it is carried out into actually living action, and the one-sided 'pathos' has become the one and only 'pathos' of a specific individual. Now if the one-sidedness is to be cancelled, it is the individual, since he has acted solely as this *one* 'pathos', who must be got rid of and sacrificed. For the individual is only this *one* life and, if this is not to prevail on its own account as this *one*, then the individual is shattered.

This sort of development is most complete when the individuals who are at variance appear each of them in their concrete existence as a totality,¹ so that in themselves they are in the power of what they are fighting, and therefore they violate what, if they were true to their own nature, they should be honouring. For example, Antigone lives under the political authority of Creon [the present King]; she is herself the daughter of a King [Oedipus] and the fiancée of Haemon [Creon's son], so that she ought to pay obedience to the royal command. But Creon too, as father and husband, should have respected the sacred tie of blood and not ordered anything against its pious observance. So there is immanent in both Antigone and Creon something that in their own way they attack, so that they are gripped and shattered by something intrinsic to

¹ Hegel simply means that, as human beings ('concretely existent'), individuals have an entirety of obligations (are under the dominion of *all* the 'ethical powers') but their overmastering 'pathos' is identified with one obligation alone, with the result that when one individual fights against another individual who is similarly overmastered by a different obligation, they are both caught in a fight against themselves.

their own actual being. Antigone suffers death before enjoying the bridal dance, but Creon too is punished by the voluntary deaths of his son and his wife, incurred, the one on account of Antigone's fate, the other because of Haemon's death. Of all the masterpieces of the classical and the modern world—and I know nearly all of them and you should and can[1]—the *Antigone* seems to me to be the most magnificent and satisfying work of art of this kind.

But the tragic denouement need not every time require the downfall of the participating individuals in order to obliterate the one-sidedness of both sides and their equal meed of honour. We all know that the *Eumenides* of Aeschylus does not end with the death of Orestes or the discomfiture of the Eumenides. (These were the Furies, the avengers of a mother's blood, and the violation of family piety, against Apollo who means to maintain the dignity and veneration of the King and the head of the family, and who provoked Orestes to kill his mother.) On the contrary, Orestes is excused punishment and both the gods are honoured. But at the same time we see clearly in this decisive conclusion what their gods meant to the Greeks when they brought them before their eyes in a combat between one another as particular individuals. To the contemporary Athenians they were only elements which were bound together into the entire harmony of ethical life. The votes of the Areopagus were equal; it is Athene, the goddess representing the whole substance of living Athenian life, who inserts the white stone which liberates Orestes, but she promises altars and worship to the Eumenides and Apollo equally.

Secondly, in contrast to this objective reconciliation, the assuaging of conflict may be of a subjective kind when the individual agent gives up the one-sidedness of his aim. But in this desertion of a substantive 'pathos' of his own he would appear as lacking in character, and this contradicts the solidity of the Greek plastic

---

[1] The boast is not unreasonable, as these lectures surely prove. 'Of this kind', *nach dieser Seite*. The meaning of this qualification has been much disputed. Did Hegel merely mean that the *Antigone* was the finest of Greek tragedies, or did he put it above Shakespeare? His meaning, however, is clear from what he says later when he contrasts Greek tragedy with modern. His point is that the *Antigone* is the finest portrayal of what he regards as the greatest tragic conflict, i.e. one where the issue is not merely personal arising from e.g. jealousy like Othello's, but one where both parties are under the necessity of transgressing; they are divided against themselves; neither of them can obey *both* the valid *laws* to which they are subject.

figures. In this case, therefore, the individual can only put himself at the mercy of a higher power and its advice and command, so that while he persists on his own account in his 'pathos', his obstinate will is broken by a god. In such a case the knots cannot be untied but, as in the *Philoctetes*, for example, are cut by a *deus ex machina*.

Finally, more beautiful than this rather external sort of denouement is an inner reconciliation which, because of its subjective character, already borders on our modern treatment. The most perfect classical example of this that we have before us is the eternally marvellous *Oedipus Coloneus*. Oedipus has murdered his father, taken the Theban throne, and mounted the marriage-bed with his mother. These unconsciously committed crimes do not make him unhappy; but of old he had solved a riddle and now he forcibly extracts [from the oracle] a knowledge of his own dark fate and acquires the dreadful realization that it has been accomplished in himself. With this solution of the riddle in his own person he has lost his happiness as Adam did when he came to the knowledge of good and evil [Genesis, 3]. The seer now, he blinds himself, resigns the throne, exiles himself from Thebes, just as Adam and Eve were driven from Paradise, and wanders away a helpless old man. In Colonus, sore afflicted, instead of listening to his son's request that he might return, he invokes on him his own Furies [or curse]; he expunges all his own inner discord and is purified within. Then a god himself calls him [i.e. to death]; his blind eyes are transfigured and clear; his bones become a salvation and safeguard of the state that received him as friend and guest. This transfiguration in death is for us, as for him, a visible reconciliation within his own self and personality. Attempts have been made to find a Christian tone here: the vision of a sinner whom God pardons and a fate endured in life but compensated with bliss in death. But the Christian religious reconciliation is a transfiguration of the soul which, bathed in the spring of eternal salvation, is lifted above its deeds and existence in the real world, because it makes the heart itself into the grave of the heart (yes, the spirit can do this), pays the imputations of earthly guilt with its own earthly individuality and now holds itself secure against those imputations in the certainty of its own eternal and purely spiritual bliss. On the other hand, the transfiguration of Oedipus always still remains the Greek transfer of consciousness from the strife of ethical powers, and the violations involved, into the unity and harmony of the entire ethical order itself.

What is further implied in this reconciliation is *subjective* satisfaction, and this enables us to make the transition to the sphere of comedy, the opposite of tragedy.

(ββ) What is comical, as we saw, is a personality or subject who makes his own actions contradictory and so brings them to nothing, while remaining tranquil and self-assured in the process. Therefore comedy has for its basis and starting-point what tragedy may end with, namely an absolutely reconciled and cheerful heart. Even if its possessor destroys by the means he uses whatever he wills and so comes to grief in himself because by his own efforts he has accomplished the very opposite of what he aimed at, he still has not lost his peace of mind on that account. But, on the other hand, this subjective self-assurance is only possible if the aims, and so with them the characters in question, either have no real substance in themselves or, if they have, then their essentiality has been made an aim and been pursued in a shape really opposed to it fundamentally and therefore in a shape without substance; and the result is that it is always only what is inherently null and indifferent that comes to grief, and the individual remains firm on his feet and undisturbed.

On the whole this is also the character of the old Greek comedy as it has been preserved for us in the plays of Aristophanes. In this matter we must be very careful to distinguish whether the dramatis personae are comical themselves or only in the eyes of the audience. The former case alone can be counted as really comical, and here Aristophanes was a master. On these lines, an individual is only portrayed as laughable when it is obvious that he is not serious at all about the seriousness of his aim and will, so that this seriousness always carries with it, in the eyes of the individual himself, its own destruction, because from beginning to end he cannot devote himself to any higher and universally valid interest which would bring him into a conflict of substance [i.e. with another such interest]. Even if he really does so devote himself, he can only exhibit a character which, owing to what it directly and presently is, has already annihilated what it apparently wanted to accomplish, and we can see at once that the substantial interest has never had a real hold on him. The comical therefore plays its part more often in people with lower views, tied to the real world and the present, i.e. among men who are what they are once and for all, who cannot be or will anything different, and, though incapable of any genuine 'pathos', have not the least doubt about what they are and what they are doing. But at the same time they reveal themselves as having something higher in them because they are not seriously tied to the finite world with which they are engaged but are raised above it and remain firm in themselves and secure in face of failure and loss. It is to this absolute freedom of spirit which is utterly consoled in advance in every human undertaking, to this world of private serenity, that Aristophanes conducts us. If you have not read him, you can scarcely realize how men can take things so easily.

The interests within which this kind of comedy moves need not be drawn at all from spheres opposed to morality, religion, and art; on the contrary, the old Greek comedy keeps precisely within this objective and substantive sphere, but it is by subjective caprice, vulgar folly, and absurdity that individuals bring to nought actions which had a higher aim. And here Aristophanes had available to him rich and happy material partly in the Greek gods and partly in the Athenians. For making the gods into human individuals has itself produced a contrast with the loftiness of their significance owing to their being so represented and particularized, particularized and humanized right down to detail, and their form can be portrayed as an empty pride in a subjective personality thus inappropriately given to them. But what Aristophanes especially loves is to expose to the ridicule of his fellow-citizens in the most comical and yet profound way the follies of the masses, the insanity of their orators and statesmen, the absurdity of the [Peloponnesian] war, and above all, most mercilessly, the new direction that Euripides had taken in tragedy. The persons in whom he embodies the objects of his magnificent ridicule are made into fools from the start by his inexhaustible humour, so that we can see at once that we are to get nothing but ineptitude from them. Take, for example, Strepsiades, who wants to go to the philosophers to learn how to be rid of his debts, or Socrates, who offers to teach Strepsiades and his son;[1] or Dionysus, who is made to descend into the underworld in order to bring a true tragedian up from there;[2] or Cleon,[3] the women,[4] and the Greeks who want to

---

[1] *The Clouds.*   [2] *The Frogs.*
[3] *The Knights.*   [4] *Ecclesiazusae* and *Thesmophoriazusae.*

draw the goddess of peace from the well;[1] and so forth. The keynote resounding in all these portrayals is the self-confidence of all these figures, and it is all the more imperturbable the more incapable they obviously are of accomplishing their undertaking. The fools are such naïve fools, and even the more sensible of them also have such an air of contradiction with what they are devoted to, that they never lose this naïve personal self-assurance, no matter how things go. It is the smiling blessedness of the Olympian gods, their unimpaired equanimity which comes home in men and can put up with anything. In all this Aristophanes is obviously not a cold or malignant scoffer. On the contrary he is a man of most gifted mind, the best of citizens to whom the welfare of Athens was always a serious matter and who proved to be a true patriot throughout. Therefore, as I have said earlier, what is portrayed in his comedies is not the complete dissolution of religion and morality but both the all-pervasive corruption which plumes itself on keeping step with the fundamental powers, and also the shape of things and the appearance of individuals, which are a mask concealing the fact that real truth and substance are no longer there and can be simply and openly handed over to the unfeigned play of subjective caprice. Aristophanes presents to us the absolute contradiction between (*a*) the true essence of religion and political and ethical life, and (*b*) the subjective attitude of citizens and individuals who should give actuality to that essence. But in this very triumph of the subjective attitude, whatever its insight, there is implicit one of the greatest symptoms of Greek corruption, and thus these pictures of a naïve fundamental 'all is well with me' are the final great outcome of the poetry of this gifted, civilized, and ingenious Greek people.

(β) We turn now at once to the dramatic art of the modern world, and here too I will only bring out in general some of the main differences of importance in relation to tragedy, drama, and comedy.

(αα) At its plastic height in Greece, tragedy remains one-sided by making the validity of the substance and necessity of ethical life its essential basis and by leaving undeveloped the individuality of the dramatis personae and the depths of their personal life. Comedy on its side brings to view in a converse mode of plasticity, and to perfection, the subjective personality in the free expatiation of its absurdity and its absurdity's dissolution.

[1] *Peace*.

Modern tragedy adopts into its own sphere from the start the principle of subjectivity. Therefore it takes for its proper subject-matter and contents the subjective inner life of the character who is not, as in classical tragedy, a purely individual embodiment of ethical powers, and, keeping to this same type, it makes actions come into collision with one another as the chance of external circumstances dictates, and makes similar accidents decide, or seem to decide, the outcome. Here there are the following chief points to discuss.

(i) The nature of the various aims which the characters have and which are to be attained;

(ii) the tragic characters themselves and the collisions to which they are subjected;

(iii) the difference from Greek tragedy in respect of the sort of denouement and the tragic reconciliation.

However far the centre of romantic tragedy is the individual's sufferings and passions (in the strict sense of that word),[1] nevertheless in human action a basis of specific ends drawn from the concrete spheres of family, state, church, etc. is never missing. For, by acting, man, as man, enters the sphere of the real world and its particular concerns. But since now it is not the substantial element in these spheres which engrosses the interest of individuals, their aims are broadly and variously particularized and in such detail that what is truly substantial can often glimmer through them in only a very dim way; and, apart from this, these aims acquire an altogether different form. For example, in the religious sphere, the dominating subject-matter is no longer the particular ethical powers made by imagination into individual gods and displayed either in their own person or as the 'pathos' of human heroes, but instead the story of Christ, the saints, etc. In the political sphere what is brought before us in all sorts of different ways is especially the monarchy, the power of vassals, the strife between dynasties or between members of one and the same royal family. Indeed, furthermore, civil and private rights and other relationships are dealt with and, similarly, even aspects of family life arise which

---

[1] i.e., presumably, as meaning something suffered, or something to which a man succumbs, the opposite of action. Hegel seems here to be emphasizing the connection between *Leiden* (suffering) and *Leidenschaft* (passion). But he is soon using 'passion' in the ordinary sense as meaning something driving a man to act.

were not yet compatible with Greek drama. For since the principle of subjectivity itself has gained its right in the [religious, political, and social] spheres mentioned above, it follows that new features appear even in them which modern man is entitled to make the aim and guide of his action.

On the other hand, it is the right of personality as such which is firmly established as the sole subject-matter, and love, personal honour, etc., are taken as ends so exclusive that the other relationships either can only appear as the external ground on which these modern interests are played out or else stand on their own account in conflict against the demands of the individual's subjective heart. The situation is more profound when the individual character, in order to achieve his goal, does not shrink from wrong and crime, even if he has not envisaged himself as unjust and criminal in choosing his end.

But instead of having this particular and personal character the ends chosen may be extensive, universal, and comprehensive in scope, or, again, they may be adopted and pursued as having substance in themselves. (*a*) As an example of the former case I will only refer to Goethe's *Faust*, the one absolutely philosophical tragedy. Here on the one side, dissatisfaction with learning and, on the other, the freshness of life and enjoyment in the world, in general the tragic quest for harmony between the Absolute in its essence and appearance and the individual's knowledge and will, all this provides a breadth of subject-matter which no other dramatist has ventured to compass in one and the same work. A similar example is Schiller's [*Robbers* where] Karl Moor is enraged by the entire civil order and the whole situation of the world and mankind in his day, and his *rebellion* against it has this universal significance. Wallenstein likewise adopts a great universal aim, the unity and peace of Germany. He failed in his aim partly because his forces, collected artificially and held together by purely external links, broke up and scattered just when things became serious for him, and partly because he revolted against the authority of the Emperor, a power on which he and his undertaking were bound to be shipwrecked. Universal ends, like those pursued by Karl Moor and Wallenstein, cannot be accomplished by a single individual by making others his obedient instruments; on the contrary, such ends prevail by their own force, sometimes with the will of the many, sometimes against it and without their knowledge. (*b*) As examples of the adoption of ends in virtue of their substantial character, I will mention only some tragedies of Calderón in which the rights and duties involved in love, honour, etc. are used by the dramatis personae as a sort of code of laws rigid and inflexible in themselves. Something similar occurs frequently in Schiller's characters, although their point of view is quite different; anyway this is true in the sense that these individuals adopt and fight for their aims by regarding them at the same time as universal and absolute human rights. So, for example, in *Intrigue and Love* Major Ferdinand means to defend natural rights against fashionable conventions and, above all, the Marquis Posa [in *Don Carlos*] demands freedom of thought as an inalienable possession of mankind.

But in modern tragedy it is generally the case that individuals do not act for the sake of the *substantial* nature of their end, nor is it that nature which proves to be their motive in their passion; on the contrary, what presses for satisfaction is the *subjectivity* of their heart and mind and the privacy of their own character. For consider the examples just cited: in the case of the Spanish dramas, what the heroes of love and honour aim at is in itself of such a subjective kind that the rights and duties involved in it can coincide immediately with what their own heart wishes. And, in Schiller's youthful works, bragging about nature, human rights, and the reform of mankind is little more than the extravagance of a subjective enthusiasm; when in his later years Schiller tried to vindicate a more mature 'pathos', this happened simply because he had it in mind to restore in modern dramatic art the principle of Greek tragedy.

In order to exhibit in more detail the difference in this respect between Greek and modern tragedy, I will direct attention only to Shakespeare's Hamlet. His character is rooted in a collision similar to that treated by Aeschylus in the *Choephori* and Sophocles in the *Electra*. For in Hamlet's case too his father, the King, is murdered and his mother has married the murderer. But whereas in the Greek poets the King's death does have an ethical justification, in Shakespeare it is simply and solely an atrocious crime and Hamlet's mother is guiltless of it. Consequently the son has to wreak his revenge only on the fratricide King in whom he sees nothing really worthy of respect. Therefore the collision turns strictly here not on a son's pursuing an ethically justified revenge and being forced in the process to violate the ethical order, but on Hamlet's personal character. His noble soul is not made for this kind of energetic activity; and, full of disgust with the world and life, what with decision, proof, arrangements for carrying out his resolve, and being bandied from pillar to post, he eventually perishes owing to his own hesitation and a complication of external circumstances.

If we turn now, in the second place, to that aspect which is of more outstanding importance in modern tragedy, to the characters, namely, and their conflict, the first thing that we can take as a starting-point is, in brief summary, the following:

The heroes of Greek classical tragedy are confronted by circumstances in which, after firmly identifying themselves with the one ethical 'pathos' which alone corresponds to their own already established nature, they necessarily come into conflict with the opposite but equally justified ethical power. The romantic dramatis personae, on the other hand, are from the beginning in the midst of a wide field of more or less accidental circumstances and conditions within which it is possible to act either in this way or in that. Consequently the conflict, for which the external circumstances do of course provide the occasion, lies essentially in the character to which the individuals adhere in their passion, not because of any substantial justification but because they are what they are once and for all. The Greek heroes too do act in their individual capacity, but, as I have said, when Greek tragedy is at its height their individuality is itself of necessity an inherently ethical 'pathos', whereas in modern tragedy it remains a matter of chance whether the individual's character is gripped by something intrinsically justified or whether he is led into crime and wrong, and in either case he makes his decision according to his own wishes and needs, or owing to external influences, etc. It is true, therefore, that character and an ethical end *may* coincide, but since aims, passions, and the subjective inner life are all particular [and not universal], this coincidence is not the *essential* foundation and objective condition of the depth and beauty of a [modern] tragedy.

Few generalizations can be made about further differences in [modern] characterization because this sphere is wide open to variations of every kind. I will therefore touch on only the following chief aspects.

A first contrast which strikes the eye quickly enough is that between (*a*) the individuals who come on the scene as living and concrete people, and (*b*) an abstract and therefore formal characterization. As an example of the latter we can cite especially the tragic figures in French and Italian drama. They originate from an imitation of classical models and may count more or less as mere personifications of specific passions—love, honour, fame, ambition, tyranny, etc. They relate the motives of their actions as well as the degree and kind of their feelings with great declamatory splendour and much rhetorical skill, but this way of explaining themselves reminds us more of Seneca's failures than of the Greek dramatic masterpieces. Spanish tragedy too borders on this abstract characterization; but in this case the passion of love, in conflict with honour, friendship, royal authority, etc., is itself of such an abstractly subjective kind, and the rights and duties involved are so sharply emphasized, that a fuller individualization of the characters is impossible, since in this as it were subjective substantiality[1] this passion is supposed to be prominent as the real interest of the piece. Nevertheless the Spanish figures often have a solidity, even if there is little in it, and a sort of brittle personality which the French ones lack; at the same time, in contrast to the cold simplicity of the action's development in French tragedy, the Spanish, even in tragedy, can make up for a deficiency in variations of character by an acutely invented wealth of interesting situations and complications.

But in the portrayal of concretely human individuals and characters it is especially the English who are distinguished masters and above them all Shakespeare stands at an almost unapproachable height. For even if some purely single passion, like ambition in Macbeth or jealousy in Othello, becomes the entire 'pathos' of his tragic heroes, still such an abstraction does not devour their more far-reaching individuality at all, because despite this determinant they still always remain complete men. Indeed the more Shakespeare proceeds to portray on the infinite breadth of his 'world-stage'[2] the extremes of evil and folly, all the more, as I have remarked earlier, does he precisely plunge his figures who dwell on these extremes into their restrictedness; of course he equips them with a wealth of poetry but he actually gives them spirit and

[1] i.e. in Greek tragedy the 'pathos' or ruling passion is 'substantial', i.e. has a moral or objective basis. In the Spanish tragedies, love may be 'substantial' in a sense, but it is only subjective after all, and therefore, so to say, or 'as it were', subjectively substantial, and the substantiality inhibits romantic individualization.
[2] *As You Like It*, II. vii. 139.

imagination, and, by the picture in which they can contemplate and see themselves objectively like a work of art, he makes them free artists of their own selves, and thereby, with his strongly marked and faithful characterization, can interest us not only in criminals but even in the most downright and vulgar clouts and fools. The way that his tragic characters reveal themselves is of a similar kind: individual, real, directly living, extremely varied, and yet, where this emerges necessarily, of a sublimity and striking power of expression, of a depth of feeling and gift for invention in images and similes produced on the spur of the moment, of a rhetoric, not pedantic but issuing from the actual feeling and outpouring of the character—take all this into account, this combination of directly present life and inner greatness of soul, and you will scarcely find any other modern dramatist who can be compared with Shakespeare. Goethe in his youth did try to achieve a similar truth to nature and an individuality of personality but without achieving the inner force and height of passion [of Shakespeare's characters], and Schiller again has fallen into a violence which has no really solid kernel in its expansive storming.

A second difference in modern characters consists in their being either firm or inwardly hesitant and discordant. The weakness of irresolution, the swithering of reflection, perplexity about the reasons that are to guide decision—all this does occur here and there in the tragedies of Euripides, but he already abandons polished plasticity of character and action and goes over to subjective emotion. In modern tragedy such dithering figures generally appear by being themselves in the grip of a twofold passion which drives them from one decision or one deed to another simultaneously. This vacillation I have mentioned already in another context,[1] and here I will only add that, even if the tragic action must depend on a collision, to put this discord into one and the same individual must always involve much awkwardness. For mental distraction into opposed interests has its source partly in a vagueness and stupidity of mind, partly in weakness and immaturity. We have some figures of this sort even in Goethe's youthful[2] productions: Weislingen [in *Götz*], for example, Fernando in *Stella*, and Clavigo [in *Clavigo*] above all. These are men in two minds who cannot acquire a finished and therefore firm individuality. It is quite different if two opposed spheres of life or two

[1] In Vol. I, pp. 237–41. [2] 1773–8.

opposite duties, etc., seem equally sacrosanct to a character already assured in himself and yet sees himself compelled to align himself with one to the exclusion of the other. In that case the vacillation is only a transitional phase and is not the nerve of the man's character itself.

Again, a different kind consists of the tragic case where someone is led astray by passion against his better judgement into opposite aims (like Joan in Schiller's *Maid of Orleans*), and now must perish unless he can rescue himself from this discord both within and in his external actions. Yet, if the lever of the tragedy is this personal tragedy of inner discord, there is about it something now sad and painful, now aggravating, and the poet does better to avoid it instead of looking for it and pre-eminently developing it.

But what is worst of all is to exhibit such indecision and vacillation of character, and of the whole man, as a sort of perverse and sophistical dialectic and then to make it the main theme of the entire drama, so that truth is supposed to consist precisely in showing that no character is inwardly firm and self-assured. The one-sided aims of particular passions and characters should certainly not come to be realized without a struggle, and in everyday life when the force of circumstances reacts against them, and other individuals oppose them, they are not spared the experience of their finitude and instability. But this outcome, which alone forms an appropriate conclusion, must not be inserted by a sort of dialectical machinery into the individual's own character, for otherwise the person as *this* personality is only an empty indeterminate form instead of growing in a living way along with determinate aims and a defined character.

It is something different again if a change in the whole man's inner condition appears itself to be a logical consequence of precisely his own peculiarities, so that what develops and emerges is something that was implicit in his character from the start. For example, in *King Lear*, Lear's original folly is intensified into madness in his old age, just as Gloucester's mental blindness is changed into actual physical blindness and only then are his eyes opened to the true difference in the love of his sons.

It is precisely Shakespeare who gives us, in contrast to this portrayal of vacillating characters inwardly divided against themselves, the finest examples of firm and consistent characters who come to ruin simply because of this decisive adherence to themselves and their aims. Without ethical justification, but upheld solely by the formal inevitability of their personality, they allow themselves to be lured to their deed by external circumstances, or they plunge blindly on and persevere by the strength of their will, even if now what they do they accomplish only from the necessity of maintaining themselves against others or because they have reached once and for all the point that they *have* reached. The passion, implicitly in keeping with the man's character, had not broken out hitherto, but now it arises and is fully developed—this progress and history of a great soul, its inner development, the picture of its self-destructive struggle against circumstances, events, and their consequences—all this is the main theme in many of Shakespeare's most interesting tragedies.

The last important point—the one we now have still to discuss—concerns the tragic denouement to which the modern characters are driven as well as the sort of tragic reconciliation with which this is compatible. In Greek tragedy it is eternal justice which, as the absolute power of fate, saves and maintains the harmony of the substance of the ethical order against the particular powers which were becoming independent and therefore colliding, and because of the inner rationality of its sway we are satisfied when we see individuals coming to ruin. If a similar justice appears in modern tragedy, then, owing to the non-universal nature of aims and characters, it is colder, more like criminal justice, owing to the greater reflectiveness of the wrong and crime into which individuals are forced when they are intent on accomplishing their ends. For example, Macbeth, Lear's elder daughters and their husbands, Richard III, the President in [Schiller's] *Intrigue and Love*, deserve for their atrocities nothing better than what happens to them. This sort of denouement is usually so presented that the individuals are shipwrecked on a power confronting them which they had deliberately defied in the pursuit of their own private ends. So, for example, Wallenstein is wrecked by the stability of the Emperor's power, but even old Piccolomini, who in [secretly] upholding the established order has become a traitor to his friend and misused the form of friendship, is punished by the death of his son who was sacrificed to the end that his father really wanted to achieve.[1]

---

[1] The son declined to follow his father's devious ways. He therefore openly deserted Wallenstein instead of pretending to follow him. He is then killed in action against one of Wallenstein's regiments.

Götz von Berlichingen too attacks an existent and firmly established political order and therefore perishes, just as Weislingen and Adelheid[1] meet an unfortunate end owing to wrong and disloyalty, although they are on the side of this legal order and its power. This subjectivity of character immediately implies the demand that the individuals must have shown themselves inwardly reconciled to their own particular fate. This satisfaction may be religious when the heart knows that it is assured of a higher and indestructible bliss in exchange for the destruction of its mundane individuality, or alternatively it may be of a more abstract and mundane kind when the strength and equanimity of the character persists, even to destruction, without breaking, and so preserves its subjective freedom, in the face of all circumstances and misfortunes, with energy unjeopardized; or, finally, it may be more concrete owing to a recognition that its fate, however bitter, is merely the one appropriate to its action.

But on the other hand the tragic denouement is also displayed as purely the effect of unfortunate circumstances and external accidents which might have turned out otherwise and produced a happy ending. In this case the sole spectacle offered to us is that the modern individual with the non-universal nature of his character, his circumstances, and the complications in which he is involved, is necessarily surrendered to the fragility of all that is mundane and must endure the fate of finitude. But this mere affliction is empty, and, in particular, we are confronted by a purely horrible external necessity when we see fine minds, noble in themselves, perishing in such a battle against the misfortune of entirely external circumstances. Such a history may touch us acutely, and yet it seems only dreadful and we feel a pressing demand for a necessary correspondence between the external circumstances and what the inner nature of those fine characters really is. It is only from this point of view that we can feel ourselves reconciled in e.g. the fate of Hamlet or Juliet. Looked at from the outside, Hamlet's death seems to be brought about accidentally owing to the fight with Laertes and the exchange of rapiers. But death lay from the beginning in the background of Hamlet's mind. The sands of time do not content him. In his melancholy and weakness, his worry, his disgust at all the affairs of life, we sense from the start that in all his terrible surroundings he is a lost man, almost consumed already

[1] Also in Goethe's *Götz*.

by inner disgust before death comes to him from outside. The same is the case in Romeo and Juliet. The soil on which these tender blooms were planted is foreign to them, and we are left with nothing but to bewail the tragic transience of so beautiful a love which is shattered by the crazy calculations of a noble and well-meaning cleverness, just as a tender rose in the vale of this transitory world is withered by rude storms and tempests. But the woe that we feel is only a grievous reconciliation, an unhappy bliss in misfortune.

(ββ) Since the poets present to us the mere downfall of individuals, they can equally well give such a turn to equally accidental complications that, however little other circumstances may also seem to produce this result, a happy outcome for the situation and the characters can be produced, and this is something which may be of interest to us. A happy denouement has at least as much justification as an unhappy one, and when it is a matter of considering this difference alone, I must admit that for my part a happy denouement is to be preferred. And why not? To prefer misfortune, just because it is misfortune, instead of a happy resolution, has no other basis but a certain superior sentimentality which indulges in grief and suffering and finds more interest in them than in the painless situations that it regards as commonplace. Thus if the interests at issue are in themselves of such a kind that it is really not worthwhile for an individual to sacrifice himself for them, since without self-sacrifice he can renounce them or come to an agreement with others about them, then the conclusion need not be tragic. For the tragedy of conflicts and their resolution must in general prevail only where this is necessary for justifying them in virtue of some higher outlook. But if there is no such inevitability, mere suffering and misfortune are not justified by anything.

This is the natural reason for plays and dramas that are midway between tragedy and comedy. I have already indicated the strictly poetical element in this kind of dramatic poetry. But in Germany touching features of civil life and family circles have been all the rage or there has been preoccupation with chivalry to which an impetus has been given since the time of Goethe's *Götz*, but what has been celebrated above all in this field and most frequently is the triumph of the subjectively moral outlook. The usual topics here are money and property, class-differences, unfortunate love-affairs, mental wickedness in trifling matters and narrow social circles, and the like, and, in general, with what we see elsewhere every day, only with this difference that in these moralizing plays virtue and duty win the day and vice is put to shame and punished or is moved to repentance, so that the reconciliation is supposed to lie in this moral conclusion where both vice and virtue get their due. Thus the chief interest is made to lie in the individual's own personal disposition and the goodness or evil of his heart. But the more the abstract moral disposition is made the kingpin, the less can it be a passionate concentration on something, on a really substantial end, that the individual is tied to, while in the last resort even a definite character cannot hold out and accomplish its aim. For once everything is shuffled into the moral disposition and the heart, there is no support any longer, given this subjectivity and strength of moral reflection, for a character otherwise firm or at least for his personal ends. The heart can break, and its dispositions may alter. Such touching plays as Kotzebue's *Menschenhass und Reue* [Misanthropy and Repentance] and many of the moral trespasses in Iffland's dramas, taken strictly, have a result which is really neither good nor bad. The chief theme usually ends in forgiveness and the promise of reform and then there appears every possibility of inner conversion and the repudiation of the old self. Here there is of course the lofty nature and the greatness of the spirit. But if the young wastrel, like most of Kotzebue's characters and like Iffland's too here and there, is a blackguard, a rascal, and now promises to reform, then in the case of such a fellow who is worthless from the start, conversion is only hypocrisy, or so superficial that it has not gripped his heart, and an end has been made of the thing in only an external way for a moment, but at bottom it can only lead to false starts when the thing is only played over and over again from the beginning.

(γγ) Finally, in modern comedy especially there is an essentially important difference on which I have touched already in connection with Greek comedy, namely whether the folly and one-sidedness of the dramatis personae appears laughable to the audience only or to themselves as well, whether therefore the characters in the comedy can be mocked solely by the audience or by themselves also. Aristophanes, the comic author par excellence, made the latter alternative the fundamental principle of his plays. But in the new comedy in Greece and later in Plautus and Terence the opposite tendency was developed, and this has acquired such universal prominence in modern comedy that a multitude of our comic productions verges more or less on what is purely prosaically laughable and even on what is bitter and repugnant. This is the attitude especially of Molière, for example, in his more subtle comedies which are not meant to be farces. There is a reason for prose here, namely that the characters are deadly serious in their aims. They pursue them therefore with all the fervour of this seriousness and when at the end they are deceived or have their aim frustrated by themselves, they cannot join in the laughter freely and with satisfaction but, duped, are the butt of the laughter of others, often mixed as it is with malice. So, for example, Molière's Tartuffe, *le faux dévot*, is unmasked as a downright villain, and this is not funny at all but a very serious matter; and the duping of the deceived Orgon leads to such painful misfortune that it can be assuaged only by a *deus ex machina*, i.e. when the police officer at the end says to him [ll. 1905-9]:

> Remettez-vous, monsieur, d'une alarme si chaude,
> Nous vivons sous un prince, ennemi de la fraude,
> Un prince dont les yeux se font jour dans les cœurs,
> Et que ne peut tromper tout l'art des imposteurs.

There is nothing really comical either about the odious *idée fixe* of such rigid characters as Molière's miser[1] whose absolutely serious involvement in his narrow passion inhibits any liberation of his mind from this restriction.

Next, as a substitute for this kind of thing, mastery in this field has the best opportunity for its cleverness by displaying its subtly developed skill in the precise portrayal of characters or the carrying out of a well-considered intrigue. The intrigue generally arises from the fact that an individual tries to achieve his aims by deceiving other people. He seems to share their interests and to further them, but this false furtherance actually produces the contradiction of falling into his own trap and so coming to grief himself. Next, on the other hand, the opposite means are commonly employed, i.e. the individual puts a false face on himself in order to put others into a similar perplexity: this coming and going makes possible in the most ingenious way endless tergiversation and complicated involvement in all sorts of situation. In inventing such intrigues and their complications the Spanish are the finest

---

[1] Harpagon in *L'Avare*.

masters and have given us in this sphere much that is attractive and excellent. The subject-matter here is provided by interests such as love, honour, etc. In tragedy these lead to the most profound collisions, but in comedy (for example, the pride which will not confess a love that has been long felt and at the end is just for this reason betrayed) they are clearly without substance from the start and are annulled comically. Finally, the characters who contrive and conduct such intrigues in modern comedy are usually, like the slaves in Roman comedy, servants or chambermaids who have no respect for the aims of their masters, but further them or frustrate them as their own advantage dictates and only give us the laughable spectacle of masters being really the servants, or the servants masters, or at least they provide an occasion for other comic situations which they contrive by external means or by their own arrangements. We ourselves, as spectators, are in the secret and we can always feel assured in the face of all the cunning and every betrayal, often very seriously pursued against the most estimable fathers, uncles, etc., and now we can laugh over every contradiction implicit or obvious in such trickeries.

In this way modern comedy displays to the spectators (partly in character-sketches, partly in comical complications of situations and circumstances) private interests and characters involved in them with their casual obliquities, absurdities, unusual behaviour, and follies. But such a frank joviality as pervades the comedies of Aristophanes as a constant reconciliation does not animate this kind of modern comedy at all. Indeed these comedies of intrigue may be actually repulsive when downright evil, the cunning of servants, the deceitfulness of sons and wards, gains the victory over honest masters, fathers, and trustees when these older people have themselves not been actuated by bad prejudice or eccentricities which would have made them laughable in their helpless folly and put them at the mercy of the projects of other people.

Nevertheless, in contrast to this on the whole prosaic way of treating comedy, the modern world has developed a type of comedy which is truly comical and truly poetic. Here once again the keynote is good humour, assured and careless gaiety despite all failure and misfortune, exuberance and the audacity of a fundamentally happy craziness, folly, and idiosyncrasy in general. Consequently there is presented here once more (in a deeper wealth and inwardness of humour), whether in wider or narrower circles of society, in a subject-matter whether important or trivial, what Aristophanes achieved to perfection in his field in Greece. As a brilliant example of this sort of thing I will name Shakespeare once again, in conclusion, but without going into detail.

Now, with the development of the kinds of comedy we have reached the real end of our philosophical inquiry. We began with symbolic art where personality struggles to find itself as form and content and to become objective to itself. We proceeded to the plastic art of Greece where the Divine, now conscious of itself, is presented to us in living individuals. We ended with the romantic art of emotion and deep feeling where absolute subjective personality moves free in itself and in the spiritual world. Satisfied in itself, it no longer unites itself with anything objective and particularized and it brings the negative side of this dissolution into consciousness in the humour of comedy. Yet on this peak comedy leads at the same time to the dissolution of art altogether. All art aims at the identity, produced by the spirit, in which eternal things, God, and absolute truth are revealed in real appearance and shape to our contemplation, to our hearts and minds. But if comedy presents this unity only as its self-destruction because the Absolute, which wants to realize itself, sees its self-actualization destroyed by interests that have now become explicitly free in the real world and are directed only on what is accidental and subjective, then the presence and agency of the Absolute no longer appears positively unified with the characters and aims of the real world but asserts itself only in the negative form of cancelling everything not correspondent with it, and subjective personality alone shows itself self-confident and self-assured at the same time in this dissolution.

Now at the end we have arranged every essential category of the beautiful and every essential form of art into a philosophical garland, and weaving it is one of the worthiest tasks that philosophy is capable of completing. For in art we have to do, not with any agreeable or useful child's play, but with the liberation of the spirit from the content and forms of finitude, with the presence and reconciliation of the Absolute in what is apparent and visible, with an unfolding of the truth which is not exhausted in natural history but revealed in world-history. Art itself is the most beautiful side of that history and it is the best compensation for hard work in the world and the bitter labour for knowledge. For this reason my treatment of the subject could not consist in a mere criticism of works of art or an instruction for producing them. My one aim has been to seize in thought and to prove the fundamental nature of the beautiful and art, and to follow it through all the stages it has gone through in the course of its realization.

I hope that in this chief point my exposition has satisfied you. And now when the link forged between us generally and in relation to our common aim has been broken, it is my final wish that the higher and indestructible bond of the Idea of beauty and truth may link us and keep us firmly united now and for ever.

TRANSLATOR'S POSTSCRIPT

(i) Hegel's quotations from the *Bhagavad Gita* on p. 367 above are subject to later correction. They were translated from the Latin version by A. W. Schlegel (Bonn, 1823). See *Enc.* § 573 and the note *ad loc.* in the edition edited by Nicolin and Pöggeler (Hamburg, Meiner *Phil. Bibl.*, 1959).

(ii) Dr. M. J. Petry informs me that the author of the *Notes* in the *Morning Chronicle*, quoted by Hegel on p. 766 above, was Hazlitt. See his *Complete Works*, vol. x, pp. 221–3.

(iii) The passage from Vasari's life of Fra Angelico, quoted on p. 878 above, may be found in, for example, Mrs. Foster's translation of the *Lives of the Painters* (London, 1851), vol. ii, pp. 34–5.

T.M.K.

March 1974

INDEX

The Index supplements and does not repeat the Tables of Contents pp. 1–612 are in Vol. I and pp. 613–1237 in Vol. II

Abbadona, 1076
Absolute, the, *see* God
Abyssinia, 42, 1106; *see also* Ethiopians
Academy of Arts, 258
acanthus, 680
accent in music, 917–18
accuracy, sole merit of mediocre artists, 772
Achilles, and Athene, 228, 1049
  and Briseis, 563
  and Patroclus, 568, 1083, 1216
  as hero of the *Iliad*, 1066
  character of, 1067–8
  clad as girl, 760, 860–1
  death of, 480–1
  embodies entire Greek spirit, 1068
  Homer's description of, 166, 173, 237, 240, 416, 1003
  in the underworld, 523, 1071
  moralizing about, 240, 1067–8
  portrait statue of, 750
  reaches his goal, 1216
  shield of, 1055
  speaks of his life, 1101
  stays away from the fight, 1053
  vulnerability of, 226–8, 497
  wrath of, 219, 557, 979, 1069, 1081, 1088, 1089
action, and event, 1063–6, 1069–71, 1088–90, 1161
  as means to an end, 988
  basic ends in, 1223
  beginning of an, 217–18
  belongs to men, 225
  can produce harmony, 1203–4
  essence of every true, 1193–4
  in drama, 1161–2, 1166–7
  inner and outer aspects of, 860
  man enters reality in, 1166
  must be by individuals, 1066, 1089
  presuppositions and consequences of, 1169
  what weakness in is, 1214
actor, art of the, 1190–1
  in drama is himself a work of art, 955
  is not a moral blot, 1189
acts, number of in drama, 1169–70
Adelung, J. C., 497
Adonis, 353
Adoration of the Kings, 594, 859, 861
adornment, reason for, 31, 258
adventures, as romantic theme, 86
  capricious, 81, 529, 556
  finitude of, 152
  in epics of chivalry, 191, 1053, 1105
  meaning of, 575–6
  of knights-errant, 257, 401, 571
advocacy, legal, 991–2
Aeginetan sculptures, 724, 785–6
Aemilius Paulus, 778
Aeneas, 230, 274, 416, 448, 1069–71, 1075, 1082, 1106
Aeschines, 1131
Aeschylus, betrayed the Mysteries, 469
  characters of, 863
  Choephori, 1225
  choruses of, 945, 1186
  conflict in plays of, 1213
  Eumenides, 227, 275, 463–4, 471, 487, 1165, 1204, 1218
  not interested in romantic love, 564
  Oresteia, 278, 1169, 1213
  plays of, deal with 'pathos' of substance, 554–5
  Prometheus Vinctus, 493
  Septum, 1060–1, 1213
Aesop, 384–8, 390, 391, 395, 447
affinity between meaning and expression, 350, 352
affluence, not unaesthetic, 257
Agamemnon, and Achilles, 228, 237, 480–1, 557–8, 1081, 1216
  and Iphigenia, 214, 1213
  as a shade, 1071
  avenged, 463
  character of, 863

INDEX

Agamemnon (*cont.*):
  House of, 218
  King of men, 1003
  'pathos' of, 568
  relation to Princes, 186, 1053
  sceptre of, 261
age and youth, interests of, 999
agreeable, as principle of dramatic success, 1197
agriculture, ends roving of nomads, 651
  in Egypt, 359, 646
  leads to ethical ties, 462
  nature of, 329-30
  taught by Ceres, 462
Agrippa, Pantheon of, 682
aims of characters in modern drama, 1224 ff.
Ajax, 214, 237, 448, 863, 1004
Alcaeus, 1151
Alexander the Great, admired Achilles, 497
  adventures of, 1106
  age of, 776, 989
  and the lentil-thrower, 44
  conquest of Persia, 1002-3, 1080
  epics after him, 1099
  his sense of self, 1068
  in medieval poetry, 274, 1106
  statues of, 750
alexandrine metre, 1012, 1174
allegorical figures, 1177
allegories, Greek gods are not, 238, 471, 487, 488
  of universal powers, 224-5
allegory, always found in art by F. Schlegel, 312
  in modern sculpture but not in classical, 712, 778
  in paintings, 859
alliteration, 1029, 1136, 1137, 1153
Amadis of Gaul, 1106
ambiguity of oracles, 457-8
America, 1062, 1101
Ammon, 357, 451
amphibia, announce the impotence of nature, 148, 628
  not beautiful, 131
Amsterdam, 162
anachronism in art, 277-9
Anacreon, 563-4, 1120-1, 1145
ancient subjects foreign to modern public, 275
Andromache, 238, 563, 1083-4
angels, hovering over birth, 825
  in Klopstock's *Messiah*, 1075, 1076, 1077, 1154
  not individualized, 225, 852, 1072, 1154
Angelus Silesius, 371
anger, seat and expression of, 715-16
animals, and human face, 729 ff.
  as symbols, 353
  cannot stand erect, 739
  classification of, 382
  differences of, 490, 577
  embalming of, 355, 446
  form of, use of sculpture, 758, 761
  growth of, 136
  identification of from single bone, 127-8
  in fables, 384-90
  in metamorphoses, 447-52
  life of, 97, 151, 167
  meaning and shape of in Greek ideas, 445 ff., 474
  mouth and head of, 728
  movement of, 122-4
  not an adequate mode of God's existence, 349
  nourishment of, 128
  organism of, 124, 129, 137-8, 145
  sacred, 324, 328, 355, 651
  shape of, determined from within, 668
    distinguished from human shape, 714-15, 723
  skin of, 145, 846
  soul of, 132-3
  species of, 148, 150
  summit of natural beauty, 132
  ugly if unfamiliar, 127
  well treated in Egyptian sculpture, 783
  worship of, repugnant to us, 357
annihilation of one's personality is harsh, 336
anthropomorphism, essential in art, 78, 820
  in Christianity, 435-6, 505-6, 519, 535
  in Greece, 341, 490
  of art, 790
Antigone, character of, 564, 1217-18
  'pathos' of, 232, 568
  story of, 221
  see also Sophocles
Antilochus, 237
antiquaries, pedantry of, 753

Antwerp cathedral, 690
Anubis, 475
ape, the sacred, 336, 337
Apelles, 720
Aphrodite accompanied by doves, 475
  and Hippolytus, 564
  Asian origin of, 474
  attribute of, 753
  birth of, 346
  captivates the heart, 227
  hair of, 496
  image of in Rome, 682
  individuality of, 225
  in song of the Pierides, 395
  lament for Adonis, 353
  no real model for, 173
  not a mother, 759
  nude in statues, 745
  portrayal of, 541, 555
  punished Narcissus, 393
  statues of, 202, 763
Apis, 313, 356, 357, 652
Apollo, actions of, 313
  and death of Patroclus, 226, 498–9
  and Niobe, 393
  and Pindar, 1131
  attributes of, 495
  Belvedere, 202, 618, 766
  dominion of, 473, 487, 489
  figures of, 757, 758, 762
  indignation of, 480
  individuality of, 225
  instigates and defends Orestes, 458, 463–4, 471, 1218
  not strictly a character, 863
  oracle of at Delphi, 361, 457
  painting of, 294
  powers of, 177
  Sauroctonus, 224, 760
  Sosianus, temple of, 768
  Tieck's statue of, 770–1
Apollodorus, 186, 207, 360, 361, 374, 760, 860
Apostles, the, 171, 174, 176, 402, 803, 851, 865, 877
apparatus of knowledge needed for art, 157, 265
appearance, and esssence, 8
  finitude of, 147–8
  fleeting, fixed by painting, 812
  not reality, required for painting, 806, 809–11
  positive and negative, 121–2
  pure, 4, 598
  produced by the spirit of the artist, 795, 801
apprehension, modes of, 36–8
apprenticeship, 593
Apuleius, 472
arabesques, 658–9, 696, 789
Arabian Nights, the, 1073, 1097, 1192
Arabs, and the pyramids, 652
  architecture of, 698
  characteristics of, 255, 398, 430, 557, 1097
  expulsion of, 587
  lyrics of, 1148–9
  poetry of, 610, 1011, 1025, 1096–7, 1098
Arberry, A. J., 1097
arch, nature of, 681, 686
  seldom used by Greeks, 681
Archilochus, 1151
architect, arrangement of columns by, 679
  needs help of craftsmen, 936
  task of, 661–2, 664
architecture, and music, 911, 916
  and painting, 850–1
  as ornament, 423
  Egyptian, 352, 356, 661
  Gothic, 619, 634, 807, 851
  now connected with sculpture, 701–2
  labyrinth of forms of, 632
  regularity in, 247–8
  riddle in, 398
Ares, *see* Mars
Argonauts, 374
Argus, 154, 224
Ariosto, adventures in, 1082
  asked about his material, 280
  contrasted with Tasso, 1108
  description of war in, 1059, 1062
  fantastic inventions of, 1075
  independence of heroes in, 1053
  painting of subjects drawn from, 856, 858
Aristophanes, acted himself, 1187
  Birds, 470
  brought comedy to perfection, 1236
  Clouds, 1221
  discloses his own personality, 1080–1
  Ecclesiazusae, 1201, 1221
  Frogs, 1221

1242 INDEX

Aristophanes (cont.):
  his attitude to Athenian life, 1180–1, 1202, 1221–2
  joviality of his comedies, 511, 1235
  Knights, 1221
  living people as characters in, 1188
  makes his characters comical in themselves, 1220–1, 1233
  Peace, 387, 447, 1222
  polemics of, 605, 1180
  Thesmophoriazusae, 1221
  what he did and did not make fun of, 1202
Aristotle, language of, 407
  Nic. Ethics, 469
  Poetics, 15, 212, 396, 403, 1060, 1164, 1169, 1174, 1178, 1197
Aristoxenus, 926
army discipline, 1054
Arnim, L. J. von, 290
art, a thing of the past, 11
  absolute Spirit not an immediate topic for, 539
  aim of, and instruction, 50–1
    and moral betterment, 51–5
    and purification of passions, 49–50, 51–2
    not arousing feeling, 46–7
    not imitation, 41–6, 155, 833
    not production of pleasure by study, 797
    not utility, 55, 102, 152
    sensuous presentation of the Absolute, 70, 105
    to bring absolutely rational into appearance, 1202
    unveiling of truth, 55, 152, 1236
  and feelings, 32–3
  and luxury, 258–9
  and morality, 52–5
  and past and present, 265 ff.
  and philosophy, 102–4, 282, 627, 628–9
  and pleasure, 51, 58–9, 107
  and religion, 102–4, 550–1, 603
  and senses, 38–9, 621–2
  and spectator, 619–20, 806, 809–11
  as instructress, 50
  as purifying force, 49–50
  attains absolute truth, 606
  basis of, 602
  'before' and 'after' of, 102–3
  beginning of, 315–16, 615–16, 624, 630–1
  belongs to same sphere as religion and philosophy, 7, 94
  boundaries of, 830
  can be studied philosophically, 13–14
  cannot dispense with the finite, 257
  caprice absent from, 704
  conditioned by place in history, 34
  confers permanence, 163, 459, 599–600, 835–6
  conquers nature, 163
  content is decisive in, 611
  contrasted with nature, 1–3, 29–30, 35–6, 37
  decadence of, 1191
  deserves serious treatment, 3–7, 11, 91
  dissolution of, 576, 607, 1236
  each one rises to perfection and falls, 614
  end in itself, 55, 102, 152, 992, 995
  essence of, 301, 400
  exists for a public, 264 ff., 276–7, 704
  great themes of, 220
  has nothing to do with abstractions, 400
  height of, 358
  history of, 14, 21, 34–5, 605–6, 615–16, 629, 780, 786
  honourable to devote money to, 258
  in modern, the artist's skill is the most important thing, 602
  integrity of, conditions for, 604
  intermediate kinds of, 628
  is mastery in portrayal of pure appearance, 598
  is merely skill after all has been revealed, 605
  is spiritual in kind, 12–13, 26, 50, 86, 94, 704
  liberates us from the finite, 1236
  martyrdom a hazardous material for, 545
  may come to perfection, 90, 103
  meaning of, 19–20
  midway between sensation and thought, 156, 163
  mitigates desires, 48–9
  most beautiful side of history, 1236–7
  most concrete form of, 87
  most important part of is discovery of situations, 199
  must be faithful to nature, 253 ff.

INDEX 1243

must be immediately intelligible, 273
must not withdraw from the external world, 245–6
must withdraw from any foreign element, 959
need for, 30–2, 333, 535, 635
need for philosophy of, 11
needs study, 27, 28, 45, 286
no longer meets our highest needs, 10, 103
not a deception, 4, 8–9
not all allegorical, 312, 400
not born but produced by the spirit, 280, 316, 319, 333, 351
not merely sensuous, 35–41, 621
not purely intellectual, 37
not the highest way of apprehending truth, 9–10, 13, 71, 101 ff., 529
not truly adequate to the spirit, 105
nothing dark in, 243
of the actor, 1190–1
Pantheon of, completion will need millennia, 90
parts of work of must be both independent and unified, 983–4
peak of, 882
perfected in artist's middle or old age, 283
perfection of in Greece, 517
philosophy of, 11, 94, 611, 629, 967–8
pinnacle of, 79
present-day unfavourable to, 10–11, 103
renews the events in Christ's life, 535
reveals truth, 1236
romantic theme of derived from religion, 550–1
seriousness of, 157
should please by solidity of content, 619
should show us an inner harmony, 222
study of should be based on original works, 869–70
task of, 152
theories of, 15
transfers external reality into a sensuous material, 247
transforms earlier material, 465, 492
ultimately annuls itself, 529
vocation of, 603, 611, 621, 623
what in general it consists in, 858

withdrawal of from the inorganic is the beginning of sculpture, 701
work of is a dialogue, 264, 619–20
Artemis, and Arethusa, 393
and Iphigenia, 218, 229–30
in song of the Pierides, 451
not a character, 863
not goddess *of* the moon, 471
parentage of, in Aeschylus, 469
portrayal of, 763
art-forms, general nature of, 300 ff., 985
summary of development of, 967–8
Arthur, King, 1106
artificiality in beginnings of art, 615
artist, activity of the, 27, 28, 39, 161
age of the, 28
as creator, 163
as magician, 848
both prophet and priest in classical art, 479, 480
does not need philosophy, 282
genius of gives freshness to tradition, 722
his cross, 146
in humour enters his material, 600
may borrow foreign materials, 275–6
means of portrayal more important than his subject, 599
musical, skill of, 909
must study and reflect, 27, 28, 45, 282, 286
not as a rule very pious, 604
not tied to traditional types, 786
obstacles in the way of the, 285–6
should be in earnest with his material, 603–4
skill of, 536–7, 575, 576, 596–600, 604, 620
sometimes not concerned for his public, 619–20
strips foreign material of ugliness, 794
the romantic, a *tabula rasa*, 605
activity of, 603–8
can master all reality, 595, 602, 606
portrays things as they are, 594
works to a commission, 606
truly existent only in his productions, 291
work of in Greek sculpture, 725
works on given material, 288
artisic taste, 7, 16, 34, 44

arts, the, difference between, 199, 205, 222, 239, 254, 276
  grounds for division of, 621
Asan Aga, 1124
Ascension, the, 535, 539, 822
assonance, 1029-30, 1136, 1137, 1150
astronomical symbolism, 330, 447
Athene, actions of display power, 313
  and Hephaestus, 460, 461
  appears to Achilles, 228, 1049
    to Odysseus, 481
    to Thoas, 229
  as representative of Athenian life, 1218
  attributes of, 496
  averts the arrow, 416
  character of, 489
  eyes of, in sculpture, 731
  judgement of, 471, 1218
  statues of, 258, 762-3, 773
  symbolic portrayal of, 357
Athens, 675, 677, 761, 764, 768, 773
  Aristophanes and, 1180-1, 1202, 1221-2
attributes, animals as indicative, 313, 474-5
Augean stables, 186
Augustus, Emperor, 1130
  age of, 1152
avarice, 1200

Babel, Tower of, 638-9
Babylonia, architecture of, 661
  art in, 636
Bacchus, an imaginative picture, 555
  attended by nymphs, 801
  attributes of, 495
  domain of, 489
  festival of, 450, 1212
  figures of, 758, 762
  in song of the Pierides, 451
  Indicus, 745, 753
  introduced from Egypt, 477
  joviality of, 1091
  Mysteries of, 469
  senseless stories about, 493
  with faun, 202, 453, 733, 801
Bach, J. S., 932, 950
bagpipes, 908
ballads, 1092, 1114, 1116, 1117, 1134
ballet, intellectual poverty of, 1192
baptism, 692
barbarians, 212, 369, 587, 1054
bard, dignity of, 1130, 1131, 1155

barrel-organ players, 956
Basedow, J. B., 297
baseness, 221-2
basilicas, 697
Batteux, C., 7, 16
Battus of Cyrene, 759
Baumgarten, S. J., 1
beat, the, in music, 249, 913-18
  in music and poetry, 1017-18, 1033, 1137
beating time, 249, 906, 913
Beatrice, 402, 564
beautiful soul, 67, 241-2
beauty, and truth, 91
  becomes spiritual in romantic art, 518
  conception of, 613
  deficiency of natural, 132-3, 143 ff.
  distinct from sublimity, 372
  essence of, 101, 112, 114
  Idea of, 21-2, 73-82, 90, 111 ff., 144
  ideal, disappears in romantic art, 526, 574
  interest in, 95
  Kant's theory of, 57-61
  lacks subjectivity, 142
  no longer ultimate, 518
  not demanded by Christian believers, 574
  not in Indian art, 334, 340
  of art and nature, 1-3, 6, 29-30, 248
  of art, Concept of, 22-5, 94
  of deep feeling, 531
  of Greek art, 482, 531
  of Greek gods like immortals among mortals, 484
  of romantic art, 531
  of soul, 532, 549
  of the ideal not a universal norm, 751
  one thing certain in, 598
  only an accessory if truth is known, 535
  pinnacle of, in Greek art, 517
  pure appearance of the Idea to sense, 111
  realm of lies between ordinary and religious thinking, 968
  requires developed technique, 615
  serenity of, 618
  spiritual, is love, 540, 542, 546
  theories of, 16 ff.
Beethoven, 893, 899, 901, 954
beggars, 557

beginnings, always abstract, 317
  always immediate and simple, 632
  of art, 315–16, 615–16, 624, 630–1
Bel, Tower of, 639–40
bells, peal of, 695
  sound of, 921
Belzoni, G. B., 652
Berlin, 401, 770, 775, 790, 821, 856, 870, 901, 949, 986
Bhagavad Gita, 367
Bible, cited:
  Genesis, 373, 445, 505, 527, 639, 743, 858, 980, 1219
  Exodus, 980
  Joshua, 909
  Psalms, 15, 307, 340, 375–6, 588, 829, 1139, 1149
  Proverbs, 980
  Song of Solomon, 413
  Wisdom, 980
  Matthew, 178, 533, 574, 595, 860, 873
  Mark, 178
  Luke, 549, 553, 828, 860
  John, 506, 553
  dominion of God in, 471
  not epical, 1045
  Old Testament, epic quality in, 1096
  Goethe on, 1058
  patriarchal life in, 1096, 1110
  we are at home in, 1058
  parables in, 391
  Prophets in, 279, 430, 1139–40
  Psalms in, 279, 430, 901, 947
  stories in, familiar to us, 274
biography, 491, 712, 989, 1066
birth, as ground of collisions, 207–12
  ought not to determine man's class, 209, 565–6
Black Sea, 341, 346, 473
bliss, after repentance, 831
  distinguished from happiness, 816
  in misfortune, 1232
  in prayer, 827
  in religious love, 816–18
blood-relationship, 463
Blücher, G. L., statue of, 401, 775
Blumauer, A., 1074
Blumenbach, J. F., 42, 146, 728
Boccaccio, 392, 564, 876, 1106
Bodmer, J. J., 274, 1075
body, and soul, 108, 118–19, 123
  spirit's, 167–8, 702, 713
  the human, *see* human form

Bohr, Niels, 1135
Boisserée, M. and S., 821, 828
books, medieval, 668
bookworms cannot understand art, 769
Bosanquet, B., 2, 17, 33, 59, 78, 85, 86
Böttiger, K. A., 621
Bowra, C. M., 1050
bracelets, 753–4
bravery, in war, 1059–60
  medieval and classical, 556, 590
  see also heroism
Brazilian plants, 295
Breda, tomb at, 790
Breitinger, J. J., 389
Brentano, C., 290
Breslau, statue in, 775
brigandage, 1125, 1126
Bromwich, Dr. Rachel, 1101
brothers, relation between, 207–8, 1060–1
Bruce, James, 42
Bruges, figure of Mary in, 790
Buffon, G. L. L. de, 293
building, difficult if no clear ground, 478
  in wood, 670, 672, 676–80
  in wood or stone, 631, 633
bull, in Egyptian religion, 313
  reverenced as sacred, 324
  symbolical meanings of, 305–6
Bürger, G. A., 1118
Burnett, J. H., 127
Büttner, C. W., 42
Byron, Lord, 1137
Byzantine architecture, 697
  painting, 800–1, 851, 876–7

Cabiri, 467
cacti, 127
caesura, 917, 918, 1014, 1018–19, 1023–6, 1033, 1136, 1150
Cain and Abel, 208, 266
cairn as a sign, 636
Calchas, 1049
Calderón, comparisons in, 414
  Devotion at the Cross, 406–7
  diction of, 1174
  metaphor in, 405
  similes in, 411–12
  tragedies of, 1176, 1225
  Zenobia, 274
Callan, H. G., 127
Callimachus, 774, 1152
Callinus, 1118, 1150

Calvinism, 324
Calypso, 1069, 1075, 1081
cameos, 778
Camoens, 273-4, 1059, 1062, 1108
Camper, P., 728
caricature, 18-19, 295
Carlyle, T., 312, 857
'carnation', 846-8, 850, 922
Carracci, A., 820
caryatids, 657
caste, 208, 212, 337, 346, 781
Castiglione, B., 281
casting, a single, 174, 296, 407
   of a bell, 1119
Castor and Pollux, 353
catacombs, 650, 681
cathedral, impression given by, 688
   interior and exterior of, 690-5
cats, sacred, 355-7, 395
cause and effect, chain of, 1073, 1087
cavalry troop, 836
cave-dwellings, 648
Caviglia, G. B., 652
ceilidh, jollity of a, 834
Celtic bard-songs, 1101
Centaurs, 453
Ceres, and Proserpine, 353, 492, 733, 755
   benefactor of mankind, 460, 462, 474, 489
   daughter of, 469
Cervantes, 196, 397, 589, 591-2, 605, 1107
Chaldean priests, 639
champagne, 27, 287
chance, in history, 988
Chanson de Roland, 571, 1106
character, as natural side of the spirit, 1060
   development of in drama, 579
   dramatic and epic, 1067, 1070
   essential to individuality, 482
   how known, 147
   how moved in epic, 1082-3
   in drama picks fruit of his own deeds, 1161
   individual, 181
   keynote of, 67-8
   meaning of, 576
   not displayed in sculpture, 705
characteristic, concept of the, 17-20, 863
   of one art-form also found in the others, 303, 313, 320

characterization in music, 897, 940, 943, 947-8
characters, in Aristophanes, 1221-2
   in comedy, whether comical in themselves, 1220, 1233-4
   in drama, should not be interests personified, 1177-8
   in Greek drama are not characters in the modern sense, 1209-10
   in modern tragedy, 1230-1
   in Molière, 1234
   in Shakespeare, 1227-8
   in tragedy, dominated by a single power, 1194-5
   vacillation of, 237-41, 1228, 1229
Charlemagne, 186, 571, 1105
Charles V, Emperor, 169
Chateaubriand, 589
chemistry, 297
chiaroscuro, 840, 848, 878, 881
child of his time, every man is, 603
children, are at the most beautiful age, 151
   are unintellectual, 308
   features of, 167-8
   figures of, 756-7
   go on all fours, 739
   in tears, 159, 828-9
   lack character, 238
   paintings of, 822-3
   sketches by, 615, 721
chin, the, in sculpture, 736-7
China, beginnings of drama in, 1206
Chinese art, formlessness of, 74
   history, 859
   horticulture, 699
   ladies, 31
   lyrics, 1149
   may have had a sense of history, 987
   on French stage, 608
   outlook and literature of, 1095
   pagodas, 248, 699
   painting, 799
   view of beauty, 44, 730
Chiron, 453
chivalry, as basic for self-reliant individuals, 186, 196
   chorus not fitted to, 1212
   dissolved from within, 591
   has higher justification, 590
   in medieval epics, 1104-6
   interests of, 1067
   knights-errant in, 191, 196, 257, 592-3

INDEX

made fun of, 1107
modern plays preoccupied with, 1232
chords, harmony of, 985
  system of, 926–9
chorus in Greek tragedy, a background, 192
  a subordinate accompaniment, 900
  accompanied by dancing, 1187
  an integral part, 1139
  assigns equal honour to all the gods, 1215
  difference of, from dialogue, 1172
  does nothing, 1080
  is lyrical, 1151, 1211
  made more intelligible by music, 1186
  meaning and significance of, 1210–11
  observations of, 1017
  perfect in Aeschylus and Sophocles, 945
  unsuitable for modern tragedy, 1183
Chorus in satyric dramas, 1203
Christian art, 200, 230, 507, 722
  churches, 308, 684 ff., 697, 702
  painting, 737, 801
  sculpture, inadequate, 802
  virtues, 751
  worship, character of, 695–6
  worship dominates Gothic architecture, 684–97
Christianity, after conversion of barbarians, 1152
  allegorical treatment of in poetry, 402
  content of, but not revealed by, romantic art, 505
  doctrine of God in, 70, 72, 75, 79, 80, 435–6, 487, 505–6, 519–22
  doctrine of Eucharist in, 324
  doctrine of Grace in, 226
  early, 555
  essentially historical, 532–3
  grief essential in, 928
  Hegel's philosophy of, 347, 487
  historical elements in, 103, 532–3
  ideal of, 191
  in *Nathan*, 392
  introduced rhyme into Latin verses, 1024–5
  moral categories of, 278
  mysticism in, 321, 364
  not constructed by imagination, 574

opposed by lovers of classical art, 506–9
renunciation in, 507–9
scarcely mentioned in *Nibelungenlied*, 1072
spread of, 587–9
the Trinity fundamental in, 343
church music, 293, 935, 949–50
  relation of to God, 798
Cicero, 1010, 1191
Cid, *Romances of the*, 159, 1102, 1117
  the, 187, 273, 570–1, 1053, 1062, 1066, 1067
Cimabue, 876
Circe, 453, 1069, 1075
circle, most regular line, 668
  of little interest, 139
civil society, 183, 195, 260, 592–3
clairvoyance, 243–3, 272
Clark, Sir K., 737, 760, 766
class differences, necessary, 565
  not tied to birth, 209, 565–6
  rational, 209
'classical', meaning of, 441
classical art, compared with romantic, 554–5
  form of, 301, 309–10
  history of, 575
  transcended by romantic art, 302
  true manifestation of art, 317
classical education, 272
classical languages, 1022, 1025
classification of the arts, 89, 621 ff.
  of symbolic architecture, 637
Claudius, M., 235
clay models for marble statues, 772
Cleopatra, 753
clothes, ancient and modern, 165–6, 746
  kind of suitable in statuary, 746–50
  passers-by preoccupied with, 717
  rationale of, 742–5
Clytemnestra, 214, 568, 1213
cold, we are often left by modern dramas, 559, 560, 568
  by severe style, 619
Coleridge, S. T., 5
Collingwood, R. G., 129
collision, as subject-matter of poetry, 994
  epic and dramatic, 1059–60, 1080
  in drama, 197, 220 ff., 1178, 1193, 1196–9, 1203–4, 1207–8
  in romances, 1092–3

collision (*cont.*):
  necessary in drama, 1159, 1160, 1164–70
  not interesting unless between things of substance, 560
  not portrayed in sculpture, 741
  situation leads to, 199
  see also oppositions
Cologne cathedral, 691, 828
colour, alone does not make a painting, 898, 965
  as material of painting, 625–6, 801–2
  can represent differences between objects, 810
  effects of, 599–600
  excluded from sculpture, 706–7, 773, 777, 805
  fundamental ones, 142, 250–1
  Goethe's theory of, 87, 108, 141, 626, 705, 809–10, 841, 924
  harmony of, 140–1, 250–1
  in painting, 87, 839 ff.
  magic of, 836, 848, 853, 889
  makes a painter a painter, 838
  masters of, 839, 840
  nature, kinds, and use of, 839–50
  play of, 836
  preparation of, 876, 920
  purity of, 142, 250–1, 924
  totality of, 985
colours of a regiment, 304, 306
columns, 666–85 *passim*
  as supports for roofs, 656–7
  Egyptian, 658
  not beautiful if only an adornment, 657
  triumphal, 657
  when beautiful, 659
comedy, characters in, 1220–2
  function of, 511
  has more scope for expressing poet's own views, 1180–1
  leads to dissolution of art, 1236
  leitmotiv of, 1207
  lower classes the best material for, 192, 1220–1
  not so concentrated as tragedy, 1167
  nullifies the null, 160
  'pathos' in is not mere folly, 233
  reveals oppositions as self-dissolving, 1163
comic, the, in Dutch and modern German pictures, 887
  principle of the, distinguished from the ironic, 67
comical distinguished from laughable, 1199–1200, 1220–1, 1233–4
commentators on poetry, 403, 1005
comparison, in Eastern art, 412
  is disappearance of symbol, 318
  like simile, 306–7
  not metaphor, 403
  often wearisome, 413 ff.
  what is the use of?, 411
composer displays caprice in instrumental music, 955, 956
  needs executants, 936
  often empty-headed, 954
  work of the, 954 ff.
concentration, of lyric, 1146, 1164, 1168
  of drama, 1164, 1167
Concept, and Idea, 106, 143 ff.
  the, as unity of differences, 108–9
conflict in drama, both sides are justified and guilty, 1196
  in drama, how resolved, 1215
  in Greek drama not a matter of guilt and innocence, 1214–15
  in modern drama, 1223 ff.
  types of, in drama, 1213–14
  see also collision
conformity to law, 5, 88, 134, 138 ff., 247–50, 660, 927, 929, 930, 1026
connoisseur, apt to be pedantic, 270
  Greek sculpture intelligible only to a, 275
  instrumental music meant for, 899
  learned idleness of, 628–9
  may be concerned with technique only, 34–5
  perverse follies of, 1184
  pretension to be a, 14
  Rumohr a serious, 106–7
Conradin, 1155
conscience is not Greek, 278, 458
consciousness, naïve, 1209
  twilight of, 467
Constantine, Emperor, 697
contemplative satisfaction, 258
content, and form of art, 70–2, 77–8, 317
  and form of independence of character, 190
  and meaning, 95
contentment, nature of, 485
contingency is unbeautiful and prosaic, 596
  of some works of art, 61

contradiction, in comedy, and its solution, 1201-3
in Indian art, 333-4
in love, 818
its resolution necessary in life, 97-100, 150
must be resolved in drama, 1197
sense of, and wonder, 315
without it nothing living can exist, 120
conversation, social, 834-5, 867, 1121, 1184
conversion, 543
convivial songs, 1121, 1147
Copson, E. T., 140
Corinth, bronze of, 774-5
Doric temple at, 678
statues in, 764
Corneille, 223, 241
Cornelius, P. von, 162
correctness, 74, 155
Correggio, at zenith of Christian painting, 814
colour in, 839
grace and innocence of, 882
his Mary Magdalene, 868
master of chiaroscuro, 848, 881
cosmogonies, 1042-3
cosmology, 343-6
Cotta, J. F., 516
cow, Myron's, 761
the sacred, 336, 337, 448
creation contrasted with generation, 344, 373
Crelinger, Madame, 581
Creon, 221, 564, 568, 1163, 1217-18
see also Antigone *and* Sophocles
Crete, 648
Creuzer, F., 310-11, 403, 452, 473, 477, 640, 642-3, 780
crime, 81, 1207
criminals, 'morally noble' ones in modern plays, 1212
Cromwell, O., 165
Cronus, 459, 460, 465, 492
cross, as a sign, 636
the artist's, 146
Crucifixion, the, 522, 820, 822-3, 859, 862, 872, 884, 935
Crusades, the, 587-9, 1025, 1108, 1160
crystals, 130, 136, 653
Cupid, a universal power, 459, 541
as emblem, 875

becomes a boy, 489
captivates the heart, 227
in love-scenes, 858
not a child of Aphrodite, 759
nude in Greek art, 745
playful statues of, 202, 767
the oldest god, 337
curiosity, 98
Cuvier, Baron de, 127
Cybele, 353, 456, 460, 641
Cyclopes, 459
Cyrus, 391

Daedalus, 360
dance, as imperfect art, 627
chief part in, 1192
complications of, 1150, 1151
in drama, 1182, 1186, 1187
in pantomime, 1039
jumping is not a, 632
-music, 906
not capricious, 124
symbolic, 330, 352-2, 495
Dante, allegories in, 312, 402
as framer of language, 1009
as judge of mankind, 564, 589, 1076
commentators on, 403
Divine Comedy, collision in, 1059
described and considered, 1103-4
slow advance of, 1086
does not describe an actual world, 1055
himself the hero of his epic, 1066, 1075
Inferno, 259, 874, 1076
love in, 591
prosody of, 1031
religious material of, 439
universal and individual in, 979-80
Darius, King, 651
death, a misfortune but not, as such, tragic, 1198
a process to life, 523-4
and sleep, 421
Greek and Christian attitude to, 522-3
how symbolized, 400, 401
immediate negation of spirit, 348 ff.
in romantic art, 523
is diremption of body and soul, 119
not mere negation, 523
presentation of, 405
the end for nature, but not for man, 1089

declamation, musical, 942-4, 951, 957, 1013, 1181-2
defectiveness of art, 79
  not always due to lack of skill, 74
  in great statues, 772
degradation of the spiritual, 393, 395, 448 ff.
Deism, 508
Delille, J., 423-4
Delos, 457
Delphi, 457, 465, 489, 1131
democracy, self-destructive if not morally sound, 1199
Democritus, 681-2
Demosthenes, 407
Denner, B., 165, 834
Denon, D. V., Baron, 658
denouement, in Greek and modern drama, 1223
  is preferably happy, 1232
  may be unhappy, 1231
  may be an inner reconciliation, 1219
  need not be tragic, 1218, 1232
  of tragic complications, 1215, 1229-31
  requires a previously developed plot, 600
dependence of man on environment, 256
Dervish, 170
Descent from the Cross, 823
desire, as practical relation to the world, 315
  instigated by art, 48-9
  not our relation to works of art, 36-7, 58, 622
d'Este, I., Cardinal, 280
destiny, man the slave of, 158
  submission to, 189
determinacy, is differentiation, 348
  of the Concept, 109
  the bridge to appearance, 75
deutsch temperament, 886
development, gradual is trivial reasoning, 630
  principle of, 177-8
devil, the, 222, 1076
dialects, 252
dialogue in drama, 1170, 1172-3
  man speaks to man directly in, 1184
Diana, *see* Artemis
  of the Ephesians, 474, 489
Diaz, Rodrigo, *see* Cid

diction, crude and polished, 1171-2
didactic poetry, gives decorative border to prose, 1092
  of Hesiod and Virgil, 1042
  prosaic in principle, 515, 1010
Diderot, D., 597, 845, 847, 1171
Dido, 1074, 1086
differences, vague in Indian thought, 342
Dike, 400, 462
dimple, not essential to beauty, 737
Diogenes Laertius, 153
Diomedes, 237, 1101
Dionysus, festivals of, 450, 1212
  see also Bacchus
Dioscuri, statue of, 768
diphthongs, 252, 1015
Disciples, the, 521, 533, 543, 820, 825, 827, 830, 860, 862, 864-5
Discobolus, the, 761, 767
discords, 250
disposition, the subjective, 193
dithyramb, 1139, 1146, 1211
divination, 383-4, 446
Divine, the, *see* God
division of subject, basis for, 72, 75, 82
  of subject, principle of, 22-3
  of the arts, 622-4
Dodona, 457
dogs, performing on the stage, 388-9
dolce far niente, 411
domesticity a poor aesthetic subject, 268
Don Quixote, *see* Cervantes
Donna Diana, 559
Doolin of Mainz, 1105
Dover sole, 127
drama, acts in should be equal in length, 250
  authorship of not disputed, 1179
  change of scene in, must be limited, 1165
  chief thing in, 1061
  and in characters of, 1067
  concerned with inner motives, 167
  conflict in, 220 ff.
  contrasted with epic, 1078-9, 1081-3, 1085, 1090, 1161
  demands production on the stage, 1165, 1192
  displays action, 18
  episodes in, 986
  God in, 1162-3

highest stage of poetry and art, 1158
historical detail dangerous for, 276
honour a dead topic in, 559
moves rapidly forward, 982
needs scenery, 1181
obsolescence of, 1177
persons in, 417–18
progress of, fettered by similes, 414
relation of to epic and lyric, 1168
should be intended for the stage, 1182–4
simile in, 416–18
subject of, 416
task of actors in, 1039
uses the other arts, 1181–2
dramatic poetry, general character of, 1038–9
dramatist, may educate, 1180
must have profound insight, 1163, 1179
sins twice if he flatters falsity in his public, 1180
work of, 605
draughtsmanship, 838–9, 876
Dresden, 762, 823, 849, 852, 858, 868, 869
drudgery is not artistic, 261
Duccio of Siena, 875
duck-bill, the, 131
Durante, F., 939
Dürer, A., 294, 838, 867, 884
Düsseldorf, school, 162, 856
statue in, 775
Dutch painters are masters of colour, 839, 843, 848
painting, 64, 161–2, 168–9, 292, 597–600, 820, 885–7
people, character of the, 168–9, 597–8
see also Netherlands
duty, 52–4, 980

eagle, attribute of Zeus, 313, 753, 758
fable of and Zeus, 386–7, 447
strength of, 128
whether symbol or not, 306
ears, treatment of in Greek sculpture, 735
Eastern art, almost all is ambiguous, 308
outlook, 978, 1098, 1205
poetry, 977, 991, 1004, 1094
Edda, the, 1026, 1101
education, modern view of, 297, 819

effects, production of to please the public, 619, 620
Egypt, columns, in, 658–9, 668
country of symbols, 354
gave gods to Greece, 444, 477, 780, 1048
Egyptian agriculture, 359, 646
architecture, 352, 356, 661, 665, 680–1
art, 74, 308–9, 354 ff., 636, 722
mythology, 472
painted idols, 707
painting, 799
religion, 313, 320, 440, 457, 459, 472, 477, 641, 654
scarab, 386, 447
sculpture, 200, 201, 708, 721, 736, 776
statues, 724, 743, 759
symbols, 362, 394–5, 403, 448
thought, 394
view of animals, 387, 445–6, 448, 452
view of facial beauty, 730
view of nature, 383
Egyptians, arch and vault unknown to, 680–1
are children in sculpture, 783
are focus of symbolic art, 353
Magic Flute gives pleasure to, 280
the first really artistic people, 354
elegiacs, 1150
elegies, 1020, 1114–15, 1146, 1150, 1152
elevation of mind, 375
Elgin marbles, 173, 724
Elis, games at, 735
statues in, 764
embalming, 355, 357, 651
emotion, bridled by music, 939
catharsis of, 1197–8
emotional moods evoked by nature, 131–2
outbursts, effect of, 741
England, 'originals' in, 294–5
English archaeologists, 358
ballads, 1117
Byzantine architecture, 697
critics, 417
drama, distinguished for portrayal of character, 1227
divided into five acts, 1170
metre in, 1174
history, 859

English (*cont.*):
  painting, 871
  pantomime, 939
  poetry, 977, 1092
  productions of Shakespeare, 277
engravings, 704
enigmatic character of symbol, 397
Enlightenment, the, art of is prosaic, 507
  is abstractly intellectual, 315
Ennius, 514
Entombment, the, 823, 859, 935
Ephesus, Ionic temple at, 679
epic, action and event in, 1064, 1069, 1079
  addressed to imagination, not vision, 1165
  as the bible of a people, 1045, 1087, 1099, 1108
  authorship of, disputed, 1179
  collateral types of, 1091–3
  contrasted with lyric, 1113–17, 1120, 1123, 1126–8, 1132–6
  could not have been prolonged indefinitely, 1050, 1087
  demands detail, 254–5, 276
  differs from drama, 167, 227, 238, 1078, 1158 ff.
  episodes in, 1081, 1086, 1095
  expresses a childlike consciousness, 1045
  finds words for a nation's deeds, 1108
  form and content of, 1064
  heroes of, 255–6
  hindrances in, 1081, 1086–7
  kinds of, discriminated, 1193
  lingers on events, 982, 1086, 1133, 1168
  medieval, 1137
  more primitive than lyric or drama, 1046
  moves tranquilly, 1044–5
  must be a unity, 1045, 1049–50
  must be a composition by one individual, 1050
  must present fact, 1044, 1047, 1064
  not a mere sequence of events, 1088–9
  parts and unity of, 985–6
  personality of author not revealed in, 955, 1037, 1048–9, 1111, 1179
  poet must be at home in his world, 1048
  poetry has no strophes, 1031
  poetry, task of, 1037
  reveals kernel of a people's life, 1094
  seems to be its own minstrel, 1049
  spurns dramatic dialogue, 1079
  successful only in primitive epochs, 1114
  what an absolute one would be, 1064–5
Epicurus, philosophy of, 423
epigrams, allied to riddles, 398
  as kind of lyric, 1116–17
  as rockets, 409
  later Greek, 555, 608, 609, 761, 1152
episodes, in epic, 1081, 1086, 1095
  in lyric poetry, 1134
epitaphs, 1117
equality, right of, 463
Erinyes, *see* Furies
Eros, *see* Cupid
Eskimos, 365, 1126
etching, art of, 839–40
Eteocles, 207, 228
eternal justice vindicated in tragedy, 1197–9
eternity, circle as symbol of, 304
  expression of, becomes sublime, 339–40
ethical life, natural and spiritual, 1213
  not given by Prometheus, 462
  stability of, 459
ethical order, as the Divine made real, 1195
  in action, 1209–10
  man's relation to, 1197–8
  upheld by Greek chorus, 1211
ethical powers, advance from opposition to harmony, 1217, 1219–20
  differentiated in reality, 1195–6
  dominant in Greek drama, 1206
  ideality of, 1209
  in heroic age, 1208
  harmonized in tragedy, 1198
  not particularized in modern drama, 1233
  particularized in individual's 'pathos', 1210
  pushed into the background in comedy, 1203
  represented by the Greek gods, 1208–9
  see also spiritual powers *and* universal powers

INDEX

Ethiopians, 42, 492, 643
  see also Abyssinia
Etruscan art, 785, 787
etymologies, quest for, 312
etymology and dead languages, 404
Etzel, King, 273, 1057, 1072
Eucharist, 324
Eumenides, the, as inner furies, 227
  as universal powers, 278
  right of, 462
  see also Aeschylus
eurhythmy, 646, 655, 663, 674, 685, 698, 894, 911
Euripides, *Alcestis*, 206
  Hecuba, 360
  Iphigenia in Aulis, 212, 218, 1183
  Iphigenia in Tauris, 212, 218, 229, 456, 1183
  Phaedra, 564, 567
  slips into expressing emotion, 1215
  took new direction in tragedy, 1221
  vacillation of characters in, 1228
Eurystheus, 186
event and action, 1063–6, 1069–71, 1088–9, 1090
Everitt, W. N., 140
everyday life not artistic, 268, 289
evil, greatness of, in drama, 244
  has no truth or interest in itself, 1212
  idiosyncrasy is on verge of, 579
  not a theme for art, 221–2
  not portrayed in antiquity, 222, 500
  portrayed in Shakespeare, 222, 1227
  powers of, 221–2
evolution, theory of, 129
excavation, 648–9, 653, 665
exits and entrances of characters in drama, 1171
expectorations, 423
eye, demands completeness, 1185
  expresses a mood, 718, 736
  how treated in Greek sculpture, 731–4
  light of, is absent from sculpture, 522, 706, 731–3
  relates man to the external world, 732
  soul seen in the human, 153–4, 433–4, 729, 732
eyebrows, 734–5

fable, meaning of, 19
  distinct from metamorphosis, 395
fabliaux, 1106
fabula docet, 50, 385
façade of a commonplace man, 581
face, analysis of parts of, 729 ff.
  colour of, 846–7
  formation of the human and animal, 723, 728–38
  portrayal of, 866, 867
facial expressions, colours suited for portrayal of, 844–5
  disclose the inmost life, 540, 727
  fleeting, 717–18
  in Fra Angelico, 878
  in pictures, 174, 703
  in recent German painting, 867
  may be beautiful but expressionless, 173
  of children and the dead, 167–8
  of children and the aged, 828–9
  permanent, 151
factories, modern, 1053, 1054
fairground entertainers, 254, 1055
fairy-tales, 216, 495
faith, anguish of, 829
  power of, 535
Falstaff, 277, 585, 592
family, idioms, 150
  life, 179
  organization, 147
  person distinguished from the, 188–9
  property, 189
  quarrels, 208, 215
  relationships, 245, 554–7
  renunciation of may be fanaticism, 546–8
fanaticism is not sanctity, 547–8
fancy and imagination, 5
fashion in clothes, 747, 749
  in hair, 737
fate, absolute power of, 1230
  as necessity, 580, 607, 1208, 1212, 1214
  in drama, 1038–9
  individuals reconciled to, 1231
  irrationality of, 500, 1216
  man's is settled by himself, 589
  of one-sided characters, 585
  rules in epic but not in drama, 1070
faun and Bacchus, 202, 453, 733, 801
fauns, 452, 508, 745, 760, 791, 1091
Fauriel, C., 285
fear, nature of, 32–3
  objects of, 1197–8
  when felt, 523

1254 INDEX

feeling, and will, 1045–6
  assuaged by music, 935
  complexity of, 924
  nature of, 32–3, 81, 119, 126, 902–4, 910
  not free but determined, 151
  not present in every bodily organ, 146
  stimulated by reading, 935
  the artist's is what painting expresses, 804
  what music expresses, 904
female characters, love in, 563, 582
Fescennine verses, 514
festivities after funeral, 353
feudalism, 186, 196, 570
Fichte, J. G., 64–6, 1065
Field Marshal, powers of, 194
figures of speech, 1008
Fildes, L. V., 156
finitude, art cannot dispense with, 257,
  of human existence, 151–2
  transcendence of, 544
Firdausi, 186, 208, 405, 1097–8
firmness of character vital in art, 240–4
flattery of art, 155
  of public, 618–20
Flemish painting, 828–9, 839, 844, 851
  see also Dutch *and* Netherlands
flesh, colour of, *see* 'carnation'
Florence, 755, 768
fluting of columns, 669, 677–80
folk-poetry, 1117, 1124, 1144
folk-song, arbitrary expression in, 1122
  belongs to periods of little spiritual development, 285
  calls for musical accompaniment, 1138, 1144
  foreign examples of, 270, 1124, 1126
  general character of, 1124–7, 1144–5
  Germanic, 582
  Herder instigated study of, 270
  melancholy, 918
  requires a singer, 1050
forehead, in sculpture, 731
forest of pillars, 688, 691
  of pinnacles, 694
  of statues in Greece, 764
forests, southern, 71
Forkel, J. N., 950
form, and content advance to perfection together, 440

infinite maintains itself in the content, 118
forms, for spiritual content, 171–4
  not to be derived from old etchings, 174
fortified dwellings, 698
Fra Angelico, 878, 881
Frazer, Sir J., 207, 374, 860
Frederick I, 775
Frederick the Great, 203, 699, 750, 918, 1156
Frederick William III, 821
free necessity, 718–19
freedom, and necessity, 930–2
  and necessity united in beauty, 115
  nature of and how realized, 97–100
  necessary for beauty, 112–13, 150
  of gods and men, 226
  of production in art, 5
  of the Concept, 151
  realized in the state, 182–4
  subjective, is required, 510
freemasonry, 649
French, aim at flattery and effects, 620
  alexandrines, 1012, 1174
  allegorical poetry, 1106
  archaeologists, 358, 644, 645, 653
  architecture followed Roman models, 683
  Byzantine architecture, 697
  didactic poetry, 1092
  drama, acts in, 1170
    aims at pleasing, 620
    anachronistic productions of, 267–8, 608
    and the unities, 1164
    characters in earlier, 1178
    characters of, are brutes, 586
      are infirm of purpose, 420
      are personifications, 238–9, 1227
    cultural delicacy of, 267
    diction of, 1171
    heroes in, 223
    often arid, 560
  enthusiasm for Dido, 1074
  enthusiasm for Gessner, 1091–2
  epigram on God, 435
  even in farces, keep public in view, 1191
  expression of passion, 235
  have an established taste, 1175
  historiography, 268
  horticulture, 700

impatient of research, 269
keep to schools of acting, 1190
language, 1024, 1030
love-poetry, 565
melodies, 931
music, absence of melody in older, 949
not fond of the humorous, 601
painters have preferred Roman subjects, 814–15
poetry, 946, 1010, 1012, 1027
Revolution, 191, 262, 908, 1110, 1156
scholars, 672
'taste', 266–7, 417, 684
vaudevilles, 1117
writers, 597
Fréret, N., 494
frescoes, 847
friendship, bonds of, 546
essentially youthful, 568–9
requires mutual aim, 541–2
friezes, 658, 663, 670, 678
frigidity, alleged of Greek gods, 485
Furies, inner, 227–8, 230
of hatred, 222
see also Eumenides
Furtwängler, A., 202

Gall, F. J., 716
Games, Greek, 735, 743–5, 761, 771, 1089, 1119, 1129, 1131
as symbol of Greek unity, 1151
gardens, man is the chief thing in, 248
purpose of, 700
see also horticulture
Gash, N., 592
gems, 774, 778
generation, contrasted with creation, 344
idea of, 373
in theogonies, 345
see also procreation
generalizing about painting is hazardous, 813
genius, and talent, 27, 41
involves mastery of the material, 775
of artist indicated in sketches, 838
of musical executants, 956–8
taste cannot comprehend, 34
genre painting, 168, 170, 293, 574, 597–600, 833–4, 869, 1115

German, anarchy in literary criticism, 1175
architecture, 619, 683 (*see also* Gothic)
art, now counterfeits daily life, 597
attitude to the scientific intellect, 1077
behaviour at opera, 901
Byzantine architecture, 697
distaste for Italian libretti, 946
drama, 1170, 1174, 1182–3
dramatists, 1175
Emperors, 1155
exactitude, 269
familiarity with foreign peoples, 270
fondness for descriptive poetry, 425
historical epics, 274
iambics, 1018–19
language, 142, 901, 918, 1020–2, 1030–2, 1155
medieval love-poetry, 564
music, 918–19
musical intellect, 949
painting, facial expressions in, 944–5
older, 161, 174, 828, 829
related to architecture, 851
people, characteristics of, 584, 1124
tolerant of humorous aberrations, 601
poetry, 235, 423, 977, 1033
Princes, 115–16, 571
prosaic view of art, 1180
theatre favours naturalness, 1190–1
view that dances in dramatic productions are frivolous, 1187
Germanic languages, 1025
peoples, 1152–3
Germany, artist in is not concerned for the public, 620
borrowed art from elsewhere, 597
drama in, 417
epic becomes idyllic in, 1109
freedom of thought in, 605
Middle Ages in, 390, 571
youthful celebrations in, 495
Gerstenberg, H. W., 259–60
Gessner, S., 191, 259, 1091–2
gestures as substitutes for words, 1188–9
Ghent, 820
ghosts, 230–1
Giants, 459
Giorgione, 858, 881
Giotto, 876–7

Glockner, H., 584
Gluck, C. W., von, 206, 277, 900, 939, 947, 1183
Gnesen, 775
God, actually existent in animals, 357
  art aims at revealing in appearance, 1236
  as dying and arising from death, 348-9
  as subject matter of painting, 793, 798, 804, 819-20
  at first is external, 104
  belief in is a universal interest, 234, 272
  better portrayed in art than in nature, 30
  characters who set themselves against him, 882
  Christian conception of, 70, 72, 75, 80, 83, 86, 175-6, 178, 325, 435-6, 453-5, 487, 505-6, 519-22, 532-51, 574, 819-20
  consciousness of, 284, 1210, 1212
  'enlightened' ideas of, 1141
  existence of in the spirit of man, 793, 798, 821
  extruded from nature, 374, 586
  first revealed in nature, 316
  his work and man's, 719
  in classical art, 454-5
  in Dante, 1103-4
  in drama, 1162-3, 1195
  in his community, 1162
  in his sight all men are equal, 818
  in symbolical art, 421, 428-31
  Indian views of, 335 ff.
  individual's subjection to, in Mohammedanism, 1205-6
  Jewish view of, 325, 430, 445, 468, 471, 486-7
  justice of, 372
  made *ens rationis* by Deism, 506-7
  majesty of, in Eastern poetry, 1148
  man may fear his power, 1198
  mythology beneath the dignity of, 309, 310
  negativity in, 348, 519, 522
  not portrayed in comparative art-form, 379, 383
  now known as spirit, 75, 104, 342-3, 505 ff.
  object of philosophy, 101
  our fate comes from, 496
  portrayal of, by Hans Sachs, 265-6
  forbidden to Jews and Mohammedans, 175
  in Christian art, 200
  in different art-forms, 623-5
  in sculpture, 712, 716
  positive and negative relation of world and man to, 320-1, 363 ff., 375-7
  present in all mankind, not only in Jesus, 521-2
  presented in Greek art, 1236
  Protestant hymns to, 1145
  quest for harmony with him, 1224
  revealed in world-history, 1236
  rules nature only through its laws, 550
  substance of the world, 320
  symbols for, 304-6
  unattainable might of, 319
  unity of spirit and nature, 453-5
  visualized in objects, 313, 323-5, 329, 454
  worshipper finds rest in him alone, 689, 751
Godfrey of Bouillon, 1068
Goethe, aphorisms of, 392
  ballads of, 1118
  bust of, 484
  character-sketch of, 1131-2
  discarded aesthetic theories, 296
  distich of, 638
  early poems, 27-8, 195, 271, 289, 370, 597, 1173, 1180
  experience in theatrical production, 1185
  fables of, 389-90
  had genius in youth, 283
  has fewer metaphors, 408
  his dramatic characters are full of life, 1178
  in youth tried to individualize characters, 1228
  later diction of, 1172
  less 'pathetic' than Schiller, 235
  living poetry of, 233
  offered prizes, 516, 860-1
  on architecture, 672-3, 684
  on Hamlet, 231
  on Old Testament, 1058
  on old women, 737
  only when aged, produced his best work, 999
  parables of, 392
  pièces d'occasion, 1118

INDEX

poems composed in manner of, 1049
prohibited performing dogs, 389
scientific work, 61–2, 129
songs of, 285, 1121, 1122, 1147, 1156–7
theory of colour, 87, 108, 141, 626, 705, 810, 924
translated Voltaire for Weimar stage, 1191
translation of Diderot, 597, 845, 847
treatment of foreign folk-song, 1124
use of classical metres, 1031
views on art, 17, 19, 21
wide interests of, 282
youthful diction of, 1171
Works mentioned or cited:
  Approaching the Classical Form, 1031
  Art and Antiquity, 761
  Autobiography, 204, 279, 849, 1058
  Blumengruss, 290
  Braut von Korinth, 509
  Cat made into a Pasty, 392
  Clavigo, 1228
  Der Kläffer, 389–90
  Der Sänger, 287
  Elective Affinities, 52, 297
  Faust, 467, 583, 834, 1224
  God and the Bayadere, 393
  Götz von Berlichingen, 196, 271–2, 296–7, 1012, 1228, 1231, 1232
  Hermann and Dorothea, 191, 262–3, 1110
  Ich hab' mein Sach, 1122
  Iphigenia, 229–30, 276, 1012, 1178, 1183, 1204
  Mahomet's Song, 409
  Philostrats Gemälde, 275, 814
  Reineke Fuchs, 187, 389, 390, 571
  Stella, 1228
  Tasso, 1012, 1178, 1204
  The Erl-King, 290, 1144
  The Fisherman, 856
  The King in Thule, 583
  The Shepherd's Lament, 289
  The Treasure Seeker, 393
  Werther, 203–4, 241
  West-östliche Divan, 275, 370, 610–11, 1058, 1145
  Wilhelm Meister, 231, 593, 857
  Willkommen und Abschied, 610
  Xenien, 409, 1117

gold, as adornment, 258
  as pictorial background, 851
  colour of, 108, 843
  in statuary, 707
  in Tower of Bel, 639
Golden Age, 259
Gombrich, Sir E. H., 847
Gorgon's head, 740
Görres, J. von, 186
Gothic architecture, 619, 634, 674, 684–98, 807, 851
  kings, 698
Gottsched, J. C., 1154
Goyen, J. van, 292
Gozzoli, B., 881
grace, 617–18
Greece, dramatic poetry really begins in, 1206
  tragedy and comedy are at their zenith in, 1208
Greek Anthology, 1117
Greek, architectural simplicity, 682
  architectural subjects, 662
  art, beautiful days of are gone, 11
  derives its material from religion, 439
  does not portray love as spiritual depth, 563–4
  does not release the external into independence, 594
  elaborated in sculpture and epic, 284–5
  gods of, 157
  is art in supreme vitality, 436
  nothing can be more beautiful than, 517
  older, 722
  polytheism in, 175
  represents gods as free, 313
  some ambiguity still in, 309–10
  superior to Egyptian, 801
  artists learnt from Egypt, 780
  bucolic poetry, 1091, 1099
  clothes, 746–7
  comedy, the new, 1233
    the old, 1220, 1221
  cyclic poets, 1088, 1096, 1099
  didactic poetry, 1099
  elegies, 1041
  epigram, 425–6, 761
  ethical life, freedom in, 437, 555
  expression of passion, 235
  feeling for personal individuality, 744

Greek (cont.):
  Games, see Games
  goddesses portrayed as childless, 759
  gods, as powers of the human heart, 228
    attributes of, 495
    battle between old and new is serious, 506
    beautiful sublimity of, 483
    best portrayed in sculpture, 486–90
    bliss of, 157, 482–5, 533, 1210, 1222
    character necessary in, 482
    cognomina of, 493
    conflict of as 'pathos' in human individuals, 1196
    created by human passions, 237
    dethroned by subjectivity, 519, 520
    do not supply native imagery to Germany, 1155
    forms for portrayal of, 171 ff.
    given by Homer and Hesiod, 394, 444, 477, 1047–8
    have no 'pathos', 232
    have no truth for us, 272
    hold sway as ethical powers, 1211
    how individualized in sculpture, 753 ff.
    how portrayed in art, 602–3
    human in shape, but not mortal, 532
    individuality of, 444, 481 ff.
    mourn over their blessedness, 485–6, 503, 757, 817
    negative in, 484–6
    no seriousness in their disputes, 1074, 1210
    not a systematic ensemble, 751
    not abstract, 72
    not always in repose, 502–3
    not to be taken symbolically, 313
    of families, and cities, 494
    origin of, in spiritual power, not history, 494
    portrayal of can be enjoyed without superstition, 499
    relation of, to men, 225–8
    represent ethical powers, 1208–9
    satirized in Aristophanes, 1221–2
    seated in imagination only, 508
    serenity of, 201–3, 223–4
    some derived, 443–4, 477–8, 1048
    sometimes laughable, 1074, 1099
    special arrangements in worship of, 494–5
    spirit and body united in, 9, 484
    statues of require environment produced by art, 655
    stories about, 309–10
    subject to fate, 178
    symbolism in, lost in later art, 496
    we can be serious about, 1196
  Hermae, 641
  houses, simple, 662, 682
  ideal, realized in sculpture, 708 ff.
  lack of fundamental religious books, 1045
  language, 408, 1015, 1020
  milieu, 437
  mimes, 1187
  music, 926
  mythology, Argonauts in, 374
    beginning of spiritual religion, 394
    derived from nature-religions, 491
    development to beauty portrayed in, 455
    familiar to us, 272–3
    how far drawn from abroad, 443–4, 477
    how far symbolical, 309–10, 432
    not material for modern art, 275
    personifies the Black Sea, 341
    stories in, connected with history and colonization, 493–4
    not arbitrarily invented, 492
    often senseless, 493
    subjects from, in Italian painting, 872
  outlook corresponds with what sculpture alone can achieve, 800
  painting, 779–802, 871
  people, is gifted, 1222
  philosophy, 423
  poetry, 977, 978, 1016, 1026, 1073, 1092
  political life, corruption of, 510–11, 1209, 1222
  portrait statues, 750
  prosody, 1024, 1028
  religion, is the religion of art, 438
    needed sculpture, 763
    partly derived from Egypt, 641
    the essential content of classical art, 79

INDEX 1259

religious ceremonies, 1139
religious outlook, 1043
royal families, 278
sacrifices, 446
satyric dramas, 1203
sculpture, all-pervasive vitality of, 173
  bas-reliefs in, 837
  forms of, not adopted by Raphael, 881
  situations of, 200–2
  skill in harmonizing details, 756
  skill in individualizing the gods, 762
  statues, public appreciation of, 724
  studied by Winckelmann, 724
  whether coloured, 706–7
  stories about origins, 631
  temples, more than satisfying, 674
  theogonies, 345–6, 459 ff., 464 ff.
  tragedy, actor in, is statuesque, 1186–7
    keeps easily to instructions of the author, 1188
    acts scarcely found in, 1169
    art of actor begins in, 1186
    characters in, are not culpable, 1215
      do not speak as they would have done in life, 273
      drawn from an older period, 264
      explained by statuary, 1195
      individualized, 863
      'pathos' of is the important thing, 579
    chorus in, see chorus
    conflicts are simple in, 1207
    deus ex machina in, 580
    effective by objective 'pathos', 1173
    how alone can be understood, 1215
    one-sidedness of, 1222
    origin of, 1139, 1212
    'pathos' in is morally justified, 568, 580
    'pathos' not personal character is important in, 579
    plastic character of its production, 1187
    related to contemporary life, 275
    romantic love not in, 564
    sometimes had happy outcome, 1204
    trilogies of, 204
    unity in, 1167
    universal interest of, 1176
    what counts in, 1206
    will never lose its effect, 1177
    written for stage but excluded from modern theatre, 1183
  vases, 871
Greeks, artistic insight of, 733, 745
  artistic taste of, 408
  demanded support of music for verse, 1138
  do not view nature as divine, 472
  just sense of, in architecture, 663, 674
  know nothing of modern conscience, 278, 458
  only to be understood in light of their sculpture, 719–20
  their amazing technical execution, 772
  their correct sense of the Divine, 466
  their supreme sense of beauty, 738
  their tragedians did not invent their material, 439
  their unity against Troy, 467
  their unity symbolized in the Games, 1151
  took religion from the East, 439
  unsurpassed in sculptural invention, 772
grief, a negation to be superseded, 96–7
  alleviated on pictures of Christ, 823
  alleviation of, 49, 203–4, 1112, 1129
  an end in itself for martyrs, 545, 548
  an unsurmountable one, 448
  as source of Ossian's poems, 1100
  can be reconciled, 81
  displayed in some statue groups, 768–9
  endured for the sake of salvation, 587
  essential for the soul's development, 815–16
  essential in the Christian religion, 928
  expressed by the lines of the mouth, 730, 736
  expression of, as starting-point of music, 938
  in Italian painting, 873
  final in Greek figures, 817

grief (cont.):
  in comparisons, 413
  in love, 817
  indicated but unexpressed, 289-90
  infinite, 522, 537, 538
  liberation from, 419-20, 1112
  may allow little room for similes, 416-17
  memories of, 415
  negative and positive elements in, 830
  not a topic for classical sculpture but sometimes in Christian, 788-9
  not merely contemplated when Passion Music is heard, 935
  of death is preliminary to life, 535
  of disunion, 435-6
  of human unworthiness, 376
  of lovers, devoid of real interest, 568
  of Virgin Mary, 542, 826
  contrasted with Niobe's, 825-6
  rather Western than Eastern, 412
  road and portrayal of, 830 ff.
  serenity may be preserved in, 158
  should be expressed in song, 1143
  spiritual, 548, 625
  suppressed by strong men, 418 ff.
  to indulge in is sentimentality, 1232
  tone of in Old Testament prophets, 1140
  transcendence of, 348-9, 523
grouping, in pictures, 861-3, 883
Grupello of Innsbruck, 775
guilt, inheritance of, 188-9
guitar, a trivial instrument, 957
Gunther, King, 497
gypsum, 776

habit, 126-7, 198
Hadrian, tomb of, 654
Hafiz, 369, 370, 410, 1121, 1145, 1148
Hagen of Troy, 238, 1072
hair, a sign of weakness, 737
  on portraits of Christ, 821
  treatment of, in sculpture, 726, 737, 755
half-columns, 671-3
Hamasa, 1097
Hamlet, character of, 231, 244, 583-4, 1225-6, 1231-2
Hammad al Rawiya, *Collections* compiled by, 1096
Hammer-Purgstall, J. von, 370, 410
hand is not a hand when severed, 121

Handel, *Messiah*, 919, 947, 949
  operas, 949
  used libretto by Metastasio, 900
handshake, reveals personality, 732
  significance of, 861
Hariri, *Collections* of, 1097
Harlequin, 939, 1190
harmless situations, 199, 201-3, 741-2, 766
harmonica, 921
harmony is qualitative, 250 ff.
  of man and environment, 255 ff.
  of object and subject, 255 ff.
Hartmann von der Aue, 221
Haydn, 900, 939
Hazlitt, W., 1237
hearing, abandoned by poetry, 963
  general, 1021
  sense of, 890, 924
Hebenstreit, E. B. G., 146
Hebrews, *see* Jews
Hecate, at Aegina, 773
Hector, 237, 240, 498-9, 1068-9, 1083-4, 1089-90, 1216
Heidelberg, 310, 780, 821
Heinse, J. J. W., 426
Heldenbuch, 254, 1056
Helen of Troy, 214, 218, 563
Helios, *see* Apollo
Hell, devils in, 864
  souls in, 874
Hellenistic poetry, 1152
Hemling, H., *see* Memling
Henry IV, Emperor, 1155
Hephaestus, cupbearer, 499
  hurled down by Zeus, 309, 462
  image of, 470
  laughed at, 1074
  made armour for Achilles, 261
  technical skill of, 460, 461, 489
Hera, *see* Juno
Heracles, *see* Hercules
Heraclidae, the, 470, 777-8
Hercules, and Omphale, 858
  and Prometheus, 460, 470
  becomes a god, 470, 816
  cast away by Juno, 474, 759
  character and independent action of, 185-6
  diverse material in stories of, 493
  hairdress of, 496
  in the *Philoctetes*, 206, 226, 1183, 1204
  labours of, 186, 309, 352, 447, 474, 758, 816

nude in statuary, 745
overthrows old ruling families, 471
portrayed youthfully, 758
sculptures of, 731, 735
self-repose of, 177
Herder, J. G., diction of, 1010
  folk-song, collections of, 1124
  instigated study of, 270
  portrait of, 749–50
  Romances of the Cid, 159, 1102, 1117
hermaphrodites, 758
Hermes, conductor of souls, 480
  escorts Priam, 226
  messenger of Zeus, 461
  slayer of Argus, 224
  statues of, 762
  territory of, 489
Herodas, 1187
Herodotus, art of, 987
  epigrams preserved by, 425, 974
  on Babylon and Media, 639–40
  on Cabiri, 467
  on Cyrus and the Persians, 391
  on Dodona oracle, 457
  on Egypt, 353–6, 358–9, 452, 641–2, 645, 647–8, 650, 652–3, 781
  on Gyges, 743
  on origin of Greek gods, 394, 444, 477, 780, 1047–8
  on Pataeci, 460
  on Scythia, 651
  refers to Aeschylus, 469
heroes of Greek tragedy grew from fruitful soil, 1211
heroic age, and drama, 1208
  and epic, 1046, 1053–6
  and organized states, 179 ff., 188, 190
  and subjective responsibility, 187–8
  best suited to ideal art, 260–1
  history begins at end of, 987
  individuals in, 194
  relics of, 494
  subsequent to folk-song, 1125
heroism, degrees of, 556
  in chivalry and Greece, 555
  in romantic art is submission, 525
  see also bravery
Hesiod, gave gods to Greece, 394, 444, 477, 780, 1047–8
  gods of, opposed by Plato, 103
  Theogony, 345–6, 446, 492, 1043
  Works and Days, 423, 1042

hexameter, suitable for epic, 1020, 1136
  unsuitable for drama, 1173
Heyne, C. G., 312, 406, 494
hieroglyphics, 356–7, 644–5, 647, 653, 721
Highlanders, pipes of, 908
hindrances in epic, 1081, 1086–7, 1134, 1160, 1168
Hippel, T. G., 584, 602
Hirt, A. L., 17–20, 631, 643, 653, 663, 671, 675–6, 678, 680–1
historical, detail in plays may satisfy reader but not playgoer, 272, 276
  exactitude unnecessary, 276, 279
  fidelity, 269 ff.
  material, advantageous for art, 255–6
    can become familiar to us, 272
    in art must belong to one's own nation, 273 ff.
  origin of classical art, 475
  origin of Greek gods, 473–4
  painting, 233, 291, 293
  treatment of mythology omitted here, 455
  treatment requires *sang-froid*, 334
historiography, 9, 33, 268, 495, 515, 866, 986–9, 993
history, and poetry, 993–5
  architect of, 1065
  can be related as an event, 1064
  can reveal meaning of events, 129
  God revealed in, 1236
  Hegel's dismissal of, 780
  in nature and the spirit, 962
  of art, 14, 21, 34–5, 605–6, 615–16, 629, 780, 786
  of the sciences, 52
  of the world displayed in epics, 1056
  prerequisites of, 987–8
Hoffmann, E. T. A., 223, 243
Hogarth, W., 134, 140
Holberg, Baron, L., 64
Holinshed, R., 208
Holy Family, as subject for painting, 819
  Grail, 571, 589, 1106
  Spirit, doctrine of, supersedes mariolatry in Protestantism, 543
holy, the, as content of architecture, 638
Home, H., Lord Kames, 16
Homer, animals in, 445–6
  at home in his world, 1048

Homer (cont.):
  author of poetic bibles, 1045
  authorship of, 1049–50
  characters of are ideal individuals, 863
  characters are rich, 1178
  Creuzer on, 477–8
  descriptions in, 253–4, 273, 498, 1002
  epics of are definite wholes, 1089, 1098
  epithets in, 1003
  have material to Phidias, 439
  gods of, as individuals, 399, 479 ff.
    blessedness of, 719
    form a determinate world, 467
    given by him to Greece, 394, 444, 477, 1104
    how related to men, 226, 228
    laughter of, 159
    opposed by Plato, 103
    rooted in the spirit of the Greek people, 478
    serenity of, 157
    sometimes laughable, 1075–6
    visit the Ethiopians, 492
    war with one another, 224
  grandeur of works of, 617
  heroes in, 237–8
  how begins the *Iliad*, 219, 1086
  interprets events as divine interventions, 480
  language of, 407, 1009, 1011
  lays no great weight on love, 563
  originality of, 298
  poems did not come to him in sleep, 283
  portrays a 'pathos' of substance, 554–5
  productive in old age, 28, 999
  similes in, 415–16.
  stories in, 447
  supposed to be non-existent, 1130
  theophanies in, 499
  to be a follower of is fine, 607
  Wolf, F. A., on, 1087
  work in, 261
  wrote later than the Trojan war, 264, 1046–7
Homeric Hymns, 1139, 1150
  poems as patterns of epic, 1051–61, 1066–75, 1078 ff.
  scholarship, 1051, 1087, 1098

honour and love, as romantic themes, 220, 239, 241, 1224–5
  conflict of, 241, 565–6, 1227, 1235
Horace, and Augustus, 1130
  Ars Poetica, 15, 50, 218, 855, 1024
  decorates prosaic matter, 1010
  Epistles, 293, 1130
  lacks warmth, 1142
  more original in *Epistles* and *Satires*, 515
  not amongst the best lyric poets, 1127
  Odes, 1015, 1115, 1118, 1120, 1130, 1135
  Satires, 748
  tries to please, 618
horror, does violence to our way of thinking, 1176
  leaves us cold, 1173
horse, in sculpture, 758
horticulture, an external adornment of a given site, 423
  art of, 627, 699–70
  at Roman villas, 683
  riddle in, 398
  see also gardens
Hottentots, 44
house, as fundamental in architecture, 655, 713
  character of, 665, 669
  origin of, 673
Hübner, J., 856–7
human, and animal body, 434
  form, alone capable of expressing spirit, 78, 340, 433–4, 705
  as symbol, 353
  cannot express nature, 341
  determined from within, 668
  distinct from animal's, 714–15, 723
  imitated of necessity by art, 434
  in sculpture, 85
  not copied precisely in portraits, 164–5
  not personified or a revelation of spirit in Egypt, 359–60
  parts of, not suitable as subject for poetry, 972
  nature, empty finitude of, 711
  in visual arts, 896
  is universal, 978
  known in Dutch paintings, 887
  organism, articulated in detail, 981
  skeleton in, 943–4
  voice, *see* voice

humanity, absolute content of art, 608
  centre of art, 432
  one with God, 504
  spirit of, 1064
  subject-matter of romantic art, 607-8
  the existence of the absolute Spirit, 543-4
Humboldt, W. von, 215
humour, as the close of romantic art, 576
  becomes flat if bizarre, 601
  Hafiz almost approaches, 1121
  makes self-transcendence of art possible, 607
  not difficult to produce, 295-6
  often easy, 601
  sort of objective, 609
hunger, satisfied only temporarily, 98
Hüon's horn, 740
hybrid kinds of art, 382
  kinds of lyric, 1038
  kinds of poetry, 1041, 1090 ff.
hybrids, in Greek art, 452-3
  not beautiful, 131
hymns, 995, 1139, 1145, 1146

iambics, 918-19, 1018-19, 1150-1, 1173-4
Icelandic poetry, 1026, 1029
Idea, the, and the Concept, 143 ff.
  develops by its own activity, 299
  given first existence in nature, 713-15
  is actual, 244
  see also the Introduction, passim
Ideal figures best placed in the past, 189-90
  freedom of the, 978
  realization of the, 613-14
  sculpture especially points to the, 718
  the, and nature, 41-6, 813
  the, is not supreme for symbolic and romantic art, 718
  the mundane is one factor in, 574
  see also Part I, passim
idealism of life, 120
  objective, 123, 124
ideas, are abstractions, 722
  as content of poetry must be adapted for linguistic expression, 969
  as such, do not make a material poetic, 965

identity of meaning and shape is produced by the spirit, 351
idiosyncrasy of the artist, 292, 294-5, 298
idyll, 1091-2, 1109-10
idyllic life, 259, 261-3, 1091
  situations, 190-1
Iffland, A. W., 597, 1190, 1216, 1233
Iliad, see Homer
illness, 119, 148, 206
image, and meaning, 306, 404
  and simile, 323, 1148-50
  of saint need not be faithful, 721-2
imagination, and artistic creation, 5, 40, 81, 89-90, 101, 164
  and fancy, 5
  cannot harmonize man and his environment, 255-6
  distinct from thinking, 1035
  Eastern and romantic, 1004
  in seeing drama staged, 1165
  power of, 411
  restlessness of Indian, 343
  spirit's life in, 715
  the poetic, 971, 1007, 1027, 1035
imitation, not the aim of art, 41-6
  not what painting provides, 832
immortality, drink of, 332
  idea of, 376
  not taken seriously in Greece before Socrates, 523
  taught by Egyptians, 355, 650
importance of possessing *this* girl, 564, 567-8
improvisers, 285
Incarnation, the, 103, 532-5
incompatibility between meaning and shape, 317-18
independence, formal, 211
  meaning of, 180 ff., 200
  of men, 226
Indian abstraction transcended in Egypt, 355
  architecture, 661, 648
  art, absurd transgression in, 215
    can be appreciated, 20
    formless, 74
    not beautiful, 340
    popularized by the Schlegels, 64
    problematic, 308-9
    the older, 636
  buildings, colossal, 354
  caste system, 209, 212, 337, 346
  cosmogonies, 1043

Indian (*cont.*):
  cremation, 650
  drama, 1206
  epics, 273, 338-9, 1072, 1095-6
  everything is miracle in, 375
  fantastic conceptions in, 349
  feebleness of, 430
  images, 759
  incarnations, 1065, 1072, 1095
  lack of historical sense, 987
  lyrics, 1149
  modes of thought, 393, 428
  mythology, 272
  outlook foreign to us, 1095
  pagodas, 641
  painting, 799
  pantheism, 364
  penances, 547-8
  people, strange to us, 1058
  poetry, 374, 478, 978, 1045
  religion, 320, 321, 459, 641, 1048, 1095
  rhymes, 1025
  sacred animals, 387, 445-7
  views of nature, 383
  war with Portuguese, 1062
individual, a totality in himself, 146-7
  and the environment, 246, 255
  and the state, 182 ff., 980
  and universal powers, 198
  as master of the objective world, 313
  as related to God, is an end in himself, 980
  can achieve little, 149, 182 ff.
  dependence of, 147 ff., 193-4
  fends for himself, 569
  firmness of character of, 240-4
  freedom of, preserved in epic, 1053-4
  how to be actual on the stage, 255
  independence of, 180, 190, 192, 195 ff.
  moved by all the gods of Olympus, 236
  predominant in painting, 803-4
  responsibility of the, 187-9, 377
  revealed in a single action, 218-19
  revealed in speech, 219
  self-contained in art, 181
  should not withdraw from externality, 245-6
  substantiality of the, 189
  supposedly determined by dark powers, 243
  weakness of the, 237
individuality, and artistic expression, 156, 164, 190
  determinacy necessary for, 197
  entails contingency, 488, 491, 502
  first constituent in development of, 650
  forms of, 144 ff.
  Greek feeling for, 744
  how far expressed in sculpture, 705
  of Greek gods, 481 ff.
  synthesis of particular and universal, 236, 241
  unity with oneself, 240
individuals, world-historical, 987-8
inexpressible, the, 291, 296
infamy a subject in romantic but not classical art, 500
infinite grief, 522, 537, 538
  the bad, 466
innocence, state of, 177, 197, 259, 1091 (*see also* idyll)
insanity as a theme in art, 243
inscriptions, 1040 (*see also* epigram)
insects, 129
inspiration, 27
instruction, art and, 50-1
instructress, art as, 50, 316
instruments, musical, 898, 919, 920-3
intellect, one-sided, 621
  the inventor of allegories, 399
  see also prosaic, prose, scientific thinking
intellectual analysis of music, 906
  categories destroy form of art, 312
  reflection may belittle heroes, 226-7
  reflection may misinterpret rich characters, 240
intellectualism of prosaic reality, 1052-3
intention, and act, 187-8, 213 ff.
  cannot summon inspiration, 287
interest, dramatic, none in modern individuals, 194
  none in the 'beautiful soul', 242
  none in the grief of lovers, 568
  of idylls, negligible, 191
interests, of an ideal kind necessary in drama, 220
  of the spiritual life, 263
interjections, 235, 903, 938
intrigue in comedy, 1207, 1212, 1234-5
invention of situations, 216
  of tools, 43, 245

INDEX 1265

Iphigenia, 212, 218, 221, 229–30, 1213
  see also Agamemnon, Euripides, Goethe
Ireland, 1101
irony, 159–61, 223, 228, 243–4, 296, 1175, 1210
Iroquois, 270, 365, 1126
Isis, and child, 784, 800
  figure of, 743
  work of, 472
Isocrates, 1131
Israelites, *see* Jews
'it is so', 158, 495, 580, 1070
Italian architecture followed Roman models, 683, 697
  behaviour at opera, 901
  Byzantine architecture, 697
  comedy, Harlequin in, 939
  commedia dell' arte, 1190
  composers, modern, 937
  drama, 417, 1227
  fondness for metaphor, 405
  improvisers, 285
  language, 142, 252, 918, 1024, 1030
  masqueraders, 576
  melodies, 931
  music, 158, 874, 918–19, 940, 949
  older church-music, 939
  opera, 939, 953, 956–7
  painters, masterly treatment of Madonna and child by, 800–1
    masterly treatment of Mary Magdalene, 549
    the earlier, superior to Raphael in expression, 812
    the masters portray suffering of soul, 823
    the older are masters of colour, 843
    the older portray love-scenes, 857–8
  painting, displays accord between character and situation, 828, 868–9, 873
    lilies in, 861
    more attractive than Flemish, 883
    portrays peace even in grief, 939
    the older, fresh interest in, 161
  people have melody and song by nature, 284, 922, 939
  poetry, expression of love in, 610
    depth of feeling in, 874
    lacks classical metre and rhythm, 1027

  sonnets and sestinas in, 1146
  suitable for setting to music, 946
  tied to national character, 977
  wealth of images in, 1011
  singers, and Handel, 949
  skill in libretto, 900
Italy, palaces in as fortresses, 698
ivory in statues, 707

Jacobi, F. H., *Woldemar*, 241–2
Jalal-ed-Din Rumi, 368, 1098
James VI and I, King, 208
Jean Paul Richter, 295–6, 408, 584, 601, 602
Jena, 69, 662
Jericho, walls of, 909
Jerusalem, 254, 1057
Jesus Christ, allegorical presentation of, 402
  appearance of, 230
  Byzantine pictures of, 872
  ideal forms for, 176
  images of, 721
  individual man but also Second Person, 574
  Mary's feeling for, 453
  object of prayer, 829
  Passion of, *see* Passion
  portrayal of, birth of, 594
    in childhood, 865, 883
    in Passion Plays, 266
    invention of forms for, 171
    love of as divine love, 541
    should not be purely ideal, 536
    situationless, 200
  salvation in, 588
  statuary of events in life of, 789
  story of, as subject of modern drama, 1223
  is real for us, 1057
  portrayed in romantic art, 103, 521, 533, 803, 820–5, 851, 877–9
  treatment of hair of in pictures, 737
Jews, arch and vault unknown to, 680
  cannot portray their God, 70, 103, 175, 373
  epic ideas and stories of, 1096
  God of, 325, 468
  lyrics of, 1148–9
  poetry of, 321, 364, 478–9
  political position of, 208, 211
  religion of, 486–7
  revenge characteristic of, 430
  their idea of facial beauty, 730

Joan of Arc, *see* Schiller, *Maid of Orleans*
John the Baptist, 173, 820, 852, 865
  the Evangelist, 852
Johnson, Dr., 1100
joiners, 786
jokes, characteristic of fable, 389-90
  in musical execution, 957
  in Parny, 508
  in stories of the gods, 499
  of Lucian, 516
  riddles as, 398
Joseph the Carpenter, 820, 825
  II, Emperor, 1156
Judea, cave dwellings in, 648
Julius Caesar, statue of, 682, 790
Juno, and Hercules, 474, 759
  attribute of, 753
  fundamental relation of, to Zeus, 475
  hung on an anvil, 224, 493
  in human affairs still majestic, 177
  jealousy of, 452
  no real women for models of, 173
  sends Athene, 228
  statues of, 762, 767
  wedlock the chief characteristic of, 489
Jupiter, *see* Zeus
justice, administration of not personal, 193
  and law and punishment, 182 ff.
  criminal, 1230
  eternal in tragedy, 1230
  of God, 372
  symbolized, 400, 401
Justinian, 697
Juvenal, 515

Kant, ethics of, 53, 57
  K.d.r.V., 935
  K.d.U., 4, 43, 57-61, 107, 134, 362-3
  philosophy of, 56-7
  Prolegomena, 13
  Understanding and Reason, 1135
Keats, 283
Kemmer, N., 1135
kettledrum, 921
keys, musical, 923, 925-6
Kleist, H. von, *Kätchen von Heilbronn*, 565, 578
  Prince of Homburg, 243, 578-9
Klopstock, F. G., and his publisher, 1131
  cult of national gods, 273, 1057, 1079
  Hegel's assessment of, 1154-7
  hymn-like poems, 1141
  love-poems, 610
  Messiah, 274, 1059, 1075-7, 1079, 1109, 1121
  metres in, 1031
  Odes, 273, 425, 1142, 1156
  Selmar and Selma, 1154
Knights errant, 191, 196, 257, 592-3
  of the Round Table, 186, 571, 1106
'know thyself', 361, 489
knowledge of rationality alone worthy of man, 311
Königsberg, statue at, 775
Koran, the, 42, 1045
Kotzebue, A. F. F., 268, 289, 423, 578, 597, 1190, 1202, 1215-16, 1233
Kügelgen, G. von, 852, 869

labyrinths, 352, 359-60, 495, 647-8
lackey, 210
La Fontaine, 233
Lamaism, 324, 387
landscape, as background, 861, 871, 880
  Dutch, 886
  has no spiritual value, 167
  in Dutch painting, 812
  interesting in art only as a human environment, 972
  is permanent, 599
  painting, 29, 233, 291, 600, 831-2, 841, 844, 846, 854, 859, 869
  reshaped by horticulture, 699
  uncommon in Italian painting, 873
  unity in difference of, 941
  what delights us in, 699
language, accentuation of, 1026
  and metaphor, 404
  'flowery', 1184
  made an instrument of art by poetry, 796, 969
  most malleable form of expression, 972
  natural and rhetorical, 1171-2
  objectivity of is only sound, 701
  poetic, becomes decoration, 1010
    different from ordinary, 1007
    most spiritual form of expression, 1170
    must be naïve, 1011
    poetry an innovator in, 1008

INDEX

poetry may elaborate intentionally, 1010
prosaic and poetic, 1000, 1007, 1009–10
rhythm in, 918–19
sounds and signs in, 304, 635, 903
use of, differentiates poetry from the other arts, 998
languages, classical and modern, 1019–22, 1032, 1137
Laocoon group, 757, 769, 817, 823
lapidary, art of the, 682
lark, song of the, 939
Lasson, G., 238, 244, 284, 385
Last Judgement, 854
Latin language, 1010, 1015, 1020–2
  lyric poets not amongst the best, 1127
  peoples, development of lyric in, 1152–3
  prosody, 1024
laughable, the, and the comical, 1199–1200
laughter, in tears, 158–9, 757
  in the elderly, 829
Lavater, J. K., 715
law, administration of, 183–4, 590
  and justice, 220
  man's relation to, 377
  of the land, 99
  prevails in organized state, 182 ff.
  stability of, 459
Leda, 218
Lely, Sir Peter, 165, 531
Leonardo da Vinci, colour in, 848
  figures in, 880
  Last Supper, 865
Leonine verses, 1025
Lessing, *Education of the Human Race*, 1065
  language of, 1171
  Laocoon, 769
  Nathan, 392, 1012, 1180
  on fables, 389
  time of, 766
letter-writing, 609, 1184
Lewes, G. H., 52, 191, 1012
libretto, 900, 902, 934–5, 937, 940, 941–9, 952, 957
life, actuality of, 144
  dialectic of, 350
  in animals, 145
  nature of, 118 ff.
  process of, 78, 96–7

light, as the element used by painting, 808–10
  connection of, with knowledge, 473
  in Zoroastrianism, 325 ff.
  nature of, 117, 521
  non-material matter, 622
  on precious stones, 580
  the spiritual, 521
lighting of pictures, 840–1
lilies in paintings of the Madonna, 861
linear instruments and their sounds, 921
lingams, 637, 641, 642
Linnaeus, 42
lion, as symbol, 76, 128, 304–6, 389
  picture of, 635
  sculptures of, 761
  slain by Hercules, 758
lips, formation of, 736
Livy, 456, 515, 1073–4, 1099
Logau, F. von, 1117
Longfellow, H. W., 221
Longinus, 15, 373
Lotti, A., 939
Louis XIV, 267, 608
  XV, 203, 608
love, as reconciliation with God, 533
  centre of chivalry, 554
  contingency of, 589–90
  does not imply transgression, 215
  expression of in painting, 856
  fundamental in religious paintings, 864
  general content of art's religious sphere, 533
  in Ariosto, 591
  in Greek and romantic art, 453
  is spiritual beauty, 540
  its portrayal of its object, 412 ff.
  knowledge of, 280
  maternal, 541–2, 801, 824–5
  not the sole basis of marriage, 210, 463–4
  of Christ, purely spiritual, 824
  of kindred, 462, 824
  of Mary for her child, 824
  of Mary Magdalene, 549–50
  religious, 816–21
  sickliness of, we would like to be spared, 857
  spiritual depth of, 533, 540–1
  true essence of, 539–40

lower classes, best material for comedy, 192, 1220–1
  domestic life of portrayed in poetry, 596
  lack of education in the, 584
  marriage with one of disgraces one of higher, 565
  subjection of, 192
Lucan, 1061
Lucian, 515–16, 605
Lucretius, 423
Lucullus, villa of, 683
Luke the Evangelist, 313
luncheon, requirements for, 1055
Luther, 296, 297, 307, 527, 775
Lutheranism, 324
lyric, and drama, 1159 ff.
  can express the praise of God, 175
  can express richness of character, 240
  concerned predominantly with feelings, 254, 276
  contrasted with epic, 254–5, 1078, 1081–2, 1113–17, 1120, 1123, 1126–8, 1132–6
  elegances of, 555
  fundamental characteristic of romantic art, 528
  general character of, 986
  kinds of discriminated, 1193
  not a subject for painting, 855–6
  poet, expresses *himself*, 1179
    is a work of art himself, 1120, 1121
    must not enter dramatic conflicts, 1129, 1138
    tries to arouse in his hearer the same mood aroused in him, 1116, 1118, 1129, 1134
  poetry, general character of, 1037–8
  leans towards music, 1038
  rhyme in, 1031
  situations expressed in, 203, 1138
  subjects expressed in, 162
Lysippus, 202

Macbeth, character of, 578, 1227
  contrasted with Hamlet, 583
  demoralization of, 579
  deserved what he got, 1230
  justification of, 208
  when his hour has struck, 420
  witches and, 231, 585
Macbeth, Lady, 244, 578–9
Macpherson, James, 255, 413, 1100

Madonna, *see* Mary the Virgin
magic, of colour, 836, 848, 853, 889
  of rhyme, 1012
  use of in plays is a mistake, 242
Mahabharata, 214–15, 346, 1045, 1905–6
maker, poet as, 396, 479, 974
Malta, 648
man, and animals, 80
  as he is, is not revealed in some modern portraits, 887
  bears and sustains contradiction, 240
  chief thing in gardens, 248
  conforms to law of his existence only when he knows what powers direct him, 973
  enters reality in action, 1166
  has vocation to achieve union with God, 534
  his supreme renunciation is denial of knowledge of God, 508
  in epic has a living tie with nature, 1053
  in the street is a poor artistic subject, 268
  manners of a cultured, 615
  must humanize his environment, 252 ff.
  must submit to necessity, 503
  must work, 259, 833
  requirements of an active, 707
  spirit of, 1064
  the destiny due to, 1163
  who *can* write poetry *ought* to be a poet, 1129
Manesse Codex, 1155
mannerism, in Laocoon, 769
  of painters, 813, 829
many-sidedness of character not illogical, 240
march of troops, 907
Marcus Aurelius, 735
mariolatry, 542–3
Marmontel, J. F., 287, 620, 947
marriage, a relationship of substance, 475, 554
  fidelity in, 559
  headaches in, 593
  not natural but willed, 463
  obligations of persist after love is dead, 464
  taught by Ceres, 462
  unity with *this* individual not the chief thing in, 567

INDEX 1269

Mars, 177, 225, 489, 498, 682, 762
Marseillaise, 908
Marsyas, 203
Martha, 828
martyrs, 191, 505, 556, 587, 830, 887
Mary Magdalene, 52, 393, 549–50, 868
Mary the Virgin, apparitions surround her in pictures, 230
  as Queen of Heaven, 825, 842
  Assumption of, 826, 829
  Byzantine pictures of, 800–1, 872
  colour of mantle of, 251, 842
  grief of, 825–6
  her life of pain and sorrow, 178
  images of, 324–5, 616, 721
  in Parny's poem, 508
  lilies of, 861
  love for her child the most beautiful subject of religious painting, 824
  maternal love of, 453, 533, 541–2, 819
  object of prayer, 829
  portrayal of, by Raphael, 156
    has one expression, 174
    her love and life, 810, 825–6, 830
    in romantic art, 521, 878
    no model available for, 173
    not now worshipped, 103, 603
    portrayed not as an individual only, 402, 868
  position of in paintings, 862
  whole being of, lies in love, 864
  worship of, 542–3
Masaccio, 878
masks of Greek actors, 1187, 1188
master and servant, 1053, 1054
Mastersingers, 254, 1056, 1127
matria medica, 3
mathematical examples, 139–40
  figures, 96
matter and form, 130
mausoleums, 650–4
Mausolus, 653
maxims, 1041, 1044
mealtimes, 123
meaning, and shape, accord between, 300 ff.
  and shape, battle between, 333, 783, *et al.*
  and shape, coincide in Greek art, 313
  and sound in prosody, 1020 ff.
  not first grasped and then illustrated, 351

of the external, 349
search for symbolic is often vain, 311–12, 691
means and end, 973, 974, 983, 984, 990 ff.
measure as synthesis of quality and quantity, 134, 135
Medici, Venus, 564, 737, 763, 766
  Villa, 753, 755
medieval pictures, 200
meditation, Indian, 346
Meleager, *Garland* of, 555
melody, 141, 1182
members of an organism, 125–6
Memling, H., 599, 821
Memnons, 638–57
memory, 189–90, 281–2, 622, 892
men, are 'natural' in conversation, 1171
  unified by cult of the dead, 651
  unified by religion, 637–8
Mendelssohn, Felix, 28, 950, 1142
Moses, 32
Mendes the goat, 452
Menelaus, 218, 416
Mengs, A. R., 19, 294, 844
Mercury, *see* Hermes
Meru, the hill, 367, 642
metal-workers, 460
metaphor, 1003–5, 1148–9, 1150
Metastasio, P. A. D. B., 900, 947
metre in lyrics, 1135–7, 1150–1
  of drama, 1170, 1173–4
Meyer, J. H., 17–19, 707, 773, 789
Michelangelo, 619, 790, 864, 865, 881
Middle Ages, allegories frequent in, 401
  art of, 20, 216
  borrowed material from antiquity, 274
  champions in, 556
  collective adventures in, 588
  dissensions in, 208
  end of the, 605, 677
  epics of, 1102–6
  German poetry in, 977
  Golden Age of is past, 10
  how colours were prepared in, 847
  lyrics in, 1152, 1154
  painting in, 800
  riddles popular in, 398
  situation in, 196, 390
  use of ivory in, 774

Middle Ages (*cont.*):
  use of wood in, 773
  virtues in, 751
  why rated highly, 571, 593
Milky Way, 474, 759
Milton, John, inferior to Dante, 1109
  lyrical expressions in, 1079
  Paradise Lost, 222, 1075, 1109
mind, distraction of is stupidity, 1228
Minerva, *see* Athene
miracle, 319, 375, 505
  -working pictures, 851
Mithras, bas-reliefs of, 330, 649
  caves, 649
  in Egypt, 642
  in Persian religion, 327
Mithridates, 859
'modelling', 840, 842, 848, 871
modern drama, characters in seek subjective satisfaction, 1225
  chorus inappropriate in, 1212
  collisions in, 566, 1223 ff.
  origin of, 1212
  subject of, 1223-4
modern Greeks, folk-songs of, 285
modesty, *see* shame
Mohammed, 42, 409
Mohammedan, Arabs, conquests by, 1097
  buildings in India, 650
  pagodas, 641
  poetry, 430, 1004, 1011, 1025, 1097-8, 1144, 1205
  poets, 364, 999
  religion, 487, 1073
Mohammedanism, attacked in Crusades, 587
  cannot picture its God, 42, 103, 175
  mystical art of, 321
  spread of, 409, 557
Molière, *L'Avare* and *Tartuffe*, 1234
monarchs, modern, 186, 193-4
monasticism, 507-9, 564
Mongols, art of, 700
monologue, 1170, 1172
monotheism, 1043
Montalvo, G. de, 1106
Moorish architecture, 634
Moors, the, 587, 1062, 1102
moral commonplaces, 268
  is easily drawn, 386
  order, ties of readily renounced by fanatics, 546-8
  outlook, 188, 258-9
  principles, 194
morality, bourgeois, 597, 886
  commonplace as substance of domesticity, 596
  nature of, 52-5
  subjective, 1195, 1215, 1232-3
  moralizing about Achilles, 226-7, 1067-8
morbidezza, 146
Moreto y Cabaña, A., 559
Morlaccia, 1124
mortality, meaning of, 475
mosaics, 807, 847, 871
Moses, 445
mother and child, different treatment of in painting, 800-1
  statuary, 759, 784, 800
mountains, Hegel's view of, 132, 158
  not suitable as a subject for poetry, 972
mouth, animal, 728
  expressive of grief, 730, 736
  expressive of mood, 718
  how treated in sculpture, 736
  purpose of, 730
  seat of speech, 736
movement in nature and in life, 122-4
Mozart, 28, 234, 283, 893, 939
  Figaro, 949
  Magic Flute, 272, 279-80, 946, 1191
  symphonies of, 900, 923
Müllner, A., 1207
Mummius, L., 774-5
mummy as an original form of sculpture, 653
Munich, 170, 202, 203, 453, 785, 821, 824, 829, 838
Mure, G. R. G., 232
Murillo, 170
Muses, the, 294, 451, 474, 478, 481, 489, 555, 745, 1104, 1130
music, almost always accompanies lyric, 1137-8
  alone provides sensuous stimulation, 1137
  amateur tries to find meaning in instrumental, 954
  and architecture, 911, 916
  and Greek lyric, 1150-1
  and rhythm and accent of poetry, 917-19
  architecture is frozen, 662
  as accompaniment in Greek drama, 1186

as complete negation of space, 804–5
assuages grief, 939
bridles emotion, 939
cadence in must end firmly, 668
can disclose inmost life of spirit, 540
cannot manifest inner life perceptibly, 815
chief thing in opera, 1191
church-, 293, 935, 949–50
content and material of, 626
deals with the inner movement of the soul, 855
declamatory, 942–4, 951, 957, 1013, 1181–2
demands a text at first, 960
difference between attitude of dilettante and expert to, 953
distinguished from poetry, 904–5, 959–69, 997 ff., 1017 ff., 1023
dramatic, 950–1
elemental might of, 908
freedom from content incompatible with art, 906
gift for composition is developed in youth, 954
harmony in, 141, 250
history of, 1093
in drama, 1187–8
inmost soul of, 938
intellectual analysis of, 906
interjections as foundation of, 903, 938
keynote of romantic art, 528
lyric poetry approaches, 1137
lyrical, 950
material of cannot be persistent, 889–90
mathematical basis of, 662, 911 ff.
may be free from subject-matter, 895, 899, 901–2
must always be reproduced anew, 909, 936
nature of, 28, 87–8
not all-powerful as such, 908–9
not indigenous in northern peoples, 284
not required to accompany cultured poetry, 1146
painting begins to swing over to, 848, 853
performance of is primarily virtuosity, 1188
poet cannot make audible, 426
power of, 906
principal business of, 904
principle of, 952
portrayal in, 795
provides reconciliation, 940
purity in notes of, 251–2
regimental, 909
regularity in, 124, 249
relation between notes in, 600
religious, 158, 946–7
style in, 293
supplements words expressing feelings, 1122
task of, 1015
time in, 907
musical accompaniment of romantic lyric, 1153
instruments, 920–3, 953–8
talent, 28
tunes, 247
musicians, are often unintelligent, 930
as executants are artists too, 936
Myron, 761, 767, 773, 774, 777
Mysteries, the, 495
mythology, an invention of fables, 309
as artistic material, is given, 725
belongs to a period earlier than abstract thought, 311–12
Germanic, 1155
historical or symbolical study of, 310–12
subjects from, used in Christian painting, 814–15
universal thoughts implicit in, 311
see also Greek

Napoleon, 485, 657, 750, 776
nation, reality of a, 1056–7
national aptitudes for specific arts, 284–5
characteristics, 235
convictions, 348
nations, European may not begin aggressive war, 1062
war between, 1061
naturalism in art, 45–6, 161, 166–7
naturalness, aimed at by Giotto, 877
demand for in drama, 277–8
favoured in German theatre, 1190–1
insisted on by Diderot, 597
of genre painting, 833–4, 879
of sculpture, 703
nature, an 'other' for man's apprehension, 315
and spirit, 136, 154, 355, 431–2, 465
artistic fidelity to, 253 ff.

nature (*cont.*):
  as first existence of the Idea, 713-15
  as self-external, 428
  as subject for painting, 832
  description of, in novels, 1054
    in poetry, 1092, 1145
  engenders only the ephemeral, 459
  environment of, in epic, 1078
  for romantic art, not a revelation of God, 524-5, 1236
    not symbolic, 524
  imitation of, 595, 596, 597
  in art must reveal the spirit, 424
  interpreted in the East as divine, 602
  lower than art, 29-30, 168
  man's relation to, 245-6, 256-7
  modern portrayals of, 253
  needs arising from should appear in art as assured, 257
  only a background in Greek art, 467
  philosophy of, 88, 94, 127, 129, 134, 154, 382, 428, 434, 621, 628, 714, 718, 795, 808, 891, 912, 921, 924
  productions of are complete all at once, 614
  -religions, 1043
  scarcely suitable as a subject for poetry, 972
  sentimental reaction to, 425
  series of formations in, 468, 490
  -worship, 316, 324, 383-4
necessity, an abstract category, 59-60
  and action, 1084
  and freedom, 931, 932
  as fate, 503, 580
  at the heart of events, 1070-3
  external, 98
  how present in beautiful objects, 115
  in civil life, 148
  objects must be proved in accordance with their, 24
  of art, 95
  of nature, 97, 100
  of the Ideal, 142
  reasonable to bow to, 211, 503
  working of, in drama, 1163
Neer, A. van der, 292
negation, double, in development of the self, 907-8
  in sound, 891
negative, and positive elements in grief, 830
  essential in life, 96-7
  essential in love, 818
  necessarily present in God, 347, 505 ff.
  not a theme for art, 221-2
  not present in Indian thought, 340, 347
  process of the self, 914
  soul must pass through, 816
  symbolized in life of nature, 353
negativity, absent from Greek art, 437, 530
  absolute, 68, 93, 109, 160
  emerges in romantic art, 442
  implicit in reconciliation, 573
  in life, 122
  in the East, 429
  necessary process for overcoming finitude, 533
  of comparative art, 431
  of irony, 66-7, 159-60
  of time, 907, 913
  spirit's, 92-3
Nemesis, 462-3, 1217
Neo-Platonists, 311, 403
Neoptolemus, 226, 1204
Nestor, 237, 480, 1049
Netherlands, churches in, 689
  painting in, 292
  see also Dutch
Newton, Sir Isaac, 392, 810, 945
Nibelungenlied, alien to the present day, 1057
  authorship of, unknown, 1049
  characters and geography of, 238, 273, 447
  contrasted with the *Iliad*, 497
  criticized, 1103
  descriptions in, 258
  fate in, 1071-2
  prolix, 1055-6
  unified by one poet, 264
  unity of, 1087
  vagueness of, 254
  valued by the Schlegels, 64
Niebuhr, B. G., 1099
nightingale, 43, 370, 828
Nile, the, 350, 352, 359, 454, 468
Niobe, 393, 768, 817, 825-6
Nisami, 1098
Nordic heart is pressed in on itself, 1144
  mythology, 1153
  myths more alien to us than Mohammedan poetry, 1102

INDEX

nose, character and significance of, 729–30, 735
notes, developed by musicians from sounds, 962
  figuration of, 908
  impermanent, 909
  music is existent in, 905
  musical are an ensemble, 903
  not closely connected with the content placed in them, 898
  not interjections, 903, 938
  numerical basis of, 923 ff., 929
  range of, 923
  without content of their own, 959
Novalis, 159
nude in sculpture, 165, 742–5
nudity, Greek view of, 742–4
  not necessary for beauty of a statue, 744–5
number as symbolical, 352, 403
numismatics, art of, 776
nuns, 829
Nürnberg, 265, 691, 789
nursery tales, 308

'objective' meaning of, 711–12, 792, 962
objectivity, and subjectivity, 705, 928
  nature of, 116–17
  of the Concept, 110
  of the work of art, 269–70, 279
  originality is identical with, 294
  unveils 'pathos', 279
oblong, more pleasing than a square, 663
Octavian, 274
odes, 1141–2, 1146, 1152
Odysseus, and the Phaeacian, 481
  carpentered his marriage-bed, 261
  character of, 237, 863
  deception of, 226
  embodies entire Greek spirit, 1068
  helped by Hermes, 452
  penetrates disguise of Achilles, 860–1
  speaks of his exploits, 1101
  succeeds at last, 1216–17
  swineherd of, 569
  wanderings of, 1068–9, 1079–81
Odyssey, see Homer
Oedipus, 188, 207–8, 214, 218, 228, 275, 361, 568, 1213–14, 1217, 1219
oils, painting in, 847–8, 883

Old Testament, 374–5, 858 (*see also* Bible)
Olympia, 258
Olympic Games, victors in, 720 (*see also* Games)
Olympus, gods of, 157, 170, 187, 224, 228, 236
omens, Greek interpretation of, 496–7
onyx, 778
opera, barbarity tolerable in, 1183
  elaborate production of, 1191–2
  everything in is expressed in song, 951
  Italian, 953
    and German, 949
  listener's attitude to, 952, 953
  music the chief thing in, 1191
  not indigenous in northern Europe, 284
  recitative in, 943
  requires oracle, 272
  style in, 293
  subjects of, 234
operetta, 951
opposites, identity of, 120
  nature of, 928
opposition, in later sculpture, 768
  not reconciled in classical art, 436
  within the spirit, 537
  see also negativity
oppositions, 117 ff., 180, 198, 201, 202 ff.
  see also collisions
oracle, 230
oratorio, 943, 949
oratory, 33, 35, 989–93, 995
ordinary thinking, 968, 975, 1001, 1006, 1135
  poetry must transcend, 1007, 1012
Orestes, 184, 212, 214, 221, 229–30, 232, 278, 463–4, 458, 487, 568, 1213, 1218
organic unity, 982–4
organism, nature of, 119–21
  the animal, 124, 129, 137–8, 148
  the human, 135–8, 148, 150, 943
Oriental, clothes, 746
  despotisms, 436–7
  imagery, 410, 412
  lack of historical sense, 987
  love of metaphor, 408
  love of riddles, 398
  view of individuality, 429–30
  see also Eastern

Ormuzd and Ahriman, 325 ff.
ornamentation in architecture, 674–5, 680, 682, 695–7
Orpheus, 277, 908
Orphic hymns, 908
Ortnit, 254
Osiris, in form of wolf, 448
  the dead become, 654
  work of, 472
Osmaston, F. P. B., vii, xiii (in Vol. I), 170, 385, 600
Ossian, 255, 413–15, 1047, 1053, 1055, 1059, 1072, 1079, 1100–1
Ostade, A. van, 599, 849
Othello, 212, 578, 1218, 1227
ottava rima, 1137, 1174
oval, beauty of, 731, 737–8
  more interesting than a circle, 139–40
Ovid, 394, 413, 447–50, 1024–5
Ozymandias, 643

paean, 1211
Paestum, Doric temple at, 678–9
painter, business of, 598
painting, and architecture, 806–7
  and poetry, 854–7, 959–69, 982
  and sculpture, 167, 703–4, 851, 853–4, 863–5
  and spectator, 805–6, 905
  approaches music, 848, 853, 895
  attitude to objects portrayed is contemplative, not practical, 835
  can portray trivialities, 596
  content and material of, 625–6, 804, 812, 889
  does not just imitate subjects from the real world, 895
  Dutch, 64, 161, 162, 168–9, 292, 597–600, 820
  equality of groupings in, 250
  execution is the important thing, not the subject painted, 598–600
  expresses personality by colour, 732
  few statements about it are universally true, 813
  Flemish, 158, 174
  genre, 168, 170, 293, 574, 597–600, 833–4, 869, 1115
  German, 161, 174, 829, 887
  gives permanence to what is fleeting, 835–6
  harmony and beauty of colours in, 250–1
  history of, 1093
  in antiquity, 799
  individual modes of treatment in, 292
  invention and execution are one in, 936
  is detailed, 255
  is work of spirit for spiritual apprehension, 805
  Italian, 161, 549, 800–1, 812, 823, 883
  manifests the inner life of the spirit, 814
  may portray the history of conversion, 549
  more abstract than epic, 173
  must keep to reality, 836–7
  of martyrs must express the bliss of torment, 546
  of statues, 731–2
  origin of, 630
  our relation to, 891
  passing glances a suitable subject for, 718
  perfection achieved by over-paintings, 839
  plastic element in, 838–9, 850–1
  principle of, 771, 789, 798–9, 802, 808–10, 815, 889
  pyramidal grouping in, 671, 862
  regularity in, 248–9
  reproached for using arabesques, 659
  restriction to two dimensions is a necessary advance, 805
  should be intelligible and recognizable, 858–61
  task of, 795
  truth to life in, 938
Palestrina, 939
Pan, 452, 832
Panofsky, E., 17, 646
pantheism, 321, 364 ff., 368, 370–1, 378
Pantheon of art, 90
pantomime, 1039, 1192
paragraph-construction, 1008
Paris, 170, 285, 649, 747, 871
Paris of Troy, 218, 563
park, character of a, 699–700
Parmenides, 1042
Parny, E. D. D., 508
Parsis, *see* Persian
Parthenon, 724, 726, 768
particularity and individuality, 476–7

parts and members, difference between, 118, 120-1
Passion, locality of the, 588
  music, 935, 950, 955
  Plays, 266
  portrayal of the, 158, 823-4, 830, 864, 878-9, 884
passion, as creator of the gods, 237
  expression of, 406 ff.
  in drama, 1163
  liberation from, 417-18
  strength of, 406
  surmounted by the best men, 417
pathognomy, 715-16
'pathos', can be surmounted, 417
  comes from the gods, 458, 497
  ethically justified, 1209, 1214-15, 1226
  gods have no, 232
  in drama, 416, 568, 1162-3, 1170, 1172, 1176, 1187-9, 1196
  individual may renounce his, 1218-19
  leads to conflict, 1213
  meaning of, 232 ff.
  of lyric poet, 1135
  one-sidedness of cancelled, 1217
  Schiller's, 506
  should be completely expressed, 289
  subjective and objective, 1170, 1173
  without one a character vacillates, 1214
patriarchal community, 182
patriotism, 566, 1154-6
Patroclus, 226, 237, 568, 1083, 1089, 1216
patron-saints, 828, 859
Pausanias, 186, 457, 465, 493, 643, 735, 753, 773, 774, 832, 1131
Peloponnesian war, 1180, 1221
penances, 339, 345-7, 547-8, 556, 830
Penelope, 563
penitence, 278, 334
people in small towns, 717
Percy, Bp. T., 1117
performance, musical, 909
  of dramas, 707-8
Pergolesi, 939
Pericles, 719
periphrasis in poetry, 1003
Persia, conquest of, 989, 1002-3
Persian, art, 308
  gardens, 700
  monuments, 643
  outlook, 348, 366, 368, 383
  absence of art in early, 362
  poets, 364, 368-70, 610, 1011, 1097-8
  religion, 320, 327, 328-30, 456-7, 649, 1045
  wars, 1160
Persians, incited to revolt, 391
  lyrics of, 1148-9
Persius, 515
person, may become selfish and evil, 711
personality, 188-9
  of poet not revealed in epic, 955, 1037, 1048-9, 1111, 1179
personification, 78, 314, 325, 340-2, 349, 353, 359, 399-400, 402-3, 434, 441, 454, 456, 458, 465, 471, 479, 482, 607
perspective, absent from Egyptian reliefs, 771
  atmospheric, 845-6
  linear, 837, 845, 849
  undeveloped in Byzantine painting, 871
Perugino, 881
Peruvians, 608
Petrarch, 276, 564, 591, 610, 874
Petry, Dr. M. J., 139, 146, 1237
Pfeffel, K., 388
Phaedrus, 385-6
Phidias, *Athene*, 773
  Castor, 768
  in Elgin marbles, 173, 724
  materials used by, 776
  plastic character of, 719
  what we marvel at in, 617
  Zeus, 439, 707, 762, 773
Philip II, 169
Philip Augustus, 1105-6
philosophical thinking, 1114, 1128, 1135
philosophy, and art, 7, 14, 100, 104, 967-8
  and identity of opposites, 120
  God the object of, 101
  Hegel's: *Encyclopaedia of the Philosophical Sciences*, 94, 434, 928, 1059, 1207
  History, 1062, 1156
  Mind, 94, 428, 434, 714, 902, 1059
  Nature, 88, 94, 129, 134, 382, 428, 714, 795, 808, 891, 912, 921, 924

philosophy (*cont.*):
  Phenomenology, 241, 1201
  Religion, 222, 356, 465, 487
  Right, 53, 64, 68, 194, 241, 243, 260, 268, 436, 508, 555, 981
  Science of Logic, 134, 928
  must be scientific, 11–12
  not required by the artist, 282
  not the only example of idealism, 120
  procedure of, 11
  proof in, 24–5
  reconciles oppositions, 54–5
  Roman, 515
  system of, 23–5
  work of, 704, 715
  wrongfully accused of pantheism, 365
Philostratus, *Eikones* of, 275, 814
Phoenicia, 448, 680
Phoenix, 237
phoenix, the, 353
Phrygia, 353, 387, 448, 460, 641
Phryne, 720
physical suffering, not artistic, 830
physiognomies, 151, 173–4
physiognomy, 715–16
physiology, 78
Piccinni, N., 947, 949
pictures, confused collections of, 859
  historical collections of, 870
pièces d'occasion, 203, 288, 995–6, 1118–20
Pierides, 393, 394–5, 451
Pigalle, J. B., 203
pilasters, 673
Pindar, alleged theogony in, 465
  attains summit of perfection, 1151
  criticized by Voltaire, 267
  lyrical enthusiasm of, 1142
  metres used by, 1017
  Odes, frequently commissioned, 288
    pièces d'occasion, 203, 1118–20, 1129–30
  rewards given to, 1131
pinnacle of art, 79, 517
pity, 1197–8, 1215
plague in Greek camp, 207, 480, 1086
plants, alleged soul of, 154
  as columns, 657–8
  compared with animals, 145
  forms of, in architecture, 656, 659, 668
  life and growth of, 136–7, 350

various forms of, 490
Plato, as plastic figure, 719
  disgusted with Athenian government, 510
  distich of, 153
  language of, 407
  Laws, 781
  opposed Homeric gods, 103
  Politicus, 460
  Protagoras, 361, 461
  the Idea in, 21–2, 143
  Timaeus, 467–8
Plautus, 514, 1203, 1233
play, 201, 204, 257
plays, modern, give scope to virtuosity of the actor but are not poetic, 1204–5
  ought not to be printed, 1184
Pliny, the Elder, 42, 630, 642, 647, 760, 767, 768, 775
Plutarch, 127, 472, 497, 683, 778
poems, become lame if addressed to or about things, 609
  how set to music, 941–2
  made dull by similes, 411
poet, first to open the lips of a nation, 1009
  not in evidence in folk-song, 1124–5
  personality of, not revealed in epic, 955, 1037, 1048–9, 1111, 1179
poetic activity, ingredients of, 396
  subjects are inappropriate for painting, 856–9
  way of visualizing things, 331
poetry, alone can express sublimity, 366
  alone can express general meanings, 422
  alone uses comparative art-form, 381
  and history, 994
  and music, 904–5, 917–19, 952, 959–69, 1017 ff.
  and prose, 161–2, 316, 331, 973, 1005–7, 1009–10, 1012
  art itself begins to dissolve in, 968
  as art of speech, 626, 796, 960
  best able to portray chivalric virtues, 554
  can be translated into other languages or prose without detriment, 964
  can portray trivialities, 596
  classification of, 1090–1

compared and contrasted with painting, 854-6, 959-69
delivers heart from dominion of passion, 1112
descriptive, 596, 855, 858, 982
develops stories of the gods, 490
didactic, not a proper form of art, 423
distinct from visual arts and music, 959-69, 997 ff.
division of, 634
does not merely record events but probes their meaning, 994
first attempts at, 616
in avoiding prose may be over-subtle, 1006-7
in West and East, 557, 978
Italian, 874
makes the gods act, 486
may describe ugliness, 205
metre and rhyme in, 249
miracles in, 988
must be spoken, 1036
must stick to reality and its meaning, 994-5
not an adornment of prose, 39, 102
not for senses but for spiritual imagination, 626
of early Persian outlook, not art, 331
organic character of, 996
originally produced unintentionally, 974
particularization of content is of highest importance, 981
particularized geographically and historically, 977-8
provides only imperfect vision of the corporeal, 815
romantic, defectiveness of, 945-6
sentences preceding difference between it and prose, 980
should avoid allegory, 401
slower than scientific thinking, 981
something made, 162, 164
subject-matter of, 166-7, 972
  must be both particularized and unified, 983-4
superior to sculpture, 703, 705
task of is to liberate the spirit not from but in feeling, 1112
the universal art, 89, 285, 627, 796, 966-7, 1037
universal teacher of humanity, 972
'poetry of poetry', 296, 858

poets praised for metaphors, 396
Pöggeler, O., 69
'police', meaning of, 592
political organization, 461
Polyclitus, 767, 774, 777
Polygnotus, 800, 814
Polynices, 207, 228
polytheism, essential in classical art, 346-7, 486
Pompeii, 800
Pontius Pilate, 266
Pontus, *see* Black Sea
portrait statues, 401, 735, 747-50, 787
portraits, by Flemish and German painters, 174, 829, 887
  commissioned, 606
  Denner's, 165, 834
  Greek, 761, 762
  interest of, 851-2
  Italian, 872, 875
  medieval tend to be sculptural, 789
  must flatter, 155, 531, 867
  not to be treated sculpturally, 851-2
  of Christ, 820-1
  of old men, 827-8
  of some masters discussed, 865-9
  painted in antiquity, 801
  some are 'disgustingly like', 43, 531
  subjects of, how clothed, 748-9
  true to nature, 574, 596, 938
  Van Dyck's, 169, 852
Portuguese, voyages of, 1108
Poseidon, 229, 470
  birth of, 492
  dominion of, 473
  not god *of* the sea, 471
  statues of, 755, 757, 762
possibility, 1207
practical activity, 31, 36, 113-14, 123
Praxiteles, 760, 768, 776-7
prayer, nature of, 827
prehistoric age, 459
prescriptions for artists not the concern of the philosophy of art, 18, 103, 161
present, the, an inadequate theme for art, 189-80, 193-4
Prester John, 1106
presuppositions, of classical art, 440-4, 491
  of honour, 558
  of romantic art are religious, 526
  of sculpture, 721-2, 779 ff., 785

Priam, 230, 237, 1071, 1084, 1089–90
priest, Greek poet as, 479, 480
priesthoods, quarrels between, 494
prima donna, 159
primary interest of men, 149
Princes, class of, 192
    German, 571
print, gives vogue to undramatic dramas, 1184–5
    unconnected with spiritual meaning, 1036
printing, art of, 839
problems, characteristic of Eastern art, 308, 320
    unresolved in Egypt, 354
procreation, 337, 343, 373, 454, 641
Prodigal Son, the, 549, 852, 869
programme music, 897
Prokofiev, S. S., 893
Prometheus, 446, 460–2, 466, 469–70
prophecy, 243
prophet, Greek poet as, 479, 480
prosaic, character of fable, 387
    circumspection not Indian, 334, 1096
    intellect misinterprets Homer, 499
    material cannot be made poetic, 423
    nature of opposition between self and reality, 511–14
    reflection on nature and man, 480
    treatment of world depends on intellectual freedom, 316
prose, and poetry, 161–2, 226–7, 316, 1005–7, 1009–10, 1012
    begins with slavery, 387
    not the judge of poetry's truth, 1166
    of life, 148–50, 163, 193–4, 245, 598
        how far a theme for art, 255, 259
    of nature, 255
    poverty of, 152
    rule of, 1005
Protestantism, abandons mariolatry, 542–3, 603
    architecture of, 684–5
    demands sure footing in the prose of life, 598
    Dutch, 598, 885
    hymns of, 1145
    Klopstock's, 1154–5
    music in, 950
Providence, Divine, 989, 1038, 1063, 1072, 1179, 1208, 1216
Psyche, 859, 875
psychology, 23

public, art exists for the delight of the, 246, 264, 617–20
    grace is an appeal to, 617–18
    is supreme tribunal for drama, 1184
    kept in view by the French, 1191
    may be impressed by a poet's flattery, 1180
    may be misled by connoisseurs, 1184
    pleasure of, whence derived, 726–7
    relation of, to dramatic music, 952
    to blame for tasteless ideas, 1180
    types of appeal to, 619–20
    what an educated one requires from drama, 1179
punishment, can be unjust, 189
    metamorphosis as, 448 ff.
    vindicates law, 183
Puranas, 1096
purity of sensuous material, 141 ff.
purposiveness, 59, 145, 655–6, 659, 665–6, 686, 688, 692
Pylades and Orestes, 856
Pythagoras, 821, 924
    'Golden Verses' of, 980, 1041

quantity and quality, 135, 138, 960
Quatremère de Quincy, A. C., 773–4

Racine, *Esther*, 267
    Iphigénie, 267
    Phèdre, 241
ram, the sacred, 395
Ramayana, 336, 337, 344–5, 346, 1045, 1058, 1059, 1061, 1066, 1087, 1095–6
Ramler, K. W., 16
Rammelsberg, cave-dwellings in, 948
Ranke, L. von, 986
Raoul-Rochette, D., 784, 800
Raphael, arabesques in, 659
    at zenith of Christian painting, 814
    beauty in his pictures, 864
    cartoons of, 812
    drawings of, 838
    in details preserves the note of beauty, 948
    letter of, 281
    Madonnas of, 156, 800, 823, 827
    manliness of figures in, 865
    originality of, 298
    outclassed in colour by Dutch painters, 812
    perfection of, 881
    portrait of a boy, 170

School of Athens, 821
shaped religious ideas, 439
Transfiguration, 860
worldliness in, 884
Rask, R. K., 1029
Ratisbon, Diet at, 1155
Rauch, C. D., 166, 401, 484, 775
reading, dramas, 707
   knack of, 1002
   poetry, 1036–7
reality and actuality, 1202, 1222
recitative, 942–4, 952, 1017
recognition, necessary in honour, 560–2
   perfect in love, 562
reconciliation, afforded in Greek and modern plays, 1204
   afforded in tragedy, 1193, 1198–9, 1203
   by thinking and in poetry, 976
   in Christianity, 1219
   in comedy, 1235
   in epic, 1216–17
   in modern drama, 1230 ff.
   is moralizing, 1233
   negativity in, 573
   never to be lacking in art, 1173
   of conflict in Greek tragedy, 1215–30
   of spirit with itself and God, 517–51 *passim*, 573–4, 687, 793, 816, 830
   provided in Italian art, 939–40
   religious, 882
   sense of, in sculpture, 767
Reformation, the, 103, 885, 1109
regularity, 5, 60, 125, 126, 134 ff., 247–50, 894
   in architecture, 656, 669, 671, 700, 915
   in music, 906–7
   to be avoided in sculpture, 739
Reichardt, J. F., 918
religion, alone substance of spiritual depth, 816
   and art, 83, 103, 104
   arises from the spirit, 310–11
   as an aim of tragic character, 1194
   as unifying force, 637–8
   begins where art ends, 574
   can never be satisfied in real life, 552
   Christian, *see* Christianity
   doctrines of, allegorized in art, 402
   not a topic for art, 234, 990, 991
   education in, 182
   effect of, 234
   expressed in the East by building, 636
   Greek, 9–10, 72, 79, 102, 103 (*see also* Greek)
   higher sphere than art, 10, 968
   life of, 100–1
   material of may clash with our ideas, 571
   need for, 95
   not the highest form, 104
   origin of art closely associated with, 314, 316
   originally imposed from abroad, 1048
   productive of symbols in worldviews, 320
   provides romantic art with its absolute theme, 550–1
   reconciliation in, 1231 (*see also* reconciliation)
   secular, of the heart, 565
   symbolical ideas in, 314
   the substantial spirit of peoples, 603
religious, ideas lose their seriousness if beautified by art, 500–1
   practices, some merely customary, 495
Rembrandt, 169
remodelling of plays necessary, 277
Renaissance, the, 1107
Reni, G., 824, 829–30
repose of the Greek gods, 176, 200 ff., 476 ff.
responsibility, imputation of, 187–9, 458
restaurant, noise in a, 907
Resurrection, the, 535, 539, 822, 859
revenge, Arabian, 430, 1097
   as source of war, 1061
   distinct from punishment, 184
   goddesses of, 463
   in heroic times, 1068
   Procne's, 450
   right of, 462
Reynard the Fox, 187, 389–90, 571
rhetoric in poetry, 1008, 1010, 1011
Rhine wine, 263
rhyme, in lyric, 1136, 1137, 1142, 1146
   interlacings of, 1153, 1174
rhythm, in lyric, 1136, 1137
   in Schiller, 1146
   in versification, 1153

Richter, G. M. A., 202, 706, 760, 767
J. P. F., *see* Jean Paul
riddles, 320, 354, 360–2, 387
'rightness' of nature, 164
rite, the Greek as distinct from the Roman, 697
Rodenwaldt, G., 202
Roland, Chanson de, 571, 1105, 1106
Roman de la Rose, 1106
Roman, architectural subjects, 662
    art, borrowed from Greece, 285, 514
        perhaps prosaic from the start, 787–8
    Catholic Church, 324, 589, 606, 885, 950, 1102
    coins, 776
    columnar Order, 676
    comedy, 1235
    drama a pale reflection of Greek, 1208
    Empire, memorials in, 654
    historiography and philosophy, 515
    history, 1099
    law, 1057
    painting, 799–802
    poetry, a decoration of prose, 1092
        different spirit of, 977
        half-prosaic, 1100
        love in, 564
    reception of Cybele, 456
    religion, 649, 1048
    satyric dramas, 1203
    state, and virtue, 185
    statuary, 172
    Villa Albani, 294
    villas, excavation of, 799
    world, dominated by abstraction, 514
        mysteries in, 472
        subjective freedom in, 317
romances, as modern popular epics, 1092–3
    knowledge derived from, 280
    lyric expands into, 1117
    nature of, 1066
    unlimited field for, 1110
'romantic' and 'modern', meaning of, 1138
romantic art, accepts things without trying to beautify them, 531
    can give free play to the ugly, 527
    content of, given from without, 505, 526
    -form, 301–2
    points beyond itself, 438
romantic drama, 559–60
romantic feeling, 369
Romaunts, 1092, 1116, 1134
Rome, gems and vases shipped to, 778
    Monte Cavallo in, 768
roofs, different sorts of depend on weather, 670
Rösel, A. J., 43
rose-window, 693
Rossini, 234, 893, 949, 957
Rousseau, J. J., 949
Rubens, at zenith of Christian painting, 814
Rückert, F., 368, 610, 1097
rules for producing art, 15, 18, 20, 26, 107, 161
Rumohr, K. F. von, 106–7, 161, 168, 171–2, 293–4, 872, 875–81
Rumpf, A., 768
Ruskin, J., 170
Russia, 212

Saadi, 1098
Sachs, H., 265–6
sacred art, 372–3
    poetry, 379
St. Ambrose, 1025
    Augustine, 297, 555, 1025
    Barbara, 827
    Francis of Assisi, 827, 877, 878
    John of the Cross, 824
    John the Divine, 864
    John's fire, 495
    Sebald, church of, 691, 789
saints, appropriate subject of ideal art, 176, 803
    attributes of, 721
    definitely individualized, 402
    images of, 258, 616, 721, 789
    in modern drama, 1223
    legends of, 230, 269
    portrayals of, 171, 174, 587, 828–30, 851–2, 859, 865, 872, 877
Sallust, 515
Salsette, 648
San Angelo, castle of, 654
Sancho Panza, 397
Sanskrit, 1015
Sappho, 563, 1151
Saracens, 187, 1062, 1082, 1086, 1088
sarcophagi, 401
satire, 1010, 1100, 1152, 1200
satyrs, *see* fauns

INDEX

savages, 257
scales, chromatic and diatonic, 925-6
Scamander, 254, 341
Scandinavia, mythology of, 272, 273
  poetry of, 1026, 1029
  riddle in, 398
  sagas of, 1040
  theogonies in, 345
scenery in dramatic productions, 1158, 1168, 1177, 1181, 1182, 1186
Schadow, J. G., 770, 775
  R., 203
  W., 162, 857
Scharnhorst, G. J. H. von, 166
Schein, pure appearance, 4, 8, 9
Schelling, F. W. J., 63, 154, 467, 628, 662
Schikaneder, E., 946
Schiller, and Kant, 53, 61
  ballads of, 1118
  diction of, 1010, 1171, 1172
  early poems, 27, 28, 195, 597, 1225
  effect of his objective 'pathos' on the stage, 1173
  falls into violence, 1228
  formation of mouth of, 736
  great themes of his poetry, 1122, 1128
  greatness of, 1156
  had genius in youth, 283
  later works of, try to revive Greek tragedy, 1225
  living poetry of, 233
  lyrics of, characterized, 1146-7
  master of his subject, 1146
  'pathetic' poetry of, 235, 290
  'pathos' of, 506
  poems of, useless for music, 901, 945
  prose dramas of, 1012
  rich in metaphor, 408
  Works, cited or discussed:
    Aesthetic Letters, 4, 62, 204
    Braut von Messina, 192, 208
    Cranes of Ibycus, 1114
    Die Horen, 17, 156
    Don Carlos, 195, 1225
    Essay on Goethe's Iphigenia, 1178
    Expectation and Fulfilment, 307
    Fiesco, 195
    Gods of Greece, 506-8
    Grace and Dignity, 62
    Ideal and Life, 156
    Intrigue and Love, 195, 1225, 1230
    Lied von der Glocke, 1119, 1147
    Maid of Orleans, 277, 566, 1084-5, 1191, 1229
    Misanthrope, 233
    Robbers, 195, 307, 1083, 1224
    Shakespeare's Ghost, 161, 268, 1202, 1215
    Wallenstein, 157, 195, 583, 1189, 1224, 1230
    William Tell, 243, 280
    Xenien, 409, 1117
Schlegel, A. W., 63-4, 344, 407, 835, 1175, 1176
  F., advocates fidelity to nature, 269
    Alarcos, 423, 560
    finds allegory in all art, 312, 400
    his work evaluated, 63-4
    irony in, 66, 1175
    Lucinde, 508
    on architecture, 662
    on the inexpressible, 291, 296
    'poetry of poetry', 296, 858
    poor versifier, 284
    terminology of, 1138
Schleissheim gallery, 824
Schlüter, A., 775
scholars, musical, 930
scholarship in art, 14, 21, 34-5 (*see also* connoisseur)
Schubert, 899, 901, 1144
science, not a topic for art, 234
scientific study, only for the few, 234
  thinking, and belief, 1004
  categories of dominate oratory, 993
  essentially abstract, 983
  essentially prosaic, 974 ff.
  limitations of, broken by German philosophy, 1077
  makes for universals, 1001
  may regard poetry as superfluous, 1003
  nature, of, 1006
  not addressed by orators, 990
  not poetic, 965, 973, 998, 1002, 1007, 1035
  works more quickly than poetry, 981
scolia, 1151
Scopas, 776-7
Scorel, J. van, 599, 826
Scotland, 1101
sculptor, invention of, 719

sculptor (*cont.*):
  must first consider where his work is to be placed, 702
sculpture, allegories common in, 401
  best adapted to present the classical ideal, 486
  consolidates the character of Greek gods, 488, 490
  expression in, 239
  figures of have conventional distinctions, 254
  Greek, all-pervasive vitality of, 173
    how it individualizes the gods, 493, 495–6
    lacks the light of the eye, 522, 797, 856
    leaves us cold, 797
    more subjective in bas-reliefs, 555
    subjectivity lacking in, 504
  history of, 455–6
  how distinguished from painting, 863–5
  in Christian art only an adornment, 763, 789
  independence of, 905
  inorganic, 633
  invention and execution are at one in, 936
  less able to portray deep feeling, 546
  more abstract than painting, 167
  most suitable subject for, 797
  needed in Greek religion, 763
  needs architectural environment, 806
  needs Greek gods, 275
  needs scholarly study, 797
  portrays repose, 176, 200
  real function of, 766
  suppresses any practical relation, 835
  von Rumohr on, 293
  works out anthropomorphism, 633
sea, as subject for painting, 832
self, comes to self-consciousness by negative process, 914
  identity, negative movement of, 907–8
  inmost, moved by music, 891
  simple, elevated by music, 906, 908
self-consciousness, how acquired, 31, 256, 914
  necessary for reality of the spirit, 712

self-preservation, 145, 146, 157
self-satisfaction, 711, 717
Seneca, 681, 1227
sensation, 36, 112
'sense', a wonderful word, 128–9
sense of beauty, 33–4
senses, the five, 38, 129, 137, 890
sensuous intuition, 101, 128
sentence-construction, 1008
sentimentalism, 830
Serapis, 762
serenity, of Greek gods, 157, 223–4, 477 ff.
  only achieved by conquering the dragons of the heart, 816
seriousness, in fable, 390
  in Greek temples, 676
  lifeless in Egyptian sculpture, 784
  not to be taken in allegory, 400
  of art, 157
  of Gothic buildings, 696
  of sculpture, 766–7
sermons, 991, 992–3
Sesostris, 642, 646
sestinas, 1145–6
sex-relations, 562–4
sfumato, 848, 853
Shahnameh, 186, 208
Shakespeare, anglicizes Romans, 274–5
  bogus disciples of, 579
  changes of scene in, 1165
  characters of, 192–3, 577, 579, 585–6, 591–2, 1178, 1188
  clowns in, 240
  compared with Voltaire, 235
  critics of, 417
  deals preponderantly with universal interests, 1176
  diction of, 1172
  dramatized English history, 274
  drew material from chronicles, 288
  firmness of characters in, 1229–30
  French attitude to, 267
  hardly any modern dramatist can approach, 1228
  historical dramas, 190, 276
  humour in, 295
  images in, 417
  material of his Tragedies, 190
  originality of, 298
  painting of subjects drawn from, 856
  perfection of comedy in, 1236

INDEX 1283

places the trivial beside the important, 594
production of plays of, 277
rich in metaphors, 408
supreme as a dramatist, 1173
unapproachable as portrayer of character, 1227
wars in his Tragedies, 1061
Plays, quoted or mentioned:
  Antony and Cleopatra, 421
  As You Like It, 1227
  Hamlet, 214, 231, 244, 583–4, 594, 1167, 1225, 1231–2
  1 Henry IV, 277
  2 Henry IV, 418–19
  Henry VIII, 419, 420
  Julius Caesar, 420
  King Lear, 222–3, 569, 592, 1229, 1230
  Macbeth, 208, 231, 244, 420, 578, 579, 583, 585, 1227, 1230
  Othello, 212, 578, 1218, 1227
  Richard II, 405, 419
  Richard III, 578, 592, 1230
  Romeo and Juliet, 69, 215, 239, 415, 581–2, 585, 592, 594, 856, 1167, 1231–2
  Tempest, 582, 585
  Timon of Athens, 233
Shakuntala, 339, 1176
shame, sense of, 742–4
Shaw, W., 1100
shrieking, not dramatic, 417
  not music, 159, 910
Sickingen, F. von, 196
Siegfried, 238, 497, 1057
signs, and symbols, 304
  conventionality of, 307–8
  natural and arbitrary, 1002, 1012
  words as, 796, 898, 903, 1000
silhouettes, 704
simile, 306, 1149
singing is not yet music, 632
single cast, 174, 296, 407, 615, 719
Sistine Madonna, 827, 862
Sisyphus, 466
situations, choice of, 853–5
  invention of, 199, 216
Sixtus, Popes III and V, 827
sizes for colours, 847, 876
skill, can collaborate with nature, 257
  of artist, 575, 581
skin, animal and human, 145–6
sky, as background, 770

colour of the, 841–2, 847
slavery, 208, 212
Slavonic peoples, 1152–3
sloth, the, 130–1
smell, sense of, 38, 137–8, 621–2, 729–30
smoke, colour of, 842
snuff-boxes, 750
society, conversation in, 834–5, 867, 1121, 1184
Socrates, and immortality, 523
  features of, 864
  in Aristophanes, 1188, 1221
  richness of character of, 719
  period of, 510
solar system, 102, 117, 121–2
Solger, K. W. F., 68–9
Solly, E., collection of, 820–1
Solon, 1041
somnambulism, 243, 579
song, and lyrics, 1142–5
  expresses national differences, 1143
  general nature of, 940 ff.
  in opera, etc., 951
  is articulated sound, 695
  Italians as people, of, 922
  love in, 280
  makes us notice its intention, 235
  may be meagre, 900
  may have simple harmonies, 931
  of birds, 903
  of the human voice, 909
  old ones die away, 1144
  poetry of awakens ever anew, 1143
  unsuited to cultured poetry, 1146
  see also vocal music
songs, German, 918–19
  Schubert's, 901
sonnets, 1145, 1146, 1174
Sophocles, acted himself, 1187
  as plastic figure, 719
  characters in tragedies of, 239, 273, 863, 1178
  choruses in, 945, 1186
  conflict in, 1213–14
  his plays concern a 'pathos' of substance, 554–5
  language of, 407
  master of living language, 1215
  not interested in romantic love, 564
  originality of, 298
  perfect beauty of, 278
  three Theban tragedies, 1167
  tragedies of, 1045

Sophocles (*cont.*):
  Tragedies, cited or discussed:
    Ajax, 1165
    Antigone, 221, 464, 471, 564, 1163, 1213
      Hegel's estimate of, 464, 1218
    Electra, 1213, 1225
    Oedipus Coloneus, 227-8, 275, 470, 1214, 1219
    Oedipus Tyrannus, 1214
    Philoctetes, 206, 226, 580, 1183, 1204, 1219
soul, and body, 118-19, 123, 434
  both negative and affirmative, 121-2
  conception of the, 1059-60
  distinguished from spirit, 714-15
  living in an organism, 985
  manifested in feeling, 125
  meaning of, 108
  not recognizable in nature, 128
  of animals, 146
  of things, 154-5
sound, and numerical relations, 924
  and speech, 627
  as double negation, 890-1
  as material of music, 626, 890, 894, 899, 901-4, 906, 908
  as objective side of language, 701
  in nature and life, 123
  in poetry, 88-9, 898, 899, 968, 1011, 1014, 1027-8
  lyric relies on, 1136-7
  nature of, 622
  not music until made into notes, 962, 965
  totality of contained in the human voice, 922
space, in epic, 1136
  negatived by music, 249, 804-5, 889-90
  negatived by time, 907
Spain, Gothic kings in, 698
spandrels, 694
Spanish, chivalry, 1097
  dominion, 885
  drama, 417, 560, 1137, 1170, 1174, 1225
  epic and romances of the Cid, 1102
  epic of Amadis, 1106
  language, 1030
  literature, rich in metaphors, 408
  painting, 871
  plays, excel in intrigues, 1234-5
  plays treat honour subtly, 1176

poetry, 564-5, 610, 977, 1010-11
romances, 273, 1117
tragedy, 1227
Sparta, 743-4, 908
spatial symbols, 352-3
species, actuality of, 144
  and genus, 299, 326
spectator, Greek chorus is not a, 1210-11
  his relation to the work of art, 619-20, 806, 809-11, 831-2, 905
  is in the secret of a comedy, 1235
  must *study* the play of colour, 841
  of action, naïve consciousness of a, 209
  see also public
speculative thinking, 965, 973, 975-7, 984, 1007, 1135
speech, alone expresses comparisons, 381
  appeals to *spiritual* vision only, 961
  as revelation of the individual, 219
  in drama, 1171-2
  mechanical, is sufficient for reciting epic, 1038
  not needed for thinking, 898
  only an external reality, 964
  ordinary, poetry must go beyond, 1012
  poetry as art of, 626-7, 796
  signs in, 898
  sole element worthy of spiritual expression, 1158, 1170
  sound of, 252, 701, 898-9, 903
sphinxes, 360-1, 638, 643-5, 649, 655-6, 783
spirit, acquires affirmative satisfaction only by first traversing the negative, 524
  and appearance, 333
  and body, 702, 713, 727
  and light, 467, 473
  and nature, unity of, in classical art, 432-3, 435, 444
  not achieved in symbolic art, 443
  as subjectivity, 710 ff.
  chief factor of, 466
  completely unfolded in its reality, 426
  concreteness of, 342-3
  distinguished from soul, 714-15
  exists only as individual consciousness, 1049

life of, 154 ff.
  may be disdained by a person, 711
  movement of from finite to infinite, 688
  nature of, 12–13
  overcomes its finitude, 528
  portrayed in painting as reflected in nature, 794–5
  power of, 1219
  pure appearance of in painting, 805
  realization of, 301
  unsatisfied urge of in Egypt, 354
spiritual powers, 213, 1163 (*see also* ethical powers *and* universal powers)
splendid vices, 555
stagecraft, 1183–4
stage production of drama, 1182 ff.
stained-glass windows, 686, 690
stanchions and columns, 667, 668–9, 672
standing erect, significance of, 739
stars, law of the, 290
'state' of mind or things, 179, 198
state, administration of is not personal, 184
  and individual, 182 ff., 980
  as actualization of freedom, 98
  as ethical substance, 581
  as unifying bond, 638
  foundation of, 829
  Greek life in, 510
  life of is a totality, 99
  manifest in individual wills, 147
  organized, 182–4
  originates with families, 494
  relations in, 555
  scope of, 95
  should combine law and conscience, 555
  stability in, 459
  subjective feeling should not be at issue in, 567
Statius, 237
statue, unconcerned about the spectator, 806
Steen, J., 599
Sterne, L., 602
Steevens, G. E., 683
Stosch, P., Baron von, 777
Strabo, 452, 460, 643–5, 647, 652, 774, 775
Strasbourg, 807
study, essential for the artist, 27, 28, 45, 286

Sturluson, S., 1026
style, prosaic and poetic, 407
  severe, ideal, and pleasing, 615–20
subjective self-consciousness, constitutive of God and man, 504
subjectivity, and objectivity, 705
  as ordinary life, 268
  as union of opposites, 236
  depth of, 178
  important in images, 409
  must be objectified, 96 ff.
  negative unity, 144
  not fully explicit in nature, 141–2
  objectified in action, 179
  of life, 122, 143
  of revenge, 184
  of spirit, 79, 93, 112
  of the Concept, 108, 928
  principle of, 519 ff., 793–4, 797–8, 802–3, 808
sublimity, 77, 303, 318, 320, 339–40, 378–80, 383, 482–3
substance, and subject, 1202–4
  of character is what sculpture portrays, 712
Suetonius, 1130
Sunna, the, 42
Swiss people, 885
symbol, ambiguity of, 306–10
  and comparison, 307
  and meaning, 352
  as sign, 304
  meaning of, 19, 303–6
  shape the chief thing in, 372
  when can and must appear, 349–50
symbolic art, defect of, 427–31, 433, 438–9
  is presupposition of classical art, 441, 443
  sees God in nature, 454
symbolic forms, 172
symbolism, accessories in, 467
  in Greek art, 432, 482
  in myths, 459
  in painting, 861
  obscurity of, 469
symmetry, 84, 134 ff., 247–50, 786, 894
syncopations, 918
Syria, 353, 641

tableaux vivants, 156, 297
Tacitus, 358, 515, 987, 1057
talent, acquires technique easily, 286

talent (*cont.*):
  as a natural gift, 40–1, 288
  distinguised from genius, 27, 283–4
  of improvisers, 285
Tantalus, 218, 466
Tartarus, 466
Tasso, *Jerusalem Delivered*, 273, 856, 1068, 1074, 1082, 1086, 1108
  lyrical expressions in, 1079
  relation between Princes in, 1053
  war in, 1059, 1062
taste, sense of, 38, 137–8, 621–2
tears, 158–9, 233
technical skills, 460–2
technique, easily mastered by genius, 286
  in classical art, 440
  of art, and feeling, 778
  of bronze casting, 775
  of Egyptian sculptors, 783
  varies with style, 615
Telemachus, 228, 1079, 1081
teleology, 983
tempera, painting in, 847–8
Teniers, D., 599
Terborch, G., 600
Terence, 46, 514, 607, 1233
Terpander, 1151
The Boy's Magic Horn, 290
theatrical performances, 271–2
Theocritus, 1091, 1152
Theodosius I, 774
theogonies, 343–6, 459 ff., 464 ff., 1043
theologians, 365
theology, 23
theoretical, activity, 31, 37–8, 113–14, 123
  and practical relation to the world, 729, 731
Thespius, 186
Thetis, 237, 261, 480–1
thinking, both subjective and objective 180
  not the content of art, 431
  not the reason for dancing, 495
  reconciles reality and truth, 976
  requires self-consciousness, 335
  types of, 965–76
Thirty Years War, 977
Thoas, 212, 229–30
Thomson, D. S., 1100
Thor, 1102
Thorwaldsen, A. B., 203
Thucydides, 407, 719, 744, 987

Tibet, 700
Tieck, C. F., 770
  L., 68, 69, 244, 426, 1175, 1180
time, annihilates everything born, 347, 459
  empty, filled by music, 907
  essence of, 249, 907–8, 913
  in music, 1016, 1018
  lyric's relation to, 1136
  negativity of, 913
  rolling stream of, 894, 906, 913, 1016
  sphere of, 904, 912
  universal element in music, 907
Tischbein, J. F. A., 749
Titans, 451, 456, 459 ff., 466–7
Titian, 866, 881
tobacco, 266
torch-thistle, 71
toreutics, 773–4
touch, sense of, 38, 621
touched, being, 233
tragedy, expression of, 158
  gives less scope than comedy for the poet's own views, 1180
  see also drama, Greek, *and* grief
Traill, D., 106
Trajan, 654, 657
transcendence of art, 80, 82, 89
  of classical art, 302
Transfiguration, the, 822, 860
transformation of earlier material by art, 442 ff., 465, 477–8
  of man from nature to ethical life, 466
transgression, as basis of collisions in drama, 204–5, 213 ff.
  in Greek tragedy has some justification, 500
transition from symbolic to classical art, 505
translations, of poetry, 964, 1013
transmigration of souls, 78, 448, 651
trees, Gothic pillars analogous to, 688, 691
triangle, as symbol, 308
Trier, 697
Trinity, the, 304, 308, 342–3
Trojan War, 207, 214, 218, 224, 237, 264, 278, 448, 467, 473, 480, 563, 979, 1047, 1057, 1059, 1081, 1088, 1160
Trophonius, cave of, 457
Troy, *see* Trojan War

truth, absolute, is what the material of poetry is to be used for, 964
absolute, nature, of, 99–100
always victorious at last, 1180
and beauty, 91–2
and the Idea, 110
comprises essential distinctions historically related, 962
demands nullity of the finite, 1216
first knowledge of, 316
nature of, 110–12, 153, 341
of the spirit, 93
the centre of art, 83
to nature and life, 165, 174, 833–4
unveiled by art, 8–9, 55, 152, 155
turgor vitae, 146, 726
Turks, 42, 70, 285, 724, 746
Tuscan columnar Order, 666, 676, 678
type, use of a fixed one is to the detriment of art, 762
Tyrtaeus, 908, 1118

ugly, accepted by the 'characteristic', 19
and beauty, 44
animals, 127, 130–1
disunion productive of the, 436
expunged by classical art, 434
lack of self-control is, 159
painting cannot wholly dispense with the, 864
portrayed in Flemish and German painting, 883–4
portrayed in poetry, 205
portrayed in romantic art, 442, 527, 538
Ugolino, 259
Uhden, W. (1763–1835), 654
Ulysses, *see* Odysseus
umlaut, 142
Understanding, the, *see* intellect *and* scientific thinking
unification, of man with God, 791
of self with world possible only in religion, 575
uniforms, 125
unity, and unities in drama, 1164–7
general meaning of, 1088
in lyric and epic, 1164
less in music than in the visual arts, 896–7
of a lyric, 1115, 1119, 1132–3, 1135
universal, and individual unified in ideal sculpture, 787

ends, 1224
powers, as the Eumenides, 278
immanent in men, 227, 232 ff.
in existence, 197–8
must be configurated in individuals, 223
pervaded by the particular, 241
revealed by art, 8
the gods themselves, 224
see also ethical powers *and* spiritual powers
universities are for the few, 234
unworthiness of man, 376

Valhalla, 273
Van Dyck, A., 169, 852
van Eyck, H., 883
  J., 599, 820–1, 823, 828, 843, 861, 883–4
Vasari, G., 878
vassals, claims of, 569–70
independence of, 390
Vates, activity of is religious, not artistic, 384
Vatican, figures in, 753
Vaucluse, 276
vaudeville, 951
Vaughan, R. A., 371
Vedas, the, 337, 1095
Velleius Paterculus, 775
Venice, painting in, 764, 839
Venus, *see* Aphrodite
verse, supposedly unnatural, 1012
versification, Italian, 874
rhythmic, 1153
victory, statue of, 770
when historically justified, 1062
Vienna, 901, 949
Virgil, *Aeneid*, 769, 1070, 1075, 1086, 1099
allegorical beings in, 399
and Dante, 874
decorates prosaic matter, 1010
Eclogues, 1091
Georgics, 405, 423, 1042
gods in are mere inventions, 1073
influence of on Tasso, 1108
interweaves actions of men and gods, 1072
travestied, 1074
tries to please, 618
virtue, Greek and Roman sense of, 183
of Christian piety, 556

virtuosity, of actor, 1205
  of musical executants, 956-8, 1188, 1191
virtuoso on guitar, 957
Vischer, P., 789
Visconti, E. Q., 754
visual arts, cannot portray pantheism, 70, 366
  cannot portray sublimity, 373
  defined, 17
  element, of, 704
  music contrasted with the, 795
  poetry contrasted with the, 997 ff.
  riddle in, 398
  separate what poetry can unite, 705
  task of, 381
  terminate, 635
Vitruvius, 631, 646, 663, 671, 672, 675, 677, 678, 679, 680
vocal music, 934 ff., 940, 953
Vogelweide, W. von der, 1127
voice, notes of the, 142
  production of, 142
  purity of, 142, 874
  the human, 159, 252, 358, 893, 909, 919, 920, 922, 934, 936, 951, 953
Volker, the minstrel, 238
Voltaire, contrasted with Shakespeare, 235
  Henriade, 274, 1061, 1075, 1109
  makes fun of Pindar, 267
  Tancred and *Mahomet*, 1191
  used drama to spread his principles, 1180
Voss, Heinrich, 1017
  J. H., dispute with Creuzer, 473
  Luise, 262, 1017-18, 1110
  on versification, 1031
vowels, 142, 252
vulgar, characters in Shakespeare, 585-6
  material in art, 168-71, 527, 832, 834-5
  scenes, 886-7
  see also Dutch painting
vulgarity of ordinary life, 245

Wagner, J. M. von, 785-6
  R., 254
Wales, 1101
wall, cost of exceeds that of columns, 657, 673
  must be perpendicular, 671
  purpose of, 666

Wallenstein, A. W. E. von, *see* Schiller
Wander, K. F., 218
wars, justification of, 1061-2
  kind of suited to epic, 1060-1
Wartburg, contests at, 398
warts, 146, 155, 165
weaving, art of, 461, 462
Weber, C. M. R. E. von, 159
Weimar, 280, 389
Welsh triads, 1101
werewolf, 1102
West, the, triumph of over the East, 1061-2
Western, outlook, 978
  poetry distinguished from Eastern, 412, 978
Wetzlar, 296
Weyden, R. van der, 828
wickedness of man, 376
Wieland, C. M., *Oberon*, 571, 740
  portrait of, 749-50
Wilkins, Sir Charles, 344
will, and impulse contrasted, 53-5
  as spirit's route to existence, 179
  guided by law and morality, 179
Wilson, H. H., 342
Winckelmann, J. J., 19, 63, 160-1, 172, 400-1, 723, 727, 733-63, 766, 769, 772, 777-8, 781-3, 787
windows, regularity or symmetry of, 125, 135
wine, 370, 376
wit, and humour, 295-6, 398, 508, 576
  artist's can master all reality, 595
  capricious, 407
  excluded from sculpture, 719
  in lyric, 1115, 1135, 1149, 1152
  of invention in reliefs, 771
  self-complacent expressed in laughter, 1200
witches, in *Macbeth*, 231, 585
  intruded into Christian art, 230
  world of, is Indian, 336
Wittenberg, statue, in, 775
Wolf, F. A., 1087
wolf, as symbol, 394
  in Egyptian and Greek thought, 448-9
  in fable, 389
Wolff, C., 1075
women, expressions of, 156
  provincial, 1198
  whims of, 1201
wonder, 315

wood as building material, 664
word, as meaning of 'epic', 1040
words, are means in prose, ends in poetry, 1000
  as ideal power, 373–4
  as signs, 304, 306, 898, 963, 964, 1000, 1036
  made so by sound, 88
  most intelligible means of communication, 997
  product of our ideas, 167
  spiritual and literal meanings of, 306, 404
  thinking, in, 898
world, finitude and grief of, 176, 178
world-spirit, aim of is grasped only by thinking, 1064
  in history, 1064–5
worship, does not belong to art as such, 103, 104
  expressed in lyric, 1139
  is prayer answered, 827
  raises the eye to heaven, 829
Wouwerman, P., 169

Xenophanes, 435, 1042
Xenophon, 510, 719, 987

youth, and age, interests of, 999
  friendship closest in, 568–9
  idealism of, 593

Zaehner, R. C., 215, 325, 367
Zelter, C. F., 950
Zeus, accompanied by eagle, 313
  amours of, 224, 452, 475, 493
  and Hephaestus, 309, 462
  and Leda, 218
  and Lycaon, 394, 448–9
  and Niobe, 826
  and Prometheus, 446, 460 ff.
  and Proserpine, 492
  and the beetle, 386, 447
  as father of gods and men, 819–20
  attribute of, 475, 496, 753, 758
  birth of, 492
  characteristics of, 487–9
  giver of Palladium, 230
  hides in shape of a ram, 395
  majesty of, 173, 177
  more familiar than Wotan, 273
  not a character, 863
  powers of, not absolute, 187
  race of, 456, 1043
  relation to other gods, 177, 187, 571
  statue of, 258, 439, 707, 745, 757, 762, 773–4
  symbolism in, 474
  temple of, at Aegina, 785
    at Olympia, 675
Zeuxis, 42
zodiac, 359, 646

The manufacturer's authorised representative in the EU for product safety is Oxford University Press España S.A. of el Parque Empresarial San Fernando de Henares, Avenida de Castilla, 2 – 28830 Madrid (www.oup.es/en or product. safety@oup.com). OUP España S.A. also acts as importer into Spain of products made by the manufacturer.

www.ingramcontent.com/pod-product-compliance
Ingram Content Group UK Ltd.
Pitfield, Milton Keynes, MK11 3LW, UK
UKHW022152230426
12049UKWH00003BA/47